THE EVOLUTION OF NATIONAL
INSURANCE IN GREAT BRITAIN

The Evolution of National Insurance in Great Britain

THE ORIGINS OF THE WELFARE STATE

BENTLEY B. GILBERT

London
MICHAEL JOSEPH

First published by
MICHAEL JOSEPH LIMITED
26 Bloomsbury Street
*London, W.C.*1
1966
© *copyright* 1966 *by Bentley B. Gilbert*

Set and printed in Great Britain by
Unwin Brothers Limited at the Gresham Press, Woking,
in Imprint type, eleven-point leaded, and bound by
James Burn at Esher, Surrey
(5922B)

CONTENTS

The author gratefully acknowledges permission to quote from the works of Rudyard Kipling and George Bernard Shaw.

FOREWORD

'I refuse,' said Winston Churchill in replying to Asquith's offer of the Local Government Board portfolio in 1908, 'to be shut up in a soup kitchen with Mrs Sidney Webb.'

It is doubtful whether young and ambitious politicians in Britain or North America today would decline so summarily a ministerial post in the social policy field. The responsibilities, status, and relative importance of 'social service' departments of government have changed since the days when many people were uncertain whether new measures of social welfare were rank socialism or first-class imperialism.

Professor Bentley Gilbert of Colorado College, U.S.A. (to whom British students of social policy will assuredly acknowledge their debt after reading this book) traces these changes during the last quarter of the nineteenth century and up to the outbreak of the First World War.

With the aid of the public archives and a massive collection of private and public papers (marred only by the withholding by the late Lord Beaverbrook of the Lloyd George papers) Professor Gilbert has given us the first definitive history of 'the new philanthropy' and the formation of social policy in the early years of the twentieth century. He examines in detail and against the wider political background of 'the condition of the people question' six great social laws—as examples of social policy rather than an attempt to offer a comprehensive definition of the term; school meals and school medical inspection, old age pensions, unemployment insurance and labour exchanges, and national health insurance.

Some arrived on the statute book almost in secret, pushed along by powerful and determined civil servants like Robert Morant; themselves the product, so to speak, of the 'administrative revolution' of the nineteenth century. Some stemmed directly from the 'Quest for National Efficiency' which dominated the politics of welfare after the disasters of the Boer War; a process of national self-diagnosis not unlike that which absorbed France in the 1950's and Britain in the early 1960's. Some were avowedly seen as a defence against socialism and the discovery by the poor of their political power; they did not represent, as Professor Gilbert remarks, 'a conscious search for a revised philosophy of poverty.' Students of the contemporary American War on Poverty will find here some analogies if not resemblances.

These were some among the many forces which stimulated political action. Those that shaped the final form and structure of legislation—often remarkably dissimilar from the first draft Bills— were equally diverse and commanding. The struggles for power between the contending parties and interests, pressure groups and lobbyists were intense, complex and bitter; the doctors, for example, were divided amongst themselves and against 'the Harley Street leadership,' sometimes they were found in alliance with the commercial insurance lobby against the great Friendly Society movement and sometimes not, sometimes they were publicly fighting the Government whilst privately welcoming State intervention.

No one who reads Professor Gilbert's absorbing account of these events can with honesty continue to subscribe to the myth that lobby pressures do not exist in Britain or are relatively ineffectual in the party political system. Nor, as students of the evolution of social policy, will they be able to continue to accept the placid, conventional, textbook account of the historical romance of 'Welfare Statism.'

February 1966   RICHARD M. TITMUSS

PREFACE

The writer of a study such as this one is immediately beset by the problem of definitions. What after all is 'social legislation'? Is not the poor law social legislation, for that matter the Elizabethan poor law, or the Education Act of 1902? Can it not be argued that any activity of a government dealing with its own people, beyond the traditional functions of the rendering justice and maintaining the peace, is social legislation? This definition would bring within the scope of social legislation such things as an Act establishing a post office or building a road.

The writer does not question the merit of these definitions, but is bound to say first that they would increase the size of this project beyond all manageable proportions, and more important would fail to note the revolution in the British government's relations with the nation's citizens that occurred after 1906. For however it is styled the legislative efforts of the New Liberalism to deal with the 'condition of the people question' *were* altogether unprecedented. Their newness was perhaps better understood at the time than since. Trade boards, the Edwardians recognized, could trace their ancestry to the Factory Acts of the eighteen forties. The Housing and Town Planning Act of 1909 was only a more ambitious version, and even less successful, of the Housing Acts of the eighteen seventies. But the series of six measures that began with the Education (Provision of Meals) Act and culminated with the National Insurance Act were based on an entirely new principle which for this writer separates true social legislation from all other forms of parliamentary activity. In these measures there occurred the transfer of income through the medium of the State from the pocket of the taxpayer, not to some general service available to all citizens, but rather to the benefit of certain designated individuals, who suffered moreover no pain or penalty on the account of the aid they received, and who were chosen principally on the basis of their need.

This transfer provides the critical element in the New Liberalism. Within this definition unsubsidized housing programmes are not social legislation, but subsidized housing is. The definition could be stretched, perhaps, to include the poor law but here the

A*

recipient of aid suffered at least severe civil penalties while receiving relief. The Victorians felt very strongly about this. Except for the performance of a service no person should receive tax money whether in cash or in kind without being made to suffer. Even at the height of the potato famine, the Irish relief committees were under orders, frequently ignored to be sure, never to give away food, and to sell it at cost only when the local workhouse was full. Meanwhile cash relief was available only through artificially provided work. The importance of the departure when these penalties were first dropped seemed great to Englishmen at the time, but has been too frequently missed since. Indeed the paucity of writing on the pre-World War I social reform and the general lack of interest in the topic of welfare legislation by political, diplomatic, and economic historians of the period is little short of astonishing. A recent biographer of A. J. Balfour, for instance, is altogether unaware that his subject led the Unionists during most of the passage of the National Insurance Act and assumes in addition that the Act was passed in 1912. (The term Unionist will be employed in this study to refer to the coalition of Conservatives and Liberal Unionists who constituted the Government from 1895 to 1905 and who were in opposition thereafter.)

This study aims to trace the forces that caused this revolutionary action, to examine the techniques by which the British State undertook to provide for that portion of the population unable to care for itself, and to elucidate, so far as possible, the thinking and backgrounds of the men who made the welfare state what it is. Social legislation is not, after all, only a matter of royal commissions and parliamentary debate, although historians tend to treat it this way. Formal planning, certainly in Britain, probably counts for less in this field than in any other type of parliamentary activity. The politician who would deal with a public welfare problem has above all others to proceed by trial and error. Unlike many other fields of government work, he cannot proceed secretly. Unlike many other matters of State, the objects of his concern have a way of retaliating against him if they feel he is mistaken. Because he is intruding into the ordinary citizen's intimate daily affairs, normally reserved only for private decisions, he becomes subject to endless and conflicting vested economic interests and personal prejudices of a sort not encountered when the Government remains within its normal spheres of activity, where it has the monopoly of decision.

This book owes its existence to many people in addition to the formal author. The writer is indebted to the custodians of the various manuscript collections he was permitted to use, to the Keeper of Public Records, and to the editors of the *Journal of British Studies*, the *Economic History Review*, the *American Historical Review*, and the *Bulletin of the History of Medicine* for permission to reprint the substance of articles which first appeared in these journals. He wishes to acknowledge also the help of certain individuals who gave him the benefit of their recollections of the Edwardian period and who answered graciously and pleasantly a large number of what must have seemed irrelevant and impertinent questions: the late Lord Beveridge who also permitted the writer to work in his residence at Oxford and to use his personal papers, and the late R. H. Tawney, Miss Rosemary Braithwaite, Mrs C. F. G. Masterman, Mr H. F. Watson of the Manchester Unity of Oddfellows, Mr H. W. Townley of the Shepherds, Mr D. H. Roper of the National Deposit Friendly Society, Mr Thomas W. Prior of the Hearts of Oak, Mr S. S. Townsend of the Prudential, Sir Henry N. Bunbury, Lord Salter, Mr S. E. Minnis, and Sir H. Guy Dain, M.D. Particularly he wishes to express his gratitude to Sir Alexander Carr-Saunders, whose memories of the Edwardian period and of the settlement house movement, and whose careful reading of the manuscript, have made this a better book than it would otherwise be. For scholarly and editorial advice besides Sir Alexander Carr-Saunders, the author is indebted to Professor Charles Mullett of the University of Missouri, Professor C. W. Vogel of the University of Cincinnati, Mr Maurice Bruce of the University of Sheffield, Major Victor Sutch of the United States Air Force Academy, and to Ellen MacVeagh and Mrs Louis Geiger of Colorado Springs, each of whom read part or all of this manuscript.

For editorial assistance, for checking consistency of bibliographical style, for the accuracy of quotation, and the detection of all too numerous infelicities in the writing, I acknowledge a heavy debt to Lois Lentz who did also much of the typing and to the staff of the Colorado College library, especially to the Research

Librarian, Miss Reta Ridings, whose unfailing and cheerful help and expert knowledge of bibliographical and statistical reference guides were invaluable.

To Mr Ernest Whybrow at the library of the Ministry of Pensions and National Insurance who gave the writer both the benefit of the vast collection of source material on early pension activity, the only complete file of the *National Insurance Gazette*, and his own recollections as an insurance agent, the author wishes to give special thanks. He must also mention the courtesy and help of Mr A. E. Fountain, librarian of the Ministry of Health, and Mr H. A. Hewitt, departmental record officer of the Ministry, now the Department, of Education.

The author acknowledges with special gratitude the financial aid provided by the Colorado College Faculty Research Committee, the American Philosophical Society and the National Institutes of Health that supported the editorial work in this project and enabled him to spend two extended periods of residence in the United Kingdom.

Finally he expresses his special thanks to Professor Richard Titmuss of the London School of Economics from whose encouragement this book grew in the first place but who by now may wish he had let well enough alone.

Colorado Springs, Colorado   BENTLEY B. GILBERT
October 15, 1965

INTRODUCTION

The story of the evolution of national insurance in Great Britain begins with the changing view of the nature of distress and poverty that began to affect the minds of reformers and social thinkers in the last quarter of the nineteenth century. This altered concept, frequently styled 'the new philanthropy,' derived less from a conscious search for a revised philosophy of poverty than from changes in British economic society combined with a growing consciousness among the poor themselves that they had it within their power to alter the conditions under which they lived. This agitation among the poor was spurred by the proliferation of socialist ideas and, after the grant of household franchise in 1885, by the appearance of politically oriented labour leaders. The new philanthropy had behind it a suspicion and fear of the lower classes that Great Britain, unlike the Continent, had not known in the nineteenth century.

But it proceeded also from a new awareness among those of the upper classes who were in daily contact with the poor that the old assumptions about poverty simply were not true. All of the poor were not lazy and improvident. Industrial society clearly did not distribute its rewards equally, or according to effort. Moreover, contrary to the mid-nineteenth century faith in the inevitable and linked betterment of the economic, moral, and social values of mankind, the condition of too many of the working class did not appear to be improving, but rather the reverse.

The new philanthropy represented a departure, not so much from the traditional Christian attitude towards the poor, or for that matter from the eighteenth-century English point of view, but from the attitudes of the immediately preceding seventy-five years. The first half of the nineteenth century witnessed the temporary triumph in Great Britain of the Puritan ethic that poverty itself demonstrated a personal failing and that the gift of alms, far from sanctifying the giver, contributed to and compounded the moral failing of the beggar. But least blessed of all was State aid. Here the donor did not receive even the comfort of the recollection of his own generosity because his payment was a compulsory one through the medium of local taxes, the poor rate.

Hence it was appropriate that a person who accepted such aid temporarily lost his rights as a citizen.

This point of view received its most perfect legislative expression in the Poor Law Amendment Act of 1834, the so-called 'new poor law,' which was supposed to end domiciliary or out-door relief, England's customary provision for most of its poor since the days of Elizabeth. Labour was no different from any other factor of production, taught the classical economists. The most efficient use of available labour within the United Kingdom demanded that the market for it should be as fluid as possible. Any restriction upon labour mobility, any inducement for the individual worker to remain in one place hindered the efficient and the profitable functioning of the nation's economic plant. Moreover any relief given to the individual workman that lessened his desperation for work increased the employer's wage bill, it was assumed, by the same amount. Logically an application for parish relief carried more than the disparagement of the individual; it constituted an interference with the perfect operation of the free economic system.

Relief therefore might, indeed ought to, be given only on the most onerous and unpleasant terms and its acceptance could be made to carry the stigma of the semi-criminal. 'The first and most essential of all conditions,' stated the 1834 Poor Law Commission, whose report became essentially the Amendment Act, 'a principle which we find universally admitted, even by those whose practice is at variance with it, is that his [the unemployed applicant for relief] situation on the whole shall not be made really or apparently as eligible as the situation of the independent labourer of the lowest class.'

> Throughout the evidence it is shown, that in proportion as the condition of any pauper class is elevated above the condition of independent labourers, the condition of the independent class is depressed; their industry impaired, their employment becomes unsteady, and its remuneration in wages diminished. Such persons, therefore, are under the strongest inducement to quit the less eligible class of labourers, and enter the more eligible class of paupers.

Here was defined the principle of 'less eligibility' that gave the premise for deterrent poor relief and the spartan miseries of the workhouse. By applying for relief the applicant gave up all claim to equality with his fellows in society. Therefore, said the Commission, 'the public is warranted in imposing such conditions on the individual relieved, as are conducive to the benefit either of the individual himself, or of the country at large, at whose expense he is to be relieved.'

In the sentences quoted above lay the force that would make the welfare state inevitable by the end of the century. A system of public relief deliberately made hideous for its recipients could not long outlast the grant of universal franchise. More important, when the demand for a new system appeared, the mere improvement of the conditions of relief, such as the mitigation of the rigours of the workhouse which occurred in some East End London unions at the end of the century, would never satisfy the reformers. For over two generations the British working class had been taught that an application for parish relief was the ineradicable mark of economic degradation. This meant that no plan for old age pensions, the feeding of school children, or health insurance that touched the poor law was acceptable to the working class. Such was the legacy of Victorian respectability. As significant in the long run was the reaction to the disciplinary and supervisory features of parochial relief. There would be little working class enthusiasm for any scheme of 'conditional relief' even unconnected with the poor law if the applicant for aid was required to submit to vocational training or show improved habits of personal cleanliness, or in return for State support to give some other sign of greater social responsibility. In this way the one great alternative to social insurance, the elaborate programme published in 1909 by Sidney and Beatrice Webb as the minority report of the Royal Commission on the Poor Laws and Relief of Distress, was removed as a possible competitor to the haphazard but unconditional welfare programmes of the New Liberalism.

The goal of the Poor Law Amendment Act had been to force the individual workman to place himself at the disposal of the British productive system. The more efficiently the economic plant could make use of his talents, it was held, the greater would be the production, and in the long run the greater the happiness for everyone. Any system of relief, public or private, that made it possible for him to withhold his labour demoralized him as an individual and robbed the national treasure. The Poor Law

Amendment Act was the means by which the economic nation protected itself from the assumed laziness of the workman.

There was still another area, no less a product of the nineteenth century than the industrial revolution, in which the upper class felt it necessary to guard itself from the poor. The era of the new poor law saw also the beginnings of modern sanitary science, and with this came the realization for the ordinary well-to-do British taxpayer that good health in the slums was an advantage to his pocketbook and that ill health there could endanger his life. The last three-quarters of the nineteenth century and the first quarter of the twentieth became, as a result, the classical age of public health and the public health physician, the period of the conquest of contagious and infectious disease. It may be argued that the era began with Edwin Chadwick's discovery that the percentage of deaths from cholera in the outbreak of 1831–2 was markedly higher in the poor districts. Perhaps it ended, for Western Europe and North America only, almost precisely a century later in 1929 with Sir Alexander Fleming's first observations on penicillin in his laboratory in St Mary's Hospital.

The sanitary legislation of the middle years of the nineteenth century had surprisingly little effect on the social and health legislation of the twentieth except in two important respects. It provided a number of 'fever' hospitals, many of which were built in London as a result of the establishment, in 1867, of the Metropolitan Asylums Board. After 1879 these institutions were permitted to admit non-pauper patients, thus becoming an embryonic municipal hospital system. Also, by emphasizing the environmental causes of sickness, the nineteenth-century interest in public sanitation directed the nation's attention towards the housing of the poor. Legislation for the abatement of nuisances and for the inspection and occasionally the demolition of unsanitary working-class houses represented in the sixties and seventies British society's response to the new discoveries in public health science.

Two men, Sir Edwin Chadwick and Sir John Simon, whose lifetimes span the nineteenth century, must be mentioned in any discussion of British health and sanitary legislation. Their appearance symbolizes the beginning of the intrusion of the 'expert' into the business of government, a field previous centuries had always assumed belonged to the aristocratic amateur. Sir Edwin Chadwick, born in 1800, was perhaps the archetype, certainly one of the first, of the impatient, domineering, officious, administrative technician, who appears to have been bred for the administration of public or private institutions of public welfare. In 1832 Chadwick had been appointed the secretary of the commission investigating the poor laws. The Poor Law Amendment Act placed the administration of poor relief at the local level in the hands of a new elective body, the board of guardians, and entrusted the supervision of the board of guardians to three national commissioners. Chadwick became the secretary of the commissioners. During his fourteen years in this office Chadwick made himself thoroughly unpopular with his own immediate superiors, with the politicians at Westminster, and with the public at large. But at the same time he introduced the British nation to the idea that health was a matter for public as well as individual concern and that whatever one might think of the people in the slums—if one thought of them at all—their physical as well as their moral well being was important. An early result of this new consciousness was the establishment, in 1836, of the office of the Registrar General of Births and Deaths under William Farr. Four years later, in 1840, poor law guardians were ordered to provide free vaccination. And in 1848 Parliament established a national Board of Health with the duty of acting as a clearing house for health statistics and with the power to require the establishment of a local sanitary board in areas with a death rate higher than twenty-three per thousand.

The Board of Health led a stormy and tortured life, partly because it had no regular minister to defend it in Parliament and partly because it had received Chadwick as its secretary. 'Mr Chadwick is in the wrong place,' wrote the *Economist* on August 5, 1854, 'a gem spoilt from bad setting. In Austria, in France, in Prussia, where people were to do nothing for themselves, ... where they were to be governed honestly, justly, kindly, but to have no self-government whatever ... Mr Chadwick would be invaluable.' The journal concluded by suggesting that he be sent to Russia to help rebuild that country from the defeat of the Crimea. Even though Chadwick resigned his secretaryship in 1854, the board was allowed to die four years later.

Chadwick had left the Board of Health realizing that his connexion with that body hurt its chances for success. Although he lived until 1890, his official life was over. His short, tumultuous, public career would resemble in the twentieth century that of Sir Robert Morant, with whom Chadwick was similar in personality, in aim, and in contempt for the easygoing and feckless political world. Chadwick's own accomplishments were limited, but he set the lines for future action. The upper classes might look at the poor with pity or with contempt, but they could no longer disregard the poor and even the death of the general board did not mean the end of public interest in sanitation and sanitary regulation.

Moreover with Chadwick's retirement his place as supervisor of the rather limited British welfare activities was taken by John Simon, a man whose personality was as agreeable and mild as Chadwick's had been cocksure and unpleasant. Unlike Chadwick, Simon was a physician. He became medical officer to the Board of Health in 1854. When the general board disappeared its health powers passed to the Privy Council. Simon continued in the service of that body until the establishment of the Local Government Board in 1871, when he became the board's first chief medical officer. He held this post until his retirement in 1876.

Largely at the instance of the medical profession, led by the recently organized British Medical Association, the Gladstone Government had appointed in 1869 a royal commission to study sanitary conditions. The report of this commission led to the establishment of the Local Government Board. The board received the powers and duties of the Poor Law Board, which had succeeded the originally established Poor Law Commission in 1847, and it received the peregrinatory health powers that had been held by the Privy Council. It was allowed to constitute new sanitary authorities and was charged with the supervision of the enforcement of the Sanitary Acts.

The establishment of the board was followed the next year by a new Public Health Act mapping out the nation's sanitary districts and providing for the unification of these districts under the supervision of the Local Government Board in order to provide for the appointment of a medical officer of health. Three years later Parliament consolidated all previous public health and sanitary legislation, with the Public Health Act of 1875. The measure became the basic statute for all public health power for the next half century.

The next year Simon retired, was appointed a crown member of the General Medical Council—designated by the Medical Act of 1858 as the judicial and disciplinary body of the medical profession—and set himself to writing his classical history of his nation's activity in environmental medical care, *English Sanitary Institutions*. This book was published in 1890, fourteen years before Simon died.

By the time of the publication of *English Sanitary Institutions* the social revolution that would bring the welfare state was under way. The ferment of the eighties that form the first chapter of this study had made the 'condition of the people' a chronic, if not a critical, political question. The poor refused any longer to suffer in silence. The aim of the eighteen-thirties had been to induce people receiving relief to work. By 1890 the old problem of pauperism had become a problem of poverty and the essentially economic dilemma was political and social: What, it was asked, can the governors of the nation do to prevent the poor from using their franchise to overturn a society based on capitalist wealth? As it turned out, the defence against socialism was social legislation.

1 The Eighties and the Nineties: The Two Nations

The stranger paused; Egremont was silent, but looked inquiringly.

'Yes,' resumed the younger stranger after a moment's interval. 'Two nations; between whom there is no intercourse and no sympathy; who are as ignorant of each other's habits, thoughts, and feelings, as if they were dwellers in different zones, or inhabitants of different planets; who are formed by a different breeding, are fed by a different food, are ordered by different manners, and are not governed by the same laws.'

'You speak of——,' said Egremont, hesitatingly.

'THE RICH AND THE POOR.'

BENJAMIN DISRAELI, *Sybil*.

Until the last quarter of the nineteenth century provision for the poor in Great Britain was founded on the poor law of 1834 supplemented by individual philanthropy. To the well-to-do 'the poor' were a race apart, inevitable but unpleasant like sin or death, to be tolerated and pitied, or to be despised if they fell into the hideous category of 'paupers.' Pauperism meant more than misfortune, it implied a moral failing. Those who accepted parochial aid were legally assumed to be guilty of sin, of laziness and improvidence. They were less eligible for the privileges of citizenship than their fellows and as such were deprived of the franchise or, in fact, of their personal freedom by being required to accept parish aid under semi-penal conditions in the poor house.

The 'respectable' working class shared the view of the well-to-do about pauperism, if not about the poor. But if the prosperous despised the individuals, the worker feared the condition. The bricklayer, the miner, the mechanic, the carpenter, knew that old age, or accident to himself, a technological improvement, the failure of his provident society or trade union, or the malfeasance of its treasurer, might throw him and his family onto the poor law. Economic security was a condition he and his fellows would never know, but he despised paupers no less than the wealthy on this account. Victorian England succeeded so well in making the term 'the poor law' a phrase of abuse that social reformers of the twentieth century were unable to cleanse these words of their disparaging connotations. As a result, when the welfare state began to grow, practically all the vast nineteenth-century apparatus of parochial relief had to be abandoned lest it taint the new reform measures.

The official services of the poor law to the poor were supplemented by a conglomeration of private, individual, to a large extent unorganized—one might say almost disorganized—humanitarian agencies. These, practically without exception, were concerned with saving the souls of the poor, which were considered to be in danger from the degradation of poverty. The interest was less in destitution in this world than in damnation in the next. In that the ordinary Victorian philanthropist found the physical welfare of the individual of secondary interest to his spiritual welfare he could trace ancestry back to Lord Shaftesbury's evangelical humanitarianism which, for instance, objected less to the fact that women worked underground in coal mines than that they did so unclothed to the waist in the company of men. Typical of the mid-nineteenth century was the 'Midnight Movement for Fallen Women' which attracted the attention of Catherine Booth, the wife of William Booth, after the couple came to London from Sheffield in 1865. The Midnight Movement sought to induce the ladies of the evening whom it could bring to prayer meetings to reform their lives through prayer with a view to going into domestic service. Help for prostitutes occupied the time of even so eminent a man as William Ewart Gladstone, who conducted a personal mission of this sort until the end of his life, and it would become a major activity, eventually, of William Booth's Salvation Army.[1]

Mid-nineteenth-century humanitarianism culminates in the Salvation Army. Booth's great organization made no distinction between the worst in the community and the best, but had no illusions about the moral condition of the poor. Booth was not

---

[1] William Booth, 1829–1912, born, Nottingham in poor circumstances; little education; 1844, apprenticed to pawnbroker; began revivalist preaching after conversion; 1849, moved to London, and became lay preacher for Methodist New Connexion; 1855, married Catherine Mumford; 1861, broke with Methodists on issue of authority; left London as itinerant, independent revivalist; 1866, returned London and founded the East London Revival Society, Whitechapel, later called the 'Salvation Army.'

concerned about the cause of poverty, and would be invariably criticized by later reformers for his lack of discrimination among individuals in the administration of charity. He knew only that the degradation of poverty led to depravity, that millions of souls were in danger on that account, and that he must do something about it. He wrote in 1891:

> Were it not that I utterly repudiate as a fundamental denial of the essential principle of the Christian religion the popular pseudo-scientific doctrine that any man or woman is past saving by the grace of God and the power of the Holy Spirit, I would sometimes be disposed to despair when contemplating these victims of the devil. The doctrine of Heredity and the suggestion of Irresponsibility come perilously near re-establishing, on scientific basis, the awful dogma of Reprobation which has cast such a terrible shadow over the Christian Church.

> For thousands upon thousands of these poor wretches are, as Bishop South truly said, 'not so much born into this world as damned into it.' The bastard of the harlot, born in a brothel, suckled on gin, and familiar from earliest infancy with all the bestialities of debauch, violated before she is twelve, and driven into the streets by her mother a year or two later, what chance is there for such a girl in this world—I say nothing about the next?[2]

To save souls, therefore, one must feed bodies. To feed the hungry, for Booth, meant that the body must be fed before the spirit. But individual spiritual redemption was always the ultimate goal.[3]

The world of which the Salvation Army had been so typical began to change almost as the Army appeared. Booth's lonely stork-like figure standing in the mist of Whitechapel before 'The Vine' public house, banging a Bible against an upraised thigh and waving an umbrella to attract attention, symbolized an age that had almost passed in 1865 when he began his work. While in the next two decades the Salvation Army would grow and flourish, England was learning that destitution was a larger problem than the Army could solve.

[2] General William Booth, *In Darkest England and the Way Out*, New York, 1891, pp. 46–7.
[3] For a good short summary see: St John Ervine, *God's Soldier, General William Booth* (New York, 1935), II, 707–11.

First of all it was becoming clear that the condition of the poor living on the very doorsteps of London's West End was more hideous than anything that had been imagined, that the West End itself was an island in a swamp of filth, and second that the problem of poverty itself had changed. Hitherto the concern had been to protect the ratepayer from the expense of pauperism and to insure a labour market unhampered by competition from charity. There was an underlying assumption that at some wage level jobs existed for all. Few men cared what a subsistence wage meant in terms of the conditions of human life.

In the last quarter of the century the poor forced themselves upon the attention of the rich. They refused to accept the argument that capitalism made wide distinctions of wealth inevitable or that respectable poverty was an honorable estate. After 1885 they had the weapon of manhood franchise which reinforced the threat of revolutionary socialism. The great and near-great, the legislator, the merchant, the man of affairs, had long known that the world in which they had made their fortune had been less kind to many of their fellow citizens than it had been to them, that England was in fact, as Disraeli had put it, 'for the few, and for the very few.' There were signs that in one way or another the revolt of the many against the few might soon begin.

The eighties would be a decade of violence more frightening because the poor attacked the established order with a kind of intolerant anger reminiscent of nothing so much as the mob fury of European capitals of 1848. The protest riots of the eighties had nothing in common with the franchise and Chartist demonstrations of the eighteen-thirties and forties and of 1866. Then the mobs' anger had been directed at particular individuals, at the reactionary politicians whom all men of good and liberal minds could likewise denounce. Now the attack was on the established order itself, directed not at individuals but at property. To satisfy the poor, the rich could do nothing but give up their wealth.[4]

[4] For those who would look for a basis for the discontent of the eighties in economic statistics, the data is disappointing and unhelpful. Trade union unemployment, to be sure, reached a high of about 10½ per cent of those employed in 1885–6, but it had been considerably greater among trade unionists at the end of the eighteen-fifties without any comparable outbreaks of violence. George D. H. Cole and Raymond Postgate, *The British Common People, 1746–1946*, University Paperback Edition, London, 1961, p. 544. Moreover, these statistics, although frequently used, are quite unreliable. Only trade union members were covered and these amounted to less than one-fourth, perhaps one-

The problem bedevilling reformers of the eighties and nineties involved what was beginning to appear as perhaps a basic weakness of capitalism: that it was possible that destitution was the inevitable result of economic growth, that Henry George's equation of progress and poverty was, after all, true.[5] If it were, could anything be done about poverty beyond the abolition of capitalism? But if something were not done for the poor, would not the poor soon use the new power of the ballot to modify capitalist society in their own favour? 'Collectivism,' Sidney Webb had warned the Royal Commission on Labour in 1892, 'is the economic obverse of democracy.' Asked why, he answered:

It appears to me that if you allow the tramway conductor to vote he will not forever be satisfied with exercising that vote over such matters as the appointment of the Ambassador to Paris, or

fifth, of the total work force and the group least likely to be unemployed. (For a discussion see: William Beveridge, *Unemployment, A Problem of Industry*, rev. ed., London, 1931, pp. 16–28.) Most surprising is the fact that the percentage in receipt of poor law relief declined steadily from the middle of the nineteenth century down to World War I.

England and Wales

Decade	Lowest Number in Receipt of Poor Law Relief	Highest Number in Receipt of Poor Law Relief
1850–1859	444 per 10,000 of population	574 per 10,000 of population
1860–1869	429 per 10,000 of population	530 per 10,000 of population
1870–1879	295 per 10,000 of population	465 per 10,000 of population
1880–1889	283 per 10,000 of population	318 per 10,000 of population
1890–1899	256 per 10,000 of population	273 per 10,000 of population
1900–1909	241 per 10,000 of population	262 per 10,000 of population
1910–1914	203 per 10,000 of population	259 per 10,000 of population

Sir Ioan Gwilym Gibbon, 'The Public Social Services,' *Journal of the Royal Statistical Society*, C (part IV, 1937), 527. It may be important that while the crude proportion of paupers in the population declined steadily after 1850, the proportion of able-bodied paupers increased from 29 per 10,000 in 1877 to 46 per 10,000 in 1906. Geoffrey Drage, *The State and the Poor*, London, 1914, p. 113.

[5] The Fabians found this equation rather satisfactory. See Beatrice Potter's statement of the problem in Beatrice Webb, *My Apprenticeship*, 2 ed., London, 1945, p. 149.

Henry George, 1839–97, born, Philadelphia; elementary education, learned printer's trade; 1857, moved to California; 1865, became a journalist in San Francisco. Developed theory of 'single tax' on land as the original source of wealth to solve the problem of poverty accompanying progress. Publications: 1871, *Our Land and Land Policy*; 1880, *Progress and Poverty*; 1883, *Social Problems*; 1887, *Science of Political Economy*.

even the position of the franchise. He will realize that the forces
that keep him at work for sixteen hours a day for three shillings a
day are not the forces of hostile kings, of nobles, of priests; but
whatever forces they are he will, it seems to me, seek so far as
possible to control them by his vote. That is to say, he will more
and more seek to convert his political democracy into what one
may roughly term an industrial democracy, so that he may
obtain some kind of control as a voter over the conditions under
which he lives.[6]

Sidney Webb, suavely lecturing, with a slight Cockney lisp, to a
royal commission composed of some of Britain's wealthiest men
headed by the Duke of Devonshire, exemplified progressive social
thought of the eighties and nineties. Scientific reform presented as
great a contrast to the evangelical humanitarianism or deterrent
poor relief of the previous age as would the Labour Party to the
Chartists. If the older groups had pitied or despised the individual,
the modern reformer hated the condition. It was a crime to be
poor, for poverty wasted the individual and so harmed society. As
the framers of the Poor Law of 1834 had assumed the individual to
be poor because he was evil, and as such might be treated with a
generous helping of salutary harshness, the social reformer of the
eighties found the individual to be evil because he was poor,
and therefore a threat to the well-being of the social organism. If
social reform could remove the degrading aspects of poverty—the
filth, the hopelessness, the deterioration of family life—the nation
might yet save itself from a threat represented by the poor. One
might not eliminate poverty, but one could eliminate slums,

[6] Royal Commission on Labour, *Minutes of Evidence, Fourth Report*, November 15, 1892, p. 268. Quoted in Helen M. Lynd, *England in the Eighteen Eighties*, New York, 1945, pp. 185–6.

Sidney James Webb, Baron Passfield, 1859–1947, born, London; working-class family; educated abroad and at Birkbeck Institute and City of London College; 1878, entered Civil Service; 1885, called to the Bar; 1885, joined Fabian Society; contributor, *Fabian Essays in Socialism*, 1889. Married Beatrice Potter, 1858–1943, daughter of a wealthy railroad director in 1892, and published with her numerous articles and books on labour and economics. Member London County Council, 1892–1910; among founders of the London School of Economics, 1895. Served on Labour Party Executive, 1915–25 and published *Labour and the New Social Order*, 1918. Labour M.P. for Durham, 1922–9; President, Board of Trade, 1924, under Ramsay MacDonald's first Government; elevated to Peerage in MacDonald's second Government, 1929; Secretary of State for Dominion Affairs and for the Colonies, 1929–30; Secretary of State for the Colonies, 1930–1.

ignorance, and squalor. It was not dangerous that the poor were lazy, but that they were dirty. In place of the evangelical preacher, who required attendance at prayers in return for a meal, the new missionary to the East End would be the inspector of drains.[7]

I

As the eighties opened, public attention was turned towards the question of social reform by the English publication in January, 1881, of Henry George's *Progress and Poverty*, the sale of which Kegan Paul reported was 'the most astonishing success he ever knew.'[8] In the same year appeared H. M. Hyndman's[9] ringing answer to Disraeli, *England For All*, followed in 1883 by *Socialism Made Plain*. In 1882 and again in 1884, Henry George visited England to promote before large audiences his idea for the taxation of the unearned increment in land value, converting to socialism, among many others, George Bernard Shaw.

The present discontent was unprecedented, commented the *Quarterly Review* in October, 1883, in a review article based on

[7] The economist Alfred Marshall put the difference clearly to the Royal Commission on the Aged Poor:

> The problem of 1834 was the problem of pauperism, the problem of 1893 is the problem of poverty; that a man ought not to be allowed to live in a bad home, that extreme poverty ought to be regarded, not indeed as a crime, but as a thing so detrimental to the State that it should not be endured.

Quoted in Charles L. Mowat, *The Charity Organization Society, 1869–1913*, London, 1961, p. 124. The evangelist did not, of course, yield without a fight and would remain the most noticeable, if not the most influential, figure in poor relief until well after World War I. The *Athenaeum*'s review of the seventh volume of Charles Booth's study of the London poor, *Religious Influences*, concluded in 1903:

> One half of London seems engaged in entertaining the other half with soup and bread with a view to its subsequent spiritual edification. In a very real meaning the impression is driven home that if but a fraction of the energy expended in London had been extended in Tyre and Sidon they would have repented in sackcloth and ashes.

Athenaeum, May 16, 1903, p. 65.

[8] Herman Ausubel, *In Hard Times: Reformers Among the Late Victorians*, New York, 1960, p. 107.

[9] Henry Mayers Hyndman, 1842–1921, born, London; well-to-do family; educated privately and at Trinity College, Cambridge. Publications: 1881, *England For All*; 1883, *The Historical Basis for Socialism*; 1896, *Economics of Socialism*. 1884, founder of Marxist 'Social Democratic Federation'; 1886, tried and acquitted for part in West End riots. During war served on Consumers' Council at Ministry of Food. Stood for Parliament several times without success.

England For All and *Socialism Made Plain*, but surveying generally the astonishing proliferation of radical writing. Even though Henry George's exceptionally popular books sounded like 'a joint production of Marat and a dissenting minister,' the present agitation could not be compared with Chartism. It was less the result of suffering than of 'speculative conviction.' If it seemed less ferocious than before, it was 'not that it has lost strength, but that it has gained in conviction.' English society, concluded the journal gloomily, may not be a house on fire, but it certainly is a house 'that is full of exceedingly inflammable materials.'[10]

Just as these unhappy reflections were published, there appeared perhaps the most influential single piece of writing about the poor that England has ever seen. In October, 1883, the London Congregational Union, sponsored by the Reverend Andrew Mearns, published over the name of William C. Preston a thin pamphlet entitled, *The Bitter Cry of Outcast London: An Inquiry Into the Condition of the Abject Poor*. *The Bitter Cry* was essentially a primitive attempt at house-to-house surveying and was by no means limited to the East End. Indeed, most of the examples cited in its few pages were drawn from streets lying west of the City. There were descriptions of hideous overcrowding in the area around Leicester Square and Seven Dials. 'In one cellar a sanitary inspector reports finding a father, mother, three children, and four pigs!'[11] In another street nearby were seven people living in one underground kitchen and a little dead child lying in the same room.[12] There were reports of one street with thirty-five houses, of which thirty-two were brothels.[13] In Euston Road an investigator found one public house for each one hundred people. Concerning wages, *The Bitter Cry* reported that the going rate for a gross of matchboxes was $2\frac{1}{2}$d., the maker finding his own paste. Children could earn 1d. to 2d. a peck for shelling peas in Covent Garden and 3d. a dozen for shirt finishing. Rents, typically, were 3s. 6d. to 4s. a week or 8d. for a night. The effect of municipal housing and sanitary regulation appeared to have been only to raise rents.[14]

Mearns followed *The Bitter Cry* in December, 1883, with an article in the *Contemporary Review* in which he emphasized that

---

[10] 'Socialism in England,' *Quarterly Review*, CLVI (October, 1883), 356–8.
[11] William C. Preston, *The Bitter Cry of Outcast London: An Inquiry Into the Conditions of the Abject Poor*, London, 1883, p. 5.
[12] *Ibid.*, p. 5.   [13] *Ibid.*, p. 7.   [14] *Ibid.*, pp. 9–10.

much of the filth, squalor and overcrowding discovered was altogether in violation of the law. The Public Health Act of 1875 and the various Housing Acts gave municipalities ample power to enforce cleanliness. He said that he had received many letters since the publication of *The Bitter Cry*. He cited one in particular from the Reverend S. Barnett, Vicar of St Jude's, Whitechapel, urging first of all enforcement of legislation already on the books. 'Cleaning can be *enforced*,' he quoted from Barnett's letter.[15] The enormous impact of *The Bitter Cry* is the more surprising because the condition of the London poor had been better described in several earlier works without public response. Henry Mayhew's *London Labour and the London Poor*, first published in three volumes in 1851 and reissued in 1861 as *Mayhew's London*, gave a comprehensive, and relatively objective, picture of the London underworld that would not be equalled until Charles Booth's great survey in the 1890's. In 1872 appeared *London, A Pilgrimage*, by Blanchard Gerrold, illustrated by Gustave Doré. In this classic work, which has proved a mine for book illustrators, Doré offered graphic proof to West End Londoners that at their very doorstep existed an inferno swarming with tormented souls.

The Victorian conscience, pricked in 1883 by *The Bitter Cry*, had been left at ease in the seventies by the far larger and less emotional classics of Mayhew and Gerrold, as well as by a host of earlier works. The reasons for this delayed awakening were first, that Englishmen were aware of the dark shape of social democracy as they had not been a decade earlier, and secondly and perhaps most important, that in August, 1883, W. T. Stead replaced John Morley as editor of the *Pall Mall Gazette* and chose to make *The Bitter Cry* pamphlet the basis of his inaugural experiment in the 'new journalism.' It was 'the first great *coup* which we made in

[15] Andrew Mearns, 'Outcast London,' *Contemporary Review*, XLIV (December, 1883), 924–33. Mearns pointed out in a note at the end of the article that he had seen some statements printed 'to the effect that two others who acted as my assistants are credited with the pamphlet.' He wished to make clear that he had been helped in the investigation by the Rev. James Monro of Limerick and in the literary work by the Rev. W. C. Preston of Hull, but the 'inception' was all his and the investigation carried out 'under my direction.' (*Ibid.*, p. 933.) The authorship of *The Bitter Cry* seems never to have been cleared up. Authorities generally are divided between Mearns and Preston, although R. C. K. Ensor attributes the pamphlet to G. R. Sims. R. C. K. Ensor, *England, 1870–1914*, Oxford, 1936, p. 127. Helen M. Lynd credits Mearns, *England in the Eighties*, p. 147. Elsie Gulley credits Preston, *Joseph Chamberlain and English Social Politics*, New York, 1926, p. 252.

the *Pall Mall Gazette*,' he wrote to Alfred Milner in 1890.[16] The influence of *The Bitter Cry* seemed endless as it was picked up and broadcast by Stead. 'Where is the man,' Stead asked, 'who will preach a new crusade against the crying evils of our time?' In response the *Pall Mall Gazette* was 'overwhelmed' with congratulatory correspondence,[17] and university men began to trickle into the East End to form what would become Toynbee Hall.[18] England suffered, said Canon Henry Scott Holland, 'one of those spasms of pity' that swept over the nation and usually died away.[19] But the effect of *The Bitter Cry* did not die away. The conditions that evoked the frightened and horrified response in the first place demanded that something be done, that Parliament take action, that further investigations be undertaken.

The following month in the *National Review*, Lord Salisbury, who would become the next Conservative Prime Minister, published what was for the time a sensational article observing that the difference between the lowest possible cost for adequate working-class dwellings and the highest possible rent the poorest of the working class could pay should perhaps be made up by government subsidy. He suggested that the government show the way by

[16] Quoted in Frederic Whyte, *The Life of W. T. Stead* (New York, n.d.), II, 13.
William Thomas Stead, 1849–1912, born, Embleton, Northumberland; father, a Congregational minister; educated at home. 1863, apprenticed in counting house, Newcastle-Upon-Tyne. 1870, regular contributor, *Northern Echo*, Liberal daily, Darlington; 1871, editor; 1880, assistant editor, *Pall Mall Gazette*, under John Morley; 1883, replaced Morley as editor with Alfred Milner as assistant editor; began 'The New Journalism' of sensation; 1890, founded *Review of Reviews*. Went down on the *Titanic*.

[17] J. A. R. Pimlott, 'Toynbee Hall and the Settlement Movement,' *Contemporary Review*, CXLVIII (April, 1935), 448.

[18] Mrs Barnett and J. A. R. Pimlott are most explicit about the influence of *The Bitter Cry* on Toynbee Hall. Henrietta O. Barnett, 'The Beginning of Toynbee Hall,' in Samuel A. and Henrietta O. Barnett, *Toward Social Reform*, New York, 1909, p. 249. J. A. R. Pimlott, *Toynbee Hall, Fifty Years of Social Progress, 1884–1934*, London, 1935, pp. 29–30. The famous meeting at St John's College, at which Samuel Barnett proposed what the *Oxford Magazine* described as a 'new Oxford Movement,' occurred on November 17, 1883, a month after the appearance of *The Bitter Cry*.

[19] Henry Scott Holland, *A Bundle of Memories*, London, 1915, p. 89.
Henry Scott Holland, 1847–1918, born, Ledbury, Herts; aristocratic family; educated privately, Eton, and 1866, Balliol, Oxford. 1870–84, Senior Studentship, Christ Church, Oxford; 1872, ordained; 1884, Canon, St Paul's. Supporter of Oxford House in Bethnal Green and Christ Church Mission in Poplar. 1890, a founder of the Christian Social Union. High Church Radical, Liberal in politics. 1895–1912, editor, *Commonwealth*, organ of the Christian Social Union; 1911, Regius professor of divinity, Oxford.

subsidizing houses for some of the worst paid of its own employees in the post office, police, and customs houses.[20] A proposal of this sort coming from the head of the clan of Cecil and the leader of the opposition in the House of Lords could not remain unnoticed. In any case, Joseph Chamberlain, the Liberal President of the Board of Trade, had no intention of permitting his party to be outflanked on the left by the Conservatives.[21] He answered in December in the *Fortnightly Review* with an article bearing the same title as Salisbury's. 'Social reform is in the air,' he said. 'Never before in our history were wealth and the evidences of wealth so abundant; never before was luxurious living so general and so wanton in its display; and never before was the misery of the very poor more intense, or the conditions of their daily life more hopeless and degraded.' Chamberlain remarked ironically that it was a sign of the times that Lord Salisbury would attack the institution of private property, but he urged his readers to understand that the wide circulation and acceptance of *Progress and Poverty* among the working classes was 'a fact full of significance and warning,' and that it was impossible to ignore 'the terrible instances quoted in *The Bitter Cry of Outcast London.* . . .'[22]

Although the more discriminating knew that the 'bitter cry' was for work, not housing, and that poverty could not be cured by cleanliness,[23] Salisbury moved in the House of Lords on February 22, 1884, the appointment of a commission to investigate the housing of the working classes. He feared, as he put it, not only a

[20] Lord Salisbury, 'Labourers' and Artizans' Dwellings,' *National Review*, II (November, 1883), 301–16.

[21] Joseph Chamberlain, 1836–1914, born, London, substantial middle-class family; educated privately and at University College School. 1852, entered family manufacturing business, moved to Birmingham, successfully expanded business interests. 1874, retired to devote full time to public life. 1869, member Birmingham City Council; 1873–5, Mayor of Birmingham. 1876, M.P., Liberal, Birmingham; 1880–5, President of the Board of Trade; 1886, President of the Local Government Board; 1886, broke with Liberals; 1895–1903, Unionist Secretary of State for the Colonies. 1903, resigned on Tariff Reform; 1906, retired due to ill health.

[22] Joseph Chamberlain, 'Labourers' and Artisans' Dwellings,' *Fortnightly Review*, XXXIV, n.s. (December, 1883), 761–5.

[23] 'The Dwellings of the Poor,' *Westminster Review*, CXXI, o.s. (January, 1884), 137–51. The *Westminster Review* printed the names of some men of 'discrimination' qualified to give information and to distribute donations to the poor. Several would soon become better known: Samuel A. Barnett, St Jude's, Whitechapel, the Rev. J. B. Brown, East London Tabernacle, the Rev. G. T. Cull-Bennet, St John's Vicarage, Commercial Road.

physical or material deterioration of the poor as a result of poor housing, but the existence of conditions 'deleterious and ruinous to the moral progress and development of the race to which we belong.'[24] Thus the immediate, tangible result of *The Bitter Cry* was the Royal Commission on the Housing of the Working Class, under the chairmanship of Sir Charles Dilke, which reported later in the year that housing in the United Kingdom was in many places certainly unfit for human habitation. The commissioners felt, nevertheless, as had many before the investigation took place, that the failure lay in administration rather than in legislation, and that although new legislation would be of use, the real need was an aroused public opinion.[25]

Public opinion would soon be aroused, although not, to be sure, over the question of housing. While Stead persisted in his revelations of the degradation of the poor in the East End, culminating in July of 1885 with the famous series, 'The Maiden Tribute of Modern Babylon,' which earned him a stay in jail, and *The Bitter Cry* continued to have an enormous sale through the year 1884, the problem of the poor, as the *Westminster Review* correctly inferred, was not housing but employment. And the winter of 1885–6 brought hard times and unemployment to a peak. The distress caused an outbreak of violence among the poor which altered for ever the relations between the two worlds of the British nation.[26] In the Trafalgar Square riot of February 8, 1886, the old humanitarianism died in a spasm of terror. The poor were no longer to be pitied and to be helped from Christian generosity. They now were a menace to be bought off, and while the various relief funds and the Salvation Army would linger and indeed thrive for a time as vehicles to transmit the ransom, the day of the indiscriminate charity they represented was over.

The Trafalgar Square riot is frequently dismissed as a mere breaking of windows in Pall Mall resulting in the next few days in

---

[24] *Hansard's Parliamentary Debates*, Series 3, CCLXXIV (February 22, 1884), col. 1690. The Prince of Wales, the future Edward VII, who became a member of the commission, made his only speech in the House of Lords upon this occasion. *Ibid.*, col. 1693–4.

[25] Quoted in George Newman, *The Health of the State*, London, 1907, p. 174.

[26] Asa Briggs has recently suggested that the publication of Arnold Toynbee's *Lectures on the Industrial Revolution* in 1884 may have helped to break down the prevailing faith in *laissez faire*. Asa Briggs, *A Study of the Work of Seebohm Rowntree, 1871–1954*, London, 1961, p. 54.

an increased contribution to the Lord Mayor's Relief Fund.[27] It amounted to a good deal more than this. The trouble began in the middle of the day of February 8, 1886, as nothing more than a demonstration of the unemployed in Trafalgar Square. The police, who were clearly unprepared for violence, attempted to press the demonstrators around the bottom of Nelson's column. For a long time they were successful in keeping the mob quiet, even though it was rallied to action by John Burns of Battersea. He stood between the lions on the base of the monument waving a red flag. When the police attempted to clear the pavement, Burns appeared in the roadway above the square in front of the National Gallery, and began to harangue the crowd. There was a 'great roar of voices as the man with the red flag mounted the stonework overlooking the Square,' where, in a stentorian voice, he declared that to hang the House of Commons, the landlords and the railway directors 'would be a waste of good rope.'[28] At this point, the mob of unemployed found themselves in competition with a demonstration of tariff reformers at the south side of the square promoting duties on foodstuffs to revive agriculture. The unemployed, crowded from the south and drawn to the upper side of the square by Burns, now began to disperse into Pall Mall, where the crowd appeared to divide, and a number of workers drifted off. But a large mass of men under no apparent leadership moved up Pall Mall and crossed Waterloo Place.[29] Almost immediately they were stung by the jeers of a number of young men standing in the windows of the Carlton

[27] For instance, Cole and Postgate, *British Common People*, p. 422; Ensor, *England*, p. 100.

[28] *The Times* (London), February 9, 1886.

John Elliott Burns, 1858–1943, born, South Lambeth; working-class family; educated South Lambeth night schools; skilled engineer, participated in trade union movement; Delegate of Amalgamated Society of Engineers to T.U.C., 1890. Dropped out of A.S.E., 1895. Joined H. M. Hyndman's Democratic Federation, 1884, before it became Social Democratic Federation that year. Dropped out of S.D.F., 1889. In addition to participating in the Trafalgar Square riots, 1886, in November, 1887, he was arrested with R. B. Cunninghame Graham on 'Bloody Sunday' for trying to force his way into Trafalgar Square. 1889, with Tom Mann, led London dock strike. 1889, bolted Social Democratic Federation and formed Battersea Labour League, essentially a personal political vehicle; 1892, independent Labour M.P., Battersea; 1895, elected as 'Socialist'; 1910, elected as Liberal. Member, London County Council for Battersea, 1889–1907; M.P., 1892–1918; President, Local Government Board, 1905–14; President, Board of Trade, 1914; resigned from the Government upon declaration of war.

[29] *The Times*, February 9, 1886.

Club. The workmen retaliated with oaths and stones, breaking a large number of windows. They did no further damage in Pall Mall, but when they turned into St James's Street they began systematically to break windows. '. . . all the clubs on the left,' reported *The Times*, 'without distinction of party, shared in the howls and the breakages—the mob apparently acting on the principle of the Revolutionary Social Democratic League, that they were now to regard all the upper classes as their enemies. . . .' *The Times* noted that an especially 'significant volley of stones' fell against the windows of the New University Club, which had recently expelled Mr Hyndman.[30]

The mob appeared to be driven to hysteria by its own noise and destructiveness. When it reached the corner of St James's Street and Piccadilly, it began to loot. The ground floor of the Bath Hotel and a jewellery shop nearby were plundered. Moving west along Piccadilly, the mob divided; part of it turned north into Mayfair, boiling up Half Moon Street, breaking windows and pillaging. 'Individual policemen were overpowered and cast down. The well-dressed public fled at the mere hubbub of voices. . . .'[31] Others continued down along Piccadilly smashing more windows, particularly at the Duke of Cambridge's on the corner of Park Lane. From here they surged into Hyde Park.

> Here the mob stopped carriages, and turned the occupants out of them, and it is stated that in one instance the coachman was stripped of his livery and some roughs jumped into the vehicle. Several of the police who ventured to interfere were pelted with stones and obliged to retreat from the overpowering numbers of the crowd.[32]

Tiring of this, the mob left Hyde Park at the then-standing Standhope Gate, passing through Dean (now Deanery) Street, where they joined the mass of men already raging through the area south of Grosvenor Square.

> Tradesmen and others residing in this street [South Audley] were almost terror-stricken by the approach of the overwhelming crowd, and to offer any resistance to their violence was altogether useless. There was nothing to be done but to stand by and see the windows crashing and the goods extracted by the marauders.[33]

[30] *The Times*, February 9, 1886.   [31] *Ibid.*   [32] *Ibid.*   [33] *Ibid.*

Some tradesmen, *The Times* reported later, were ruined. Messrs Purvis and Bishop, for instance, clockmakers in South Audley Street, reported damage and loss of £4,000. They had been forced to stand by and watch the plundering.[34] The crowd gradually flowed north through Mayfair along North Audley Street, where the merchants had prudently shuttered their windows. Upon reaching Oxford Street, the men began to drift back towards the East End.

London had never experienced anything like the riot of February 8. Most frightening was the fact that hitherto there had always been respect for private, if not government property. The West End, reported *The Times*, 'presented an appearance hitherto unknown to London in modern times. The Chartist demonstration of 1848 was sufficiently alarming, but there was no preaching the gospel of revolution even then, and there was certainly no such application of its principle as was witnessed on Monday.'[35] Especially frightening was the ferocity and boldness of the mob and its unwillingness to heed the orders of the police. Indeed, it was remarked that the mob noted the timidity of the police and grew even bolder as it found the authorities unwilling to interfere. 'Such a state of excitement and alarm has rarely been experienced in the metropolis. . . . In the West End yesterday there was something little short of panic. There seemed to be a general sense of insecurity. . . .'[36] Above all was the indiscriminate anger of the mob against individuals whose only offence was the appearance of wealth.

It is said that in Piccadilly the first attempt was made upon a carriage which in this instance carried the wife of an ex-Cabinet Minister, but appreciating the peril of the situation she gave instant orders to the coachman who, whipping up his horses, forced an opening through the crowd and escaped. The occupants of other carriages in Hyde Park were not so fortunate. The carriages were stopped, windows smashed, and jewels violently torn from the necks of ladies wearing them, who were then

[34] *The Times*, February 10, 1886.
[35] *Ibid.* For a generally good account of the riots by a participant, see Henry M. Hyndman, *The Record of an Adventurous Life*, London, 1911, pp. 400–7. Hyndman makes some mistakes of detail. He dates the riots, for instance, in 'the autumn of 1886.'
[36] *Ibid.*

turned out of their vehicles. Some of the footmen, on seeing the carriages surrounded, never waited to ascertain whether their services were of any value, but got down and bolted precipitately. Seeing some of the vehicles damaged, the police on duty prevented the carriages from entering the Park, and many were thus happily saved from the outrage and loss which others had suffered.[37]

By February 10, *The Times* was filled with letters complaining of the lack of action by authorities. There were attacks on the Home Secretary, Hugh Childers, who had been in office only five days. Why hadn't the police done something? There were indignation meetings among West End merchants, two hundred being present at a meeting in the Grosvenor Riding School in South Street under the chairmanship of Lord Dorchester, whose residence facing Standhope Gate had narrowly escaped attack. An immediate scapegoat was Sir Edmund Henderson, Chief Commissioner of Police of London. His resignation was eventually requested to 'quiet the disturbed nerves of well-to-do Londoners.'[38] Reports of the riot in the European press betrayed a certain gratification that London now tasted the danger European capitals had long known. A report from Madrid on February 9 noted smugly that in no other city would a riot of working men have produced such an effect. 'Here we have the Civil Guard, which is a guarantee against such surprises. . . .'[39]

The Times leader of February 9 had closed by remarking that a fund had been established at Mansion House for the relief of the unemployed. 'The Lord Mayor's Fund, dispensed by skilled almoners, should be supported so long as it is shown it does not pauperize.'[40] The fund had, in fact, been established some weeks earlier, but contributions had come in slowly. Within the next few days, however, it jumped up to £70,000. This sum was dispensed with an undiscriminating prodigality that not only prevented any effective use of the money itself but went a long way towards discrediting the principle of voluntary charity.[41]

[37] *The Times*, February 10, 1886.

[38] Lord George Hamilton, *Parliamentary Reminiscences and Reflections, 1886–1906* (London, 1922), II, 14. See Childers' statement to the House of Commons, *Hansard*, CCCII (February 22, 1886), cols. 909–10.

[39] Quoted in *The Times*, December 10, 1886.   [40] *The Times*, February 9, 1886.

[41] C. L. Mowat describes the distribution of the Mansion House Fund in 1886 as a 'catastrophe.' Mowat, *Charity Organization Society*, p. 132.

The attempt of the West End to pay ransom to the East End, represented by the Lord Mayor's Fund, was only the most dramatic, by no means the most important, result of the Trafalgar Square riot. The need, the clear demand of the mob, was for employment. Men did not want charity, but work. On the day after the riot, Lord Brabazon wrote to *The Times* saying that he had received a cheque, apparently within hours after the beginning of the riot, for £1,000. He had sought the assistance of Mr Arnold White, 'whose experience in such matters is well known,' and was at the moment putting seventy to eighty men to work laying out gardens and playgrounds. Brabazon himself suggested emigration as the final answer.[42]

A second proposal, widely supported and more immediately practicable, was for the establishment of labour registries. Many writers of letters in the days immediately following the riots proposed that philanthropic organizations offer their services to bring employers and unemployed workmen together. At the time of the riots there were two registries, at Egham and at Staines, already in operation. These, having opened in 1885, found their services called upon with reasonable frequency. In the next several weeks sixteen more registries were opened in London but disappointingly little use was made of them. A report published a year later, in March, 1887, showed that two had had no applications for work whatever, and although 1,061 men had applied through registries only 674 had been found situations. Furthermore, of the 674 men placed, 325 passed through the Egham registry.[43]

The Trafalgar Square riots mark, nevertheless, the serious

[42] *The Times*, February 9, 1886. Lord Brabazon would continue to promote emigration both in the interest of peopling the empire and in solving the problem of unemployment. See, for instance: Lord Brabazon, 'State Directed Colonization,' *National Review*, X (June, 1887), 525–37. Emigration and the white empire would become an important constituent of the imperialist creed by the turn of the century.

Arnold White, 1848–1925, popular authority and polemicist on social questions; wrote as 'Vanoc' in the *Referee*. Agent for Baron de Hirsch in the czar's negotiations for Jewish land colonization in Argentina. Supported National Service and naval reform after the Boer War. An intimate friend of Lord Fisher. Four times unsuccessful candidate for Parliament.

[43] The registry at Egham, Surrey, appears to have been the first true labour exchange in Great Britain. It was founded by Nathaniel L. Cohen in February, 1885. Cohen was an active promoter of exchanges in the months after the Trafalgar Square riots. See his letters to *The Times* of February 9 and May 8, 1886, and Nathaniel L. Cohen, 'Free Registries and the Marketing of Labour,' *National Review*, X (March, 1887), 60.

beginning of the movement towards private labour exchanges in Great Britain. While skilled workers were suspicious of them, and employers used them only as a last resort, the exchanges came now to be a fixture of urban working-class existence. The Salvation Army became an active sponsor of labour exchanges during the nineties, opening its first office in January, 1890. The Army would remain important in the field until the advent of municipal exchanges with the passage of the Labour Bureau (London) Act of 1902.

The most significant result of the mob violence of February 8 was Joseph Chamberlain's Local Government Board circular issued on March 15, 1886, which encouraged local authorities to undertake public work as a means of relieving unemployment. This circular expressed for the first time, however reluctantly and hesitantly, the acceptance by the government of the principle that unemployment was a problem of society, not the result of want of virtue, or of laziness in an individual.[44]

After refusing to see Burns and Hyndman, who proposed to question him about what the Local Government Board planned to do for the unemployed, Chamberlain announced on February 9, the day following the riot, that he believed public works were 'not within the province of the Local Government Board.'[45] Nevertheless a little more than a month later appeared his circular permitting, although not requiring, the local authorities to set up works projects to relieve unemployment. Chamberlain specified: (1) that the work provided should not have the stigma of pauperism, (2) that it should be of such kind that the unskilled could perform it, (3) that it should not compete with existing employment, and (4) that the pay should be slightly less than that given for comparable private employment.

The circular was reissued the next year, again in 1891, 1892, 1893, and in 1895. In 1895, point four was dropped. Although there can be no doubt that much of the work performed under authority provided by the Local Government Board circular was

---

[44] The circular, wrote a spokesman of the Charity Organization Society, was the 'first breach in the unity of the Poor Law.' William A. Bailward, 'Some Recent Developments of Poor Relief,' *Economic Journal*, XXII (December, 1912), 544. See also Joseph L. Cohen, *Insurance Against Unemployment*, London, 1921, pp. 161–2.

[45] 'The Demagogues and the Local Government Board,' *The Times*, February 10, 1886.

costly and useless,[46] Chamberlain's departure set the pattern for government attempts to solve the unemployment problem for the next twenty years which culminated in the Unemployed Workmen Act of 1905. For the first time the Government took responsibility for the welfare of citizens in some other form than through the deterrent poor law, and even though the failure of the Unemployed Workmen Act would discredit artificially provided employment as a means for solving the problem of poverty, the precedent of government responsibility by then was too strong to be denied.[47]

The wave of fear that swept over London with the riots of February subsided, although slowly. But if terror died away, distrust did not. Lord Elton's assessment of the demonstration on February 8 deserves to be repeated.

> This was not the last riot in Trafalgar Square at which the Socialists would assist. But hereafter even head-breaking would be but head-breaking: never again the glimpse of chaos, the sudden dread which had clutched for a moment at the heart of London. London would not lose its head again, although there would remain, no doubt, many citizens who privately believed that the revolution might yet be.[48]

[46] A Mansion House conference in 1888 examined the experience of the Public Gardens Association in finding work for the unemployed. Altogether work had been offered to 456 men. Of these, sixty-two had failed to appear, 134 had been dismissed for misconduct, absence, or incapacity, 164 were designated as 'unhelpable,' and ninety-six of the 456, or 22 per cent, were usefully aided. Cited in Mowat, *Charity Organization Society*, p. 135.

[47] R. C. K. Ensor has pointed out, 'it is symptomatic that the word "unemployed" used as a noun is first recorded by the *Oxford English Dictionary* from the year 1882; the word "unemployment" from 1888.' Ensor, *England*, p. 112.

[48] Godfrey Elton, *England Arise, A Study of the Pioneering Days of the Labour Movement*, London, 1931, p. 135. W. S. Adams recalls that his father kept in his desk the red and white armband and the baton that he had been issued in the mid-eighties when he enlisted with other young stockbrokers to serve as a special constable in case of working-class revolution. William S. Adams, *Edwardian Portraits*, London, 1957, p. 6. Twenty-one months later, on November 13, 1887, Trafalgar Square was the scene of a second riot, designated usually as 'Bloody Sunday.' The aim on this occasion was simply a protest at the nakedness of Irish Nationalist M.P., William O'Brien, who in prison refused to wear prisoner's garb and was punished by the guards by being deprived of his own trousers. 'O'Brien's Breeches!' was the cry, not unemployment. Sir Charles Warren, the new head of the Metropolitan Police, prudently refused a parade permit and ordered out the Horseguards as well as the police, this time in force. The authorities took no chance of losing control of the crowd. The Horseguards rode briskly through the mob and numerous heads were split, eventually causing a

2

While the majority of the inhabitants of London's West End were being made aware for the first time of the poor's impatience with their lot, some members of the middle class were already planning solutions to the problems of destitution. Before the end of the century the organizations that represented scientific social reform in Great Britain had sorted themselves into three groups. First, not perhaps in size but in influence on the New Liberalism, was the settlement house movement, founded and to some extent symbolized by Canon Samuel A. Barnett of Toynbee Hall.[49] The second, the Fabian Society, was until the end of the century largely a planning and agitational group, confining its direct political activity chiefly to local government. Although the Fabian Society had an influential and intellectual following, it saw poverty, and the social reform that poverty made necessary, only as an incidental by-product of the capitalist system, which it sought to overthrow. The third, the Charity Organization Society, had been in existence since 1869 and was the first representative in England of non-evangelical, professionally-minded social work. Each group had some effect on social legislation. Of the three, the settlement house movement typifies best the transition from the old to the new humanitarianism and should be described first.

One Englishman who neither feared nor despised the poor, who was neither sentimental nor scientific, who had nothing in common either with the Salvation Army or the Fabian Society, demanding neither prayer nor washing of hands before a meal, was Samuel A. Barnett. Barnett had been one of the little group who sought in 1869 to end wasteful and competitive giving to the poor by found-

couple of deaths. Joseph Burgess, *John Burns: The Rise and Progress of a Right Honourable*, Glasgow, 1911, pp. 99–103. In 1887 Burgess was a correspondent for Stead on the *Pall Mall Gazette* which, of course, supported the strikers. The state of public opinion by this time was such that the *Gazette* suffered severely in advertising and circulation for its stand. J. W. Robertson-Scott, *The Life and Death of a Newspaper*, London, 1952, pp. 148–9.

[49] Samuel Augustus Barnett, 1844–1913, born, Bristol; wealthy merchant family; educated at home and Wadham College, Oxford. 1865, curate at St Mary's, Bryanston Square; 1869, a founder Charity Organization Society; 1873, vicar at St Jude's, Whitechapel; 1894, Canon of Bristol; 1906, Canon of Westminster. 1875, promoted the Artisans' Dwellings Act; 1875–1904, Poor Law Guardian, Whitechapel Parish; 1884–1906, Warden of Toynbee Hall. Publications: 1888, *Practicable Socialism*; 1907, *Religion and Progress*; 1911, *Religion and Politics*.

ing the Charity Organization Society. Three years later, at the request of Bishop Jackson of London, he had accepted the parish of St Jude's in Whitechapel. It is the 'worst parish in my diocese,' he was told, 'inhabited mainly by a criminal population, and one which has, I fear, been much corrupted by the dole.'[50]

Barnett realized the danger in the separation of classes in England and sought to bridge the gap between the two worlds into which the nation was divided. Religion, he argued, was the one force that could bring together the antagonistic estates and turn them into fellow workers.[51] Years before the outbreaks of the eighties, he had come to understand the meaning of poverty to those in that condition, the helplessness it bred, and the resentment against those who neither felt nor understood it. He saw the masses as his personal responsibility. 'The sense of sin has been the starting point of progress,' he was fond of saying.[52] Ignorance bred suspicion; suspicion bred hostility. His personal mission to the East End was an attempt to show the poor that someone from the outside did care, not only for their spiritual redemption but for their practical grievances.

Religion for Canon Barnett was not theology, but love and energy. It meant calling the attention of the authorities to the plight of his neighbours in Whitechapel, or taking Sir Richard Cross, Disraeli's Home Secretary, on a tour of the East End to show him the condition of slum property which resulted in an amendment to the Artisans' Dwellings Act. It meant vigorously and continually protesting to the local authorities the laxity in enforcement of sanitary and police regulations. Everywhere the researcher turns, there in the background appears the smiling, homely, wispily bearded face of the 'pale little clergyman from Whitechapel' whom Georges Clemenceau designated as one of the three greatest men he met in England. There is Barnett converting Charles Booth to old age pensions in 1883,[53] breaking the monopoly of the Charity Organization Society on social work in 1886, counselling statesmen on social reform. One can sympathize with the plaint of Beatrice Webb, then Beatrice Potter. 'How can I make my readers see, as they are engraved on my memory, the figures of

---

[50] Pimlott, *Toynbee Hall*, p. 15.

[51] Samuel A. Barnett, 'Class Divisions,' *Commonwealth*, VIII (November, 1903), 349.

[52] Pimlott, *Toynbee Hall*, p. 1.

[53] Webb, *Apprenticeship*, p. 179.

B*

Samuel and Henrietta Barnett, and the impression they made on philanthropic workers and social investigators of London in the "80s"?'[54]

The influence of Samuel Barnett on the next generation of British social reformers can hardly be overestimated. In the establishment of Toynbee Hall, his greatest achievement, he created an outpost of educated enthusiasm in the East End, where the best young men England bred could live and carry on and enlarge his work of bringing the poor out of their dangerous isolation. In Toynbee Hall he built a permanent institution to bridge the gap between the East and the West, one that would permit young men from the universities to serve God by serving their fellow men, by providing leadership, energy, and intelligence to mitigate the hopeless daily round of the poor. By making art, culture, and education available, he let some of the light of civilization into darkest London. Finally, perhaps most important of all, in educating the poor, men of Toynbee Hall were themselves educated and carried with them into the universities, the civil service, and the House of Commons a knowledge of the realities of poverty derived from intimate daily contact with the slums.

The idea of East End settlements for the moral guidance of the poor by no means originated with Samuel Barnett. Individuals, notably John R. Green and Edward Denison, under the influence of Christian Socialism, had settled in the slums in the sixties. Salvation Army missions had become common in the seventies. In 1878, six years after Barnett had gone to St Jude's, Bishop Jackson sent Walsham How to the East End as a specially designated 'Bishop of East London' to effect a spiritual revival,[55] and in 1882 the Church Army appeared as a sub-committee of the Church Parochial Mission Society.[56]

In this tradition then, but as a personal project, Samuel Barnett began to collect about him in the late seventies and early eighties a heterogeneous set of young men, brilliant Oxford scholars, generally with a connexion at Jowett's Balliol, like Alfred Milner and Arnold Toynbee, and self-educated working-men such as the deeply religious and devoted Frederick Rogers. Around this

[54] Webb, *Apprenticeship*, p. 180.
[55] Pimlott, 'Toynbee Hall,' *Contemporary Review* (April, 1935), 447.
[56] Albert E. Reffold, *Wilson Carlile and the Church Army*, 3rd ed., London, 1928, p. 78.

nucleus of volunteers, Barnett proposed in 1883 to build a permanent institution to carry on his work among the poor. Reform could not be conducted from the outside, concluded Barnett, in making a formal proposal for a university settlement on November 17, 1883, at St John's College, Oxford. It was essential to 'live within sight of the poor.'

Many schemes of reform I have known, but, out of eleven years experience, I would say that none touches the root of the evil which does not *bring helper and helped into friendly relations*. Vain will be higher education, music, art, or even the Gospel, unless they are clothed in the life of brother men—'It took the life to make God known.' Vain, too, will be sanitary legislation and model dwellings, unless the outcasts are by friendly hands brought in one by one to habits of cleanliness and order, to thoughts of righteousness and peace. 'What will save East London?' asked one of our University visitors of his master. 'The destruction of West London,' was the answer, and, in so far as he meant the abolition of the space which divides rich and poor, the answer was right. Not until the habits of the rich are changed, and they are again content to breathe the same air and walk the same streets as the poor, will East London be 'saved.'[57]

Barnett's paper, appearing at a time when *The Bitter Cry* turned all attention towards the poor, resulted during the winter of 1883–4 in the formation of a committee at Balliol College to plan a permanent association to found and maintain a university settlement in East London. In February, 1884, it offered Barnett the post of warden and took steps to purchase the premises of a disused boys' industrial school immediately adjacent to St Jude's Vicarage in Commercial Street for the site of a permanent structure. Later in the summer Charlotte Toynbee gave permission to call the new settlement Toynbee Hall in honour of her husband, Arnold Toynbee, who had died in April of 1883.

The settlement movement grew rapidly in the years after the founding of Toynbee Hall so that by the end of the century about thirty houses had been established, of which almost half were in provincial cities, Liverpool being the most active in this field. Not

[57] Samuel A. Barnett, 'Settlements of University Men in Great Towns,' paper read at St John's, Oxford, November 17, 1883, Appendix A; Pimlott, *Toynbee Hall*, pp. 266–73.

all followed the pattern of Barnett's foundation. For instance, Oxford House in Bethnal Green, the product of a committee organized at Keble College in 1884 under the leadership of Dr E. S. Talbot, warden of Keble, and Canon Henry Scott Holland, sought to do religious as well as social work. Mansfield House in Canning Town and Browning Hall in Walworth became centres for Nonconformist activity as Newman House in Southwark served the Catholics.[58]

In all its varying patterns, settlement work became fashionable. It commanded the time of young men with assured careers before them, and the money and patronage of the leaders of the nation. The overall effect of the movement on society was in the long run very great, less perhaps because of any immediate accomplishment in the East End than because young men from settlements went on to careers in which they were able to improve the lot of the poor through legislation and political administration. Examining the biographies of the not-very-large group of men who were the effective architects and carpenters of English social legislation in the first decade and a half of the twentieth century, the researcher finds that nearly without exception these men—junior Members of Parliament, private secretaries to Prime Ministers, permanent secretaries of ministries, junior civil servants—had settlement house experience and continuous settlement house contact in their background. They knew the hostility that poverty breeds to all activity of government. They understood what would become the principle of all subsequent British reform legislation: that there was no practicable way to enforce personal responsibility for health, steady employment, retirement, or children's welfare, if those who failed to make provision for themselves were to be supported by the State. If relief were to be given whatever the answer, it was no use, they argued, to ask the applicant for an old age pension why he had not saved for his retirement, or the unemployed worker whether he drank, or the sick head of a family

---

[58] Oxford House grew much more slowly than Toynbee. In 1889, when Arthur Foley Winnington-Ingram became Head, there were only three residents in a disused church school building. The permanent building was opened in 1894. On the early days of this foundation see: Arthur Foley Winnington-Ingram, *Fifty Years' Work in London, 1889–1939*, London, 1940, pp. 5–14. Winnington-Ingram became Bishop of London in 1901. For an excellent recent discussion of the religious side of the settlement movement see: K. S. Inglis: *Churches and the Working Class in Victorian England*, London, 1963, pp. 155–65.

why his home was dirty. Yet not to give aid was to return to the principle of the deterrent poor law. To give help only to those who demonstrated worthy behaviour meant to deny it to those who did not, and a society that was no longer sure what was the cause of poverty could not arrogate the right to make moral judgments about the worthiness of those who needed economic help. State aid, if given at all, had to be given to all who applied, worthy or unworthy, as a right.

On this basis Barnett had proposed as early as 1883 a pension of 8s. or 10s. a week for all citizens with only the test that they managed to stay out of the workhouse until the age of sixty. 'If such pensions were the right of all,' he had written in the *Nineteenth Century*,

> none would be tempted to lie to get them, nor would any be tempted to spy and bully to avoid paying them. So long as relief is a matter of desert, and so long as the most conscientious relieving officers are liable to err, there must be a mistake both on the side of indulgence and neglect.

> Pensions would be no more corrupting to the labourer, who works for his country in the workshop, than for the civil servant who works for his country at the desk, and the cost of pensions would be no greater than is the cost of infirmaries and alms houses. In one way or another the old and the poor are now kept by those who are richer, and the present method is not a cheap one.[59]

3

The preceding paragraphs have attempted to define the social philosophy of the settlement movement in order to draw a distinction between it and the scientific framework of prevention of poverty that would become the competing philosophy of the Fabian Society. The aim in this is not to suggest that either group represented a reaction to the other, but simply to propose the not-particularly-novel thesis that the Fabian principle of 'conditional relief'—those who receive aid from society must pay for it by improved social behaviour—had far less impact on the legislation of the New Liberalism than did Barnett's 'Practicable Socialism.' The Fabians, to be sure, approved of much that was done, and

[59] Samuel A. Barnett, 'Practicable Socialism,' *Nineteenth Century*, XIII (April, 1883), 557.

deluged Liberal ministers and civil servants with literate and closely-reasoned memoranda, but with the exception of Robert Morant who was himself a product of Toynbee Hall, and Richard Burdon Haldane, they were unable to gain any considerable influence over the Liberal establishment. With unimportant exceptions, the social legislation of the New Liberalism provided benefits as of right.

Fabian proposals before the turn of the century were directed toward the elimination of the capitalist system through the device of taxation and the promotion of municipal ownership. Although some Fabians, notably Beatrice Webb, were well acquainted with the problems of the poor, their programme aimed at altering the system that caused poverty rather than alleviating the condition itself. Their proposals dealt with employers of labour rather than with workers. They were social reformers in the literal sense, only incidentally interested at this time in what would come to be known as welfare legislation.[60] During the nineties, for example, the most ambitious excursion by the Fabians into bread and butter national, as opposed to local, social politics was their celebrated promotion of the radical platform at the Newcastle

---

[60] James Keir Hardie's opinion of National Health Insurance is typical of the reaction of the advanced theoretical socialist to welfare legislation in the period before World War I. Speaking to his constituents at Merthyr in 1911 in favour of the minimum wage for miners, he upbraided the Asquith Government for offering palliatives instead of the reform of the capitalist system. What was the answer received, he asked, when a minimum wage of 30s. for all and 8s. per day was demanded for those who worked underground in unhealthy conditions.

No, say the Liberals, but we will give you an Insurance Bill. We shall not uproot the cause of poverty, but we will give you a porous plaster to cover the disease that poverty causes.

Emrys Hughes, *Keir Hardie*, London, 1956, p. 200.

Not long before he died, G. D. H. Cole admitted that this premise had been disproved by events.

It used to be widely argued that no large improvements in the 'condition of the people' could in fact be achieved as long as capitalism remained in being, and that socialism alone could arm the Government with power to bring about an effective redistribution of incomes. But this view has been blown upon by the undoubted advances made by the workers under capitalism in the United States, and even in Great Britain. It used to be supposed that capitalism could exist only with the aid of a large reserve of unemployed labour, and that it was necessarily subject to the periodical alternations of boom and slump due, in the last resort, to maldistribution of consuming power.

G. D. H. Cole, 'The Growth of Socialism,' Morris Ginsberg, ed., *Law and Opinion in England in the 20th Century*, Berkeley, Calif., 1961, p. 91.

Conference of the Liberal Party in 1891. Even here the evidence is dubious. Bernard Shaw wrote a letter to Edward Pease boasting that he had tricked the Liberals into accepting the Fabian programme written by Sidney Webb.[61] After the election of 1892 Webb himself wrote a bitter attack on the party for giving up the programme, attempting to show that where Liberal candidates had been successful, for instance in London, it was on the basis of the Newcastle programme.[62] But on the whole scholars have agreed that Fabian influence, if important at all, was only one of several pressures on the unhappy Liberals, who were casting about desperately for some platform that would catch votes.[63]

Later Fabian influence was undoubtedly great and the unfortunate modern tendency to denigrate its impact on English politics is as mistaken as were the sweeping statements twenty years ago that the Fabians had practically written the Beveridge report by 1909.[64] Nevertheless, except to look forward to the eventual reconstruction of the productive system when the labour market could be organized and unemployment abolished, before the turn of the century the group showed almost no interest in the problem of poverty.[65]

Yet if the Fabians were uninterested in the prosaic administra-

[61] Quoted in Margaret Cole, *The Story of Fabian Socialism*, London, 1961, p. 46.

[62] 'The Fabian Society' (Sidney Webb), 'To Your Tents, O Israel,' *Fortnightly Review*, LIV, n.s. (November, 1893), 569–89.

[63] Cole, *Fabian Socialism*, pp. 45–7; A. M. McBriar, *Fabian Socialism and English Social Politics, 1884–1918*, Cambridge, 1962, pp. 238–41. Joseph Clayton, in his too-much-neglected history of English socialism, says of the Fabian breach with the Liberals:

It is probable that the Fabian Society exaggerated the advantage of capturing moribund political associations and getting resolutions passed; certain of the wires so industriously pulled were without figures to be made to move.

Joseph Clayton, *The Rise and Decline of English Socialism*, London, 1926, p. 47.

[64] For example: George Bernard Shaw, 'Fabian Failures and Successes,' and William A. Robson, 'The Influence of Fabianism on British Social Policy,' in the *Fabian Quarterly*, No. 41, April, 1944; G. D. H. Cole, *A History of Socialist Thought* (London, 1956), III, 207.

[65] Tom Mann's minority report to the Royal Commission on Labour in 1894, written by Sidney Webb, provides an illustration of early Fabian proposals for dealing with the poor. Considered by the Webbs themselves a very radical document, it proposed a large number of legal restrictions on employers aimed at improving the condition of labour. But for those who had no work, it suggested only empowering of poor law guardians to acquire land to be tilled by unemployed men. Beatrice Webb, *Our Partnership*, London, 1948, p. 41.

tive problems involved in handling relief in metropolitan slums, they found in the London County Council a laboratory for testing theories which they hoped would eventually make unnecessary the labours of Barnett and the Salvation Army. The administrative county of London came into existence in 1888 with the County Councils Act that set up elected councils to handle local government throughout England and Wales. At that time the Unionists had agreed that the special problems of London would require further legislation. The real organization of parties in the government of the metropolis did not occur until the council election of 1892. The two parties, the Moderates and the Progressives, were loosely allied with the Conservatives and Liberals, but the most potent influence among the LCC Progressives was Fabian socialism. The Fabians succeeded in permeating the Progressive forces of the London County Council in a way never approached in the Liberal Party, and in London government Sidney Webb scored some of his greatest political successes.[66] From 1892 to 1908—until the third year of the New Liberalism when the Progressives at last lost their majority on the London County Council—political reformers found opportunities for action denied them at the national level. In the LCC, reform politics and reform politicians had, if not a legislative body they could always dominate, at least a forum in which reform could get a respectful hearing.

In working for the Progressive victory in the LCC elections of 1892, the Fabians obtained, through Lord Rosebery's friendship with Thomas Wemyss, the support of the new Liberal journal, the *Speaker*. (In 1894 Wemyss was knighted on Rosebery's recommendation.) But the Progressive platform was Webb's *The London Programme*, proposing basically the application of 'gas and water socialism' to the metropolis.[67] Even though among the majority of Progressives elected in 1892 there were only six Fabians in a total

[66] For a full discussion of Fabian activity in the LCC, see McBriar, *Fabian Socialism*, pp. 187–233. For the Liberal–Progressive connexion, see also Sir Ioan Gwilym Gibbon and Reginald W. Bell, *History of the London County Council, 1889–1939*, London, 1939, p. 91.

[67] *The London Programme*, published in 1891, appeared also as a series of Fabian Tracts, numbers 30–37. The contents of the platform is well outlined by the titles of the individual tracts: 'The Unearned Increment'; 'London's Heritage in the City Guilds'; 'The Municipalization of the Gas Supply'; 'Municipal Tramways'; 'London's Water Tribute'; 'The Municipalization of London Docks'; 'The Scandal of London's Markets'; 'A Labour Policy for Public Authorities.'

council of 118, the Fabians were led by Sidney Webb sitting for Deptford, who could usually be assumed to be the principal author of the report of any committee upon which he sat. Under his leadership the Fabians on the London County Council, who never numbered more than eight and who in 1895 dropped to three, succeeded in making municipal socialism in London important enough to appear a menace to the Salisbury administration.[68]

In the long-promised London Government Act of 1899, the Unionists tried to prevent the extension of municipal socialism by wiping out the thirty vestries and twelve district boards that were the administration of metropolitan London and entrusting their duties—supervision of markets, public health, maintenance and repair of streets, housing—to twenty-eight newly created metropolitan borough councils and to the ancient city corporation. By giving these powers to the metropolitan borough councils, each with taxing authority, and denying them to the London County Council, the Unionists compartmentalized the government of the metropolis and hoped to protect the wealth of the West End from raids for the improvement of the East End.[69]

The London County Council was important to reformers as an arena in which they could be politically effective in a decade increasingly dominated by excitement over imperialism. In addition, activity in the LCC deserves notice by historians because the elements of the Progressive programme that came nearest to realization before the South African War were those that would appear during the conflict to be at the root of the most disturbing and potentially dangerous of all social problems: the general unhealthiness of the urban population. In the nineties the physical well-being of city dwellers was assumed to vary inversely with population density. The solution to the problem of urban crowding—the means of breaking the monopoly of the urban landlord—seemed most simply to be found in the improvement of metropolitan transportation, the municipalization of trams, a regular system of water transport on the Thames, and the extension of the

---

[68] Salisbury referred to the LCC as a place where 'socialist and collectivist' experiments were tried, and where the 'revolutionary spirit' lurked. A *Punch* cartoon in November, 1897, showed the LCC as a rather dandified Frankenstein monster looming over Salisbury, its creator. *Punch*, CXXX (November 27, 1897), 247.

[69] Elie Halevy, *A History of the English People in the Nineteenth Century, Imperialism and the Rise of Labor, 1895–1905*, V (New York, University Paperbacks, 1961), 241.

network of underground trains. The LCC had acquired, as its first municipal enterprise, in 1891, the ownership of street railways, but it had specifically abjured at that time the right of their operation. However, pressure from the Progressives resulted in 1896 in a request to Parliament for power to operate the trams. Under the direct management of the Progressive chairman of the LCC Highways Committee, who hoped to paint London red with electrified municipally-owned tram routes, city operation of tramcars became a conspicuous success of the metropolitan reformers.[70]

The LCC experimented with water transport and with a works department in an attempt to break the power of municipal contractors. Here it was less successful—both would be abolished before the war—but reformers could take heart in the fact that London had moved from the unenviable position of being one of the worst-governed large cities in the world, which it had been in the eighties, to one of the best by the end of the century. When, therefore, the crisis over national efficiency and specifically the deterioration of national physique became an issue during the South African War, it was on the local level that reformers expected first to take action.

Local government activity during the nineties occupied the Fabians almost to the exclusion of other political spheres. Certainly after the Liberal Party failure to enact the Newcastle Programme and Sidney Webb's ill-tempered attack upon his former colleagues in 'To Your Tents, Oh Israel!' connexions between the Fabians and the national Liberal Party became strained. Not until 1901, when the Webbs found themselves deeply involved in the intrigues of the clique of Liberal Imperialists, with R. B. Haldane and Lord Rosebery, did the Fabians attempt to renew their influence in national politics.[71]

---

[70] A. G. Gardner, *John Benn and the Progressive Movement*, London, 1925, p. 245. The first electric municipal tram ran between Westminster and Black-friars on May 15, 1903; but the metropolis did not obtain the right from Parliament to run a line across Westminster Bridge until 1906. The principal opponent of North–South service was Lord Halsbury, who fought to keep uncluttered the view from Parliament House terrace with the same determination he would display in opposing House of Lords reform.

[71] Rosebery made, however, a handsome figurehead president for the Fabian-dominated London Reform Union, which functioned as the agitational committee of the LCC Progressives, and he won Progressive gratitude for his services in the cause of reform as chairman of the council itself.

4

At least until the end of the eighties, the most influential determinant of serious English middle-class opinion about the care of
the poor was neither the Fabian Society nor Toynbee Hall, but the
Charity Organization Society. The society had appeared in 1869,
growing out of the Society for the Prevention of Pauperism and
Crime, as a reaction to the myriad of amateur Victorian charities.
By falling over each other to feed the poor without mitigating the
condition of poverty, these had built up, as Canon Barnett and
every other professional worker knew, a sharp and seasoned
clientele among the wastrels and loafers of the East End. Adopting
the recommendations for systematic investigation of applicants for
relief worked out in the first quarter of the nineteenth century by
the pioneer Scottish social theoriest Thomas Chalmers, the Charity
Organization Society attempted to apply a standard of public
social responsibility as a criterion for granting aid.[72] By making no
a priori assumption about the moral worth of those who applied to
it, accepting in effect the possibility that at least some of the poor
were not in want through a defect of behaviour or character, the
C.O.S. marked an early departure from the strictly deterrent
principle of poor relief. But on the other hand the society always
distinguished carefully between those who were 'helpable' and
those who were not. Those who could be returned to responsible
society were offered carefully measured portions of loans, advice,
and gifts. Those who were beyond the societies' resources to help,
however worthy they might be, or however piteous their case, were
consigned to the poor law relief, which the society hoped to see
again as unbendingly austere as the 1834 Poor Law Commission
intended it should be. The Charity Organization Society assumed
that the most carefully administered aid would be wasted on the
majority of those in poverty, who were basically of weak character
and corrupted by indiscriminate charity. A good relieving officer,
it followed, would be suspicious and hard-hearted in order to
preserve the society's limited means for the few worthy cases.
'Want of employment,' wrote the secretary of the C.O.S., Charles
S. Loch, in the early nineties, 'in nine cases out of ten in which the
plea is used, is not the cause of distress. It is, as often as not,

[72] On Chalmers' influence on the C.O.S. philosophy of granting relief see:
Karl de Schweinitz, *England's Road to Social Security*, Philadelphia, 1947, pp.
100–13; 140–53.

drink.'[73] The C.O.S. opposed, therefore, all forms of public support that did not trouble to distinguish between the deserving and the undeserving poor, those who could be redeemed and those who could not, the elect and the damned. In this the society was as stringent as the most orthodox Calvinist divine. It fought every attempt to weaken the poor law and when they were proposed, the society would oppose old age pensions, unemployment insurance, and health insurance, and in doing so would separate itself from the central trend of twentieth-century social reform.[74] Nevertheless, in the eighties, with its insistence on systematic, private, carefully supervised relief granted only after an exhaustive investigation and tailored to the exact needs of the particular case, the C.O.S. collected among its supporters many of England's progressive thinkers on the problem of poverty.

Samuel Barnett, a founder and active member of the Charity Organization Society, left the national organization in 1886 on the question of the usefulness of state activity, although he would remain a member of the C.O.S. committee in Whitechapel. Barnett's revolt was an important matter for English social reform. Wrote Beatrice Webb: 'The breakaway of Samuel and Henrietta Barnett in 1886 from the narrow and continuously hardening dogma of the Charity Organization Society sent a thrill through the philanthropic world of London.'[75] In fact the split took another decade to harden. In 1895, when Barnett was an international figure, he attempted to gain Charity Organization Society support for state-provided old age pensions. On July 15, 1895, he read a paper entitled, 'A Friendly Criticism of the C.O.S.' He argued that the society considered hard selfishness and miserly savings as the highest virtue to be desired over hospitality and generosity. Barnett's paper brought him into an angry argument with C. S. Loch, who announced that the paper was a personal attack upon himself.[76]

[73] Quoted in Ervine, *God's Soldier*, p. 708.

[74] Charles Stewart Loch, 1849–1923, born, Bengal; father with Indian Civil Service; educated at Trinity College, Glenalmond, and Balliol College, Oxford. Secretary, Council of London Charity Organization Society, 1875–1914; Tooke Professor of Economic Science and Statistics, King's College, London, 1904–8; member Royal Commission on Poor Laws, 1906–9. Accounted self Liberal in politics, but actively opposed social legislation of New Liberalism. Knighted 1915.   [75] Webb, *Apprenticeship*, p. 178.

[76] Mowat, *Charity Organization Society*, pp. 127–9. See also: Henrietta O. Barnett, *Canon Barnett* (Boston, 1919), II, 267–8.

The Charity Organization Society represented perhaps the most that private philanthropy could accomplish in helping the deserving poor. The society strove in the eighties to force public recognition of poverty as a social evil, depriving a man in the condition not only of his morality but of his claim to membership in the race of civilized human beings. Yet in the nineties the public began to see the poor in other than individual terms. Instead of the dying child in a filthy basement or the forgotten old woman in a poor house ward, the British upper classes began to understand the numerical extent of poverty and came to learn, as Canon Barnett had learned, and as the Fabians had never doubted, that the dimensions of the problem were beyond the resources of any private agency. The Salvation Army could perhaps reform a drunkard, the Charity Organization Society could by judicious loans and gifts help a family over the period of hard times when the bread-winner had fallen ill, but the great ocean of distress could not be reduced by bailing with teaspoons.

The nature and the extent of poverty, as opposed to the condition of the individual poor, was investigated, calculated, and publicized by Charles Booth, a practical businessman, representative of an age that regarded itself above all as practical and willing to face facts.[77] Booth gave late Victorian Britain a detailed statistical picture of the condition it was accustomed to approach only through the dismaying description of individual examples.

Booth's survey appears to have been impelled in the first place by the sensationalism of the writings on the poor of the mid-eighties. Victorian sentimentality could fasten on an example of poverty and miss the mass of destitution. Booth set out to discover whether the sensationalism of Stead and *The Bitter Cry* overstated the case.[78] His aim, he emphasized in the conclusion of his first paper on the subject, 'The Inhabitants of the Tower Hamlets

---

[77] Charles Booth, 1840–1916, born, Liverpool; middle-class family; educated at the Royal Institution School; chairman, Alfred Booth & Co., Ltd., Liverpool, shipper. Politically a Conservative; President, Royal Statistical Society, 1892–4; Privy Councillor, 1904. Conducted investigation of working and living conditions in London, 1891–1903; began publicly to advocate a universal tax-supported old-age pension in 1891; helped found The National Committee of Organized Labour for Promoting Old Age Pensions in 1898, retired from active participation because of health. Close friend of S. A. Barnett; married Mary Macaulay, cousin of Beatrice Webb, niece of T. B. Macaulay.

[78] Helen F. Hohman, *The Development of Social Insurance and Minimum Wage Legislation in Great Britain*, Boston, 1933, p. 361.

(School Board Division) Their Conditions and Occupations,' was to break up the problem of distress into the manageable divisions it must have 'to be solved or even to be adequately stated.'

> The question of those who actually suffer from poverty should be considered separately from that of the true working classes, whose desire for a larger share of wealth is of a different character. It is the plan of agitators and the way of sensational writers to confound the two in one, to talk of 'starving millions,' and to tack on the thousands of working classes to the tens or perhaps hundreds of distress. Against this method I strongly protest, and I do so all the more that I am deeply in earnest in my desire that the conditions under which the mass of the people live should be improved, as well as that of those who now suffer actual distress. To confound these essentially distinct problems is to make the solution of both impossible; it is not by welding distress and aspirations that any good can be done.
>
> We need to begin with a true picture of the modern industrial organism, the interchange of service, the exercise of faculty, the demands and satisfaction of desire. It is the possibility of such a picture as this that I wish to suggest, and it is as a contribution to it that I have written this paper.[79]

Booth's dramatic finding was that only 65 per cent of the inhabitants of Tower Hamlets were above the poverty line. Twenty-two per cent were on the line, while 13 per cent fell below. Booth admitted he was surprised by the fact that 35 per cent of the population was living more or less in want. His survey had in effect justified the claims of some of the sensationalists he had hoped to refute. In the discussion, Professor Leone Levi detected immediately the weakness in Booth's paper that would lead to his definition of the 'poverty line,' which the Simeys have suggested was 'perhaps his most striking single contribution to the social sciences.'[80] What, Professor Levi asked, was a poor man? Was not Booth guilty of the same inaccuracy he attacked? Did the high proportion of poverty he discovered indicate anything about

[79] Charles Booth, 'The Inhabitants of Tower Hamlets (School Board Division) Their Condition and Occupations,' *Journal of the Royal Statistical Society*, L (June, 1887), 375–6.

[80] T. S. and M. B. Simey, *Charles Booth, Social Scientist*, London, 1960, p. 88.

conditions beyond the narrow section of the community in which
it was found?

> Quite recently there had been published a paper called the
> 'Bitter Cry of Outcast London,' which implied the existence of
> a very extensive amount of poverty in London; but when they
> came to see how far such poverty extended, it might be found
> that it only applied to some hundreds or perhaps thousands of
> persons amidst nearly four millions of people. He wondered also
> whether the paper gave an accurate idea of the word 'poor.'
> Who was a poor man? The author had stated that a certain
> number were very poor who were in receipt of from 18s. to
> 20s. a week. An income of 18s. or 20s. a week, even with four or
> five persons in a family, where there was generally more than one
> person earning something, ought not to leave the recipient in a
> condition of poverty. The view that such persons were poor was
> not justified by the cost of living; and if the expenses of such
> people included drink and unnecessary luxuries, there was no
> ground for sympathy with their poverty. It is a misnomer to
> call a person poor where, out of an income of 20s. a week, he
> spends 10s. or 12s. in a wasteful manner.[81]

The Tower Hamlets investigation, and the second investigation
and paper that followed it, 'The Conditions and Occupations of the
People of East London and Hackney, 1887,'[82] which confirmed the
finding that one-third of the population of East London was in
want, led directly to the general inquiry that would be the seventeen volumes of *The Life and Labour of the People in London*.

It would be easy to misconstrue, without diminishing, the
importance of Booth's survey. All people interested in the welfare
of the poor did not as a result become social scientists, nor did
those who had previously denied the existence of large-scale
poverty become willing to agree that one-third of the people of
London were living below the 21s. per week that he established in
his first volume as the poverty line for a family of five.[83] Nevertheless, the history of British social reform can be, and frequently

---

[81] 'Discussion on Mr Booth's paper,' *R.S.S. Journal* (June, 1887), 394.

[82] Charles Booth, 'The Conditions and Occupations of the People of East
London and Hackney, 1887,' *Journal of the Royal Statistical Society*, LI (June,
1888), 276–331.

[83] See, for instance: 'Depression Corrected,' *Edinburgh Review*, CLXXXII
(July, 1895), 1–26.

has been, divided into periods before and after Booth. Booth's importance lay in bringing home to the mass of thinking Englishmen the fact that the relief of distress, because of the sheer numbers involved, could not be the relief of individuals. This applied whether the particular solution to the problem of destitution was, as the Fabians hoped to see it, the prevention of destitution, or, as it eventually became, the alleviation of the effect of destitution. In either case, it was a task involving millions, one that could not be left to private charitable agencies, still less to the individual distribution of alms. Booth forced a nation that took pride in its unwillingness to think in theoretical terms to forget individual cases of hardship and examine the numerical dimensions of poverty. This was, to be sure, the Fabian approach. Beatrice Webb, who worked as an investigator for Booth, had often been described as 'hard' because of her unwillingness to deal with cases of individual suffering. Booth taught the entire nation to be practical, rather than sentimental, about poverty. Although *Life and Labour* probably increased the popularity of sensational descriptions of the condition of poverty, if the number of detailed reports that appeared in the next few years may be taken as an indication, thoughtful people nevertheless began now to plan ways to protect society from the deteriorating effects of widespread poverty, to plan on such a scale that effect could be given to the schemes only by the State.[84]

[84] In 1892 Frederick Engels found it appropriate to publish for the first time in Great Britain in English his first important work, *The Condition of the Working-Class in England in 1844*. The book had been published in the United States in translation in 1886 but had apparently made no impression in Great Britain. In a preface written for the English edition in January, 1892, Engels reiterated Booth's emphasis on the distinction that had to be made between the well-to-do working-class 'engineers, carpenters, joiners' who had profited much from the capitalist system. 'These are the model working men of Messrs Leone Levi and Giffen,' who were always cited by those who sought to deny the existence of real poverty in England, but, he continued in a passage that might have been written by Booth himself,

as to the great mass of working people, the state of misery and insecurity in which they live is as low as ever, if not lower. The East End of London is an ever-spreading pool of stagnant misery and desolation, of starvation when out of work, and of degradation, physical and moral, when at work.

> Frederick Engels, *The Condition of the Working-Class in England in 1844*, London, 1892, p. xv.

Engels' book was among the early, but by no means the first, examples of the almost innumerable outpourings of eyewitness descriptions of the poor that fill the next twenty years. Arnold White, for instance, made a career of being an

These proposals—old age pensions, either state-supported or contributory, labour exchanges and work projects, state-aided emigration, the return of city unemployed to vacant land where they would be taught farming, usually known as land colonization —will be considered in greater detail in later chapters. Generally for English social reformers the decade of the nineties was a period of planning and of hope. Toynbee Hall continued to grow in influence, and if it did not accomplish all that Canon Barnett planned for it, the settlement movement as a whole flourished and new houses appeared yearly. The dock strike of 1889 marked the beginning of effective union organization for unskilled labour, which, unlike the old New Model unions, was interested in politics. In 1892 three labouring men won election to the House of Commons as independent candidates, James Keir Hardie for South-West Ham, John Burns for Battersea, and J. H. Wilson for Middlesbrough. Although the return of prosperity by the middle of the decade, the preoccupation of the electorate with the question of Irish Home Rule, and the over-optimism of the Independent Labour Party in attempting to field twenty-eight candidates in the election of July, 1895, resulted in the defeat of all I.L.P. candidates, social reformers hoped still to see the accomplishment of some of their aims within a few years.

The nineties generally must be regarded as a time of agitation, of organization, of no conspicuous failure, because very little was attempted. The fear and urgency that had pressed reformers during the depression of the eighties had disappeared. Yet generally reformers were optimistic. The death duties in William Vernon Harcourt's budget of 1894 looked like socialism to Liberals raised in the Gladstone tradition. Booth's investigations, Joseph Chamberlain's apparent success in interesting the Unionists in old age pensions, the enactment of old age pension legislation by Germany in 1889 and by New Zealand in 1898, the Workmen's Compensation Act of 1897,[85] the amendments to the poor law

expert on the poor. See his *Tries at the Truth*, London, 1891; *The Problems of a Great City*, 3rd ed., 1895; *Efficiency and Empire*, London, 1901; *The Great Idea*, London, 1909.

[85] The Workmen's Compensation Act amended the Employers Liability Act of 1880, which had simply been the legislative statement of common law liability. The new Act swept away for employers in certain large and hazardous industries the legal defences of contributory employee negligence and common employment. Employers in the designated industries were required either to self-insure or to procure insurance coverage from a commercial carrier. This Act

which broadened its application and narrowed the definition of pauperism[86]—all seemed to promise hope for future reform. Finally, there was the increased awareness of leaders of both parties that unless Britain's traditional political leadership found a way within the capitalist system to satisfy the economic demands of the now fully-enfranchised working class, the traditional parties, and perhaps the capitalist system itself, might be superseded by something else.

Then suddenly, in October, 1899, the cheerful anticipations of reformers were sucked away by the war in South Africa. The English working man, who for a decade had been carefully instructed in his rights and opportunities, could not be interested in explanations of pension annuities and employers' liability when offered either the glamour of fighting for the Queen in South Africa, or well-paid, war-stimulated employment at home. The South African War disrupted what appeared to be the orderly evolution of English politics towards social reform. But before the conflict was half over, discoveries resulting from the war itself about the condition of Britain would make immediately imperative social reform on a far wider scale than ever had been envisioned.

provided an important security for the working man but inasmuch as the government participated only as a regulatory agency, it was not a departure in the direction of true social legislation. Rather, it should be viewed as a continuation of the tradition of industrial protective measures begun by the Factory Acts.

[86] These were the Medical Relief (Disqualification Removal) Act of 1885, which permitted a citizen to receive medical treatment under the poor law without incurring the political disenfranchisement of pauperism, and the Outdoor Relief (Friendly Societies) Act of 1894, which authorized Poor Law Guardians to disregard any sums up to 5s. per week from a friendly society received by an applicant for relief. The discretionary authority became a requirement in 1904.

2 *The Condition of the People*

Nations have passed away and left no traces
And history gives the naked cause of it——
One single, simple reason in all cases;
They fell because their peoples were not fit.
RUDYARD KIPLING, *Land and Sea Tales.*

In the last two decades of the nineteenth century pressure for
welfare legislation had come mostly from groups outside politics,
from social workers and political philosophers concerned with the
'condition of the people.' Besides the overt threat of violence
represented at its peak by the Trafalgar Square riots of 1886, they
had had as a weapon only the force of public opinion made effective
after 1885 by substantial manhood franchise. They could warn
politicians that unless the government acted, the labouring
classes would eventually displace the traditional parties with a
party of their own. They could seek to make this threat real by
education and agitation among the lower classes. The work of the
National Committee of Organized Labour for Promoting Old Age
Pensions, which attempted to mobilize working-class opinion in
favour of non-contributory pensions, provides an example of this.
Nevertheless, until the Boer War, so far as they attempted direct
political action, reformers generally had to try to influence
politicians through the traditional means of petitions, lobby delegations, and constituency manifestoes. The occasional front bench
man who proclaimed himself a social reformer was likely either to
be of second rank—Sir John Gorst—or to be suspected of
opportunism and demagogery—Joseph Chamberlain. The fact was
that social reform promised little political profit. There were
prospects that the return might improve in the future—the reformers themselves were most optimistic by the end of the decade.
But in the nineties, beyond the Newcastle Programme, Gorst's
pronouncements during the election of 1895, and Chamberlain's
success in keeping the Unionist Government busy appointing
commissions to consider, but not to approve, old age pensions,
reform legislation received little attention inside Westminster.

The immediate effect of the South African War in October, 1899, was to throw serious reformers into despair. The Government could reasonably plead it had no money to spend on social legislation. The orgy of imperialism that accompanied the conflict turned the attention of the working man away from the condition of the society in which he lived, and deprived reformers of the only weapon they had. But after the military disasters of the first six months of the war came revelations of defective organization in the army and of inadequate education among the officers. Most important were the rumours of widespread weakness and positive physical disability among the working classes volunteering for military service. It seemed the time had come to re-examine the old assumptions about the inevitable superiority of the British social system and of the British race. Were English ways of doing things any longer invariably the best? Were the ancient Anglo-Saxon people who had painted the map red now decaying? Did a nation forced to spend three years and £250,000,000 to defeat a handful of unorganized farmers have the right to call itself the greatest power on earth? The menace implicit in these unhappy reflections was that of armed, organized, vigorous, Imperial Germany.

What Germany had that Great Britain did not came to be termed 'national efficiency.' The noun 'efficiency' could take many qualifying adjectives. There could be political, educational, commercial, industrial, and above all, physical efficiency. In the name of efficiency academicians questioned whether Greek had any usefulness as a university requirement except to secure a monopoly of university places for the public schools. Soldiers discussed whether it was as necessary a language for military officers as German. Politicians debated whether the way to improve output in decaying industries should be greater competition or tariff protection. Businessmen decired the small number of technicians and scientists produced annually. At the centre of the problem, nevertheless, lay the matter of physical efficiency. Great Britain was wasting her human resources. A great empire needed a martial and vigorous race. Instead there was a declining birthrate and a deteriorating, incapacitated manhood.

The quest for national efficiency, therefore, gave social reform what it had not had before—the status of a respectable political question. Imperialism and the 'condition of the people question' became linked. Only an efficient nation could hold a vigorous, expanding empire. The Boer War did not bring Victorian imperialism to an end, as some writers have suggested, nor did the Liberal victory in 1906 show that Britain was tired of adventure.[1] Rather, the war and its aftermath turned imperialism inward and directed its energy, its violence, and its intolerance back onto England. Imperialism metamorphized, and imperialists, with the same uncompromising vigour they had displayed in the conquest of Africa, took up national service, physical training and the Boy Scouts, tariff reform, maintenance of the House of Lords veto and of the Irish union. Most important for this study, they adopted national efficiency, which brought them to the question of the physical condition of the people.[2] The white man's burden had to be carried on strong backs.[3]

[1] 'The Imperialism of the nineties had burnt itself out in the Mafeking bonfires, and the Conservative overthrow of 1905 recalled, in its grounds and its magnitude, the defeat of 1880.' G. M. Young, *Victorian England, Portrait of an Age*, Oxford Paperback edition, London, 1961, p. 183.

[2] *The Islanders*, written in 1902, exemplifies the transition from imperial to domestic questions. Here Kipling used the shame of imperial weakness and domestic fecklessness to promote universal military training.

> And ye wanted your fathomless power,
> And ye flaunted your iron pride,
> Ere ye fawned on the Younger Nations
> For the man who could shoot and ride!
> Then ye returned to your trinkets;
> Then ye contented your souls
> With flannelled fools at the wicket
> Or the muddied oafs at the goals
> Given to strong delusion,
> Wholly believing a lie,
> Ye saw that the land lay fenceless
> And ye let the months go by
> Waiting some easy wonder,
> Hoping some saving sign—
> Idle—openly idle—
> In the lee of the forespent Line
> Idle—except for your boasting—
> And what is your boasting worth,
> If ye grudge your year of service
> To the lordliest life on earth?

[3] The space devoted in Hansard's index to the topics 'Housing,' 'Unemployed,' and 'Poor Law' may be revealing as a crude statistical comparison of Parliamentary interest in the poor before and after the South African War. Together the three headings had in 1904 ten and one-half columns of entries. Six years before in 1898 there was no heading of 'Unemployed' and the other two had together one and three-quarters columns.

I

At the beginning of the war the popular enthusiasm for imperialism caused black discouragement not only for advocates of social reform but for all who deplored cheapness and vulgarity, who prized English moderation in behaviour and fair play in competition. The clearest manifestations of the martial temper were the unrestrained mob celebrations that occurred upon the announcement of victories. The more subtle, the more profound, the more dangerous results came with the erosion of Victorian standards of deportment in society and, more important, in politics. A ferocity and intolerance appeared in public life—notable perhaps first in the 'Khaki Election' of 1900 and achieving a dangerous climax in the struggle over Irish Home Rule—that would destroy the old easy balance of British parliamentarianism and bring that system close to ruin.

The nation witnessed a demonstration of the popular hysteria lurking close to the surface of English phlegm in the celebration that occurred on May 18, 1900, at the report of the relief of General Robert Baden-Powell and his men, who had been besieged in Mafeking in the extreme north of the Cape Colony. The news set off spontaneous celebrations of a sort altogether unknown to Englishmen of the day, and the word 'mafficking' drifted into the language, a description of extravagant behaviour of crowds. The announcement of the town's relief appeared in the windows of the newspaper offices in Fleet Street at about nine o'clock in the evening. Within half an hour the streets of central London from Mansion House west to Piccadilly were black with people shouting, singing, and weeping. At the Lyceum, Eleanora Duse's presentation was interrupted to allow the manager to read the dispatch and to lead the audience in singing 'God Save the Queen.' By midnight, usually sober men were riding cabs through the quiet streets of suburban London between rows of darkened villas, shouting the news. Coming as it did after months of nothing but discouraging reports from the field, there was, to be sure, some excuse for rejoicing, but the event was beyond understanding. Walking down Lower Regent Street towards Pall Mall, Soames Forsyte was disgusted and horrified.

This was—egad!—Democracy. It stank, yelled, was hideous!
. . . It wasn't English. And all this about the relief of a little

town about as big as—Watford,—six thousand miles away. Restraint, reserve! Those qualities to him more ideal almost than life, those indispensable attributes of property and culture, where were they? It wasn't English! No, it wasn't English![4]

'One might have thought that we had won the greatest victory of all time. Baden-Powell became the idol of the Press and the crowd. . . .' concluded Lord Newton sadly.[5]

In October, 1900, the insanity appeared again with tragic consequences, upon the return of the City Imperial Volunteers. When they marched through Ludgate Circus on the way to St Paul's for a Thanksgiving service, the crowd was so great that two people were crushed to death. The rest of that day was given up as before to blind celebration, accompanied now, however, by destruction of property. 'Hooliganism,' then a new word, was first widely used to describe the behaviour of the mob on this occasion.[6]

Rhetorical and political violence in the world of society, letters, and government matched the physical violence in the streets. As Rudyard Kipling was the literary voice of imperialism, Professor J. A. Cramb was its philosopher. In his lectures at Queen's College delivered during April and May of 1900, Cramb proposed a Darwinian evolution of the national organism into a higher imperial form.[7] 'In political life,' said Cramb, 'in the life-history of states, as in religious, as in intellectual and social history, change in

[4] John Galsworthy, *The Forsyte Saga*, New York, 1922, p. 527.

[5] Lord Newton, *Retrospection*, London, 1941, p. 107.

[6] See R. H. Gretton, *A Modern History of the English People, 1880–1922*, London, 1930, pp. 539–40. For a critical appraisal, Henry Scott Holland, "The Return of the C.I.V.'s,' *Commonwealth*, V (December, 1900), 349–51.

[7] Caroline Playne suggests that Cramb was as influential in England as Friedrich von Bernhardi and Houston Stewart Chamberlain were in Germany. Caroline Playne, *The Pre-War Mind in Britain, An Historical Review*, London, 1928, pp. 199–203. Cramb, however, was without the anti-Semitism of Chamberlain, although his writing was clearly influenced by Chamberlain's *Foundation of the Nineteenth Century*.

John Adam Cramb, 1862–1913, educated Glasgow and Bonn; appointed to Luke Fellowship in English Literature at Glasgow, 1885; lecturer in modern history, Queen Margaret College, Glasgow, 1888–90; professor of modern history, Queen's College, London, 1893–1913. Published: *Reflections on the Origins and Destiny of Imperial Britain*, 1900; *Germany and England*, 1914.

Lord Roberts' biographer designates Cramb as the most important supporter, with L. S. Amery, of the campaign for compulsory military training that occupied so many imperialists between 1900 and 1914. Many of Lord Roberts' speeches were written by Cramb. David James, *Lord Roberts*, London, 1954, pp. 450, 459.

growth of what we now name Evolution, are perpetual, continuous, unresting.' A nation must advance or recede. '. . . imperialism is the supreme, crowning, form . . .' and was demonstrated now in the war in the Transvaal between '. . . the moribund principle of nationality . . .' and '. . . the vital principle of the future.'[8]
The war for empire, said Cramb, had made the empire.

The deeds on the battlefield, the spirit which fires men from every region of that empire and from every section of that society of nations, the attitude which has marked that people and that race towards the present war, are not without significance. Now at last the name English People is co-extensive and of equal meaning with that of the English race.[9]

The patriotic frenzy that accompanied the Boer War created a climate of opinion in England that made any criticism of the conflicts or discussion of the shortcomings of English society politically, and even physically, hazardous.[10] To point out the new coarseness and ostentation of the world of society, to suggest that some of the nation's leaders were stupid, lazy, or incompetent in office, or to attempt to show the heedless English working class that its patriotism was used to further the political ends of others, was to risk being branded as disloyal and 'Pro-Boer.' Beatrice Webb's reflections at Torquay on January 31, 1900, provide a catalogue of the miseries of English reformers in the early days of the war.

The last six months, and especially the last month at Plymouth, have been darkened by the nightmare of war. The horrible consciousness that we have as a nation, showing ourselves to be unscrupulous in methods, vulgar in manners as well as inefficient, is an unpleasant background to one's personal life—a background always present, when one wakes in the night and at intervals of leisure during the day. The Boers are, man for man,

---

[8] John A. Cramb, *Reflections on the Origin and Destiny of Imperial Britain*, London, 1900, pp. 132–40. Lecture of May 29, 1900.

[9] Cramb, *Imperial Britain*, p. 149.

[10] David Lloyd George, for instance, narrowly avoided injury on December 18, 1901, when he attempted to address the Birmingham Liberal Association at Birmingham town hall. Several policeman were hurt attempting to defend the Welsh radical, who escaped from the building in a policeman's uniform. A young man in the crowd, Harold Ernest Curtin, died in the hospital of a broken skull. *The Times*, December 19, December 21, 1901.

our superiors in dignity, devotion and capacity—yes *in capacity*. That, to a ruling race, is the hardest hit of all.

I sometimes wonder whether we could take a beating and be better for it? This would be the real test of the heart and intellect of the British race: much more than if we win a long and costly conflict. If we win, we shall soon forget the lessons of the war. Once again we shall have 'muddled through.' Pecuniary self-interest will be again rehabilitated as an Empire-building principle. Once again the English gentleman, with his so-called habit of command, will have proved to be the equal of the foreign expert with his scientific knowledge.

To us public affairs seem gloomy; the middle-classes are materialistic, and the working classes stupid, and in large sections sottish, with no interest except racing odds, whilst the Government of the country is firmly in the hands of little cliques of landlords and great capitalists and their hangers-on. The social enthusiasm that inspired the intellectual proletariat of ten years ago has died down and given place to a wave of scepticism about the desirability, or the possibility, of substantial change in society as we know it.

If we found ourselves faced with a real disaster, should we as a nation have the nerve and persistency to stand up against it? That is the question that haunts me.[11]

Henry Scott Holland's anguish bordered on physical pain. He wrote to Mary Drew, W. E. Gladstone's daughter, in 1900:

One word out of my misery. The Boers are not wicked to aim at paramouncy. . . . I know that horrible Raid was the primary cause of their doing so. But oh! that they could have saved themselves from being made desperate by that crime! How awful is our plight! I gang like a ghaist! Dust and ashes.[12]

For G. M. Trevelyan the pain was less of the conscience than of fear for the nation. England need not fear a yellow peril, wrote George Macaulay Trevelyan in December, 1901, in the *Nineteenth Century*, but there is a 'white peril.'[13]

[11] Beatrice Webb, *Our Partnership*, London, 1948, pp. 194–5.

[12] S. L. Olland, ed., *A Forty Years' Friendship, Letters from the Late Henry Scott Holland to Mrs Drew*, New York, 1919, pp. 193–4.

[13] The decline in tone of the popular press, for instance, as much as the arguments of David Lloyd George, influenced George Cadbury to buy the *Daily*

Art, literature, religious leadership, political common sense, have in our island gone down before the tide in one generation. The material luxury alone seems likely to survive the general wreck, and the relation that luxury bears to higher efforts of the mind and spirit is inverse.[14]

No wonder that while unveiling the statue of Gladstone in Manchester in 1901, John Morley, with tears in his eyes, quoted Wordsworth:

> Earth is sick
> And heaven is weary of the hollow words
> That States and Kingdoms utter when they talk
> Of truth and justice.[15]

Liberal unhappiness was darkest during the Khaki Election of October, 1900. The public was apathetic about politics—the turnout was the smallest of any of the four elections in the twentieth century before World War I—and the appeal of reform seemed to have disappeared altogether. The Liberals' protestations of patriotism, their promises of a better world, their serious discussions of issues, simply were not listened to. C. F. G. Masterman's report was typical.

> We had descended on a prosperous provincial town. There, we argued, exhorted, entreated, lamented. We praised our soldiers in the war, talked proudly of our Empire, spread a Gargantuan banquet of social reform—housing, temperance, education. We waxed pathetic over the millions illegally overcrowded in London, six times the Outlanders in the Transvaal. We mourned over the children contaminated by the public house. We darkly prophesied the results of foreign competition and our imperfect education.

The opponent 'slapped his chest' and 'muttered concerning Lord Roberts and the Army and was elected.'[16]

News as an outlet for responsible anti-war Liberal opinion. A. G. Gardiner, *The Life of George Cadbury*, London, 1923, pp. 210–17. The *News* immediately had to face a serious and organized boycott of advertisers because of its stand on the war. By the end of 1901 the syndicate that bought the paper was on the verge of breaking up.

[14] George Macaulay Trevelyan, 'The White Peril,' *Nineteenth Century*, L (December, 1901), 1054.

[15] John, Viscount Morley, *Recollections* (New York, 1918), II, 93.

[16] C. F. G. Masterman, 'For Zion's Sake, The Wail of a Social Reformer,' *Commonwealth*, V (November, 1900), 322.

So great was the support of imperialism that radicals were defeated in solidly labour constituencies. W. C. Steadman, for instance, the anti-war secretary of the Barge-Builders' Union, lost in Stepney to a Conservative through a pamphlet linking him to John Ellis, Liberal M.P. for Rushcliffe. Ellis had failed, on technical grounds, to obtain an injunction against a Unionist poster branding him a pro-Boer. The Conservative pamphlet in Stepney, therefore, stated 'Mr Justice *Bicknell* refused to interfere with a poster describing Mr *Ellis* as a *Traitor* because of his communication with *Kruger. Ellis and Steadman are Pals*. Are they not *Both Traitors* and *Pro-Boers?*'[17]

The Unionist victory was overwhelming. They received a higher proportion of the total vote than any Government would achieve again until 1931. Four hundred and two Conservatives and Liberal Unionists were elected to be opposed by 268 Liberals, Labourites, and Irish Nationalists. Not again until 1955 would an incumbent Government increase its majority at a general election.

The Khaki Election had been called on the assumption that the war in South Africa was over. But while organized resistance had been broken, the Boer Commandos stubbornly remained in the field, and Britain had to continue large-scale, expensive, military operations for another nineteen months, until May, 1902. During this period, the growing internal disharmony between the 'Liberal Imperialists' and the 'Pro-Boers' in the Liberal Party and the multiplying reports about the low state of British national efficiency seemed for a time about to bring into existence a new political alignment, a party of national efficiency, that would have as its chief task the revival of British energy and prestige. This was not to be, however, for the chosen leader of this party, Lord Rosebery, was not equal to the task, and had not the courage to match his intellectual and literary eminence. In the end, the Unionists were diverted by Joseph Chamberlain's proposal for an imperial economic unit based on preferential tariffs. This no Liberal could support, be he imperialist or not. National efficiency could not be achieved by increasing the price of the working man's bread.

Hence, national efficiency carried by the Liberal Imperialists

---

[17] Walter Grant Inman, 'The British Liberal Party, 1892–1939,' unpublished Ph.D dissertation, Clark University, 1939, pp. 278–9. There was, in addition, the Unionist slogan, 'A vote for the Liberals is a vote for the Boers.'

united with the older social reform enthusiasm of the Pro-Boer radicals to produce in 1905 the New Liberalism. The careers and opinions of the men who formed the heterogeneous Cabinets of Sir Henry Campbell-Bannerman and Herbert Asquith deserve some examination. Together these men would end the predominance of Gladstonian economics among the Liberals and lay the foundations of the welfare state.

2

The beginnings of scientific philanthropy were discussed in the previous chapter. It drew its inspiration from the settlement houses and from the traditions of Christian socialism. The movement had friends, or at least connexions, in the trade unions. It was willing to use national efficiency as an argument for social reform, but it attacked poverty as a social evil of itself. Many of its adherents, C. F. G. Masterman, G. K. Chesterton, Cyril Jackson, Percy Dearmer, Charles (later Bishop) Gore, Noel Buxton, G. P. Gooch, G. M. Trevelyan, were held together by membership in the Christian Social Union which Canon H. Scott Holland had founded in 1890 to provide a non-socialist outlet for Christian social–political activity.[18] Besides the C.S.U., the anti-imperialist radicals frequently had a journalistic connexion with Henry W. Massingham. Massingham had been editor of the *Daily Chronicle* from 1895 until November, 1899, when he resigned in protest against his paper's imperialist policies, taking with him Vaughan Nash and Harold Spender.[19] After a short sojourn on the *Man-*

[18] The Christian Social Union was only an indirect descendant of mid-nineteenth century Christian socialism. It was founded, in fact, as a reaction to the extreme socialism of the Guild of St Matthew, which attempted to carry on the work of Kingsley. The C.S.U. never inquired into the politics of its members, although they were almost exclusively Liberal. By 1905 the C.S.U. had fifty-four branches and was particularly influential at the ancient universities and in the settlement house movement, from which many of its members had originally come. Although membership at its peak never exceeded four thousand, it included many whose influence on the Asquith Government would be critical, and its two magazines, the *Commonwealth* and the *Economic Review*, were widely read. See Donald O. Wagner, *The Church of England and Social Reform Since 1854*, New York, 1930, pp. 272–9, for the early evolution of the C.S.U. For the condition of the C.S.U. in 1905, see T. C. Fry, 'The Christian Social Union,' *Economic Review*, XV (October, 1905), 385–402. See also G. K. Chesterton, *Autobiography*, Grey Arrow edition, London, 1959, pp. 150–2.

[19] Vaughan Nash, 1861–1932, born, Clifton; educated privately; resident Toynbee Hall, 1887–9; entered journalism, 1893. Editorial staff, *Daily Chronicle*,

chester Guardian, the trio went to the *Daily News,* which George Cadbury had bought to give a voice to radical anti-imperialism.

Many of the writers who worked for Massingham on the *Daily News* also wrote for J. L. Hammond on the *Speaker.* The *Speaker* had been acquired from Sir Thomas Wemyss in 1899 by a group of young pro-Boer Liberals—Hammond, who became editor, Hilaire Belloc, Philip Comyns Carr, F. Y. Eccles, F. W. Hirst and John Simon. Eventually, in March, 1907, the *Speaker* evolved into the *Nation* with Massingham as editor, and nearly every member of the C.S.U.–*Daily News*–*Speaker* group, plus Henry N. Brailsford, L. T. Hobhouse, and J. A. Hobson as contributors. With many of its regular staff in Parliament, and frequently in the Government or at the elbow of leading radical politicians, the *Nation* operated as the official spokesman for the Lloyd George wing of the Cabinet in the way J. A. Spender's *Westminster Gazette* served Asquith, Grey, and Haldane. The famous 'Nation Lunches,' held weekly on Monday or Tuesday at the National Liberal Club provided a clearing house for ideas on Liberal social reform. Massingham himself, Mrs Masterman remarks, had more influence than most ministers in the early years of the Campbell-Bannerman ministry.[20]

1893–9, with Harold Spender and H. W. Massingham, and dismissed with them for criticizing Boer War; correspondent for *Manchester Guardian* in India during famine of 1900; editorial staff, *Daily News,* 1901. Vice-Chairman, Development Commission, 1912–29; Secretary, Ministry of Reconstruction, 1917–19; private secretary, Prime Minister Campbell-Bannerman, 1905–8; private secretary, Prime Minister Asquith, 1908–12.

Edward Harold Spender, 1864–1926, born, Bath; father noted physician; brother, J. A. Spender; educated, Bath College, University College, Oxford; resident, Toynbee Hall, 1887–8; novelist and journalist; wrote for *Pall Mall Gazette,* 1891–3, *Westminster Gazette, Daily Chronicle, Manchester Guardian, Daily News,* the *Nation.* Dismissed from *Daily Chronicle* with Nash and Massingham, 1899, for criticism of Boer War. Disciple of Lloyd George; defeated United Labour candidate for Parliament, 1922; member, Fabian Society. Father of Stephen Spender.

[20] Lucy Masterman, *C. F. G. Masterman,* London, 1939, p. 78. Unfortunately, there is no biography of Henry W. Massingham, nor any connected story of the evolution of the group around the *Nation.* For parts of the story, see John L. Hammond, *C. P. Scott of the Manchester Guardian,* London, 1934, pp. 79–80. The fullest printed source on Massingham at the *Speaker* and the *Nation* is Masterman, *C. F. G. Masterman,* pp. 58–9, 78–81. For Massingham at the *Nation,* see also Henry W. Nevinson, *More Changes, More Chances,* New York, 1925, pp. 214–22. See J. A. Hobson's estimate of the influence of the *Nation* Lunches: J. A. Hobson, *Confessions of an Economic Heretic,* New York, 1938, pp. 82–3.

Henry William Massingham, 1860–1924, born, Old Catton, Norwich; father,

Among the most important of the philanthropist reformers was Charles Frederick Gurney Masterman, who edited an influential collection of essays entitled *The Heart of the Empire*, which fairly exemplifies the point of view of the group.[21] Besides Masterman, Frederick Pethick-Lawrence, Reginald Bray, Noel Buxton, Philip Wilson, A. C. Pigou, G. P. Gooch, and G. M. Trevelyan contributed essays. The aim of the book, Masterman explained in the preface, was to force recognition of the danger to the empire resulting from unsolved problems of the metropolis of London, which was the 'Heart of the Empire.' Those who sought the welfare of the empire could not be indifferent to or remain ignorant of the condition of the people in the world's largest city. Masterman was distressed that progress toward reform seemed to have stopped. In the eighties much effort had been directed toward making reform possible. Government machinery had at last rid itself of old restrictions. Household franchise, militant trade unionism, strikes and riots suggested, as all competent observers could see, that class politics and social reform were coming. But if a man had gone to sleep in the mid-eighties and awakened in 1901, he would not believe what he saw. A 'wave of "imperialism" has swept over the country,' said Masterman, 'and all those efforts, hopes, and visions, have vanished as if wiped out with a sponge.' The Independent Labour Party and settlement houses were 'relics.' The 'Age of Slumming' had passed. The 'Age of Settlements' had passed. The 'Age of Philanthropy' had passed. 'People have become tired of the poor.' And the poor, for their part, had no interest in improving their condition. The town-bred man,

Methodist preacher; educated, King Edward VI's School, Norwich. Entered journalism, 1877; Editor, *Daily Chronicle*, 1895–9; resigned over Boer War; associated with *Manchester Guardian*, *Daily News*, and *Speaker*, 1900–7; editor, *Nation*, 1907–23. Lost much of his admiration for Lloyd George over the Marconi Scandal in 1911.

[21] Charles Frederick Gurney Masterman, 1874–1927, born, Wimbledon; educated, Weymouth College and Christ's College, Cambridge; journalist, author, and politician; contributor, *Independent Review*; literary editor, *Speaker*, *Daily News*, and *Nation*; Liberal M.P. for West Ham, 1906–11; for Bethnal Green, 1911–14; for Rusholme Division, Manchester, 1923–4. Parliamentary Under-secretary to the Local Government Board, 1908–9 (served with John Burns); Under-secretary of State to the Home Office, 1910; Financial Secretary to the Treasury, and Chairman, National Insurance Commission, 1912–14; P.C., 1912; Chancellor of the Duchy of Lancaster with a seat in the Cabinet, 1914–15; unable to win by-election for Cabinet seat; required to resign; Director, Wellington House (propaganda department), 1914–18; Director, literary department, Ministry of Information, 1918.

physically stunted and easily excited, sought stimulus in drink, betting, and a new press that catered to his love of sensationalism and need for excitement. The mindless revelry at the relief of Mafeking was typical.[22] Moreover, indifference to the condition of the people of London represented indifference to the welfare of the empire.

> The centre of Imperialism, as Lord Rosebery is never tired of reiterating, rests in London. With a perpetual lowering of vitality of the Imperial Race in the great cities of the Kingdom through overcrowding in room and in area no amount of hectic, feverish activity on the confines of the Empire will be able to arrest the inevitable decline.[23]

Masterman's preface and introductory essay were followed by statements by the other contributors on specific problems— housing, the condition of children, industry, the Church, and the damage done to old-fashioned standards of behaviour and morality by the all-encompassing preoccupation with empire. Imperialism, concluded G. P. Gooch in his essay, was based on assumptions of superiority which were not valid. Patriotism had become militaristic savagery. The hero of Mafeking, General Robert Baden-Powell, in his book, *Aids to Scouting*, had exhorted England's young men: 'Better than football, better than any other game, is man-hunting.'[24] The nation gave a pension to a soldier, but not to a man who served his country by a life of honest industry. Nations, Gooch suggested, could 'go mad.' England had, as had the United States. 'The Philippine War,' he concluded, 'goes far to cancel the debt of liberty that the world owes to the United States.'[25]

Through *The Heart of the Empire*, as through all the writing of the philanthropist reformers, ran the theme: imperialism, far from being a symbol of national greatness, was a promoter of national decadence, for it diverted attention and resources from the one project that did betoken the national greatness, the improvement of the condition of the people.

[22] Charles F. G. Masterman, ed., *Heart of the Empire*, London, 1901, pp. 3–8.
[23] *Ibid.*, p. 24.
[24] George P. Gooch, 'Imperialism,' in Masterman, ed., *Heart of the Empire*, p. 318.
[25] *Ibid.*, p. 329. For a discussion of the origins of *The Heart of the Empire*, see G. P. Gooch, *Under Six Reigns*, London, 1958, pp. 85–6. Gooch points out that three of the contributors became Cabinet ministers and one an archbishop.

3

The first political manifestation of the concern for national efficiency appeared early in 1901 with an attempt to organize a political combination among reformers of both parties that would have efficiency as its chief object. The leader of the new alignment was to be the Earl of Rosebery—a sincere reformer, but a reluctant leader—whose interest in the cause he represented began to decline the moment a group ready to support him appeared. Lord Rosebery had raised the banner of national efficiency, even though he did not use the term, a little more than a month after the Khaki Election. While most reformers were mourning the defeat of their cause, and the Unionists, securely in power, were celebrating the expected end of the war, Rosebery used the occasion of his rectoral address at the University of Glasgow on November 16, 1900, to address the nation.[26] His speech was an admirable summary of most of what would become the programme of national efficiency. Empires could be lost through neglect and complacency, he said. English institutions needed modernization. The empire needed men from the universities trained in modern languages, not Latin and Greek. Most important, cities were destroying the people.

> An Empire such as ours requires as its first condition an Imperial Race—a race vigorous and industrious and intrepid. Health of mind and body exalt a nation in the competition of the universe. The survival of the fittest is an absolute truth in the conditions of the modern world.

[26] *The Times*, November 17, 1900. Rosebery's biographers say practically nothing of his part in promoting the ideal of national efficiency. Lord Crewe gives it almost no importance. Marquess of Crewe, *Lord Rosebery* (London, 1931), II, 575. Robert Rhodes James refers to Lord Rosebery's 'vague' and 'curious doctrine of "Efficiency".' Robert Rhodes James, *Rosebery*, London, 1963, pp. 431–2. This attitude is not surprising. Commentators at the time assumed the speech was the beginning of a campaign by Rosebery to resume the Liberal leadership and discussed it in these terms. *The Times* leader the following day and a letter from H. W. Massingham in the same paper took almost no note of Rosebery's call for efficiency. *The Times*, November 17, 1900.

Archibald Philip Primrose, Fifth Earl of Rosebery, 1847–1929, born, London; his mother was a daughter of fourth Earl Stanhope and a great-niece of William Pitt. Educated at Eton, Christ Church, Oxford. Under-secretary of the Home Office for Scottish Affairs, 1881–3; Lord Privy Seal, 1885; Secretary of State for Foreign Affairs, 1886; 1892–4; Chairman London County Council, 1889–90 and 1892. Prime Minister, 1894–5. Resigned Liberal leadership, 1896. Declined high office in 2nd coalition Cabinet, 1916. His wife was Hannah Rothschild, heiress of Baron Meyer Amschel de Rothschild.

If nations are to survive, he concluded,

> . . . they must constantly sharpen their intelligence and equip-
> ment. They need constant co-operation and vigilance with
> commerce; of the teachers with the taught, and with the age in
> which they teach.

What is empire, he asked, but predominance of race?[27]

At Glasgow Rosebery had been speaking for himself. Whether
he realized that national efficiency could provide a platform upon
which to bid for the Liberal leadership can never be determined.
Nor, to be sure, is there any certainty that Rosebery even desired
the party leadership that might have been his if he chose to claim it.
His behaviour suggests he was not sure himself. Lord Rosebery
was a man, Bernard Shaw remarked later, 'who never missed an
occasion to let slip an opportunity.' Nevertheless, whatever were
his personal feelings on the matter, there began to grow around
Rosebery in the next year an enthusiastic group of imperialist social
reformers who hoped to make him the head of a revived Liberal
Party that would carry the banner of national efficiency.[28]

The titular leader of the Liberal Party was Sir Henry Campbell-
Bannerman, a man of kindliness and determination who passion-
ately opposed the war and imperialism. He had, on this account,
experienced some cooling in his relations with H. H. Asquith,
Edward Grey, and R. B. Haldane, his chief lieutenants in the
party, who believed in the concept of empire and supported the
prosecution of the war.[29] However, until well into 1901, Campbell-
Bannerman attempted to serve the Liberals as a mediator, 'a
smoother,' holding together the imperialist and anti-imperialist

---

[27] *The Times*, November 17, 1900.

[28] Rosebery had a reputation for interest in social reform. Henry W. Massingham wrote in 1923 that most of the Liberals who supported Rosebery for Prime
Minister in 1893 were attracted by the possibility of strong leadership in the
field of domestic social reform rather than by his imperialism, and were convinced of the unwisdom of continuing the Gladstonian tradition in economics.
During the Boer War, this reputation helped Rosebery acquire followers—for
instance, the Webbs—among reformers who knew nothing of his views and
intentions. H. W. Massingham, 'Morley the Humanist,' *Fortnightly Review*,
CXX (November, 1923), 699.

[29] R. B. Haldane was promoting Rosebery for the Liberal leadership well
before the Glasgow speech. See, for instance, Beatrice Webb's description of a
pro-Rosebery 'anti-little England' party at Haldane's on March 16, 1900. Webb,
Partnership, p. 198. Mrs Webb pretended at this time not to take the movement
seriously, but the couple continued to be invited.

C*

wings of his party, even though, by declining to take a stand, he brought upon himself attacks of the press that threatened his own leadership. Then in mid-summer of 1901, C. B. left his middle position and denounced, fiercely and publicly, the war in South Africa and by implication all who approved of it. His biographer, J. A. Spender, argues that it was only sympathy for Boer families suffering in British concentration camps that caused the departure. Nevertheless, the suddenness and violence of the new stand, particularly when contrasted with his former studied moderation, suggests that Campbell-Bannerman saw in Rosebery a threat he could not ignore. On June 14 at a banquet of the National Reform Union in the Holborn Restaurant, Campbell-Bannerman concluded a denunciation of the Unionist conduct of the war with the accusation that the Government was using 'methods of barbarism' by confining the Boer civilians in concentration camps. Here Campbell-Bannerman threw down a challenge to the members of his own party who supported the Government policy in South Africa. The imperialists replied almost immediately by announcing a dinner to be held at the Hotel Cecil on July 19 in honour of Asquith, which could only be interpreted as a clear attack upon Campbell-Bannerman's leadership. On July 9, at a meeting at the Reform Club, Campbell-Bannerman tried to forestall the open split the dinner would cause with an impassioned appeal to the Liberal M.P.s for loyalty. The meeting concluded with expressions of confidence and high personal regard for Campbell-Bannerman, but he realized he had failed in his appeal for support. The next day he addressed a petition to Asquith begging him to postpone the July 19 event. Of the dinner he said,

> . . . it cannot be doubted that it originated in a desire to emphasize a sectional difference, and in issuing invitations many men have been excepted on this ground.
>
> Will you let me appeal to get it postponed to a later time when all the party will join in. . . .[30]

The night before the Reform Club meeting, on July 8, Richard

[30] Henry Campbell-Bannerman to H. H. Asquith, July 10, 1901, Asquith Papers, box 10, ff. 5–6. This letter seems to dispute the contention of Campbell-Bannerman's biographer, J. A. Spender, that the Reform Club meeting re-established the future Prime Minister 'firmly in the confidence of the country.' J. A. Spender, *The Life of the Right Hon. Sir Henry Campbell-Bannerman, G.C.B.* (Boston, 1924), I, 346.

Burdon Haldane visited Sidney and Beatrice Webb and pleaded with Mrs Webb to see that Sidney came to the dinner.

'We are fighting for our lives,' said Haldane to me: 'Both Asquith and I would attach much importance to Sidney's being present at the dinner: we do not like to press it because the whole movement may be a failure.'[31]

The same day she noted,

... G. B. S. writes us urging us to plunge in with Rosebery as the best chance of moulding a home policy.[32]

Sidney agreed to attend, and so the Webbs joined the movement for national efficiency. Undoubtedly they looked forward to making Lord Rosebery the decorative leader of a party of social reform that they could hope to control as they had guided the Progressive Party on the London County Council.

In September, 1901, Sidney Webb published an article in the *Nineteenth Century*, 'Lord Rosebery's Escape from Houndsditch,' in which he outlined a programme for the new group. This widely-quoted statement expressed the disquiet that England had felt since the beginning of the war. While most critics had been content to diagnose the ills of the nation without offering remedies beyond such unspecific advice as the Prince of Wales' injunction to 'Wake

[31] Webb, *Partnership*, p. 218.
Richard Burdon Haldane, 1856–1928, 1st Viscount of Cloan, cr. 1911, born, Edinburgh; evangelical family; father former Fellow of Oriel College, Oxford, retired to Cloanden, Scotland, as gentleman farmer; educated at Edinburgh Academy, Universities of Göttingen and Edinburgh; called to Bar, 1879; Q.C., 1890, specializing in cases concerning Dominions. Liberal M.P. for East Lothian, 1885–1911; Secretary of State for War, 1905–12; Liberal-Imperialist; worked for Liberal League under Lord Rosebery; helped Sir William Harcourt draft and defend the Finance Act of 1894 (estate duty); while at War Office reorganized army along modern lines; accepted peerage, 1911, to aid Liberal leadership in Lords while Lord Crewe was in India; Lord Chancellor, 1912–15; because of his previous visits to Germany and other German associations he was wrongfully accused of pro-German sympathies, which although groundless, made Asquith unable to keep Haldane in Cabinet during 1st coalition; later left Liberal Party over lack of interest in educational policy and reappeared as Lord Chancellor, 1924, of first Labour Government; led Labour opposition in House of Lords, 1925–8. Participated in the formation of the University of London from University College as a member of its Council; a founder, with the Webbs, of the London School of Economics, 1895; supported establishment of provincial universities, Workers' Educational Association and British Institute for Adult Education.
[32] *Ibid.*, p. 220.

up,' Webb told what needed to be done and suggested Lord Rosebery would be able to do it. Most important, he established the principle that the true imperialist must be a social reformer. His article was read and pondered, if not approved, by reformers of all political complexions, many of whom differed from Webb in outlook and had no desire for Lord Rosebery as their leader.[33]

What, Webb asked, is in the minds of Englishmen today? It is

> . . . a burning feeling of shame at the 'failure' of England—shame for the lack of capacity of its governors, shame for the inability of Parliament to get through even its routine business, shame at the absence of grip on and resourcefulness in our statesmen, shame for the pompous inefficiency of every branch of our public administration, shame for the slackness of our merchants and trades that transfers our commercial supremacy to the United States, shame for the supineness which looks on unmoved at the continued degradation of our race by drunkenness and gambling, and all the horrors of the sweated trades, as rampant today in all our great centres of population as they were when officially revealed fifteen years ago. This sense of shame has yet to be transmitted into political action. Lord Rosebery's quick political wit seizes this fact, and rightly pronounces that 'The country is ripe for a domestic programme,' which shall breathe new life into the administrative dry bones of our public offices. The party leaders and statesmen . . . [will get support only if] . . . above all other considerations they stand for a policy of National Efficiency.[34]

[33] For instance, Canon Barnett wrote to his brother Frank (no date but '1901'):

> Last Saturday a lot of old Toynbee Hall men discussed Webb's article. Harold Spender opened, and, as is usual with pro-Boer people, put that side to the front. This diverted talk, and the mind of the men did not get at Webb. Read the article. To me the scheme is like the Catholic Church without the Pope, like a garden of flowers without roots. National efficiency is what we all desire, but how is it possible till individuals have some motive for efficiency which will inspire and guide the conduct of each? All along the line this generation consumes what others have created, and Webb's care of efficiency is born of a faith which many men now disown. Rosebery hit the mark when he went for 'mental indolence.'

Henrietta O. Barnett, *Canon Barnett* (Boston, 1919), II, 183.

[34] Sidney Webb, 'Lord Rosebery's Escape From Houndsditch,' *Nineteenth Century*, L (September, 1901), 366–86.

The basis of imperial strength, said Webb, must be racial strength. He linked with national efficiency what would be perhaps his most famous contribution to social thought, the ideal of the national minimum—a basic competence below which society ought not to permit any of its members to fall. 'The statesman who is really inspired by the idea of National Efficiency will stump the country in favour of a "national minimum" standard of life . . .,'[35] said Webb. This statesman '. . . would be able to expand our uneven and incomplete Factory Acts into a systematic and all-embracing code, prescribing for every manual worker employed a minimum of education, sanitation, leisure, and wages as the inviolable starting-point of industrial competition.'[36] He applauded Asquith's speech at the Hotel Cecil banquet of July 19 when the Liberal leader had proposed that a society be judged by the 'material and moral minimum it prescribed for its members.' What, Asquith had then asked,

> is the use of an Empire if it does not breed and maintain in the truest and fullest sense of the word an Imperial race? What is the use of talking about Empire if here, at its very centre, there is always to be found a mass of people, stunted in education, a prey of intemperance, huddled and congested beyond the possibility of realizing in any true sense either social or domestic life?[37]

Gladstonian Liberalism—'Peace, Retrenchment, and Reform'—was dead, pronounced Webb. Socialist thought was spreading over the land like a river at the flood, not deep but wide—a kind of seeping socialism. For their own advantage, and for the country's, the Liberals must adopt a new creed.

Thus, in the last six months of 1901, Sidney Webb lent his considerable influence to incorporate national efficiency as a permanent part of the movement for social reform. But by linking his political fortunes with Rosebery he destroyed for himself, his wife, and practically for the Fabian Society, the possibility of guiding or shaping the reform activity he supported.[38]

---

[35] Webb, 'Rosebery,' p. 376.   [36] *Ibid.*   [37] *Ibid.*
[38] R. C. K. Ensor suggests that Webb lost even more than a connexion with the Liberal administration and the opportunity to influence legislation.

The fact was that between 1895 and 1905 the Webbs had a clear opportunity of placing Sidney in a position, where the office of President of the Local Government Board or of the Board of Trade would have been his for the choosing in the Campbell-Bannerman Cabinet. They lost it, not for want of trying,

The third event in the short history of Lord Rosebery's flirtation with the party of national efficiency was his Chesterfield speech at the end of 1901. Unionist commentators assumed that in view of Campbell-Bannerman's repeated attacks upon the supporters of the war, the Liberal Imperialists must by this time begin to look for a new leader. Surely Rosebery would announce his resumption of power.[39] The speech hardly justified the great interest it had evoked. Rosebery did indeed say that the watchword for the Liberals must be 'efficiency.' He told what he would do if he were in office—there would be 'war office reform,' 'naval improvement,' more efficient promotion of trade and industry, 'extension of education,' 'housing reform.' He agreed that the temperance problem 'means much in the physical degeneracy of our race.' He noted that the Germans handled all these problems well. But nowhere was there a challenge to Campbell-Bannerman nor a clear invitation to the Liberals to come to him.[40]

Nevertheless, in the next few weeks the party of national efficiency seemed about to appear. The Liberal Imperial Council transformed itself into the Liberal League with the platform of carrying out the policies of the Chesterfield speech. Rosebery became president of the league. Asquith, Sir Edward Grey, and Henry Fowler were vice-presidents. Yet even then Rosebery was slipping away. In the last days of December and the first days of January, each of the leading Liberals visited him. Campbell-Bannerman, eager for a compromise, offered to make him Liberal leader of the House of Lords.[41] Rosebery declined. He denied

but because they tried in the wrong way and put their money on the wrong horses.

The trouble, essentially, says Ensor, lay with the character and nerve of Rosebery, and the misrepresentation of these qualities to the Webbs by Haldane.

. . . for the future lay with the Radicals. Haldane sought to disguise this from Webb by representing the Roseberyites as the 'collectivist' wing of the party. He was only too successful, and Webb's fortunes were cast with the Roseberyite group. On 28th [sic. 19] July, 1901, he took part with them in an anti-Campbell-Bannerman dinner, and this was followed in September by a much-quoted article. . . . 'Lord Rosebery's Escape From Houndsditch.' Thus the Webbs fatally antagonized all shades of radicals. . . .

R. C. K. Ensor, 'Permeation,' in Margaret I. Cole, ed., *The Webbs and Their Work*, London, 1949, pp. 65, 66.

[39] *The Times* leader: '1901, Review of the Year,' December 31, 1901.

[40] *The Times*, December 17, 1901. The most that *The Times* could say of the speech was that it had won him 'a leading position in politics. . . .'

[41] R. W. Perks ('Imperial Perks') to H. H. Asquith, January 2, 1902, Asquith Papers, box 10, ff. 46–8.

there were any differences between himself and Campbell-Bannerman on the Boer War, but said he could never agree to Irish Home Rule. Campbell-Bannerman reported to Asquith that Rosebery had said, 'the appeal he made at Chesterfield was not to the party but to the country.'[42] Already the party was dissolving. Within three months the Webbs saw their mistake. On March 19, Mrs Webb wrote:

> Having done our level best to stimulate the 'Limps' into some kind of conviction, and having most assuredly failed, we now return to our own work. Three months' peaceful and strenuous effort in the country seems a delightful prospect. And between me and this diary, I think the 'Limps' will be glad to be rid of us! Our contempt for their 'limpness' and our distrust for their reactionary views are too apparent.[43]

Thus, while Lord Rosebery drifted off to plough again his lonely furrow, contact between the Webbs and the Liberal Party grew more and more tenuous. Haldane, to be sure, remained a friend, but the Webbs' support of the Education Act of 1902 lost for them whatever affection remained among the rest of the Liberal leadership. After the formation of the Campbell-Bannerman Government in December, 1905, Sidney and Beatrice Webb tried to re-open the lines of communication between themselves and the Liberal ministry.[44] Masterman, Winston Churchill, and a number of other junior Liberals received invitations to dine at 41 Grosvenor Road. The Webbs supplied Haldane with helpful memoranda to place before the Cabinet. They pumped R. L. Morant for ministerial gossip. But the reformers in the Cabinet regarded them with suspicion if not dislike. Finally, after the appearance of a competing social programme derived from the minority report of the Royal Commission on the Poor Law, most Liberal reformers looked on the Webb team as a positive menace.

[42] H. Campbell-Bannerman to H. H. Asquith, January 7, 1902, Asquith Papers, box 10, ff. 52–3.

[43] Webb, *Partnership*, p. 232.

[44] See, for instance, Sidney Webb to John Burns, December 11, 1905, on hearing of Burns' appointment as President of the Local Government Board. 'A thousand Congratulations!' It was 'splendidly courageous' of him to accept it. 'You will be cruelly denounced for not doing impossibilities, but you have survived that sort of thing before.' He would always be 'entirely at your service.' B.M. Add. MSS 46287, Burns Papers, Vol. VII, f. 289.In private, the Webbs rather despised Burns. Webb, *Partnership*, pp. 325, 393–4.

The Webbs had many faults. Insincerity and lack of realism were not among them. Their inability to turn the party of Liberal imperialism into a party of social reform under Rosebery did not discourage them. By word and action they continued to promote national efficiency. Their most valuable service to the cause may have been the organization, about six months after their break with Lord Rosebery, of a group designed to be an inter-party brain trust or general staff for imperialism and social reform—the 'Coefficients.' The first meeting occurred in November, 1902, at the Webb residence. This was followed soon, on December 8, 1902, by a dinner in the flat maintained by Grey and Haldane in Whitehall Court. For the next six years the group met more or less regularly at Ship Tavern in Whitehall and finally at Saint Ermin's Hotel in Westminster. Besides Webb, Grey, and Haldane, the group included at various times influential Unionist journalists, Leo Maxse of the *National Review*, J. A. Garvin of the *Observer*, and W. F. Monypenny of *The Times*. There were politician-journalists—L. S. Amery, a Unionist, and C. F. G. Masterman, a Liberal, and established politicians such as Lord Hugh Cecil and Josiah Wedgwood. There were scholars—H. J. Mackinder, W. A. S. Hewins, Michael Sadler, Bertrand Russell—and Social-ists, besides Webb, William Pember Reeves and H. G. Wells, and finally, among others, Lord Milner.[45]

The Coefficients were united by disgust at the fecklessness, aimlessness, and ostentation of English society, demonstrated at its worst in the Boer War, and the stark contrast presented by Germany. Their political bond, Liberal and Conservative alike, was opposition to the destructive competition of untrammelled free enterprise and a belief that a moderately authoritarian State could organize the nation's resources for the collective good. As did all English imperialists, the group divided over Chamberlain's announcement on tariff reform in May, 1903. About the necessity of protection for social planning, Conservatives and Fabians were

[45] The best sources on the Coefficients are Leopold S. Amery, *My Political Life* (London, 1953), I, 223–4, and Herbert George Wells, *Experiment in Autobiography*, New York, 1934, pp. 650–5. For a discussion of the membership and aims of the Coefficients by a modern historian, see Bernard Semmel, *Imperialism and Social Reform*, Cambridge, Mass., 1960, pp. 74–82. The Coefficients are the Pentagram Circle in Wells' *The New Machiavelli*, to which Remington was introduced by 'Crupp' (Leopold Amery). Their influence caused Remington to change from the Liberal to the Conservative Party in search of a 'new aristocracy.'

more nearly of a mind than Liberals. Nevertheless, the group lingered on as a dining club and a forum for the expression and exchange of ideas among men too influential to be ignored by the press or by either party.[46]

4

Soon after the Khaki Election of 1900, the national temper had begun to change. By 1901 English patience with heedless imperialism had nearly disappeared.[47] For a nation that had accepted uncritically the doctrine of imperial expansion, 1901 was a year of disillusion and disappointment. Added to the obstinate unwillingness of the Boers to surrender before the power of an empire continually proclaimed as the greatest in the word was the embarrassment of the concentration camp system for civilian Boers that was uncomfortably similar to the odious Spanish practices in Cuba between 1896 and 1898. Moreover 1901 brought the decennial census which showed that Germany, who seemed to be able to do all things with efficiency, was increasing the gap between her population and Great Britain's. The slightly more than ten million margin of 1871 had grown only to eleven million in 1881. By 1901 it had leaped to fifteen million.

The growing disparity in population seemed to be matched by German expansion and British decay in manufacturing, commerce, and technical and military education. Article after article in Conservative and Liberal journals alike attacked the ignorance, the complacency, the 'inefficiency' of the class that traditionally devoted itself to the management of the nation's affairs.[48]

[46] Surprisingly, Mrs Webb, whom H. G. Wells credits with the suggestion for the Coefficients (Wells, *Autobiography*, p. 651), does not mention the group in the published portion of her diary.

[47] An almost unbroken series of Unionist election defeats began within a year after the Khaki Election. No government in the twentieth century would even approach the net loss of twenty-four seats in five years which the Unionists sustained between the Khaki Election and their resignation in December, 1905. Furthermore, the trend was uniformly to the left, for in the same period the Liberals lost six seats to Labour, who lost none themselves.

[48] For a sampling of early writing on various forms of inefficiency, see: 'The Crisis in British Industry,' *The Times*, November 18, November 21, December 3, December 14, December 16, December 24, December 26, December 28, December 30, 1901; G. G. Colton, *Public Schools and Public Needs*, London, 1901; 'Yolet Capel,' 'England's Peril,' *Westminster Review*, CLVII (February, 1902), 163–70; T. Miller Maguire, 'The Technical Training of Officers,'

At the end of the year, on December 5, the Prince of Wales—
the future George V—just returned from a world tour, made a
widely-quoted speech at the Guildhall in which he told of the
affection for Great Britain that he had found in the empire, but
concluded with the warning: 'The old country must wake up if
she intends to maintain her competitive pre-eminence in her
colonial trade against foreign competitors. (hear, hear.)' Although
the competition referred to was commercial, the speech was
usually interpreted as an injunction to greater British activity in all
fields.[49]

The supporters of national efficiency were frequently less interested in government welfare activity to improve the condition of
the people than in the establishment of institutions to promote
discipline, sobriety, and vigour among the population—compulsory military service, the Boy Scouts, physical training in State
schools, temperance legislation.[50] For many the answer seemed to
lie in the return to a hierarchical society. There was much nostalgia
for the devotion and sense of responsibility associated with a well-
established aristocracy. There were attacks on the 'smart set' and
the 'financial intrigue' of 'foreign Jews' (to be distinguished from
English Jews) who were undermining the economic and social
position of the traditional ruling classes. The social Darwinian
ethic was continually evident in the association of high and loose
living, neglect of duty, and careless breeding, with a degenerating
race.[51]

National Review, XXXVI (January, 1901), 684–91; Charles Warren, 'Some
Lessons From the South African War,' *National Review*, XXXVIII (October,
1901), 181–96. Particularly for Leo Maxse and the *National Review*, the quest for
national efficiency became something like a crusade.

[49] See *The Times* leader, December 6, 1901. It was widely suggested that
colonial markets could be best held, and colonies strengthened, by assisted
emigration of Englishmen to them. Both Lord Rosebery and Joseph Chamberlain, who were significantly paired on the platform to follow the prince, emphasized the importance of populating the empire with the British race. *The Times*,
December 6, 1901.

[50] After the Anglo-Japanese alliance, many Englishmen found their ideal in
the Japanese code of *Bushido*, which provided precisely the combination of self-
denial, valour, and sober but energetic obedience that was felt to be lacking in
England. The quick Japanese defeat of Russia made a great impression. See
Leopold S. Amery, *My Political Life* (London, 1953), I, 218; Frederick Le Gros
Clark, *Social History of the School Medical Service*, London, 1948, p. 5.

[51] See Arnold White, *Efficiency and Empire*, London, 1901, *passim*.; Robert
Blatchford, *Britain for the British*, London, 1902, *passim*.; H. G. Wells' description of the 'new aristocracy' in *The New Machiavelli*.

For many Englishmen, national efficiency meant, above all, physical efficiency. The greatest weakness revealed by the Boer War was the widespread physical disability among working-class men who offered themselves for service in the army. Because this was the first time in half a century that large numbers of English males had been weighed, measured, and tested for physical weakness, no one could be certain whether the conditions discovered were new—whether the apparent unhealthiness was the result of an urban, industrial environment or of progressive racial degeneracy. But to a nation wedded as the British were to the idea that greatness and survival were symbolized by physical vigour, the apparent symptoms of national decline and racial decay were terrifying. The possible distinctions between unfavourable inherited physical characteristics and weakness caused by unhealthy environment were not clear to many. Unscientific publicists such as Arnold White could advocate in a single work sterilization of the unfit and compulsory military service and physical exercise for the improvement of the race.[52]

The importance of the facts concerning the poor physical condition of British industrial workers penetrated the popular consciousness only slowly. During 1901 the nation received warnings, which were generally disregarded, from two major writers on the subject. Arnold White, attempting to prove his assertion about the general physical deterioration of the race, pointed out that three out of five soldiers attempting to enlist in the army at the Manchester depot in 1899 had to be rejected as physically unfit. He was the first to use this famous example of the disability of the industrial working classes.[53] A few months later, B. Seebohm Rowntree, in his study of the living conditions among the working classes in York, noted that of 3,600 recruits applying between the years 1897 and 1900 at the York, Leeds, and Sheffield military depots, 26½ per cent were rejected as unfit and a further 29 per cent were only provisionally accepted as 'specials.' If the physical fitness of working men in the rest of the country was no better, Rowntree remarked, at least one-half of the manpower of England would be unavailable for military duty. Rowntree concluded:

Even if we set aside considerations of physical and mental suffering, and regard the question only in its strictly economic

[52] White, *Efficiency and Empire*, *passim*.　　　[53] *Ibid.*, pp. 101–2.

and national aspect, there can be no doubt that the facts set forth in this chapter indicate a condition of things the serious import of which can hardly be overestimated.[54]

Perhaps because White was regarded by serious thinkers as an empire-promoting sensationalist and Rowntree's study conversely had in it so much other material that was new, the remarks on the physical condition of army recruits in these two widely-read books made no impression on the public. General recognition of the fitness problem came only in January, 1902. In that month, General John Frederick Maurice, the son of Frederick Dennison Maurice, writing under the pseudonym, 'Miles,' published an article in the *Contemporary Review* entitled, 'Where to Get Men.'[55] General Maurice argued that the current shortage of recruits that was causing so much anxiety among military authorities was the result, not of the system of voluntary recruiting, the low pay, or of any lack of patriotism, but of the fact that relatively few among the men applying for the army were able to meet even the drastically reduced wartime physical requirements. The environmental conditions of English working-class life, argued General Maurice, were dangerously reducing the reserve of physically qualified men from which soldiers had to be recruited. Expressing Arnold White's ratio, he said:

> What I want to insist upon is, that a state of things in which no more than two out of five of the population below a certain standard of life are fit to bear arms is a national danger which cannot be met by any mere scheme of enlistment, and that true patriotism requires that that danger be recognized.[56]

General Maurice's article appeared only four months after Webb's 'Lord Rosebery's Escape From Houndsditch,' two months after the Chesterfield speech, and two weeks after the

---

[54] B. Seebohm Rowntree, *Poverty, A Study of Town Life*, London, 1901, pp. 216–21. The unwillingness of informed opinion to accept the statistical findings of social surveyors is illustrated by a lead article in *The Times* in late summer of 1902 on a series of Rowntree lectures at Cambridge. The paper questioned Rowntree's assertion that 52 per cent of children in York showed traces of malnutrition and suggested an inquiry in another town would show the opposite. In any case, the article concluded, what did Rowntree plan to do about it? 'Irremediable Poverty,' *The Times*, August 23, 1902.

[55] 'Miles' (Major-General Sir John Frederick Maurice), 'Where to Get Men,' *Contemporary Review*, LXXXI (January, 1902), 78–86.

[56] *Ibid.*, p. 81.

Prince of Wales' 'Wake Up, Britain,' speech, at the moment when Lord Rosebery seemed at last about to step forward and take the leadership of a party of national efficiency. It set off a frightened and angry popular discussion that linked together in men's minds, so they could not again be separated, the questions of public health and national welfare. As a working-class revolution resulting from poverty and unemployment had appeared to threaten the social structure in the eighties, so national physical deterioration became a clear danger after the Boer War, not only to the structure of domestic society, but to the very existence of Great Britain as a world power. Particularly for those who feared Germany and hoped to see national military service in England, the matter of widespread physical deterioration in the British race became, during the next nineteen months, the most important aspect of national efficiency.[57]

A year after his first contribution, General Maurice published a second article in the *Contemporary Review*, 'National Health, A Soldier's Study.'[58] He referred to the controversy that had arisen since his first article and emphasized that the physical condition of recruits was even worse than recruiting statistics indicated because patriotism was bringing a better class of volunteers. At the same time requirements had been relaxed and recruiting sergeants had been urged not to reject summarily any applicant who might conceivably pass a physical examination.

General Maurice drew heavily on the Booth and Rowntree investigations and called attention to the observations of Samuel Barnett, who had pointed out that the Jewish women in Whitechapel, living under slum conditions as bad as any in London, enjoyed a far greater life expectancy than Christian women. Christian women customarily went off to work, while Jewish

---

[57] See, for instance, the *Spectator*, October 18, 1902; 'Episodes of the Month,' *National Review*, XL (November, 1902), 342–3; George F. Shee, 'The Deterioration in the National Physique,' *Nineteenth Century*, LIII (May, 1903), 797–805. Shee presented some frightening comparative statistics with physical condition of recruits in 1845. The number of recruits under the standard height for military service, 5 feet 6 inches, was greater in 1900 than it had been fifty-five years earlier. In 1845, 105 men per thousand were under the standard height. In 1900 565 men per thousand were under the standard height, and the army in 1901 had been given permission to enlist men down to a minimum of five feet tall. *Ibid.*, p. 798.

[58] Major-General Sir John Frederick Maurice, 'National Health, A Soldier's Study,' *Contemporary Review*, LXXXIII (January, 1903), 41–56.

women did not. Maurice urged, as Charles Booth had long urged, a national inquiry into the conditions of working-class life. Such research would do God's work as the Christian Socialists had sought to do it, and was absolutely vital for national welfare. Concluded General Maurice:

> If by any similar investigation we could ascertain the true meaning of those figures, the 5–2, which I have given, it may be that we should be able to achieve a real step towards the securing of national health and thereby to the maintaining of a virile race able to hold for us and to hand down to our children's children the precious heirloom which has been handed down to us by virile forefathers.[59]

Within weeks after Maurice's second article, the Inspector-General of Recruiting laid before Parliament a special report on the man-power problem. Referring specifically to Maurice's articles, the Inspector-General suggested that the allegations of the last eighteen months concerning the physical condition of recruits were substantially true, that the army felt the class from which it drew soldiers was in fact suffering progressive physical deterioration, and that this was a matter of grave concern.[60]

[59] Maurice, 'National Health, p. 56.

[60] *Cd. 1501*, 'Report of the Inspector-General of Recruiting,' 1903. Because of widespread acceptance of the two out of five proportion of militarily fit men to all men examined, the results of physical examinations during World War I may be of interest. In 1920 the Ministry of National Service published a report describing the physical condition of men called up under compulsory service after the institution of conscription in 1916. Those examined were divided into four grades: I. Those who attained normal health; II. Those less fit than Grade I, but who had fair hearing and sight and no marked disease, and who could undertake moderate exercise; III. Those with marked disabilities, but who could do clerical work. For instance, those with varicose veins, flat feet, hernia, etc.; IV. Those whom the army would not take. The total number of examinations in England and Wales for the year ending November 1, 1918, was 2,425,184.

Number of Men in Grade:		Per cent of total:	
I	871,769		36·0
II	546,276		22·5
III	756,859		31·5
IV	250,280		10·0
	2,425,184		100·0

In effect, nine men were accepted for military service from each ten examined. However, these men were examined in the last year of the war, when physical requirements were lowest.

On the other hand, in the largest cities, the percentage of unfit and physically

By the spring of 1903 discussion of possible physical deterioration was no longer confined to imperialist and philanthropic
circles. The report of the Inspector-General of Recruiting had
made concern for the condition of the people a patriotic duty.
Only the most incurable optimist could deny that social reform
had become an inevitable concomitant of national greatness.
Furthermore the discussion was no longer political and moral, it
was scientific. The state of the nation was a reflexion of the state of
the race. The state of the race had to be determined on the average
by the condition of the working class. In a lead article on July 25,
1903, the *British Medical Journal*, which hitherto had taken no
official position on the subject, noted that the 1901 census showed
that of 2,673,676 children in England and Wales between the ages
of ten and fourteen, 138,130 boys and 7,262 girls were at work.
(There were, in fact, 142 ten-year-old charwomen.)[61] If, said the
Journal, the stunting effect of work upon children was combined
with lack of sunshine, outdoor exercise, or fresh air, and if family
earnings were insufficient to obtain

> the minimum necessities for the maintenance of physical
> efficiency in the family, as, according to Mr Rowntree and Mr
> Charles Booth, happens to be the case in more than a quarter of
> our town populations, it is easily conceivable that the British
> race will deteriorate.

This was not a matter for the future, but a present crisis, concluded
the *B.M.J.*

> Now, more than at any time in the history of the British
> people, do we require stalwart sons to people the colonies and to
> uphold the prestige of the nation, and we trust that the searching
> inquiry which the Duke of Devonshire's speech seems to fore-
> shadow, if it does not dispel the fears engendered by the
> memorandum of the Director-General [*sic*, Inspector-General],
> may, at any rate, be a means of arresting the physical decline of
> the nation.[62]

marginal recruits was significantly higher than the national average. For instance,
between January and October, 1918, 160,545 men were examined in the London
region. Of these, 77,900 or 48·5 per cent were put in grades III and IV, i.e.,
60,031 or 37·4 per cent in grade III, 17,869 or 11·1 per cent in grade IV.
Quoted in George C. N. M'Gonigle and J. Kirby, *Poverty and Public Health*,
London, 1936, pp. 27–33.
    [61] 'National Health and Military Service,' *British Medical Journal*, July 25,
1903, pp. 207–8.   [62] *Ibid.*, p. 208.

The 'searching inquiry' promised by the Duke of Devonshire, the Lord President of Council, began on September 2, 1903, with the appointment of the Interdepartmental Committee on Physical Deterioration. The long delay in undertaking an investigation illustrates the extreme reluctance with which the Balfour administration approached social reform. Their unwillingness to attack the problem of the physical condition of the people, a complicated and probably expensive aspect of public welfare, was reinforced by the normal diffidence that inevitably arose in any inquiry that would involve criticism by civil servants of activities of their own departments.

The physical welfare of the working population involved wide areas within the competence of the Local Government Board and the Home Ministry. Neither department, it would appear, desired an investigation at all.[63] The Government had intended originally to use an interdepartmental committee only to discover whether 'the allegation concerning the deterioration of certain classes of the population as shown by the large percentage of rejections for physical causes of recruits for the army' ought to be the subject of investigation by a royal commission. But by the end of the parliamentary session of 1903, it had become clear that even an interdepartmental committee of docile civil servants would be bound to find a royal commission necessary. A Government that had no desire for investigation at all wished still less to see its works, or the lack of them, criticized by a body of non-political, independent experts. The original terms of reference, therefore, were enlarged, and the decision to investigate the need for an investigation became an inquiry into the question of physical deterioration itself. The enlarged terms of reference ordered the interdepartmental committee:

(1) To determine, with the aid of such counsel as the medical profession are able to give, the steps that should be taken to furnish the Government and the Nation with periodical data for an accurate comparative estimate of the health and physique of the people; (2) to indicate generally the causes of such physical deterioration as does exist in certain classes; and (3) to point out the means by which it can be most effectually diminished.[64]

[63] Almeric Fitzroy, *Memoirs* (London, 1925), II, 259.
[64] *Cd. 2175*, 'Report of the Interdepartmental Committee on Physical Deterioration,' 1904, p. v.

The committee, thus charged with conducting a broad investigation that normally would have been assigned to a royal commission, was made up of two civil servants from the English, and one from the Scottish, Board of Education, the Inspector of Marine Recruiting, the Inspector of Reformatory and Industrial Schools for the Home Office, and a physician from the General Register Office. The chairman was Almeric Fitzroy, Secretary of the Privy Council. He was a sincere social reformer, but one who was also a gentleman of unimpeachable Unionist connexions.[65]

The report of the Interdepartmental Committee, published July 29, 1904, can have been no surprise to anyone who had read the works of Charles Booth and B. Seebohm Rowntree. It told the same dreary tale of poverty, malnutrition, and disease. An important exhibit was the Johanna Street School in South London, not ten minutes' walk across Westminster Bridge from Parliament Square. Dr Alfred Eichholz, Medical Inspector of Schools for Lambeth, reported that in this institution about 90 per cent of the students were hindered in their studies because of some physical defect.[66] Basically, the trouble was that the children did not get enough to eat. They got bread and tea for breakfast, bread and margarine for lunch, and about a penny's worth of food, usually fish fried in cottonseed oil, for supper. This fare might occasionally be supplemented by vegetables picked up under a barrow. Eichholz estimated that not more than twelve of some 200 of the students' parents he knew did not drink.

Witnesses confirmed Arnold White's original charge about the physical condition of men attempting to enlist in the army at the Manchester depot. Of 12,000 men examined in 1899, 8,000 had been rejected as virtual invalids and only 1,200 were found after service in the army to be physically fit in all respects.[67]

[65] Noting that a committee appointed to inquire into public health contained no Medical Officer of Health nor any representative of the Local Government Board's public health authority, Gilbert Slater remarked, 'Dog does not eat dog, nor do Civil Servants in one department of the national service readily cast aspersions on those in other departments, or depreciate the value of their work.' Gilbert Slater, *Poverty and the State*, London, 1930, pp. 170-1. The exclusively official character of the committee was noted also by Sir John Gorst, who would nevertheless become a champion of the report. *Hansard, Parliamentary Debates*, 4 ser., CXL (August 10, 1904), col. 48.

[66] *Cd. 2175*, p. 19.

[67] *Cd. 2210*, 'Minutes of Evidence, Report of the Interdepartmental Committee on Physical Deterioration,' 1904, p. 123.

An official of a rural friendly society in Wiltshire stated that environmental sanitary conditions and knowledge of health care were no better in the country than in town. The river flowing from Chippenham was full of sewage and the local residents did not seem to care. Among countrymen, the witness reported, information of the most elemental rules of infant care simply did not exist. For obstetrical attention the poor never went to a licensed midwife, and if a mother died in childbirth the baby was allowed to die and was buried with her. They 'simply do not know what to do with it,' the witness concluded.[68]

Charles Booth testified concerning the common working-class accident of smothering infants while asleep, 'overlaying' it was usually called. Booth argued that in too many cases these tragedies, usually assumed to be the result of drunken parents sleeping with their children, were actually homicide. Infants were murdered for their insurance, which was sold to the parents by zealous industrial insurance salesmen who visited the home after the report of the birth of a child.[69]

Withal, there was no proof that the race was deteriorating. There was much unfitness due to environmental conditions and lack of proper nourishment, but the unfitness disappeared when these conditions were removed. On the other hand, there were no adequate anthropometrical surveys covering the whole population. A uniform and continuous system of physical inspection of children appeared as one of the most important of the committee recommendations.

The committee's recommendations may be grouped as follows: (1) The State should consider the extension and enforcement of regulations over environmental health conditions: the enforcement and extension of building and sanitary regulations in factories and homes, control over the distribution of food and the handling of milk. (2) Mothers should be taught proper child care; girls should be instructed in cookery and dietetics; curbs should be introduced on adult drinking and juvenile smoking. (3) Specifically, the State should make an effort to encourage physical training and exercise. (4) The committee emphasized the importance of an adequate system of school medical inspection, and (5) of a State-sponsored

---

[68] Cd. 2210, 'Minutes of Evidence, Report of the Interdepartmental Committee on Physical Deterioration,' 1904, p. 199.

[69] Ibid., pp. 47-8.

system for feeding necessitous schoolchildren to insure that children could take full advantage of the education offered by the State.[70]

5

The report of the Interdepartmental Committee on Physical Deterioration awakened scientific controversy over the condition of the people in a way unknown in England since the days of sanitary reform in the eighteen-seventies. Central to the problem of poverty appeared the problem of ill health among the poor. A man made stunted and weak, listless and ignorant by poverty could not escape from the slums to a healthy environment. Sickness caused poverty and poverty, sickness. During the Boer War the nation came to understand what the Charity Organization Society, the settlement house movement, and the Fabian Society had tried to teach in the eighties—that the evil of poverty lay not in its effect on the individual, but on society. Poverty, if it produced national weakness, was a danger to the empire. If, as the Webbs put it, 'the result of destitution was the creation of new destitution. . .,'[71] the question now presented to biological science was: For the sake of the nation and empire, at what point could the chain of circumstances be broken?

The physical deterioration report seemed to suggest beginning with children. Whether anything could be done for those who had grown into weak and malformed adults remained for the future; humanity and national interest alike dictated that society turn its attention to the lot of those not yet grown. Yet even the nature of the problem was unclear. Essentially, the debate among experts on physical deterioration revolved around two not precisely contradictory points of view. First of all there was the question of whether racial physical deterioration was actually taking place. If it were, if progressive evolution had become degeneration, nothing could be done. If, as seemed probable, the proliferation of un-

[70] *Cd. 2175*, pp. 84–93. These findings reinforced the recommendations of the Royal Commission on Physical Training (Scotland) which had reported in 1903 before the Interdepartmental Committee on Physical Deterioration, *Cd. 1507*, 'Royal Commission on Physical Training (Scotland),' 1903. Although of higher rank, this investigation received virtually no attention until the interdepartmental committee made its report.

[71] Webbs, *Local Government*, p. 551.

talented and malformed children continued, while the intelligent and well-fed failed to reproduce themselves, no amount of reform legislation aimed at cleaning up the slums would improve the general condition of the race. This, basically, was the view of Karl Pearson and Sidney Webb.[72] For these men the only possible solution was State action, not in favour of the depressed classes, but in favour of the talented classes, to encourage larger families. Webb called for 'a revolution in the economic incidence of child-bearing' and his campaign for the 'endowment of motherhood,' for mothers' pensions, was the result.[73] A number of the more enthusiastic, perhaps less conscientious Darwinists, for instance, Arnold White and H. G. Wells, as well as writers in widely-read periodicals of fashion of the type of the *Queen*, found the obvious solution in 'the sterilization of failures.'[74]

Opposed to the Darwinists, less in the solution than in the statement of the problem, was the medical profession. Generally, the doctors refused to admit that the race was deteriorating. In some cases they were suspicious of the report of the physical deterioration committee itself.[75] Nevertheless, the profession was well-acquainted with the physical condition of the working classes, and doctors generally supported measures designed to extend knowledge of hygiene and domestic science among the poor through training in State schools. The British Medical Association, once its interest had been aroused, gave much attention to the committee report and became particularly active in bringing

[72] See Pearson's letter to *The Times*, August 25, 1905, entitled 'National Deterioration,' in which he speaks of the 'approaching crisis' resulting from the decline in birth rate among the talented. Any schoolmaster, he argued, admitted that it was already showing up. 'The dearth of ability today must indeed depress thoughtful Englishmen. . . .'' For a fuller discussion of Pearson's writing, see Semmel, *Imperialism and Social Reform*, pp. 35–52. See also, *The Times*, October 11, 1906, October 16, 1906, a two-part article by Sidney Webb, 'Physical Degeneracy, or Race Suicide.' Webb pointed out that between 1896 and 1905, although the population of London County had increased by 300,000, the total number of children in the three- to five-year age bracket scheduled for school fell from 179,426 in 1896 to 174,359 in 1905.

[73] See: Sidney Webb, *The Decline in the Birthrate*, Fabian Tract 131, 1907.

[74] On Wells' proposals in this area, see: William J. Hyde, 'The Socialism of H. G. Wells in the Early Twentieth Century,' *Journal of the History of Ideas*, XVII (April, 1956), 217–34. George Bernard Shaw agreed with Wells on the need for eugenic protection of the race, although the two agreed on little else.

[75] See, for instance, the *Lancet*, August 6, 1904, 'The Report of the Privy Council Upon Physical Deterioration,' pp. 390–2.

pressure on the Government to begin physical exercise and medical inspection among schoolchildren.[76]

A leading spokesman for the medical point of view, who became at this time one of the best known physicians in the kingdom, and who would, within two years, be appointed Chief Medical Officer to the Local Government Board, was Arthur Newsholme.[77] Newsholme was impatient with the Darwinist argument that medical science, particularly sanitary science, was saving the lives of thousands whom nature had long since declared unfit and who ought to be eliminated according to the laws of survival. Over and over he repeated his denial of what Huxley had called 'the gladiatorial theory of existence.' Competition for survival, Newsholme claimed, had been replaced among humans by co-operation for survival. Omission of measures for sanitary regulations only increased the number of chronically unfit while eliminating a few of the congenitally unfit. A man given to homely, forceful analogy in argument, he suggested that the Darwinists no doubt opposed sunshine, for as one of the most potent givers of health, it was certainly keeping many unfit alive and therefore ought logically to be shut out.[78]

[76] Through November and December of 1903, and January of 1904, the *British Medical Journal* published a continuing series on the question of national physical deterioration. While unwilling to recommend direct State welfare activity, the *Journal* did propose a wide range of regulatory measures: reduction of licenses of public houses, physical training in schools, care of poor children's teeth by the poor law medical service, charitable funds to be used to supply meals for underfed schoolchildren, and physical inspection in schools.

[77] Arthur Newsholme, 1857–1943, M.D., London, 1881; Medical Officer of Health, Brighton, 1888–1908; Editor of *Journal of Hygiene*; prolific writer on public health, Chief Medical Officer, Local Government Board, 1908–19; lectured at the Johns Hopkins University, 1920–1. Editor, *Public Health* until February, 1908; C.B., 1912; K.C.B., 1917.

[78] For examples of Newsholme's arguments, see: 'Alleged Physical Degeneration in Towns,' an address to the University Extension Club, Brighton, November 27, 1903, in *Public Health*, XVII (February, 1905), pp. 293–300. (Newsholme was at this time editor of *Public Health*, the magazine of the Medical Officers of Health.) See also, an address on 'Social Evolution and Public Health,' to the York Medical Society, October 21, 1904, *Lancet*, November 12, 1904, pp. 1331–5. Although no particular friend of the British Medical Association, Newsholme gave the B.M.A. credit for 'forcing the hand' of the Board of Education towards medical inspection. Sir Arthur Newsholme, *Fifty Years in Public Health*, London, 1935, p. 392. Newsholme was himself the author of the lead article in which the B.M.A. formally proposed medical inspection of schoolchildren, eight months before the physical deterioration report. 'The Organization of the Medical Inspection of Schools,' *British Medical Journal*, November 14, 1903, p. 1288.

While the dispute boiled among the experts on the presence and nature of physical deterioration, the lay public continued to discuss the matter as the prime constituent of national efficiency. The principal topic now was whether the Government could be induced to implement the findings of the physical deterioration committee, particularly in reference to the feeding and medical inspection of schoolchildren. Many imperialists sought in addition to use improvement of the English physique as an argument for the establishment of military training.[79]

In the political world, leadership in the promotion of the physical deterioration report fell to Sir John E. Gorst, who hoped to use the committee findings to force a revival of Tory Democracy. Gorst had resigned from the Balfour ministry early in 1902 when he found he would not be given charge of the Education Bill of that year. Since 1903 he had sat as an independent member. His political life was clearly ending at the time of the interdepartmental committee, but he used the vestiges of his popularity in the promotion of its report. In doing so he quickly killed what was in any case a dying parliamentary career.[80] But by his continued attack on

---

[79] The drive for National Service was linked with physical deterioration by the publication at almost the same time of the Report of the Royal Commission on Militia and Volunteers, which recommended military training for all. *Cd. 2061.* 'Report of the Royal Commission on the Militia and Volunteers,' 1904. The coincidence in time of publication may not have been altogether fortuitous. For an example of the use of the theory of physical deterioration in the promotion of National Service, see Henry Birchenough, 'Compulsory Education and Compulsory Military Training,' *Nineteenth Century*, LVI (July, 1904), 20–7.

[80] Sir John E. Gorst, M.P., 'Physical Deterioration in Great Britain,' *North American Review*, CLXXXIV (July, 1905), 1–10, and John E. Gorst, 'Children's Rights,' *National Review*, XLV (June, 1905), 705–15. Also on the condition of the people generally, see: John Gorst, 'Social Reform,' *Nineteenth Century*, LIII (March, 1903), 519–32; John Honeyman, 'Sir John Gorst and Poor Law Reform,' *Westminster Review*, CLXI (June, 1904), 648–52; Sir John Gorst, 'Governments and Social Reform,' *Fortnightly Review*, LXXVII, n.s. (May, 1905), 843–55.

John Gorst, 1835–1916, born, Preston; family, Lancashire County landowners; educated, St John's College, Cambridge; civil servant in New Zealand, 1860–3; called to Bar, 1865; defeated candidate for Hastings, 1865 (Conservative); M.P. for Cambridge City, 1866–8; 1868, reorganized Conservative Party on a popular basis, but did not receive an administrative appointment after the party's victory in 1874; M.P., Chatham, 1875; with Lord Randolph Churchill, A. J. Balfour and Sir Henry Drummond Wolff in 'The Fourth Party.' Q.C., 1875; Solicitor-General, 1885–6 (post carried a knighthood); Under-Secretary of State for India, 1886–91; 1891–2, Financial Secretary to the Treasury; Vice-President of the Committee of the Privy Council on Education, 1895–1902; M.P., Cambridge University, 1892–1906; left Conservative Party

the Government in the Commons and in the press for its failure to show any interest in the condition of the people, Gorst contributed materially towards making social reform politically profitable for the Liberals after 1905.

The Government's attitude towards the physical deterioration committee recommendations appears to have been determined solely by considerations of economy. Gorst's successor as under-secretary of the Board of Education (the official title after 1902 was 'Secretary to the Board of Education'), William Anson, was most sympathetic towards proposals for feeding and medical inspection of schoolchildren, even though he and Gorst personally were on the worst possible terms. But the Balfour Cabinet had resolved in May, 1904, before the interdepartmental committee had reported, to give no sanction to the local authorities to increase rates (local taxes) for the purposes of social welfare. Prime Minister Balfour had told Anson curtly that so far as children's welfare was concerned he 'could be as sympathetic as he liked but there would be no increase in rates.'[81] By the beginning of 1905, however, public discussion outside of Parliament and Gorst's clamour in the press made it imperative that the Government manifest at least the appearance of concern for the condition of schoolchildren.[82]

over tariffs; defeated as Liberal candidate, Preston, 1910; outspoken critic and reformer of British state education; his recommendations were incorporated in the Education Act of 1902; supporter of Toynbee Hall and close friend of Barnett's; was one of men listed by Asquith to go to House of Lords in 1911.

[81] R. L. Morant to Balfour, December 3, 1904, British Museum, Add. MSS 49787, Balfour Papers, Vol. CV, f. 123. This memorandum was the result of Anson's suggestion that the Government should use the King's Speech to make some statement about physical deterioration. See also Anson's memorandum of February 3, 1905, Public Record Office, Cab. 37/74, No. 24, for an expression of Anson's private attitude on school feeding.

[82] Unionists affected to regard Gorst as a revolutionary whose presence in politics represented a danger to the British system of government. Gorst's proposal to throw upon local authorities the duty of feeding as well as educating children at school, said The Times in a lead article on January 2, 1905, should be stigmatized as a 'dangerous and far-reaching change in our social system.'

Sir John Gorst presents a not unusual combination of cynicism and sentimentalism. He is very lacking in sympathy with other people's ideals, aspirations, and efforts, and he is very much wedded to his own notions. On this question he contentedly accepts all the exaggerations that may help to make out a case for sentimental legislation.

If instead of quickening parental sense of duty, we are going to weaken it, we shall have to begin with the newborn babe. It is a race of fatherless and motherless foundlings to which Sir John Gorst's proposals point.

The Times, January 2, 1905.

The Cabinet decision of 1904 not to commit any funds for this purpose was energetically supported by influential leaders among the Unionists. As Gorst was likely to ask awkward questions in the debate on the King's Speech, which was to contain no reference to the report, the Cabinet decided on February 9, 1905, to appoint a second committee to investigate the findings of the physical deterioration committee. This decision was heartily approved by Anson's immediate chief, the Marquis of Londonderry, who circulated the next day a memorandum suggesting the lines upon which the new investigation should be conducted. The committee should consist exclusively of civil servants, said Londonderry, to

> ... avoid the difficulty of having ['unsuitable' scratched out in original MS] persons pressed upon us who might approach the subject with preconceived conclusions, and this committee should meet as soon as possible, so that in the event of any serious debate on the Address we may be aided in resisting premature or too far-reaching proposals by referring to the lack of specific information and practical suggestions. . . .

One could always propose waiting for the committee report.

Most important were terms of reference, Lord Londonderry went on. The committee must 'not be at liberty to make far-reaching proposals that the Unionist Party would decline to support. . . .' Anything, for instance, that would require new legislation or increased rates should be resisted. On the other hand, he warned, the terms could not be too narrow or the Government 'would be accused of [parking?] discussion while taking no really effective steps to discover or bring about any practical remedies for the evils now generally admitted to exist.'

Personally he was against anything that would increase local taxes and suggested

> that it would be politic to state this explicitly for the reassurance of many anxious members of the Unionist Party. This would limit researches of the committee as would the decision to refuse the right to recommend new legislation, but no doubt there were many other points of great value that the committee could formulate suggestions about.[83]

[83] Lord Londonderry to Cabinet, MS Memorandum, February 10, 1905. (Subsequently printed with deletions. P.R.O. Cab. 37/74, No. 28.) Ministry of Education, Private Office Papers, 'Education (Provision of Meals) Bill, 1906, Papers Leading Up to Bill.'

Following these suggestions, the Balfour Government refused to take advantage of the splendid electoral weapon offered by the Interdepartmental Committee on Physical Deterioration and left the field of social reform entirely open for the Liberals when they came to power in December, 1905.[84] In place of action, Londonderry appointed on March 14, 1905, a committee of civil servants to review the work of the previous committee of civil servants who had formed the Interdepartmental Committee on Physical Deterioration.

The Interdepartmental Committee on Medical Inspection and Feeding of Children Attending Public Elementary Schools was ordered, as Londonderry had proposed: 'to ascertain what is now being done in medical inspection and to inquire into methods employed, the sums expended . . .' on feeding, and to report whether it 'could be better organized, without any charge upon public funds. . . .'[85] With the exception of H. Franklin Parsons,

[84] After he left office, Arthur James Balfour, whose motives about many things were complex and profound, was at pains to emphasize his interest in welfare legislation, although his biographer, Mrs Dugdale, leaves the topic unexplored. At Whittingame in December, 1910, with old age pensions in operation and very popular, and national insurance a probability for the next year's session, he intimated his feelings to his sister-in-law, Elizabeth Balfour, who transmitted them in a series of letters to Beatrice Webb. Mrs Webb had written that she felt David Lloyd George, then Chancellor of the Exchequer, cared more about social reform than Balfour ever had. Betty Balfour quoted her brother-in-law:

'I was very interested in Mrs Webb's letter, but I do not pretend to understand it. I cannot begin to think what she meant by it.' I tried to explain but of course failed—'By what word or deed has Lloyd George proven that he cares more for soc-reforming the welfare of the people than I do—I have no doubt he is sincere—and is sorry that people are poor—but not a bit more than the rest of us and how are this party likely to find time for dealing with social reform more [fully?] than we should have done with no constitutional revolution hanging around our necks?'

Elizabeth Balfour to Beatrice Webb, December 14, 1910, Webb Papers, Section II, subsection 4, group e, f. 91.

The explanation continued on Christmas night. Mrs Balfour reported:

Arthur says: 'that what he was *not* sympathetic with was the political attitude which made men advocate schemes not because of a motive of sympathy or desire to reform but simply to win electoral advantage—more votes.

He, like Gerald—said that the S. African War had made it imperative for the Conservatives to pass old age pensions. 'Joe's war had stopped Joe's pensions.' They could not raise revenue out of the kind of taxes put on by Lloyd George.

Elizabeth Balfour to Beatrice Webb, December 25, 1910, *Ibid.*, f. 94.
[85] *Cd. 2779*, 'Report of the Interdepartmental Committee on Medical Inspection and Feeding of Children Attending the Public Elementary Schools,' 1906.

D

Assistant Medical Officer of the Local Government Board, the committee was made up entirely of members of the Board of Education inspectorate. Its report, rendered in November, 1905, was as pallid as Lord Londonderry could have wished. The committee was unable to determine how successful school feeding would be, but suggested that experiments be tried. It argued that local authorities should be 'kept regularly informed of feeding,' and should be represented on feeding agencies '. . . unless there is good reason to the contrary. . . .'[86] The committee found that school medical inspection, where it was conducted by the school medical officers, was most beneficial, but noted that because of poverty, or more often, apathy and indifference, defects discovered by the medical officer frequently were not remedied.

Gorst's attack on the Government, anticipated by Londonderry's memorandum of February 10, began with the opening of Parliament four days later. Gorst inquired what the Government intended to do toward implementing the interdepartmental committee's investigations. Society, he said, separated parents and children by compulsory education, but did not adequately care for the child. The State, which obliged a child to attend school, was itself obligated to see that he was in a condition to learn.[87] Gorst insisted on keeping the physical deterioration report before Parliament and the nation. He would, he said a few days later, 'bring the subject to the attention of the House at every opportunity. He would bring it up on the Irish Estimates, the Scottish Estimates, and the English Estimates, and he would entreat the Government for the sake of the nation and Empire . . . not to neglect the recommendations of the Committee.'[88]

The Government, of course, planned nothing beyond the ancient subterfuge of another committee of investigation. New legislation, the ministers retorted, required careful study. Moreover, no department admitted responsibility for hungry or unwell schoolchildren. Maintenance of paupers was not the business of the Board of Education, Gorst was told, and the Local Government Board, which supervised the poor law, insisted it had nothing to do with schools.[89]

[86] Cd. 2779, pp. 84–5.
[87] Hansard, CXLI (February 14, 1905), cols. 141–5.
[88] Ibid. (February 23, 1905), col. 1145.
[89] Ibid., CXLIII (March 22, 1905), cols. 874–5.

Early in April, 1905, Gorst, Thomas J. MacNamara,[90] who, with Will Crooks, provided most of Gorst's support, the Countess of Warwick,[91] and a physician, Dr Robert Hutchison, visited the notorious Johanna Street School in Lambeth. Anson had visited the institution a few days earlier and had refused in Parliament to admit that he found anything amiss.[92] Now among the students Gorst and his followers selected twenty boys whom Dr Hutchison was able to certify were suffering from malnutrition so acute that it made effective school work impossible. The group then visited the Lambeth Board of Guardians and made application for relief in the name of the boys. The guardians, suitably impressed by a visit from two Members of Parliament and a peeress bearing one of the oldest names in England, immediately issued orders for the out-of-doors maintenance of all necessitous children within the Lambeth Union.[93] With the example of this concession, the reformers forced a debate in the House of Commons on April 18 on the resolution that 'local authorities should be empowered . . . for insuring that all children at any public elementary school . . . shall receive proper nourishment before being subjected to physical or mental instruction. . . .' At the discretion of the guardians, any cost would be recoverable.[94]

In the course of the debate, Anson announced that the Local Government Board was about to issue a circular to all guardians permitting them to give poor law relief to schoolchildren upon

[90] Thomas James MacNamara, 1861–1931, born, Montreal; father a sergeant in British Army; educated, St Thomas's School, Exeter, and Borough Road Training College for Teachers; strong Nonconformist; elementary school teacher; editor, *The Schoolmaster*, publication of National Union of Teachers, 1892–1907; President, N.U.T., 1896; Liberal M.P. for North Camberwell, 1900–24; Parliamentary Secretary, Local Government Board, 1907; Privy Council, 1911; member, London School Board, 1896–1902; Minister of Labour, 1920–2.

[91] Frances Evelyn Greville, Countess of Warwick, 1861–1938, born, London; aristocratic family; educated at home; married, 1881, Francis Richard Charles Guy Greville, Lord Brooke, who later acceded to title as Fifth Earl of Warwick; converted to socialism by Robert Blatchford, who, in the *Clarion*, had criticized the extravagance of a ball given at Warwick Castle in 1895; woman of great beauty, friend of Edward VII; established a school at Dunmow for encouragement of rural occupations; established a college to train women in horticulture and agriculture at Studley Castle, Warwickshire; defeated as Labour candidate for Parliament, 1923, by Anthony Eden, her eldest son's brother-in-law.

[92] *Hansard*, CXLIII (March 20, 1905), cols. 455–6.

[93] For Gorst's story of this excursion, see: Sir John E. Gorst, *The Children of the Nation*, New York, 1907, pp. 86–7.

[94] *Hansard*, CVL (April 18, 1905), col. 531.

application from the school manager or teacher. The relief, he said, could be given either as out-of-door maintenance or as a loan. A copy of the circular together with a letter from him would shortly be sent to all schools.[95] Poor law maintenance of the children, Anson admitted, would put parents under the legal disabilities of pauperism, but he was unsure whether maintenance given as a loan only would do the same. Conditions among school-children were not invariably so bad as they seemed, concluded the Secretary to the Board of Education, loosing a final barb in the direction of John Gorst. An emotional observer, he remarked, might see malnutrition among children who were not in fact underfed. 'Charitable people were often misled by appearances, and something of the kind seemed to have occurred to the distinguished party visiting the Johanna Street School.'[96]

Anson announced that the vote on the resolution would not be treated as a party question. As a result the Government was defeated, and the resolution passed, 100 to 64. Ministerial members present, A. J. and G. W. Balfour, Walter Long, and Anson, together with Joseph Chamberlain, all voted against the resolution. None of the Liberal leaders was present.[97] Thus, over a year before it was sanctioned by Parliamentary enactment, the State undertook to feed necessitous schoolchildren and so gave effect to one of the first recommendations of the physical deterioration report.

A resolution passed by a minority of an ageing House of Commons advising the Government to permit local authorities to give food to hungry infants hardly counts as an act of revolution. Nor, finally, were the new powers of any conspicuous use to the children they were intended to benefit. The poor law inspectors and the guardians administered the order with a systematic ineptitude more appropriate to the Chinese Empire than to Edwardian England.[98] The importance of the Relief (School Children) Order

---

[95] *Hansard*, CVL (April 18th, 1905), cols. 562–3.

[96] *Ibid.*, col. 561.

[97] *Ibid.*, cols. 567–8

[98] The Local Government Board circular, the Relief (School Children) Order, 1905, stipulated that the new powers given for the out-of-doors maintenance of hungry schoolchildren were 'not to apply to widows' children or to children residing with other relations of the family, or to blind, deaf, and dumb children, or to children with absent parents.' These categories were excluded because the guardians already had powers for their relief under previous orders. There apparently was no explanation for this in the original order or later. Thus with extraordinary single-mindedness the guardians struck from their relief rolls

of 1905, like the importance of Chamberlain's circular of 1886, was that it provided the symbol of a movement, minute but clear, towards State intrusion into those affairs which the Victorians usually assumed were of individual responsibility. A corner of the Victorian ideal of self-help had been chipped away. The principle ungraciously and reluctantly accepted by the Local Government Board of the Balfour Ministry in April, 1905, would be confirmed in the Education (Provision of Meals) Act of 1906, which will be discussed in the next chapter. But by the time of the passage of this Act, there was little new that either opponents or supporters of the measure could say. On however small a scale, State provision of meals had begun. The question only remained whether society should attempt to punish the parents for neglect of the child by casting the father into the legal category of a pauper, or by proceeding against him for recovery of the cost of the food provided for his child. Neither measure, in fact, would ever provide sufficient incentive to force truly indifferent parents to care properly for the physical condition of their children, and no punishment could compel a parent without money to buy food. In many cases, therefore, the alternatives were not whether the State or the parent should feed the child, but whether the State should feed the child or permit him to go hungry. The same intractable logic would soon be applied to medical care for schoolchildren and to State maintenance for the aged in the form of non-contributory old age pensions. Finally, after provision for the helpless at the beginning and the end of life, British society established, through compulsory health insurance, the principle that the physical welfare of the mature working man was a matter of State concern. An efficient nation could not afford to permit its people to suffer the consequences of their own improvidence. So began the evolution of national insurance.

large numbers of children whom in many cases they had already been feeding. For a biting commentary on this extraordinary administrative mistake, see Cd. 4499, 'Report of the Royal Commission on the Poor Laws and Relief of Distress, Volume III, Being the Minority Report,' 1909, pp. 160–1.

3 The Children of the Nation

Advice to children
Take the utmost care to get well born and well brought up.
This means that your mother must have a good doctor. Be careful
to go to a school where there is what they call a school clinic,
where your nutrition and teeth and eyesight and other matters of
importance to you will be attended to. Be particularly careful to
have all this done at the expense of the nation, as otherwise it will
not be done at all, the chance being about forty to one against your
being able to pay for it directly yourself, even if you know how to
set about it. Otherwise you will be what most people are at present:
an unsound citizen of an unsound nation, without sense enough
to be ashamed or unhappy about it.

GEORGE BERNARD SHAW, 'Preface on Doctors'
from *The Doctor's Dilemma*.

The passage of the Education (Provision of Meals) Act of 1906
and the Education (Administrative Provisions) Act of 1907,
establishing medical inspection in State schools, marked the
beginning of the construction of the welfare state. For the
historian, feeding was the more important measure, not because
it was wider in scope or more beneficial, but simply because it
occurred first. Charles Pipkin's estimate of a third of a century ago
seems even more transparently true sixty years after the establishment of school meals.

It would be difficult to place too much emphasis on the new
principle of state action which the Education (Provision of
Meals) Act, implied, for in a nation jealous of individual rights
and proud of its conservative instincts it was nothing less than a
revolutionary principle.[1]

Although the introduction of school medical inspection and the
subsequent founding of the school medical service entailed a far
larger official establishment, the spending of much greater sums of
money, and had no doubt a more salutary effect on the physique of

[1] Charles W. Pipkin, *Social Politics and Modern Democracies* (New York, 1931),
I, 72-3.

Englishmen than did the mere provision of meals in school, it seemed at the time to be less revolutionary. Precedent for State interest in the health of its citizens existed in the sanitation legislation of the last quarter of the nineteenth century, the Contagious Disease Acts, and the appointment by local authorities in many places of medical officers of health. (Appointment of a medical officer of health became compulsory upon the local authorities only in 1909 with the Housing and Town Planning Act.) Moreover, the school medical service came into being only as a result of administrative order. The Members of Parliament who voted for the Education (Administrative Provision) Act in 1907 could scarcely have contemplated, and certainly did not discuss, the establishment of the comprehensive system of medical care for children that finally evolved from their action.

In contrast to medical inspection, the Bill to establish the feeding of schoolchildren became the centre of violent controversy. Here Parliamentary discussion was little concerned with the methods of administration. Even the staunchest, true-blue Tory could make few objections on the basis of wasteful finance or authoritarian administration to the timid measure that received the royal assent at the end of 1906. Rather, the controversy was entirely upon principle. Should the State, it was asked, be permitted to enter the most elemental of all fields of parental responsibility, the provision of meals for children, without punishing the parents in some way for neglect of duty? Even this question, however, generated little heat inside the House of Commons. The Unionist M.P.s, seriously shaken by their resounding electoral defeat in January, 1906, and embarrassed by their own Local Government Board order for poor law feeding of schoolchildren, were unwilling to risk further charges of disregard for the plight of the poor. But while politicians declined to test further the wrath of an aroused electorate dominated now by the working class, Unionist groups from outside of Parliament showed no such reluctance. Hence, even though the measure in question was paltry and thin, the principles of social welfare were thoroughly debated in connexion with the provision of meals.

I

The first recognition that the physical welfare of schoolchildren should be a matter of national concern rather than an object for private charity occurred in France in the ebullient days following the revolution of 1848. In 1849 the National Guard of the Second Arrondissement of Paris established what were termed *Caisses des Écoles*, or school funds, in their district to encourage school attendance, give prizes, and to look out generally for the pupils' welfare. Very soon these funds had as their principal duty the feeding of children attending the schools. In the years after the French defeat of 1871 the school funds everywhere established *Cantines Scolaires*. With a declining birth rate, France could not afford to neglect a single potential citizen. In this period also, larger French municipal governments began to make regular contributions towards school feeding. By the end of the century the department of the Seine, which included the municipality of Paris, was paying the *Cantines* about one million francs annually towards the provision of meals, of which nearly two-thirds were now given free.[2]

British interest in the feeding of schoolchildren, as a separate philanthropic project, dates from the eighteen-sixties. In February, 1864, the first of the relatively few stable school meal associations appeared in the Destitute Children's Dinner Society, which had as its chief object the feeding of children at a ragged school in Westminster. This society and others like it grew rapidly in the years at the end of the decade under the stimulus of the interest in education aroused by the Forster Education Act of 1870.[3] The disorderly competitive expansion of the school feeding associations and the desire by many reformers to force at least a minimum of parental responsibility resulted in attempts in many places to demand a nominal fee, usually a penny, for a student's meal. The Charity Organization Society, which came into being in 1869, was foremost among the groups seeking to insure that school feeding gave no encouragement to the parents to rely upon charity.

The Charity Organization Society's point of view was characteristic of most of the philanthropic groups which undertook school feeding at the end of the century. Generally the C.O.S. assumed it would be possible to do in school feeding what Octavia Hill seemed to be successfully accomplishing in housing. Under proper

[2] For an excellent discussion of the early history in France of the provision of meals, see M. E. Bulkley, *The Feeding of School Children*, London, 1914, pp. 249–51.

[3] Fifty-eight dining rooms opened between October, 1869, and April, 1870. Bulkley, *School Children*, p. 4.

supervision, inexpensive, healthful dinners, like inexpensive, healthful living accommodations, could be made to pay for them- selves. Most successful of the self-supporting dinner experiments were those of Sir Henry Peck, who began at Rousdon in Devon- shire in 1876 to provide five hot meals per week at a cost to the schoolchild of one penny each. Peck's undertaking was a great success and became practically self-supporting. The obvious flaw in the proposal for charges—one that the C.O.S. reformers never succeeded in repairing—was how to deal with the ragged, hungry infant who appeared and said that he had spent his penny, that he had lost his penny, or that his parents could not afford a penny. Was he to be turned away hungry, or was he to be fed? He was, of course, fed and as a result the next day more children and still more children appeared without pennies. The programme then incurred a deficit, which could be overcome only by appealing for general charitable support.

With the coming of hard times and social disorder in the eighties more and more self-supporting school dinner programmes began to supplement their incomes by appeals to charity, and the number of programmes supported completely by voluntary funds increased. Among these, the *Referee* Funds promoted by G. R. Sims and Arnold White of the *Referee* newspaper staff were most important.[4] By the end of the eighties, therefore, school feeding was being carried on by a large number of competing associations, some of which were wholly supported by charity and gave their meals free, while others collected, with greater or less success, a small fee from the children. Although Sir Henry Peck had tried vainly to form a committee of the five most important school feeding organi- zations, throughout the decade of the eighties school feeding went on without plan or coordination.

In 1889, the London School Board appointed investigators to survey the institutions attempting to feed hungry schoolchildren. As might have been expected, the committee uncovered a great variation of interest and activity. In some districts, committees competed with each other; in many more there was no provision at

---

[4] George Robert Sims, 1847–1922, educated, Hanwell Military College and the University of Bonn; wrote under pseudonym 'Dragonet' in the *Referee*, 1877–1922. Journalist, drama critic, and dramatist, and writer on social ques- tions; associate of Arnold White; books helped turn attention of nation toward the condition of the poor; *Social Kaleidoscope*, 1880; *How the Poor Live*, 1883; *In London's Heart*, 1898; *Living London*, n.d., *The Cry of the Children*, n.d.

D*

all. The London investigators calculated that overall 43,888 school-children or 12·8 per cent of the children attending London schools were habitually in want of food and of these less than half were provided for.[5] The result of the London School Board investigation was the formation in 1889 of the London Schools Dinner Association. This organization attempted to bring onto its board representatives of all the large feeding societies while main-taining liaison with the London School Board by putting seven board members onto its executive committee. The attempts of the L.S.D.A. to organize school feeding were relatively unsuccessful. One researcher has estimated that in 1905 when poor law feeding began, there were over 300 charitable feeding bodies in the United Kingdom.[6] Furthermore, the London Schools Dinner Association was unable to elicit much co-operation either from the London School Board, which allowed its representation to dwindle to three, or from the poor law guardians who carefully avoided all participation in school feeding until ordered to enter the field in 1905.

Throughout the nineties the only clear trend noticeable in the gradually enlarging movement towards the feeding of school-children was the decline in self-supporting dinners. By 1895 only about 10 per cent of the feeding associations were still trying to collect a fee from the students.[7] Charitable feeding, however supported, was still on too small a scale to diminish appreciably the great mass of hunger with which the English education authorities were faced. The L.S.D.A., for instance, spent £1,233 in 165 schools in 1900, and £1,286 in 181 schools in 1901.[8] The associa-tion in 1901 had provided 660,000 meals, or slightly more than one meal per year for each child attending State schools within the jurisdiction of the London School Board. In the same year the chairman of the London School Board, Lord Reay, reported that while £1,286 had been spent by the London Schools Dinner Association, only £1,186 had been received in donations. This was, he noted, the third year in which the L.S.D.A. had incurred a deficit.[9]

[5] Bulkley, *School Children*, p. 16.

[6] Frederick Le Gros Clark, *The Social History of the School Meals Service*, London, 1948, p. 4.

[7] Bulkley, *School Children*, p. 19.

[8] Annual Report, London Schools Dinner Association, *The Times*, December 11, 1901.   [9] *Ibid.*

With the Boer War in progress and their budgets constantly in need of replenishing, the supporters of voluntary feeding used the appeal of patriotism and national efficiency to stimulate contributions for their projects.[10] Lady Burdett-Coutts, writing on behalf of the still-active Destitute Children's Dinner Society, now operating mainly in Hackney and Bethnal Green, reminded the West End that the East End school dining rooms helped to provide the empire with soldiers.

The children do credit to the dinners, and the dinners will do credit to the children and will help them to grow up strong, hardy men and women—a credit to their own special locality and to the empire at large. In connection with this remark I am tempted to revert to the observation I made in my letter to you a year ago, that many of the men fighting for their country in South Africa were lads who in their childhood found their share of food and comfort in our dining rooms, where the foundation of their manhood was laid.[11]

Even the stimulus of war-inspired interest in physical fitness did little to enlarge the voluntary programme of school feeding. One may presume that by the turn of the century old-fashioned voluntary humanitarianism had done as much as it could in this area. Even though an immensely wealthy lady from the West End might look on with satisfaction as hungry infants in the East End gulped the food provided for them, charitable efforts really could have little permanent effect. As it turned out, the revelations of the next few years swept away any lingering complacency.

2

The military disasters of the South African War that caused Britain's anxious quest for national efficiency have been discussed in the previous chapter. But not until nearly a year after the end of hostilities was school feeding suggested by an official body as a way to stem alleged physical deterioration of the country's human resources. This came in March, 1903, when the Royal Commission on Physical Training (Scotland) recommended that education authorities be empowered to co-operate with voluntary agencies to

[10] Letter to *The Times*, December 11, 1901.
[11] *The Times*, December 14, 1901.

provide suitable food for schoolchildren without cost to public funds. The commission recommended that when income from voluntary contributions was inadequate, public authorities be given power to pay for meals and to secure reimbursement from parents. Unfortunately, the importance of these recommendations was vitiated by the commission's hesitancy in giving power to education authorities themselves to provide food.[12] On this matter the Interdepartmental Committee on Physical Deterioration, reporting eighteen months later, was far more outspoken. As has been seen, it urged without equivocation that municipal and voluntary agencies combine to feed habitually undernourished schoolchildren.[13]

By 1905 John Gorst's well-publicized excursions into the slums of London and the mounting disquiet over the report of the interdepartmental committee forced the government to order poor law guardians to feed necessitous schoolchildren. The Relief (School Children) Order of 1905 was of great importance in establishing the precedent of State aid for feeding while at the same time it probably diminished the number of children who finally were fed. By driving the guardians into the business of feeding, the government caused many parents whose children were genuinely undernourished to withdraw them from school dining rooms for fear of being designated as paupers. In addition, there were certainly many thousands of hungry schoolchildren whose parents, while not technically destitute, found it difficult to provide adequate meals. The incredibly inept administration of the order caused these children, as well as many others whose parents were legally paupers, to be dropped from relief rolls.

One city that attempted most seriously and intelligently to give effect to the Local Government Board order was Bradford. Its administrative difficulties may provide a measure of national accomplishment in the field. In Bradford the method of feeding was worked out between the local education authorities and the board of guardians, and approved by the city council in July, 1905. Feeding began on September 1, 1905. Between that date and March 23, 1906, the Bradford guardians provided 101,932 meals. They attempted to offer meals six days a week. The Local Govern-

[12] *Cd. 1507*, 'Royal Commission on Physical Training (Scotland),' 1903.
[13] *Cd. 2175*, 'The Interdepartmental Committee on Physical Deterioration,' 1904, pp. 84–93.

ment Board order had stipulated that the cost of meals could be recovered, so far as possible, from the parents, or from charitable contributions. Only in the last resort was rate aid to be used. The Bradford guardians conscientiously attempted to follow these instructions. But while they received £728 from the Lord Mayor's Fund and £595 14s. 4d. from the rates, £2 19s. 3d. was recovered from parents. Of this amount, £1 19s. 3d. came in voluntarily, and £1 after court proceedings.[14]

In many other towns the local education authority and the guardians were unable to come to any agreement on the method of feeding. The guardians refused frequently, for reasons of their own, to admit that the students sent to them by the schools were actually destitute. In Manchester, for instance, of 3,301 names sent by the Manchester Education Authority to the Chorlton Union, the guardians struck off all but 468. Of 2,562 names sent to the Manchester Union, the guardians accepted 629.[15] Moreover, many fathers refused to allow their children to receive the tickets for meals when they discovered that the tickets came from the poor law guardians.[16]

The Relief (School Children) Order gave perhaps its greatest service by destroying forever any vestige of the possibility that the poor law guardians would be permitted to take part in the reforms of the next decade. While there was no agreement in 1906 among Labour Representation Committee candidates, radical Liberals, and all other aspirants to the House of Commons who demanded feeding and medical inspection of schoolchildren, all were certain it should not be done by the poor law.[17] On the other hand, the Liberal Party leadership had been noticeably absent from the vote on the resolution of April 18, 1905. Nor did it say anything on school feeding either during or after the election of January, 1906. Many Gladstonian Liberals would have argued to continue poor

[14] 'Special Report and Report from the Select Committee on the Education (Provision of Meals) Bill, 1906; and the Education (Provision of Meals) (Scotland) Bill, 1906,' *Parliamentary Papers*, Reports from Committees, 1906, VIII, Part III, 288, p. 299, Appendix 10.

[15] 'Report of Select Committee,' para. 1173–91.

[16] *Cd. 4499*, 'Report of the Royal Commission on the Poor Laws and Relief of Distress, Vol. III, Being the Minority Report,' 1909, p. 161.

[17] Sir John Gorst may have made one of the most important of his many contributions to social reform by obtaining from the Trades Union Congress in 1904 a resolution in favour of school feeding. Gertrude M. Tuckwell, 'Trades Union Congress, 1904,' *Commonwealth*, IX (October, 1904), 307–8.

law feeding on a somewhat broader scale, but no more.[18] Thus, there was some consternation when a lucky draw on the private members' ballot at the beginning of the 1906 session enabled William T. Wilson, Chairman of the Amalgamated Society of Carpenters and Joiners, and a newly-elected Labour M.P. from Lancaster, to introduce, within days of his arrival in London, a Bill for the feeding of schoolchildren by the local education authorities.

The Board of Education itself was completely unprepared for any decision on State provision of meals. Its permanent secretary was the formidable Robert Laurie Morant, one of the great civil servants of the twentieth century, whose part in the social reform activities of the next eight years would be of critical importance.[19] On February 23, Morant wrote his opposite number on the Local Government Board, Sir Samuel Provis, that someone, 'I think a Labour Member,' was going to introduce a Provision of Meals Bill 'or something of that kind.' Morant admitted he personally knew very little about the Bill but he thought it would be useful for the Board of Education and the Local Government Board to consult about it. 'I find that my President's mind is practically a blank on the subject.' It would be necessary soon for the Government to decide what line to take and, although it would certainly be a Cabinet matter, 'the Party is probably considerably divided.'[20] Two days later, on February 26, Morant prepared a memorandum for the President of the Board of Education, Augustine Birrell. He reviewed the history of school feeding, citing the evidence of the physical deterioration committee, and the Local Government Board order of April, 1905.[21] Less than a week later, on March 2,

[18] Clark, *School Meals*, p. 6.

[19] Robert Laurie Morant, 1863–1920, born, Hampstead; father, Robert Morant, an artist; educated, Winchester and New College, Oxford; tutor to royal family of Siam and organized public education there, 1886–94; returned to England and engaged in social and educational work in East London; resident, Toynbee Hall, 1895–6. Private Secretary to Sir John Gorst, 1899, during Gorst's term as Vice-President, Committee of Council on Education; Assistant Private Secretary to Duke of Devonshire when the Duke was Lord President of Council, 1902; Permanent Secretary, Board of Education, 1903–11; Chairman, National Health Insurance Commission, 1912–19; First Permanent Secretary, Ministry of Health, 1919–20. K.C.B., 1907.

[20] R. L. Morant (unsigned) to Sir Samuel Provis, February 23, 1906, Bill File, Education (Provision of Meals) Act, 1906, Ministry of Education.

[21] Memorandum for the President of the Board of Education, February 26, 1906, *Ibid*.

with only Augustine Birrell present for the Government, the House of Commons gave Mr Wilson's Bill its second reading.[22]

The second reading speech offered little that had not been said before. Birrell, in some discomfort, answered Wilson's explanation of his Bill by saying that the education authorities, when faced by a hungry child, 'must either feed it or turn it away; and as the Minister for Education he could not be responsible for the latter alternative. As everybody was agreed that the child could not be taught before it was fed, then fed it had to be.' He stated further that the local education authorities appeared, on the experience of France, to be the appropriate body for conducting the feeding.[23] Finally at the end of the discussion, John Burns, who had just arrived, promised government time for the Bill. Thus, tardily, the Liberal administration made its own a measure it did not really want but could not decently oppose. Even with Government support, the Bill moved forward only slowly. It was referred to a select committee which reported in July when Parliament was about to recess.[24] As a result the measure did not receive a third reading until December and was finally given the royal assent on December 21, 1906.

The Education (Provision of Meals) Act of 1906 as it emerged from Parliament was far more modest in scope and hesitant in the granting of power than had been the measure introduced at the beginning of the year by enthusiastic Labour M.P.s. Basically it permitted, but did not require, the local education authorities 'to take such steps as they think fit for the provision of meals for children in attendance at any public elementary school in their area. . . .' To this end, authorities might work through any local associations already providing meals (to be styled 'School Canteen Committees') or they might acquire for themselves any necessary facilities. The education authorities could pay for the meals by soliciting private contributions through any voluntary organizations available. They could charge students receiving the meals a reasonable fee and seek to recover the cost of meals from parents as a civil debt. As a last resort they could support the meals from public funds, providing that no rate for the purpose might exceed one halfpenny in the pound.

[22] Hansard, Parliamentary Debates, Series 4, CLII (March 2, 1906), cols 1390–448.   [23] Ibid., col. 1440, et seq.
[24] PP, 'Education (Provision of Meals) Bill, 1906; and the Education (Provision of Meals) (Scotland) Bill, 1906.'

Section IV of the Act marked the point of contest between the new radicalism and the old conservatism. This paragraph stipulated that notwithstanding any failure by any parent to pay for the meals provided for his child the parent should not suffer any losses of civil rights or privileges. In effect, meals, in the last analysis, were to be provided free. With this mild proposal the welfare state began.

In the House of Commons the Provision of Meals Bill had been attacked only by the slightly eccentric Harold Cox, who reminded the Members that when the Lambeth Board of Guardians investigated the parents of the hungry schoolchildren uncovered by Gorst's famous expedition to the Johanna Street School, some families were found with incomes up to 72s. per week.[25] But outside the Commons, in the House of Lords, in the Unionist press, and in other quarters less vulnerable to direct working-class retaliation, the Bill was freely denounced.[26] Generally the Opposition's attitude was that although the Bill meant little in itself, it constituted a vital departure from the principle of limited State activity. To its opponents the Bill took the State into an area that it had hitherto carefully avoided, but one which might logically lead to full protection by society against all hazards of modern life.[27] Never before had the British State offered to support its citizens without reciprocal deprivation of right for those who applied for relief. Even though poor law relief had grown continually more generous and more comfortable, it carried with it still the stigma of parochial charity. Those who applied for it were 'less eligible' for political franchises than their fellow citizens. Now this stigma was gone. The State might, to be sure, attempt to recover the cost of meals through legal action. But if it were unsuccessful, no further penalty would accrue to the parents. In the introduction to the second edition of his *Law and Opinion in England*, written in 1914, Professor A. V. Dicey designated the feeding of school-

[25] *Hansard*, CLII (March 2, 1906), cols. 1413–14.

[26] The Lords amended the School Feeding Bill to exclude Scotland. This act provoked Sir Henry Campbell-Bannerman's only intervention in debate on the Bill with a denunciation of the Lords for the invasion of the Commons' prerogative.

[27] See, for instance: Sir Arthur Clay, 'The Feeding of School-Children,' in J. St Loe Strachey, ed., *The Manufacture of Paupers: A Protest and a Policy*, London, 1907, pp. 15–23. Clay was a leader of the Charity Organization Society. Most of the articles in this collection appeared in the *Spectator*, of which Strachey was editor, between May and July of 1906.

children as the first of the socialist measures that culminated in what was to him the deplorable National Insurance Act of 1911. The privileges of citizenship, Dicey argued, were the corollary of the successful fulfilment of private and domestic obligations. Now, for the first time, failure on the one hand carried no deprivation on the other. The Liberals and Conservatives who supported the Education Act of 1870 could hardly be called socialistic, said Dicey, and perhaps would not even have approved of the Education Act of 1891 by which education became entirely free.

It is certain that they would have condemned the Education (Provision of Meals) Act, 1906. No one can deny that a starving boy will hardly profit much from the attempt to teach him the rules of arithmetic, but it does not necessarily follow that a local authority must therefore provide every hungry child at school with a meal; still less does it seem morally right that a father who first lets his child starve, and then fails to pay the price legally due from him for a meal given to the child at the expense of the rate-payers should, under the Act of 1906, retain the right of voting for a Member of Parliament. Why a man who first neglects his duty as a father and then defrauds the State should retain his full political rights is a question easier to ask than to answer.[28]

3

Despite predictions that the English working class, their character undermined by the prospect of gifts from the State, would everywhere demand the provision of meals, the number of local education authorities conducting school feeding grew slowly. By the fiscal year 1911–12, only 131 of the 322 education authorities in England and Wales had begun the service. Of these, seventeen were depending entirely upon voluntary contributions for their support; nineteen were using rate money for the administration of meals only; and ninety-five were using rate money for food. The immediate effect of the School Feeding Act had been to reduce the flow of voluntary contributions from £17,831 in 1908–9 to £3,064 in 1911–12.[29]

[28] Albert V. Dicey, *Lectures on the Relation Between Law and Public Opinion in England During the 19th Century*, 2nd ed., London, 1930, pp. xlix–l.
[29] Bulkley, *School Children*, pp. 54–5.

Overall it is clear that so long as the provision of meals was entirely at the discretion of local government officials, and costs came entirely from local treasuries, education authorities would be reluctant to enter the field. Moreover, the semi-official, semi-voluntary system of administration was bound to be inefficient and slipshod. The pre-war peak for school feeding was reached in 1912–13. In that year about 100,000 children were fed in the county of London and 258,000 in the rest of the country. In the next year, the last fiscal year before the war, 85,000 children were fed in the capital and 225,000 in the rest of the country. The abnormally large number in 1912–13 was attributed by the Chief Medical Officer at the Board of Education to the coal strike. The fact that numerous authorities dropped the programme the next year suggests that feeding had about reached the limits of its normal expansion under the terms of the Act of 1906.[30]

The powers granted the local authorities to recover in court from the parent the cost of meals provided for children proved to be almost totally unworkable. Up to March 31, 1909, of the total of over £66,000 spent, only £295 was recovered from parents, over half of it by court order. In this, Bradford, as usual, was the most active. The Bradford authorities had proceeded against 194 parents in court and had received the amount claimed in 54 cases for a total in and out of court of £150. Four other authorities had obtained more than £10. Four had received between £5 and £10. Thirty-four local authorities had received less than £5. Sixty-eight had recovered nothing. Charges, when made, were usually between 1½d. and 2d., although the cost of meals frequently was above 2d.[31] The businesslike London County Council, which served 7,335,469 meals in 1909–10 and which had expected to recover £1,000 from parents, was actually able to get 1s. 10d. In its next fiscal year, more realistically, it budgeted to recover £20 and did recover £4 14s. 8½d.[32]

The practical inability of the education authorities to recover costs from parents able to pay them caused some authorities to

---

[30] Cd. 7730, 'Report of the Chief Medical Officer for the Board of Education for 1913,' 1914, pp. 244–5. It was easier to ascertain the number of meals given than the number of individual children benefited.

[31] Cd. 5131, 'Report on the Working of the Education (Provision of Meals) Act, 1906, up to the 31st March, 1909,' 1910, p. 9.

[32] Henry Iselin, 'The Story of a Children's Care Committee,' Economic Review, XXII (January, 1912), 44.

substitute what was frequently termed 'a food test' to prevent the abuse of the school feeding programme. This was, in fact, simply a return to the deterrent principle of the poor law. Food of the plainest sort would be given under conditions made austere, if not disagreeable, by design. The rigorous application of this system in an undesignated East London district had resulted in its canteen committee feeding ordinarily about one-third the number of children handled in the surrounding area. The feeding was done not at the school but in a parish room, only between the hours of 8.15 and 8.45. Porridge and milk, sometimes bread and milk, were provided. As the education authority expected, parents were reluctant to send their children for meals under these conditions. 'I can give them better at home than what you gives them,' 'It ain't worth while to tell lies about a bit o' porridge,' were typical comments reported by a member of the care committee.[33]

In summary, any care committee that attempted to prevent abuse of its services prevented also a considerable amount of necessary feeding. Far from diminishing the parental sense of responsibility, or perhaps because of the controversy surrounding it, the institution of State feeding of schoolchildren appears to have quickened parental pride or, perhaps more accurately, quickened the desire of parents to appear to care for their families. Parents would not permit their children to take simple meals. A line of demarcation soon grew up, not between parents who paid for meals and those who did not, but between parents whose children took meals at school and those who were fed at home. Once a parent agreed to permit his child to be fed by the education authorities, he was never willing to pay for a meal other children were getting for nothing. Hence there was an almost uniform failure of the local authorities to recover any costs.[34]

It cannot be surprising, therefore, that in the years before the First World War the ordinary, unimaginative county or borough council had little incentive to require its education committee to begin the difficult and unrewarding business of school feeding. Aware of this, the Board of Education acted, just before the war

[33] Iselin, Children's Care Committee,' p. 43.

[34] In the year 1909–10, 503 children in eleven areas were withdrawn from feeding altogether when the parents were asked to pay for the meals. *Cd. 5724*, 'Report on the Working of the Education (Provision of Meals) Act, 1906, for the Year Ending 31st March, 1910,' 1911, p. 5.

broke out, to provide a financial inducement to the local authorities to undertake the provision of meals. The result of this effort was the Education (Provision of Meals) Act of 1914, a measure described even in the sober prose of the board's chief medical officer, Sir George Newman, as an 'event of outstanding importance.' This measure brought the hesitant, introductory phase of school feeding to an end. Perhaps the most important of several changes it effected was the grant of power to the Board of Education to compel local authorities to undertake the feeding of necessitous schoolchildren. With the power of compulsion came, on the one hand, the removal of the halfpenny limitations on the amount of rate money to be used for school feeding, and on the other, the authorization of a regular grant-in-aid from the Exchequer, given effect by a Board of Education circular of June 25, 1914. This promised help to a maximum of 50 per cent of the total cost of meals provided by the local authority. Finally, the measure authorized feeding during vacations, and by giving the school medical officer sole responsibility for determining which children should be fed, it reasserted the original intent of school feeding: that feeding should be undertaken solely for the benefit of the physique and learning ability of children and not considered in any way a measure of poor relief.

The evolution of school feeding, like that of nearly every other reform measure of the New Liberalism, was interrupted by the First World War. While the conflict disproved some of the economic presuppositions (for instance, the fear of national physical deterioration) that had caused the measure to be enacted, it also destroyed the world for which it had been intended. The massive intrusions of the State into wide areas both of economic activity and of personal regulation between 1914 and 1918 made ridiculous the furor over its assumption of the right to feed hungry schoolchildren. Nevertheless, at the time it had been made, the departure was recognized for what it was, a breach in the wall of absolute personal responsibility for one's own fate. Here for the first time the State used its power on behalf of a particular segment of the population who were selected on the sole criterion that they were poor, who had rendered the State no service, who were afflicted by no contagious disease except the disease of poverty, and who finally were to suffer no penalty or disenfranchisement on account of the aid they received. The Act, in effect, recognized that poverty was of itself a danger, and that if it could not be prevented it must be alleviated.

4

The establishment of the school medical service excited little of the public controversy that surrounded the provision of meals. Medical inspection was not, to be sure, born without a share of the pain and bitterness that seem inevitably to accompany the creation of new social institutions, but in this instance the struggle was among experts. Although no less unpleasant on that account, the contest primarily was over technique and personnel, not principle. Partly, this happy circumstance resulted from the fact that the medical service itself came into being only as a corollary of medical inspection, which was all the Education (Administrative Provisions) Act of 1907 specifically authorized. Even the authorization for inspection was buried among more than a dozen other clauses dealing with uninteresting and involved housekeeping details of State school administration. Thus, the medical service grew unnoticed and quietly from ministerial order.

Also, medical inspection had already built some tradition as a public service. At the time the Liberal Government took office in December, 1905, eighty-five of a total of 336 counties, county boroughs, non-county boroughs, and urban districts in England and Wales employed medical officers for educational purposes.[35] In most cases, to be sure, the duty of these medical officers was the inspection of the school premises rather than of the scholars—a public health, not a personal health function—but by 1907 forty-eight education authorities already had begun medical inspection of students.[36]

Most important, however, the school medical service came peacefully because it came secretly. In the school medical service, Parliament and the British nation were the victims of a political-administrative trick by which the evolution from personal medical inspection to personal medical care was blurred and disguised so that not even the House of Commons, let alone the public, had the opportunity to discuss the change in any detail. The perpetrator of

[35] Sir Lauder Brunton, 'Introduction,' in T. N. Kelynack, ed., *Medical Examination of Schools and Scholars*, London, 1910, p. xv.
[36] F. Le Gros Clark, ed., *National Fitness*, London, 1938, p. 18.

this deception was Robert Morant, the Permanent Secretary to the Board of Education, who was supported in his stratagem by most serious English social reformers. Chief among these was Margaret McMillan, in whom the cause of better physical care for school-children found a persistent champion.[37]

In many ways the beginnings of the school medical service should date from the election of Margaret McMillan to the Bradford School Board in 1894. The physical condition of students in this northern city was appalling. There may be no more dramatic evidence of circumstances of life of the English lower classes at the end of the nineteenth century than the familiar photographs of working-class children gathered in by the Education Act of 1880, which had finally made education compulsory. In these terms, G. A. N. Lowndes, the historian of English education, has described what Miss McMillan saw when she came to Bradford in November, 1893.

> Anyone who studies with a seeing eye and the aid of a magnifying glass . . . will easily detect the matted hair of the girls—although you will not see the vermin; the sore eyes—although you will probably not realize that many of the children were blind by the end of their school days through the continual effort to see the blackboard; the open mouths, symptoms of adenoids; the 'tallow candles' pendant from the nostrils of little children who had probably never heard of handkerchiefs, let alone possessed one; the evidence of rickets. . . .
>
> What he will not be able to perceive, however strong the magnifying glass, is how many of the children had been sewn into their clothing perhaps with pads of cotton wool underneath, for the whole of the winter months; the number deprived of their birthright of sleep by the nightly attention of bedbugs; the barefooted urchins turning cartwheels in the snow to attract pennies of the carriage gentry; the bags of sulphur sewn round

[37] Margaret McMillan, 1860–1931, born, New York City; after father's death returned with her mother to live with grandparents in Scotland; educated in Inverness, Frankfurt-am-Main, Lausanne and Geneva; companion and protégée of Lady Meux while training for the stage; slightly involved in support of the dock strike of 1889. Member, Bradford (Yorks) School Board, 1894–1902; promoted medical inspection in Bradford and London; established clinics at Bow and Deptford; established first open-air nursery school at Deptford, 1914; founded Rachel McMillan College, Deptford, 1930, to train nursery school teachers. C.B.E., 1917.

the hems of the teacher's trailing skirt to prevent the vermin climbing, sidling, or leaping up.[38]

When Margaret McMillan arrived in Bradford, the city was still seething from the bitterness of the famous lockout at Lister's mills which had lasted for nineteen weeks through the hard winter of 1890–1. Such widespread suffering had been unparalleled since the days of the hungry forties. In the end the workers had been defeated and the mill owner was elevated to the House of Lords. The immediate consequence of this bitterness was the organization of the Independent Labour Party, which was first proposed at a meeting on January 13, 1893, held in the Peckover Street chapel in Bradford. Margaret McMillan immediately joined the new party. It may be significant that both school feeding and medical inspection received an early and potent impulse from Bradford, and that both of these movements had around them, as had the I.L.P. itself, an atmosphere and an appeal that invited support of stern, north-country, Nonconformist radicals.[39]

The year before Miss McMillan's election to the Bradford School Board that body had appointed on an experimental basis the second school medical officer in the country, Dr James Kerr.[40] (London had appointed the first in 1890.) School medical inspection began in the United Kingdom in 1894 with the examination by Dr Kerr of some 300 children at the Usher Street School in Bradford. The early inspections were principally for cleanliness and obvious physical disability.[41] Later, Bradford added examinations

[38] G. A. N. Lowndes, *Margaret McMillan, The Children's Champion*, London, 1960, p. 55.

[39] Max Beer, arguing with George Bernard Shaw in 1904, had denounced I.L.P. doctrine as 'non-conformism sicklied o'er with the pale cast of socialist thought.' *Clarion*, December 16, 1904, quoted in Phillip Poirier, *The Advent of the Labour Party*, London, 1958, p. 226. In the election of 1906, the Labour candidates stressed their Nonconformity more than their socialist qualifications. *Ibid.*, p. 277.

[40] James Kerr, 1862–1941, born, Glasgow; educated Manchester Grammar School, St John's College, Cambridge, and St Bartholomew's Infirmary, London; member, honorary medical staff, Bradford Infirmary, and member, medical staff, Bradford eye and ear hospital; medical superintendent, Bradford School Board, 1893–1902; Medical Officer (Education), London School Board and London Education Committee, 1902–11; Secretary, Second International Congress on School Hygiene, 1907.

[41] Kerr discovered that of the first 300, over 100 had not had their clothes off for over six months. Lowndes, *McMillan*, p. 56. For the results of the earliest medical inspections in Bradford and elsewhere see: James Kerr, 'School

of eyes and teeth, and finally, dental and medical treatment. The first school clinic was established in the Bradford town hall.[42]

In the first years of the twentieth century, while Kerr and Margaret McMillan were still in the north, the rather casual public interest in the health of schoolchildren suddenly became a widespread fear over the apparent physical deterioration of the British working class. A healthy working-class child was precious in a way he had not been before. One result was the proliferation of infant welfare centres and milk depots in the poor areas of London, laid out on a pattern of similar establishments in France that had been founded a quarter of a century earlier. (France had established universal school medical inspection in 1887.) John Burns was particularly active in this endeavour in Battersea, where he worked with Dr George F. McCleary, who became Medical Officer of Health for Battersea in 1901.[43] McCleary and Burns established the first milk depot in London in 1902.

In November of 1901, when the search for national efficiency was beginning to be a popular public topic and Lord Rosebery seemed about to emerge as the leader of a revived British nation, Earl Grey wrote a letter to *The Times* in reference to its new series, 'The Crisis in British Industry,' in which the paper had asked 'whither we are tending as a nation.' Grey, who was an ardent imperialist and a close friend of Milner, Chamberlain, and Cecil Rhodes, answered that it might be true that the real crisis lay in what industry did to its servants. He feared for the 'third generation' reared in the slums 'of smoke enveloped cities.' The 'human reservoirs of the country' could eventually dry up. In one of the

Hygiene, in its Mental, Moral, and Physical Aspects,' *Journal of the Royal Statistical Society*, LX (September, 1897), 613–80.

[42] Lowndes, *McMillan*, p. 56.

[43] McCleary represented an early attempt at Fabian permeation of the affairs of John Burns. He is 'the best qualified man I have ever known. . . . But what I wish to add is that he is a staunch Fabian and a convinced teetotaller,' wrote Sidney Webb, recommending him to Burns. Sidney Webb to John Burns, March 4, 1901, B.M. Add. MSS 46287, Burns Papers, Vol. VII, f. 286. McCleary succeeded George Newsholme as editor of *Public Health* in January, 1908, which office he held until 1912 when he became principal medical officer of the National Health Insurance Commission. At the time of his retirement in 1932 he was deputy senior medical officer of the Ministry of Health. He was also a prolific writer on public health subjects. On his work in Battersea, see: G. F. McCleary, *The Early History of the Infant Welfare Movement*, London, 1933, pp. 73–5; *The Maternity and Child Welfare Movement*, London, 1935, pp. 8–9, 39.

very early references to Arnold White's discovery of the two-out-of-five ratio of acceptable recruits in Manchester, Grey expressed the fear that 'our successors will not be able to bear the burden of empire.' He proposed 'an annual stock taking' of the national physical condition, which would feature a thorough weighing and measuring of British schoolchildren.[44] In common with much of the early pressure for medical inspection, Grey's concern was less for the welfare of the country's children than to discover trends in national physical characteristics and so to provide data unavailable to a country without compulsory military service.

The Times leader on the same day dealt with Grey's letter in terms that are a fair example of the British upper-class reaction to reports of national physical weakness before the report of the physical deterioration commission. It does not follow, said the newspaper, that 'slender physique is associated with a low order of vitality.' As irrefutable evidence for this assertion the paper cited the story of Jack the Giant Killer. The slums did, to be sure, produce many people who were 'incapable of being turned to good account.'

> Such people are the offspring of alcoholics, or the victims of diseases which certain forms of 'anti-ism' have done much to protect and perpetuate in our midst. . . .

These people were often in jail or in the workhouse and:

> When at liberty, they propagate their kind; and the state of the descendant is usually more helpless than that of the progenitor.

The newspaper was not sure what ought to be done if it *were* discovered that city influence was harmful. But in any case, it concluded: 'All such questions belong to the future. . . .'[45]

The Times' careless remarks about the unimportance of working-class physique would be disputed by an official body within six months after the original statements were made. In March, 1902, with General Maurice's first article on recruiting already in print, the Government appointed a royal commission to investigate physical training and education in Scotland. The commission's appointment had been prompted by the fact that British children had little opportunity for systematic exercise in school and, as they

[44] *The Times*, November 26, 1901.   [45] *Ibid.*

rarely stayed in school beyond the age of twelve, whatever possibility there was of supervised physical education disappeared early. The commission's terms of reference specified that it recommend a plan for some continuation course of physical training that would 'contribute towards the sources of national strength.'

The appointment of the commission was overshadowed in the spring of 1902 by the controversy surrounding the great Education Bill of that year. Nor, at the time of its publication in March, 1903, did the commission's report receive much attention. Yet this document contained the first scientific evidence of the effect of slums on physique. The children in Edinburgh schools in poorer areas were nearly two inches shorter and ten pounds lighter than the British average, and this disparity increased with age.[46] Moreover, the commission recommended—well outside its terms of reference —that a regular system of student medical inspection be established in all schools with, as has been mentioned, the provision of some form of school feeding in those institutions that needed it.

The Royal Commission on Physical Training was a factor leading to the appointment of the Interdepartmental Committee on Physical Deterioration.[47] It was not considered conclusive by itself, however, and only in July, 1904, when the more detailed and comprehensive investigation of the interdepartmental committee confirmed its findings and brought forward, among others, the same recommendations for feeding and medical inspection, did the Royal Commission on Physical Training receive the attention it deserved. During the ensuing months, the physical condition of children was a topic of general public interest. The British Medical Association had officially endorsed medical inspection on November 9, 1903. Medical and educational experts, and lay philanthropists, demanded inspection with a good deal more unanimity than they had displayed for school feeding.[48] Medical inspection

[46] Cd. 1507, 'Royal Commission on Physical Training (Scotland),' 1903, p. 25.
[47] It was specifically mentioned in the first terms of reference given the committee.
[48] Typical of this attitude was the 'National League for Physical Education and Improvement' formed in the first six months of 1905 by a group of medical officers of health, and including later a number of extremely influential public figures—R. B. Haldane, General F. D. Maurice, Bramwell Booth, Lord Alverstone, the Lord Chief Justice, and the Bishops of Ripon and Southwark. A delegation from this group privately visited the Board of Education on February 27, 1906, to press for the inclusion of medical inspection, and reluctantly, feeding, in the Education Bill that was at that time being prepared. Ministry of

did not, after all, deprive parents of responsibility. It could be justified both in terms of the need of the individual scholars and of the British race. Although much the same could be said of school feeding, this reform, while held to be desirable, was embarrassingly difficult to implement without what seemed unwarranted intrusions upon parents' rights.

5

The thesis that systematic medical inspection originated as a humanitarian measure in Bradford and grew as a means of combating, or investigating, the frightening problem of racial physical deterioration after the outbreak of the Boer War has been contradicted by Sir George Newman, who became the Chief Medical Officer to the Board of Education in 1907 and would be one of the builders of the school medical service.[49] Writing at the end of his life, Newman argued that medical inspection had been from its inception an educational and not a medical project.

> ... its primary purpose was not to create a healthy people, but to enable every school child to take full advantage of the education provided him by the State. This principle had been alleged as the basic ground for the school-feeding statute passed by Parliament the year before. Nonetheless, it was the primary reason also for the medical inspections and treatment of the school child. It was this common sense foundation which commended it alike to the Members of Parliament, to their constituents, and to payers of rates and taxes. Thousands of children were compulsorily sitting in schools in 1906 ... who could not by reason of lack of

Education, Private Office Papers, Medical, General, 'Formation of the Medical Department.' On the formation and activities of the National League, see: *Public Health*, XVII (February, 1905), 274–92; *The Times*, June 20, June 29, 1905.

[49] George Newman, 1870–1948, born, Leominster, Herefordshire; Quaker background; educated, King's College, London, and University of Edinburgh; lecturer at King's College, London, 1896–1900; emeritus lecturer, St Bartholomew's Hospital; Medical Officer of Health, Finsbury and Bedfordshire County; Chief Medical Officer, Board of Education, 1907–35; succeeded Arthur Newsholme, Chief Medical Officer to Local Government Board, 1919; continued as Chief Medical Officer to Ministry of Health with rank of Permanent Secretary in 1920 when the L.G.B. was absorbed into the Ministry of Health; combined this post with C.M.O. at Board of Education until retirement in 1935. Kt., 1911; K.C.B., 1918.

food receive proper advantage from the education provided. Likewise, tens of thousands of other children in school were failing to gain advantage from their education by the State for reason for their lack of health. Hence, the two Acts for school feeding and medical inspection and treatment were complementary. They were, at initiation, strictly and properly education Acts.[50]

There is much to be said for this point of view. Certainly Sir John Gorst and a number of other early promoters of the physical deterioration report had argued their case along these lines.[51] But in opposition to Newman, it must be pointed out that children had been 'compulsorily sitting in schools' for over a quarter of a century before the advent of feeding and medical inspection. It was only among the reformers and educationalists themselves that feeding and medical inspection appeared as an educational measure. Elsewhere, like the appointment of the physical deterioration committee that prompted the measures, they were presented as ways of strengthening the nation and empire. Even reformers themselves made public pronouncements about medical inspection and feeding that were argued in terms of physical and national rather than educational efficiency. The Liberal radical, T. J. Macnamara, apologized if his proposal for children's care sounded like 'rank socialism, in reality it is first-class imperialism.'[52] In thinking of national strengths, asked Leo Chiozza Money in his extremely influential book, *Riches and Poverty*, why are not sturdy and upright boys and girls 'as well worth consideration as the resistance of an armour plate, the trajectory of a rifle bullet or the virtues of smokeless powder?'[53] Indeed, Newman himself used the argument of national efficiency in promoting medical inspec-

[50] Sir George Newman, *The Building of a Nation's Health*, London, 1939, pp. 194-5.

[51] See, for instance: Sir John E. Gorst, 'Children's Rights,' *National Review*, XL (June, 1905), 705-15; Frances Evelyn Greville, Countess of Warwick, *A Nation's Youth*, London, 1906, *passim*.

[52] Thomas J. Macnamara, 'The Physical Condition of Working-Class Children,' *Nineteenth Century*, LVI (August, 1904), 307-11.

[53] Leo Chiozza Money, *Riches and Poverty*, London, 10th ed., 1911, p. 199. *Riches and Poverty* went through ten editions between October, 1905, and March, 1911. On its unexampled influence, see Charles Furth, *Life Since 1900*, London, 1956, p. 28, and E. H. Phelps Brown, *The Growth of British Industrial Relations*, London, 1959, p. 53.

tion. He noted that in 1905, 120,000 infants under one year had died.

> In view of the marked decline in the birth rate which is taking place, the loss becomes very grave. We are burning the candle at both ends. Few children are born and yet there is the sacrifice continually going on. Secondly, the circumstances and diseases which kill 120,000 infants every year, maim and injure the children that survive. Some only survive a few months, but others linger on and even grow up to adult age. Nevertheless it cannot be doubted that many of them are as brands plucked from the burning, and bear the mark of death upon them. It is idle to wonder at physical degeneration if the majority of the nation's infants have before they grow up to pass under such unfavourable influences as are able to kill 150 in every thousand. A high infant mortality must therefore be taken, as Sir John Simon said, to denote a prevalence of those causes and conditions which, in the long run, bring about a degeneration of the race.

For remedies, he proposed:

> *First* and foremost regular medical inspection. Every child should be submitted to medical inspection at least three times during its school life, and those requiring it should be kept under more frequent observation. The price of efficiency is eternal vigilance.[54]

In the last analysis, Newman, Margaret McMillan, and Sir Robert Morant were interested in medical inspection only as an avenue to medical treatment. Every reformer knew the mass of unhealthiness among schoolchildren that Kerr and Margaret McMillan had discovered at Bradford. They knew that the physical defects uncovered by school medical inspection would not, or could not, be treated by the mass of working-class parents; that the children would have to be treated either by charity at the voluntary hospitals or by the poor law. For nearly two decades, ever since some school boards had begun to demand certificates of health when a child was brought to school, the problem of medical treatment had been critical. Unless a voluntary hospital were available to take the child as a charity case, the only resort for the working class was the poor law medical officer, which technically

[54] George Newman, *The Health of the State*, London, 1907, pp. 109–10, 147.

made the parents paupers. School medical inspection, in effect, forced parents onto parish relief. Understandably, the school boards were reluctant to do this, and the alternative, widespread unhealthiness among the children, was usually the result. Therefore, as long as treatment was unavailable, or carried with it the taint of pauperism (although the legal penalties for medical relief had practically disappeared), there was little interest in uncovering defects. Medical inspection without treatment meant little for the welfare of the child.

But for the ordinary upper-class Englishman, the opposite was the case. For him the Boer War and the fear of racial decline had made medical inspection a matter of pressing interest. He wished to know the direction the national physique was moving, and to him this was important whether or not any treatment followed. He would ignore the health of the working man as long as he assumed it to be good. When he became suspicious that it was not, he found the need for exact data imperative. The reformers capitalized on this interest in inspection, for they knew unhealthiness would indeed be found, and that treatment would then be provided.

Margaret McMillan left Bradford in November, 1902. (In the same year Kerr was appointed Medical Officer (Education) for London.) At a farewell reception in Bradford she met Joseph Fels, to whom she transmitted her own sympathy for unhealthy schoolchildren, as George Lansbury eighteen months later would introduce him to the paradox of idle men in the city and idle land in the country in a nation that imported food, and to the remedy of rural labour colonies.[55] Fels promised at this time that he would support the establishment of clinics for schoolchildren when Miss McMillan came to London. After further discussion in London the two, in November, 1904, approached the education committee of

[55] Joseph Fels, 1854–1914, born, Halifax County, Virginia; parents German immigrants; education irregular, left school in 1869 to enter a small business with his father in Baltimore, Maryland; entered soap manufacturing independently in Philadelphia, 1873, and developed the process of Fels-Naphtha Soap which brought him great wealth. Began to withdraw from business by mid-nineties and devoted practically the whole of the last ten years of his life to social causes. Particularly interested in the single-tax, although mostly through humanitarian concern for popular welfare rather than from economic motives. Underwrote expenses of delegates to Russian Social Democratic Congress meeting in London in 1907 in amount of £1,700; note alleged to have been repaid by Soviet Government after Fels' death. Credited James Keir Hardie with stimulating his interest in social service. Also supported Zionism; described by Beatrice Webb as 'a decidedly vulgar little Jew.'

the London County Council with a proposal for school clinics which Fels proposed to endow with £5,000. The education committee was willing to accept the money without the clinics but, upon learning it could not have one without the other, refused both.[56] After her rebuff by the London Education Committee Miss McMillan, in alliance with the National Union of Teachers through T. J. Macnamara, and the National League for Physical Education and Improvement through Sir Lauder Brunton, became part of the general movement demanding the establishment of a system of medical inspection. Her aim, however, was always the cure rather than the discovery of disease. And her outstanding contribution to the health of children lies in her work in the establishment of school clinics.

6

Despite pressure from the outside, and notwithstanding the obvious interest in all sections of the House of Commons, the Government did not include a provision for medical inspection in the great Education Bill of 1906. Thus, as a few months earlier with feeding, there was some embarrassment when Mr H. J. Tennant, Liberal M.P. for Berwickshire, proposed on July 16, 1906, during the committee stage of the Bill an amendment requiring local education authorities to 'make arrangements for attending to the health and physical condition' of schoolchildren.[57] Tennant stated specifically in answer to a question that his amendment did not intend to include treatment.[58] The Government discomfort at Tennant's amendment was evident in the flurry of debate that followed. Although the ministry was prepared to accept some form of medical inspection, the broad terms of the amendment, even with Tennant's protestations to the contrary, clearly opened the door to medical treatment and so took the Liberal leaders further than they cared to go. Augustine Birrell, for the Board of Education, quickly agreed to the principle of medical inspection and promised an amendment to the Bill at the report stage. However, the amendment finally put down stated only that the local education authorities must 'provide for the medical

---

[56] Mary Fels, *Joseph Fels, His Life-Work*, New York, 1916, pp. 203–4.
[57] *Hansard*, CLX (July 16, 1906), col. 1376, *et seq.*
[58] *Ibid.*, col. 1390.

inspection of every child' when admitted to school and at such other times as necessary.[59] Macnamara and Charles Masterman attempted to induce Birrell to admit that inspection would be continuous. Birrell declined, arguing that this would be medical treatment.[60]

The government substitute for Tennant's amendment died with the rest of the Education Bill at the end of the year. Its importance stands as a demonstration of the Campbell-Bannerman Government's intentions on medical inspection during the first year of its tenure. The Birrell amendment provided medical inspection only and would not have permitted the extension of education authority health activity through administrative order.

At the end of 1906 Birrell left the Board of Education for the Chief Secretaryship of Ireland, and Reginald McKenna succeded him at education. Even before the appointment was announced, Robert Morant was in contact with his new chief laying plans for legislation that would found a school medical service.[61] In McKenna, Morant had an unimaginative minister, who knew nothing of education, whose talent, whose interest, and whose best work would be entirely in the area of finance, and who had no understanding of the implications of school medical inspection. Writing a generation later, Sir Lawrence Brock, who joined Morant in 1912 on the National Health Insurance Commission and served with him until the permanent secretary's death in 1920, told of Morant's plan.

> Morant knew . . . but did not tell his Minister, that medical inspection would reveal such a mass of disease and defect that no Government subsequently would be able to resist the demand

[59] *Hansard*, CLX (July 16, 1906), col. 1398.

[60] *Ibid.*, cols. 1398–9.

[61] Before the appointment was announced, Campbell-Bannerman had written McKenna, '. . . will you communicate with Morant at the Edn Office— he is gasping for you for some very urgent matters.' H. Campbell-Bannerman to Reginald McKenna, January 17, 1907, quoted in Stephen McKenna, *Reginald McKenna, 1863–1943*, London, 1948, pp. 43, 46.

Reginald McKenna, 1863–1943, born, London; father a civil servant, educated at King's College, London, and Trinity Hall, Cambridge; admitted to Bar, 1877; contested Clapham, 1892; M.P., Liberal, North Monmouthshire, 1895–1918. Financial Secretary to Treasury, 1905; President, Board of Education, 1907–8; First Lord of Admiralty, 1908–11; Home Secretary, 1911–15; Chancellor of the Exchequer, 1915–16; Chairman, Midland Bank, 1919–43. Offered Chancellor of the Exchequer by Andrew Bonar Law, with a safe seat in Parliament; upon refusal, post taken by Stanley Baldwin.

of the Local Education Authorities to provide treatment. Morant told me himself that he foresaw what would happen and *meant it to happen* because without the horrifying results of inspection there was no chance for a Bill authorizing treatment. Up to this time the State had not provided treatment, except under the Poor Law, for anything but infectious diseases.

. . . .

It was Morant's action that broke down the barrier established by the Public Health Act of 1875. He started and set in motion a vast social revolution probably without then foreseeing the ultimate result of his action.[62]

Morant's main concern in the next few months was to produce his measure for the health of children quietly, bury it among a mass of other details, and get it passed without debate. In June, he explained his plans to Margaret McMillan, with whom he was in constant communication.

. . . I have for some time past come to feel that for the good of the children and the public, what subjects are taught and how much they are taught *do not matter anything like so much nowadays* as attention (a) to the *physical*-condition of the scholars and the teacher and (b) to the physiological aspect of the school. . . . Between us we shall do something, I am sure, if we can avoid raising a public hubbub against our efforts, and I have found it an immense help to have a talk with you. I trust we may have many more together.[63]

Morant's concern had been increased by the appearance on March 1 of a Private Member's Bill to require school playgrounds and medical inspection introduced by Walter Russell Rea, Liberal of Scarborough.[64] Rea simply used the inspection clause of the 1906 Bill which would have excluded any provision for treatment. His Bill caused a considerable anxiety among Liberals of all shades of opinion. It disturbed the radicals by being more limited in scope than they intended inspection to be, and the rest of the party because as a Private Member's Bill it was non-political and

[62] Quoted in Violet Markham, *Friendship's Harvest*, London, 1956, pp., 200–1. Brock was at this time private secretary to T. J. Macnamara.
[63] Quoted in Albert Mansbridge, *Margaret McMillan, Prophet and Pioneer*, London, 1932, p. 64.
[64] Rea's father was a managing director of the Taff Vale Railway.

E

so offered the Unionists the opportunity to retrieve their reputation as reformers. Both Balfour and Anson supported it, and as a result the measure quickly passed through the second reading, committee, and report stages.[65]

Hence, for the second time the Government was in the awkward position of having to provide a substitute of its own for the initiative of a private member on medical inspection. Bearing the Unionist jeers as well as he could, McKenna asked Rea to withdraw his Bill,[66] and on July 31, 1907, Morant's proposal, the Education (Administrative Provisions) Bill, received its second reading. Clause 13 of the measure combined the wording of Birrell's and Tennant's amendments on medical inspection of the previous year. The clause specified that the local education authorities were to 'provide for the medical inspection of children' at appropriate times during their school career, and also 'to make such arrangements as may be sanctioned by the Board of Education for attending to the health and physical condition of children educated in public elementary schools. . . .' On the words 'arrangements . . . for attending to the health,' borrowed from Mr Tennant's amendment, hung the establishment of the school medical service.

The Unionists were somewhat suspicious of the wording of the Bill. Anson called attention to the 'extreme vagueness' of the paragraph about treatment and asked what was meant by it. The Parliamentary Secretary, Thomas Lough, answered hesitantly describing a 'small hospital outside the school.' The Unionists offered an amendment requiring the Local Education Authority to attempt to recover the costs of any treatment made necessary by inspection in the manner laid down by the Education (Provision of Meals) Act. McKenna answered this, not altogether truthfully, saying that a provision for recovering charges would compel the local education authorities to offer treatment, which was not the intent of the measure.[67] Generally the Government insisted that it had no intention of compelling medical treatment, and that in any case the decision lay with the local authorities, as would any decision on financing the treatment.[68] But the matter was little discussed. The entire debate on Clause 13 did not occupy a score

[65] *Hansard*, CLXX (March 1, 1907), cols. 426–31; CLXXVI (June 14, 1907), cols. 33–63.

[66] *Ibid.*, CLXXIX (July 31, 1907), cols. 1102–3.

[67] *Ibid.*, CLXXX (August 12, 1907), cols. 919–21.

[68] *Ibid.*, cols. 921–2.

of pages in *Hansard*. On August 28, without ever having excited the 'hubbub' Morant had feared, the Bill requiring school medical inspections and permitting treatment became law.

7

While the Parliamentary politics of the school medical service were of the most routine sort, its administrative politics illustrate perhaps better than any other foundation of the New Liberalism the vast power possessed by a truly energetic and imaginative civil servant who is armed with a coherent plan and is supervised by an amateur, inexperienced, and transient minister. This is not to suggest that an able minister who troubles himself about the details of the running of his department cannot leave his stamp clearly upon legislation, even in the tenure of a few months. Certainly Winston Churchill proved this in his attack upon unemployment during his short stay at the Board of Trade. But the presidents of the Board of Education during the establishment of the school medical service, Reginald McKenna in 1907 and Walter Runciman from 1908 to 1911, were fleeting, indistinct figures. For practical purposes the head of English education was Sir Robert Laurie Morant. Almost as soon as the House of Lords had disposed of the Education Bill of 1906, for which his enthusiasm understandably was limited, he began to plan for measures to guard the health of English children. In this the central, but by no means only, agency would be the school medical service. He calculated precisely the sort of innocuous legislation that would best accomplish his aim. He had seen to the politics of its passage. With this complete in the late summer of 1907, he began to prepare plans for a medical department to be established under the Board of Education which in the future could be merged into a general public health agency of the sort soon to be proposed, as he well knew, by the minority report of the Royal Commission on the Poor Laws. He had planned this with Beatrice Webb in the spring of 1907. On April 27 she wrote:

> Dined alone with Morant to talk over the handing-over of Poor Law children of school age to the education authorities— infants to the public health authority. He agrees to both, and is much pleased with the latter idea because it chimes in with his

notion of taking ordinary infants away from the school, and placing them under the public health authority. He would like to go to the L.G.B. and we must see whether it could be managed. He says he will be forced to start a medical department because of the incapacity of the L.G.B. to do the necessary work.[69]

The integration of the school medical service with other local authority medical services was an ideal solution that would have to wait until the establishment of the Ministry of Health, at the end of Morant's life. For the immediate future the best he could do was to establish the strongest possible medical service in the Board of Education and attempt to undermine the resisting power of John Burns and his permanent secretary, Sir Samuel Provis, at the Local Government Board.[70]

The critical appointment to the new post of Chief Medical Officer to the Board of Education went to George Newman, who was at that time Medical Officer of Health for Finsbury. Newman had been a friend of the Webbs for several years and was an important writer in the public health field. His handbook for medical officers of health, written with Sir Arthur Whitelegge, *Hygiene and Public Health*, had been standard since the eighteen-nineties and his appointment had been under consideration at the Board of Education well before the Education (Administrative Provisions) Bill became law.[71] He found the idea of building a new department quite as exciting as did Morant himself. 'I do hope all is as it should be,' he wrote the permanent secretary on August 8,

> and if it is, as Card. Newman used to say, we will do a work in England. To assist in a bit of solid building and good construction concerning the physical condition of the English people is worth spending oneself for![72]

The two men agreed that the medical department should be a 'small dept.—of good men and no juniors.'[73]

[69] Beatrice Webb, *Our Partnership*, London, 1948, pp. 378–9.
[70] The first act in this campaign was to secure the appointment in January, 1908, of Arthur Newsholme as Chief Medical Officer to the L.G.B. On this, see: Webb, *Partnership*, p. 394.
[71] Webb, *Partnership*, p. 385.
[72] George Newman to R. L. Morant, August 7, 1907, Ministry of Education Private Office Papers, Medical, General, Formation of the Medical Department.
[73] Newman to Morant, August 18, 1907. *Ibid.*

Unfortunately, Newman, like Morant, was a man with many enemies. His appointment to the central post in children's health in England and Wales meant passing over several members of the powerful body that had for many years been most active in the medical inspection of schoolchildren—the London Education Committee. Some members of the London medical inspectorate they could dismiss with a sugared letter. One was Dr Alfred Eichholz, school medical inspector for Lambeth, and the discoverer of the conditions at the notorious Johanna Street School. Wrote Morant to Eichholz:

> From the beginning I have always had you in mind, and hoped that the establishment of the Bureau, whenever it came off, would be an opportunity for recognizing the admirable services . . . you have always rendered—you will . . . understand the determinative effect of the political and other reasons which have influenced the President. . . .[74]

On the same day Morant wrote to Newman telling him he had been appointed at an annual salary of £1,200. It would, Morant said, be hard to write up a newspaper announcement.

> It will also be difficult to put in as much as I should like of your own personal qualifications, without seeming to show too definitely the comparatively small list of personal qualifications in the same directions that are possessed by Dr Eichholz.[75]

But a far more serious competitor for the new post of Chief Medical Officer was the Medical Officer (Education) for the London Education Committee, Dr James Kerr. Kerr had come to this post after his pioneering work in Bradford and was at this time perhaps the best-known man in England in school medicine.

Kerr's most important disqualifications were political. He represented the anti-Webbian faction in the struggle that had been boiling within the education committee of the London County Council since that body had replaced the old London School Board under the London Education Act of 1903. The London School Board had been a stronghold of the National Union of Teachers,

[74] Morant to Alfred Eichholz, August 28, 1907. Ministry of Education Private Office Papers, Medical, General, Formation of the Medical Department.
[75] Morant to Newman, August 28, 1907. *Ibid.* Eichholz was nevertheless appointed to the Board of Education inspectorate, and finally became chief medical inspector at the Board of Education in 1919.

many of whose members, particularly the influential T. J. Macna-mara, had been active supporters of medical inspection. The London Education Act was perhaps Sidney Webb's greatest triumph in local government, but it fatally divided the radical majority among the Progressives in the London County Council, with which the Webbs and the Fabians had worked since the early nineties. As the result, when the London Education Committee began its work in 1904, Webb lost his post as chairman, although the Progressives held their majority on the LCC for three more years.[76]

The split between the radicals and Fabians was over more than personalities. The radical majority of the London School Board was also strongly Nonconformist. It had bitterly opposed the Education Act of 1902, which had been chiefly Morant's work, and the London Education Act of 1903, which had been Webb's.[77] The climax to the dispute came eventually in the controversy over the Holmes circular, in which Morant permitted his name to be put to a document carrying a number of disparaging comments about local school inspectors, nearly all of whom were former teachers and staunch members of the National Union of Teachers. As a result, the N.U.T., to its great delight, participated in 1911 in driving Morant from the Board of Education.[78]

The radical-Nonconformist-N.U.T. oligarchy in the huge London education system identified Robert Morant with Sidney

[76] On this break-up of the Progressive majority see: A. M. McBriar, *Fabian Socialism and English Politics, 1884–1918*, Cambridge, 1962, pp. 216–17.

[77] The radical alliance had been nearly strong enough to frighten the increasingly weak Balfour ministry into dropping the London Bill. Webb, *Partnership*, p. 263.

[78] The 'Holmes circular' was a memorandum, first made public on March 14, 1911, written by the chief inspector of elementary schools at the Board of Education, E. G. A. Holmes, discussing the 'uncultured and imperfectly educated' condition of the local education inspectors. This paper was circulated over Morant's signature and although Holmes accepted full responsibility for it, Morant received the blame and the view expressed probably coincided with his own.

The members of the local inspectorate were almost invariably former board school teachers and members of the National Union of Teachers with whom Morant had struggled since he replaced George Kekewich as permanent secretary during the planning of the Education Act in 1902. The furor over the Holmes circular represented, therefore, the accumulation of bitterness against Morant going back nearly a decade. On the activity of the N.U.T. and T. J. Macnamara's publication, *The Schoolmaster*, in forcing Morant's resignation in 1911, see: Bernard M. Allen, *Sir Robert Morant*, London, 1934, pp. 260–3. Allen leaves much unsaid. See also: Markham, *Harvest*, pp. 188–9.

Webb. They rightly suspected Morant of intending to use Webb's proposals for unification of all health, hygiene, and sanitary activities under a single local public health authority, thus depriving education authorities of control over the service. In James Kerr they had an eminent and obviously qualified candidate for the critical post of Chief Medical Officer to the Board of Education. Kerr, they knew, would see to it that the school medical service remained under the local education authorities, and would prevent its merger into a larger service in which the dominant administrative figure would be the medical officer of health.[79]

The London Education Committee radicals had as an ally the British Medical Association, a body with a tradition of hostility to the medical officers of health and an even greater fear that a Fabian-planned school medical service would grow into a complete State health service.[80] The doctors reacted immediately to the

[79] Kerr's first report to the London County Council after the passage of medical inspection gives an adequate summary of his ideas on the proper place of the school medical service.

> Any public provision for protecting and aiding growth and development of children during the years of school life—three to sixteen years of age— should be entirely committed to the Education Authority. This would allow such matters as feeding, teaching, cleansing, medical treatment, or social protection of school children, when these duties become a public care, to be administered by one authority, and by bringing all the various problems into a correct relation and perspective would also effect considerable financial economy.
>
>   .   .   .   .
>
> Fortunately this is the line taken by all recent legislation in matters concerning children.

> Report for the twenty-one months ending December 31, 1908. Quoted in *Nature*, LXXXIII (April 7, 1910), 170-1.

See also Archibald Hogarth's arguments for the separation of the services in: A. H. Hogarth, *Medical Inspection of Schools*, London, 1909, *passim.*, which is dedicated to Kerr. At the time of publication Hogarth was a resident of Toynbee Hall.

[80] The following estimate of the public position of the medical officer of health, by a well-established consultant, may be not untypical.

> . . . the Medical Officer of Health is a power in the land. The rich are particularly well satisfied with him, and he is too well satisfied with himself.

> He goes about preventing diseases that the clinician cannot cure and carrying the gospel of cleanliness. The results of his work lend themselves to easily understood statistics.

> Herbert De Carle Woodcock, *The Doctor and the People*, London, 1912, p. 51.

The *Medical Directory*, *1912*, shows Woodcock to be an M.D., F.R.C.P., a holder of honorary appointments at several London hospitals, and a consultant in diseases of the lung.

announcement in *The Times* of September 13, 1907, that the Board of Education had decided to establish a medical department 'on a broad public health basis' with George Newman at its head. The next week the *British Medical Journal* carried a long article applauding the principle of the school medical service. The journal asserted incorrectly that the programme had been forced upon an unwilling education department by public opinion led by the B.M.A., and concluded with a harsh personal attack upon Morant.

> We do not question Sir Robert Morant's devotion to duty, but we think it is clear that he has failed to move with the times, and that the policy which he seeks to impose upon the education authorities of this country is antiquated and reactionary.

Continuing, the *B.M.J.* expressed 'keen disappointment' in the appointment of Newman, because

> the person designated by medical and public opinion for the office was Doctor James Kerr, who may be justly called the founder in this country of this new department of preventative medicine.[81]

In the same issue of the magazine a still more immoderate denunciation of the new medical department appeared in the form of a letter from Dr Archibald H. Hogarth, an Assistant Medical Officer (Education) for the London County Council under Kerr. Newman, Hogarth asserted, was a medical officer of health and so 'knows nothing' of school hygiene; he had, indeed, 'been pitchforked into office.' In the summer of 1906, said Hogarth, the former President of the Board of Education, Augustine Birrell, had promised Kerr the 'first refusal' of the Chief Medical Officer's post. Then in January, 1907, after the appointment of McKenna, Morant had told Kerr that the idea of a separate medical department had been 'entirely dropped.' Moreover, the new president, McKenna, had never been given the opportunity to interview Kerr. Morant had 'behaved as an autocrat' and should be over-ruled by higher authority. Behind the new health proposals of the Board of Education, said Hogarth, was the Society of Medical Officers of Health, which wanted to 'subordinate medical inspection of schools to the general sanitary administration of the coun-

---

[81] *British Medical Journal*, September 21, 1907, pp. 760–1.

try.' This system, he concluded, had been condemned by all countries with medical inspection. Argentina had dropped it in 1883.[82]

The comments in the *British Medical Journal* sent Newman into a rage. Hogarth was a former student of his, he wrote to Morant on September 20. The letter, Newman thought, was 'impertinent;' Kerr had taught him 'bad manners.' He had already drawn a draft of an answer saying that the article and the letter were incorrect.[83] Later the same day Newman wrote again to Morant saying he had received a letter from Arthur Newsholme urging him not to reply. Commenting on the charge that he was inexperienced in school medical inspection, he remarked that during his time in Finsbury he had applied to Kerr for permission to conduct medical inspections in that borough and had been refused.[84]

The Board of Education's unfriendly relations with the London Education Committee and with the B.M.A. made more important the mobilization of support among the medical officers of health. During the next few weeks, while Newman and Morant were preparing what would become in November the famous Board of Education Circular 576 ordering the commencement of medical inspection, Newman leaned heavily upon the support and advice of Dr Newsholme. Early in the second week of October, Newman informed Morant he was going to Brighton to see Newsholme to show him the draft circular.

> He is the editor of the M.O.H. monthly journal, *Public Health* and we want to have this definitely on our side all along. The Soc. wanted me to be Joint Ed. w. Newsholme. He and I are v. great friends—so I think this can be assured.

Public Health was a very influential magazine, continued Newman. He said he would help to edit it, but assured Morant he would not commit the board to anything.[85] Morant replied the

[82] *British Medical Journal*, pp. 771–2. Letter dated September 16, 1907.

[83] George Newman to Morant, September 20, 1907. Ministry of Education, Private Office Papers, Medical, General, Formation of the Medical Department. The fact that this note is dated a day before the official publication date of the *B.M.J.* suggests that the journal had appeared before its official date of publication.

[84] Newman to Morant, September 20, 1907. *Ibid.*

[85] Newman to Morant, October 7, 1907. *Ibid.*

E*

next day saying that he had written to Newsholme, that he warmly approved of Newman's visit, and that he expected Newsholme 'may give us useful hints.'[86] Upon his return the next day, Newman reported that his visit had been a great success:

> I wish you would see him someday. He does not know you and he may be v. useful in stating our case in the press if the need arise. Happily for us, he warmly approved of my notes for the circular. I am glad you wrote him.[87]

While Newman was consulting Newsholme, Morant was strengthening the position of the medical department by consulting other people on the wording of the order inaugurating medical inspection. On October 28, he wrote to Margaret McMillan:

> I want to ask if you would come and see me for a good talk in Whitehall on the inauguration of Medical Inspection under the new Act and help me by going through my draft circular with me, for I am very anxious to keep the zealous interest of those who care for this new development so we may get it started right, and that it shall neither hang fire nor get started on the wrong and futile lines.[88]

A few days later he submitted the draft to C. F. G. Masterman, asking advice in flattering terms, and urging him not to be misled by Kerr's attacks upon medical inspection.[89]

Board of Education Circular 576, which had been the subject of so much anxious consideration, appeared on November 22, 1907. The Act had stipulated that medical inspection would go into effect on January 1, 1908. Now, in its first set of regulations, the Board of Education proposed that for the year 1908 the local authorities should concentrate upon examining all students entering school, that is, all students at age five. During 1909 the authorities should try to examine those leaving in that year. This would mean about two million examinations each year. After this, local education authorities should examine each child at least three, and preferably four times—once upon entering school at age five, a second time at about age seven or eight, a third time at about age

---

[86] Morant to Newman, October 10, 1907. Ministry of Education, Private Office Papers, Medical General, Formation of the Medical Department.

[87] Newman to Morant, October 11, 1907. *Ibid.*

[88] Quoted in Mansbridge, *McMillan*, p. 68.

[89] R. L. Morant to C. F. G. Masterman, November 4, 1907. Ministry of Education, Private Office Papers.

ten, and also, if possible, upon leaving school, at age thirteen or fourteen.[90]

While the circular was under preparation, the unedifying controversy between the Board of Education Medical Department and the London Education Committee continued and grew more bitter.[91] This rather squalid discussion could be well ignored except that it illustrated, and to some extent caused, the almost total alienation for the next four years of the London education system from the national authorities. As a result, the largest school system in the United Kingdom did not participate in the inaugural phase of medical inspection or medical treatment.

Margaret McMillan, who had expected that compulsory medical inspection would finally bring success to her long crusade for school clinics, was unable to extract the most elemental co-operation from the London Education Committee. Very reluctantly she was lent the upper room of an L.E.C. infant school in Bow for a student treatment centre in the autumn of 1908. But she received nothing more. The London school authorities neither gave funds for its support—these were finally provided from the apparently bottomless purse of Joseph Fels—nor after the centre was established did they send students for treatment. The clinic was little used, and the two physicians who had been retained had little to do. Therefore, students who did attend had to be charged 7s. 6d. a visit. As anyone could visit the out-patient clinic of a voluntary hospital for 5s., Miss McMillan's experiment in Bow was a failure. In 1910 she abandoned Bow and moved to Deptford, the borough Sidney Webb had represented on the LCC for twenty years. Here, under the auspices of the Greenwich Borough Council, she established a public clinic for children. This was open to anyone and not limited to students from schools. Here she was flooded with patients, whom she charged 2s. 6d. per visit. In the years before the war the Deptford clinic added mental treatment, a specialized baby clinic, as well as a wide range of health activities, including physical drill and outdoor camps for boys and girls. On this foundation grew Margaret McMillan's reputation as a friend of English children.[92]

[90] The most convenient source for the Board of Education Medical Department circulars is the *British Medical Journal Supplement* for the appropriate date.

[91] See the *British Medical Journal*, September 28, October 5, October 12, 1907.

[92] On the Bow and Deptford clinics see: Fels, *Joseph Fels*, pp. 206–8; Lowndes, *McMillan*, p. 62.

A far more important result of the ill-feeling between the London Education Committee and the Board of Education was that until the removal of Dr Kerr in 1911 London schoolchildren received little benefit from the pioneering works of Morant and Newman. After 1907 Kerr virtually disappeared from medical circles concerned with public health and schoolchildren's welfare. Particularly he avoided all public appearances with medical men around the Board of Education, nor did he respond, except in the most cursory way, to medical department circulars. He refused to establish school clinics and, of course, declined to support Margaret McMillan's work in any way. Children whose need for medical care was too apparent to be ignored were sent to the voluntary hospitals, with which, fortunately, London was well provided.

In his fight to keep the school medical service purely a function of the local education authorities and altogether separate from the control of medical officers of health, Kerr generally had been supported by the British Medical Association. But by sending schoolchildren needing treatment to the voluntary hospitals he was taking an action that the B.M.A. strongly opposed. As will be discussed in connexion with national health insurance, the B.M.A. regarded the voluntary hospitals with a mixture of admiration and suspicion. The hospital represented, to be sure, the summit of medical skill, but their out-patient clinics, originally intended for treatment of the indigent, were becoming serious competitors for doctors practising among the working classes. Any large number of students sent there by an official body would either overcrowd facilities theoretically reserved for the poor or if the Government sought to pay for the children treated by the hospitals, its money payments would inevitably be followed by some form of official control. Therefore, the B.M.A. insisted that students whom the school authorities ordered to seek medical treatment should be treated at the cost and in the facilities of those authorities.

In the end, three years after the beginning of compulsory medical inspection, the British Medical Association came to feel that the situation in London was approaching a scandal. By driving doctors into opposition, Kerr caused his own downfall. The change in attitude of the British Medical Association became public in a speech made by an eminent surgeon, Sir Victor Horsley. At Clifford's Inn on March 16, 1911, Horsley, addressing a small medical gathering, expressed the growing resentment in the profession against the studied neglect of the health of London schoolchildren. Medical inspection as it was carried out in the capital, he said, was not what was intended by the framers of the Administrative Provisions Act. The present behaviour of this 'great municipal body . . . amounted to a breach of faith with the nation.' Citizens of London, he said, had a right to complain of the present situation. The present medical staff was nowhere near sufficient, nor was it intended to be. 'Merely to take selected schools, and, by inspecting a few children, arrive at an idea of what was happening in the mass, was not the intention of the Act of 1906.' [*sic*.] The whole organization as it stood was 'ridiculous' and 'inadequate.' The LCC, he concluded, had no interest in changing things and was merely trying 'to fend off the time for a decision. . . .'[93]

Horsley's speech came a few days after the consideration by the London Education Committee of a report of its Children's Care Sub-Committee which had proposed to expand the system of payments to voluntary hospitals for the treatment of children. Earlier in the year, under pressure from the B.M.A., the Board of Education had severely criticized arrangements of this sort,[94] and when the report was rendered to the London Education Committee, Reginald Bray moved an amendment to put all children's medical care under the medical officers of health. Kerr's supporters on the L.E.C. defeated the amendment and approved the report nineteen to ten.[95] It was this intransigence, one may imagine, that caused Horsley's speech and brought the question of the London school medical service to a crisis.

In the House of Commons five days later, Leo Chiozza Money asked the new President of the Board of Education, Walter Runciman, whether he had seen a report of Horsley's address.[96]

[93] *The Times*, March 17, 1911.
Victor Alexander Haden Horsley, 1857–1916, physiologist and surgeon, pioneer in neuro-surgical techniques; advocate of temperance reform and female suffrage; first Chairman of the Representative Body of the B.M.A. when the new system of government was organized in 1902; several times Liberal candidate for Parliament; became an outspoken supporter of national health insurance and as such was repudiated by the B.M.A.

[94] *Ibid.*, February 22, 1911.

[95] *Ibid.*, March 2, 1911.

[96] Walter Runciman, Viscount Doxford, 1870–1947, born, South Shields; father, first Baron Runciman, in shipping business; educated privately and at Trinity College, Cambridge. Contested Gravesend, 1898; entered Parliament for

Runciman, whose life at this time was being made hideous by the Holmes circular—the existence of which he had publicly denied a few days earlier in terms that would have appeared unequivocal to all but the most subtle minds—answered vaguely that he had seen the report but that he was not sure he agreed with it. In the next few months the B.M.A. carried on an unremitting attack against their former allies on the London Education Committee. At the end of June, Horsley led a large deputation of doctors to see Runciman and to demand that the board force the L.E.C. to 'carry out their duty in accordance with the terms of the Act of 1907.'[97] Two weeks later, in a lead article, the *British Medical Journal* criticized the municipal government of London in terms that approached the libellous. In the capital, said the *B.M.J.*:

> It is indisputable . . . that neither medical inspection nor treatment of school children is being properly carried out. This, indeed, is a very mild statement, for it might not be untruly said that the medical inspection and school treatment provided are in the nature of a farce, and that in both connexions, the London County Council is endeavouring to hoodwink the public.[98]

The affair came to an end quietly; Kerr's defeat was accomplished with true municipal political finesse by the abolition of his post. At the beginning of November, the Board of Education informed the London Education Committee that it would withhold its sanction to the plan proposed the previous March for widespread treatment of students at voluntary hospitals.[99] Under this pressure, and with the implied threat of further prohibitions and the

---

Oldham defeating Winston Churchill, 1899; defeated by Churchill, 1900; M.P., Liberal, for Dewsbury, 1902–18; West Swansea, 1924–9; St Ives, Cornwall, 1929–31, and as a Liberal National, 1931–7; House of Lords, 1937–47. Parliamentary Secretary to the Local Government Board, 1905–7; Financial Secretary to the Treasury, 1907–8; President, Board of Education, 1908–11; President, Board of Agriculture, 1911–14; President, Board of Trade, 1914–16 and 1931–7; Lord President of Council, 1938–9. Entered family shipping business upon graduation from Cambridge, 1892; head of unsuccessful mission to Prague, 1938, to mediate dispute between Czech Government and Sudeten Germans.

[97] *The Times*, June 28, 1911.

[98] 'The Board of Education and the London County Council,' *British Medical Journal*, June 15, 1911, p. 132.

[99] *The Times*, November 9, 1911. One private facility, however, that was specifically approved at this time was Margaret McMillan's Deptford clinic.

subsequent withholding of grants, the London Education Committee surrendered. The Children's Care Committee was abolished, and the council committed all 'school medical work' to the Medical Officer of Health for London County, who would discharge his duties through six new assistant medical officers in the department of the Public Health Committee of the LCC.[100] The post of Medical Officer (Education) disappeared.

In this way London acceded to the Board of Education and its principle of unification of all children's medical services. Just as this occurred, Sir Robert Morant and Walter Runciman left the Board of Education. Runciman's translation to the Board of Agriculture, occurring with a large number of other changes, may not have derived from anything more than Earl Carrington's clear incompetence and Asquith's desire, at a time when the Government was under heavy siege, to keep a defender who had outlived his usefulness in education. But it is hard not to wonder whether some of the strong anti-Morant forces in the London Education Committee were not influenced by the departure of Robert Morant from the Board of Education just before their decision to topple their own chief medical officer. The coincidence in dates is too strong to be disregarded.[101] Even though Morant was not implicated in any except the most formal way in the Holmes circular, he was a formidable and ancient enemy of the National Union of Teachers and of its domination of London education. The researcher must at least admit the possibility that the intimation of his departure helped to dissolve the pro-Kerr majority of the previous March on the L.E.C.

Thus, London came into step with the rest of England. Under a stronger minister or less controversial permanent secretary, this consummation might have occurred sooner. The sufferers were Dr James Kerr and the people of London.[102]

[100] *The Times*, December 18, 1911.

[101] Morant's departure from the Board of Education and his appointment to the national health insurance administration was announced to an astonished House of Commons on November 28, 1911. The reorganization of the London Education Committee took place two and one-half weeks later.

[102] Kerr remained in the employ of the LCC until 1928, first as 'Medical Research Officer' until 1924, and then as 'Consulting Medical Officer.' Neither of these posts survived his tenure of them. Both *The Times* and *Public Health* ignored Kerr's death in 1941.

8

Except for the chronic friction with the London Education Committee, the Board of Education and the Fabians appeared to move forward rapidly in 1908 and 1909 in their campaign to unify local authority health and education services. During 1908, while Morant was laying the foundation for the school medical service, the Webbs, whose administrative ideas were identical with his own, were writing the minority report of the investigation of the poor law, recommending in many areas things Morant was already doing. Morant hoped, in one direction, eventually to divest the education authority of all responsibility for the medical treatment, but not the medical inspection, of schoolchildren. He intended to combine all medical services of the local authority under a single administrative committee of the county and borough councils. Indeed, his plans in this direction had caused much of the opposition to Newman's appointment. Conversely, he intended to put the education of all children, whatever their status, under the local education authorities. This proposal would become a key provision of a minority report of the Royal Commission on the Poor Laws.

When one considers how intelligent, informed, and well-connected were the reformers attempting to rebuild English welfare institutions from the inside, it is surprising that more was not accomplished. But for the energy and resourcefulness of Winston Churchill, David Lloyd George, and C. F. G. Masterman, the architects of the alternative programme of the New Liberalism, the refusal of John Burns to do anything, and Morant's sheer bad luck in the Holmes circular, the history of English social reform might have been altogether different.

The reformers achieved an early victory in January, 1908, when John Burns appointed Arthur Newsholme to the post of Chief Medical Officer to the Local Government Board. With Newman at the Board of Education and Newsholme at the Local Government Board, Fabian reform had a dependable team to work together for the unification of health services regardless of the opinion of temporary political ministers. An early product of the new co-operation was the appearance on August 17, 1908, of Board of Education Circular 596, which showed clearly the orientation intended for English public health activity.

Circular 596, as important as a Parliamentary statute, provided the charter for the school medical service in the way Circular 576 had inaugurated school medical inspection. But whereas the circular of the previous November had required local education authorities, in peremptory terms, to begin medical inspection in the following year, warning them that efficiency in this activity was to be considered part of their overall efficiency for grant purposes, Circular 596 could only urge, not require, the local authorities to make available means for medical treatment. Even though Morant and Newman had always seen medical treatment as the ultimate goal of medical inspection, the two men had to act cautiously. If, as they hoped, medical treatment were to be incorporated with other forms of public health activity under a single local health authority, the local education authorities could not reasonably be ordered to push ahead to spend funds on facilities that might soon be taken from them. Therefore, while Circular 596 proposed eight different means by which the education authorities might care for the health of their students—several, such as attention to school sanitary arrangements and informing parents of the defects discovered in medical inspection, might have occurred to even the most obtuse school official—the significant provisions were those laying down the lines for future action. Local education administrators were informed that the Board of Education was 'prepared to consider' plans for the establishment of school clinics. Of far greater significance for the future was the statement that the Board of Education particularly hoped

that . . . powers conferred on the education authority may have the result of greatly extending the influence and the scope of the work hitherto performed solely by the sanitary authority.[103]

Probably the greatest importance of Newman's and Morant's plans for the eventual concentration of all public health activity does not lie in any immediate achievement for the Board of Education. Rather they deserve notice for the impact of their administrative pattern upon the minority report of the Royal Commission on the Poor Law. The extent of the Morant–Newman–Newsholme contribution to the minority report is, of course, impossible to assess precisely. But it appears to have been very large. The Webb papers and Mrs Webb's diary show that she was in almost constant

[103] Board of Education Circular 596, August 17, 1908.

touch with these men, particularly during the first half of 1908, on all matters of child welfare. Behind the back of his departmental chief, Morant especially gave her confidential data for the minority report, not only from his own department but from the Local Government Board, and kept her up to date on ministerial gossip.[104]

In an address at the annual dinner of the Society of Medical Officers of Health in November, 1909, nine months after the report was published, Sidney Webb himself acknowledged the health reformers' work on the minority report. Even discounting a considerable amount of Webbian hyperbole, there remains the speaker's clear assertion that the pattern of integration of preventative health activities of the M.O.H.s under the local authorities provided the germ of the idea for a generalized 'framework of prevention of destitution' recommended in the minority report. When they began to testify, the entire complexion of the poor law investigation changed, Sidney Webb flatteringly told the medical officers of health.

> Up to that point it had been a question of how to deter people from applying. The medical officers of health brought in the ideas of searching out cases, of insisting on treatment at the incipient stage, of regarding even one 'missed case' as an evil and a public danger; and the Commission came to see what was wanted was not the relief of destitution but its prevention. It was this new principle learnt from the medical officers of health that the Minority Report worked out into a complete scheme.

. . . .

No one knew better than a medical officer of health that the only way of preventing [destitution] was to arrest the operation

---

[104] I started to dictate you a letter about the report on the Poor-Law schools, but was prevented through Runciman turning up here to do some Office Work for the first time since he has been president.

The report on poor law schools was, in fact, a Local Government Board report, which he suspected the board would not want the Royal Commission to see. R. L. Morant to Beatrice Webb, May 22, 1908, Webb Papers, Section II, Subsection iv, Group D, Item 15.

For conditions in the Local Government Board see also: Sir Arthur Newsholme to Beatrice Webb, May 4, 1908, *Ibid.*, Item 7; R. L. Morant to Beatrice Webb, May 10, 1908, *Ibid.*, Item 9.

of the specific causes, either before the appearance of the disease, or at any rate in its most incipient stage. Thus the prevention of destitution due to disease, child neglect, mental defectiveness or unemployment, was obviously the task of the Health, Education, Lunacy, and Unemployment Authorities respectively.

Webb concluded:

It was because the medical officers of health had been the first missionaries of this gospel, without quite claiming the full share of the credit to which they were really entitled, that he was very glad to be present that night. It was very largely to them that we had to look for the success for the scheme formulated in the Minority Report. He could not help thinking that the medical officers of health were doing more than any other public officers in England—to make England even a more productive nation than it would otherwise be.[105]

At the same dinner Morant, in one of his very few public statements (he said jokingly that he was only 'thinking aloud'), boasted that the coalition of services everyone hoped to see had already begun.

In the first place there had been a linking up between Health and Education. This linking up between the two services was needed both centrally and locally. Centrally, as they knew, the Education Department when it required a Chief Medical Officer came to that society and selected for that post a medical officer of health, in the person of Dr Newman, whose admirable work for the Board, for local authorities, and for the country had fully justified the choice and the policy.

Part of the new unification, Morant remarked, had come from the 'close touch with the Local Government Board' and in 'the happy co-operation which existed between Dr Newman and Dr Newsholme.'[106]

[105] Sidney Webb, address to the annual dinner of the Society of Medical Officers of Health, October 8, 1909, in *Public Health*, XXIII (November, 1909), 65–6.

[106] *Ibid.*, pp. 66–7. Towards the end of his address Morant reiterated the point made earlier in this chapter in connexion with Newman: that the over-riding goal of the school medical service was the improvement of the race rather

9

During his speech at the M.O.H. dinner in 1909, Morant had warned his hearers to 'advance slowly' towards health reform, not 'to exasperate people' even though 'there might be short-cuts to reform. . . .'[107] He was referring here specifically to the local authorities—one may imagine he had in mind the recalcitrant metropolis—but the school medical service had, in the British medical profession, a potential enemy and permanent critic, perhaps even more influential and better entrenched than the powerful London County Council. As quickly as anyone, the doctors had seen that in the long run the requirement for medical inspection would inevitably make necessary a provision for medical treatment. Without waiting for the first frightening reports that surely would come after medical inspection, the Medico-Political Committee of the British Medical Association began, early in 1908, to study possible methods of medical treatment for indigent schoolchildren.[108] As in the case of school feeding, the doctors were aware that the alternative to some form of public facility for school medical treatment was not treatment by by the parents, but no treatment whatever. This latter possibility quite properly they were unwilling to consider, and so had addressed themselves to consideration of the various public and charitable medical institutions available.

The dilemma over the school medical service would anticipate on a small scale the violent internal and public struggle that beset the medical profession three years later over national health insurance. In 1908 the British Medical Association's attitude towards any form of salaried practice was coloured by the fact that it had only begun to recover from a large-scale, unpleasant self-appraisal of possible unethical practices conducted by a proportion

than the narrower aim of putting schoolchildren in the physical condition to learn.

. . . we have now to think of the English people in competition with other races, and if we neglected the health of the race—if we deliberately left open the three roads to destitution of which Mr Webb had spoken . . . we should lose in the racial competition of this world.

Public Health, XXIII (November, 1909), 67.

[107] *Ibid.*, p. 68.

[108] See 'Report to Divisions' of the Medico-Political Committee of the British Medical Association, *British Medical Journal Supplement*, July 18, 1908, pp. 41–2.

of its own members.[109] This investigation, usually referred to as
'The Battle of the Clubs,' was the result of the association's long
overdue attempt to bring to an end a particularly pernicious form
of contract medical care.

Although widely varying in form, 'club practice' involved
basically the agreement by a doctor to treat all members of some
organization or casual group in return for a fixed fee, paid either as
a stipulated salary or as an amount per head per year for each
patient treated. Medical competition kept both salaries and
capitation fees so low that a doctor in club practice was confronted
with the options of depriving himself and his family of a viable
income; or in order to increase his income with a capitation fee, of
soliciting a larger number of patients than he could conscientiously
serve; or in the case of a salary, of neglecting his club patients
while searching out private, fee-paying patients. These alternatives,
equally detestable, demonstrated the fact that in the years before
World War I many doctors in Britain practised under what were
nearly sweatshop conditions. This fact rendered them, incidentally,
highly vulnerable to the appeal of the generous and regular income
afforded by national health insurance. As it affected the immediate
problem, the existence of this type of medical practice made
imperative the interception by the Medico-Political Committee of
the B.M.A. of any move to establish a competing State medical
department that might further reduce the incomes of doctors in
working-class areas.

In attempting to define its attitude towards the school medical
service, the doctors found, as they would again in 1911 and 1912,
that their economic interests as entrepreneurs in a highly competitive enterprise conflicted directly with their calling as healers.
Basically there were four practicable means for the treatment of
schoolchildren and the Medico-Political Committee examined
each of them in turn. First, children could be given medical care
under the auspices of the poor law. The objections here were two.
It was certain, in the first place, that many respectable parents
would resist any form of aid offered in connexion with the poor
law, even though this despised form of medical care was
rapidly improving, and thus many children's ailments would

[109] 'An Investigation into the Economic Conditions of Contract Medical
Practice in the United Kingdom,' *British Medical Journal* Supplement, July 22,
1905, pp. 1–96.

remain unattended. Second, if treatment through the poor law were made universal, and somehow respectable, many parents would remove their children from the market for private practice.

Nor could the Medico-Political Committee accept, as a second possibility, the proposals for wider use of the existing semi-charitable, semi-insurance based dispensaries and infirmaries supported by eleemosynary organizations of the sort of the Salvation Army and the Church of England. In these, most of which were situated conveniently in working-class neighbourhoods, families paid a stipulated weekly or monthly fee and received stipulated medical treatment without further payment. Many doctors, and the Medico-Political Committee, regarded these institutions as little better than medical clubs and did not wish to see this system of practice extended under State patronage.[110]

A third alternative, the suggestion of the Charity Organization Society, was that schoolchildren needing treatment be sent to voluntary hospitals. The voluntary hospitals had been established, typically in the eighteenth century, to provide charitable medical care for the working class.[111] By the end of the next century their out-patient clinics were almost the only resort for the working class in need of specialist treatment, and were becoming, for that portion of the population too proud to use the poor law and too poor to join some form of medical insurance plan, the normal place for consultations on even minor ailments. The voluntary hospitals were staffed by the best men in the British medical profession, who gave their services without charge. Appointment as an 'honorary' at a well-known voluntary hospital was the badge of arrival in the British medical profession. It separated the specialist and the consultant from the general practitioner, to whom hospital facilities were closed. The honorary was reimbursed for the time given to the treatment of the poor in the morning by the large fees charged the well-to-do patients attracted by the eminence of

[110] It should be noted that the majority report of the Royal Commission on the Poor Law suggested the expansion of these institutions as the means of providing medical care for the working class. As a result of this recommendation from the majority, the British medical profession found little to support in either of the commission reports. For comments see: Alfred Cox, 'Seven Years of National Health Insurance in England,' *Journal of the American Medical Association*, LXXVI (May 7, 1921), 1309.

[111] On the history of the voluntary hospitals, see: Brian Abel-Smith, *The Hospitals in England and Wales, 1800–1948*, Cambridge, Massachusetts, 1964.

his name, who came to his Harley, Wimpole, or Rodney Street office in the afternoon.

Besides their services to the poor, the best voluntary hospitals served also as teaching institutions. Through his students, the young doctors who 'walked the wards' with him, the well-known specialist built a professional empire. Those who learned their skill at his side treating the poor would carry on his work after his retirement. The Medico-Political Committee was well aware that voluntary hospital out-patient facilities were becoming increasingly overburdened by the attendance of people well able to afford the fee of a private doctor. The hospitals' charitable activity in this sense competed directly with general practice. Moreover, as seemed to be happening in London, the hospitals could engage in the treatment of schoolchildren only at the jeopardy of their financial, and eventually administrative, independence. Hence the profession firmly opposed all suggestions, both for the school medical service and later for national health insurance, that the State rely upon the voluntary hospitals to make up the inadequacies of its own planning.

The final proposal examined during 1908 by the Medico-Political Committee envisioned the establishment of clinics within the schools themselves or, as an ideal, private treatment by the doctor of each family's choice. Some form of reimbursement from public funds would have to be worked out for those parents unable to pay a private physician.[112] In their report submitted at the end of the year to the Regional Divisions of the British Medical Association for discussion and recommendation, the committee proposed school clinics as the least dangerous alternative. Specifically, the report insisted that any provision for school medical aid should not be connected either with existing charitable relief or with the poor law.[113]

The position finally taken by the British Medical Association on the school medical service followed generally the recommendations

[112] The Medico-Political Committee did not consider the possibility to which the minority report of the Royal Commission was pointing, of a full-grown State public and personal medical service combining all preventative and curative functions in a single department.

[113] *British Medical Journal* Supplement, July 18, 1908, pp. 41-2. The Chairman of the Medico-Political Committee was Dr J. A. MacDonald, who would appear in 1911 as Chairman of the Council of the British Medical Association and the leading negotiator with David Lloyd George over national health insurance.

of the committee. The divisions agreed that although the best possible scheme would be the referral of students needing treatment to private practitioners, who might if necessary be paid out of public funds, at least in the towns the most practical arrangement would be a room in the school, as the report put it, 'to be designated "school clinic",' where private physicians might treat children needing help. In sparsely populated areas a doctor's surgery might be similarly assigned. Except to insist that parents who were able to pay for treatment of their children should be forced to do so, and that there should be no poor law treatment or charity treatment, the divisions were not specific on how clinics should be financed. Contrary to the recommendation of the Medico-Political Committee, the divisions agreed the provident dispensaries might be used if 'remuneration were adequate,' which, as all doctors knew, it almost invariably was not.[114]

The difficulties of the medical profession in its search for a way to provide treatment for the manifold ailments of working-class children without permitting charity to cut into already competitive private practice, but also without agreeing to a large-scale salaried State medical service, illuminated for the first time the elements of a problem that would recur in every consideration of State medical activity until the establishment of the National Health Service in 1948. In some ways, it would be the key problem of the welfare state. If the health of a child was of concern to no one except his parents, no outside agency need have any but a philanthropic interest in his physical condition. But if, as the Boer War seemed to have proved, an unhealthy schoolchild was a danger to all society, then it was in society's selfish, non-humanitarian interest to see that the child was treated. However, if medical care was provided by the State, what would become of those men who had made a living selling what treatment the working class could afford? And if the service was made free, who would ascertain that families well able to pay for private treatment did not take advantage of it? Yet if those who were able to pay were forced to do so, the necessary investigation of family means might differ very little from the awkward and humiliating tests that accompanied relief granted under the poor law.

The trouble is that medical relief, of all social services, lends itself least well to a test of means. The amount of money necessary

[114] *British Medical Journal* Supplement, May 15, 1909, p. 246.

to bring an indigent widow up to a minimum standard of human dignity varies little from one case to the next. The amount of food that one hundred hungry children can eat is readily measurable in quantitative terms. But the expense of illness bears no relation whatever to a patient's means and varies widely among individuals. And because in the last analysis the doctor is bound to give his services to whatever extent necessary, whether or not the patient can afford them, without distinguishing between eligible or ineligible patients or illnesses, a limited State medical service has always a tendency to expand.

In 1908 the doctors' dilemma was made more complicated by 8 Edw. 7, Cap. 67, popularly known as the 'Children's Act.' The Children's Act was a huge inchoate measure, more than seventy pages long. At the time of its enactment the Liberals attempted to give it a good deal of attention, although in fact it was chiefly a consolidating statute providing a few new penalties for old crimes, codifying a large amount of previous legislation, and adding a number of minor innovations. Generally, it aimed at protecting the legal rights of children—infants put out to nurse, children smothered accidentally or otherwise while sleeping with their parents (this was causing 1,600 deaths per year) and, most important for the school medical service, making an offence the neglect of medical treatment necessary for a child's welfare.[115] By defining it a misdemeanour for a parent not to provide medical treatment for the ills of his child, the State put itself under obligation to provide facilities for treatment for those children whose parents were unable to afford it for themselves. But it followed that if free clinics were established by the local authorities, and parents were required by law to attend to the medical needs of their children, large numbers of parents, many of whom were not indigent, might take advantage of the treatment provided. This could become extremely expensive for the local authorities and for the ratepayers who supported them. Worse, it would be financially disastrous for the doctors in working-class districts who would see many of their patients go off to competing medical care provided without charge by the local education authority.

Faced with the prospect of having their ratepayers mulcted for vast amounts by the requirement of medical treatment, and under

---

[115] For a brief survey of the intent of the Children's Act see: *Hansard,* CLXXXIII (February 10, 1908), cols. 1432–8.

pressure from the local medical profession to keep any free treatment provided solely for the poor, many local authorities were reluctant to establish a school clinic at all. In 1909 Parliament attempted to provide some inducement by the passage of the Local Education Authorities (Medical Treatment) Act which gave legal sanction to local authorities to attempt to recover costs of medical treatment from parents as a civil debt. This Act put the school medical service on the same non-deterrent basis achieved in 1906 by school feeding: parents were required to pay for the aid given their child if they could; if they could not, they suffered no civil penalty.

Although the Local Education Authorities (Medical Treatment) Act of 1909 carried the principle of non-deterrent social welfare much farther and offered far greater opportunity for ultimate growth than had the feeding of schoolchildren in 1906, the Act received no public attention whatever. By this time the State had, in old age pensions, so far extended the principle of non-deterrent welfare legislation that any complaint over measures to give rate-supported medical aid to a few thousand sickly schoolchildren would have seemed eccentric indeed.[116]

A second measure to force local authority to provide school medical treatment came in 1912 with the beginning of a system of Exchequer grants as bonuses to the L.E.A.s doing the most in school medical treatment. The education estimates for 1912–13 provided £60,000 for this purpose. The money was allotted on the basis of the efforts that the local authorities were already making in the use of rate money, on the extent of their co-operation with voluntary agencies, and by consideration of such special needs as extreme poverty or sparse population.[117]

10

As a conclusion to this discussion of school medical inspection, a survey of the problems faced by local medical authorities may be of some value. Like many difficulties in social welfare, the elements of

[116] The Local Education Authorities (Medical Treatment) Act was hurried through the House of Commons without debate. For an explanation of the Act see: *Official Report, House of Lords Debates*, Series 5, III (July 29, 1909), cols. 842–4.

[117] *Official Report, House of Commons Debates*, Series 5, XXXVII (April 12, 1912), cols. 189–90.

the problems were essentially administrative. That is, they were less the result of the inequities in society than of the steps themselves taken to correct social inequities. Social welfare legislation creates its own problems. Accordingly, medical inspection brought up the question of medical treatment, and medical treatment involved State invasion of areas that existing medical institutions had always considered their own. Almost everyone agreed that it was of no use to inspect a child to discover disability if the diseases discovered went untreated. Yet all agreement disappeared on the question of how treatment should be administered and paid for.

When the individual parent was informed that his child needed glasses, or dental work, or a tonsillectomy, or an adenoidectomy, he asked reasonably who would bear the cost of these treatments, and complained in stout English terms when told this was not the affair of the education authority. Dr Newman's annual reports before the war reflect the acerbity of the statements received from local school medical officers whose lives daily were haunted by the complaints of working-class parents who had been advised to provide treatments for their children which they could not afford.

Where it was possible, the local school medical officer tried to pass on the duty of seeing that some treatment took place to the 'Children's Care Committee' which each school administration attempted to organize. In most places these were simply the successors of the old 'School Canteen Committees' that had received semi-official status with the Education (Provision of Meals) Act of 1906. Now, with their duties broadened, this rather typically English, semi-official, semi-voluntary body was charged with the duty of advising parents on how to secure treatment for their ailing children.[118]

Despite the watchfulness of the British Medical Association, the school medical service in its early years caused serious difficulties for the voluntary hospitals. Large numbers of schoolchildren and anxious parents appeared, having been directed there by school medical officers who knew nowhere else to send them. The hospital problem was described by Dr Newman in his last report before the war.

> Without any corresponding advantage to the medical and surgical staff, a large number of school children have been

[118] Newman, *Nation's Health*, p. 205.

presented for treatment suffering for the most part from conditions which indeed require careful and skilled attention, but which are devoid of any clinical interest.[119]

Pressure from the leaders of the profession who served as honoraries in the voluntary hospitals combined with encouragement from Parliament and from Whitehall to induce local education authorities to set up school clinics. By March 31, 1914, 241 of 317 education authorities (the number of education authorities varied as mergers and new creations took place) were giving some form of medical treatment on their own. Perhaps more significant, at the end of the same period 53 local education authorities were contributing funds to about 100 voluntary hospitals for the treatment of schoolchildren.[120] In some cases these payments were regular contributions; in others, more commonly, the local education authority paid a fee for each case treated by the hospital. By this time, 84 authorities had established altogether 150 dental clinics.[121] Characteristically, the largest and most progressive school clinic was in Bradford. In 1910 when the movement for clinics had only begun and when the leadership of the medical profession still despaired of any initiative in this direction among the local authorities,[122] the Bradford clinic had 15,984 attendances and actually treated 3,520 children.[123]

The feeding and medical inspection of schoolchildren were the first elements of the welfare state. To be sure it is possible to argue, as will be seen later in this study, that provision of work relief that culminated in the Unemployed Workmen Act was—as the Charity Organization Society regarded it—the first breach in the unity of the poor law. But this measure ranks at best as an unsuccessful experiment in social legislation. Moreover, it did not

---

[119] Cd. 7730, 'Annual Report for 1913 of the Chief Medical Officer of the Board of Education,' 1914–16, p. 98. The Parliamentary papers for the first two years of the war are bound as a single series.

[120] Ibid., pp. 105, 108.   [121] Ibid., p. 183.

[122] For instance, the Lancet, commenting in a lead article on Dr Newman's first annual report as Chief Medical Officer of the Board of Education, noted the great success of medical inspection but concluded:

The grave remaining question, that of the treatment of the many ailments disclosed by medical inspection is still surrounded by difficulties from which a way of escape has to be discovered.

Lancet, January 22, 1910, p. 248.

[123] Public Health, XXV (December, 1911), 112.

give aid, but rather the opportunity for work. The transferral of wealth through the medium of the State did not occur. However, many observers quickly recognized in the feeding of school-children the evolution of a new principle. The old dictum of Liberalism, that each individual in a free society was responsible for his own welfare, and that he might ask society for aid only at the expense of his freedom, had been dissolved. To be sure, the outcry was less vehement than it might have been. The State was acting on behalf of children, who were at once society's most defenceless class and most valuable resource. Only a few implacable political logicians of the sort of A. V. Dicey could object to a measure permitting the local authorities to spend the proceeds of a penny rate upon the feeding of hungry infants in school. Yet the dyke had been breached and the trickle of 1906 became in the next few years a roaring flood which swept away the few figures who stood against all unconditional State aid.

By the time of the enactment of medical inspection, opposition to the idea embodied in the legislation had practically disappeared. For many, the physical condition of the working-class child had come to represent the pivot which turned the fate of British civilization. Like a pyramid stood on its point, the destiny of the empire seemed to depend in the long run on the results of some two million physical examinations conducted each year in State schools. This agreement on the absolute importance of the health of schoolchildren, reflected in all discussions of the subject, in the Conservative press and in the debates in Parliament, made certain that in some form health care for children would have to be provided.

Indeed, the opposition attitude apparent in the consideration of the feeding and medical inspection Bills signalized a permanent change in the politics of welfare legislation. Party contention over the principle of social reform practically vanished. In politics nine-teenth-century *laissez-faire* orthodoxy fell without a fight. Of the great measures discussed in the rest of this study—old age pensions, unemployment insurance and labour exchanges, or national health insurance—none was opposed by the Unionists on the grounds that the proposals constituted an invasion of individual responsibility, even though over the last, the political struggle was fierce. A. J. Balfour's party, which had itself witlessly thrown away the opportunity to become the champion of social reform, changed front upon the Liberals' adoption of that programme as a part of their platform. Indeed, on old age pensions, which may represent the greatest of all missed opportunities for the Unionists, the Opposition deliberately tried to out-promise the Government. On other measures, the most the Unionists could do was to nibble at the edges of the Liberal programmes, forcing concessions of detail that made some of the measures, notably health insurance, awkward if not almost impossible to administer. Finally, by preventing the completion of the Liberal programme through the struggle over Irish Home Rule, they prevented the Liberals from gaining popular acceptance as the party of social reform, and so perhaps insured the party's final extinction.

4 Old Age Pensions

'Christmas Eve in the Workhouse'

It's Christmas Eve they tell me, but
  in a workhouse ward
One day is like another and both
  is mortal long.
What sort of grand rejoicing could
  the like of us afford,
That's poor old pauper women
  who could never raise a song?

Peace and good will the angels
  sing
To Christianable people
You'll hear the merry bells
  ring out
From every Dublin steeple.

       W. M. LETTS, also attributed to G. R. SIMS.

By the enactment of old age pensions the Liberal Government gave effect to one of the oldest demands of the social reformers. Indeed the Old Age Pension Act of 1908 may stand as a symbol of the early welfare state. This is not to say that pensions, at least in the form in which they were finally passed, were the most useful, or the most influential of the welfare measures of the New Liberalism.[1] But certainly at the time, non-contributory pensions were regarded as a wildly extravagant piece of class law making. Moreover, as an exemplary piece of social legislation, as a way of transferring wealth from one income group to another, tax-supported old age pensions were of almost unequalled effectiveness. The government demanded only that in order to receive a pension the recipient be old and in reduced circumstances. After pensions, the timid measure for feeding schoolchildren seemed insignificant as a threat to the English sense of social responsibility.

Politically, by their failure to enact pensions the Unionists let

---

[1] The General Register Office reported that in 1911 eleven pensioners died from starvation. Geoffrey Drage, *The State and the Poor*, London, 1914, p. 18n.

slip their best opportunity to establish themselves as the true friends of the working man in the tradition of Tory democracy. Pensions were the one social reform of the pre-war period that was at once universally popular with the working class and also approved by respectable social thinkers. Other reforms, for instance unemployment insurance, more salutary in the long run, were less popular. Still others, like Labour's annual right to work Bill—which would have required local authorities to provide work for any unemployed person asking for it—were regarded by middle-class philanthropists as socialist dogmatics. For Joseph Chamberlain, pensions could perhaps have provided the catalyst necessary for tariff reform. At least they would have tempered the image of Balfour's party as concerned with nothing more than capitalist imperialism. Although it is not quite true to say, as A. J. Balfour remarked in December, 1910, that the South African War 'killed' the possibility of pensions,[2] still the war did destroy any interest among Unionist Party leaders in non-contributory, tax-supported pensions. The £250,000,000 spent fighting the Boers made further expenditure on social reform, even such modest proposals as the feeding and medical inspection of schoolchildren, let alone a tax-supported pension, appear to be out of the question financially, while friendly society opposition made a contributory pension scheme out of the question politically.

Finally, the consideration of old age pensions had elicited from the outset suspicion and hostility from the British friendly society movement. For over half a century these societies had regarded themselves as the principal guardians of domestic working-class welfare. To the friendly societies old age pensions represented a threat of government competition in the same way that the school medical service had seemed a danger to the British medical profession. Beginning with the planning of pensions, the role played by the societies in all consideration of social legislation would grow increasingly larger. It may not be too much to say that the necessity of placating the societies was an important determinant of the form both of old age pensions and of national health insurance.

[2] See: Betty Balfour's letter to Beatrice Webb, Chapter II, p, 97

I

Certainly there was nothing new in the idea of old age pensions, although until the end of the eighteenth century pensions had usually assumed a service rendered. A gift of a pension had presumed some form of patron–client relationship. However, toward the end of the eighteenth century the connexion between old age and poverty was too obvious to be missed. As a consequence, in 1772 the House of Commons passed a Bill for voluntary annuities, which would be assisted and guaranteed from the poor rate. The assumption here would dominate thinking on pensions for many years to come: that money spent on pensions for the aged would be recovered to a considerable degree by savings in poor law maintenance of the same people.

In the early decades of the nineteenth century, under the impact of the writings of Malthus and Ricardo, the popular attitude towards the poor changed and at the same time interest in old age pensions declined. The underlying principle of the new deterrent poor law was that an application for State relief implied a moral failure on the part of the applicant. Those who received aid should be punished in the workhouse and thus impelled to mend their ways, it was felt, or at least deterred from further application. The disgrace was still present, however, when relief was given in the applicant's own home, if in effect the punishment was absent. This generally-held attitude destroyed nearly all interest in State-provided pensions between the mid eighteen-thirties and the eighteen-nineties and would, in fact, colour the attitude of many men towards non-contributory pensions even after the Act establishing them had been passed. Pensions not paid for by the recipient, it was argued, were no different from any other form of State relief. Universal State-supported pensions simply meant the pauperization of everyone in old age. As a result of these opinions, when discussion of the matter revived in the last decades of the century, the plans first proposed were uniformly for contributory, insurance-based pensions.

The man responsible for beginning the movement that led eventually to the Old Age Pensions Act of 1908 was the Reverend Canon William L. Blackley, who proposed in an article in the *Nineteenth Century* in November, 1878, a plan for each working man while he was between the ages of eighteen and twenty-one to

F

contribute £10 to an annuity fund.[3] Blackley asserted that the sum of £10 paid in would be sufficient to provide 8s. per week sick pay during the rest of the man's life and a pension of 4s. per week at age seventy. By law the employer would be made responsible for seeing that the sum was paid in. Blackley made his appeal, like nearly every early proponent of pensions, contributory or tax supported, as a way of relieving the poor rates. Although he used no statistical evidence to support his argument, data produced later by Joseph Chamberlain and others would prove that the aged were the largest and most rapidly-growing single category of poor law clients.

The Blackley scheme immediately came under attack from two directions. On one side was the newly-formed Charity Organization Society, a steady opponent of pensions throughout the period under study, although it came eventually to accept voluntary contributory pensions under State auspices. It was impossible to legislate thrift, the society argued, and for the workman at subsistence wages, the cost of compulsory insurance would be thrown upon the employer.[4]

Fear of the effect of an insurance contribution on the working-man's wages was also the basis of the attack by a far more powerful opponent of the Blackley scheme, the friendly society movement. The societies in the next few years would put the Blackley scheme quietly to death. As moulders of opinion among the best paid and most responsible British workmen, they were unsurpassed even by the trade unions, whose membership until well into the first decade of the twentieth century was scarcely half as large.[5] More-

[3] William Lewery Blackley, 'National Insurance: A Cheap, Practical, and Popular Means of Abolishing Poor Rates,' *Nineteenth Century*, IV (November, 1878), 834-57.

William Lewery Blackley, 1830-1902, born, Dundalk, Ireland; father a land-owner; educated in Brussels and at Trinity College, Dublin; curate of St Peter's, Southwark; held various benefices in Surrey and Hampshire until 1889; honorary canon of Winchester, 1883; vicar of St James the Less, London, after 1889. Director of Clergy Mutual Insurance Company; active in promotion of pension funds for clergy.

[4] See, for instance: 'Friendly Societies and the Limits of State Aid and Control in Industrial Insurance,' lecture by Sir George Young, May 2, 1879, pamphlet published by Charity Organization Society.

[5] In 1898, for instance, British and Irish friendly societies reported to the Registrar of Friendly Societies a total membership of 4,203,601. Sir Edward Brabrook, *Provident Societies and Industrial Welfare*, London, 1898, p. 55. In the same year the trade unions with headquarters in Great Britain and Ireland

over, in contrast to the unions, there was no antagonism between the friendly societies and employers. They strongly supported the capitalistic system, were conservative politically, and had long maintained regular parliamentary agents. Thus, although Blackley founded in 1882 the National Providence League to promote his plan and succeeded in interesting numerous politicians and poor law guardians in his scheme, the select committee of the House of Commons which examined the proposal reported in 1887 that it was unable to agree that the scheme was actuarily sound and declared itself 'disposed to wait on the further development of public opinion. . . .'[6]

In fact, as Blackley himself well knew, his proposal had been destroyed by the friendly societies' pressure in Westminster. Blackley had little esteem for the societies, recalled one of the organizers of the National Providence League,

> . . . and perhaps had too low an opinion of their power for good, and thus aroused the opposition and animosity of many of these Societies. This was unfortunate, as no movement in favour of a National Insurance could possibly be carried out against the determined opposition of these bodies, numbered by millions and highly organized, like the Friendly Societies.[7]

Blackley himself misunderstood the basis of friendly society opposition to his plan. In a bitter speech at the end of 1891, he described his attempts to come to terms with the societies. He admitted that he had

> . . . received very strong objections from the friendly societies

reported a total membership of 1,608,000. Brian R. Mitchell, *Abstract of British Historical Statistics*, Cambridge, 1962, p. 68.

[6] 'Select Committee on National Provident Insurance,' *Parliamentary Papers*, 1887, Vol. XI, p. ix.

[7] Sir James Rankin, M.P., 'Introductory Chapter,' in M. J. J. Blackley, *Thrift and National Insurance as a Security Against Pauperism, with a Memoir of the Late Rev. Canon Blackley and a Reprint of His Essays*, London, 1906, p. 40 (paperback pamphlet). For an example of friendly society opinion on the Blackley scheme see: J. Frome Wilkinson, *The Blackley National Providence Insurance Scheme: A Protest and an Appeal*, London, 1887 (paperback pamphlet). Besides Wilkinson, an active friendly society opponent of the Blackley scheme was the Registrar of Friendly Societies, John Malcolm Ludlow. Ludlow's biographer speculates on the reasons for his subject's resistance to the insurance proposals, although in fact Ludlow's attitude was general throughout the entire friendly society movement. N. C. Masterman, *John Malcolm Ludlow, Builder of Christian Socialism*, Cambridge, 1963, pp. 231–2.

against the sick pay part of his proposal. That part only of the proposal could interfere with the great friendly societies and it was only the great friendly societies that ever ventured to enter the field against him, because the bad societies simply made a stalking horse of the great ones, their own unsoundness depriving them of any *locus standi*. The friendly societies made very violent objection to any interference with their sick pay. Their average sick pay was 12s., and his proposal was only for a minimum of 8s., but practically they did not provide pensions at all, and therefore his proposal as to pensions would never be proved to interfere with friendly society action. But even if his pension proposal did affect (as it would not) the good of any particular society, the good of the whole nation should be considered first. The Parliamentary Committee refused to entertain the idea of compulsory sick pay, and the National Providence League joined him in thinking it was a very advisable thing to bow his head before the storm; but then he thought they might reasonably go to the leaders of the friendly societies and say, 'we give up the sick pay altogether, and as our pension proposals do not interfere with pensions you do not give, we ask you to join us in getting for our old people in their old days something that will keep them.' He met with no response. He had asked their assistance, but he never had an answer.[8]

Blackley's mistake, demonstrated in this statement, lay in his assumption that the friendly societies feared *only* a government-sponsored sickness benefit that would compete with their own. In fact, the societies feared any form of competition for the limited savings of their working-class clientele, irrespective of the benefits offered. If the law forced the working man to divert his surplus earnings into a government programme, the sort of benefits received made no difference; the working man simply would leave the society. The importance of this consideration in the last decade of the century lay in the fact that although the movement as a whole was large and politically potent, many societies were in desperate financial condition.

[8] 'Discussion of Charles Booth's Paper, resumed December 22, 1891,' *Journal of the Royal Statistical Society*, LV (March, 1892), 65–6.

2

The British friendly society movement was in many ways the most powerful single vested interest encountered by the social reformers of the New Liberalism.[9] The importance of these institutions for the rest of this study necessitates some discussion of their situation in the British working-class world.

The societies were a typical manifestation of the Victorian ethic of providence and self-help. Although there had been legislation concerning them in the eighteenth century, the classical age for the foundation of friendly societies was the second and third quarters of the nineteenth century. During this period the movement grew rapidly, both in number of societies and in membership, so that by the end of the century the Registrar of Friendly Societies reported the existence of nearly 24,000 registered societies and branches, with about four and one-quarter million members.[10] Friendly societies formed a vast network over Great Britain. Every middle-sized town had scores of national societies represented among its population, as well as uncounted, and uncountable, local societies.[11] For the most prosperous class of Victorian artisan, membership in a friendly society was almost mandatory. It was the symbol of his

[9] Repeatedly in the next twenty years, speakers in government and business referred to the influence of friendly societies at Westminster. See, for instance, the speech of David Paulin, not a friendly society man, but managing director of the Scottish Life Assurance Company, in his inaugural address as president of the Actuarial Society of Edinburgh. Friendly societies, said Mr Paulin,

> have become so influential a force in national life that no government would care, or dare, to introduce legislative proposals affecting the welfare of the people in times of sickness and of old age, without their co-operation and approval.

> David Paulin, *Old Age Pensions and Pauperism*, Edinburgh, 1896, p. 17 (paper-back pamphlet).

[10] Brabrook, *Provident Societies*, p. 55. These statistics are far from reliable. New societies continually appeared and old ones went out of existence. There were, besides, unknown but very large numbers of unregistered societies, some prosperous and well-established, like those among the workers at the Swindon shops of the Great Western Railway, but more frequently small, casually organized clubs formed among the clientele of a public house. By the end of the century, lapses in membership and transfers from one society to another were frequent, and the societies invariably tended to overestimate their own membership.

[11] Rowntree estimated that 636 societies had members among the 76,000 people in York. B. Seebohm Rowntree, *Poverty, A Study of Town Life*, London, 1901, p. 358.

independence and respectability. It combined for him the social and moral aspects of a fraternal lodge with the opportunity for leadership and increased status in the narrow world of the nineteenth-century English working man. Also the society guaranteed a measure of financial independence to its members. In return for a contribution of between 4d. and 8d. a week, the society gave sick pay, ordinarily around 10s. a week, medical care usually provided by a physician under contract to the society, and a death benefit of £10 or £15, enough for a 'respectable' funeral.

In the early days of their organization the social and edificatory attractions of the societies probably accounted for their great popularity. Invariably, their constitutions emphasized the principles of Victorian morality and character improvement. Many of them were open only to members of a certain religious sect, frequently Nonconformist, and nearly all societies were powers in the chapels. Some offered membership only to teetotallers, and many barred public-house keepers, who were also surprisingly poor insurance risks.[12] They maintained, of course, close connexions with the New Model trade unions, were staunchly anti-socialist, favoured a strictly deterrent poor law, and so far as they supported a party interest—in fact prohibited by statute—were likely to be adherents of Gladstonian Liberalism. Like the industrial society to which they were a response, they tended to be centred in the midlands and the north of England, and the lowlands of Scotland. A large number had their headquarters in Manchester, and of the largest societies, only one, the Hearts of Oak, had its main offices in London. In fact, the societies seemed to distrust the capital. Their colourful annual conventions or conferences, occurring generally during Whitsun week, almost never took place in the metropolis.

As important as their north country base was the economic orientation of the friendly societies. They made no appeal whatever to the grey, faceless, lower third of the working class. Friendly society membership was the badge of the skilled worker. Some of the societies, for instance the Hearts of Oak, maintained a minimum income limit (in the case of the H. of O. 25s. per week).

---

[12] The death rate among publicans in the eighties was three times that of clergymen, and only slightly better than the mortality of street sellers and general labourers. Noel A. Humphreys, 'Class Mortality Statistics,' *Journal of the Royal Statistical Society*, L (June, 1887), 277.

Friendly society membership was not for the crossing sweeper, the dock labourer, the railroad navvy, any more than it was for the landowner, the Member of Parliament, or the company director.[13] The census of 1891 in England, Wales, and Scotland showed 8,517,700 men over the age of nineteen, which may be taken as a normal entering age for the societies.[14] Assuming, therefore, a friendly society membership in the two kingdoms and Wales of between four and a quarter and four and a half million with some duplication (friendly society membership in Ireland was negligible, about sixty thousand), it follows that nearly half the adult males in Great Britain were members of societies. Up to a point, the proportion increased with age.

As politicians of both parties were fond of saying, sturdily independent friendly society members were the backbone of the English nation. They represented a solid voting block, fully conscious of its power, that no government could afford to ignore. Like Victorian England itself, the movement was rich, influential, and conservative. But as the Queen's reign neared its end, a frightening number of societies were in financial trouble.

From one point of view, the societies' difficulties may be said to be the result of their success. They had grown too large. At the end of the century the two largest societies, the Manchester Unity of Odd Fellows and the Ancient Order of Foresters, each had well over 700,000 members, while the Hearts of Oak had 400,000. A number of societies of the second rank counted memberships between 50,000 and 150,000. In organizations this large the sense of fraternity was bound to decline, even though all of the large societies except the Hearts of Oak were organized into lodges to provide fellowship and the social surveillance that would protect each lodge's individual insurance fund. Unfortunately in the last

[13] Rowntree found 10,662 friendly society memberships, with some duplication, among the 75,812 citizens of York, a city containing a fairly representative segment of English social classes from top to bottom. This provides a ratio of friendly society members to population of 1 to 7·6 or a percentage of 14·4 per cent. In the slums of East London and Hackney, Charles Booth estimated only about 50,000 friendly society members among a total population of 891,539. This provides a ratio of almost 1 to 18 or a percentage of friendly society members in the depressed sections of East London of 5·6 per cent. Rowntree, *Poverty*, p. 357; Charles Booth, *Life and Labour of the People of London* (London, 1892), I, 106.

[14] Mitchell, *Historical Statistics*, pp. 12–13. The societies usually accepted no one below the age of sixteen, and their relatively high cost prevented young men from joining during the first few years of work.

quarter of the nineteenth century the legal independence of the individual lodges, and with it much of the conviviality and club atmosphere that had meant so much at first, began to disappear. In 1886, a decision of the High Court (Schofield *vs.* Bause) terminated the right of local lodges to secede from the central body without permission. The tightening of central regulation that followed, and perhaps the growing interest in temperance around the turn of the century—which ended for many lodges the use of society funds for food and beer at meetings —resulted in a decline in the powerful local loyalties that had made the movement what it was.[15]

The increasing urbanization of Great Britain also had its effect in that the lodge in a metropolitan environment had now to compete with the far more sophisticated attraction of English cities. The appeal of the pub increased, now that the lodge meetings no longer served beer. The glamour of the music hall, and later the cinema, dimmed the homely amenities, the singing and ritualized conviviality of the friendly society lodge. The improvements in urban transportation broke the sense of physical isolation that half a century earlier had driven the workman, perhaps newly-arrived from the village, into a lodge in the search for friendship. Why go to a 'sing-song,' lamented a friend and supporter of the friendly society movement at the time of national health insurance,

> to hear Bob Turner the blacksmith sing some song fifty years old when they can go to the 'tuppenny gaff' next door and hear the latest music hall artist or hear Mme Melba or Harry Lauder repeated on the gramophone . . . he can get into a tram and go and see his friend at the other end of the town and every year see fresh openings for social intercourse which did not exist fifty years ago.[16]

[15] The friendly societies of England have at last found their historian in P. H. J. H. Gosden, whose excellent book was partially sponsored by the Manchester Unity. Unfortunately Gosden does not carry his history beyond 1875. P. H. J. H. Gosden, *The Friendly Societies in England, 1815–1875*, Manchester, 1961.

[16] W. J. Braithwaite (unsigned) in *Westminster Gazette*, December 12, 1911. On the decline of the social aspects of friendly society membership, see also the testimony of Walter P. Wright, Grand Master of the Manchester Unity, before the departmental committee on women's illness. *Cd. 7690*, 'Report of the Departmental Committee on Sickness Benefit Claims Under the National Insurance Act,' 1914, Appendix III, Qu. nos. 31, 648–9.

The result of all this was not that friendly society membership declined in the last decade and a half of the nineteenth century, but that attendance at lodge meetings fell off sharply. Significantly the most rapidly-growing society around the turn of the century was the completely centralized Hearts of Oak, which ran all its business from London without any local organization whatever.

The success of the Hearts of Oak exemplifies the new orientation in the friendly society movement. Although membership in most societies continued to grow, the new brothers looked upon the organization and society membership in purely economic terms. Friendly society membership was desirable, if one could afford it, because the society benefits were more generous in proportion to contributions than were similar benefits offered by the profit-making insurance companies. This was the case partly because the societies received statutory exemption from certain taxes and selected their applicants more carefully than did commercial insurance companies.[17] But the society member benefited also because much of the organization's work was done free of charge by officers of the local lodges. This old type of friendly society man—the backbone of the movement, for whom the lodge was the centre of life, for whom the chief attraction of the society was the fellowship of sober, prosperous, respectable working men like himself, who would say with pride that not once in his career had he been 'on the funds'—was becoming rare. And with his disappearance the friendly society movement, whatever the membership figures showed, began to decay.[18]

[17] Under the Friendly Society Act of 1896 no friendly society could sell an annuity worth more than £50 per year, nor a death benefit worth more than £200, although these limits were raised by legislation in 1908 to £52 per year and £300 respectively. But registered friendly societies received exemptions from income, corporate property, and stamp taxes. These attractive privileges caused the establishment of a number of what were actually commercial insurance companies organized as friendly societies. These firms, usually referred to as 'collecting' friendly societies, had no stockholders, but were run for the benefit of their officials who, unlike officials of true friendly societies, were paid large salaries. Their fraternal activity was virtually non-existent. They made little effort to sell sickness benefits, which demanded a substantial amount of supervision, and concentrated on the promotion of death benefits through door-to-door agents. The important differences between the collecting friendly societies and the true friendly societies have been missed in many histories where the distinction is important. For instance: Sir Arnold Wilson and G. S. Mackay, *Old Age Pensions, An Historical and Critical Study*, London, 1941, pp. 17, 24.

[18] After the turn of the century even some of the largest societies, the Foresters and the Manchester Unity, began to show a net loss in membership which they

F*

By the eighteen-nineties, then, the English friendly societies were losing the fraternal spirit that had so long characterized the movement. And it was precisely as this occurred, in the area where the economic and the fraternal aspects of the friendly society movement overlapped, that the second weakness of the societies became apparent. Friendly societies were beset by an actuarial danger that many of them were unable to understand and that they could scarcely recognize—that medical science was causing an increasing number of their members to live into old age and so to demand sick pay in amounts that their reserve funds had never been calculated to support.

The extent of the societies' financial difficulties was demonstrated on a large scale in 1898 in a report made for the Rothschild Committee, which had been appointed to study old age pensions. This survey included returns from thirty-four societies with 22,608 branches (valued separately) with 2,351,150 members. Of those willing to reveal their financial status, 5,049 societies and branches reported an actuarial surplus and 12,448 revealed a deficit. Some large organizations were in desperate straits. The Grand United Order of Odd Fellows, with 241,771 members, showed a reserve deficiency of 6s. 6d. in the pound and even the giant Foresters, with 726,403 members, had a deficiency of 2s. 5d.[19]

The financial malaise that began to creep over the friendly societies in the last fifteen years of the nineteenth century, and which had by the early twentieth infected even the largest and most stable societies, was the result of conditions inherent in the friendly society movement. They were bound by the principles of brotherhood and loyalty to their increasingly large numbers of ageing members. But these same members, whom every ethic of fraternity demanded that the organization support so long as there was a penny of income available to do so, had long since exhausted the funds accumulated to pay their sickness benefits.

sought to hide by padding their membership statistics with the inclusion of foreign members. See: Alfred W. Watson, 'Some points of interest in the operation of Friendly Societies, Railway Benefit Societies, and Collecting Societies,' *Journal of the Institute of Actuaries*, XLIV (April, 1910), 171.

[19] C. *8911*, 'Report to the Lords of the Treasury of the Committee on Old Age Pensions,' 1898, Appendix X, p. 187. A reserve deficiency meant that present reserves plus calculated future income and interest were insufficient to cover calculated future claims.

Basically, the difficulty was that friendly society actuarial tables were calculated on the assumption that a substantial proportion of their members would die before middle age without ever making any large claim upon the sickness benefits that would have been accumulated on their behalf during the first quarter century or so of their active working life.[20] But by the eighties and nineties, medical and sanitary science and an improved standard of living for at least two-thirds of the English population was, unhappily for the friendly societies, keeping alive into old age large numbers of men who would have been dead fifty years before.[21] Yet while the death rate among friendly society members fell dramatically in the eighties and nineties, sickness claims among the same groups, that is those over forty, rose above expectation in almost the same proportion. The friendly societies were experiencing a phenomenon that would not be fully understood until after World War I, that increased length of life did not necessarily mean better health, that in fact correlation was almost negative. The normal assumption of rural and village England in which the friendly societies had originated was that a man worked until he died. This condition had now been replaced by the reverse: increasingly large numbers of friendly society members could not work, but did not die.[22] The quick-killing illnesses of the first half of the nineteenth century—typhoid fever and cholera, accident and septic infection —that typically swept away thousands of men in the prime of life to the profit of the friendly societies were now superseded by the lingering chronic illnesses of tuberculosis, cancer, and all respiratory and circulatory diseases that were enhanced by the impure air

[20] Friendly society actuarial calculations were almost invariably based upon Dr William Farr's English Life Table Number I, founded on mortality between the years 1838–54. Farr calculated that for each million births 651,903 men would reach the age of twenty and of these 531,697 would still be alive at age forty.

[21] Tatham's English Life Table Number VI based on mortality between 1891 and 1900 showed that out of each million male births, 711,714 were alive at age twenty and 615,964 at age forty. This constitutes an increase in the survival rate over forty of 15·8 per cent in fifty years.

[22] One of the earliest actuaries to discover the dangerous trend in friendly-society mortality and sickness claims was George F. Hardy, who would serve as a government actuary during the planning of national health insurance and as actuarial adviser to the Royal Commission on the Poor Laws. In a paper read before the Institute of Actuaries on April 30, 1888, Hardy charted the experience of the Essex Provident Society, a large country friendly society, between years 1876 and 1880, and compared its mortality and sickness experiences with the

and dirt of industrial cities. Any savings that the friendly societies accrued from the postponed payment of death benefits were lost many times over in increased claims for sickness benefit. The increasing vitality of the community was bankrupting the insurers of health.

A dramatically increased survival rate into middle age was the experience of Englishmen of all classes. But available statistics demonstrate that friendly society members as a selected group were enjoying even a greater reduction in their death rate and had long enjoyed far greater longevity than the population at large.[23]

actuarial tables used by the two largest national societies, the Manchester Unity and the Ancient Order of Foresters.

Age Groups	Numbers at Risk	Expected Sickness in Weeks		Actual Sickness Weeks	Deaths Expected and Experienced		
		M.U. Table	A.O.F. Table		M.U. Table	A.O.F. Table	Ex- per.
15–24	610·5	441	510	325	4	4	3
25–34	2,598	2,300	2,398	2,443	21	22	19
35–44	5,411·5	6,362	6,884	7,083	60	65	53
45–54	6,553	13,009	13,355	14,493	112	125	91
55–64	7,737·5	30,294	29,901	36,331	240	260	181
65–74	2,681	34,257	35,354	53,975	228	248	196
75–84	958	17,780	18,341	33,575	120	122	118
85–94	46·5	1,303	1,192	1,750	11	11	10
	27,596	105,746	107,935	149,975	796	857	671

George F. Hardy, 'Friendly Societies,' *Journal of the Institute of Actuaries,* XXVII (October, 1888), 311.

[23] Deaths Per Year Per One Hundred Exposed to Risk

Experience	At Age: 25–29	30–34	35–39	40–44	45–49	50–54	55–59	60–64	65–69	70–74
Manchester Unity 1893–7	0·46	0·55	0·70	0·96	1·18	1·70	2·84	3·63	5·48	8·20
Hearts of Oak 1883–96, 1899– 1901	0·40	0·54	0·71	0·97	1·28	1·63	2·33	3·23	5·38	8·51
Rational Association 1892– 1901	0·42	0·48	0·63	0·82	1·11	1·51	2·32	3·40	5·06	7·87

Surveys after the establishment of health insurance suggest the death rate in the largest friendly societies taken at almost any age between twenty and eighty averaged about one-third fewer deaths per year per hundred members exposed to risk than did the general average of the British population.

A second influence apparent at the turn of the century, in addition to the greater survival and longevity among friendly society members, was a declining national birth rate,[24] which resulted in a diminished rate of growth of the pool of young lives from which societies drew their members. These conditions taken together made inevitable a sharp and frightening advance in the average age of membership of all societies which itself resulted in

Expe-rience	At Age:									
	25-29	30-34	35-39	40-44	45-49	50-54	55-59	60-64	65-69	79-74
Life Table No. VI 1891-1901 General Popu-lation	0·61	0·76	1·02	1·30	1·66	2·19	2·98	4·15	5·91	8·71

E. C. Snow, 'Some Statistical Problems Suggested by the Sickness and Mortality of Certain of the Large Friendly Societies,' *Journal of the Royal Statistical Society*, LXXVI (April, 1912), 451, Table V.

Life Expectancy in More Years of Life for Selected Groups			
Life Expectancy at Age	For Friendly Society Members	For Commercial Insurers	For English Peers
20	43·89	39·84	38·47
30	37·22	33·17	30·87
40	30·09	26·06	24·45
50	22·79	19·41	17·92
60	16·23	13·47	12·56
70	10·81	8·34	8·15
80	6·69	4·75	5·08

From Nieson, *Contributions to Vital Statistics*, 3rd ed., London, 1857, pp. 40, 41. Quoted in Joseph Chamberlain, 'Old Age Pensions,' *National Review*, XVII (February, 1892), 735.

[24]

Census Period	Birth Rate Per 1,000 Population
1851-60	34·1
1861-70	35·2
1871-80	35·5
1881-90	32·4
1891-1900	29·9

an almost frantic scramble for new members. In five years, for instance, between 1892 and 1897, the percentage of membership over sixty in the relatively new and rapidly-growing Hearts of Oak went from 1·58 per cent to 3·04 per cent and in about the same period the mean age of Hearts of Oak members advanced from 35·18 years in 1892 to 36·65 years in 1900.[25] The rapid trend towards ageing was even more marked in the older societies. Between 1892 and 1897 the proportion of members of the Manchester Unity in the sixty to sixty-nine age bracket increased by nearly 1 per cent.[26] The society found that in 1897 it had among its nearly 800,000 members twenty-three times as many men over sixty-five as it had had at the time of its first valuation in 1846-8.[27]

While by the middle nineties British friendly societies were in an increasingly difficult position financially, the degree of danger varied widely with individual societies. The older and smaller societies generally were the nearest to bankruptcy. But even when the larger and better-run organizations began to uncover the causes of the appalling growth in reserve deficiencies among their lodges, they were in many cases unable to take the steps necessary to insure solvency. Viewed historically there were five factors hindering the solution by the friendly societies of the problem of their older members: First, before the war no one was sure of the exact relationship between lengthening life and sickness. The warning implicit in the statistics of Hardy's paper to the Institute of Actuaries in 1888 was misunderstood, and although David Lloyd George pointed out to the House of Commons in 1911 during the second reading of the National Insurance Bill that longer life did not mean greater health, no positive statement of this fact seems to have appeared until after World War I.[28]

[25] Snow, *J.R.S.S.*, April, 1913, pp. 447, 448.　　　　　[26] *Ibid.*

[27] Alfred W. Watson, *An Account of an Investigation of the Sickness and Mortality Experience of the I.O.O.F., Manchester Unity, During the Five Years, 1893-1897*, Manchester, 1903, pp. 16-20.

[28] The first discovered by this researcher are in Collis and Greenwood's standard work. Edgar L. Collis and Major Greenwood, *The Health of the Industrial Worker*, London, 1921, p. 77. E. C. Snow's statement of 1913 may be taken as typical of the best informed opinion before the war.

The data, of course, are not sufficient to dogmatize upon, but there is such general—though rough—agreement between comparable material that we appear to be justified in concluding that high mortality is not associated, in general, with excessive sickness.

Snow, *J.R.S.S.*, April, 1913, p. 484.

A second factor was that while friendly societies, even the best managed, did not understand precisely the reason for their actuarial deficiencies, even more difficult for the smaller societies was the task of making clear to steel workers or coal miners in the lodge meeting the meaning of actuarial deficiency. To hard-handed men for whom statistics were a mystery, a society was solvent if more money came in each year than was paid out. Future liability and compound interest were beyond their comprehension. The fact that the society was mortgaging the contributions of its young members to meet the present claims of older brothers who had exhausted their reserves could not be explained. For this reason Sir Edward Brabrook, the Registrar of Friendly Societies after 1891, sought to help the leaders of the admirable institutions under his care by suggesting that the principles of friendly societies' finance be taught in the State schools.[29]

A third reason for the failure of societies to take steps to meet their problems was the relief afforded their reserves by the rising interest rate that prevailed in the United Kingdom in the Edwardian period. From the time of the beginning of statutory friendly society valuations in 1875 to the end of the century, actuaries at each quinquennial valuation had had to assume an increasingly lower rate of interest. But in the twentieth century, partly because of the vast government borrowing for the Boer War, interest rates rose. Because with the tables then used an increase of $1\frac{1}{2}$ per cent in assumed interest could shoulder nearly one-third of a society's future liability for sick pay for a man at thirty years of age, the really desperate actuarial position of many of the societies was obscured from even well-informed members. The rising price of money in the last decade before the war increased the value of the societies' reserves without mitigating in any way the causes of the societies' danger.[30]

[29] For instance: Sir Edward Brabrook, 'Friendly Societies,' *Nineteenth Century*, LX (December, 1906), 998–1002.

Edward William Brabrook, 1839–1930, educated at the school of William Pinches; barrister, 1866; Assistant Registrar of Friendly Societies, 1869–91; succeeded Ludlow as Chief Registrar, 1891–1904. Interested in anthropology. Held many offices in scientific societies. C.B., 1905.

[30] On the effect of the rising interest rate on societies, see: Gilbert Slater, *Poverty and the State*, London, 1930, p. 36. On the experience tables used at the turn of the century, a society's future liability for sick pay for a man of thirty assuming a $2\frac{1}{2}$ per cent interest rate was £65 10s. per pound per week of sick pay. If the interest rate was 4 per cent, the necessary reserve fell to £43 14s. 10d.

Without an understanding of the problems of the movement, society membership could hardly be expected to take the necessary steps to reduce benefits and increase contributions in order to protect reserves. But, in fact, as a fourth reason for the societies' difficulties, the leaders themselves were often unable to explain the burden of elderly members, because many society records and statistics were so inadequate that the true actuarial position was unclear. Only occasionally could a great organization undertake a three-year examination of its sickness experience comparable to Alfred Watson's investigation for the Manchester Unity, and so by a large and expensive project accomplish what should have been possible by a routine report.[31] Watson's complaint about the inadequacy of the early records even in the large and well-run Manchester Unity may be assumed to apply still more to the smaller societies with less professional advice.[32]

A fifth element, perhaps most important of all, preventing the societies from taking the necessary steps to bring themselves into solvency, was the fierce competition among the societies within the friendly society movement. A result of the breakdown of the social aspect of the friendly societies had been the virtual disappearance of all loyalty to any particular organization. An individual working man joining a society as a young man was concerned principally with the rate of sickness benefit offered, and he would change his membership quickly should his society make any large increase in

Brabrook, *Provident Societies*, p. 87. Bank rate varied about a median of 3 per cent from the mid-eighties until 1901, and a median of 4 per cent thereafter until the war. During the two and one-half years from February, 1894, to September, 1896, it remained steadily at 2 per cent. It rarely touched and never went below $2\frac{1}{2}$ per cent again. After 1911, during the great pre-war surge of capital exports, it tended to move in the range of $4\frac{1}{2}$ to 5 per cent. Mitchell, *Statistics*, p. 458.

[31] On the origins of the Watson investigation see: Alfred W. Watson, 'The Methods of Analysing and Presenting the Mortality, Sickness, and Secession Experience of Friendly Societies, with examples drawn from the Experience of the Manchester Unity of Odd Fellows,' *Journal of the Institute of Actuaries*, XXXV (July, 1900), 268–332.

Alfred William Watson, 1870–1936, born, Nottingham; grandfather, Reuben Watson, actuary to the Manchester Unity; educated, Nottingham High School; actuary to the Manchester Unity, 1893–1911; chief actuary to national health insurance joint committee, 1912–19; chief government actuary, 1917–death. Married daughter of R. W. Moffrey of the Manchester Unity. K.C.B., 1920.

[32] Watson, *Investigation*, p. 39. Part of the societies' difficulty was that British official statistics upon which they had to depend were themselves the worst of any European nation. See: Arthur L. Bowley, 'The Improvement of Official Statistics,' *Journal of the Royal Statistical Society*, LXXI (September, 1908),

contributions or diminution of benefits.[33] Not surprisingly, friendly societies were most reluctant even to discuss the wholesale changes in their financial structure necessary to return themselves to solvency.[34] They were caught between the demands of brotherhood, which obligated them to maintain an old member throughout his life, and the rivalry for younger members that prevented the changes in contributions and benefits making this financially possible to accomplish.

Most commentators of the nineties who were not officials of the societies themselves were suspicious of the rapid growth in claims that seemed to be driving the societies to ruin. Old age is not sickness, remarked the Registrar of Friendly Societies, Sir Edward Brabrook, in his book on provident institutions, and ought not to be compensated by sick pay. But, he continued, many societies were construing the terms of sickness 'with undue liberality greatly to the damage and loss of their younger members.'

> The societies which have thus, by over-generous treatment, protected such of their members against pauperism as would otherwise have fallen into that condition, have done so at the risk of their own stability; and as accurate views are more and more prevailing on the actuarial conditions of financial success in the friendly societies, it is becoming more and more obvious that the reform of limiting sick pay to a given age will have to be adopted.

Yet, Brabrook continued, the necessary reform of limiting sick pay could not come because:

> At present the societies appear to be waiting for each other

459–95. This situation would come forcefully to the government's attention in its attempt to make actuarial calculations for unemployment insurance.

[33] A survey made in 1908 by the Registrar of Friendly Societies showed that during 1905 the 26,917 societies or branches of societies in Great Britain and Ireland, with a total membership of 5,899,918, had admitted 458,854 new members. Membership termination had included 64,528 through death and 338,235 through secession and lapse for an annual lapse rate of 5·76 per cent. 'Memorandum of the Chief Registrar of Friendly Societies,' December 12, 1908, Braithwaite Papers, Part II, Item 2.

[34] Not until 1909, after the establishment of old age pensions, did the Annual Movable Conference of the Manchester Unity dare to order an investigation to ascertain the effect on its reserves of ending sickness benefits at age seventy when the insured became eligible for a State pension. R. W. Moffrey, *A Century of Odd Fellowship*, Manchester, 1910, p. 181.

before effecting the reform voluntarily, as the present system is still too attractive to the members for a society rejecting it to meet the competition of those which would maintain it.[35]

Nor could the societies afford to require new entrants to contribute towards old age pensions, for this would mean an increase in contributions, which would put any society making the requirement in an unfavourable competitive position. In a confidential report to the Rothschild Committee, Alfred Watson criticized in plainest terms the societies' unwillingness to save themselves.

> Old age, as distinguished from sickness, was not contemplated as a period of special necessity when societies were established, and reformers subsequently have had a sufficient task (and one by no means yet accomplished) in inducing the payment of adequate contributions for the limited benefits promised.

No one seemed able, Watson continued, to force society members to switch from sickness benefits to pensions, and societies were simply afraid to require new applicants to subscribe to pensions.[36]

While Watson's investigation, published in 1903, sounded the alarm—for many societies too late—about the bankruptcy toward which they were rushing, the investigations of the societies during the consideration of old age pensions in the nineties was the first announcement of the movement's difficulties both for the societies themselves and for politicians interested in the welfare of the aged. The precarious solvency of the societies made it certain that a

---

[35] Brabrook, *Provident Societies*, pp. 112, 113.

[36] 'Confidential Memorandum submitted by Alfred W. Watson on Friendly Societies and Old Age Pensions,' n.d. (printed January 21, 1897), p. 1 in Accession No. 19740 ('Miscellaneous Collection of Papers and Pamphlets relating to Old Age Pensions') Ministry of Pensions and National Insurance Library.

In 1890 the Foresters established a voluntary pension plan. By 1898, from among its 700,000 members, three had subscribed. 'Questions to Friendly Societies, printed return of a Survey made for the Committee on Old Age Pensions by B. Holland, Secretary,' October, 1897, p. 2, in Accession No. 19740.

The reply to Bernard Holland's questionnaire from the secretary of the Independent Order of Rechabites, Salford Unity is probably typical of the ordinary friendly society member's attitude towards pensions. After saying that 99 per cent of his 221,000 members were against pensions he remarked:

> There is too much tomfoolery and humbug about all this State business. If we cannot manage better than the State we had better shut up shop altogether. . . .

> *Ibid.*, p. 17.

compulsory contributory pension scheme, which would compete for working-class savings, would be resisted at all costs. But here was a paradox, for although societies were at once vulnerable and extremely sensitive to any State programme on behalf of elderly people, whether under the poor law or otherwise, a tax-supported old age pension, unlike a contributory one, was the one form of government welfare activity that would be a positive advantage to them. The societies were, in fact, already giving an old age pension in their sick pay and a government programme that relieved them of this burden without cost to themselves would have the effect of providing a large contribution to their reserves.[37] Such a programme should have been welcomed, but surprisingly it was not. The societies were suspicious of any government intervention into their area and comprehended only slowly the benefits to them of a tax-supported pension.[38] The tradition of Victorian *laissez*

[37] Early in the nineties one of the most prosperous societies, the Hearts of Oak, investigated the cost of giving its membership a pension. The actuaries discovered that a four shilling pension at age sixty-five would require an addition to reserves of £902,071. If the age were reduced to sixty, this figure became £2,068,531, or nearly seven years' contributions from the society's 153,000 members. Ralph Price Hardy, 'An Enquiry Into the Methods of Representing and Giving Effect to the Experience of a Friendly Society: with an account of the Hearts of Oak Benefit Society and its Experience for the years 1884–91,' *Journal of the Institute of Actuaries*, XXXI (January, 1894), 109–10. This article also gives an excellent general history of the Hearts of Oak Society.

The friendly societies had long looked on the poor law as a competitor and had strongly supported the Out-door Relief (Friendly Societies) Act of 1902, which made it mandatory for poor law guardians to disregard any friendly society sick pay up to 5s. when granting relief. This had been permissive since 1894. Relief given by some of the more generous guardians was frequently larger than the sick pay that could be afforded by some of the nearly bankrupt friendly societies. See: Conference Report of the Annual Meeting of the Southeastern and Metropolitan Poor Law divisions, *The Times*, December 14, 1901. In their attempts to eliminate poor law competition, the societies were opposed by the Charity Organization Society, which invariably resisted any expansion of parochial relief. See: W. H. Long to Cabinet, April 29, 1092, 'Out-Door Relief (Friendly Society) Bill, *Confidential*,' Public Record Office, Cab. 37/61, No. 77.

[38] Not until 1896 did a major society approve any form of government pensions. In that year the Grand United Order of Odd Fellows, the most nearly bankrupt of the large societies, passed a resolution at its annual meeting at Cardiff, subsequently forwarded to the Rothschild Committee, stating that 'in the opinion of the conference the solution to the old age pension question is through the State. Therefore, we the delegates, in conference assembled . . . call upon the Government to provide an old age pension fund from which a pension of not less than 5s. per week shall be paid to all members of friendly societies, on reaching the age of sixty.' Even though burdened by a reserve deficiency of 33 per cent, the Grand United passed this resolution only by 84 votes to 50. *C. 8911*, Appendix X, p. 202.

faire was too strong. They were bound by the weight of their own tradition and unable to free themselves even to take the action necessary for survival. In effect they preferred insolvency to immorality.

3

In the decade of the nineties, the friendly society power that had destroyed the Blackley scheme with almost contemptuous ease would frustrate a more wily, more potent, and in every way more formidable opponent, Joseph Chamberlain, and in doing so would increase the movement's reputation for political influence. Chamberlain's reasons for the espousal of the cause of old age pensions must remain cloudy. From his correspondence with Jesse Collings and with members of Lord Salisbury's Cabinet, one receives the impression that his basic motive was a conviction that pensions were likely to come in any case and that if they did he wished to be associated with them.

In the last decade of the century this was a reasonable assumption. Social reform was in the air. In 1889 the German Reichstag had passed its 'Law of Insurance Against Old Age and Infirmity,' and by the end of the next year Sir John Gorst, one of the earliest and most ardent admirers of German social welfare institutions among the Unionists, began to propose a full-scale social welfare programme for his party.[39] Perhaps more significant for Chamberlain, since 1889 the National Liberal Federation had been urging on the Liberal Party the programme of reform legislation that would become, in 1891, the Newcastle programme. Hence, in April, 1891, Chamberlain, always jealous of every man's reputation as a social reformer, published the first of his several pension plans.[40]

It can be argued that as soon as Chamberlain discovered the difficulties to be encountered in a contributory pension scheme— friendly society opposition and the understandable hostility among British workmen to a payment that would bring benefits only years in the future—he gave up its serious consideration. Nevertheless, Chamberlain's name had been associated with this

[39] For a résumé of Gorst's programme see: *Review of Reviews* (New York), III (April, 1891), 266–70.

[40] 'Provident Insurance' (Reprint of a speech made at the Town Hall, Portsmouth, April 2, 1891), Birmingham, 1891, in Joseph Chamberlain Papers, JC6/4. See also: *The Times*, April 22, 1891.

reform long enough to force him, during the rest of his parliamentary career, to go through the motions of promoting a programme he no longer believed politically feasible, however desirable. After he began his tenure as Colonial Secretary his papers suggest that his private interest in pensions centred chiefly in insuring that the Unionist Party gave the appearance of concern for the topic. By the end of the decade, the real force behind the promotion of pensions had moved elsewhere and the men whose steady propaganda eventually brought the enactment of this reform had long since given up the expectation of help from the brilliant Unionist leader.

Chamberlain's importance lay in showing what could not be done in the way of pensions. By demonstrating that friendly society opposition and lack of working-class enthusiasm would make the passage of any contributory plan impossible, he eliminated the only important alternative to free pensions provided from general taxation. However, by putting off contributory pensions, he postponed all pensions for fifteen years and delayed a genuinely comprehensive contributory scheme until 1925.

Chamberlain's pension proposals varied throughout the period of his interest in them, but basically he proposed a voluntary contributory plan in which participation was encouraged by a State subsidy. Ideally a man would begin his pension account before age twenty-five with a deposit of £5. Any such depositor would receive a State credit of £15 more plus State guaranteed interest. This account of £20 would be kept open by forty annual payments of £1, providing a total basic capital of £60. No arrears of more than £5 would be permitted. Sixty pounds, Chamberlain calculated, paid in over a period of four or more decades with compound interest, would provide a man 5s. per week at age sixty-five for life, or 5s. per week for twenty-six weeks to the widow of a contributor who died before age sixty-five, plus 2s. per week for each child until twelve years old. Women could also become contributors making a smaller contribution and receiving a smaller pension.[41]

In conception Chamberlain's plan was an outgrowth of the

[41] Chamberlain's plan, like Blackley's, suggests an amateur's fascination for the compound interest table upon which many schemes for the effortless acquisition of riches have been based. One pound per year paid in over forty-five years with 4 per cent compound interest would accumulate to £125·87. At 5 per cent this would be £167·69.

Blackley scheme. He secured several members of Blackley's old National Providence League, most important of whom was Sir James Rankin, a Conservative M.P. who became the secretary of a committee of pension reformers in the House of Commons. This committee, usually referred to as the Committee of 100, included members of both parties and represented the most that Chamberlain attempted towards the formation of an organization to promote his programme.

Problems for Chamberlain's scheme appeared almost immediately. The Committee of 100 was soon apprised of the friendly society opposition to their pension plan, and within nine months had admitted that friendly society support would be essential to the success of the programme. Moreover, by the end of the year, Chamberlain's monopoly of the pension field was challenged by Charles Booth, who announced his advocacy of universal, non-contributory, tax-supported pensions in a paper read before the Royal Statistical Society on November 17, 1891.[42]

Chamberlain sought to counter the greater appeal of Booth's plan by arguing that at bottom it was no less contributory than his own in the sense that contributions were in fact made through general taxation, and that by being universal it would be ruinously expensive. Also, in comparing his own programme to Booth's, he took pains to point out that his own involved a far smaller amount of State supervision, and in the long run would be more palatable to the friendly societies. Immediately after Booth's announcement he wrote

. . . it is certain that the Friendly Societies would strenuously resist a proposal which would throw the whole business into the hands of the State, and would exclude them altogether from any future share in it. The influence of the Friendly Societies is so great, and so much regard would properly be paid to their opinion, that the second point established in the discussions of the House of Commons Committee was that it was essential to obtain the co-operation [for any programme] of at least the larger Societies. Up to this time, the evidence and assurance of such co-operation have not been forthcoming; but it must be remembered that no definite plan has yet been laid before the

[42] Charles Booth, 'Enumeration and Classification of Paupers, and State Pensions for the Aged,' *Journal of the Royal Statistical Society*, LIV (December, 1891), 600–43.

managers of these Societies. We may hope, however, that a fair and reasonable proposal, which would not put a limit to their extension, nor involve any increase in control or supervision of their affairs, nor interference with the existing management, would be welcomed by the able leaders of this great movement.[43]

Chamberlain's rather naïve hope that friendly societies were interested in his old age pension scheme was quickly put to rest. In April, Thomas Scanlon, a prominent member of the National Conference of Friendly Societies, referring to his article of February and remarking derisively on the 'suspicious juncture' in Liberal Unionist affairs (a coming election), informed him curtly that a contributory old age pension was out of the question so far as the societies were concerned.

> . . . if the friendly societies, with their superior organization and unique means of reaching the people, find it impossible to make such a scheme succeed, there is not much hope that any other agency will be found equal to the task.

Pensions, Scanlon continued, would do nothing to help the problem of pauperism, in which both Chamberlain and Booth professed to be interested. Certainly, he agreed, the industrious poor had a claim on society, but that claim must be handled through 'the adjustment of the relations between class and class. . . .'[44]

Chamberlain received a further warning in July from his expert in working-class matters, Jesse Collings, who wrote in reply to a request for suggestions about what should go into the Queen's Speech that he questioned the popularity of contributory pensions and preferred for a beginning a non-contributory plan.

> I don't think . . . that the scheme you have in mind will create much enthusiasm except among the better and more educated class of men who look forward. The name, however, 'Old-Age Pensions,' would be most powerful and the scheme itself [gain?] in favour. It would not touch those already old. I fancy it must come to a *general superannuation scheme*, taking in everyone after 65 years old. It would be costly (17 millions I believe Booth puts

[43] Joseph Chamberlain, 'Old-Age Pensions,' *National Review*, XVIII (February, 1892), 734.
[44] Thomas Scanlon, 'Mr Chamberlain's Pension Scheme: A Friendly Society View of It,' *Westminster Review*, CXXXVII (April, 1892), 357, 360, 363.

it at) but that could be got over. A 'General Superannuation Bill' would be a good cry. It is certain to come. Your scheme would run as well and would be aided by it; the advantages under it being in addition to the general scheme.[45]

Chamberlain's concern that the Queen's Speech show a proper interest in old age pensions proved unnecessary. A general election in July returned a small Liberal majority and in August, 1892, W. E. Gladstone formed his fourth ministry. Gladstone's interest in his last few months of office was home rule for Ireland, not social reform. But the Liberals were bound to pay at least some attention to the Newcastle programme, the rising unemployment that had overtaken the country in 1891, and the Unionist interest in pensions. The result, among several others, was the Royal Commission on the Aged Poor, the 'Aberdare Commission,' which maintained a strict neutrality among opposing philosophies, and perhaps also insured a sterile investigation, by including as members both Joseph Chamberlain and Charles Booth.

With his characteristic sense of political theatre, Chamberlain, although a commission member, received permission also to appear before the commission in favour of his pension plan. Chamberlain's testimony seemed aimed at insuring that the Liberals would not undertake old age pensions, while presenting himself at once as an advocate of pensions and of limited and prudent government. A well-conducted pension scheme, he argued, would make possible a return to truly deterrent poor law principles, which was impossible if the worthy and unfortunate poor had no alternative to parochial relief. To the complaint that a voluntary pension scheme did no good for the very poor, Charles Booth's 'submerged tenth,' who never had the opportunity even to begin a pension account, he answered firmly that the very poor did not in any case live to be sixty-five years old and cited the returns from the Birmingham workhouse as proof.[46]

At the same time Chamberlain warned the Liberals against proceeding with old age pensions in the face of friendly society opposition.

They are in touch with the thriftily-minded section of the

---

[45] Jesse Collings to Joseph Chamberlain, July 22, 1892, Chamberlain Papers, JC5/16/30.

[46] See: 'Notes of Evidence by the Right Hon. J. Chamberlain, M.P.,' (printed memo, 6 pp.), Chamberlain Papers, JC6/4.

working class. Their criticism of any scheme would be very damaging: their opposition might be fatal. They have very great Parliamentary influence and I should myself think twice before attempting to proceed in the face of hostility from so important and so dangerous a quarter.[47]

Before the Aberdare Commission reported, Chamberlain made a last attempt to win friendly society support for a pension programme. In a speech on December 6, 1894, in Birmingham, he appealed to the societies with most uncharacteristic humility. He had thought, he said, that the societies would welcome pension proposals as a solution to their difficulties and he was surprised and disappointed when the leaders 'warned me off as though I were an intruder on their private domain, and a poacher on their preserves.'

There was perhaps still some misunderstanding about his intentions, he suggested, and on this account he was glad to have the opportunity, almost his first, to explain his proposals to a large number of friendly society men. The friendly societies, he said, would have to solve soon the problem 'of their present unsound financial system. If they continue to give old age pay in the form of sick pay, the result will be bankruptcy.' He proposed that the government and the societies go into partnership, the societies giving each member a 2s. 6d. pension which the government would match to make a 5s. total. 'Is that the proposal of an enemy?' he asked. 'Is it not, at any rate, worthy of serious and impartial, I would say, of favourable, consideration?'[48]

Any lingering hope that the new proposal for partnership between the State and the friendly societies might bring society support for voluntary, contributory pensions was almost immediately dashed by a harsh reply from J. Lister Stead, at that time the assistant secretary of the Foresters, who was emerging as a leading spokesman of the friendly society movement.[49] Any State

[47] Quoted in Wilson and Mackay, Old Age Pensions, p. 28. In his notes of evidence, Chamberlain was even more blunt. See: Chamberlain Papers, JC6/4.

[48] Joseph Chamberlain, 'Old Age Pensions and Friendly Societies,' National Review, XXIV (January, 1895), 593–603. Commenting to the Rothschild committee two years later, Alfred Watson warned that Chamberlain's new proposal was unrealistic. The requirement to raise even 2s. 6d. per member 'would exclude the great majority of present members of friendly societies from the scheme on account of the actuarial unsoundness of the societies . . .' and even good societies would be hurt. Watson, Confidential Memorandum, pp. 3–5.

[49] James Lister Stead, 1864–1915, born, Leeds; no relation to F. H. or W. T. Stead; educated in State schools; journalist before becoming Assistant Secretary

aid, said Stead, retarded the teaching of thrift, although no doubt 'this remark applies less to Mr Chamberlain's scheme than to that of Mr Charles Booth, whose proposals in the words of Canon Blackley, "would be a form of universal pauperization. . . ." ' In regard to Mr Chamberlain's complaint that he had never had the opportunity to present his full programme to the friendly societies, Stead continued, the Unionist leader 'omitted to mention' that he and some other members of the Committee of 100 had met the National Conference of Friendly Societies in March, 1892. At that time he had explained his scheme. The National Conference had made no comment but had agreed to submit a printed outline of the scheme to the various societies at their meetings during 1892 'and in no instance, I believe, were Mr Chamberlain's suggestions of State aid accepted.' The proposal had finally been turned down by the National Conference at its meeting in London on March 29, 1893.[50]

After the spring of 1895 with the most equivocal, almost meaningless, report of the majority of the Aberdare Commission, suggesting that pensions be left in the hands of friendly societies, and the most unequivocal refusal of all co-operation from the societies themselves, contributory old age pensions were dead as a political issue.[51] They were highly useful as a symbol of the Unionists' solicitude for the working man, but no one, including Chamberlain himself, thought of them as anything more than an easy answer to an inconvenient question.

In July, 1895, the Unionists returned to office and Chamberlain, to the world's surprise, accepted the post of Secretary of State for Colonies, where in the next eight years he would epitomize British imperialism at its zenith. Within six months he was deeply involved in proving his innocence of complicity in the Jameson Raid in the Transvaal in South Africa and his concern for domestic welfare legislation understandably declined. But for four years Chamberlain had reiterated the Unionist interest in social

of Ancient Order of Foresters, 1889; Chief Secretary of Ancient Order of Foresters, 1897–1915. Member of English Insurance Commission, 1911–15.
    [50] J. Lister Stead, 'Friendly Societies and Old Age Pensions, A Reply to Mr Chamberlain,' National Review, XXV (March, 1895), 59–60.
    [51] C. 7684, 'Report of the Royal Commission on the Aged Poor,' 1895. The deliberations of the Aberdare Commission, the Simeys remarked, 'ended in ruin.' T. S. and M. B. Simey, Charles Booth, Social Scientist, London, 1960, p. 167.

reform. He had made social legislation an important part of his party's election platform.[52] It was therefore inconceivable that any government of which he was a part should not manifest a solicitude for the working man. As a result, almost precisely a year after he took office, in July, 1896, Lord Salisbury's Government appointed a Treasury Committee under Lord Rothschild to examine possible plans for old age pensions.[53]

The Cabinet's sincerity in this action is open to question. Probably it never intended the Committee on Old Age Pensions, or 'The Rothschild Committee' as it was usually called, to find old age pensions feasible, or even desirable. The committee's terms of reference prohibited the examination of any but contributory schemes. As a result it was able to consider only four of the one hundred plans submitted to it. Conversely, there was no danger that the committee would accept a contributory scheme, for its two most expert members were Alfred Watson, recently appointed chief actuary of the Manchester Unity, and Alfred Chapman, parliamentary agent of the Foresters. The latter society's High Court had reacted to the Rothschild Committee's appointment by passing a sweeping resolution on August 6 condemning all pensions as 'detrimental to the best interests of the Friendly Societies.'[54]

Although Chamberlain had stated optimistically at the time of the committee's appointment that he found it 'impossible to have a committee more likely to produce something that would be satisfactory,' it came as no surprise that the committee, after taking two years to examine four schemes, found itself 'unable to agree upon any of them.'

After the report of the Rothschild Committee, most public commentators assumed that pensions were dead. Friendly societies would not permit contributory pensions; the Booth scheme was out of the question because of its cost. Thus, although

[52] See: J. L. Garvin, *The Life of Joseph Chamberlain* (London, 1933), II, 607–10.

[53] A far more concrete result of Chamberlain's work was the important and highly useful Employer's Liability Act of 1897, which although technically in the care of the Home Office was managed in the House of Commons by Chamberlain.

[54] *The Standard*, August 7, 1896. The resolution passed 329 to 56 amid loud cheers.

everyone approved of pensions, there would be no pensions.[55] But, in fact, the new drive for pensions, one that led eventually to the enactment of that reform, was getting under way and, by the spring of 1899, it would be causing serious discomfort to the Government.

4

The event that caused this revival was the adopting by the colony of New Zealand of a plan of non-contributory old age pensions in the autumn of 1898. Since 1896, the Agent-General of New Zealand in the United Kingdom was William Pember-Reeves, a man well known in radical and Fabian circles.[56] In the summer of 1898, just after the report of the Rothschild Committee and while pensions were under consideration in the New Zealand Parliament, Reeves was asked by the Reverend Francis Herbert Stead, warden of the Browning Hall settlement house in York Street, Walworth, to speak to a small group of supporters of Booth's pension plan. Reeves declined at the time, saying that he could not come while the Bill was still political, but after its passage he agreed to speak and a meeting was set for Sunday, November 20, 1898.[57] The

---

[55] 'The universal scheme of Mr Booth, by reason of its immense cost, is felt to be as yet beyond the range of the possible. The report of the Rothschild Committee is a sentence of death for schemes dependent upon deferred annuities or direct money contributions by the recipients.' 'Old Age Relief,' *Edinburgh Review*, CXC (October, 1899), 388.

Booth's scheme 'is now practically abandoned by its own author....' Henry W. Wolff, 'Old Age Pensions,' *Economic Review*, IX (July, 1899), 326–7.

'The Booth Scheme, indeed, though apparently propounded with complete gravity by its author, may not unfairly be considered as a kind of *reductio ad absurdum* of the pension idea.'

Edward Bond, 'Is the Unionist Party Committed to Old-Age Pensions? III,' *National Review*, XXXIII (July, 1899), 727.

[56] William Pember Reeves, 1857–1923, born, Canterbury, New Zealand; educated, Christ's College Grammar School, Christchurch, New Zealand; admitted to New Zealand Bar; entered journalism, editor of the *Canterbury Times* and *Lyttelton Times*; Member New Zealand Parliament, 1887–96; Minister of Education, Labour and Justice, 1891–6; Agent-General and High Commissioner for New Zealand, 1897–1908; Director of the London School of Economics, 1908–19.

[57] Francis Herbert Stead, *How Old Age Pensions Began to Be*, London, n.d. [1910], pp. 11–14.

Francis Herbert Stead, 1857–1928, born, Howdon-on-Tyne; father Congregational minister, brother of W. T. Stead; educated at home, Owens College, Manchester, Airedale College, Bradford; Universities of Glasgow, Göttingen and Berlin; studied divinity; reporter for *Northern Daily Express* and *Northern*

meeting was advertised throughout Walworth with the Browning Hall brass and reed band carrying placards through the streets and distributing handbills. Charles Booth sent a message of congratulations.

The Reeves talk was a great success and, encouraged by the universal popularity of non-contributory old age pensions, Stead began to lay plans for a national campaign. Immediately afterwards he wrote to Booth asking whether he would attend an organizational conference at Browning Hall. Booth agreed and the meeting was planned for December 13, 1898. Stead secured the vitally necessary co-operation with labour through the prestige lent by the presence of Charles Booth and through his own friendship with G. N. Barnes of the Amalgamated Society of Engineers.[58] During the meeting Stead asked Booth to lend his name and presence to a series of conferences to be arranged in the north that would aim at interesting labour in pensions. The next day Booth wrote saying that if the meetings could be arranged:

> I shall be very glad to attend to do my best to interest the audiences in my argument as to the provision of Old Age Pensions by the State.
>
> . . . .
>
> It would be understood that the meetings are to be private, by invitation of representative working-class leaders, and without reporters. The time has not come for public meetings on the subject.[59]

The conferences in the north, which began the national campaign for non-contributory old age pensions, were handled

Echo, 1874–6; studied for Congregational ministry, 1876–84; pastor, Gallowtreegate Church, Leicester, 1884–90; member Leicester School Board, 1888–90; Warden, Robert Browning Settlement, Walworth, 1894–1921; continued in journalism, assistant editor, *Review of Reviews*, 1894–1912.

[58] George Nicoll Barnes, 1859–1940, born, Dundee; working-class parents; left school at eleven to work in a jute mill; moved to London, apprenticed in a machine foundry in Lambeth; joined Amalgamated Society of Engineers; took part in 1887 riots in Trafalgar Square; Assistant Secretary A.S.E., 1892; General Secretary, 1896–1908; defeated as I.L.P. candidate, Rochdale, 1895; M.P., Labour, Blackfriars division, Glasgow, 1896–1922; Minister for Pensions, 1916–18; Minister without Portfolio, 1919; War Cabinet, 1917, and resigned from Labour Party when it withdrew from coalition in 1918; Minister Plenipotentiary, Paris Peace Conference, 1919; resigned from Government, 1920. P.C., 1916; C.H., 1920.

[59] Stead, *Old Age Pensions*, p. 23.

generally by trade union leaders to whom Stead had reported on the meeting of December 14 in a confidential circular. The first meeting was at Newcastle, a town always regarded as a barometer of working-class opinion, on January 17, 1899, and was organized by Thomas Burt. This meeting was private, but Booth's address was such a success, although he was an uninspiring speaker, that thereafter they were thrown open to the public. Further meetings were scheduled in Leeds, Manchester, Bristol, Glasgow, and Birmingham.

Inevitably the new agitation affected politics. 'I hear the Opposition are talking of an Amendment to the Address on Old Age Pensions,' wrote Chamberlain to Salisbury on January 31, 1899, about two weeks after the Newcastle meeting.

> This would be awkward for many of our men and should be avoided if possible. I am afraid the Speaker would not rule it out of order even if a Bill were brought in by a private Member so Balfour will have to be prepared for it.[60]

'I expect trouble over the Old Age Pension question. I wish it could be kept off the Address,' he wrote to Balfour three days later.[61]

Chamberlain's embarrassment increased rapidly in the next few weeks. The final meeting of the series had been set, not without design, for Birmingham on March 25, 1899, and was arranged by George Cadbury.[62] Cadbury wrote to the Colonial Secretary on March 16 inviting him to attend. Chamberlain, who by this time must have regarded the pension reformers as only slightly less dangerous than the South African Boers, replied on March 18 that his 'work in London' would make it impossible for him to come, but that he looked forward to the results with interest.

---

[60] Joseph Chamberlain to Lord Salisbury, January 31, 1899, Chamberlain Papers, JC11/6.

[61] Joseph Chamberlain to A. J. Balfour, February 2, 1899, Chamberlain Papers, JC5/5/81.

[62] George Cadbury, 1839–1922, born, Edgbaston, Birmingham; family wealthy chocolate makers and strong supporters of Society of Friends; educated at day school, Edgbaston; entered family business at sixteen. Became interested in social work from measures to promote health, education and housing of workers in family business. Maintained through life interest and activity in the Society of Friends, settlement house work. A life-long campaigner against sweated labour.

While most persons are agreed as to the greatness of the evil with which we have to deal, there is marked difference of opinion as to the lines on which a remedy can be found, and any discussion which is calculated to throw light on this important question will be most valuable.[63]

Three days later, on the occasion of a motion by Lionel Holland to give a second reading to a Bill for a non-contributory old age pension of 5s. per week at age sixty-five to all who had insured against sickness and funeral expenses (i.e., friendly society members), Chamberlain announced the appointment of a select committee to look into pensions after the Easter recess. The Government, he said, was aware of the problem of the aged and anxious to find a remedy. '. . . we shall not be satisfied,' he concluded, 'until we have done something to make the condition of the aged poor more satisfactory than it is at the present time.'[64]

Thus the campaign for old age pensions achieved its first victory by forcing the appointment of the Select Committee of the House of Commons on the Aged Deserving Poor, the 'Chaplin Committee.' Introducing Stead to the audience in Birmingham three days later, Cadbury referred to him as the man who had brought the most powerful Government of modern times 'to its knees.'[65]

There were over seven hundred people present in the Examination Hall of the Technical School in Birmingham on March 25, to hear Charles Booth's final public speech in the inaugural series that would eventually bring old age pensions. His argument on this occasion illustrates the case for non-contributory pensions that would be made throughout the next eight years. Old age pensions,

---

[63] Stead, *Old Age Pensions*, p. 52.

[64] *Hansard, Parliamentary Debates*, Series 4, LXIX (March 22, 1899), cols. 68, 81.

Holland was a Conservative and cousin of the Rothschild Committee secretary, Bernard Holland. After the unsatisfactory Rothschild report he had written a stinging attack on the Government for duplicity in the matter of pensions. Lionel Holland, 'The Report on Old Age Pensions,' *National Review*, XXXI (August, 1898), 868–85. In 1899 Holland left the Conservatives over pensions and in 1906 as a Liberal contested Chamberlain's home constituency of Edgbaston in Birmingham.

About one hundred Unionist M.P.s had petitioned the Government a few weeks earlier to make a 'definite attempt to fulfil the pledges on pensions given by so many of them.' C. A. Whitmore, 'Is the Unionist Party Committed to Old-Age Pensions? I,' *National Review*, XXXIII (July, 1899), 713.

[65] Stead, *Old Age Pensions*, p. 75.

he said, reduce pauperism and eliminate the hideous living conditions he had discovered in the London investigation. In Stepney 32·8 per cent of pauperism was caused by old age, and in St Pancras 23·4 per cent. He calculated that of all who died over age sixty-five, 40 per cent had received parish relief during the last year of their lives and noted that Canon Blackley's investigation of 26 parishes had come to almost precisely the same conclusions— 42·7 per cent.[66]

The argument, then, for any pension was that it would reduce society's expenditure on the maintenance of its aged poor. But as society had already begun to insure itself, Booth opposed any scheme that might reduce the usefulness of provident organizations already in existence. Hence he opposed any contributory scheme because:

> It is impossible to conceive any plan by which contributions can be drawn from the masses of the people alongside of Friendly Society contributions without interfering with the Friendly Societies; nor could the Government enter into a sort of partnership with the Friendly Societies without in some way interfering with them, which is not only undesirable but would never be accepted.

Besides this, Booth noted, friendly societies did not provide for women nor, finally, would a governmentally-sponsored contributory scheme accomplish anything until the present generation had grown old. A tax-supported scheme, Booth pointed out, would not discourage, but encourage, thrift, for it would make the friendly societies more solvent. They were now converting sickness allowance into what were practically old age pensions at the cost of their solvency. With a true old age pension: 'There would be far less of insolvency and lapses. . . .' and all forms of 'industrial and friendly endowments would be encouraged.'[67]

In the months following the Birmingham meeting the enthusiasm of old age pension supporters mounted rapidly. On May 1, Charles Booth published his *Old Age Pensions and the Aged Poor*, in which for the first time he presented a detailed plan arguing for a universal 7s. pension to be paid at age seventy. The cost he esti-

---

[66] This is fully described in Booth, 'State Pensions for the Aged,' *J.R.S.S.*, December, 1891, pp. 609, 615, 631–2.

[67] Stead, *Old Age Pensions*, pp. 33–44.

mated would be £16,000,000 per year.[68] About a week later the organization that finally brought old age pensions had its first meeting. This was cumbersomely entitled 'The National Committee of Organized Labour (Trade Unions, Trade Councils, Federations of these bodies, Friendly Societies, and Co-operative Societies) on Old Age Pensions, based on the Principle that every old person on attaining a given age should be entitled a free Pension from the State; and charged with the Instruction to promote the legal enactment of this Principle.' The National Committee, as it will hereafter be called, had its first meeting on May 9, 1899, at Browning Hall. It was made up of seven local committees based in London, Northumberland and Durham, Yorkshire, Lancashire, west of England and South Wales, Scotland, and the Midlands.[69] The first meeting departed immediately from Booth's plan by reducing the amount of pension proposed from 7s. to 5s. There was some fear that Booth would now leave the movement, but he cheerfully replied that, as they had not endorsed his specific proposals, he could now in better conscience contribute to the expenses of the labour leaders present and promised £50.

Booth was pressed to take the chairmanship of the committee, but he said he thought it should go to a labour leader. As a result, J. V. Stevens of Birmingham was appointed chairman. Stevens held this office until 1902 when he was succeeded by G. N. Barnes. Far more important than the chairmanship was the appointment, in July, 1899, of the paid organizing secretary of the National Committee. This post went to Frederick Rogers, at that time secretary of the small Vellum Binders Union. Rogers, one of the absolutely unknown figures in the history of the welfare state, had been joint secretary with Alfred Milner, under the chairmanship of Samuel Barnett, of the University Extension Society in East London since 1877. He would become in February, 1900, the first chairman of the Labour Representation Committee.[70] The

[68] His earlier book, *Pauperism a Picture, and the Endowment of Old Age an Argument*, London, 1892, had presented indeed the picture and an argument, but hardly a plan.

[69] On the formation of the National Committee see: Stead, *Old Age Pensions*, pp. 63–4.

[70] Frederick Rogers, 1846–1915, born, Whitechapel; self-educated; secretary Vellum Binders' Union; active in workers' education, member of Bethnal Green School Management Committee, promoter of university extension with S. A. Barnett, Alfred Milner and Arnold Toynbee; member of LCC; first

G

National Committee included a number of the most influential names in the labouring movement—besides Barnes, Francis Chandler, Will Crooks, J. R. Clynes, Thomas Burt, and Frederick Maddison. It established its headquarters at Browning Hall and began the systematic promotion of old age pensions in the fall of 1899, a campaign that would continue until the enactment of pensions nine years later.

From the headquarters in London went out a stream of pamphlets and suggestions for addresses urging pensions. G. N. Barnes' *The Case Briefly Stated* was the first and ran eventually to 100,000 copies.[71] Stead himself drew up a leaflet entitled *Hints for Helpers*, in which the advice offered to the National Committee workers fairly illustrates the means employed in the fight for pensions. 'Approach public bodies,' he urged. 'Get to know whether the local board of guardians has voted on the Pensions question.' If it had not, and the worker felt the board might be favourable, an able guardian was to be urged to put the resolution before the body. Influential newspaper editors of any party could be a help. 'Lay on their consciences the sad plight of more than a million aged poor.'

> Invoke religious bodies, in the name of the poor and them that labour and are heavy laden. Wait upon ecclesiastical leaders such as the chief local dignitary of the Roman Catholic Church, of the Church of England, and of dissenting bodies.
> Caution! Keep yourself carefully from entangling alliances with any political parties.[72]

Public reactions to the work of the National Committee varied. Politicians generally were wary of opposing pensions in the abstract while being equally wary of committing themselves to any particular system. Rogers remarked that 'officers of friendly societies, or co-operative stores, and deacons of dissenting chapels, were often more conservative in their ultimate thinking about the aged than were members of the Primrose League.'[73] Rogers early got a

Chairman of Labour Representation Committee, 1900–2; Treasurer, 1902–3. A devout Anglo-Catholic; active in Christian Social Union.

[71] For Barnes' description of the pension agitation, see: George N. Barnes, *From Workshop to War Cabinet*, New York, 1924, pp. 66–8. Barnes gives most of the credit for old age pensions to Stead and Rogers.

[72] Stead, *Old Age Pensions*, pp. 79–80.

[73] On the conservatism of working-class bodies see also: Mary Booth, *Charles Booth: A Memoir*, London, 1918, p. 124.

promise of support for pensions in the House of Lords from Archbishop Temple and of extraparliamentary support from Cardinal Vaughan for the Roman Catholics. On the other hand, the most prominent Methodist clergyman in the country, Hugh Price Hughes, refused any public support.[74] Surprisingly, Canon Blackley not only never supported the National Committee, but conducted a 'slashing attack' on Rogers late in 1899 when he read a paper to a church congress in the Albert Hall to which he had been invited by Bishop Mandell Creighton. Rogers had no way to reply, but had his answer made by his good friend, Henry Scott Holland.[75]

Although to the public, pensions seemed to have dropped from sight by the late summer of 1899, to the Government, as the appointment of the Chaplin Committee indicated, the work of the National Committee was deeply disturbing. It is not surprising, therefore, that the committee report, rendered on July 26, 1899, made the first official recommendation for a pension scheme. The Chaplin Committee proposed a 5s. payment provided partly out of poor rates and partly from the Exchequer to be made after a careful investigation of the applicant's need and character by the local board of guardians. A departmental committee immediately set to work to determine the probable cost.[76] Within the generally accepted meaning of the term, the proposal of the Chaplin Committee was not an old age pension. Rather the committee simply made a distinction between the 'deserving' and, as Balfour chose to call them, the 'not deserving' poor, giving to the former outdoor relief on improved terms, which would be styled a pension. This, Balfour admitted in December, 1899, was the best solution he could think of. If it did not satisfy pension advocates, he remarked, at least it would not frighten too much those who opposed pensions.[77]

As autumn approached, pension advocates were enthusiastic and

[74] Frederick Rogers, *Labour, Life, and Literature: Some Memories of Sixty Years*, London, 1913, pp. 224, 247, 248, 250.

[75] *Ibid.*, pp. 233-4.

[76] Chaplin's scheme would have excluded all earning less than 10s. per week who received poor relief in the past twenty years, as well as those unable to pass a stringent thrift test. As a result less than one-third of those over seventy would have been pensionable.

[77] A. J. Balfour, 'Pensions and the Deserving Poor,' December 12, 1899, P.R.O. Cab. 37/51, No. 96. Most influential Unionists refused categorically to sanction any pensions that were not connected with the poor law. See: Michael Hicks-Beach, 'Aged Poor,' November 18, 1899, P.R.O. Cab. 37/51, No. 89.

optimistic. Frederick Rogers, appointed in the same month that the Chaplin Committee reported, was told that his term of office was one year on the assumption that he would not be needed thereafter.[78] In September the National Committee secured from the Trades Union Congress in their annual meeting at Plymouth a unanimous resolution, demanding a pension of unspecified amount beginning at age sixty, paid as of right to all citizens. This resolution the T.U.C. repassed every year until pensions became law. In 1901 they were joined by the national organization of co-operative societies, which passed an identical resolution. And in March, 1902, at Manchester, after being shown that the increasing rate of bankruptcies among friendly societies was making their members almost as liable to pauperism in old age as the rest of the work force, the National Conference of Friendly Societies passed a hesitant resolution stating:

> That it is the duty of the state to provide an old-age pension of not less than 5s. a week to all thrifty and deserving persons of 65 years of age and upwards where unable to work and in need of the same.[79]

The friendly societies' ancient fear of government competition was manifest in the concluding statement of their resolution that 'the cost of the same shall be raised without any interference with the funds of the thrift societies.'[80] The stipulation that applicants for pensions be 'thrifty and deserving,' which would have tended to restrict pensions to members of friendly societies, was not accepted by the T.U.C. and the co-operatives.

Even though the advocates of old age pensions were able to obtain resolutions of support for their project from the leadership of influential labour organizations, the interest of the average British working man in this reform, and all others, disappeared in October, 1899, with the outbreak of the Boer War. The Government, to which the National Committee had appeared a menace in 1899, found itself by the next year able to disregard all demands for expenditures for welfare projects, whether of rate or Exchequer money. The ordinary government attitude may be illustrated by a

[78] Stead, *Old Age Pensions*, pp. 71, 76–7.

[79] For a description of the arguments used to bring a friendly society endorsement of pensions see: G. N. Barnes, 'Immediate Social Reform, What the Government Could Do,' *Commonwealth*, VII (May, 1902), 137–8.

[80] Stead, *Old Age Pensions*, p. 130.

memorandum to the Cabinet of March 12, 1902, from the then President of the Local Government Board, Walter Long, making suggestions on how to handle one of the several pension Bills introduced that year. The Bill in question was based simply on the recommendations of the Chaplin Committee, presided over by Long's predecessor at the board. Long noted that the members' names on the back of the Bill 'are all supporters of the Government and it will be very difficult, if not impossible, to secure its direct rejection.' But, he suggested:

It might be practicable to induce some such member as Sir Edgar Vincent, or Mr Cripps, to move some amendment based on the heavy burden which the Bill would impose both on the taxpayers and the rate payers and thus to defeat the measure.

Otherwise, Long suggested, he might himself 'refer to the financial difficulties, and express the inability of the Government to accept the liability of. . . .' etc.

Another plan would be, assuming the Second Reading to be inevitable, to insist upon the Bill being referred to a select committee for the purpose of its being examined in the light of the Report of Sir Edward Hamilton's Committee, but looking at that report there might not be much for a Select Committee to investigate.[81]

Next year, when Chaplin's plan was again introduced, the Government, as Long had suggested, resorted to a select committee which included several members of the Chaplin Committee (among them David Lloyd George). Understandably the committee reported again the Bill they had already considered with the sole change of removing the guardians from the administration of pensions.[82] Echoing Long's statement of the year before the committee concluded, perhaps wearily, that all materials for the hypothetical consideration of pensions had been exhausted and that remaining problems could be solved only by experiment.

Almost alone in the Government, Joseph Chamberlain attempted to maintain a semblance of Unionist interest in the subject. He

[81] Walter H. Long to Cabinet, March 12, 1902, 'Aged Pensioners Bill,' P.R.O. Cab. 37/61, No. 60, pp. 1–2.

[82] 'Report and Special Report from the Select Committee on the Aged Pensioners Bill,' 1903.

himself disliked the Chaplin scheme, recognizing it for what it was.[83] In 1901 after most of his colleagues had relegated pension agitation to the level of a minor annoyance, Chamberlain, addressing the annual conference of the National Order of Odd Fellows in Birmingham, made a last appeal to the friendly societies to produce a scheme that would enable the Government and the societies to share the burden of pension payments.[84] Less than a year later, as if in answer, the National Conference of Friendly Societies passed its first resolution demanding a pension supported entirely by taxes.

Any lingering hopes of a compromise plan for contributory pensions were destroyed by the National Conference resolution. But neither was there any likelihood that the Balfour ministry would find money for a non-contributory pension. In the spring of 1903, in the first budget after the conclusion of the South African War, the Government repealed the registration duty on imported small grains and dropped the income tax by 4d. in the pound, giving up a total revenue of £12,000,000 per year.[85] With these events in the background, and with the election on March 11, 1903, of Will Crooks, Labour candidate and enthusiastic member of the National Committee, for the solidly Unionist constituency of Woolwich, Joseph Chamberlain on May 15 announced the beginning of his campaign for the re-establishment of British tariff protection with the aim of promoting imperial unity through preferential reductions on dominion products. Although he certainly never promoted his scheme as an avenue to social reform, and insisted privately that consolidation of the empire was his only interest, Chamberlain suggested in the House of Commons only a week after making the original proposal at Birmingham that the Government might soon have the necessary funds for pensions, but that this would 'involve a review of the fiscal system which I have indicated as necessary and desirable at an early date.'[86] A few

---

[83] Joseph Chamberlain to Cabinet, November 17, 1899, Chamberlain Papers, JC6/4.

[84] Stead, *Old Age Pensions*, p. 125.

[85] Stead regarded this budget as the result of a formal Cabinet decision to end all consideration of pensions. Stead, *Old Age Pensions*, p. 165. There is no evidence that this was the case.

[86] See, for instance, his letter to the Duke of Devonshire on September 21, 1903, quoted in: Bernard Holland, *The Life of Spencer Compton, Eighth Duke of Devonshire* (London, 1911), II, 355.

Hansard, CXXII (May 22, 1903), col. 1553. He made this admission in

days later, on June 3, he admitted the connexion between tariffs
and pensions even more clearly in a letter quoted by F. H. Stead.

> As regards Old Age Pensions, I would not myself look at the
> matter unless I felt able to promise that the provision of such
> pensions to all who have been thrifty and well-conducted would
> be assured by a revision of our system of import duties.[87]

For Chamberlain, tariffs provided the solution to several problems at once. A pension paid for by tariffs on food would be in fact
a contributory scheme without appearing to be so. It would not
interfere with working-class savings in the friendly societies. At the
same time it would promote through imperial preference the other
project closest to Chamberlain's heart, the economic consolidation
of the empire. An eminent convert to this point of view, who saw
the connexion between tariffs and pensions, was the founder of the
movement for non-contributory pensions, Charles Booth.[88]

In the balance, Chamberlain's proposal for import duties did
nothing to advance the cause of old age pensions. Among the
Unionists, tariffs so divided the party that hope for major legislation of any sort disappeared.[89] Conversely, tariffs provided a
cement that enabled the parliamentary Liberals to hide, if not to
repair, their own divisions, and so to become less dependent upon
radical support. Hence, the revival of Liberal power did little to
increase the hope of pension supporters, or for that matter of
reformers generally. The party leadership consistently refused to
make any commitment to the National Committee.[90] Many of
those who would vote for the Liberals in the next election, wrote
the secretary of the Christian Social Union, Percy Dearmer, in

response to a searing attack by David Lloyd George, who persistently reminded
the Colonial Secretary of his commitment to pensions.

[87] Stead, *Old Age Pensions*, p. 164. In 1907, when pensions were clearly under
consideration by the Liberals, Leopold Maxse, editor of the *National Review* and
a strong advocate of tariff reform, wrote in their support suggesting that pensions
would make import duties inevitable. 'Episodes of the Month,' *National Review*,
XLIX (March, 1907), 20.

[88] Booth's conversion to protection astonished many of his friends. See:
Beatrice Webb, *Our Partnership*, London, 1948, p. 279. Booth by this time had
practically withdrawn from active participation in the work of the National
Committee.

[89] Even inter-party groups of social reformers such as the Coefficients suffered
fatal divisions.

[90] See: Stead, *Old Age Pensions*, p. 186; Rogers, *Labour*, p. 261.

October, 1904, would do so not out of love for Campbell-Bannerman or from

> ... hope for anything but words from that popular preacher Lord Rosebery, but from sheer despair. Lucky are those who have a Labour candidate, for they have a simple and unmistakable method of protest; and it seems to me that the only thing to save the House of Commons from complete putrefaction will be to get it plentifully salted by Labour members.[91]

Generally, 1904 was a gloomy year for the supporters of pensions, but the solidly middle-class walls of old-fashioned Liberalism were crumbling. Already the planning had begun of the co-operative electoral arrangements with the Labour Party that would effect the return of a large number of working men pledged to social reform. There is no need here to describe again the constituency truce effected by the Liberal Whip, Herbert Gladstone, during 1904 and 1905. By preventing three-cornered electoral fights in the 1906 election, Gladstone contributed largely both to the overwhelming Liberal victory and to the sensational success of candidates sponsored by the Labour Representation Committee.[92] For this study the importance of Gladstone's work lies in the fact that by permitting the election of a large number of Labour candidates, the Liberal Whip brought into the House of Commons a delegation of men who were uniformly committed to old age pensions, and thus gave an unmistakable demonstration of the working-class support for this measure to Liberal leaders who had themselves refused to make any promises on the subject.[93]

The Liberal gesture of welcome to the parties of the left had been made only with the greatest reluctance. Although Liberal writers and politicians had been urging some form of electoral accommodation with Labour since the turn of the century, the most practical suggestion came from Harold Spender writing in the *Daily News* on January 31, 1903. Spender argued that the truce, when it came, should be handled at the constituency level. By May of that

---

[91] Percy Dearmer, 'Politics and the People,' *Commonwealth*, IX (October, 1904), 291.

[92] For the importance to Labour of the truce with the Liberals, see: Philip, Viscount Snowden, *An Autobiography* (London, 1934), I, 217–18. Speaking of 1910, Snowden stated that without the electoral agreements 'not half a dozen' Labour members would have been returned.

[93] See Asquith's statement in the House of Commons on 1907 Budget Speech.

year, Herbert Gladstone had begun to exhort local Liberal associations to recognize Labour and to discard the air of patronage that many of them seemed to adopt when dealing with the working class.[94] The event that made the Liberal–Labour truce possible, at least acceptable, to the old-fashioned constituency associations, occurred on July 24, 1903, in the election of Arthur Henderson for the Barnard Castle Division of Durham. Henderson defeated the official Liberal candidate in a constituency that had been consistently Liberal for a generation. His return was no defeat for the national Liberal executive, which had not supported Hubert Beaumont, the candidate of the local Liberals. Rather, it was a defeat for the autonomy of Liberal constituency associations.[95]

But it may also be argued that Henderson's victory was a demonstration of the creeping paralysis that was invading the roots of the Liberal Party in the constituencies.[96] There the Liberal oligarchies were out of touch with the national leadership and indeed with the working-class voters in their own areas upon whom their continued political success depended. An old family name or a well-entrenched local candidate could, to be sure, hold the working men's loyalty to Liberalism. But when a change had to be made, the local association could not be sure of maintaining automatic attachment to the old party. Working men were no longer interested in peace, retrenchment, and reform, wrote an anonymous labour organizer in the month following the election of John Johnson, a Durham miner's agent, for the traditionally solid Liberal seat of Gateshead.

> What Liberalism in the North really needs . . . is a recognition of the fact that its old war cries are out of date, and that new ones must be found which really voice the aspiration of

[94] For a detailed story of this work, see Philip P. Poirier, *The Advent of the Labour Party*, London, 1958, pp. 185–91; Frank Bealey and Henry Pelling, *Labour and Politics, 1900–1906*, London, 1958, pp. 150, 151.

[95] On the general implications of the Barnard Castle election, see: Frank Bealey, 'The Electoral Arrangements Between the Labour Representation Committee and the Liberal Party,' *Journal of Modern History*, XXVII (December, 1956), 353–73.

[96] Also symptomatic of what was happening to Liberalism was the death, a little more than six weeks after the Barnard Castle by-election, of the *Newcastle Leader*, the last Liberal morning paper between Dundee and Darlington, leaving the *Northern Echo* of Darlington as the only important voice of radical Liberalism in the north of England.

G*

democracy by whose votes they hope to return to power. Warning after warning has been given them, all in vain.[97]

The northern working man did not understand the economics of tariff reform and as a traditional little Englander was not attracted by the plea of imperial unity. Chinese coolie labour in South Africa was irrelevant. He wanted to see the right to strike restored to trade unions and he wanted social reform.[98] In summary, for the Liberal Party the election of Arthur Henderson was a lesson and a stimulus to action as the Taff Vale judgment had been to the trade unions. It demonstrated to Liberal politicians the power of labour, as the House of Lords decision had shown to trade unions the importance of politics. It gave, therefore, the Labour Party the means to enter the House of Commons in force in 1906, and while the new working-class M.P.s were able to impose their will on the House only to a limited extent, the working-class votes that put them there clearly had to be bought back and quickly. Part of the price was old age pensions.[99]

5

The sensational increase in the number of working men in the House of Commons (twenty-nine M.P.s sitting under the auspices of the Labour Representation Committee and twenty-four more unaffiliated labouring men sitting officially as Liberals) appears to have taken the Liberal Government by surprise.[100] On January 20, almost as soon as the last polls were complete, Herbert Asquith

[97] 'The Awakening of the North,' *Commonwealth*, IX (February, 1904), 37.

[98] See also: Richard Bell, 'The Reign of Labour,' *National Review*, XLII (October, 1903), 188–97. The central labour argument was that a nation that could afford £250,000,000 for an imperialist war could afford pensions. Meeting, appropriately, in Bradford in February, 1904, the Labour Representation Committee made old age pensions a part of its official programme.

[99] The Liberals themselves showed no interest in social reform legislation during the general election of January, 1906. On most issues, the party was content to attack the Unionist record without proposing alternatives. For the Liberal issues see the pamphlet: *Ten Years of Tory Government*, London, 1906. For some reason, a few writers of history still insist that the Campbell-Bannerman Government came to power pledged to social reform. For instance: H. E. Raynes, *Social Security in Britain, A History*, 2nd ed., London, 1960, p. 181.

[100] It surprised labouring men themselves. Will Crooks in a rather boastful article in December, 1905, had predicted that thirty or forty workmen would be elected. 'The Prospects and Programme of the Labour Party,' *National Review*, XLVI (December, 1905), 621–2.

wrote to the Prime Minister asking whether he had given any thought, in view of the new importance of labour, 'to the items of the unions?' He suggested specific mention of amendments to the Workmen's Compensation Act and a Trade Disputes Bill for the King's Speech.[101] Campbell-Bannerman answered the next day, agreeing that there would have to be some mention of workmen's compensation and trade disputes and that he would ask Herbert Gladstone to deal with them. But, the Prime Minister suggested, there was also the need for a measure that would be at once agreeable to the working class and yet of wide application, not specifically for the trade unions.

> ... if we have two sops for Labour, we ought to have some other Bill beside Educ. of general interest, to balance them. Otherwise will not the [enemy blaspheme?] or will colour be given to their assertion, which seems to be their main weapon now, that we are in the hands and at the mercy of Labour (which=socialism).[102]

The conclusion appears unassailable that old age pensions first came under consideration by the Liberal leadership as a way to provide the necessary 'balance' in the party's programme. In any case, well before the end of 1906 Asquith had put Treasury civil servants to work investigating ways and means.

Although Thomas Burt, one of the most eminent of the Liberal working men in Parliament, announced in September that he had 'reason to believe' that the present Government would establish old age pensions,[103] the younger radicals clustered about Massingham's *Speaker* and the Christian Social Union were beginning to conclude by autumn that their party's leadership needed more pressure.[104] In fact, the Liberal Government was divided within itself. On one side was the 'official Liberal' point of view, which tried to maintain the old Gladstonian conventions of limited and economical government with interest in education, temperance reform, franchise reform, abolition of the Lords' veto, disestablishment of the Welsh Church, and free trade. On the other was what

[101] British Museum Add. MSS. 41,210, Campbell-Bannerman Papers, Vol. V, f. 259.

[102] H. Campbell-Bannerman to Herbert Asquith, January 21, 1906, Asquith Papers, Box 10, ff. 200–1.

[103] Thomas Burt, 'Old Age Pensions,' *Nineteenth Century*, LX (September, 1906), 378.

[104] See, for instance: 'Old-Age Pensions,' *Speaker*, September 8, 1906.

C. F. G. Masterman referred to as the 'social reformist' wing of the party—those who were in touch with the trade unions and who sought to direct Liberal attention to the condition of the people.[105] The inner history of 8 Edw. 7, Ch. 40, the Old Age Pensions Act that became law on August 1, 1908, is principally the story of forcing upon the traditional Liberals in the Cabinet the conviction that pensions were not only theoretically desirable, but politically essential, if the reputation of the Liberals as a party of social reform were to be improved.

Old age pensions moved a large step forward in the last month of 1906 when it became clear that the Education Bill to which the Government had devoted the largest amount of parliamentary time that year would not pass the House of Lords in the form even approximating that given it by the House of Commons. Education had been the one measure of 'general interest' Campbell-Bannerman had mentioned in January as necessary to mitigate the impression of excessive government preoccupation with the affairs of labour. Failure here would have to be made up in some other area. Thus between the end of October when the second chamber reconvened and began to amend the Education Bill, and December 17 when the Government finally dropped the measure, old age pensions moved from the category of a possible, to a likely, Liberal measure. Stead himself felt that the victory came on November 20, 1906, when he and Frederick Rogers, in the company of a deputation of nearly eighty Labour and Liberal M.P.s, interviewed Campbell-Bannerman and Asquith and received what Stead regarded as private assurances that the Liberal ministry would undertake an old age pensions bill.[106] Stead's report on the deputation, published the next day in *The Times*, quoted Campbell-Bannerman as saying that he 'entirely agreed with everything that had been said,' that the scheme would have to be universal and contributory, and that only money was necessary. Asquith assented, saying that nothing 'was nearer his heart' than old age pensions.[107]

---

[105] See: C. F. G. Masterman, 'Liberalism and Labour,' *Nineteenth Century*, LX (November, 1906), 706–18. For critical comments on the internal divisions of the Campbell-Bannerman and Asquith Cabinets, see: Viscount Haldane of Cloan, *An Autobiography*, London, 1929, pp. 216–18; and Webb, *Partnership*, p. 380.

[106] Stead, *Old Age Pensions*, pp. 219–23.

[107] *The Times*, November 21, 1906.

The decision to consider pensions seriously brought up serious problems. The basic question in non-contributory old age pensions was finance. Asquith, who was the chief spokesman for the Government on the matter, had always used government economy as the excuse for the Liberal failure to take action. On February 15, 1906, he had told a deputation of the parliamentary committee of the T.U.C., the first of many deputations on the subject he would receive that year, that while he and the Prime Minister were most sympathetic towards pensions, he saw 'no means of possessing the necessary funds' to put pensions into effect.[108] However, at the end of the year, faced with the clear inability to fulfil one of the most important Liberal election promises, money had to be found. The cost of a non-contributory pension was universally assumed to be high, but no one knew how high, nor could anyone ascertain what relief would accrue to local taxation by the award of pensions to hundreds of thousands of elderly people who previously had been drawing poor law relief. Finally, at least as important stood the question of the effect of pensions, even non-contributory ones, upon the friendly societies. How far had their suspicion of government action in this field been allayed? What did the rather equivocal resolution of the National Conference of Friendly Societies mean in terms of the attitudes of over four million jealously independent—and in a very large measure Nonconformist—society members, who presumably were already discontented with the Liberals over the failure of the Education Bill? These questions the Government set out to answer in December, 1906.

Most of the early spade work on pensions was carried out by Treasury officials under the direction of Asquith's then private secretary, Roderick S. Meiklejohn.[109] In the middle of December, Meiklejohn produced a long statement for the Cabinet that summarized the non-political arguments for pensions and introduced the topic at the Cabinet level. Pensions were a weapon in the attack on pauperism. Of the English population between ages

[108] Stead, *Old Age Pensions*, p. 201.
[109] Roderick Sinclair Meiklejohn, 1876–1962, father a doctor and Deputy Inspector of Hospitals and Fleets for Navy; educated, St Paul's School and Hertford College, Oxford; entered civil service in the War Office, 1899; Treasury, 1902; private secretary to Sir Edward Hamilton, 1903–4; Duke of Devonshire, 1904–5; H. H. Asquith, 1905–11; Deputy Comptroller of Supply Services at Treasury, 1911–29; First Commissioner of Civil Service, 1929–39. C.B., 1911.

sixty and sixty-five, 6·1 per cent were paupers. After sixty-five this proportion leaped to 18·3 per cent.[110] As a consequence a substantial part of the expenditure on pensions by the national government would be recovered by the local authorities in the reduction of the cost of maintenance of elderly paupers. Moreover, the saving in money did not count the more important reward in pride and self-confidence that would accrue by relieving nearly one-third of Britain's elderly citizens who had to spend some period of their retired life dependent upon parochial relief. This was indeed the basic argument for pensions: there was no public provision other than the poor law for the maintenance of the English working class in old age.

Concerning the ancient question of the friendly societies and their older members, Meiklejohn noted that the Manchester Unity and the Foresters had already established pension schemes, but that hitherto the interest among the membership had been small, although there was some indication that it was growing.

> In other directions Friendly Societies do in fact give much assistance to their members in old age by allowing them to draw sick pay, although not strictly entitled to benefit. This practice must in the long run affect the financial stability of the Friendly Societies, as in the actuarial calculations upon which the subscriptions for sick benefits were based, it was never contemplated that old age was to be treated as sickness. In fact some of the older Societies have been ruined by the practice. . . . It follows, therefore, that if the State undertook a superannuation scheme the Societies would be relieved considerably and could devote themselves more securely to their normal objects.[111]

Nevertheless, noted the memorandum, 'a noticeable feature in Old Age Pension propaganda has been the opposition which has existed among the representatives of the friendly societies.' The societies had always argued that pensions would compete with themselves and would sap the independence of the working classes. But it was hard to see, thought Meiklejohn, how the societies could object to a non-contributory pension. The Chief Registrar of Friendly Societies had been asked to make an inquiry to determine

[110] 'Old Age Pensions,' n.d. (printed December 14, 1906), p. 1, P.R.O., Cab. 37/85, No. 96. This document may also be found in the Asquith Papers.
[111] *Ibid.*, p. 2.

what provisions, if any, the societies made for superannuation of their members and whether they would object to a State plan.

After the encouraging promises made by members of the Government in November, 1906, Stead and Rogers were disappointed by the failure of the King's Speech on February 12, 1907, to include any reference to pensions.[112] G. N. Barnes promptly moved an amendment to the address regretting the absence of any such reference in view of the election pledge of many members. By pushing the matter to a division he would have enabled the Labourites and the radicals, who would surely have been supported by the Unionists, to administer an embarrassing rebuke to the Liberal leadership. Asquith avoided this unpleasantness by a soothing speech reaffirming that while he 'ardently desired' pensions, he had made no pledge about them. He reminded the reformers that a vote for the amendment would be a vote of censure for the Government.[113] Some pension supporters had by this time begun to doubt whether the Government would act other than verbally in support of the project.[114]

The Government was seriously concerned by the appearance in March, 1907, of a new pension proposal from Charles Booth. In a book, *The Aged Poor: A Proposal*, Booth suggested a universal pension of 7s. per week for men and 5s. for women to all citizens over the age of seventy, with an additional pension of the same amount for those between sixty and seventy who could show need. Booth argued that his pension would practically eliminate all outdoor relief for these groups and would hence be relatively inexpensive in terms of new cost. Meiklejohn disputed this, calculating for Asquith that the total cost of all poor relief to those over seventy was no more than £2,537,730, while the net cost of pensions to the same group, let alone those under seventy, would be at least £15,500,000, even with the assumption that £2,750,000 would be saved because of pensions not claimed by the well-to-do.[115]

Quite possibly it was the fear of being forced to adopt a universal pension scheme of incalculable cost that caused Asquith on April 18, 1907, during the introduction of his second budget, to make his

[112] Stead, *Old Age Pensions*, pp. 225–6.
[113] *Hansard*, CLXIX (February 13, 1907), cols. 216–17.
[114] Stead, *Old Age Pensions*, p. 227.
[115] 'Mr Booth's Latest Scheme,' April 4, 1907, Asquith Papers, unsorted, ('Papers on Old Age Pensions').

cryptic and equivocal promise for the future establishment of pensions about a month after the appearance of Booth's plan. Here the Chancellor reaffirmed his now-familiar concern for pensions, while emphasizing that neither he nor any of his colleagues had given 'any pledge at the elections on the subject of what is called old age pensions.'[116] Despite this, said Asquith:

> It is our hope—I will go further and say it is our intention, before the close of this Parliament, yes, before the close of the next session of this Parliament, if we are allowed to have our way (it is a large 'if')—to lay the firm foundations of this reform. . . .[117]

What the Chancellor meant by the 'firm foundations of this reform' he did not specify. His continual references, both public and private, to the financial difficulties of pensions suggested to many at the time that the Liberal pension plan, when it came, would be contributory. There are no documents among the Asquith papers to suggest that the Chancellor ever planned, or even seriously considered, a contributory pension scheme, but such a plan must have appeared attractive.[118] Nevertheless, Asquith's vagueness in his budget statement evoked an immediate response from the friendly societies. A little more than a month after budget day, in the third week of May, the major societies held their annual Whitweek conferences. Here was manifest all the old suspicion of government action and fear of government competition that Chamberlain had known. Pensions were described as a 'sop' and a system of 'general outdoor relief without the penalty of pauperism' by James Harford Hawkins, Grand Master of the Manchester Unity, in the society's annual conference at Folkestone. Several societies reminded the Government that Chamberlain had attempted to overcome, and had been baffled by, friendly society opposition, while stipulating that if pensions ever came they must be administered through the agency of the societies.[119]

---

[116] *Hansard*, CLXXII (April 18, 1907), col. 1191.   [117] *Ibid*.

[118] Reginald McKenna, discussing the proposal with Mrs Webb a few days later, stated that the plan under consideration was non-contributory. McKenna strove to give the Webbs the impression he was drawing up the plan. Webb, *Partnership*, pp. 379, 384. This appears most unlikely. He may have been involved during his time at the Treasury in 1906, but by the spring of 1907 he was at the Board of Education helping Robert Morant prepare for school medical inspection.

[119] Among Asquith's papers a long article from the *Morning Post* of May 21,

Even while opposition from the friendly societies solidified, pressure on the Government from other sources to enact pensions increased. On May 10, 1907, Mr W. H. Lever (the manufacturer of Lifebuoy soap, sitting at the time as the Liberal member for the Wirral division of Cheshire) introduced a Private Member's Bill providing a universal pension of 5s. a week payable upon application to persons of sixty-five years of age. Funds for the pension would be supplied by special income tax graduated from 2d. in the pound on incomes of £52 a year and increasing beyond the then standard rate of 1s. in the pound on incomes above £160 per year. Mr Lever's Bill never proceeded beyond the second reading, although the sympathy of the House of Commons for his principle was shown by the passage of the second reading 232 to 19, with many senior Liberals including the Chief Whip voting for the measure.[120]

Discontent with the Government's inability or unwillingness to pass measures demanded by the working class was now approaching a peak. In July, 1907, it burst into the open with two by-elections that not only made inevitable the passage of old age pensions but which inaugurated also a series of electoral disasters that would turn the Liberals to full-fledged social reform as a way of holding the party together. In the first eighteen months of office, the Liberal by-election record had generally been good. Of fifteen elections in seats with Liberal incumbents, the party had won twelve. Of those lost, one simply went to a miner who was unopposed by the Liberals as the result of an electoral arrangement, and another was regained by the Conservatives who had held it until 1906. But in the spring of 1907 the political climate was clearly changing. Even when they won, Liberal candidates no longer commanded safe majorities. There was a feeling 'of unreality about all the government proposes,' wrote Joseph Clayton in May, 1907. Everyone was doubting that old age pension promises would amount to anything.[121] A few weeks later came disaster. On

1907, containing the speeches of various society leaders were given. Several of the speeches, notably one by G. F. Howard of the Ancient Order of Shepherds, rejecting pensions outright, were outlined with red pencil. Asquith Papers, unsorted ('Papers on Old Age Pensions' on box).

[120] *Hansard*, CLXXIV (May 10, 1907), cols. 470–501.

[121] Joseph Clayton, 'The Failure of Liberalism,' *National Review*, XLIX (May, 1907), 390–4. Although he was writing in perhaps the most powerful opposition organ, Clayton was no Unionist, but the editor and proprietor of the brilliant guild socialist paper, *New Age*.

the fourth and the eighteenth of July the Liberals suffered totally unexpected defeats at Jarrow in Durham and Colne Valley in Yorkshire. There was much here to compare with Henderson's victory at Barnard Castle four years before. These too were in the north where the greatest turnover of voters had occurred in 1906. Both seats had also been held by old, well-known Liberal north country families. Sir Charles Palmer, of the Palmer Iron and Shipbuilding Works at Jarrow, had represented north Durham since 1874, and had been one of the very few Liberals unopposed in 1895 and 1900. In 1906 he had won the seat by 3,000 votes, a third more than his opponent. The election on July 4 caused by his death resulted in the loss of over half the Liberal vote so that the party was defeated even by the Conservative candidate, and the Labour candidate, Pete Curran, so heavily defeated before, was elected by a majority of 768.

The Liberal disaster on July 18 at Colne Valley was even more humiliating. Here the incumbent was Sir James Kitson, the manager of the Monkbridge Iron Works throughout his life. He had held the seat since 1892, defeating Tom Mann by over three to one in 1895, and had caused the vacancy by permitting himself to be raised to the peerage. The winner was Victor Grayson, a socialist eccentric who had not only refused to adopt the Labour Party platform, but who had neglected also to obtain trade union endorsement. The vote represented unmixed protest against the Liberal Government.[122]

In many ways the defeats by Labour in the summer of 1907 were more frightening than had been the great increase of Labour Party membership at the general election in 1906. Then the two parties had co-operated against the Unionists. Now the working class was demonstrating that the Liberal majority had been gained largely as a protest against the long and heedless Unionist tenure. The new Labour members meant nothing, of course, in terms of the Liberal parliamentary majority, but they symbolized the unrest of the working-class voter, for whom the old-fashioned Liberal slogans about economic opportunity and political equality were as out of date as the nineteenth-century Tory symbols of the crown, the land, and the Church.

The new attitude was clearly voiced by Alfred Gill, a member of

[122] For a discussion of this election, see Henry Pelling, *A Short History of the Labour Party*, London, 1961, pp. 22–3.

the Executive Committee of the textile workers, M.P. for his native city of Bolton, and president of the Trades Union Congress in 1907. In his address to the T.U.C. annual meeting at Bath on September 3, a little more than a month after the July defeats, Gill exulted and gloried in the power of labour. The Trade Disputes Bill, almost alone among the Liberal measures of 1906, had survived the House of Lords, he boasted, because the second chamber 'did not care to enter into battle with the organized workers.' Now, he said, labour wanted old age pensions. It was now the first plank in the T.U.C. platform. The pensions must be universal, non-contributory, and non-discriminatory. Labour would accept nothing less than 5s. per week beginning at sixty. Pensions, said Gill, would not cost as much as people said, but in any case this was unimportant.

It was no part of their duty to show how the money could be found. That was the function of a Chancellor of the Exchequer. If he would turn his attention to the unearned increment which had accrued to landlords from the land, the mining royalties which in other countries went to the State, but which were here appropriated by the landowner, the large fortunes which were left, and which had been made by the industry of the workers, he would find sources which could be legitimately tapped. Whatever was done, their course was clear. They must insist on the matter being dealt with in such a manner that the aged might end their declining years in peace and comfort. (Cheers)[123]

Three days later the T.U.C. passed a resolution introduced by G. N. Barnes, stating that the Congress 'demands' that the Chancellor of the Exchequer make provision in his budget for an old age pension to begin on January 1, 1909.[124]

In introducing his resolution, Barnes had taken note of the 'paltry scheme' recently made public by Lord Avebury, and had urged the Congress to reject it soundly by adopting his own resolution. The statement referred to a letter appearing in *The Times* on September 3, signed by Lord Avebury, a distinguished banker and man of science, accompanied by Sir William Chance,

[123] *The Times*, September 4, 1907. *The Times* leader that day remarked that the Chancellor of the Exchequer would be grateful 'for more practical advice' on where to find the money for pensions.

[124] *The Times*, September 7, 1907.

W. A. Bailward, Sir Edward Brabrook, and a number of others representing the Charity Organization Society–deterrent poor law point of view on social reform. The letter contained a proposal for a voluntary contributory pension plan administered through the friendly societies. Money paid in contributions to the societies would be deposited with the government, which would guarantee a fixed and profitable rate of interest. The letter cited James Harford Hawkins' address to the Manchester Unity at Folkestone on the previous May 20 as evidence that the societies would accept such a plan.

Avebury's suggestion was important, not only because it elicited a good deal of attention from the political opposition, who saw in it a last chance to head off tax-supported pensions, but because some members of the Government considered the proposal briefly as a means of avoiding the frighteningly high cost of tax-supported pensions.[125] Finally, perhaps most significant, was the fact that Avebury's plan (apparently Sir Edward Brabrook actually devised the scheme) was precisely that used in the much larger national health insurance scheme, which would have been out of the question financially on any other than a contributory principle.

Clearly the cheapness and simplicity of a contributory, voluntary pension plan administered by the friendly societies appealed to the politician in Herbert Asquith. Such an administration would avoid the creation of a large new bureaucracy. The contributions would obviate the need for increases in the budget. Friendly society suspicion of any government encroachment in their field would be allayed, and yet the ruinous burden of their elderly members would be lifted, at least in the future.

Roderick Meiklejohn was against all contributory schemes. Although the Leeds high court of the Foresters had carried unanimously a resolution that all new entrants to the society should subscribe for a 5s. pension, he wrote to Asquith on September 12, that it was significant that this requirement had not yet been adopted by the society's central high court. Moreover, he continued, the proposer of the motion, the permanent secretary of the Foresters, J. Lister Stead, had declared that the society did

[125] *The Times* published a laudatory three-column leader on Avebury's plan the day the letter appeared. The paper thought the programme ought to be tried but doubted that it would be. All political parties had already been forced to 'pledge themselves beyond recall' to tax-supported pensions, concluded *The Times*. *The Times*, September 3, 1907.

not intend to take the place of the State in providing old age pensions, but only to supplement a State system were it inaugurated. 'It is fairly certain, however,' said Meiklejohn,

> that the adoption of a scheme along the lines of Lord Avebury's would compete very seriously with Friendly Society business. It is true that the terms which the State would offer the societies (say 4 per cent) are advantageous but it would compel them to separate the funds intended for Old Age Annuities from the general body of funds. . . .
>
> No doubt the opposition of the Friendly Societies would disappear if the State voted them subsidies as is done in France and Belgium but as the Societies now do their work efficiently without such aid it would be difficult to defend such a policy.[126]

Roderick Meiklejohn was not the only one who opposed the idea of contributory pensions. In the Cabinet itself R. B. Haldane, who took a more active interest in pensions than he did in any other proposal of Liberal social reform, had produced a memorandum immediately after the appearance of the Avebury letter. On one hand he argued against Booth's universal pensions on the grounds that the requisite £26,000,000 to pay for them was out of the question, while at the same time he asserted that Lord Avebury's proposal would do the very poor no good for they would never qualify.[127] Basically Haldane thought of pensions not as a gratuity for old people but as a financial weapon with which to eradicate indigency at every age level. Pensions could also support others in need—the widow and the disabled who did not need institutional care.

From the pensionable, he thought, should be excluded children, the sick and infirm, those who would work but could not find it, and those for whom employment was available but who would not work. All care of children would be concentrated in a new local education authority. The sick would be lodged in hospitals managed by a health authority. For the genuinely unemployed there were to be labour exchanges and for the loafer, the workhouse. If any individual in these categories was receiving a pension, the sum should be paid to the institution caring for him.

[126] R. S. Meiklejohn to H. H. Asquith, September 12, 1907, Asquith Papers, unsorted ('Papers on Old Age Pensions').
[127] 'Old Age Pensions, Confidential,' September 6, 1907, Asquith Papers, unsorted ('Papers on Old Age Pensions').

Behind all of this was, of course, the thinking of Sidney and Beatrice Webb. In the next few months, Haldane bombarded his colleagues with the terse and factual arguments of his friends that a year and a half later would emerge as the framework of the prevention of destitution in the minority report of the Royal Commission on the Poor Laws.[128] For a means test they would substitute, in effect, a behaviour test.

Basically, the Webbs hoped to see State pensions fitted into the general scheme of reform of the poor law they were preparing. They wanted pensions made universal, that is, without any means or character test, simply because they felt it would be administratively 'quite impossible to exclude past paupers from pensions and practically impossible to exclude existing paupers.'[129] A previous criminal record should be no bar to a pension. It simply would add to the sentence. Withholding a pension from an unworthy person would not make him a good citizen.

> What is necessary (and required also for other reasons) is power to the local authority compulsorily to remove to an appropriate institution (as now for insane, & infectious disease cases) anyone found incapable of keeping himself decently clean and healthy: in short to prevent a public nuisance.[130]

The Webbs hoped to use the certain popularity of pensions as a weapon for promotion of their own plan for the break-up of English poor law institutions. They assumed, in common with most politicians in and out of the Government, that the crowning reform of the Asquith administration would be the complete overhauling of the system of parochial relief. When this occurred they hoped to see pensions made a part of the new scheme, to be used as an instrument of social control, rather than as a way for the lazy and improvident to avoid having to improve his behaviour.[131]

[128] Sidney Webb, 'Suggestions as to Old Age Pensions,' September 29, 1907; Sidney Webb, 'Some Arguments on Old Age Pensions,' n.d. (submitted with a Haldane letter dated December 17, 1907). Both of these memos are in the Asquith Papers, unsorted.

[129] S. Webb, 'Suggestions,' September 29, 1907. Inserted at this point in the margin of this typescript in Beatrice Webb's handwriting was the comment: 'But good financially.'

[130] *Ibid.*

[131] For a discussion of these considerations with an early outline of what would be the chief recommendations of the minority report, see Sidney Webb to R. B. Haldane, December 12, 1907, Asquith Papers, unsorted ('Papers on Old Age Pensions').

6

Uniformly, those demanding non-contributory pensions demanded also that they be 'universal.' This meant that pensions would be paid as of right to all meeting certain basic conditions of residence and citizenship and only those over the prescribed age who chose not to apply would fail to receive them. This was the ideal pension that Charles Booth had advocated from the beginning. It ought to be a perquisite of citizenship, he had always argued, like the right to petition Parliament or to use the courts. However, the nation whose pension plan provided the most important example for British advocates—indeed the nation whose adoption of pensions had caused the formation of the National Committee in 1899—was New Zealand, and that dominion placed a limit of £34 as the maximum independent income that a person claiming a full pension would be permitted to receive. Moreover, New Zealand required also considerable evidences of good character and industry from those applying for pensions.[132]

Once the essential desirability of non-contributory pensions was admitted, the question of eligibility and, hinging upon that, the question of finance, were basic. Here the precedent of New Zealand became important. On April 1, 1908, Asquith set out for the Cabinet in the final report of the committee of the Cabinet on pensions the logic behind the measure that eventually became the Old Age Pensions Act.[133] The three principles of British old age pensions, said Asquith, were that they must necessarily be experimental; that they must not 'mortgage finances'; and that in view of the approaching report of the Royal Commission on the Poor Law the system should be ready to 'harmonize' with changes in national systems of poor relief.

Contributory schemes were out of the question because a voluntary one would not help those who needed pensions most, and a compulsory one would not work because

. . . there is no practicable machinery by which, in a country such as this (whatever may be the case in Germany), it could be worked in face of the hostility of such competing collecting

[132] The dominion excluded Chinese and other orientals from pensions, even though they met all of the tests of eligibility.

[133] 'Old Age Pensions, Report of Committee of Cabinet, *Secret*,' April 1, 1908, Asquith Papers, unsorted ('Papers on Old Age Pensions').

bodies as the Trade Unions, Friendly Societies, Insurance Companies, &c.

If the scheme were to be non-contributory, the Chancellor continued, the cost would have to fall on the Exchequer, that is, upon national taxation. To put any burden upon local taxes would mean to distribute unequally the burden of pensions as the pensioners themselves were unequally distributed. The result, said Asquith, repeating almost *verbatim* an argument in Sidney Webb's memorandum of September 29, 1907, might be attempts by the local authorities to try to reduce the number of pensioners within their jurisdiction through some renewal of the pre-1834 Law of Settlement.

However, if the whole burden was to fall upon the national treasury, ' "universal" schemes, such as that put forward by Mr Charles Booth, are out of the question.' They were too expensive, said Asquith, and worse, no one could tell how expensive. No one knew how many of the middle and upper classes would fail to claim pensions. A universal scheme, thought Asquith, might cost £16,000,000 at age seventy or £27,000,000 beginning at age sixty-five, which sums 'are obviously prohibitive.'

If the scheme were to discriminate among applicants and choose the most worthy, the relevant conditions would be age, means, status, and character. The age, he continued, would have to be higher than sixty-five simply to reduce the number of pensions payable. All figures were, of course, conjectural, but assuming a 10s. per week income limit, he calculated there would be 1,137,984 people pensionable at sixty-five, and 860,881 pensionable if the age were raised to seventy. So far as status was concerned, continued the Chancellor, the pensioner would have to be a British citizen of some standing, say ten or twenty years. Convicted criminals would, of course, be excluded, but what of paupers? The reduction of pauperism had been the first, and the most widely used, argument in favour of old age pensions. Moreover, it cost nearly as much per week to maintain a pauper in the workhouse, almost 5s., as was contemplated for old age pensions. (The ordinary grant of outdoor relief, with attendant expenses, was less than half this amount.) But even though the basic moral justification for any State pension was that it would remove inoffensive old people, whose only crime was inability to work, from a degrading situation that had been designed to deter people from applying for relief, Asquith concluded that for the immediate future at least those presently receiving poor law relief would be ineligible for pensions. 'It appears to us,' he concluded,

> in view of the forthcoming report of the Poor Law Commission, to be the best plan, for the moment and provisionally, to exclude at any rate all actual paupers from the scheme.[134]

So far as a test for character was concerned, Asquith himself, echoing again the thinking of the Webbs, urged that there be no test short of actual conviction of a crime, although he admitted that misconduct after the grant of a pension might be another matter.

With these exclusions, then, for age, means, status, and character, Asquith estimated that the number pensionable at sixty-five would be reduced to 936,984, who could be given a 5s. pension at a cost of £12,180,792 or, at seventy, there would be 572,381 who would cost £7,440,953. This was the pension scheme he recommended to the Cabinet in his last days as Chancellor of the Exchequer, upon which he and his staff at the Treasury had been working for the past half-year.

Basically, Asquith's report represented a compromise between the pressures of those who were attempting to promote a simple universal pension scheme, with no exclusions and few administrative problems, and those for whom thrift represented the highest form of morality and to whom any form of indiscriminative welfare activity, public or private, was an anathema. On one side were the National Committee, the trade unions, the Webbs, the prestige, if not the person, of Charles Booth, and the radical Liberal reformers in general. On the other, less numerous, but hardly less influential, where what was left of Gladstonian Liberalism—north country manufacturing families, many leaders in the friendly society movement, a large number of higher civil servants, and the Charity Organisation Society.

---

[134] 'Old Age Pensions, Report of Committee of Cabinet, *Secret*,' April 1, 1908, Asquith Papers, unsorted ('Papers on Old Age Pensions'). It has been suggested occasionally that the exclusion of paupers from pensions was the result of a continuing tradition of deterrence into the legislation of the New Liberalism. Asquith's statement here makes clear that the exclusion of paupers was only an expedient until the Government could make up its mind, as the Webbs hoped it soon would do, about fitting pensions into the reconstruction of all poor relief. As it turned out, this was never accomplished.

The Charity Organisation Society had fought State pensions of all kinds from the beginning.[135] As pensions appeared more and more inevitable, the society sought to narrow the coverage of proposed plans and to insert stipulations of the sort it normally imposed on the character and good behaviour of applicants. In this the society received strong support from the permanent staff of the Local Government Board which included, as every reformer knew, many crusaders for old-fashioned *laissez faire* Liberalism. It had been pressure from the civil service for the return to a strictly deterrent poor law, led by the head of the poor law division, James Stuart Davey, that had caused in the first place the appointment of the Royal Commission on the Poor Laws. Now, the people who had wished to see the workhouse test imposed on every applicant for parochial relief sought to make as stringent as possible the conditions for the award of State-financed old age pensions.

Well before the end of 1907, the National Committee recognized that the pension under consideration at the Treasury would be far from universal. Stead, who was continually suspicious of the underground activities of the opponents of reform in the civil service, addressed a strong, rather crude, letter to Asquith on December 14. In it the warden of Browning Hall asked the Chancellor of the Exchequer whether 'the pressure of forces which move in darkness and operate under cover of fiscal difficulties' would be permitted to dilute Asquith's promise of November 20, 1906, that old age pensions, when they came, would be universal, non-contributory, and separate from the poor law. Stead reminded Asquith of the growing strength of the Labour Party, noting that the workers were 'disgusted' with both Liberals and Conservatives. He suggested there was danger that the Government might have to 'repeat the experience of Jarrow and Colne Valley in most of the great Industrial Centres.' Workers in many places, he said, were most disappointed that pensions were only a 'meagre beginning. . .' He asked whether the effect of such a Bill might not be to make 'the masses of the people wonder whether any great Social Reform

---

[135] Loch organized 'The Committee on Old-Age Pensions' with W. A. Bailward as secretary and Sir William Chance as treasurer, which sought to organize a counter-movement to the National Committee. See, for instance: Frederick Rogers and Frederick Millar, *Old Age Pensions Are They Desirable and Practicable: Pro and Con*, London, 1903. More typical is: *Old Age Pensions, The Case Against Old-Age Pension Schemes*, London, 1903. (A collection of papers by members of the committee, mostly by Loch, Bailward and John Martineau.)

can be secured on a Free Trade basis' with the result that they would turn to 'other executants of the national will.'[136]

Now that the Government was committed to pensions, Asquith was in a position to ignore even the most ill-tempered letters from the National Committee.[137] The National Committee and the trade unions could not reasonably oppose a Pension Bill, even a meagre one. They would have to take whatever portion the Government chose to offer, and then agitate for its extension. Pensions of any sort were bound to be popular. Indeed, for some hardened realists among the Liberals, the rights and wrongs of pensions were irrelevant; it was a matter of buying votes.[138] But Stead's fears that Asquith would be subject to pressures to raise eligibility and reduce coverage of pensions were perfectly justified. Once serious planning of the Bill began in the autumn of 1907, the Treasury was continually beset with memoranda from the Local Government Board (John Burns had expected to frame the Bill himself) proposing various restrictions on pensions. The board proposed, for instance, that all who had received poor relief for twenty years be declared ineligible for pensions.[139] The board argued that Asquith's maximum income limit of 10s. per week was too high and urged a maximum limit of 7s. 6d.[140] Finally, the board succeeded in inserting in Clause 8 (1) of the Bill the provision that members of the local pension committee, which would have the authority to administer the tests of industry written into the measure, need not be made up exclusively of members of the appointing authority, that is members of the local borough, urban district, or county council. Stead assumed this provision to be a means for securing the appointment to the committee of members of the Charity Organisation Society, who would be interested in the strict application of character tests.[141]

---

[136] F. Herbert Stead to H. H. Asquith, December 14, 1907, Asquith Papers, unsorted ('Papers on Old Age Pensions').

[137] Stead's letter was simply endorsed in pencil, 'I thanked, 17/12, R.S.M.'

[138] David Lloyd George wrote to his brother in precisely these terms on May 6, 1908, the day before Asquith's budget speech, which contained the first full-scale description of the Pension Bill. 'It is time we did something that appealed straight to the people—it will, I think, help to stop this electoral rot, and that is most necessary.' William George, *My Brother and I*, London, 1958, p. 220.

[139] R. S. Meiklejohn to H. H. Asquith, November 27, 1907, Asquith Papers, unsorted ('Papers on Old Age Pensions').

[140] Report of Committee of Cabinet, April 1, 1908, p. 5.

[141] Stead, *Old Age Pensions*, p. 256.

So far as they were willing to sanction government activity at all, the Charity Organisation Society and its allies would have supported a voluntary, contributory pension, along the lines of the Avebury scheme. The fact of an individual working man's continued contribution into a friendly society fund would have, by itself, provided a sufficient test of thrift.[142]

The influence of the Charity Organisation Society upon the Old Age Pensions Bill would undoubtedly have been greater had the society been able to effect an alliance with the friendly societies, whose belief in the restriction of government activity in the welfare field was as firm as its own. The friendly societies, which had played so great a part in destroying the movement toward old age pensions in the eighteen-nineties, were uncharacteristically quiescent in the last years before the passage of the Pension Act. This can only be attributed to the widening realization of the precariousness of the societies' economic situation and to the reluctant understanding among major society leaders that a non-contributory pension, although opposed in principle, represented at least a partial means of rescue. Hence the friendly society movement was divided on pensions in the years between 1906 and 1908 and took little part in the controversy toward shaping them.

The officials of the large societies were aware that pensions would have to come and that they would benefit the societies, but they dared not say so. In the last of several surveys of major societies in January, 1908, the Chief Registrar asked: 'Will, in your opinion, the passing of a Non-Contributory Bill conferring Old Age Pensions have an injurious effect on Friendly Societies?' One hundred and fifty-one societies replied. Of these, sixty-seven answered yes, sixty-four no. Twenty societies, while returning the form sent to them, refused to answer the question. Among these was the Manchester Unity. The other of the largest societies, the Foresters, answered that a non-contributory pension would not hurt them, but that a contributory scheme would. The ambivalence of society opinion may be illustrated by the statement of the Northumberland and Durham Miners' Relief Fund, which replied: 'The scheme of Old Age Pensions is one that we could not say anything in opposition to; its effect upon the Society will be detrimental.' While the number of societies for and against the

---

[142] This test became a government amendment to the Bill.

Bill were almost equal, the largest societies either approved the measure or at least declined to oppose it.[143]

Thus the friendly societies, whose attitudes towards old age pensions had been so important a determinant of government policy in the past, gave up any chance to influence the old age pension scheme that finally was established. The societies quickly understood that they had both lost prestige and damaged the position of their members by standing aloof from the planning of old age pensions. Particularly, they failed to get an exemption of friendly society benefits when calculating income for old age pensions. A very important result of this awareness for the future was the societies' early determination to participate from the beginning in the planning of national health insurance.[144]

7

The long-awaited public commitment to old age pensions occurred at last in the speech from the throne on January 29, 1908.[145] The statement itself excited little controversy; Balfour did not comment upon it in his answering address. Of interest was the fact that the pension announcement occurred in the portion of the King's Speech invariably addressed only to the members of the House of Commons, reserved for mention of the estimates. As Stead had urged, the Government was giving notice that pensions were a money Bill, not to be tampered with by the House of Lords. The only criticism came from Arthur Henderson, who inquired whether the proposed pensions were to be universal and reminded Asquith that during the famous interview on November 20, 1906, he had stated that the 'only satisfactory method of dealing with the question was a universal plan. . . .'[146]

The public presentation of the Old Age Pensions Bill occurred in two stages. The first was on May 7, 1908, in Asquith's explanation

[143] 'Circular letter issued by Chief Registrar of Friendly Societies to the principal Societies with questions on the proposed non-contributory scheme of Old Age Pensions,' January 17, 1908 (printed June 15, 1908), *Accounts and Papers*, 1908, LXXVIII, 177.

[144] For a general discussion of the lessons learned by the friendly societies on old age pensions, see: *Resolutions of the Annual Meeting of the National Conference of Friendly Societies*, October 14, 15, 1909, 'Report of Parliamentary Agents W. Marlow and W. G. Bunn,' pp. 25–7.

[145] *Hansard*, CLXXXIII (January 29, 1908), col. 4.

[146] *Ibid.*, col. 167.

of the budget, which he undertook even though he was now Prime Minister, and the second on June 15 when David Lloyd George moved the second reading of the measure.[147] Asquith's speech in many places repeated almost *verbatim* the April 1 Cabinet Memorandum and generally carried out the intent of that memorandum in explaining the logic behind the form of the Bill. Both he and David Lloyd George emphasized that the Bill they were presenting was only the beginning, a foundation upon which a larger framework of old age security would eventually be built after the means for dealing with paupers had been settled.

The Bill itself was simple. As introduced it provided for the payment of an old age pension of 5s. per week to all individuals who had reached the age of seventy, who had been a British subject and a resident of the United Kingdom for twenty years, and whose income did not exceed £26 per year. Married couples, estimated to be one-fourth of the total number of pensioners, would receive 7s. 6d., rather than twice the pension of a single individual, and would be permitted a maximum of £39 per year.

The applicant for pensions was required to prove that he had not been in prison within ten years (amended in 1911 to two years), that he was not a lunatic, that he was not receiving poor relief and, in addition, that he had not received poor relief that disqualified him as a parliamentary elector (in effect all but medical relief) at any time since January 1, 1908. Finally the applicant had to prove that he had been 'habitually' employed in the trade of his choice.

Pensions were to be paid on Friday through the Post Office. The Act specified that the receipt of a pension would not deprive the pensioner of any civil franchise, right, or privilege. The determination of eligibility was the responsibility of local pension committees, which would be appointed by every county council, and by the council of every borough and urban district with a population of 20,000 or more. The findings of the committee could be reviewed by the pension officers appointed by the Treasury. The Act would apply also to Scotland and Ireland.

Unionist opposition to the Bill was weak and embarrassed by the party's own failure on pensions. The leadership had agreed on June 4 not to move an amendment against the Bill, but to accept it

[147] *Hansard*, CLXXXVIII (May 7, 1908), cols. 453–76; *Ibid.*, CXC (June 15, 1908), cols. 564–86.

as an instalment on a future contributory scheme.[148] Far from
attempting to prevent the passage of the Old Age Pensions Bill,
the Unionist tactic generally was to try to extend its coverage.
Fear that government pensions would harm friendly societies
represented the chief argument of the first opposition speaker,
Henry Chaplin, during the second reading. Chaplin noted that the
Manchester Unity the previous week had passed a resolution
approving the pensions but arguing that no one should be deprived
of a pension because of friendly society benefits.[149] Eventually the
Unionists moved as their chief attempt to wreck the Bill an
amendment to exclude the first £40 of friendly society sick benefits
from any calculation of income for purposes of pensions. While this
amendment was under discussion, Henry Chaplin attempted to
add a further amendment excluding income from any private
provision made for sickness or infirmity, including individual
savings.[150] The debate on this amendment demonstrated the very
real disappointment and chagrin among the Unionists for having
failed to deal with old age pensions. A. J. Balfour, in an uncharacteristically passionate speech, charged the Government with
being 'determined to sacrifice the friendly societies upon the altar
of logic. . . .' For this he was sharply called to order.[151]

The Old Age Pensions Bill was modified in two important ways
by the House of Commons. The first was the elimination of the
flat cut-off of £26 per year, or 10s. per week for eligibility for pensions. Lloyd George had suggested during the second reading that
he might be prepared to consider an amendment for a sliding scale
if, as it appeared, this was the desire of a large number of members.[152] An amendment to this effect was introduced during the
committee stage and received support from many members of
both major parties. However, the effect of the amendment was to
reduce the maximum income to be permitted a recipient of the
full pension from £26 per year to £21 or slightly more than 8s. per
week. In the other direction it extended the maximum income for a
reduced pension to £31 10s. At the old limit of £26 the pensioner
would receive 3s. The major resistance to this change came from
Labour members who argued that they and their supporters

[148] Austen Chamberlain, *Politics From Inside*, London, 1936, p. 118.
[149] *Hansard*, CXC (June 15, 1908), cols. 590–6.
[150] *Ibid.*, CXCI (June 30, 1908), cols. 633–60.
[151] *Ibid.*, col. 654.   [152] *Ibid.*, CXC (June 15, 1908), col. 569.

regarded a 5s. pension for those who had an income of not more than 10s. per week as an absolute minimum and that a reduction of the maximum to 8s. shillings was a breach of faith. The amendment was eventually carried by a large majority with the Liberals and Unionists voting together against the Labour Party.[153] The introduction of the sliding scale may be taken as the principal contribution of David Lloyd George to the Old Age Pensions Bill. Asquith had argued strongly against this provision in his April 1 memorandum on the basis that pensions were already small, and that to provide for the payment of amounts of less than 5s. would be unreasonable.[154]

The other large change made by the House of Commons in the Bill as introduced was the elimination of the reduction of pensions for couples in one household. In this, as in the introduction of the sliding scale, David Lloyd George received pressure from both sides of the House. The chief argument against the provision was that it would greatly increase the cost of pensions. Asquith had estimated that one-quarter of all pensioners would be couples falling within the class receiving the reduced pension of 3s. 9d. each, instead of 5s.[155] Lloyd George agreed only reluctantly to abolish the reduced pension with the proviso that the party would support him on all other measures of economy.[156] One may assume that this rather considerable expansion of the cost of the programme reinforced the Government's determination to make no concession on the amendment to exclude friendly society benefits when calculating an applicant's income for pension purposes, even though since 1902 it had been mandatory for boards of guardians to do precisely this when granting poor law relief.

The only other amendments of significance were the limitation to two years after January 1, 1908, of the period during which a previous acceptance of poor law relief disqualified an applicant for pensions and in addition two others put down by the Government and passed without discussion under closure.[157] The first of

[153] *Hansard*, CXC (June 23, 1908), cols. 1583–1626.

[154] Report of Committee of Cabinet, April 1, 1908, pp. 9–10.

[155] To increase by one-third the pensions of one-quarter of all pensioners would mean to increase the total cost of the programme by over 8 per cent.

[156] *Hansard*, CXC (June 24, 1908), col. 1791.

[157] Lloyd George explained that the acceptance of the two-year limitation was in the nature of a promise by the Government to overhaul the poor law before the end of the period. *Ibid.*, CXCI (July 7, 1908), cols. 1543–4.

these made specific the right of pensioners to receive poor law medical relief without losing eligibility for pensions, and the second permitted contributions to friendly societies to fulfil the industry test required in the Bill. The exclusion of poor law medical relief as a disability was in line with the growing importance of the poor law medical service. Since 1885, with the Medical Relief (Disqualification Removal) Act, poor law medical relief had carried none of the civil disabilities that ordinarily accompanied parochial relief except, until 1918, the loss of franchise in voting for boards of guardians. Consequently, the poor law medical service had grown in importance and efficiency so that by 1908 it was the ordinary resort for large numbers of elderly people who without this provision, which was actually an amplificaiton of a section of the original Bill, would have lost their pensions when they became sick.

The acceptance of friendly society contributions as an adequate fulfilment of the industry test may only be interpreted as an obeisance to the societies and a recognition of their general discontent with the Old Age Pensions Bill. In any case, the industry test proved to be unworkable and was dropped as a requirement in 1919.[158] The tactic of the Opposition in the House of Commons had been to attempt to extend the Old Age Pensions Bill beyond the limits of prudent finance. 'To overballast the ship so that it would sink,' remarked David Lloyd George on several occasions. The Unionists had no wish to see the Liberals receive credit for a programme that should long since have been their own. But still less did they desire to appear in the constituencies as the opponent of a programme so sure to be popular as old age pensions. Hence, their opposition in the lower chamber was feeble and irresponsible.

The House of Lords showed no such hesitation. There the Bill was roundly criticized both on the grounds of expense and as a vast extension of charity that would lead to the demoralization of the working classes. An amendment by the Earl of Wemyss to delay further consideration of the Bill until the Royal Commission on the Poor Laws had reported was rejected 123 to 16. But two other amendments of importance were carried, one by Lord Cromer to end the granting of new pensions on December 31, 1915 (although all existing pensions would be continued), and one by Viscount St Aldwyn to delete the House of Commons amendment

---

[158] *Hansard*, CXCI (June 29, 1908), cols. 481–2.

that had ended the disqualification of previous recipients of poor law relief on December 31, 1910.[159]

The peers' action had been, of course, anticipated by the pension supporters and Asquith's unusual designation of pensions as a money Bill had been designed to deal with this contingency. Accordingly, upon the official advice of the Speaker that the Lords' amendments contravened the privileges of the House of Commons, their changes in the Old Age Pensions Bill were rejected.[160] The Act received the royal assent on August 1, 1908.

8

The Act had stipulated that the payment of pensions would begin on January 1, 1909. All evidence attests their profound importance in helping to lift the burden of hopelessness and insecurity from the lives of the aged. To the aged poor it seemed unbelievable that one could collect 5s. simply by coming to the post office on Friday. Particularly in the country villages, unsuspecting post-mistresses found themselves showered with apples and flowers from pensioners' gardens in gratitude for the simple act of distributing money.[161]

'Often 'ave we thought as 'ow it would be a-best for us to go,' the husband of an old couple over ninety told an investigator from the *Nation*,

> and sometimes a-most 'ave I prayed to be took; for we was only a burden to our children as kep' us; for they be good and wouldna let us go on the parish so long as they could 'elp it. But now we want to go on livin' forever, 'cus we gives 'en the ten shillin' a week, and it pays 'em to 'ave us along with 'em. I never thought

[159] *Hansard*, CXCIII (July 28, 1908), cols. 1093–4, cols 1118–20.

[160] *Ibid.*, CXCIII (July 31, 1908), cols. 1970, 1974. The Commons' action provoked a fierce attack upon the lower house by Lord Lansdowne, the Unionist leader in the House of Lords, whose ferocity was a harbinger of the bitterness that would grow up over the Parliament Act. The Commons' action was a 'most extreme interpretation of the doctrine of privilege,' said Lansdowne. The Lords followed this with an unprecedented action, passing a resolution condemning the lower chamber for its designation of the Old Age Pensions Bill as a money Bill inasmuch as it 'involves questions of policy . . . with which this House has been in the past accustomed to deal.' *Hansard*, CXCIII (July 31, 1908), cols. 1914, 1919.

[161] See, for instance, the passage in Flora Thompson's *Lark Rise*. Quoted in Maurice Bruce, *The Coming of the Welfare State*, London, 1961, p. 155.

we should be able to pay the boy back for au 'is goodness to me and the missis; but times change sir.[162]

Nowhere were pensions more appreciated than in Ireland. Indeed, their enactment was considered by J. L. Garvin to be 'a concrete guarantee of the union.'[163] Unfortunately, there had been no official registration of births in Ireland prior to 1865. Parish records were in the hands of the Church of England, which the Irish peasantry did not attend, and Roman Catholic baptismal and confirmation records were chaotic and incomplete. As a result, pensions frequently had to be granted on the sketchiest evidence. Augustine Birrell, who as Irish Secretary was also president of the Irish Local Government Board, and had therefore the duty of supervising pension administration in the other island, tells of the remarkable number of people who recalled their parents telling them that they had been born in the year of 'the big wind.' This was 1839, which would make them just eligible for pensions.[164]

The generosity of the pension administration in Ireland came quickly to the attention of British observers. At the end of March, 1910, the Postmaster-General reported that 411,489 pensions were being paid in England and Wales as of December 31, 1910, 76,889 in Scotland, and 180,974 in Ireland. The astonishing factor in these statistics was that while 44·7 per cent of all those of seventy years or older were receiving pensions in England and 53·8 per cent in Scotland, 98·6 per cent of the total population over seventy did so in Ireland. As pensions were to go only to those who earned less than 10s. a week, or at least less than 12s. per week, this figure suggested that only 1·4 per cent of the population of Ireland over the age of seventy was earning sufficient income to make them ineligible for pensions. Moreover, since all estimates agreed that nearly one-third of all those over seventy were on relief at any one time, and the Pension Act stipulated that anyone who had received relief between January 1, 1908, and December 31, 1910, should be excluded from pensions, clearly a large number in Ireland were receiving pensions who were not entitled to them.[165]

---

[162] Hugh Aronson, 'Liberalism in the Village,' *Nation*, May 18, 1912.

[163] J. L. Garvin to John Sandars, January 27, 1910, British Museum, Add. MSS. 49795, Balfour Papers, Vol. CXIII, f. 51.

[164] Augustine Birrell, *Things Past Redress*, London, 1937, pp. 210-11.

[165] See: Noel A. Humphreys, 'Old Age Pensions in the United Kingdom,' *Journal of the Royal Statistical Society*, LXXIV (December, 1910), 71-3.

With the ending of the period of disqualification for those who had received poor relief during 1909 and 1910 the pension situation in Ireland began to approach the ludicrous. John Bradbury, at that time a junior civil servant in the Treasury, discovered that the pension return of March, 1911, the first after the removal of the poor law disqualification, showed 201,783 pensioners in Ireland receiving what would amount on a yearly basis to pensions worth £2,585,428.[166] The new census of 1911, remarked Bradbury without comment, indicated that in the whole island, without regard to questions of poor relief or income, there were only 191,720 people over seventy.[167]

The best theoretical argument for old age pensions had always been that pensions would reduce pauperism among the aged by providing an alternative to the degradation of the poor law and would aid the ratepayer by shifting the costs of parochial relief to the Exchequer. There were many, nevertheless, who had warned before and during the passage of the Bill that a substantial reduction in the cost of the poor law was unlikely. A very large proportion of paupers over seventy, it was pointed out—certainly the most expensive proportion—were those receiving indoor relief in the workhouse, or more frequently in the workhouse infirmary, because they were unable to care for themselves and had no relatives.[168]

[166] John Swanwick Bradbury, 1872–1950, born, Manchester; educated Manchester Grammar School and Brasenose College, Oxford; entered civil service at Treasury, 1897; national health insurance joint committee, 1911–13; Joint Permanent Secretary to Treasury, 1913–19; Principal British Delegate to Reparations Commission, 1919–25; Chairman National Food Council, 1925–9. Immortalized name 'Bradburys' with Treasury notes issued upon outbreak of war to meet demand for currency, which were signed by him. Created Baron, 1925.

[167] Memorandum by John Bradbury, undated, Public Record Office, Treasury, Bradbury Papers, T170/5.

[168] The Local Government Board made an intensive investigation of three unions in the summer of 1908 to ascertain the effect of old age pensions on the poor law. The general finding was that because the usual grant of outdoor relief in these parishes was between 2s. 6d. and 3s. 6d. per week, all recipients of relief would, of course, apply for a 5s. pension. As the number on outdoor relief over seventy years of age was about 73 per cent of the total, the saving on outdoor relief would be important. But with indoor relief the situation was altogether different. Of those over seventy in the workhouse, very few said they would leave for a grant of pensions; and of those who looked forward to leaving, fewer still, the parish officials intimated, could be trusted away from supervision. See memorandum by E. B. Wothered, June 11, 1908, Bill File, Old Age Pensions, Ministry of Pensions and National Insurance Library.

The effect of pensions was indeed practically to eliminate out-door relief to those over seventy. Between the years 1906 and 1913 the number receiving parish relief outside the workhouse in England and Wales fell by 159,533 or 94·9 per cent.[169] But with indoor relief the effect of pensions was far less marked. Here the fall in absolute numbers was 12,171, for a decrease between 1906 and 1913 of 19·8 per cent.[170] In fact, in some counties—Middlesex, Westmorland, Brecknock, and Pembroke—the number of indoor paupers actually increased.[171]

Perhaps, however, the best indicators of the impact of old age pensions on pauperism are the figures of local authorities' expendi-ture for poor relief. Here the effect is noticeable, but certainly not large. Expenditure for poor relief by English and Welsh local authorities had grown fairly steadily in regular increments from £10,700,000 in 1903 to a pre-war peak of £12,500,000 in 1911. In 1912, the first year to feel the full effect of the ending of pauper disqualification for pensions, the figure fell to £11,900,000, but it increased again to £12,300,000 for both 1913 and 1914.[172] The saving even of £600,000 between 1911 and 1912 obviously meant

[169] *Cd. 7015*, 'Old Age Pensioners and Aged Pauperism,' 1913, p. 3. The year 1906 is used in these calculations because before the advent of old age pensions no separate statistics were kept on the age of paupers. In that year a special return was prepared for the Royal Commission on the Poor Laws.

[170] On March 31, 1906, there had been 168,096 persons over the age of seventy on outdoor relief and 61,378 on indoor relief in England and Wales. At the beginning of the years 1910 to 1913 these figures were:

Years	Outdoor Relief Over Age Seventy	Indoor Relief Over Age Seventy
1910	138,223	57,701
1911	93,177	55,261
1912	9,530	49,370
1913	8,563	49,207

Ibid., p. 3.

[171] *Ibid.*, p. 9. There was little co-operation between guardians and pension committees. Geoffrey Drage pointed out that it became the custom for aged paupers to allow their pensions to accumulate during periods in the workhouse and then to draw a lump sum during a short, and riotous, period at liberty. Clearly this was done on a large scale in Ireland. Drage, *The State and the Poor*, p. 100. For a full discussion of the impact of pensions on poor relief based principally on the figures in *Cd. 7015*, see: Helen L. Witmer, 'The Influence of Old Age Pensions on Public Poor Relief in England and Wales,' *Social Service Review*, IV (December, 1930), 587–607.

[172] Mitchell, *Historical Statistics*, pp. 416–18.

little when the national expenditure on pensions in the latter year had grown to £11,700,000.[173]

During the passage of the Old Age Pensions Bill, every government speaker had emphasized that the measure under consideration was only a beginning. Almost immediately, therefore, well before the impact of pensions could be assayed, men in and out of the Government were thinking and planning for their extension. Among the most interested were the friendly societies, which continued to press for the exclusion of society benefits from income calculations. The societies realized immediately that non-contributory pensions did them no harm and potentially could do them a great deal of good.[174] The societies urged also that the pensionable age be reduced from seventy to sixty-five.[175]

But perhaps the person most interested in the extension of the pension programme was David Lloyd George. Although he had had nothing to do with the formulation of the measure, he appears to have envisioned immediately the possibility of a vast extension of the pension principle, in one form or another, to other classes of the population who were as susceptible to pauperism as the aged. Citizens over seventy were unquestionably worthy of State support, but they represented by no means the only group unable to maintain themselves. At the end of his second reading speech introducing the Bill, the Chancellor had mentioned 'the problems

[173] Expenditures on pensions far outstripped the six or seven million pounds Asquith had estimated in the April 1 memorandum. By 1914 the Government was spending £12,500,000 on pensions, not far short of the £16,000,000 he had estimated to be the 'prohibitive' cost of a universal pension at age seventy. 'Report of Committee of Cabinet,' April 1, 1908, p. 3.

[174] Alfred Watson suggested early in 1909 that the immediate effect of pensions, particularly in rural districts, might be to slow down the search for employment among the elderly and so to keep up, or perhaps increase, claims on sickness benefits. The task of those interested in the welfare of the friendly societies, he said, was to begin to press for the official ending of sickness benefits at seventy, or at least for their conversion into whatever annuity was appropriate for available reserves. He expected that society leaders would soon begin to do this and that 'all kinds of sentimental objections would be set up . . .' and for a time at least nothing would be done. Vyvyan Marr, 'Some Financial Considerations of the Old Age Pension Scheme,' *Journal of the Institute of Actuaries*, XLIII (July, 1909), discussion, 277.

[175] For representative attitudes on pensions after the passage of the Act, see, The Presidential Address of George Wilde, Secretary of the Grand United Order of Odd Fellows, before the National Conference of Friendly Societies: October 14, 1909, *Resolutions of the Annual Meeting of the National Conference of Friendly Societies*, October 14–15, 1909, p. 9. See also, Secretary's Report, *Resolutions of the National Conference of Friendly Societies*, October 13–14, 1910.

of the sick and infirm,' and of the unemployed, with which 'it is the business of the State to deal; they are problems the State in both these cases has neglected too long.'[176] These equally deserving and more numerous groups in society might soon be demanding State-aided maintenance. If given on a non-contributory basis, this would have been monumentally expensive. This knowledge may have driven David Lloyd George to the consideration of a wide extension of contributory pensions, even though during the second reading debate he had condemned this form of welfare at length.[177]

The German plan for contributory pensions of 1889 had included provisions for support in case of the chronic invalidity of the wage earner and for the return of the working man's contribution to his widow and orphans under the age of fifteen, should he die before pensionable age. Whether Lloyd George had his attention drawn to the German programme by Churchill, which seems likely in view of the intimacy that had grown between the two men since Churchill's entrance into the Cabinet in the spring of 1908, or whether Lloyd George was affected by the widespread interest in the German pension plan without any particular adviser in the subject, his famous journey to the Continent in the third week of August was clearly instigated by a desire to study the German pension system. The entire British national insurance programme would come out of it; everything indeed except an extension of pensions. But its original aim was certainly pensions for widows and orphans and for the wage earner when he was disabled before the regular pension age. All of these appeared as part of the original health insurance scheme.

Lloyd George had confided the intention of his journey to no one. There was a good deal of speculation in the European press and within the British Cabinet that he had undertaken an unauthorized diplomatic mission aimed at reducing naval tension between the two countries. On August 21, he was forced to telegraph the Prime Minister, assuring him that he did not

propose approaching anyone on the international question. I am confining my investigation exclusively to invalid and other

[176] *Hansard*, CXC (June 15, 1908), col. 585.
[177] *Ibid.*, cols. 567–8.

pensions but I have discovered a good deal about the situation. . . .[178]

By the time of the Chancellor's return, the original simple pension scheme had grown to form a large social insurance plan
including health insurance as well as unemployment insurance.
But for Lloyd George and his intimates, pensions were at the
beginning, the core of the programme.[179]

The story of the establishment of health and unemployment
insurance constitutes the remainder of this study. They were
chiefly the work of two men who had had little contact previously
with the advanced social reformers and socialist intellectuals who
had been the promoters of the measures so far discussed.[180] The
National Insurance Act of 1911 was, to be sure, far more than an
extension of the Old Age Pensions Act of 1908, but the principle
of social insurance, 'the magic of averages' as Winston Churchill
would call it, came from Germany, whither Lloyd George had
gone first to find an answer to the problem of the extension of old
age pensions. Social insurance was a departure from the course of
development of all previous English reform. It had been decisively
rejected for pensions. Now these two politicians, not hitherto
prominent among the inner circle of social reformers, would use it
to begin a second phase of the New Liberalism, and in doing so lay
the foundations of the British welfare state.

[178] David Lloyd George to H. H. Asquith, August 21, 1908, Asquith Papers,
Box 11, ff. 146–7. This telegram was in reply to one from Asquith the previous
day telling Lloyd George not to speak to the emperor on the subject of modification of the German naval programme as his imperial majesty had become rather
sensitive about it.

[179] See the references to contributory pensions in George Allardice, Baron
Riddell, *More Pages From My Diary, 1908–1914*, London, 1934, p. 6.
As he became more deeply involved with national insurance the Chancellor
apparently came to resent non-contributory pensions. In a conversation with
Arnold White on September 7, 1911, he remarked that if half the money
'squandered' on non-contributory pensions had been spent on housing, some
people might have been helped. The reader should remember, however, that
White, a notorious sycophant, was sending the notes of his conversation to
Austen Chamberlain, who was a strong supporter of contributory pensions.
Arnold White to Austen Chamberlain, October 4, 1911, Austen Chamberlain
Papers, AC9/21.

[180] David Lloyd George had, however, sat on both select committees on
pensions in 1899 and 1903.

exchanges and unemployment insurance. Social thinkers now began to attend the problems of the mature worker, whom politicians had always agreed should be left, except for the workhouse, to shift for himself, no matter what legislative protection was given to women, children, and the elderly. Finally, in the attack on unemployment the New Liberalism moved to a second, pioneering, stage. The issues of child welfare and old age pensions, driven through Parliament by momentum built up long before Sir Henry Campbell-Bannerman came to power, were now resolved. The new measures were more experimental, more creative, and more hazardous. Their form owed little to extra-parliamentary discussion, as had, for instance, old age pensions. They owed nothing, indeed contradicted, the proposals of Sidney and Beatrice Webb and the minority report of the Royal Commission on the Poor Laws, which was published in February, 1909, just as the new phase of reform was beginning. They were almost entirely the results of the energy and enterprise of men in the Liberal Government, who saw in social reform the way to glory for themselves and the party. In attempting to deal with unemployment, British politics entered what Winston Churchill termed 'an untrodden field.' The discovery made there was social insurance.

When the nation's leaders accepted the proposition that unemployment, not the unemployed, was the evil with which society had to deal, the problems of idleness lost some of their moral overtones. But at the same time the problems themselves became harder to solve. If one assumed an unemployed man was a bad man, there was no question of what to do with him. He could be shut up in the workhouse. But if it was generally accepted that he was only an unfortunate man for whom economic society at the moment had no place, the evil lay in society and not in the man. Reasonably, therefore, the nation might be asked to help the unemployed workman, either by finding him work, or supporting him until work appeared. Indeed, it was in society's interest to do this, for an unoccupied man could quickly become demoralized and vicious, as all London knew after the Trafalgar Square riots.

Chamberlain's circular immediately after the riots marked the first official recognition of the new attitude towards unemployment. More important, the circular established the precedent of work relief as the normal means of attacking the problem. Between 1886 and the Unemployed Workmen Act of 1905, official policy towards the idle man, so far as a policy existed, was to provide him with work of some kind. Whether the work offered was useful, or profitable, or interesting, or dignified, mattered very little. There was only one stipulation. The work should not pauperize.

Sometimes entangled, sometimes in competition with the State relief activities were a large number of independent, privately financed projects for aiding the unemployed. Particularly numerous between 1890 and 1905, these generally sought to prevent the destruction of character that was assumed to accompany idleness by taking the individual from the slums and subjecting him to some form of moral and vocational education. A man might be taught a new trade or methods of agriculture. In any case he would be required to keep regular habits of life, and be given duties to perform. Most of his pay would go directly to his family, if he had one. The first and most ambitious of the philanthropic labour plans was General Booth's 'Darkest England' programme, first publicized in 1890.[2] This involved a three-stage programme of rehabilitation, culminating in agricultural training, to make possible the emigration of Great Britain's surplus workers. The idea of repopulating the English countryside with sturdy farmers who could become colonists for the Queen's empire had considerable appeal to many who, while only slightly interested in social reform, hoped for a greater Britain, self-sufficient in food and as populous as Imperial Germany.[3]

Behind the public and private interest in unemployment—as important as Christian humanitarianism, the fear of the working-class vote, or the upper-class concern for national efficiency—lay the overriding fact that the poor law of 1834 simply no longer worked. This had long been clear to experienced social investi-

[2] William Booth, *In Darkest England and the Way Out*, New York, 1891.

[3] For instance, there was the 'New Party' that clustered about Lord Milner, including

. . . socialists of the old school and people like Lord Willoughby de Broke, whose pride in his own 'Englishness' found its echo in Harry [Dr Harry Roberts]; F. S. Oliver; Lord Milner, looking for a perfect party of all sensible men, 'people who were once Socialists' as he described it; and Lady Edward Cecil—earlier Violet Maxse and later Lady Milner. The New Party was to be a really national one, aiming at agricultural reform and the rebirth of English country life . . . and was described by Willoughby de Broke with characteristic boyish enthusiasm as 'The Party, the Patriotic, Tory, National, British Character Party.'

Winifred Stamp, '*Doctor Himself*,' *An Unorthodox Biography of Harry Roberts, 1871–1946*, London, 1949, p. 103.

gators; by the early twentieth century it had become apparent to the literate public as well. Two-thirds of a century of political compromise, of attack by philanthropists and of counter-attack by business men and classical economists, had so weakened the deterrent principle that pauperism, while still degrading, was becoming less painfully uncomfortable, and the workhouse itself had the virtues neither of cheapness nor efficiency. The decayed principle of 'less eligibility' still served to make miserable some portion of the last years of one-third of the United Kingdom's old people, but fear of some aspects of the poor law among some classes of able-bodied workers seemed to be diminishing. The new attitude was clearly manifest in the growing availability of poor law medical facilities after the passage of the Medical Relief (Disqualification Removal) Act of 1885. Also, after the turn of the century, while the total percentage of paupers in the population declined fairly steadily, the number and percentage of able-bodied inmates of workhouses increased, particularly in London.[4] The workhouse was derisively called, 'The best club, there is no subscription to pay.' Thousands of workmen converged each winter in order to partake of the 'substantial comforts and agreeable promiscuity' of the several East End unions in which sympathetic working men had come to dominate the boards of guardians.[5] Yet in the country, thousands of aged men and women quietly starved themselves in order to avoid applying for parochial aid. This system of relief could hardly be commended.

Despite the fact that there was no indication that the worthy poor were better cared for, or that the able-bodied loafers received

---

[4] In the decade 1870–9 the lowest number of people relieved in any one year was 295 per 10,000 population; the highest was 465. Using the same ratio for the decade 1900–9 the low figure was 241 and the high 262. Ioan G. Gibbon, 'The Public Social Services,' *Journal of the Royal Statistical Society*, C (Part IV, 1937), 537.

In the decade between 1891–2 and 1900–1 the mean number of able-bodied paupers receiving indoor relief in England and Wales increased 6·5 per cent. But in the decade between 1895–6 and 1905–6 the increase was 21·2 per cent. For London alone this figure was 38·4 per cent. Lord George Hamilton, 'A Statistical Survey of the Problems of Pauperism,' *Journal of the Royal Statistical Society*, LXXIV (December, 1910), 28. On the development of poor law medical relief see: Sidney and Beatrice Webb, *English Local Government, English Poor Law History: Part II: The Last Hundred Years* (London, 1929), I, 329–31, 336.

[5] Geoffrey Drage, *The State and the Poor*, London, 1914, p. 87, and paper read by Thomas Mackay before annual conference of the South East and Metropolitan Poor Law Division, *The Times*, December 14, 1901.

more salutary discipline, the *per capita* cost of the poor law rose steadily in the decades before World War I. In 1871–2 the poor law in England and Wales had cost £8,700,403, or 7s. ¼d. per head of population. In 1905–6 the cost was £14,685,938 or 8s. 7¼d. per head of a population one-quarter larger.[6] Between the decade from 1871–2 to 1879–80 and the decade from 1896–7 to 1905–6, the mean annual expenditure per pauper increased from £9 8s. 11d. to £14 13s. 11d., or more than 50 per cent.[7] This system could not be retained. It punished those who needed help. It helped those who deserved punishment. And it grew ever more expensive. The poor law offered no facility upon which to build an institution for the care of unemployed. It tainted everything it touched. Either it would have to be returned to the position of a semi-penal custodian of genuine loafers planned for it by the commissioners of 1832, leaving the worthy poor to be cared for in some other way, or it would have to be swept away altogether.

These considerations generally underlay the appointment at the end of 1905 of the Royal Commission on the Poor Law;[8] and the famous reports of that investigation embody the alternatives of reconstruction or abolition of the Act of 1834. In the event the Liberal administration discovered a third option. It chose to retain the poor law substantially as it existed (although the Government hoped to abolish the general mixed workhouse and establish a system of classification of applicants for relief according to worthiness) but to reduce pauperism by attacking its causes piecemeal. This was the programme of the New Liberalism. Among its achievements none showed more legislative skill and daring than the measures enacted to deal with unemployment.

2

The history of State attempts to provide relief work for unemployed men, at least until the formation in 1904 of the London joint committees for the unemployed, can be disposed of briefly. First of all, they were invariably emergency activities and were on far too small a scale to have any impact on the employment market. During the winter of 1892–3, for instance, when Chamberlain's

[6] Hamilton, 'Statistical Survey,' *J.R.S.S.* (December, 1910), 17.
[7] *Ibid.*, p. 22.
[8] Webb, *English Poor Law History: The Last Hundred Years*, II, 470–1.

circular was reissued by Henry Fowler, the Liberal President of the Local Government Board, the seventy-seven most active of the ninety-six authorities which provided relief work employed altogether 26,875 persons.[9] This number can hardly be counted as significant in a winter when the number of unemployed men must have reached at least 750,000.[10]

The story of municipal work relief culminates with the London joint committees of 1904 and the Unemployed Workmen Act of 1905. Some recent historians have given these ventures a good deal of importance, suggesting that they mark a 'turning point' by the 'acceptance of a measure of national responsibility' for the unemployed. Properly they represent the most ambitious and the final attempt to deal with temporary unemployment by means of work relief.[11] Their failure turned serious social thinkers—most important among them, Sidney Webb and William Beveridge—to the search for other alternatives to the poor law. From this search, from the social conceptions of Webb and Beveridge, and from the legislative craftsmanship of Winston Churchill and Hubert Llewellyn Smith, came labour exchanges and unemployment insurance. The London joint committees for the unemployed and the Unemployed Workmen Act were thus an ending rather than a beginning.[12]

[9] William Beveridge, *Unemployment, A Problem of Industry*, 2nd ed., London, 1931, p. 155.

[10] The trade unions reported in 1893 an unemployment rate of 7·5 per cent. The census of 1891 showed 10,100,000 occupied males in Great Britain. The rate of trade union unemployment was invariably lower than that of general workers. Brian R. Mitchell, *Abstract of British Historical Statistics*, Cambridge, 1962, pp. 60, 67.

[11] Maurice Bruce, *The Coming of the Welfare State*, London, 1961, p. 163. See also, President of the Local Government Board Gerald Balfour's second reading statement on the precedents for the Bill. *Hansard, Parliamentary Debates*, series 4, CXLVII (June 20, 1905), col. 1118.

[12] William Henry Beveridge, First Baron of Tuggal, 1874–1964, born, Rangpur, Bengal; father member of the Indian Civil Service; educated, Charterhouse and Balliol College in Oxford; fellow, University College, 1902–9; sub-warden, Toynbee Hall, 1903–5; leader writer, *Morning Post*, 1906–8, Civil servant, Board of Trade, 1908–9; Ministry of Food, 1916–19; Director London School of Economics and Political Science, 1919–37; Master, University College, Oxford, 1937–45. M.P., Liberal, Berwick-on-Tweed, 1944–5; defeated 1945, accepted peerage and Liberal leadership in the House of Lords. Chairman, Statutory Committee on Unemployment Insurance, 1934–44; Chairman, Interdepartmental Committee on Social Insurance and Allied Services, 1941–2, the report of which was the famous 'Beveridge Report.'

Hubert Llewellyn Smith, 1864–1945, born, Bristol; family in grocery

The last phase in the history of work relief began in November of
1903 with an appeal by Canon Barnett and Cosmo Lang, then
Bishop of Stepney, for contributions to a revived Mansion House
Fund. When hostilities in South Africa ended, unemployment
began again to grow. The proposal now was not for work relief of
the ordinary kind but rather for help in the placing of men on
'farm colonies,' which had become particularly popular since the
beginning of the war.

In 1903 the idea of returning men to the land was by no means
new. As has been mentioned, the Salvation Army, joined soon by
the Church Army, had proposed work on the land in the dark days
of the late eighties as a restorative for men demoralized by unemployment. In May, 1891, the Salvation Army had bought 1,052
acres as a 'workmen's agricultural university' at Hadleigh,
Essex.[13] After the outbreak of the Boer War the popular reaction
against the shiftlessness, materialism, and unhealthiness that
accompanied city life brought support from various political
sources for the revival of British agriculture and the rehabilitation
of British manhood through settling the unemployed on the
land.[14]

The appeal for funds of the winter of 1903–4 raised about
£4,300, which was spent to send 467 heads of families to the
Salvation Army's Hadleigh colony. The men themselves were paid
nothing, but the family of each one of them received relief averaging about 23s. 3d. per week. The work on the colony itself was of

business, Quaker background; educated Bristol Grammar School and Corpus
Christi College, Oxford; resident, Toynbee Hall, 1887–9; associated with Ben
Tillett during dock strike, 1889. Entered Board of Trade, 1893; member, Royal
Commission on Secondary Education, 1894–5; Permanent Secretary, Board of
Trade, 1907–19, developed war-risk insurance and served as General Secretary
at Ministry of Munitions, 1915; chief, economic section of British delegation at
peace conference, 1919; director, New Survey of London Life and Labour,
1928–35; K.C.B., 1908.

[13] Albert E. Reffold, *Wilson Carlile and the Church Army*, 3rd ed., London, 1928,
pp. 128–31. Also Robert Sandall, *The History of the Salvation Army* (London,
1955), III, 136–45. Also, W. H. G. Armytage, *Heavens Below: Utopian Experiments in England, 1560–1960*, London, 1961, pp. 320–1. Recent research has
suggested that the original idea for land colonies was W. T. Stead's, who was
introduced to Booth by Arnold White. K. S. Inglis, *Churches and the Working
Class in Victorian England*, London, 1963, p. 204.

[14] See, for instance, Earl Nelson, 'Back to the land,' *Nineteenth Century*, L
(July, 1901), 59–66. Herbert Samuel, *Liberalism, An Attempt to State the
Principles and Proposals of Contemporary Liberalism in England*, London, 1902,
p. 130.

the most elementary sort—turning over land with spades, cutting trees, chopping wood.

The land colony scheme of 1903–4 had been limited to the East End boroughs of Stepney, Poplar, Bethnal Green and Shoreditch. A member of the Poplar Board of Guardians was George Lansbury, whose commodious, non-deterrent workhouse provided the term 'poplarism' that was coming to mean open-handed, unpunishing, rate-supported relief. Early in 1904, Lansbury became acquainted with Joseph Fels, to whom he introduced the idea of land colonies and who soon formed his own organization, the 'Vacant Lands Cultivation Society.' In March, Lansbury accepted on behalf of the Poplar guardians one hundred acres at Laindon in Essex, which were purchased by Fels and renamed 'Poplar Gardens.' Fels' generosity thus brought local authorities into the business of land colonization, and Lansbury became a firm supporter of this type of relief.[15]

By the end of the summer it was clear that conditions of employment would be even worse in the winter of 1904–5 than they had been the previous year. To plan for the emergency, a meeting under the chairmanship of Walter Long, then President of the Local Government Board, convened on October 14, 1904.[16]

[15] George Lansbury, 1859–1940, born, Oxford; father a railway subcontractor, later moved to Whitechapel; education, elementary school; travelled to Australia, 1884–5; member of Social Democratic Federation, 1884–1910; became member of the Independent Labour Party, Poor Law Guardian, Poplar, 1891–1932; Borough Councillor, 1903–40; signed minority report of the Royal Commission on the Poor Law; M.P., Labour, 1910–12, and 1922–40 for Bow and Bromley; First Commissioner of Works, 1929–31; leader of the Labour Party, 1931–5, after the defection of Ramsay MacDonald. Ardent supporter of women suffrage, had resigned seat in 1912 to fight election on this issue; identifies self as 'C. of E. teetotaller, and non-smoker.'

Mary Fels, *Joseph Fels, His Life-Work*, New York, 1916, p. 40. Armytage, *Heavens Below*, p. 377. Lansbury generally took credit for being the originator of land colonies. His biographer does not mention the Salvation Army's Hadleigh establishment. Raymond Postgate, *The Life of George Lansbury*, London, 1951, pp. 68–71. The Laindon colony was styled an 'open-air workhouse' by opponents of the Poplar system. R. C. K. Ensor, 'The Poplar Poor Law Enquiry,' *Speaker*, August 4, 1906.

[16] As early as January, 1904, Lansbury had suggested the formation of a central London authority for dealing with the unemployed. The Local Government Board, he said, would be asked to appoint such an authority, which would have the powers of all London guardians. This new body, he thought, should be able to acquire land outside the metropolis to grow food for the use of public agencies. George Lansbury, 'The Unemployed,' *Commonwealth*, IX (January, 1904), 5–6.

On the recommendation of this conference, there were appointed in twenty-seven of the twenty-eight metropolitan boroughs and in the city of London, committees composed of representatives of the borough councils, the local Boards of Guardians, and delegates from the various private charitable associations. The committees' work would be co-ordinated by a central committee, which would number seventy members and include persons nominated by the Local Government Board.[17] The central committee was charged also with operating by far the most extensive land colony scheme yet established—1,300 acres at Hollesley Bay near Felixstowe, Suffolk, purchased by Joseph Fels for £40,000, and rented to the London committee.[18]

The local joint committees were to examine applicants for relief, segregating respectable men temporarily unemployed from the improvident wastrel. The latter would be consigned to the poor law while the committees would endeavour to find work for the rest. In the first six months of their existence, to March 31, 1905, the joint committees registered and classified nearly 46,000 men (the committee records are not complete), of whom only about 11,000 were offered poor law relief. Most of the work provided was in and around London, frequently in parks and gardens with the County Council or the Home Office as the employer. The President of the Local Government Board, Gerald Balfour, estimated the next year that £110,000 had been spent in 1904–5 by the metropolitan authorities in work relief. The same work handled normally, he said, would have cost £80,000.[19] Beyond a few small contributions from local authorities, the funds spent by the joint committees came from public charity. There was no grant from the Exchequer.

The London unemployed scheme was scarcely in operation before the Government began to consider extending it to the rest of the country.[20] The resulting Unemployed Workmen Act, which received the Royal Assent on August 11, 1905, marks the culmination of the work relief experiments that between 1886 and the advent of the New Liberalism represented the most enlightened means of dealing with the unemployed. Though the Act would remain in force until the war, so far as its usefulness in diminishing

[17] Beveridge, *Unemployment*, p. 161.
[18] Armytage, *Heavens Below*, p. 378.
[19] *Hansard*, CXLVII (June 20, 1905), col. 1118.
[20] See: Walter H. Long, 'The Unemployed, *Confidential*,' January 24, 1905, Public Record Office, Cab. 37/74, No. 17.

pauperism was concerned, it was clearly a failure by 1907. But even in failure the measure has importance, for with its inability to lessen appreciably the hardship of the worthy unemployed, reformers turned to the consideration of other remedies than work relief, some suggested by the Act itself. The Unemployed Workmen Act required the establishment of a Distress Committee in every metropolitan borough and in every other urban district in the United Kingdom with population of 50,000. The committee would be composed of representatives of the local authorities and guardians and other 'persons experienced in the relief of distress.' In London many of the duties of the borough Distress Committees were given to the statutory successor of the old central committee for the unemployed, restyled ambiguously 'The Central London (Unemployed) Body.'

The Distress Committees were specifically charged by the Act with separating the worthy unemployed from the loafer. The latter would be consigned to the poor law. But, stipulated the Act:

> If the distress committee are satisfied that any . . . applicant is honestly desirous of obtaining work, but is temporarily unable to do so from exceptional causes over which he has no control, and that this case is capable of more suitable treatment under this Act than under the poor law they may endeavour to obtain work for the applicants. . . .

In the Distress Committees, the United Kingdom had at last a body of experts in each substantial municipality charged by law in very broad terms with the responsibility for relieving, not punishing, the unemployed. The committees (the Distress Committees and the Central Body together in London) had the power to use nearly all the remedies so far discussed in this study. They might aid a man to emigrate or to move from one area to another. They could establish labour exchanges and unemployment registers to bring employers and workers together. They could put men to work on their own account if no work were available with other employers and they could establish farm colonies to the end of returning men to the land. (In London these powers were reserved for the Central Body.) A number of the provincial committees did, in fact, acquire land for cultivation and the Hollesley Bay colony remained active under the management of the London Central Body.

Although the Distress Committees were only the statutory successors of the London joint committees of the previous winter, at the insistence of Walter Long they had been given the power, denied their predecessors, to call upon the local authority for funds to the extend of a halfpenny rate, or with the consent of the Local Government Board, up to one penny in the pound. However, their normal source of income was expected to be voluntary contributions. The ancient tradition that human distress was the responsibility of the locality forbade any payment from the national treasury.[21] Moreover, money from rates could not be used for the payment of labour in cases where the committees acted as the direct employers of men.

The conclusions to be drawn from the operation of the Unemployed Workmen Act may be divided into three categories. As a laboratory for experiments in social reform, the Act was most helpful. Farm colonies received a serious trial over a long period of time, and although George Lansbury disagreed, most reformers realized early their limited usefulness. Beveridge doubted whether the ideal conditions of Hollesley Bay would provide much training for the hardships of agriculture in Canada.[22]

Secondly, the Unemployed Workmen Act demonstrated conclusively that work relief did almost nothing to alleviate hardship for the best type of unemployed worker, the man whom everyone was trying to keep from the poor law. By early 1907, William Beveridge, a member of the Central Body of London, asserted that after two winters of operation of the Act: 'The attitude of nearly all those engaged in its administration may fairly be described as one of growing hopelessness.'[23] Two years later in his book,

[21] The President of the Local Government Board pointed out that the London Central Committee had spent within three months the £45,000 it had raised through voluntary contributions. Walter H. Long, 'The Unemployed, *Confidential*,' February 16, 1905, p. 1, P.R.O. Cab. 37/74, No. 31. The Liberal Government, which promised in the King's Speech in 1906 to amend the Act, failed to do so, but broke precedent by making a £200,000 grant from national taxation towards the costs of the Distress Committees.

[22] William Beveridge, *Power and Influence*, New York, 1955, pp. 45–6, Hollesley Bay is now a Borstal. For a socialist opinion see: James Keir Hardie. 'Dealing With the Unemployed,' *Nineteenth Century*, LVII (January, 1905), 46–60. Keir Hardie felt land colonies were not of much use except perhaps as therapy for the down and out. They did not do much, he thought, to help the respectable workman. *Ibid.*, p. 52.

[23] William Beveridge, 'Labour Exchanges and the Unemployed,' *Economic Journal*, XVII (March, 1907), 80. Advanced Liberal radicals had begun to

Unemployment, A Problem of Industry, he demolished the rationale of work relief that underlay the Unemployed Workmen Act. Here he defined the unrecognized problem of 'underemployment.'

The characteristic and conspicuous result of trade depression is, not to reduce to destitution men formerly in regular employment (though this no doubt also happens to some extent), but to precipitate into distress men who are always on its verge. For poverty of this type the sixteen weeks of work relief is obviously no remedy. To men of this type a reduction of earnings brought about by a shortening of hours is no deterrent. The problem as conceived by the authors of the Unemployed Workmen Act was that of a definite breach in employment hitherto continuous —a disaster analogous to those caused by famine or war—a chasm over which a bridge might be thrown from firm ground to firm ground. The actual problem had none of this convenient definiteness of outline. The passage of the unemployed percentage from two to seven and back again to two does not mean the extrusion of five thousand specific individuals out of every hundred thousand in one year and their reabsorption the year after. It means for practical purposes, the gradual and barely perceptible worsening, for three or four years, conditions of life which are always bad and their gradual and imperceptible return in the next three or four years, to being not worse than usual.

. . . .

The Unemployed Workmen Act has done a good deal in collecting information. It has done a little to co-ordinate existing agencies and improve in minor points the administration of special relief. It has not had any appreciable impression upon the problem. Its main service has been to demonstrate beyond question its own essential inadequacy and the inadequacy of all measures which like itself, leave industrial disorganization untouched and deal only with the resultant human suffering.[24]

attack the Act almost from the moment it had been passed. 'The Unemployed,' *Speaker*, June 23, 1906, pp. 264–5.

[24] Beveridge, *Unemployment*, pp. 189–90, 191. A report before the British Association for the Advancement of Science about a year after the passage of the Unemployed Workmen Act set out in some detail the type of workmen who were using the scheme and in doing so anticipated Beveridge's larger work on the 'underemployed.' As a result of sampling 'typical' districts, it had been

For Beveridge the State's function was to provide consistent year-round support to working men in the labour market. State power would have to be available to regularize the employment of casual labour, the men who were constantly underemployed, who needed help in good times as well as bad. The State ought not to provide social welfare, but social service—the organization of the labour market.

Beveridge knew, at least by 1906, the agencies through which the labour market should be organized. These were the labour exchanges. So exchanges rank as the third important result of the Unemployed Workmen Act. Labour exchanges were by no means new in Great Britain; they were commonplace in Germany. The Unemployed Workmen Act had specifically empowered the Distress Committees to establish them and to use rate money for their operation. But many trade unionists distrusted exchanges, feeling they could become a recruiting depot for strikebreakers. Socialists also looked on them as a palliative. Unemployment would be abolished not by the organization of the labour market, they argued, but by the organization of industry itself, in effect nationalization. George Lansbury, Beveridge's colleague on the London Central Body, was particularly outspoken against exchanges although, as has been mentioned, he was most enthusiastic about farm colonies. He wrote to Beveridge early in 1907:

> . . . I am only waiting for Burns' reply, and if that reply says small holdings are off, then I'm off too. I have no interest in the Central Body as a Body to perpetuate relief works or to emigrate men and women to Canada; and as you know, I look upon labour exchanges as an experiment. I, English public-like, think anything can be got done but the right thing. I am satisfied that here in England the unemployed question is not to be settled by an attempt to make labour fluid; that is an impossibility in modern commercial operations. It will be settled, I am convinced, by some kind of state employment. . . .
>
> I write this because I gather from your letter that you are

discovered that 56 per cent of those applying for work were already casual labourers, 37 per cent were at the moment out of work because of 'inefficiency, age or bad character,' 41 per cent were described as being of 'indifferent' efficiency. Only 22 per cent were described as being of 'good character,' 16 per cent had been union members, 14 per cent had been friendly society members. These percentages, of course, overlap. C. J. Hamilton, 'The Unemployed,' *Report of the British Association for the Advancement of Science*, 1906, p. 651.

feeling just a little sick: you are in my company in that respect, but perhaps it is from another point of view.[25]

Beveridge had been a member of the Employment Exchange Committee of the Central Body and so had practical knowledge of the working of exchanges. During 1906 and 1907, in articles in Fabian Ware's *Morning Post*, in the *Economic Journal*, before the British Association, and in innumerable other articles and pamphlets, he set out to destroy the popular conception of exchanges as a slightly eccentric humanitarian experiment like public baths. They should be as commonplace a government service as the post office, he argued. Most important, Beveridge succeeded in interesting Sidney and Beatrice Webb in the proposal so that the Webbs planned to make the use of labour exchanges compulsory, and to establish them as the central institution in the framework of social controls that would prevent destitution. Through the Webbs, Winston Churchill, in search of a remedy for unemployment, came to know William Beveridge. And soon after Churchill's appointment as President of the Board of Trade, the couple persuaded him to offer Beveridge an appointment in the ministry. On July 3, 1908, Beveridge entered government service, bringing with him the idea for labour exchanges.[26]

3

Public politics were little affected by the controversy among experts about the usefulness of the Unemployed Workmen Act. This was partly the result of the rapid improvement in employment conditions towards the end of 1905. Trade union unemployment fell dramatically from 5 per cent in 1905 to 3·6 per cent in 1906.[27] More important, party controversy was dominated by the resignation of the Balfour Government, the formation of the Campbell-Bannerman administration, and the approaching general election— all of which were conditioned by issues arising from the war in South Africa. Neither of the great parties, for reasons of its own, wished to put the condition of the people question before the voters. The Unionists had scarcely any record to stand on. The

[25] George Lansbury to W. H. Beveridge, January 11, 1907, Beveridge Papers, unsorted.
[26] Beveridge, *Power and Influence*, p. 68.
[27] Mitchell, *British Historical Statistics*, p. 65.

Liberal social reformers did not dominate the party, and party leaders themselves were unwilling to accuse the Unionists of failing to take action in areas about which the Liberals were not agreed. Hence, the Liberals avoided, not altogether to the satisfaction of the voters, any discussion of social reform. 'I had excellent meetings in Glasgow,' wrote Campbell-Bannerman to Asquith less than a week before the Liberals took office. But

> I found that much mischief was being done by the notion that we had little or nothing to say about the unemployed. So I risked one foot upon that ice, but was very guarded and only spoke of enquiry and experiment.[28]

Whether or not neglect of social problems contributed to the remarkable increase in Labour representation that marred the complete Liberal victory in January, 1906, the Campbell-Bannerman administration soon took steps to demonstrate that the working-class voter could look to Liberalism as well as Labour for friendship and patronage. It was, however, the Labour Party voter much more than the Labour Party Member of Parliament who influenced Liberal social policies between 1906 and 1910. Although some of the new working men in the Commons were influential and personally popular, for instance David Shackleton, G. N. Barnes, and Arthur Henderson, a few, notably Keir Hardie, were subjected occasionally to studied discourtesy.[29]

[28] Henry Campbell-Bannerman to H. H. Asquith, December 1, 1905, Asquith Papers, Box 10, ff. 172–3.

[29] For instance, on September 23, 1906, the Liberal leader in the House of Lords, the Marquis of Ripon, wrote to Campbell-Bannerman saying he had received a complaint from Sir Christopher Furniss, 'a near neighbour,' about the public behaviour of James Keir Hardie. While admitting he was 'a bit of a Socialist,' Ripon suggested that Keir Hardie 'is a little bumptuous and might be better for a mild snub which you would know so well how to administer in the most judicious manner . . .' Ripon to Campbell-Bannerman, September 23, 1906, British Museum, Add. MSS 43518, Ripon Papers, XXVIII, f. 106.

David James Shackleton, 1863–1938, born, Accrington; working-class family; left school at age nine; worked in cotton mill until 1892 and participated in the organization of the textile workers. M.P., Labour, for Clitheroe, Lancashire, 1902–10; member Parliamentary Committee of the T.U.C., 1904–10; President of the T.U.C., 1908–9; resigned from Parliament to become a civil servant; teetotaller and non-smoker; K.C.B., 1917.

James Keir Hardie, 1856–1915, born, Lanarkshire; father a carpenter, mother a domestic servant; self-educated, worked from age seven as an errand-boy, entered mine at age ten, with his brothers blacklisted by mine-owners in 1876 for trade union activity; 1878, correspondent for the *Glasgow Weekly Mail*, continued in union activity and journalism. Contested Mid-Lanark in 1888 as

The measures enacted by the Campbell-Bannerman administration on behalf of the nation's children and the nation's elderly have already been discussed. Taken together, they comprise a respectable two years' record for a Government distracted by other important legislation to which—unlike reform—it was absolutely committed. But by the end of 1907, Liberal energies were beginning to wane. The party's impotence in the face of the House of Lords' continuous rejection or mutilation of Bills that had passed the Commons by large majorities caused disappointment and humiliation. This was accompanied by a revival of militant Unionist tariff reform agitation that resulted in a series of by-election losses.[30] Whether or not these defeats could be explained as simply the return to the fold of normally Unionist seats lost in the electoral aberration of 1906, the result was a marked decline in Liberal morale. To add to the party's difficulties by the end of 1907, the American depression, 'The Rich Man's Panic,' reached Great Britain. In 1908, trade union unemployment leaped up to 7·8 per cent, the highest figure it had touched since the grim year of 1886.[31] Then early in April, Prime Minister Campbell-Bannerman resigned, to die within the month.

In the reconstruction of the Government that followed, Herbert Asquith shifted the balance of power in the Cabinet towards the left. Radical reformers now received posts of influence, and ministerial personnel unsympathetic to reform were retired. David Lloyd George took Asquith's place at the exchequer. Winston Churchill, a Liberal of only five years' standing, refused the Local Government Board, perhaps the Admiralty, and eventually took the Board of Trade.[32]

an independent Labour candidate and helped form a few months later the 'Scottish Labour Party'; elected 1892 for South West Ham and helped form in 1893 the Independent Labour Party; defeated in 1895; elected for Merthyr Burghs, 1900; M.P. I.L.P., 1900–15. A founder of the Labour Representation Committee, 1900; Labour Party leader, House of Commons, 1906–7.

[30] Between January 17, 1908, and March 2, 1909, the Unionists gained eight seats from the Liberals without losing a single one themselves.

[31] Mitchell, *British Historical Statistics*, pp. 65–6. In the autumn of 1908 a Home Office White Paper reported that 46 people had died of starvation within the administrative county of London during the winter of 1907–8. *Daily News*, September 3, 1908.

[32] Churchill wrote Asquith on March 14, that he liked the Colonial Office under Lord Elgin even without a seat in the Cabinet. He felt he had special knowledge there. Asquith had suggested the possibility of the Admiralty, but Churchill professed to be unenthusiastic even for a 'glittering post in the

Churchill's unwillingness to accept the Local Government Board portfolio caused the appointment of Charles Masterman there as under-secretary. Masterman reluctantly agreed to take the post with the understanding that the board would be reorganized and that the permanent secretary, Samuel Provis, would leave.[33]

Asquith's new Cabinet appointments, especially the emergence of David Lloyd George, opened a new phase of radical reform. Unquestionably, the desires of ambitious young men to establish reputations for themselves was an important force behind the legislation of the next few years. But the final conception was larger. The State would become, in the truest sense, the servant of all the people. Not only would the helpless be protected at the beginning and at the end of life, but the able-bodied workman in his prime could give of his best secure in the knowledge that the

Ministry.' He was still less enthusiastic, however, about the Local Government Board and, while expressing himself at some length on the problems there needing attention, he admitted he had no special knowledge of its functions. He had never piloted an important Bill through Parliament. 'That kind of work exhausts me.'

> There is no place in the government more laborious, more anxious, more thankless, more choked with petty and even squalid detail, more full of hopeless and insolvable difficulties. . . . I shall be confronted by hundreds of earnest young men who have thought of nothing else all their lives. . . .
>   Winston Churchill to H. H. Asquith, March 14, 1908, 'Secret,' Asquith
>   Papers, Box 11, ff. 10–15.

More succinct was his famous remark about the Local Government Board, which appears to have originated with Edward Marsh, at that time Churchill's private secretary, 'I refuse to be shut up in a soup kitchen with Mrs Sidney Webb.' Edward Marsh, *A Number of People, A Book of Reminiscences*, New York, 1939, p. 163. Violet Bonham Carter in her memoir of Churchill states that Churchill refused the Admiralty and asked for the Local Government Board. Violet Bonham Carter, *Winston Churchill, An Intimate Portrait*, New York, 1965, p. 123. The researcher can only say that contemporary evidence shows the opposite.

Asquith, at the time of this letter, was not yet Prime Minister, but everyone within the inner circle of the Ministry knew that Campbell-Bannerman had only weeks to live.

[33] C. F. G. Masterman to H. H. Asquith, April 13, 1908, Asquith Papers, Box 11, ff. 95–6.

Masterman had been pleading with the Liberals well before the awakening of Churchill on the subject to take up social reform as the best, perhaps the only, way to keep the party together. See, for instance: C. F. G. Masterman,'Politics in Transition,' *Nineteenth Century*, LXIII (January, 1908), 1–17.

Burns' biographer states that Masterman definitely was not wanted at the Local Government Board. William Kent, *John Burns, Labour's Lost Leader*, London, 1950, p. 183.

fruit of his labour would not be swept away by the unpreventable disasters of general unemployment or sickness.

The reform legislation after 1908 was a clear departure from what had gone before. School meals, medical inspection, and old-age pensions had been familiar and fully-debated issues long before Parliament took them up. They did not need to be introduced to the public. They had already accumulated substantial groups of supporters when the Liberal Government came to power. But now circumstances were different. In the spring of 1908, when Churchill began his campaign to solve the problem of unemployment, he was pushing the Liberal Party forward into unknown and possibly dangerous territory.

Churchill opened his programme with a letter to the *Nation* on March 7, 1908, and in his already mentioned letter to Asquith on the Local Government Board a week later. In both the public and the private statements, Churchill sought to induce his party to adopt social reform as its central dogma.[34] The Liberal Party would not abandon its historic championship of individual political freedom, he wrote, but 'it has become acutely conscious of the fact that political freedom, however precious, is utterly incomplete without a measure at least of social and economic independence.' The party's future task was the solution of the social problem. Writing privately to the Prime Minister, Churchill was more explicit about the problems needing immediate attention: They were: unemployment, housing, rating reform, electoral reform, and old-age pensions administration. Churchill admitted he had much to learn about reform and that the projects he had marked out would probably bring him into collision with some of his best friends. Most important was John Morley, 'who at the end of a lifetime of study and thought has come to the conclusion that nothing can be done.' Nevertheless, he insisted, the Liberals must take up the 'minimum standard.' This, he felt, was a worthy project that could engross all the energies of the Government and would result in the entire transformation of the state of life of the English working man.

At the bottom of everything lay the problem of unemployment.

[34] *Nation*, March 7, 1908. Churchill's statement was disguised as a letter of congratulation to H. W. Massingham on the first anniversary of the *Nation's* founding.

Any attempts to grapple with the evils of unemployment must be concerted between all departments. Youth must be educated and disciplined and trained from fourteen to eighteen. The exploitation of Boy Labour must be absolutely stopped. The Army must be made to afford a life-long career of State Employment, to at any rate a larger proportion of its soldiers on leaving the colours. Labour must be decasualized by a system of Labour Exchanges. The resultant residieum [sic] must be curatively treated exactly as if they were hospital patients. The hours of labour must be regulated in various trades subject to seasonal and cyclical fluctuations. Means must be found by which the State can, within certain limits, and for short periods, augment the demand of the ordinary market for unskilled labour so as to counterbalance the oscillations of world-trade. Underneath, though not in substitution for, the immense disjointed fabric of social safeguards and insurance which has grown up by itself in England, there must be a spread—at a lower level—a sort of Germanized network of State intervention and regulation.[35]

Social reform was, as Churchill entitled his letter to the *Nation*, 'The Untrodden Field of Politics.' This territory the Liberals must enter. 'The nation,' Churchill concluded in his public letter, 'which is greater than either party, demands the application of drastic corrective and curative processes, and will crown with confidence and honour the party which has the strength and wisdom for that noble crusade.'[36]

Manifest in Churchill's thinking here was the influence of the Webbs. Mrs Webb, indeed, gave her husband credit for the *Nation* letter.[37] After 1905, Churchill and Masterman were among the few Liberals who attended the austere suppers at 41 Grosvenor Road. Neither man had been involved in the Rosebery debacle of 1901, Masterman because he was not in Parliament and Churchill because he was then a Conservative. The Webbs undoubtedly suggested to Churchill the possibility of social reform and so helped to focus the undisciplined political energies that seemed for a time to threaten his career.[38] Certainly the Webbs introduced

[35] Churchill to Asquith, March 14, 1908, Asquith Papers.
[36] *Nation*, March 7, 1908.
[37] Beatrice Webb, *Our Partnership*, London, 1948, p. 404.
[38] For instance, in February, 1906, in the debate on the censure of Lord Milner for permitting mistreatment of coolie labour. On the reactions to

him to Beveridge and to the usefulness of labour exchanges. But after turning Churchill's great energy towards the social problem and seeing him take Cabinet office, they lost him. For in the spring of 1908 began his important partnership with David Lloyd George, whose hostility towards Sidney Webb dated at least from the Education Act of 1902. Almost certainly Lloyd George's famous inspection of the German social insurance system was the result of Churchill's enthusiasm for German efficiency in the care of the working population. Both men continually adduced the German example as they sought to make Liberalism the party of reform and efficiency.

'There is a tremendous policy in Social Organization,' wrote Churchill to Asquith at the end of 1908.

> The need is urgent and the moment ripe. Germany with a harder climate and far less accumulated wealth, has managed to establish tolerable basic conditions for her people. She is organized not only for war, but for peace. We are organized for nothing except party politics. The Minister who will apply to this country the successful experiences of Germany in Social Organization may or may not be supported at the polls, but he will at least have left a memorial which time will not deface of his administration. It is not impossible to underpin the existing voluntary agencies by a comprehensive system—necessarily at a lower level—of state action. We have at least two years. [The Unionists at this time were scoffing at the suggestion that the House of Lords would ever reject a Finance Bill.] We have the miseries which this winter is inflicting upon the poorer classes to back us.[39] And oddly enough the key class of legislation which is required is just the kind the House of Lords will not dare to oppose. The expenditure of less than ten millions a year, not upon relief, but upon machinery, a thrift-stimuli would make England a different country for the poor.

Churchill's behaviour on this occasion see: Alfred Gollin, *Proconsul in Politics, A Study of Lord Milner in Opposition and in Power*, London, 1964, pp. 93–4.

[39] A confidential memorandum the previous month had shown trade union employment in September to be 9·4 per cent. Winston Churchill, 'Memorandum on the State of Employment and Trade During the First Nine Months of 1908,' November 2, 1908, p. 1, P.R.O., Cab. 37/96, No. 143.

The priorities for action were:

    I. Labour Exchanges and unemployment insurance;
   II. National infirmity insurance, etc.;
  III. Special expansive State Industries—Afforestation—roads;
  IV. Modernized Poor Law, i.e. classification;
   V. Railway Amalgamation with State control and guarantee;
  VI. Education compulsory until seventeen.

All of these measures could be carried, Churchill argued. They would not only 'benefit the State, but fortify the party.' Even if the programme were a failure it would be a good way to go down.

> I say—thrust a big slice of Bismarckianism over the whole underside of our industrial system, and await the consequences, whatever they may be, with a good conscience.[40]

When this letter was written, unemployment and health insurance as well as labour exchanges were already under departmental consideration, but, as Churchill knew, many members of the Cabinet were far from convinced about the expediency of a party commitment to reform. Indeed, the welfare legislation of the New Liberalism never commanded whole-hearted support of the Asquith Cabinet. Perhaps for this reason, Churchill's short career as a radical is of exceptional importance. The first measure of the new phase of reform, labour exchanges, was his. And before he left the Board of Trade for the Home Office, unemployment insurance was well under way. Thus, for over a year, while David Lloyd George led the attack on the second chamber, Churchill, in Cabinet memorandum and public address, maintained the commitment to social welfare legislation among colleagues for whom 'reform' meant no more than one man one vote, Welsh disestablishment, Home Rule, or mending the House of Lords.

4

Work on a labour exchange Bill, presaged by Beveridge's appointment, did not begin until late August, 1908, after the Chancellor of the Exchequer returned from his inspection of the German welfare system. Then the project moved forward rapidly. Within weeks the

---

[40] Winston S. Churchill to H. H. Asquith, December 29, 1908, Asquith Papers, Box 11, ff. 249–54.

Trades Union Congress and the National Conference of Friendly Societies were notified officially, and confidentially, that the ministry was considering a national system of employment exchanges and that it would soon begin discussions of a comprehensive programme of social insurance. On October 14, 1908, Churchill, Lloyd George, Louis Harcourt, Sidney Buxton, Herbert Gladstone, Reginald McKenna, and John Burns were appointed to a Cabinet Committee on Unemployment.[41] On November 4, Churchill and Lloyd George met Sidney Webb, Arthur Henderson, David Shackleton, and 'four other Trade Union leaders' at the Board of Trade to discuss 'the general Rules which should govern Labour Exchanges in practice.' A little more than two weeks later, a committee of trade union leaders, C. W. Bowerman, Will Thorne, W. C. Steadman, with Shackleton as chairman, left England for Germany to study the effect on labour organization of old age pensions, sickness insurance, and labour exchanges.[42]

Late in November the House of Lords' rejection of the Licensing Bill injected a new awkwardness into Liberal plans. Second chamber reform might have to take precedence over social reform. 'We shall send them such a budget in June as shall terrify them,' growled Churchill to Lucy Masterman at dinner in the House of Commons on November 26. Stabbing furiously at his bread, he continued:

'They have started the class war, they had better be careful.' I asked him how long he thought the government had to live. 'If they thurvive the next budget, two or three years. That'll be the teeth.'[43]

[41] Lucy Masterman, *C. F. G. Masterman*, London, 1939, p. 111.
Burns opposed the appointment of any committee to deal with the problem, maintaining that the Local Government Board needed no help.

[42] For the Fabian reaction to the Liberal programme see: Webb, *Partnership*, p. 418.
Winston S. Churchill, 'Unemployment Insurance: Labour Exchanges, Confidential,' November 30, 1908, p. 6, P.R.O., Cab. 37/96, No. 159. Some manufacturers in Britain, as in Germany, had for many years been suggesting government-sponsored welfare legislation as a way of breaking the labour leaders' hold over union members provided by the organizational welfare programmes. See, for instance, the letter by 'W. B.' to *The Times*, November 20, 1901, in reference to *The Times*' widely discussed series on national economic efficiency, 'The Crisis in British Industry.'

[43] Masterman, *C. F. G. Masterman*, p. 114. The Cabinet considered a dissolution over the Licensing Bill. H. H. Asquith to Edward VII, December 9, 1908, Asquith Papers, Box 6, ff. 71–2.

A great deal, therefore, depended on whether the peers chose to be entrapped by the snare of the 1909 budget. If they rejected the budget, the Government would have to resign and politics would dissolve into the fury of a general election. If they chose to be careful, the Government could expect at least two more years of relative calm in which much could be done. By the end of the year political rumour assured the Liberals that next year's Finance Bill would survive the House of Lords. On December 26, 1908, Churchill wrote to Asquith that he heard in private that Lord Landsdowne, the Unionist Leader in the House of Lords, was giving assurances that the peers would never reject any budget. Therefore, wrote Churchill, Asquith would soon be making plans for two more complete sessions. Churchill hastened to offer the schedule for social reform. He suggested beginning with labour exchanges.

After the Budget Statement, Insurance schemes will be in the air. I don't think I will press my Unemployment Insurance plan until Lloyd George has found a way of dealing with Infirmity or (which is possible) has found there is no way. The Insurance policy must I feel be presented as a whole; for it would never do to exact contributions from masters and men in successive layers. One [slot?] must suffice. I therefore would desire to begin with a simple project of Labour Exchanges, wh. might be announced in the King's Speech, and wh. to prevent overlapping of machinery would be passed so as subsequently to support the Unemployment Insurance Scheme. The Bill would either be introduced in two parts, the second part (Unemployment Insurance) would have blank schedules and not be immediately proceeded with, or a memorandum would explain in general terms the second and complementary part. The negotiations and conferences with the interests affected, wh. are essential to the smooth development of such a scheme, could take place during the autumn of 1909, and the whole policy could receive legislative form in 1910 either as one-half of a big Infirmity Insurance Bill or (if that fails) as the second part of the Labour Exchange Bill. Nothing will in fact be lost by getting the Labour Exchanges under weigh, and everything will be gained and the opportunities for discussion and bargaining with the trades and workmen especially concerned. This is the course of action wh. Lloyd

George and I after much debating think best, and I should like to know what view you take upon it.

Churchill concluded by saying that he would be in London practically continually after January 5, 1909, working on the Labour Exchange and Sweated Trades Bills. He hoped to have them both ready for the next Cabinet.[44]

Liberals were much relieved at the end of the year by the report of the T.U.C. leaders who had visited Germany to examine that country's sickness and accident insurance plans and labour exchanges. Generally, Shackleton and his colleagues approved of the system, although they felt sickness insurance needed over-hauling. Most important, the report laid to rest the ancient trade union fear that government insurance would deprive labour leaders of the hold over their members provided by union welfare benefits. The report concluded:

> The introduction of state insurance of workmen against sickness, invalidity, and old age had in no way exercised an injurious effect upon the Trade Unions of the country.[45]

The unofficial public announcement that the Liberal Government was considering social reform appeared in an article by Harold Spender in the *Contemporary Review* for January, 1909. Spender had accompanied Lloyd George to Germany during the famous inspection trip of the previous summer and would, until the war, act as amanuensis of the radical wing of the Cabinet,

---

[44] Winston S. Churchill to H. H. Asquith, December 26, 1908, Asquith Papers, Box 11, ff. 239–44.

[45] D. J. Shackleton, Chairman, C. W. Bowerman, W. Thorne, W. G. Steadman, Secretary, 'Workmen's Insurance Systems in Germany, Strictly Confidential, December, 1908' (printed December 28, 1908), p. 4, Braithwaite Papers, Part II, Item 1. Bealey and Pelling describe Shackleton as much more of a Liberal than a Labour Party man, a 'Liberal Trade Unionist.' Frank Bealey and Henry Pelling, *Labour and Politics, 1900–1906*, London, 1958, p. 119. Churchill reminded Asquith in the letter of December 29, 1908, that the party was much indebted to Shackleton. Nine months later, Shackleton would further serve the Liberals by wresting from the Trades Union Congress, of which he was President, a resolution in support of unemployment insurance. In this he was strongly opposed by Keir Hardie. *The Times*, September 8, September 9, 1909. When Churchill became Home Secretary, Shackleton resigned from Parliament and was appointed 'Senior Labour Adviser' to the Home Office. After a term on the National Health Insurance Commission he was made in 1916 permanent secretary to the new Ministry of Labour.

and of Lloyd George in particular.[46] In his article, Spender noted the growth of unemployment during the year of 1907. Unemployment, he quoted Winston Churchill as saying, was the 'Achilles heel' of British labour. The socialists offered programmes for the cure of unemployment, said Spender, but there was less potential danger from a socialist scheme than from the possibility that the middle class would satisfy itself by defeating a socialist scheme without doing anything of its own. Spender echoed Churchill's words to Asquith a few days earlier.

> It is not enough for the social thinker in this country to meet the socialist with a negative. The English progressive will be wise if, in this at any rate, he takes a leaf from the book of Bismarck who dealt the heaviest blow against German socialism not by his laws of oppression . . . but by that great system of state insurance which now safeguards the German workman at almost every point of his industrial career.

The way to fight socialism, then, was with social reform. England already had some private provision for economic distress, but all was uncoordinated.

> Some day, perhaps, a statesman will emerge who will introduce a method and an order into the whole system. If, indeed, the Friendly Societies should become friendly to such reform— and there seems some likelihood of that event—there would seem to be no reason why the present Chancellor of the Exchequer should not take the task into his hands of putting in order the whole affair of insurance of all persons under the age of seventy. He might thus, if political circumstances and national finance allowed, be able to deal at one stroke with the three crying evils of invalidity, sickness, and unemployment.[47]

[46] Spender continued to serve Lloyd George as a species of publicity agent until after the Welshman resigned as Prime Minister in October, 1922. Some time after this, the date is not entirely clear, the two men quarrelled. The writer is indebted to Mr Stephen Spender for this information about his father.

[47] Harold Spender, 'Unemployment Insurance,' *Contemporary Review*, CXV (January, 1909), 26, 28. A few months later, J. A. Hobson published *The Crisis of Liberalism*. Here he spoke of the 'new crystallization of Liberal policy' that was occurring.

> The full implication of this movement may not be clearly grasped, but Liberalism is now formally committed to a task which certainly involves a new conception of the State in its relation to the individual life and to private enterprise.

I

In February, 1909, the reports of the Royal Commission on the Poor Law were published. Among the several areas of agreement between the majority and minority commissioners were recommendations for the establishment of labour exchanges. Then on April 29, 1909, the Chancellor of the Exchequer introduced his famous 'War Budget.' He announced at this time that part of the unprecedented amounts of money he intended to raise would be used to pay for sickness and unemployment insurance.[48] However, the meaning of these statements was lost in the storm of anger over the unprecedented measures of taxation.

The Labour Exchange Bill had its final shape when Lloyd George made his budget speech. The measure, in both conception and execution, owed little to any influence outside the Board of Trade. In his memoirs, Lord Beveridge implies that labour exchanges were the result of the poor law royal commission report, to which the Government had access by the autumn of 1908.[49] In their *English Local Government*, Sidney and Beatrice Webb say flatly this was the case.

> In 1909, accordingly, the government instantly acted on the unanimous recommendation of the Poor Law Commission in favour of the Exchanges, and promptly got passed the Labour Exchanges Act, enabling a National Labour Exchange to be set up. . . .[50]

Beveridge goes on to state that labour exchanges, while necessary to unemployment insurance, would have been established even had unemployment insurance not been under consideration.[51] This may be so, but Churchill's correspondence with Asquith in December, 1908, shows that labour exchanges were for the Cabinet simply a small part of a very large legislative package, most of which owed nothing to either the majority or minority report. Moreover, the first official notice of the Board of Trade's intentions on unemployment argued that insurance was necessary

This was not socialism, Hobson continued, and Liberalism would never forget its ancient obligation to individual liberty, but the right of self-development must 'be adjusted to the sovereignty of social welfare.' John A. Hobson, *The Crisis of Liberalism: The New Issue of Democracy*, London, 1909, pp. xi–xii.

[48] *Official Report, House of Commons Debates*, series 5, IV (April 29, 1909), col. 485.

[49] Beveridge, *Power and Influence*, p. 74.

[50] Webb, *English Local Government*, p. 663.

[51] Beveridge, *Power and Influence*, p. 75.

to provide a 'motive for the voluntary support of Labour Exchanges,' rather than the other way around.[52] The Government proceeded with labour exchanges after the budget speech because they were relatively cheap and uncontentious. Unemployment and health insurance, which had been planned to come along soon after, were delayed for two years by the struggle over the budget and the House of Lords reform.

The Government, in any case, had no need to depend upon the formal royal commission reports to ascertain the opinions at least of the signers of the minority report. Almost from the beginning of the commission's work, Beatrice Webb had been leaking documents to members of the Government[53] and from the beginning the Webbs had been invited to submit their views on insurance and exchanges. Sidney Webb's memorandum, dated December 13, 1908, illustrates the wide differences between the Webbs' and the Board of Trade's conception of the proper scope of labour exchange activity. Whereas the Government thought of exchanges only as a premise upon which an available working man and an available position could meet if both sides chose to make use of the service, the Webbs argued that the use of labour exchanges should be made compulsory, while unemployment insurance, when it came should be voluntary. If employers could hire workers only through labour exchanges, and working men could find jobs nowhere else, the Government could easily control malingering on unemployment insurance. Under these conditions, said Webb, there would be no doubt that a man applying for unemployment insurance was genuinely without work. On these grounds,

> . . . my wife and I had come to the conclusion that compulsory insurance was impracticable unless we had a compulsory labour exchange; and that, along with a compulsory labour exchange, compulsory insurance was unnecessary.
>
> . . . . .
>
> Hence our proposal is:—1. National labour exchange compulsory on employers of casual labour as defined. 2. Trade union insurance, voluntary and optional but encouraged by subvention

[52] Churchill, 'Unemployment Insurance: Labour Exchanges,' pp. 2–3.

[53] 'Memorandum by Mrs Sidney Webb, Highly Confidential,' n.d. (Printer's mark shows December, 1907), Asquith Papers, unsorted, 'Papers on Old Age Pensions' on box.

of fifty percent. of the out-of-work payments of the preceding year. 3. Decasualization of labour by 'dovetailing' all short jobs and discontinuous employments. 4. Maintenance of such men as are in distress, and for whom labour exchanges cannot discover places; but under carefully graduated conditions.

For men who had not insured or saved, Webb proposed vocational training centred on the labour exchange, compulsory attendance at labour depots, farm colonies for those unable to find work in cities, and finally, detention settlements for those who remained stubbornly unemployable. Webb concluded:

> We cannot help thinking that the compulsory labour exchange, plus subsidized voluntary insurance and maintenance under disciplinary training for uninsured men in distress, solves more difficulties than compulsory insurance plus a voluntary labour exchange. And we cannot help believing that it will prove more difficult to get employers and the trade unions to consent to compulsory insurance than to a compulsory labour exchange.[54]

Three weeks after the budget speech, on May 20, 1909, Winston Churchill introduced the Labour Exchanges Bill in a nearly empty House of Commons. The day before, on the occasion of a resolution calling attention to the poor law report, he had taken the opportunity to explain the general theory of labour exchanges and to make a statement of the Government's unemployment policy.[55] Here he reiterated the importance, frequently missed in the next few years, of the administrative connexion between labour exchanges and unemployment insurance. The failure to enforce an adequate test of willingness to work on workers claiming benefit had brought down the unemployment insurance schemes abroad. A similar failure could destroy any future unemployment insurance experiment in England.[56]

The Commons paid little attention to the Labour Exchanges Bill. The Unionists were burning with outrage over the budget, and had no time for such matters. The debates were badly attended;

[54] Sidney Webb, 'Unemployment Insurance Criticisms, *Confidential*,' December 13, 1908, pp. 8–12. Beveridge Papers, unsorted.

[55] *H. of C. Deb.*, V (May 19, 1909), col. 499 *et seq.*

[56] Two years later, on the eve of the National Insurance Bill, *The Times* was still explaining, as if for the first time, the importance of the labour exchange test. *The Times*, March 31, 1911.

there were no divisions, and no Unionist of importance, except Andrew Bonar Law, spoke on the measure.[57] Some tepid criticism from the Labour Party constituted nearly all the opposition the measure received.[58]

The Labour Exchanges Act received the royal assent on September 20, 1909. It was a spare and simple measure of six clauses empowering the Board of Trade to establish and maintain labour exchanges in places that needed them and to make regulations for their management. A fund would be established from which money could be lent to working people travelling to places where work had been found them through a labour exchange. The Act stipulated that no person should be required to accept any particular appointment found through a labour exchange. Nor would an application for work be prejudiced because the applicant had previously refused employment at a firm engaged in a trade dispute. The Board of Trade was empowered to take over any labour exchanges presently in existence. The power of local authorities to establish labour exchanges under the Unemployed Workmen Act of 1905 was fixed to expire one year after the commencement of the Labour Exchanges Act unless special permission was given by the Local Government Board after consultation with the Board of Trade.[59] When the labour exchange department of the Board of Trade came into existence on February 1, 1910, with William Beveridge as its first director, it took over the operation of 61 labour exchanges already in existence. Of these, 19 had belonged to the Central (Unemployed) Body of London.[60] This number practically doubled by the end of 1910. By the end of 1913, in response to the increased use of the exchange service as a result of

[57] H. of C. Deb., VI (June 16, 1909), cols. 994–1063.

[58] In the Manchester Guardian of May 21, 1909, James Keir Hardie wrote that there was 'nothing new' in labour exchanges. This should have come in with the last Government under the Unemployed Workmen Act. Similarly, in the Labour Leader of June 18, 1909, G. N. Barnes concluded that even with labour exchanges, 'the number of unemployed will probably not be lessened by a single person.' Quoted in Simon Maccobey, English Radicalism: The End?, London, 1961, p. 46.

[59] In the 1930 edition of his book, Unemployment, A Problem of Industry, William Beveridge points out proudly that there had been no amendment of the original Labour Exchanges Act down to that date, whereas the unemployment insurance scheme had been amended many times. Beveridge, Unemployment, p. 295.

[60] John Barton Seymour, The British Employment Exchange, London, 1928, p. 9.

unemployment insurance, there were 430 labour exchanges in the United Kingdom and in addition 1,066 small branch agencies in rural areas and in villages set up exclusively to handle unemployment insurance.[61]

A man in search of employment who signed the 'unemployment register' at an exchange with appropriate statements about his capabilities and desires would be maintained as a 'live register' for six working days. Each week he was required to renew his registration or have his name transferred to the dead file. Exchange services were free of charge for men unemployed or under notice of discharge. Services were available with a fee to men who desired to change jobs. The exchanges usually offered facilities for non-alcoholic refreshment for men attending them waiting for jobs, and some had lavatory facilities for wash up and brush up. The fund to advance travel money to men moving to new jobs obtained through the exchange service appears to have been little used in the years before the war. By July of 1912, when the exchanges had been in operation over two years and were filling 3,000 places daily, only £6,500 altogether had been advanced as travel assistance, although the workers who had received such aid had paid back by that time all but £415.[62]

The generally good economic conditions in the years immediately before the war make difficult any estimate of the impact of labour exchanges on overall unemployment. During the twenty-four months from July, 1912, to July, 1914, after unemployment insurance had doubled the use of the exchanges, trade union unemployment averaged 2·1 per cent, the lowest figure for any time since records had been kept, except 1899, when the rate was 2 per cent.[63] Perhaps of more significance, the percentage of able-bodied pauperism appears to have been unaffected by the establish-

[61] Cd. 6965, 'Proceedings of the Board of Trade Under Part II of the National Insurance Act, 1911,' 1913, p. 3. Quoted in Arthur C. C. Hill and Isador Lubin, The British Attack on Unemployment, Washington, 1934, p. 32. Also, see Beveridge, Power and Influence, p. 79. There is considerable disagreement among scholars about the precise number of labour exchanges in existence on February 1, 1910, and the numbers that were established in the next few years. Maurice Bruce, for instance, reports that '83 exchanges were opened on February 1st, 1910.' Bruce, Welfare State, p. 168. Beveridge's figures in Power and Influence, indeed, do not agree with those in Cd. 6965, which he himself wrote.

[62] Winston S. Churchill, speech to constituents at Dundee, September 11, 1912. Quoted in National Insurance Gazette, September 28, 1912, p. 341.

[63] Seymour, Employment Exchange, p. 17.

ment of labour exchanges. Local Government Board reports for 1908 show that 3·2 able-bodied paupers per thousand of population received relief. In 1909, the rate was 3·5; in 1910, when labour exchanges were established in February, the rate rose to 3·6; in 1911, it fell again to 3·5; in 1912 it was 3·3.[64]

Nevertheless the use of labour exchanges increased rapidly and steadily from the time of their establishment until the war. Between 1911 and 1914, registrations by unemployed workers increased 68 per cent. During the same period, vacancies reported by employers increased 87 per cent and vacancies filled increased 78·5 per cent.[65]

AVERAGE NUMBER OF VACANCIES FILLED DAILY BY EXCHANGES IN THE UNITED KINGDOM

First five months of 1910—Daily average—903—Exchange service begins February 1, 1910

Second six months of 1910—Daily average—1,495
First six months of 1911—Daily average—1,723
Second six months of 1911—Daily average—1,964
First six months of 1912—Daily average—2,083
Second six months of 1912—Daily average—2,858—Unemployment Insurance contributions begin
First six months of 1913—Daily average—2,913—Unemployment Insurance benefits begin
Second six months of 1913—Daily average—2,893
First six months of 1914—Daily average—3,092[66]

The most important statistic of the success of the labour exchanges may be that about 10 per cent of the vacancies filled lay outside the region of the exchange to which the man had originally applied.[67] By this amount, therefore, the fluidity of the labour

[64] Local Government Board Report for 1912–13. Quoted in Drage, *The State and the Poor*, p. 102. Seymour, *Employment Exchange*, p. 18.
[65] Seymour, *Employment Exchange*, p. 10.
[66] *Ibid.*, p. 12.
[67] *Ibid.*

market had been increased. The exchanges showed the way to end the ancient system of 'tramping' from street to street in London, or village to village in the country, which from time immemorial had accompanied the search for work. Exchanges were not what Arthur Henderson had scoffingly called them in the unemployment debate of May 19, 'the right to work bill in penny numbers.'[68] They created, to be sure, not a single extra job, but they made it possible for the workman to offer himself for employment anywhere in the country. They rigorously guarded the rights of trade unions by permitting the workman to refuse any engagement offered him at less than the union rate of wages. They observed strict neutrality in labour disputes, closing their services to employers in the search of 'black leg' labour. They made a small departure in the direction of the true competition, so dear to the hearts of classical economists, in that most imperfectly competitive of all markets, the labour market.

In the reasonably complete achievement of the limited aims of the Labour Exchanges Act, Beveridge reported one failure—his inability to force the decasualization of dock labour. The thesis of *Unemployment* had been that the most widespread hardship among the working classes was less the total loss of employment than continual and chronic underemployment, and intermittent employment. This condition was the result of employers taking advantage of the mass of partly organized and unskilled labour that collected like sediment at the bottom of the labour force in metropolitan centres. Because employers could depend on working men being available when needed, because of the high degree of replacability among unskilled dock workers, dock companies tended to hire men only as needed and to lay off immediately when the need for labour declined. The dock labourer and the railroad navvy, who was in the same marginal position, held down wages and working conditions of all other labourers.

Beveridge hoped to use employment exchanges and unemployment insurance as a weapon to force regularization of dock labour. He looked forward to extending unemployment insurance to the dock labourers under special conditions that would encourage employers to give some security of tenure to their working men and to end the casual dock gate system of recruitment and discharge according to the needs of the day. He was able to introduce

[68] *H. of C. Deb.*, V (May 19, 1909), col. 519.

an amendment to this effect into the Bill to amend Part II of the National Insurance Act in 1913. Unfortunately, before the Bill was carried, John Burns replaced Sidney Buxton as President of the Board of Trade, and Burns allowed the amendment to die. With it died the initial step towards the organization of the labour market, a project long promoted by the Webbs, who had encouraged Beveridge in his work along these lines.[69]

5

The system of national labour exchanges was an important innovation for Great Britain. But the exchanges were not unprecedented; the financial commitment was minor and no one seriously suggested they could do any harm. Hence the establishment of exchanges was an easy matter. But limitations of liability did not apply in the case of unemployment insurance.

Voluntary local unemployment insurance plans existed in many cities in Europe by the first decade of the twentieth century, and about eighty of the largest British trade unions, representing about three-quarters of a million workers, offered some form of this benefit to their members.[70] Among the most promising of the European schemes was a programme first tried by the municipality of Ghent in 1901—subsequently adopted by many town governments in Belgium, the Netherlands, Denmark, and Germany—which offered a subsidy from local taxation to unemployment insurance plans operated by trade unions.[71]

But only the canton of St Gall in north-east Switzerland had ever attempted compulsory unemployment insurance. The experience was not encouraging to English planners. Within two years after its establishment in 1895, the plan was bankrupt. St Gall had demanded contributions towards insurance from the worker, but not from the employer. This system proved to be unpopular, and because contributions were not deducted from wages by the employer, workers quickly fell behind in their payments to the

[69] Beveridge, *Power and Influence*, p. 79.

[70] For a discussion of trade union unemployment insurance before 1911, see: Beveridge, *Unemployment*, pp. 223–9.

[71] For a survey of European voluntary unemployment insurance plans, see: Joseph L. Cohen, *Insurance Against Unemployment*, London, 1921, pp. 75–155. Surprisingly, this excellent work has almost nothing on the important but short-lived St Gall plan.

I*

insurance fund. It became the practice for a man to pay nothing into the insurance fund until he lost his job. He then would make up all his arrears in a single payment and begin to collect unemployment insurance.

In addition, St Gall never succeeded in establishing an adequate system of supervision of claimants for benefit. Men who fell sick were often able to draw unemployment benefit for weeks, although they were not available for work. The unemployed were permitted to refuse, for frivolous reasons, the offers of work made through the labour registry maintained in connexion with the scheme. In this way the fund quickly built up a clientele of loafers, many of whom succeeded in drawing the maximum allowable benefit (sixty working days a year) for each of the two years the plan was in effect. In the first year of operation the premium income of the St Gall unemployment insurance fund amounted to 92·93 per cent of benefits paid. In the second year, income was 40·91 per cent of payments. The scheme was formally abandoned on June 30, 1897.[72]

The immediate motivation behind the Board of Trade's decision in 1908 to investigate the possibilities of compulsory unemployment insurance must remain obscure. Several authorities had proposed insurance at the time of the Unemployed Workmen Act. D. F. Schloss had investigated all types of European schemes for the Board of Trade in 1904, and W. H. Beveridge had done the same for the Royal Commission on the Poor Law in 1907, although neither the majority nor the minority report considered compulsory insurance to be desirable or possible.[73] The Webbs mildly supported the subsidization of trade union programmes on the Ghent system.

Very likely the idea presented itself without prompting from anyone when David Lloyd George and Harold Spender returned from Germany on August 26, 1908, full of enthusiasm for social insurance in general. Germany did not, of course, have national unemployment insurance, but neither man, probably, was expert

[72] The best source on the St Gall plan is: David F. Schloss, *Insurance Against Unemployment*, London, 1909, pp. 8–19.

[73] H. V. Toynbee, 'The Problem of the Unemployed,' *Economic Review*, XV (July, 1905), 291–305. Percy Alden, *The Unemployed, A National Question*, London, 1905. *Cd. 2304*, 'Report to the Board of Trade on Agencies and Methods for Dealing With the Unemployed in Certain Foreign Countries,' 1904, by D. F. Schloss.

enough to know why.[74] Certainly Lloyd George discussed social insurance many times during the next few weeks with Winston Churchill, who already understood in some measure the possible uses of insurance to social reform. It may well have occurred to the two men to try to find out why unemployment insurance could not be established as a complement to labour exchanges and health insurance, which were already under consideration. This theory receives some support from a statement by Lloyd George to Alexander Murray, the Liberal Chief Whip, in 1910. The Chancellor was at that time attempting to have the Unemployment Insurance Bill transferred from Churchill's successor at the Board of Trade, Sidney Buxton, to himself. He told Murray the unemployment insurance had been his idea in the first place. He had thought much about it after his return from Germany. But

> I had a weak moment . . . when Winston was at the Board of Trade. I told him of my plans. He promptly went off with them to his own Department; and got permission from Asquith to frame a Bill on the lines that I had proposed, and to introduce it himself.[75]

In any case, informal investigation of possible plans of unemployment insurance began at the Board of Trade early in the autumn of 1908, at almost the same time that labour exchanges were getting under way. The close connexions between the two Bills did not imply, however, any similarity of substance. Labour

[74] The Imperial Labour Department investigated existing insurance programmes fully in 1906 and concluded that national unemployment insurance was not feasible. *Die estehenden Einrichtungen zur Versicherung gegen die Folgen der Arbeitslosigkeit im Ausland und im deutschen Reich*, 1906, I.

[75] Arthur C. Murray, *Master and Brother, Murrays of Elibank*, London, 1945, p. 88. To an extent, Sidney Buxton confirmed this boast by saying during the second reading of the National Insurance Bill that the 'first idea' for unemployment insurance had come from Lloyd George. *H. of C. Deb.*, XXVI (May 24, 1911), col. 272. In a speech at Albert Hall, Swansea, on October 1, 1908, the Chancellor, quoting liberally from Chiozza Money, pointed to the contrast between the great wealth and the widespread poverty of England. Now that the State had taken care of old people, he said, it must begin to look after the widow, the orphan, the sick, and the unemployed. In the same month, Lord Riddell recorded in his diary a long talk with Lloyd George about unemployment, in which L. G. suggested the establishment of a fund built by a levy upon employers and workmen in prosperous times to support the unemployed during depressions. Lord Riddell, *More Pages From My Diary, 1908–1914*, London, 1934, p. 3. This in essence is the plan of unemployment insurance.

exchanges were uncomplicated and inexpensive. Their problems were administrative. The very idea of a nationwide scheme of unemployment insurance was wildly experimental. It involved legislative attack upon a problem of unknown dimensions. Except for a few trade union figures, there were no statistics on how many men were unemployed at any time, or for how long, or whether the incidence of unemployment varied with age, or what period of uninterrupted employment the average British worker could expect.

The men responsible for the planning of unemployment insurance were William Beveridge and the permanent secretary of the Board of Trade, Sir Hubert Llewellyn Smith. The forbidding shortage of data of any kind about the project at hand dictated that they solicit expert non-official opinion on how unemployment insurance might best be run. These suggestions, collected in the last months of 1908, came from a wide range of social thinkers— Sidney Webb, whose proposal for voluntary unemployment insurance coupled with compulsory labour exchanges has already been quoted at some length, Professor W. J. Ashley, and G. N. Barnes, among a number of others.[76] Generally the unofficial advisers approved of the insurance idea but showed great reluctance to give specific suggestions for its implementation. Several felt that worker contributions towards insurance would be unpopular. Trade union men objected that government-sponsored insurance would weaken the unions' hold over their men.

On April 26, 1909, with the framing of the Labour Exchanges Bill virtually complete, 'a committee of the cabinet was appointed to consider and report upon the question of insurance against Unemployment.'[77] Formal preparation of an Unemployment Insurance Bill now began.[78] To enact within two years the reform programme which Churchill had elaborated privately to Asquith in December, 1908, and which Lloyd George had outlined publicly in his budget speech of April 29, 1909, unemployment insurance would have to be passed into law in the session of 1910. This the

---

[76] These statements were printed for the Cabinet in May, 1909. They are to be found in the Beveridge Papers.

[77] H. H. Asquith to Edward VII, April 26, 1909, Asquith Papers, Box 6, ff. 106–7.

[78] 'Memorandum on a Scheme for Unemployment Insurance and Draft Heads of a Bill for the Establishment of Unemployment Insurance, Secret,' n.d., P.R.O., Cab. 37/39, No. 69. (Covering note dated April 17, 1909.)

radicals intended to accomplish.[79] During the rest of the year, therefore, Beveridge and Llewellyn Smith worked steadily on the formulation of the principles around which a parliamentary Bill would grow.[80] While the measure was by no means complete when work on social insurance was interrupted by the budget crisis, plans were far advanced. Unemployment insurance was not born in the atmosphere of haste and improvisation that surrounded health insurance.

Unemployment insurance was founded upon three principles, each of which would prove with experience to have been essential to the success of the scheme. First, the programme would be narrow in coverage. In the absence of any useful actuarial data it could not be otherwise. Beveridge and Llewellyn Smith had hoped in 1908 to safeguard the programme further by making benefits proportionate to contributions, and contributions proportionate to earnings.[81] In any event, the scheme would carefully exclude all doubtful risks and would make no attempt to insure other than temporary, predictable unemployment. This meant, Beveridge later explained, that the scheme would be confined to trades in which cyclical unemployment was the rule. The measure as originally conceived would do nothing for declining trades, nothing for trades, such as the dock workers, in which casual labour was customary. It excluded trades in which large numbers of women were employed, especially married women for whom work might be incidental. It excluded trades that normally put workers on short time rather than laying them off—coal mining and cotton spinning.[82]

Secondly, it would be impracticable for political reasons to

[79] Winston S. Churchill, 'The Budget and National Insurance,' speech May 23, 1909, at Free Trade Hall, Manchester, quoted in Winston S. Churchill, *Liberalism and the Social Problem*, London, 1909, p. 311.

[80] As the year advanced, work fell more and more heavily on Llewellyn Smith. On September 24, 1909, Beveridge was appointed Director of Labour Exchanges.

[81] William Beveridge, 'Notes on Unemployment Insurance,' October 29, 1908, Beveridge Papers, unsorted. For the earliest planning of unemployment insurance, see also: Beveridge, *Power and Influence*, pp. 82-4. It is worth noting that half a century later the Labour Party proposed at last to abolish the ancient principle of the flat rate payment to the national insurance fund and establish graded contributions and benefits.

[82] William Beveridge, 'Memorandum to the Royal Commission on Unemployment Insurance, March 31, 1931,' quoted in *Social Service Review*, VII (December, 1933), 660-1.

exclude trade unions from the scheme, as Beveridge and Llewellyn Smith had wished to do in 1908. Indeed, such actuarial data as existed on unemployment insurance came from the trade unions that ran schemes of their own. It followed that trade union unemployment insurance would have to be incorporated into the government plan on terms that the unions would accept. But practical politics dictated also that the government plan be not limited to trade unions (the 'Ghent scheme,') as the minority report of the Royal Commission on the Poor Laws proposed.

Finally, unemployment insurance would have to be contributory if it were not to be ruinously expensive. Yet here again appeared the curious opposing pressures to which social legislation seems to be particularly vulnerable. Trade unionists and radicals feared that any insurance contribution by an employer would be added to his wage cost and so would be paid finally by the worker. They sought, therefore, to make any government contribution as large as possible. The State, they argued, would recover its cost from a reduced poor law expenditure.[83] But many Liberal leaders were dubious whether the nation would agree to a large and permanent plan of unemployment relief, when scarcely three years before the Government had declined to make any payment to the Unemployed Workmen Act on the plea that unemployment was a local problem not to be relieved by general taxation.

The chief departmental controversy to occur in formulating unemployment insurance turned on the attitude the plan should take towards unemployment resulting from personal failing. In this skirmish, Llewellyn Smith engaged his own political chief, Winston Churchill. Largely at the permanent secretary's insistence, unemployment insurance remained stringent in the admission of individual claims for its small benefits. Llewellyn Smith did not expect that the application of insurance should be confined forever to the few trades selected at the beginning. He foresaw that the scheme might be extended widely among other callings. Indeed he intended that it should once sufficient actuarial data had been collected. But he always insisted that workers within a given insured trade, who lost employment through their own misconduct —laziness, drunkenness, or carelessness—should be ineligible for unemployment insurance. He admitted that in excluding this type

---

[83] See, for instance: G. N. Barnes' comments on the unemployment insurance scheme in 'Unemployment Insurance Criticisms,' p. 13, Beveridge Papers.

of man, he barred from insurance benefit the sort most likely to become unemployed. His argument was not based on morality; rather, he contended that misconduct was an individual, not a group, hazard. Hence it was incalculable and uninsurable. The scheme might do a few things well. It would be wrecked if forced to do too much. In April, 1909, the permanent secretary wrote:

> If a practicable scheme of insurance against unemployment can be devised, it is clear that so far as it goes it affords the most obvious and natural remedy for the evils arising from unemployment so far as caused by fluctuation either cyclical or seasonal in the general labour market, and not from the decay of particular trades or personal defects in the individual workman. Insurance is not a direct remedy for 'underemployment', and probably could not be applied under present conditions to the purely casual employments, though when combined with labour exchanges it may do a good deal to discourage casual engagements within insured trades.[84]

Opposing Llewellyn Smith was Winston Churchill, who insisted the State had no right to refuse benefits to a man who paid for them, whatever was the cause of his unemployment. In a memorandum to his subordinate on June 6, 1909, the President of the Board of Trade propounded with characteristic force the principles he felt ought to determine benefits under unemployment insurance. Here he contradicted both the ancient poor law view that as unemployment was *per se* immoral, a man accepting relief might be punished for doing so, and the modern Webbian doctrine of 'conditional relief'—that in return for support the relieving authority might supervise the individual's economic and social behaviour. The protection of the unemployment insurance scheme against abuse by the wastrel was a grave problem, wrote Churchill, but the safeguards ought to be mainly automatic and impersonal. Who, after all, would be the judge of misconduct?

> The best and truest safeguards are those which unite the self-interest of the individual with the interest of the fund. The spirit of the Insurance Scheme is not to weaken the impulse of self-preservation, but to strengthen it by affording the means of

[84] H. Llewellyn Smith, 'Memorandum on a Scheme for Unemployment Insurance,' April, 1909, p. 3. P.R.O., Cab. 37/99, No. 69. It is also in the Beveridge Papers.

struggle, and the fear of running through benefits, or passing out of the Insurance Scheme altogether, must be constantly operative.

The scheme should be so arranged, the President continued, that a man who is malingering will gradually lose benefits or find it more costly to reinstate them. But this should work automatically, not as the result of personal investigation.

> I do not feel convinced that we are entitled to refuse benefit to a qualified man who loses his employment through drunkenness. He has paid his contributions; he has insured himself against the fact of unemployment, and I think it arguable that his foresight should be rewarded irrespective of the cause of his dismissal, whether he lost his situation through his own habits of intemperance or through his employer's habits of intemperance. I do not like mixing up moralities and mathematics.

The fund would have to be protected, argued Churchill, not by personal judgments or officers of administration, but by

> clear ruthless mathematical rules. A disposition to over-indulge in alcohol, a hot temper, a bad manner, a capricious employer, a financially unsound employer, a new process in manufacture, a contraction in trade, are all alike factors in the risk. Our concern is with the evil, not with the causes, with the fact of unemployment, not with the character of the unemployed. In my judgment, if a man has paid to the fund for six months he should have his benefit in all circumstances, including dismissal for personal fault even of the gravest character; two securities being the low scale of benefits, and the solid rigid qualifying period.
>
> In my view the Insurance Office must stand the racket to the full, on the worst possible hypothesis within the conditions it prescribes, and its condition should be based upon the assumption that the least satisfactory possibilities will result.

Churchill concluded with a paragraph that may stand as a classic statement of the principle of social insurance and of the essentially unconditional nature of the British welfare tradition.

> These are the reflections which occur to me this morning upon the paper on malingering, and I will only add one other of

a general character. We seek to substitute for the pressure of the
forces of nature, operating by chance on individuals, the pressures of the laws of insurance, operating through averages with
modifying and mitigating effects in individual cases. In neither
case is correspondence with reality lost. In neither case are
pressures removed. In neither case is risk eliminated. In neither
case can personal effort be dispensed with. In neither case can
inferiority be protected. Chance and average spring from the
same family, both are inexorable, both are blind, neither is
concerned with the character of individuals or with ethics, or
with sentiment. And all deviation into these paths will be disastrous. But the true economic superiority of the new foundations of averages, over the old foundation of chance, arises from
the fact that the processes of waste are so much more swift
than those of growth and repair, that the prevention of such
catastrophes would be worth purchasing by diminution in the
sense of personal responsibility; and, further, that as there is
no proportion between personal failings and the penalties
extracted, or even between personal qualities and those penalties,
there is no reason to suppose that a mitigation of the extreme
severities will tend in any way to a diminution of personal
responsibility, but that on the contrary more will be gained by
an increase of ability to fight than will be lost through an abatement of the extreme consequences of defeat.[85]

The steady progress towards the completion of an unemployment insurance Bill ended suddenly on November 30, with the
House of Lords' rejection of David Lloyd George's Finance Bill.
The Cabinet had resolved early in September to dissolve Parliament should the peers take this unprecedented action. Accordingly,
Parliament was sent home on December 3, and a general election
took place the next month. Now the Liberals lost the overwhelming
majority they had gained in 1906. They returned with 275 members to the Unionists' 273. The Government majority depended,
therefore, on the eighty-two votes of the Irish Nationalists. At the
first Cabinet meeting after the election, only hours after the
publication of the final polls, Prime Minister Asquith read a letter
from the Nationalists stating 'that the Irish party would vote

[85] Winston S. Churchill to H. Llewellyn Smith, 'Notes on Malingering,' June
6, 1909, Beveridge Papers, unsorted.

against the Budget unless assurances were given that a Bill would be passed in the present year' dealing with the second chamber veto.[86] While several Cabinet members preferred defeat on the budget and resignation to dictation from the Irish, and Asquith thought it necessary to prepare the King for the Government's imminent departure, cooler heads prevailed. Thus, for the next eighteen months the radical programme formulated in 1908 and 1909 was sidetracked by the tremendous debate over the House of Lords reform. Then, after an interval for the passage of the National Insurance Act of 1911, the contest resumed over Irish Home Rule, forcing the United Kingdom to the verge of civil war. Radical reform ended with the National Insurance Act, a measure of incalculable importance, but not one intended by the radicals to be their last achievement.

During the first nine months of 1910, therefore, little was accomplished in unemployment insurance planning. Although Sir Hubert Llewellyn Smith's presidential address to the Economic and Science Statistics Section of the British Association at Sheffield on September 1, 1910, may be regarded as a semi-official announcement of what was coming, the speech showed little progress over the previous year.[87] He dealt exclusively with arguments for unemployment insurance as a principle showing that loss of employment was a reasonable insurance risk, provided the insurer had to deal only with claims of economic origin. It was 'absolutely necessary in the public interest,' he felt, to exclude claims resulting from personal misbehaviour.[88] The permanent secretary concluded his speech by listing what he termed ambiguously, 'the essential characteristics of any unemployment insurance scheme.' These may serve as a summary for the discussion of insurance planning. Any programme, Llewellyn Smith argued, must be compulsory. Otherwise, 'the bad personal risks

[86] H. H. Asquith to Edward VII, February 10, 1910, Asquith Papers, Box 6, ff. 180–1.

[87] Sir Hubert Llewellyn Smith, 'Economic Security and Unemployment Insurance,' *Economic Journal*, XX (December, 1910), 513–29. In many passages the speech repeated almost *verbatim* Llewellyn Smith's memorandum to Churchill of April, 1909. David Lloyd George revived consultations on health insurance at approximately the same time. The coincidence of date is probably accidental, however, for the Cabinet did not decide to join unemployment and health insurance in one Bill until January, 1911.

[88] Llewellyn Smith, 'Economic Security,' *Economic Journal*, December, 1910, p. 518.

against which we must always be on our guard would be certain to predominate.' The reasoning here, it should be noted, contradicts precisely the assumptions made about voluntary old age pensions only two years before. The Liberals had then argued that a voluntary contributory pension plan would be used only by provident and thrifty workers and so would not reach those who needed it most. Now the same Government argued that only the improvident and unemployable would insure against unemployment were the plan to be made voluntary.

Llewellyn Smith asserted that by keeping the insurance plan contributory and by insisting on a certain number of weeks of contribution before benefits became payable, the worst risks would be eliminated.[89] Generally, he recapitulated the arguments of Churchill's memorandum of June, 1909—that the plan's operation in giving benefits to the genuinely unemployed, in excluding the loafer, in avoiding over-use, in encouraging regular employment, should be largely automatic. Maximum benefits must be kept low and minimum contributions relatively high. Benefits would have to be considerably below wages to avoid encouraging unemployment. In every case, the scheme ought to encourage regular employment and not discourage self-insurance. It would have to be tried out first in the trades that lent themselves most readily to insurance; and the Treasury, in order to give stability and to justify a certain amount of State supervision, should contribute to the insurance fund.[90]

The address to the British Association was widely assumed to be the proclamation of a forthcoming Bill on unemployment insurance. *The Times* the next day commented most favourably on the plan. Particularly the newspaper approved of the stipulation that unemployment resulting from personal misconduct would be excluded from benefits. Lack of personal efficiency, asserted the newspaper, ought not to be permitted to impair the standard of national efficiency. Socialists, the paper predicted, would disapprove. 'The principle of discrimination, on which Sir H. Llewellyn Smith so strongly insists, is odious to Socialism.'[91]

[89] As finally worked out in the Bill, twenty-six weeks of contribution were required before any benefits were payable and no worker could at any time claim more than one week of benefit for each five weeks of contribution.

[90] Llewellyn Smith, 'Economic Security,' *Economic Journal*, December, 1910, p. 527.

[91] *The Times*, September 2, 1910.

In the next eight months the plan that became Part II of the National Insurance Bill took shape as a parliamentary measure. The trades to be insured were building, construction of works, shipbuilding, mechanical engineering, iron founding, construction of vehicles and finally sawmilling when carried on in connexion with any other insured trade. These trades were in every case highly organized. But unionization by itself conferred no eligibility for government insurance. A number of highly organized trades, for instance mining and transport, were excluded, although the Board of Trade was given power to extend the Act and to determine the eligibility of marginal occupations.

A workman in an insured trade would have 2½d. deducted from his pay for each week of employment. To this sum the employer would add a further 2½d. to make a total contribution of 5d. that would be paid to the government by the purchase of revenue stamps at the post office. The stamps affixed to a card became the workman's receipt for his contribution toward unemployment insurance.

Llewellyn Smith had asserted from the beginning that any scheme of contributory unemployment insurance would require sweetening by a government payment. An exchequer subsidy for unemployment relief was a serious innovation and the centre of some debate. Its amount was not fixed until shortly before the Bill was introduced. Originally, contributions had been set at 2d. per week equally for worker, employer, and State. But this ratio was changed early in April, 1911, on the plea that one-third of the total contribution was too large a burden for the State to bear and that the total sum was inadequate to support the contemplated benefits. The worker's and employer's contributions were raised to 2¼d. each and the Treasury payment set at one-quarter of the total amount collected from the worker and employer, in effect an average of 1¼d. per man, per week.[92] Then before the Bill was introduced, this proportion increased to one-third of the total working man's contribution, an average of 1⅔d. per man, per week.

The amount of the unemployment benefit posed a still more difficult problem. The Board of Trade could never forget that

[92] Sidney Buxton, 'Unemployed Insurance Bill, *Confidential*,' April 3, 1911, P.R.O., Cab. 37/106, No. 46, and 'Unemployment Insurance Draft Bill, 1911,' p. 5 (typescript, unsigned, dated in pencil, '8 April, 1911'), Bill File, National Insurance Bill 1911: 'Part I, to Second Reading (Commons),' Ministry of Pensions and National Insurance.

unemployment insurance was absolutely experimental. The loafer might use it to subsidize his idleness. The selfish man might try to recover every penny he had been forced to pay in. The government would not be protected by the pressure of working-class solidarity and union fellowship that kept trade union claims down. Tormented by these speculations, insurance planners had difficulty settling upon the rate of benefit. Their fears were more acute because there was to be no accumulation of a permanent insurance fund like that proposed for health insurance. Instead, only a small fund would be established to meet immediate claims. Should this prove inadequate, the resources of the Treasury were by statute made available to pay benefits to eligible men who would otherwise be denied them because of insufficient income to the insurance fund. The possibility that His Majesty's Treasury might be tapped for millions of pounds because an ill-considered piece of legislation had given large numbers of citizens the right to call upon it, caused shudders among civil servants and politicians alike. Hence, the continual adjustment of the rate of the benefit.

As it turned out, the politicians had more courage than the civil servants. In the draft Bill of April 8, 1911 (which even at this late date appears to be a reasonably tentative proposal—although entitled 'Unemployment Insurance Draft Bill', it is more of an explanatory memorandum) the benefits proposed were 7s. per week for the first five weeks and 6s. per week for the next ten weeks. Four weeks later, when the Bill was introduced in the House of Commons as Part II of the National Insurance Bill, benefits had increased to 7s. per week for fifteen weeks in all insured trades except 'in the case of workmen engaged in building or the construction of works,' where the benefits would be 6s. for fifteen weeks. This safeguard had been introduced, Sidney Buxton explained later, because data on unemployment in the building trades was more than usually unreliable.[93] The Commons sensibly threw out this unfair distinction and set the unemployment benefit uniformly at 7s. per week, after a one-week waiting period for a maximum of fifteen weeks within any twelve-month period. This was, in fact, the major amendment to the unemployment section of the National Insurance Bill.[94]

[93] *H. of C. Deb.*, XXXI (November 16, 1911), cols. 2108–9.
[94] Lord Beveridge's memory is clearly at fault in his statement in *Power and Influence* concerning the amount of the unemployment benefit. He recalls:

The language of the clauses concerning involuntary unemployment was far from precise. The Bill stipulated that the applicant for benefit who lost his employment through 'misconduct' or who had left employment 'without just cause' could be denied benefit for six weeks. But even here the workman denied benefit could appeal the decision of the local unemployment officer through a hierarchy of referees, during which time he would be paid benefits. As eventually defined, regulations rarely denied payments to any eligible worker and, more important, never used its power to improve working-class habits of life. No notice was taken if a workman squandered his insurance compensation in drink or gambling. The right of a freeborn Englishman to be dirty if he wished remained inviolate.[95]

A workman unemployed because he was on strike was not eligible for benefit under insurance. However, the Bill maintained neutrality in labour disputes by stipulating that although a worker receiving benefits should be always available for work in his own trade at the customary wage, he would not lose benefits if he declined a job with a firm engaged in a labour dispute.

The Bill provided that a man consistently unable to find employment in his own skill might, at the option of the insurance officer, be tested for skill in his professed trade. If the test uncovered remediable defects in the man's knowledge of his craft, the insurance fund could pay for his retraining. This forward-looking provision, which reflects the thinking of the Webbs, received a good deal of interdepartmental criticism. Particularly opposed was

When our draft Bill proposing 7s. a week as the rate of unemployment benefits came before the Liberal and Radical Cabinet of 1910, the only serious criticism reported to us was that the rate of benefit was dangerously high. Could we not cut the rate to 5s. a week? But we stuck to our 7s.

Beveridge, *Power and Influence*, p. 83.

[95] Writing of Churchill's and Lloyd George's unemployment and health plans in the spring of 1909, Beatrice Webb had remarked:

We do not see our way to support their insurance schemes. We shall not go against them directly, but we shall not withdraw criticisms in the Minority Report. If their schemes can be carried out we should not much object. Both have good consequences. But we still doubt their practicability, and some of the necessary conditions strike us as very unsatisfactory. The *unconditionality* of all payments under insurance schemes constitutes a grave defect. The State gets nothing for its money in the way of conduct, and it may even encourage malingerers. However, we shall honestly try not to crab the Government Schemes: they are thoroughly well-intentioned.

Webb, *Partnership*, p. 430.

Horace Munro, Permanent Secretary of the Local Government Board, who had succeeded Sir Samuel Provis in 1910 and who appears, with his predecessor, to have been chiefly responsible for the almost complete sterility of John Burns' tenure as President. Munro argued that the opportunity for education would only increase the number of competent workers without increasing the number of places available for them.[96] Despite Munro's objections, the provision remained in the Bill, becoming section 100 (1) of the Act.

Organized labour had always been suspicious of government welfare activities that would invade a province regarded by the unions as their own. The Board of Trade, therefore, sought to draw the unions in the insured trades into the insurance scheme. Any trade union, whether or not it had offered unemployment insurance previously, might elect to become an administrator for the government. Union members were not, to be sure, exempted from paying the required $2\frac{1}{2}$d. into the insurance fund, but a member had the right to draw his benefit through the union office rather than through the ordinary government agent, the labour exchange.

Most important, the government encouraged unions to offer larger unemployment benefits than the minimum paid by the State scheme. The measure provided for reimbursement to unions of three-quarters of the cost (raised by the House of Commons from an original two-thirds) of whatever unemployment benefit the organization paid. Hence, if a union paid no more than the regular minimum of 7s., it would receive from the insurance fund only three-quarters of that amount—5s. 3d. In order for the union to receive the full 7s. that the insurance fund stood ready to pay on behalf of every unemployed union member, the organization would have to offer an extra unemployment benefit of not less than 2s. 4d. from its own funds supported by its own dues. Put another way, in order to give their members the full return from the $2\frac{1}{2}$d. that each man paid to the insurance fund, trade unions had to pay benefits of not less than 9s. 4d., three-quarters of which represented the 7s. from the State fund, and one quarter the 2s. 4d. from the union treasury.

[96] Sir Horace C. Munro to Sir Hubert Llewellyn Smith, April 8, 1911, Bill File, National Insurance Bill, 1911, 'Part I, to Second Reading (Commons),' Ministry of Pensions and National Insurance.

Added to this incentive to treat the government payment only as a floor upon which private plans might build, the Bill stated that any 'association' (normally a trade union) whether in an insured trade or not, could recover from the Board of Trade one-sixth of the cost of any unemployment benefits it paid up to a maximum of 12s. a week. This provision was clearly in the nature of a bribe, an attempt to induce unions outside the insured trades to set up trial insurance schemes. The fact that the subsidy came directly from the Treasury and not from the insurance fund emphasized the non-actuarial nature of this experiment. The provision represented, nevertheless, an inducement to unions already under the government scheme further to increase the amount of their benefit. If a union paid the maximum 12s. benefit, 7s. would come as the regular government payment from the insurance fund. Of the remaining 5s. presumably drawn from its own dues, one-sixth, that is, 10d., could be recovered under the Treasury subsidy. Thus a trade union could offer its members a 12s. unemployment benefit, coming alarmingly close to the minimum wage for agricultural labourers, at a cost to itself of only 4s. 2d. A subsidy of this size was unlikely to be resisted. Any trade union opposition to unemployment insurance had been effectively bought off.[97]

The actuarial premises of unemployment insurance were, as will be seen, altogether different from those of health insurance. First of all, the planners of unemployment insurance assumed that the incidence of unemployment would not vary substantially through the course of an individual's lifetime. In any case, if such variation did exist, no data was available upon which to compute it. In health insurance, a young man was expected to build a fund during the vigorous and active time of his life to be drawn upon in the sickness of old age. This may be termed the 'lineal' concept of insurance. The money paid in by the insured, or more accurately, paid in by the entire group of insured of the same age entering insurance at the same time, would be held drawing interest to meet the ever-increasing claims as the group grew older. At the beginning of its insured life, the group's contributions would exceed its claims; later, the amounts would be equal, and finally, claims would outstrip contributions. Ideally, the group's credit in the fund would

---

[97] For a lucid discussion of the premises and implications of unemployment insurance finance, see: A. S. Comyns Carr, W. H. Stuart Garnett, and J. H. Taylor, *National Insurance*, London, 1912, pp. 106–10, 441–2.

last until the precise moment the final member passed from insurance.

Such a fund, a claims reserve, was unnecessary with unemployment insurance. The Board of Trade assumed that the frequency of claims within their particular type of insurance would be determined not by age, but by the economic circumstances of the individual's particular trade, or by the general conditions of the business world. Llewellyn Smith had eliminated all personal factors of misbehaviour or inefficiency. The unemployment scheme insured *only* against the universal, impersonal, economic forces that affected employment. These, everyone assumed, or rather hoped, were reasonably constant and predictable. Thus, if the health scheme, because of the nature of the risk insured, is thought of as lineal insurance, the unemployment plan can similarly be designated as 'lateral' in concept. Contributions from the men at work at a given moment would pay benefits to those out of work. The unemployment fund need only be large enough to pay the immediate claims likely to be made upon it. In the long run, the amount of money coming in and the amount going out ought to balance. The reserve had only to cover short run fluctuation in the amount of employment. The unemployment insurance fund thus was put without hesitation on the 'dividing out' basis against which the planners of health insurance, W. J. Braithwaite and John Bradbury, struggled for so long with David Lloyd George.[98]

In the absence of an accumulated claims reserve fund, the unemployment insurance administration received the right to call upon the Exchequer in the case of larger than calculated unemployment, or if, as was held to be possible, there occurred a run on the unemployment fund before contributions had built it up. Should the unemployment fund appear unable to meet the demand of eligible claims, the Treasury could advance whatever sums were required to discharge its liabilities to a maximum of £3,000,000. Should the fund remain insolvent, the Treasury could order the Board of Trade to lower benefits to a minimum of 5s. or to increase contributions from employers and workmen to a maximum of 3½d. each.

[98] See: Sir Henry Bunbury, ed., *Lloyd George's Ambulance Wagon, The Memoirs of W. J. Braithwaite*, London, 1957, pp. 120–7, 311–12. In his discussion of the dividing-out problem in the introduction to the Braithwaite memoirs, Richard Titmuss points out that the health insurance reserves taken over by the national insurance fund in 1948 amounted to £885,000,000. *Ibid.*, p. 46.

The Treasury in this way operated as a reserve fund for unemployment insurance.

As the Treasury added one-third to the amount of the employed contributions—that is, one-third of 5d.—the total amount going into the insurance fund for each employed workman would average $6\frac{2}{3}$d. per week.[99] The Board of Trade, charged with managing the scheme, diverted for this purpose one-tenth of the income to the insurance fund, or $\frac{2}{3}$d. per man, per week. (This included labour exchange expenses in connexion with insurance.) Administrative expenses in excess of this amount would be paid by the Treasury. Hence, the insurance fund had available for the payment of benefits, theoretically, 6d. per man, per week. ($2\frac{1}{2}$d. plus $2\frac{1}{2}$d. plus $1\frac{2}{3}$d., minus $\frac{2}{3}$d.) It follows that the planners of unemployment insurance assumed that fourteen men would be employed for each man drawing a 7s. benefit. In effect, the fund could afford to have $7 \cdot 14$ per cent of the men in insured employment drawing benefits at any one time. But because benefits were not payable during the first week of unemployment, the fund actually assumed an unemployment rate of $8 \cdot 46$ per cent. This corresponds almost exactly with the average unemployment rate estimated by Mr Thomas G. Acland of the Board of Trade, who calculated that the average British working man was unemployed $26 \cdot 8$ days per year or, put another way, that $8 \cdot 6$ per cent of workmen were unemployed at any one time.[100] As Mr Acland's estimate covered the entire British working force, general labourers, dock workers, and casual labour of all sorts, the insurance planners could feel with justice that they erred on the side of safety by using his general rate for the unemployment in the carefully selected fields to be covered by the unemployment insurance experiment.

Such were the rather primitive actuarial calculations of the unemployment insurance scheme. Their lack of sophistication was less a consequence of any conscious policy of H. Llewellyn Smith and William Beveridge than the result of the practical absence of data on British unemployment. Between the able-bodied paupers, who were reported in 1910 to be $3 \cdot 5$ per thousand of population,

---

[99] The State contribution to unemployment insurance was estimated to cost £660,000 per year. The Act provided that if the plan were extended to other trades the cost to the State was not to increase beyond £1,000,000 per year.

[100] Carr, *National Insurance*, p. 108.

who represented perhaps the dregs of the available work force of Great Britain, and the trade union unemployed, the cream of the labour movement, who numbered 45 per thousand members, lay an incalculable mass of working men. Presumably this mass constituted the majority of the working class, although who these people were, how many millions of them there were, how frequently they were unemployed, no one knew.[101] They made impossible the production of a universal scheme of unemployment insurance at once. Hopefully, all of them would be brought in eventually, trade by trade, as the scheme grew. The war and post-war depression destroyed this prudent, limited liability, approach to unemployment insurance.

6

The legislative history of the unemployment insurance sections, Part II of the National Insurance Bill of 1911, is almost without interest. The violent parliamentary struggle over health insurance overshadowed unemployment insurance. Part II received little notice in the papers and the pressure for time for Part I left small occasion for a discussion of unemployment. Health insurance was debated in Committee of the Whole House, while unemployment was dealt with by a Standing Committee. *The Times* noted that the Standing Committee established a 'record' by getting through all twenty-three clauses of Part II in six sittings.

> This is in part due to the very careful preparation of this part of the Bill in the Board of Trade. . . . It is due in part also, to the friendliness of the members of all parties who met in the committee room. . . .[102]

Only extreme Tories, such as Henry Chaplin, attacked unemployment insurance publicly, then only on detail. Chaplin, in common with the Webbs, doubted the need for compulsion.[103] Part II emerged from Parliament practically unchanged except in the details that have been noted. Its manager, Sidney Buxton, received none of the obloquy that was heaped on the head of David Lloyd George. Lord Beveridge remarks that the 'surprisingly easy

---

[101] Drage, *The State and the Poor*, p. 102. G. D. H. Cole and Raymond Postgate, *The British Common People*, University Paperbacks Edition, London, 1961, p. 544.
[102] *The Times*, November 17, 1911.   [103] *Ibid.*, October 30, 1911.

passage' of the unemployment insurance clauses was due to the fact that no one opposed the measure in principle and 'no one outside the Board of Trade knew enough to criticize it in detail.'[104]

After its quiet passage the unemployment insurance plan went into effect without the tumult and revolution that attended the beginnings of health insurance. Administrative agencies already existed in the trade unions and labour exchanges. The payment of contributions started on July 15, 1912, the same date that contributions began under health insurance, and benefits became payable on January 15, 1913, again in connexion with the health programme.[105]

The very short period given unemployment insurance to operate in the world for which it was designed makes any conclusion about its success more than usually tentative. The researcher may, nevertheless, be justified in setting out a few observations derived principally from statistical evidence. Clearest of all are the effects of the dubious and incomplete unemployment data with which the planners had to work. The number of workers to be covered was overestimated by one-quarter of a million. Two and one-quarter million men finally came under insurance instead of the expected two and one-half million. Secondly, even though the eighteen months from January, 1913, when benefits began, until the outbreak of war, were a time of exceptional prosperity, it is clear that the insurance fund could have carried far greater unemployment than workers in the then insured trades were likely to suffer. In the first full insurance year, running from July, 1913, to July, 1914, the fund received 1,100,000 claims representing probably half as many individuals. This figure reduces to an average of about 20,000 claims per week. Because the average period of unemployment in this period was slightly more than two weeks and the Act stipulated a one-week waiting period before benefit was paid, the ordinary unemployed worker would have been on benefit for slightly more than one week. It may be assumed, therefore, that at any one time

---

[104] Beveridge, *Unemployment*, p. 270. The researcher can only remark that Unionist ignorance of the infinitely more complex health insurance scheme did not protect it from their attack.

[105] The writer is unable to understand the statement in Viscount Simon's most unhelpful memoirs that the Bill had contemplated paying benefits from January 1, 1912, but that this date was changed to July 1 because of the coincidence with the holiday of Hogmanay in Scotland. Viscount Simon, *Retrospect*, London, 1952, p. 88, n. Neither date is correct.

there were about 40,000 unemployed in the insured trades, 20,000 on benefit, and 20,000 more in the statutory one-week waiting period, among a total insured of 2,250,000. This provides a daily unemployment rate of slightly less than 2 per cent, which corresponds closely to the overall trade union unemployment, both in and out of the insured trades, of 2·1 per cent for 1913.[106] Insurance profited greatly from the fact that most unemployment in the pre-war period was of short duration. Nearly half the unemployed were unable to draw benefit because they were back at work within a week. No one appears to have realized that the relief to the funds provided by this waiting period would grow proportionately smaller as the periods of unemployment lengthened. For example, if the average period of unemployment doubled—increased from two weeks to four—the number on benefit would triple. In the period before the war the ratio of contributions to benefits that had been calculated to balance at one to fourteen, was in fact one to one hundred. It is not surprising that in August, 1914, after twenty-five months of contribution, the insurance fund possessed a surplus of £3,185,000.[107]

The subsidy of one-sixth of the cost of benefits offered as an inducement to organizations outside of the insured trades to set up unemployment insurance schemes did little to extend insurance. Before the war, Lord Beveridge reports, only 11,000 workmen employed outside the insured trades had been brought into unemployment insurance by this provision.[108] On the other hand, trade unions within the insured trades used the subsidy considerably, as the government had hoped they would. Down to

---

[106] Mitchell, *Historical Statistics*, p. 65. Many of the statistics above are drawn from Beveridge, *Unemployment*, pp. 270–2. Surprisingly, the publication of unemployment statistics from the insurance programme did not begin until after the war. The only returns on monthly unemployment discovered by this investigator derive from a study of John Hilton, the Director of Statistics of the Ministry of Labour. Hilton's data, by calculating its rate from the total number of men who were unemployed for any period during a given month, indicates a higher rate of unemployment than shown here. John Hilton, 'Statistics of Unemployment Derived from the Working of the Unemployment Insurance Act,' *Journal of the Royal Statistical Society*, LXXXVI (March, 1923), 190. Trade union statistics, on the other hand, reported only the number unemployed on the last day of each month. On the origin and limitations of trade union unemployment statistics, see: Thomas G. Acland, 'Report on the Scheme for Insurance Against Unemployment Embodied in Part II of the National Insurance Bill,' May 4, 1911, *Journal of the Institute of Actuaries*, XLV (July, 1911), 459.

[107] Beveridge, *Unemployment*, p. 271. 　　　　　　[108] *Ibid.*, p. 272.

1916, when the Committee on Retrenchment recommended that the one-sixth subsidy be cut to one-twelfth, 483 unions with a membership of 1,180,000 had received payments. Payments for the year 1914–15 totalled £114,600.[109]

Of the two and one-quarter million men insured by the unemployment scheme, about 25 per cent insured through the trade unions. Of the total insured under the Act, only about 20 per cent had been insured before.[110]

The trade unions, which had uniformly insisted that they be made partners in any scheme of unemployment insurance, discovered when the Act was in operation that the State was quite prepared to treat them fairly. They found also that the burden of accounting for State funds made their new privileges less desirable than they had expected. This was particularly true for the smaller unions that had not offered their members unemployment insurance before the passing of the Act. The unions were required, for instance, to maintain a 'Vacant Book' in which the unemployed workman who lived within three miles of the union office registered daily in order to claim unemployment benefit. (If a workman lived beyond a radius of three miles, he was permitted less frequent appearances at the union office.) The maintenance of the vacant book necessitated the stationing of a full-time clerk at the union office. Moreover, to apply the work test, a union official had to be appointed to receive notice of vacancies to maintain a file of available engagements. Six months after the beginning of benefits, a survey of 200 unions revealed that the smaller ones were already tending to keep their vacant books at the local labour exchange, thus virtually giving up the business of administering unemployment insurance.[111]

Two sections of the Act representing tentative steps towards the organization of the labour market turned out in practice to be

[109] Cohen, *Insurance*, pp. 274–5.

[110] Ioan G. Gibbon, 'The Working of the Insurance Act,' *Economic Journal*, XXIII (December, 1913), 630. These figures suggest that very few, only about 5 per cent, of the new insured under the Act chose to insure through trade unions.

[111] U.I. 191. 'Repayments to Association Under Section 106, particulars of the Associations Which Have Given Notice of Their Intention to Apply for a Repayment Under Section 196 of the National Insurance Act, 1911, and Which Have Adopted Systems Deemed by the Board of Trade to be Satisfactory,' June, 1913, pp. 6–7, Central Offices for Labour Exchanges and Unemployment Insurance, Board of Trade.

almost impossible to administer. The first, offering retraining at State expense to men who appeared to need such aid, remained altogether a dead letter.[112] A second provision sought to induce employers to keep men at work. It offered a refund of one-third of the amount an employer had paid to the fund on behalf of any man if he kept the individual at work continuously throughout the year and paid at least forty-five contributions. This part of the Act proved to be unworkable because of clerical cost. The Government dropped it in the amending Bill of 1920.

The measures taken in 1909 and 1911 to solve the problems of unemployment never had a chance to prove themselves under the economic conditions for which they were designed. Although William Beveridge concluded from the pre-war experience that an unemployment fund of £5,000,000 would have been sufficient to provide benefits for a period of depression such as Great Britain suffered in 1907 and 1908, the great depression of the twenties and thirties destroyed for a time the unemployment plan as a scheme of insurance and forced the Government to provide direct, tax-supported unemployment relief coupled with a means test, the famous 'dole.' With this experience behind him, Beveridge insisted in Assumption C of his report of 1942 that any plan for unemployment insurance should be coupled with a consistent government policy of the maintenance of full employment.[113]

With the attack on unemployment, the national Government of Great Britain entered for the first time the life of the ordinary, adult, male, able-bodied workman. Welfare legislation hitherto had concerned itself with the helpless, either at the beginning or at the end of life. Invariably, previous attempts to cure unemployment had been administered by the local authorities and, more important, had been of the nature of relief. Now the crown provided permanent service agencies to which the mature workman might apply for aid and direction not only in emergency, but indeed to prevent emergency. For the average English workman, who did not pay

---

[112] Sir Frank Tillyard states that he 'never heard of the retraining provision ever being used.' Sir Frank Tillyard and F. N. Ball, *Unemployment Insurance in Great Britain, 1911–48*, Leigh-on-Sea, 1949, p. 35.

[113] The Beveridge Plan for unemployment insurance was calculated on an unemployment rate of 8·5 per cent, the figure used in the National Insurance Act of 1911. Unemployment insurance between the wars had had to assume an unemployment rate of 15 per cent. For a discussion, see *Cmd. 6404*, 'Social Insurance and Allied Services,' 1942, by Sir William Beveridge, pp. 163–5.

6 National Health Insurance

The passage of national health insurance as Part I of the National Insurance Act of 1911 brought the culmination and the end of the social welfare programme of the New Liberalism. David Lloyd George's massive plan to provide medical care for the British worker was beyond comparison the most expensive, the most ambitious, and the most controversial of the measures so far discussed in this study. However, it does not follow that health insurance represented a masterpiece of legislative craftsmanship comparable, for instance, to unemployment insurance. Nor did it have the influence on later British legislation possessed by Part II of the National Insurance Act. The awkward system of administration through private insurance organizations, and indeed the insurance of medical care itself, were discarded in 1946 in Aneurin Bevan's National Health Service Act, although social insurance would remain the basic institution of the Labour welfare programme.

But the Act is important as one of the measures generating the almost unprecedented political bitterness that brought Great Britain to the verge of civil war in the years before 1914. Moreover, by its sheer size, the Act demonstrated nearly all the problems encountered by a politician attempting to secure the passage of welfare legislation. Here, perhaps, lies the greatest importance of national health insurance for the historian. Social legislation is not a 'matter of State' in the traditional sense. It is outside the customary functions of government. The government is not dealing with other governments, nor with its own people in its customary role as ruler, keeper of the peace, or judge of disputes. Rather, in social legislation, the government is undertaking to do for the citizen what the citizen is unwilling, or unable, to do for himself. Normally, social legislation involves the government's appropriation of the function of some institution or person in society whose task has been performed inadequately. It may replace the parent in feeding schoolchildren, or the physician in treating working-class schoolchildren. It may take over part of the function of the friendly societies in the care of the elderly, or of the trade union in

K

insuring workers against unemployment. A government, particularly a democratic one, attempting to do these things, is of course
resisted by the persons and institutions whose functions it is
appropriating. These pressures may sometimes be sufficient to
prevent the government taking action at all, as in the case for
many years of old age pensions. Or conversely, the affected institutions may succeed through the ordinary channels of political
influence in dominating the project upon which the government
had originally embarked.

The latter result is exemplified by national health insurance. The
scheme that became law in mid-December, 1911, bore practically
no resemblance to the plan originally conceived in meetings with
the friendly society representatives in October, 1908. Partly this
was so because of the exceptional adaptability and flexibility of the
mind of David Lloyd George, combined with an equally exceptional ignorance of the principles of insurance. But the total
reconstruction of the Liberal Government's first plan for health
care for workers was more clearly the result of the powerful and
conflicting political pressures exerted by the three great social
institutions most affected by health insurance—the friendly societies, the commercial insurance industry, and the British medical
profession.

The story of the growth of national health insurance is to a great
extent the story of lobby influence and pressure groups.[1] To be

---

[1] There is an astonishingly persistent belief that lobby pressures do not exist
in Great Britain. For instance: 'The party is too strongly in control of English
politics for members to be liable to influence by lobbyists. . . . There is hardly a
loophole between the constituencies and Parliament through which the lobbyist
can slide to extort concessions.' Herman Finer, *The Theory and Practice of
Modern Government* (London, 1932), II, 774–5.

   With a sophisticated electorate, quick to react against any suspicion that it is
being 'got at' by a vested interest, with a highly disciplined party system that
frowns on political deviations, and in the background a tight-fisted treasury,
pressure groups, however powerful or wealthy, have formidable barriers to
surmount before they can affect the course of public affairs. . . .
         G. R. Strauss, 'Pressure Groups I Have Known,' *Political Science
         Quarterly*, XXIX (January–March, 1958), 46.

'The British lobby is domesticated.' Compared with America it behaves
'more soberly and responsibly.' S. E. Finer, *Anonymous Empire, A Study of the
Lobby in Great Britain*, London, 1958, p. 92. On the other hand modern
scholarship has begun to revise these opinions.

A recent important writer has suggested that British pressure groups have
in some ways an easier task than those in the United States. Samuel H. Beer,
'Pressure Groups and Parties in Britain,' *American Political Science Review*, L

sure, it is a political story, but one in which the significant political activity took place in committee rooms, before constituency and interest group delegations, and in Whitehall ministerial offices, seldom in the House of Commons. The formal struggle at Westminster palace only reflected this outside activity, sometimes not too accurately.[2] Moreover, the bitterness apparent in the struggle over national health insurance between the traditional political parties was less the result of strengths or weaknesses in the Bill than the residue of Unionist anger and disappointment at their defeat over the Parliament Act.

I

The primary impulse for health insurance grew out of David Lloyd George's interest in the extension of old age pensions. He considered any extension of this system to be possible only on a contributory basis. With this in mind, accompanied by Harold Spender and Sir Charles Henry, the Chancellor travelled to Germany in the third week of August, 1908, to study the German system of contributory old age and invalidity pensions. His plans, certainly discussed with Winston Churchill before his departure, were to round off the British non-contributory scheme with pensions for widows and orphans and for incapacitated or chronically ill working men under the age of seventy. As he explained to the Executive Committee of the National Conference of Friendly

(March, 1956), 9. The belief in the absence of pressure groups has been termed 'a widely accepted myth about the British political system.' R. T. McKenzie, 'Parties, Pressure Groups, and the British Political Process,' *Political Quarterly*, XXIX (January–March, 1958), 6. See also John H. Millett, 'British Interest-Group Tactics: A Case Study,' *Political Science Quarterly*, LXXII (March, 1957), 71–82.

[2] Sidney and Beatrice Webb may well have been thinking of health insurance when they wrote in 1920:

The able civil servant and expert Minister are always trying to placate . . little groups of outsiders and to make arrangements with those who really understand and are interested in the issues involved in new legislation or administrative work, so as to prevent these issues being raised in Parliament. In short, the real government of Great Britain is nowadays carried on, not in the House of Commons at all, nor even in the Cabinet but in private conferences between Ministers with their principal officials and representatives of the persons specifically affected by any proposed legislation or by any action on the part of the administration.

Sidney and Beatrice Webb, *A Constitution for the Socialist Commonwealth of Great Britain*, London, 1920, p. 69.

Societies on November 17, 1908, his proposed scheme of national insurance

> was the logical and inevitable outcome of the Old Age Pensions Act and that having made provision for those over 70 years of age, the Government desired to make provision for the workers of both sexes who are incapacitated before reaching the pension age. The importance of the question was emphasized by both the Majority and Minority Reports of the Poor Law Commission.[3]

In Germany the Chancellor received every courtesy. He arrived in Berlin on August 21, and spent the day at the Imperial insurance office talking with the minister, Theobald von Bethmann-Hollweg, whose friendliness for England was well known and who would the next year become Imperial Chancellor. On August 23 Lloyd George left Berlin for Hamburg, where he interviewed members of the German Seamen's Association. He returned to England on August 26, 1908, landing at Southampton. On the train between the port and Waterloo Station, the Chancellor announced his great enthusiasm for the German insurance system.

'Were you impressed with the German pension system?' asked a correspondent of the *Daily News*.

> I never realized on what a gigantic scale the pension system is concocted. Nor had I any idea how successfully it worked. I had read about it, but no amount of study at home of reports and returns can convey to the mind a clear idea of all that state insurance means to Germany. You have to see it before you can understand it. It touches the German people in well nigh every walk of life. Old age pensions form but a comparatively small part of the system: Does the worker fall ill? State insurance comes to his aid. Is he permanently invalided from work? Again

---

[3] 'Report of the Committee,' *Resolutions of the Annual Meeting of the National Conference of Friendly Societies*, October 14–15, 1909, p. 41. Lloyd George was fond of adducing the Poor Law Commission reports in an unspecific way to provide support for his statements about poverty, but he did not begin reading them until March, 1911. Sir Henry N. Bunbury, ed., *Lloyd George's Ambulance Wagon, the Memoirs of William J. Braithwaite, 1911–12*, London, 1957, pp. 72, 136.

Despite innumerable statements to the contrary, their effect on the health insurance scheme was minor.

he gets a regular grant whether he has reached the pension age or not.

The *Daily News* remarked that Lloyd George's inquiries had been particularly directed towards discovering whether German methods could be adopted in Great Britain. The Chancellor was asked whether he had changed his mind on non-contributory pensions. He answered that he had not.[4] Lloyd George concluded by saying he was still not sure whether German pension methods could be adapted to Great Britain and that in any case he intended to study Belgian and Austrian pension systems as well.[5]

Once back in England, the Chancellor lost no time beginning the preliminary planning for his scheme of social insurance. In addition to Churchill, who was beginning at the same time to lay the groundwork for unemployment insurance, his enthusiasm appears to have infected other members of the Cabinet. On September 10, David Shackleton, then president of the Trades Union Congress, read a letter before the annual meeting of his organization in Nottingham from the Home Secretary, Herbert Gladstone, who reported that he hoped to appoint a royal commission on compulsory State insurance.[6]

Gladstone's announcement startled also the parliamentary agents of the National Conference of Friendly Societies, who realized now that the Government was in earnest about entering the field of social insurance. For the friendly societies, this was a far more dangerous form of competition than had been old age pensions. The two agents, William Marlow of the Foresters and

[4] *Daily News*, August 27, 1908.
For some reason Peter De Mendelssohn denies that Lloyd George learned anything from the German pension system. '. . . the story that Lloyd George based his comprehensive scheme of State Insurance on an "intensive study" of conditions in Germany must surely be a myth.' Lloyd George, says De Mendelssohn, took a 'summer holiday' in Germany and was more impressed by military preparations than by social insurance. Peter De Mendelssohn, *The Age of Churchill: Heritage and Adventure, 1874–1911*, New York, 1961, p. 429.

[5] These investigations got under way immediately, as did the T.U.C. investigation of German social insurance described in the previous chapter, and the reports were made in December. See: (a) 'Memorandum prepared in the Treasury on Invalidity and Old Age Insurance in Germany'; (b) 'Report on the System of Workmen's Insurance in Austria-Hungary by Mr A. F. Whyte,' November, 1908; (c) 'Report by Mr P. A. Chance upon the Provisions Made in Belgium For Old Age Pensions, Infirmity, Sickness, and Unemployment'; Braithwaite Papers, Part II, Item 1.

[6] *The Times*, September 11, 1908.

W. G. Bunn of the Hearts of Oak, immediately sent a letter to David Lloyd George asking him to use his influence to secure friendly society representation on any commission appointed, arguing that 'the establishment of such a system in England must "kill" voluntary organizations like ours. . . .' The letter expressed disappointment that 'the remarks made to Mr Bunn and I [sic] when we were received by you at the Treasury, based upon the knowledge of our work during the past 50 to 100 years . . .' had been so completely altered by a week's mission in Germany.[7]

In their report to the National Conference in 1909 Marlow and Bunn did not give a date for their letter, but one may assume it was sent soon after Shackleton's announcement of September 10. In any case, Lloyd George reacted almost immediately both to the immediate threat of competition in the welfare field from Herbert Gladstone and to the threat of resistance to government activity from the friendly societies. On October 1, at Swansea, he made a speech which may be regarded partly as a public announcement of health insurance, but which may have been also an attempt to make sure that the reins of any government activity on the social problem should be in his hands. At the same time, he hoped to bring pressure on a still reluctant Cabinet to move forward in this field. Finally, the Swansea speech was a statement of the programme of the second instalment of Liberal reform.

Idleness was always a problem, said the Chancellor, among both the rich and the poor. Betting and drink harmed all classes equally. But there was another problem, he continued, the problem of those

> who through no fault of their own are unable to earn their daily bread, the aged and infirm, the broken in health, the unemployed, and those dependent on them. The aged we have dealt with during the present Session. We are still confronted with the more gigantic task of dealing with the rest—the sick, the infirm, the unemployed, the widows and orphans.

---

[7] *Resolutions of the Annual Meeting of the National Conference of Friendly Societies*, October 14–15, 1909, Report of Parliamentary Agents, p. 26. The reference to a meeting at the Treasury suggests that Lloyd George had discussed social insurance with Bunn and Marlow before the trip to Germany. On the other hand, this might well have been in connexion with old age pensions, which the friendly societies were still seeking to modify. Letters went also to John Burns and Gladstone.

No modern society, Lloyd George insisted, could allow its people to starve.[8]

Immediately after the Swansea speech—the date is not entirely clear, but early in October—the Chancellor interviewed Marlow and Bunn. On October 13 he met the friendly society leaders a second time, including on this occasion R. W. Moffrey, parliamentary agent of the Manchester Unity. Together the three men represented the largest societies in the movement, having about one-third of the total membership. At this meeting the Chancellor asked the men to inform the National Conference of Friendly Societies of the Government's interest in social insurance.[9]

The National Conference did not welcome the government proposals. The suspicion of government activity manifest over old age pensions had not died. When the Chancellor met the three society leaders again on October 27, after the annual meeting of the National Conference at Bristol, he was made to understand, as so many government leaders had learned before, the hostility of friendly societies to government intrusion in their field.[10] Lloyd George's reaction was characteristic of the man and typical of the way he would handle all problems during the evolution of the national health insurance programme. He invited the parliamentary agents to request all of their colleagues on the executive committee of the National Conference to meet him.

There followed now three meetings between the Chancellor of the Exchequer and the entire executive committee of the National Conference. These meetings occurred on November 17, December 1, and December 15, 1908. In them the Chancellor was able to persuade the friendly society leaders to assent in principle to the idea of State insurance and from the last conference evolved a

[8] David Lloyd George, *Better Times*, London, 1910 (A collection of speeches made between April 4, 1903, and June 30, 1910) pp. 50-3.

[9] The preceding account has been taken from Marlow and Bunn's report to the annual meeting of the National Conference in October 1909 cited above and from a letter sent by W. G. Bunn, shortly before he died, to the Hearts of Oak annual meeting in June, 1911, by which time relations between the societies and the Chancellor had cooled considerably. W. G. Bunn, 'Original Scheme of State Insurance,' June 9, 1911, *Hearts of Oak Benefit Society, Delegate Minutes, 1910–1912*, Annual Meeting, 1911, p. 35.

[10] The Directors of the Manchester Unity passed a resolution in November, proposing that each district lodge make a formal protest to their M.P. against national insurance 'which would strike a blow at the principles of individualism and self help . . .' Independent Order of Odd Fellows, Manchester Unity, Quarterly Report, February, 1909, pp. 121-2.

skeleton plan of State insurance that the Government and the societies agreed to submit to a committee of actuaries for an estimate of cost. At this last meeting the societies also received a number of promises about the Government's intentions on welfare legislation that they regarded as binding upon the Chancellor. Because of the eventual breakdown of amicable relations between the friendly societies and the Government, and as a statement of the thinking of the Liberal leaders in undertaking health insurance, these statements are of great importance. As later reported to the annual meeting of the National Conference of Friendly Societies by the parliamentary agents, they were:

1. The Government are not proposing to start an opposition establishment to the Societies.

2. They are anxious to bridge the period up to 70 years of age, when pension begins, for those who are handicapped in the race through physical disability and invalidity, and also to assist widows and orphans, tuberculosis cases, &c.

3. They are not inclined to continue support to those who refuse to make any provision and expect other people to bear their burdens, willing to tap every source of relief, but contribute nothing.

4. They are not proposing to enforce Government interference more than now exists.

5. They do not ask for control of funds of Societies nor for management of investments thereof.

6. They do not ask the morale of the present Society members should be lowered in any way by the admission of undesirable persons.

7. They cannot countenance any but sound permanent Societies.

8. They have generously granted a positive assurance that nothing shall be considered as binding upon the Societies in any way unless and until the scheme is before them to consider, and express their views upon, before a Bill is introduced.[11]

These were the assurances made to the leaders of the powerful British friendly society movement with its long tradition of political conservatism and hostility to all government activity. The Government was proposing to use the friendly societies to fill in

[11] *Annual Meeting of N.C. of F.S.*, 1909, Report of Parliamentary Agents, p. 27.

the gaps left by existing welfare legislation. Should the societies co-operate, or not? Bunn and Marlow argued persuasively that they should, that indeed the danger was greater if they did not.

Summarized, the position is that we are convinced we lost ground over the Old-Age Pension Scheme by standing aloof from it until it was an accomplished fact. The earnest desire of our brethren to participate in working thereon as committeemen, the positive need for exemption in all cases where our brethren are penalized when claiming its privileges, are the basis from which we draw this deduction. We believe it would have been to the advantage of the Societies had we been represented on the Poor Law Commission also, and with these ideas firmly rooted in our minds, we did not intend to be isolated from any movement in which the Societies were so greatly affected as National Insurance was likely to prove.

We were convinced that the efforts to explain our principles to the Chancellor will be found conducive to the best interests of the great thrift movement, and that an honour of no mean character has been conferred upon the Societies by their representatives having been invited to consult with a Minister who is apparently as eager to help on the work as we ourselves claim to be.

The Charity Organisation Society has written to the widow of the Rev. Canon Blackley who is only too willing to again bring out her late husband's scheme, and with the startling fact that although there are nearly 10,000,000 wage-earners outside these Societies, our numerical strength is not increasing as it should do, there is every reason why we should carefully consider the proposals that will lead us to meet the increasing needs of the future.[12]

Not for the last time in dealing with national insurance, David Lloyd George's charm and persuasive genius had succeeded in making supporters of potential enemies. Without any knowledge of the details of the plan under consideration, the leaders of the friendly society movement in the National Conference agreed to recommend that the constituent organizations permit their facilities to be incorporated into a national scheme of welfare insurance.

[12] *Annual Meeting of N.C. of F.S.*, 1909, Report of Parliamentary Agents, pp. 26-7.

K*

Since April 20, 1909, the plan that had evolved from the conferences of 1908 had been in the hands of actuaries George F. Hardy, president of the Institute of Actuaries in 1908, and Frank B. Wyatt.[13] This embryo scheme of insurance had already undergone some evolution during the meetings and would be further modified before the actuaries finished, but as the first stage of health insurance it deserves examination. During the first two meetings, the Chancellor had proceeded with the plan he had originally brought back from Germany: that basic benefits would be sickness, invalidity, and widows' and orphans' pensions. Simply stated the scheme provided for the protection of the wage earner or his survivors against the threat of destitution in the case of a permanent loss of family income. All working men not in friendly societies would be required to join the State programme, the benefits of which were to be kept small and limited in scope. The more important goal, stipulated in the first report, was

> to leave other benefits such as payments on death, medical and dispensary, hospitals and sanatoria, to the friendly societies as inducements to persons to join them rather than any State scheme.

> Friendly Societies are admittedly composed of the cream of the industrial classes, and it may be safely assumed that they will be fully able to adapt the working of the societies to the new conditions and to compete successfully with any State scheme.[14]

[13] For a description of the personal characteristics of Hardy and Wyatt see: Bunbury, ed., *Ambulance Wagon*, p. 77. At the December 15 meeting it had been agreed that friendly society actuaries should participate in the planning of the Bill. Subsequently the societies had named Ralph Hardy, Samuel Hudson, and Alfred Watson. However, in the spring of 1909 when the time came to begin work, Ralph Hardy was abroad and G. F. Hardy and Wyatt declined to work with Samuel Hudson, who was not a member of the Institute of Actuaries, even though he was approved by the Treasury as a friendly society actuary. Upon learning this, Watson himself withdrew, so the basic actuarial calculations for national health insurance were worked out by government appointees alone. See: Parliamentary Agent's Report, R. W. Moffrey, Agent, *Independent Order of Odd Fellows, Manchester Unity, Friendly Society, Annual Movable Conference held in Central Baths Hall, Bradford, May 31–June 4, 1909*, pp. 136–7.

[14] '*Memorandum of the Chief Registrar of Friendly Societies*, Strictly Confidential (Founded on the Proceedings at Conferences Between the Chancellor of the Exchequer and the Committee of the National Conference of Friendly Societies, Held 17th November and 1 December, 1908),' p. 7, Braithwaite Papers, Part II, Item 2.

But the plan of December 1, described in the registrar's memorandum, was expanded at the last meeting on December 15 to include in addition a medical benefit, a maternity benefit, and some form of sanatorial treatment. Also by the end of the series of meetings, the society representatives and the Government had agreed on stipulated values for the benefits. When finally transmitted to the actuaries, the cost of medical attendance and medicine had been set at 4s. a year per insured. The maternity benefit would be £1. The sickness benefit would amount to 5s. per week for twenty-six weeks, the invalidity benefit, 5s. per week indefinitely. A widow would receive 5s. per week so long as she had children dependent upon her under the age of sixteen, and orphans would receive 1s. 6d. per week until the age of sixteen, whether a mother was surviving or not. The sanatorial benefit amounted to 1s. per year per insured member towards the construction and maintenance of a building.[15]

The plan given the actuaries in the spring of 1909 had by no means undiluted support of the members of the conference that produced it. Besides the general unspecific fear of all friendly society members that minimum government benefits would grow too large and so compete with those they offered their own members, the particular provision of the widows' and orphans' pension caused an immediate protest. This pension had been the motive for Lloyd George's original trip to Germany. Together with the invalidity pension aimed at insuring the income of the injured or chronically ill wage earner, it had been seen from the beginning as the basis of the insurance scheme. The amount of the pension had been kept low in order not to compete with friendly society sickness benefits. But even so, on December 15 the Government was apprised of a serious objection to widows' pensions that

[15] The statement of the original scheme of health insurance as agreed upon in December, 1908, can be found in detail in the letter from W. G. Bunn to the annual meeting of the Hearts of Oak, dated June 9, 1911, cited above, and in 'Report of the Actuaries in Relation to the Proposed Scheme of Insurance Against Sickness, Invalidity, etc.,' March 21, 1910, Braithwaite Papers, Part II, Item 4. It is most conveniently available, however in less detail, in an article by the Rev. J. Frome Wilkinson, published when relations between the Government and the friendly societies were most hostile. J. Frome Wilkinson, 'The National Insurance Bill: *Respice, Auspice, Prospice*,' *Contemporary Review*, C (October, 1911), 501–18. Wilkinson's article gives also the only accurate published account of the early negotiations that this researcher has discovered.

would eventually become a basic controversy in the evolution of national health insurance.

In addition to sickness benefits, friendly societies normally offered a sum at the death of the insured to pay for his funeral. There was no more degrading aspect of the poor law, and no greater fear among the English working class, than the fear of death as a pauper. Burial by the parish had always been the ultimate humiliation and the assurance of a respectable funeral was often the first motive for the formation of a friendly society. Playing upon this fear, commercial insurance companies had built up a gigantic and immensely profitable business offering funeral benefits on far less favourable terms than the friendly societies. Funeral benefits had never been considered as part of the State insurance scheme, but at their last meeting one of the most influential members of the National Conference, J. Lister Stead, secretary of the Foresters, argued that by offering a widows' and orphans' pension the government was, in fact, invading this field. 'The providing of allowances to widows and orphans suggests difficulties,' wrote Stead.

> In reality it is a matter of providing a benefit at the death of the husband and the payment of the benefit in instalments, weekly or otherwise, for a limited period does not take the provision out of the category of a death benefit. From the outset it has been understood that 'death benefits' were to be excluded.

Stead admitted that the absence of a widows' and orphans' pension might be taken as a 'weakness in the scheme' and urged that if such a benefit were included it ought to be made unconditional and definite and certainly not dependent upon the circumstances of the widow. But, he argued, as indeed the actuaries eventually discovered, a widows' and orphans' pension would be expensive, taking perhaps half the total contributions.[16] Stead's reservation about widows' and orphans' pensions would be amply justified in the future. But this benefit remained in the scheme given to the actuaries three months later, although Lloyd George was careful thereafter never to mention that part of his proposed programme and to refer to it always simply as a plan of insurance for 'sickness, invalidity, etc.'

[16] 'Notes by Mr J. Lister Stead on Suggested Scheme of Insurance with Estimates of Probable Cost. *Handed in at Conference of December 15th, 1908*,' p. 2. Braithwaite Papers, Part II, Item 3.

In the early months of 1909 with rumours of the Government's interest in national insurance now widely circulating, stimulated by articles as Harold Spender's statement of January, 1909, in the *Contemporary Review*,[17] individual friendly societies, to the dismay of the National Conference, began to pass resolutions against State insurance.[18] Responding during the budget speech on April 29, 1909, Lloyd George, after describing German social insurance in the most enthusiastic terms, warned the friendly societies that they could not by themselves do all that was necessary to provide for the social welfare of the nation. Said the Chancellor:

> At the present moment there is a network of powerful organizations in this country, most of them managed with infinite skill and capacity, which have succeeded in inducing millions of workmen in this country to make something like systematic provision for the troubles of life. But in spite of all the ability which has been expended upon them, in spite of the confidence they generally and deservedly inspire, unfortunately there is a margin of people in this country amounting in the aggregate to several millions who either cannot be persuaded or perhaps cannot afford to bear the expense of the systematic contributions which alone make membership effective in these great societies. And the experience of this and of every other country is that no plan or variety of plans short of an universal compulsory system can ever hope to succeed adequately in coping with the problem.[19]

Immediately after the budget speech the National Conference asked Lloyd George for a statement on insurance that could be communicated to the friendly societies during their annual Whit week Conferences, which would be held in the last days of May

[17] See Chapter V, pp. 256-7.

[18] To reassure the Chancellor, the National Conference passed a resolution on March 3 deprecating activity by its constituent societies until the details of the Government's scheme were known. Copies of this resolution were sent to all societies in the conference, to the press, and to David Lloyd George two days later.

[19] *Official Report, House of Commons Debates*, Series 5, IV (April 29, 1909), cols. 485-7. The President of the National Conference, George Wilde, noted these remarks in his presidential address to the annual meeting of the National Conference in October. George Wilde, Presidential Address, *Resolutions of the Annual Meeting of the National Conference of Friendly Societies*, October 14-15, 1909, pp. 11-12.

and the first days of June. Although their letter was described as an 'urgent communication,' the National Conference received no reply from the Chancellor until May 26, by which time it was too late to transmit the Chancellor's letter to the societies. Moreover, the Chancellor asked the societies to appoint a 'small representative body' that would 'have powers to discuss with me the details of a scheme of State insurance against sickness and invalidity, etc.' There was some consternation both in the National Conference and in the member societies about the constitution and purpose of the 'small representative body' that had been requested. No one in the friendly society movement wished to delegate the responsibility for final approval of the Government's insurance plan. Therefore the executive committee sent a letter to Lloyd George asking for an explanation of his request and also for some indication of when the societies could expect the report of the government actuaries. Again, nearly a month passed. Not until June 28, 1909, did the National Conference receive a note from W. H. Clark, Lloyd George's secretary, saying that the actuaries were discovering the problem more complicated than it had appeared and that so far as the requested plenipotentiary committee was concerned, the aim was simply to organize a group which had the power to speak on behalf of the societies to deal with the Chancellor. This 'as you doubtless remember, was not the case in regard to the Committee with whom the Conferences have been carried on hitherto.' So far as the Chancellor was concerned, this plenary body could be the National Conference itself.[20]

Two months later, in about the middle of August, the executive committee again addressed a note to the Chancellor asking when the actuaries' report would come. This time W. H. Clark answered immediately, on August 20, 1909, commenting once more on the difficulty of the actuaries' problem, and admitting that the report could not be ready before October. 'In these circumstances,' Clark concluded, the Chancellor 'fears it would be of no use for him to have a further meeting with the Committee at present.' With this uncordial rejection, negotiations between the British friendly

[20] This letter is printed in full in *Delegate Minutes, 1910–1912*, Hearts of Oak Benefit Society, Annual Meeting, p. 67. The Hearts of Oak did pass a motion unanimously authorizing conference representatives to appoint some of their number to deal with Lloyd George.

society movement and the Chancellor of the Exchequer recessed for over a year.[21]

2

Although in the autumn of 1908 after the Swansea speech, *The Times* had expected a Bill to be introduced the next year—perhaps coupled with the Finance Bill as old age pensions had been[22]—for practical purposes all work on sickness insurance ceased after the introduction of the budget, not to be begun again until the late autumn of 1910. It may be appropriate at this point, therefore, to survey briefly the facilities for medical care available to British working men and the conditions of practice encountered by doctors who treated them.

In assessing the medical provision for the thirty-nine million people in the British Isles with incomes under the tax limit of £160 per year, the most immediately noticeable fact is that there was no 'system' of medical care at all.[23] As in charity in the eighties, as in education until 1902, there were a wide variety of overlapping, often competing, invariably uncoordinated, medical institutions. This group, representing over five-sixths of the population, earning about one-half of disposable consumer income, by their numbers controlled English vital statistics and constituted the portion of the nation on whose behalf national health insurance would be established. Of the wide range of health facilities available to them,

[21] Details of the correspondence between the executive committee of the National Conference and the Chancellor are printed in: 'Report of the Committee, George Wilde Prs.; J. E. Gilcrist V.P.; Wm. Marlow and W. G. Bunn, Parl. Agents; J. Lister Stead; R. W. Moffrey; Jonathan Duncan; John McNicol, Sec. October 14, 1909,' in *Annual Meeting of N.C. of F.S.*, 1909, pp. 43–5. Those named on the committee were the men who participated in the negotiations of November and December. The Clark letter of August 20 appeared in *The Times* on August 25.

[22] *The Times*, November 16, 1908.

[23] In a highly influential book first published in 1905, and running through ten editions in the next five and a half years, Sir Leo Chiozza Money estimated that there were 39,000,000 'poor' people living in families which received not more than £160 per year total income. Altogether they received £935,000,000 for an average of slightly more than £2 per family per week. He calculated that there were 1,400,000 rich persons in the United Kingdom who in 1908 and 1909 received £634,000,000 and 4,100,000 comfortable people receiving a total of £275,000,000. Leo Chiozza Money, *Riches and Poverty*, London, 1911, 10th ed., p. 47. Recent research has suggested that Sir Leo may have underestimated, in fact, the concentration of wealth at the top of the social scale. E. H. Phelps-Brown, *The Growth of British Industrial Relations*, London, 1959, p. 53.

some were excellent, many were bad, but all were inefficient in promoting the physical welfare of the people they were designed to serve. Partly this was the case because the best of them, the voluntary hospitals, due to their geographical distribution, were available only to a small portion of the working population. On the other hand, the most widespread health facility for the working class, the poor law infirmaries, carried the taint of deterrent parish relief, even though medically some of them were far advanced and the formal disabilities of pauperism had practically disappeared.

Beside these two major provisions for institutional care, an ordinary working-class neighbourhood might have a provident dispensary, operated either as a private enterprise by a group of doctors or by a charitable institution or, in a few cases, by a group of friendly societies. Normally the dispensary would offer fairly rudimentary general practitioner service with medicine for a fixed regular contribution or, more frequently in private dispensaries, for 6d. per visit. (These frequently were known in fact as 'sixpenny dispensaries.') Finally there were the individual medical practitioners, operating either in singlehanded practice or as an official of a friendly society or trade union, or with a medical club. A friendly society doctor normally was paid a contractual fee per year for each member under his care, a 'capitation fee.' If employed by a medical club, the doctor would be under agreement to provide service to any member of the group in return for a regular contribution averaging 1d. per week.[24]

Among the facilities listed above, by far the best, where they were available, were the voluntary hospitals. These foundations, originally established to provide medical care for the poor—in some cases tracing their origins to monastic establishments—were unfortunately available only to the populations of larger towns. Theoretically their services, both in-patient and out-patient, were either free or at least cost only a small amount as determined by the almoner. The voluntary hospitals provided practically the only

[24] During the passage of the National Insurance Bill, Canon Barnett listed for the *Westminster Gazette* the medical facilities available in Whitechapel. They were: the London Hospital; two free dispensaries; a provident dispensary; a poor law dispensary with three doctors; a private 'sixpenny dispensary'; a number of singlehanded G.P.s charging about 1s. 6d. or less for advice and drugs; and an unknown number of medical clubs plus the friendly societies and the medical officer of health. Samuel A. Barnett, 'Medical Benefit and the Insurance Bill,' *Westminster Gazette*, August 2, 1911.

specialist service available to the British working class. But, as the struggle over the school medical service demonstrated, by the end of the first decade of the twentieth century the out-patient clinics of the great voluntary hospitals were also offering serious competition in ordinary medical service. For at most a nominal fee they treated many workers whom the underpaid G.P. in the slums felt should be attending his own surgery. Thus the ordinary British doctor fought any extension of voluntary hospitals' services, as in the case of the school medical service, constantly urging that the voluntary hospitals be required carefully to restrict their services to those so poor they could not afford a private physician.

Far larger in terms of the number of beds available than the voluntary—usually referred to then as 'general'—hospitals were the poor law infirmaries. By the time of the coming of national insurance these establishments had outgrown all other forms of institutional medical care and a few were even beginning to approach some voluntary hospitals in technical efficiency. The social stigma attached to them, of course, remained. But this grew less as their facilities improved, particularly as labouring men gained control of boards of guardians. The use of the poor law medical service also increased as the definition of medical relief was broadened. With the rapid development of operative surgery, the definition of 'relief absolutely necessary for the health of the applicant' came to mean a great deal more than it had in 1834.[25]

In addition to the increasing generosity of boards of guardians in

---

[25] For a discussion see: *Cd. 4499*, 'Report of the Royal Commission on the Poor Laws and Relief of Distress,' 1909, p. 237.

Hospital Facilities Available, England and Wales, 1915

Number of Institutions	Number of Beds
General Hospitals—594	31,329
Special, Fever, Smallpox Hospitals—1,340	52,775
Poor Law Infirmaries—700	94,000

Harry Roberts, *A National Health Policy*, London, 1923, p. 89.

In 1906 the statistics in some principal cities were:

	GENERAL HOSPITALS Number of Beds	POOR LAW INFIRMARIES Number of Beds
London	10,224	16,300
Liverpool	1,172	2,000
Manchester	1,270	3,250
Birmingham	838	2,200
Leeds	450	1,000

Cd. 4499, p. 255.

working-class districts, a final, and perhaps most important, factor in the rapid upgrading of poor law medical facilities was the sheer overcrowding of facilities in the voluntary hospitals. Because of the nature of their sources of income, the voluntary hospitals, however splendid their reputation, could not expand rapidly enough to meet the needs of a growing population. But expansion of some medical facilities was absolutely necessary if the British population was to get the benefit of the new medical and surgical techniques that medical science each year was discovering.

It was inevitable that patients not accepted by voluntary hospitals would have to be accommodated by poor law infirmaries, which, supported by tax funds, could grow more readily. The difficulty was that despite the Medical Relief (Disqualification Removal) Act a person treated at a poor law infirmary, however well-to-do, became technically a pauper. He was included in the statistics of pauperism and deprived of his vote for the local board of guardians.[26]

In summary, institutional medical facilities available to the British workers at the time of the passage of the National Insurance Act were either too small for the demands made upon them or declassing to the users. In the last analysis, neither set of institutions could be expanded as they existed. Both in different ways represented attitudes towards the poor of another age. Finally, each presented a problem that national health insurance failed to solve.

Perhaps a more dangerous form of competition to the private physician, in that they were more widespread and usually far less efficient medically than the voluntary hospitals, were the provident, charitable, and endowed dispensaries. These institutions served the English working class in the slums of the great cities and also in the county towns and villages where no voluntary hospitals existed. A few of the dispensaries were two centuries old, but most were founded in the nineteenth century in the revival of religious charitable activity that had produced the Salvation Army and the settlement house movements.[27] A substantial number of dis-

---

[26] For a discussion relying mainly on the reports of the Royal Commission on the Poor Laws see: William M. Frazer, *A History of English Public Health*, *1834–1939*, London, 1950, pp. 302–3.

[27] For a good discussion of nineteenth-century church medical missions see: Kathleen J. Heasman, 'The Medical Mission and the Care of the Sick Poor in Nineteenth-Century England,' *Historical Journal*, VII, No. 2 (1964), 230–45.

pensaries were supported in part by the local parish, although under pressure from the medical profession nearly all of them attempted to make some charge to patients who appeared able to pay. Many dispensaries had been established by philanthropic organizations such as the Charity Organisation Society. The C.O.S. dispensaries and others like them required a regular monthly contribution from those in the neighbourhood who customarily used their services.[28] The provident dispensary had been from the beginning the facility for working-class medical care preferred by the Charity Organisation Society, and in the seventies it set up the Metropolitan Provident Medical Association to promote their establishment in working-class areas. Through provident dispensaries the society hoped to enforce self-help in working-class medical care as it tried to encourage parental responsibility for children by charging a penny for school dinners.[29] The majority report of the Royal Commission on the Poor Laws— to which the Charity Organisation Society stood in about the same relation as did the Fabian Society to the minority report— recommended the extension of the system of provident dispensaries for the medical care of the working class.

The provident dispensaries were perhaps more dangerous to the G.P. than the voluntary hospitals. Having little prestige and far smaller financial resources, they found it harder to discriminate between the legitimate poor and the thrifty member of the lower middle class who used their services because they were cheap. Moreover, they were easy objects of local pressure. Clement F. Rogers, curate of a London suburban parish that regularly contributed to the local charitable dispensary and had therefore to pass upon parishioners applying to use the dispensary services, told how he had refused to approve aid to the servant of a local tradesman with the result that the tradesman had withdrawn his subscription both to the dispensary and to the church. Rogers said he knew that the doctors in his neighbourhood hated the dispensary, for it

---

[28] Contributions were ordinarily 2½d. per week for a married couple with an additional ½d. for each child. Gilbert Slater, *Poverty and the State*, London, 1930, p. 200.

[29] See: C. S. Loch, 'Cross Purposes in Medical Reform,' n.d. [late 1870's], published by the Metropolitan Provident Medical Association; Sir Charles Trevelyan, 'On the Extension of Provident Dispensaries Throughout London and its Environs,' 1878, published by the Charity Organization Society (paperback pamphlets).

treated many who were well able to pay. Among those to whom he gave letters recommending charitable treatment, only one in twelve, he felt, actually needed free treatment. Moreover, he argued, the moral degradation of begging and lying for letters was worse than the mere degradation of charity.[30]

Variations of the provident dispensaries were the medical clubs and 'sixpenny dispensaries' which, appearing in many forms, represented the medical profession's attempt to meet the competition of institutionalized medical care, either charitable or State-supported. Medical clubs were sometimes organized by the workers in a particular factory or mill. A good one could offer, besides medical care, most of the benefits of a registered friendly society, that is, sickness, maternity, and death payments.[31]

But too often a medical club was the adjunct of a casually-run benefit society, more frequently called a 'slate club,' organized by the clientele of a public house. At worst, it was promoted by the doctor himself. In theory a medical club was simply a form of prepaid group medical insurance run by a layman. Similarly, the doctor himself might permit the prepayment of a small regular fee —3d. a week per family appears to have been customary in the north—by his poor patients. The more well-to-do, he hoped, would pay his regular fee for a surgery visit. (Canon Barnett discovered this was 1s. 6d. in Whitechapel.) Again in theory, there was no canvassing or solicitation to join a medical club. In fact, none of these suppositions was entirely true. Subscriptions to a slate club were normally picked up weekly by a collector working on commission. Although the collector was not supposed to solicit members, he frequently did, and a doctor desperate for patients was in no position to forbid the practice. A variation of this form of

[30] Clement F. Rogers, 'Joints in Our Social Armour, the Cruelties of Charity,' *Commonwealth*, VII (November, 1902), 349–52.

[31] See Lady Bell's well-known description of medical care among the iron workers at Middlesbrough. Three hundred and eighty of 700 workers in the largest plant in the town were in sick clubs. In addition there were branches of nearly 200 friendly societies in the town. Lady Bell (Mrs Hugh Bell), *At the Works: A Study of a Manufacturing Town*, London, 1907, pp. 85–9, 119, 122.

Trade unions also gave sick pay and death benefits to some extent. The Chief Registrar of Friendly Societies reported that in 1908 English and Welsh unions spent £449,778 on sick pay and £114,315 on death benefits. The figures represent 12·6 per cent and 3·2 per cent respectively of all union expenditures that year, and are together a little less than half the amount spent on unemployment benefits. 'Report of the Chief Registrar of Friendly Societies for the year ending 31st December, 1909,' *Parliamentary Papers*, 1910, No. 171, pp. 37–8.

practice was medical clubs organized by the agents of the few collecting friendly societies that offered medical benefits. These men organized clubs for their own profit and paid the physician a percentage of each subscription, taking the remainder for themselves.[32]

Among the various systems of group practice, unquestionably the friendly societies were the best. Here at least the doctor was spared the indignity of competing for patients. Because the lodge paid a substantial sickness benefit, its interest was in returning the ailing brother to work as quickly as possible. Hence the doctor was remunerated either by salary or capitation fee, never by the visit. In addition a good society might occasionally provide a small infirmary to which the society doctor could take his patients.[33]

But there was as much variation in friendly society practice as there was variety in the condition of the friendly societies themselves. Furthermore, friendly society practice contradicted the essential tenet of medical ethics, that of mutual choice by patient and healer. Friendly society practice was contract practice; the doctor was an employee of the society. His patients did not choose him; nor could he refuse service to any of them. He would treat as many members as the society chose to send him, or lose the contract to a younger, presumably more energetic, doctor. Withal there was keen competition among general practitioners for the 3s. to 5s. that friendly societies paid per member per year. First of all, noted Dr Alfred Cox, who became eventually medical secretary of the British Medical Association, friendly society appointments were a likely introduction to the member's family. One doctor in the Gateshead area, where Cox himself began practice in 1891, was reputed to have made as much as £500 per year from the societies, 'and it was no secret that many of the appointments were obtained by bribery and corruption.' Jobs were auctioned off to the lowest bidder.[34]

[32] For descriptions of this type of medical practice see: Alfred Cox, *Among the Doctors*, London, 1950, pp. 56–7, and 'Report of the Session of the General Medical Council,' *The Times*, November 29, 1901. This report deals in full with the important disciplinary case of Dr Robert Rendall, who was accused of canvassing among members of the Liverpool Victoria Collecting Friendly Society in Great Yarmouth.

[33] For a discussion of the various types of friendly society and club practice see: Sir Edward Brabrook, *Provident Societies and Industrial Welfare*, London, 1898, pp. 71–3.

[34] Cox, *Doctors*, p. 60. See also: Cox's testimony to the departmental com-

The profession's difficulties with contract practice came to a head between 1903 and 1905 in the famous 'Battle of the Clubs.' This began in Cork, Ireland, with the typical Irish weapon of the boycott of doctors in group practice. In Cork this was successful, partly because friendly societies were weak in Ireland. As a result the attack on friendly societies spread to England. In 1905 the British Medical Association published a report on friendly society practice which, although it had little permanent effect, did much to solidify doctors' opinions against the societies and so had considerable impact upon the drafting of national health insurance.[35] Generally the report of the B.M.A. demanded that an income limit be established to prevent well-to-do friendly society members from using the society doctor on the same terms as poorer members. It also hoped to place control over society medical practice completely in the hands of the profession.

The struggle between the societies and the medical profession continued for four years, reaching a stalemate at a meeting on July 16, 1909, convened at the invitation of the B.M.A. and chaired by Sir Edward Brabrook. Representing the doctors were J. A. MacDonald of the Medico-Political Committee of the B.M.A. and James Smith Whitaker, Medical Secretary of the association. Appearing for the societies in their capacity as members of the executive committee of the National Conference were brothers Marlow, Bunn, and Moffrey. The points of difference between the friendly societies and the medical profession were

mittee on sickness benefit under national health insurance, Cd. 7690, 'Report of the Departmental Committee on the Sickness Benefit Claims under the National Insurance Act,' Appendix, Vol. III, 1914, Q 307.

Alfred Cox, 1866–1954, born, Middlesbrough; educated, State schools and University of Durham; general medical practice, Gateshead, 1891–1908; Deputy Medical Secretary to B.M.A., 1908–11; Medical Secretary, 1912–32; Vice-President B.M.A., 1933.

[35] 'An Investigation into the Economic Conditions of Contract Medical Practice in the United Kingdom,' British Medical Journal, Supplement, July 22, 1905, pp. 1–96. This report was basically the compilation of answers to a questionnaire by the 1,548 doctors engaged in club practice who had responded to a request for information by the B.M.A. It may be notable that this figure was the return from 12,100 forms sent out. The writers of the report did not appear to understand the difference between true friendly societies and the collecting societies, which normally were responsible for the medical clubs. Ibid., p. 16. For an example of a specific case see: 'The Battle of the Clubs,' Lancet, January 6, 1906, and January 13, 1906, pp. 58–60, 121–2, describing the situation of the doctor working for the Macclesfield General Burial Society.

clearly stated in the report of the parliamentary agents to the National Conference the following October. The conference agreed on only one resolution: that it would 'be desirable to give members of societies the option of obtaining medical attendance from any medical man willing to grant it on society terms.'[36]

Above all the friendly society feared the loss of control over the branch surgeon, whose certificate of illness was the basic evidence for the payment of the sickness benefit. If the society could not control the doctor, they could not control the disbursal of their funds. This matter was of great importance in the planning of national health insurance.

Secondarily, hardly less significant for the future was the question of the income limit. A large proportion of the members of friendly societies were well able to pay private medical fees. The societies offered medical treatment at bargain prices. This the profession was determined to stop. But equally, the societies, fighting for membership, were determined not to restrict benefits. It was a good deal more difficult to obtain new members than to replace an unsympathetic friendly society doctor. Hence the meeting of July 16 achieved little. The differences between the friendly societies and the medical profession were unresolved as the early discussions of national sickness insurance began.

In making a general assessment of the medical services available

---

[36] For the future, this resolution was important, for it embodied the germ of the 'panel system' that eventually would be incorporated in the national health insurance scheme. Beyond this, Marlow, Bunn, and Moffrey were unwilling to go. To accept the recommendations of the report of the B.M.A. of 1905, they argued, would be to

> destroy the principle of trust now held for the Branch Surgeon, who is the officer upon whom we rely for safeguarding the funds from malingering &c.
> ... although a member might choose a Doctor and desire to change on their lines (only after a complete year upon any one roll), he could be rejected directly by anyone who chose to consider him an undesirable patient.
> ... this is aimed against those gentlemen who do our work, by those who want some of it, or could do with it.
> The profession allege that we have members who join these Societies solely to get cheap medical benefits, as though a man would pay between £2 and £3 per annum to get a doctor for a few shillings. ...
> To give this due effect we should cease to provide medical benefits as one of the objects of these Societies, and therefore receive no contribution from the member, and lose all power over sick members' claims.

> *Annual Meeting of N.C. of F.S.*, 1909. Report of the Parliamentary Agents, p. 24.

to the lower five-sixths of the British population, the researcher can only be struck by the fact that despite the undoubted competition among medical practitioners, despite the prevalence of friendly societies among the upper strata of the British working class, despite the rapid improvement in poor law medical facilities and the heroic efforts of out-patient clinics in the voluntary hospitals, the standard of medical care enjoyed by the ordinary English workman, and particularly his family, in the first years of the twentieth century was low. This fact can be attested by endless statistics, but perhaps the most dramatic evidence was discovered by B. Seebohm Rowntree in his investigation of York. Rowntree found that in almost any category—crude death rate, deaths of children under five years, or deaths of children under one year— the variation between the figures in the wealthiest areas and the poorest areas was regularly and dramatically higher at the lower end of the economic scale. Infant death rate—on the assumption that this statistic represents a sensitive indicator of medical efficiency—was over two and a half times higher in the poorest working-class districts than among the servant-keeping class.[37]

Perhaps a still more damaging indictment of working-class medical care lay in the fact that infant mortality remained relatively stationary in the last quarter of the nineteenth century, even though, as friendly society difficulties showed, the general standard of living was rising and longevity was increasing markedly. There were, indeed, three more deaths of infants under one year per one thousand births in the period 1896–1900 than in the period 1871–5. Paradoxically, infant and paranatal mortality showed no response to improved economic conditions, and indeed tended to fall in periods of hard times like the eighties and to rise in the relatively prosperous nineties. Conversely, deaths among children, pre-

---

[37] Deaths under one year in York per 1,000 children born—

in poorest working-class districts	247
in middle working-class districts	184
in the highest working-class districts	173
among the servant-keeping class	94
Average for York	176

B. Seebohm Rowntree, *Poverty: A Study of Town Life*, London, 1901, p. 206.

sumably less a function of medical care than of general environment, dropped regularly if slowly throughout the period between 1875 and 1915 as did deaths at any age in the population.[38]

In many ways the worst thing to be said of the medical services available to the British population, emphasized in 1910 by the Webbs in their influential book, *The State and the Doctor*, was that given the uncoordinated, unarranged, overlapping character of British medical facilities, the mere increase in the number of doctors or indeed of poor law hospitals would do nothing to improve over-all medical care for the poor. In effect, the *system* itself was at fault. There may have been, to be sure, a shortage of good hospitals, but clearly there was no shortage of doctors; if anything, competition among medical men was ruining the standards of medical practice. Yet at the same time, noted the Webbs, uncertified deaths, that is, deaths without a physician in attendance, were as high as 5 per cent of all deaths in England and ran to 20 to 30 per cent in Scotland. The two largest killers of the adult population, syphilis and tuberculosis, both diseases given to long, drawn-out periods of chronic illness, were scarcely treated. Worse, there was growing up a double standard for medicine. One standard was based upon the voluntary hospitals and the specialists and consultants who practised in them. The other standard centred upon poor law infirmaries and the underpaid, working class, general practitioner with his parlour surgery. The increasingly depressed condition of the G.P. tended to push the two levels of medical practice farther apart each year.[39]

[38] *Infant and Child Mortality Statistics*

Years	Mortality Per 1,000 Births Under One Year	1–2 yrs.	Deaths at Varying Ages Per 1,000 Survivors 2–3 yrs.	3–4 yrs.	4–5 yrs.
1871–5	153	59	28	19	14
1876–80	145	58	27	17	13
1881–5	139	53	23	15	12
1886–90	145	53	22	14	10
1891–5	151	52	21	14	10
1896–1900	156	49	19	13	9
1901–5	138	41	16	11	8
1906–10	117	35	14	9	7
1911–15	110	35	14	9	6

Sir George Newman, *The Building of a Nation's Health*, London, 1939, p. 314.

[39] Sidney and Beatrice Webb, *The State and the Doctor*, London, 1910, pp. 211–27. This book is largely a recapitulation of the medical recommendations

It would be wrong, however, to assume that national sickness insurance came under consideration because of David Lloyd George's awareness of the inadequacies of British medicine. His aim from the beginning was the improvement of the living standard of the British population. Specifically he hoped to eliminate the dependence upon the poor law as the only organized official means possessed by British society for the maintenance of its indigent members. To this end, he had conceived an extension of the State pension plan to those men not yet old, but who were unable to support their families because of chronic illness or accident, or to widows with children.[40] But the evil to be treated was pauperism, not sickness. Sickness was important to the Chancellor only as a cause of pauperism. The important benefits in national insurance, those originally considered in 1908, were the sickness and disability benefits. The idea of treatment of the illness itself appeared only after consideration of insurance had been under way for many weeks. Lloyd George's scheme, from this point of view, was a social, not a medical, measure. The Chancellor's only interest was in supporting the breadwinner during his illness. Thus under national health insurance there never was, and never would be, much provision for the treatment of dependants, for the family income was not dependent upon them. Again, there would be little concern, although more than is generally realized, with the provision of hospital care. All these things were expensive, and the aim of national insurance was, at bottom, to replace lost income, not to cure sickness. There was interest in sickness only so far as it was

of the minority report of the Royal Commission on the Poor Law. Surprisingly, syphilis does not even figure as a cause of death in the tables printed in Whitelegge and Newman's handbook for medical officers of health. See: Sir Arthur Whitelegge and Sir George Newman, *Hygiene and Public Health*, 12th ed., London, 1911, Appendix tables VI and VII.

[40] Lloyd George was obsessed with the idea of personal economic security. 'You people can never understand what it is to be hungry or out of work,' he once told Harold Spender. Spender, who perhaps knew the Welshman better than any of his colleagues, wrote that this emotion was the origin of national insurance. Harold Spender, *The Prime Minister*, London, 1920, p. 354. Commenting after the war upon the career of S. A. Barnett, Lloyd George remarked to Spender that with all the good intentions of the settlement house movement, no one could understand poverty unless, like himself, they had been born and bred in that condition. Harold Spender, 'Barnett the Sower,' *Contemporary Review*, CXV (January, 1919), 35.

Lucy Masterman has remarked to the writer that she too noticed in Lloyd George this deep and sincere sympathy for the poor.

desirable to put the breadwinner back to work as quickly as possible.[41]

National health insurance would later be criticized by many reformers for lack of attention to the wider aspects of health, for the lack of a broad range of benefits, and for its willingness to end its medical provision with service by a general practitioner 'of ordinary competence and skill.' The charge has come particularly from Fabians and medical officers of health whose thoughts on health proceeded in precisely the opposite direction from those of the Chancellor. Whereas for Lloyd George poverty was the evil that sickness caused, for these groups sickness was the evil that poverty caused. The poor acted as a focus for disease among the general public. There was much in this attitude reminiscent of the furor that had spread over England after the physical deterioration report. Poverty was bad, not because of what it did to those in that condition, but because it represented a danger to the nation at large.[42]

David Lloyd George was, of course, aware that his plan did not accomplish all that the most advanced health thinkers of the nation wished to do. He admitted many times that he would be delighted to make his programme a complete one, noted Dr Alfred Cox in a description of Britain's medical service for American doctors. But to do so would greatly increase the expense and

---

[41] The first report of the actuaries, rendered March 21, 1910, put the position clearly.

> Married women living with their husbands need not be included [in the insurance scheme] since where the unit is the family, it is the husband's and not the wife's health which it is important to insure. So long as the husband is in good health and able to work, adequate provision will be made for the needs of the family, irrespective of the wife's health, whereas when the husband's health fails there is no one to earn wages.
>
> > 'Report of the Actuaries in Relation to the Proposed Scheme of Insurance Against Sickness, Invalidity, etc.,' March 21, 1910, p. 51, Braithwaite Papers, Part II, Item 4.

[42] Poverty and disease are allied by the closest bonds, and nothing can be simpler and more certain than the statement that the removal of poverty would effect an enormous reduction in disease.

> Quoted in Sir Arthur Newsholme, *The Last Thirty Years in Public Health*, London, 1936, p. 70.

For other comments on the shortcomings of this aspect of national health insurance see: William A. Brend, *Health and the State*, London, 1917, pp. 223–5, a widely-quoted source. R. A. Lyster, M.O.H. for Hampshire, 'Public Health and the Poor Law,' *Public Health*, XXII (December, 1908), 105, gives a pre-Royal Commission statement of this attitude.

would perhaps jeopardize its main aim, the prevention of pauperism. 'The British National Health Insurance system,' concluded Dr Cox, 'is open to many criticisms, but it is not fair to blame it for not being what it never pretended to be.'[43]

3

In his last communication to the executive committee of the National Conference of Friendly Societies on August 20, 1909, Lloyd George's secretary, W. H. Clark, had suggested that the actuaries' report might be ready by October. That month, and the next, came and went without any further correspondence between the friendly societies and the Treasury. Then, on November 30, the House of Lords finally rejected Lloyd George's budget. Three days later the House of Commons declared the action of the upper house to be 'a breach of the Constitution and a usurpation of the rights of the Commons,' and on December 15 Asquith dissolved Parliament.

During the election the National Conference requested each of its constituent societies to demand from prospective candidates a pledge, among several others, that 'before any attempt is made to pass into law any scheme of State Insurance against sickness, invalidity, old age, &c., the Friendly Societies shall have ample opportunity of considering such schemes. . . .' They were to make sure the candidate would use his 'best efforts to secure that, in any legislation on the subject, the interests of existing Friendly Societies and their members will not be prejudiced.' This letter was sent to all societies on December 14, 1909, and without exception every candidate questioned gave the requested guarantees.[44]

[43] Alfred Cox, 'Seven Years of National Health Insurance in England,' *Journal of the American Medical Association*, LXXVI (May 7, 1921), 1350.

For Lloyd George's own statement on his aims, see the first paragraph of his speech explaining the National Insurance Bill during the first reading. *H. of C. Deb.* XXV (May 4, 1911), col. 609. According to the Royal Commission on the Poor Law, said the Chancellor, 30 per cent of pauperism was attributable to sickness. In fact, the majority report had stated:

It is probably little, if any, exaggeration to say that, to the extent which we can eliminate or diminish sickness among the poor we shall eliminate or diminish one half of the existing amount of pauperism.

Cd.4499, p. 289.

[44] Report of Executive Committee, *Resolutions of the Annual Meeting of the National Conference of Friendly Societies*, held in Town Hall, Reading, October 13-14, 1910, pp. 21-2.

On March 21, 1910, the long-awaited report of the actuaries was presented to the Government. This report, based upon the plan of insurance worked out on December 15, 1908, provided a basic government-guaranteed system of benefits that was intended simply to encourage contributors to become members of friendly societies. 'Existing members of Benefit Societies,' said the report,

whose present contribution in respect of recognized benefits is equal to, or in excess of, the contribution required of them under the Scheme, and all future members who may voluntarily become contributors for benefits in excess of those provided by the Scheme, would be permitted to pay their contributions direct to their Societies as at present, and would be exempt from deductions from wages. . . .[45]

Even after its many promises on the subject, the Government was slow to submit the actuarial report to the friendly societies. R. W. Moffrey wrote the Chancellor on April 23, 1910, reminding him of his promises. W. H. Clark replied on May 2, saying that the Chancellor was in a position to do nothing about insurance at present. 'Owing to delays in the passage of the Finance Act and to the present political situation the Government are precluded from taking any steps in this matter. . . .'[46]

Despite his uncommunicativeness at the beginning of May, the Chancellor invited the committee of the National Conference to meet him. This meeting took place 'in the middle of June' when the discussion centred on the actuaries' report. The meeting clearly was inconclusive. The members of the National Conference separated feeling they knew little more than before.[47] Moreover, the delegates to the National Conference were now beginning to receive pressure from local societies for their inability to publicize the details of a plan so important to the societies.[48]

[45] 'Report of the Actuaries,' March 21, 1910, p. 54, Braithwaite Papers, Part II, Item 4. (Underlining in original document.) This report is summarized, with some misleading changes, in Bunbury, ed., Ambulance Wagon, pp. 73-7.

[46] Report of the Parliamentary Agent, Independent Order of Odd Fellows, Manchester Unity, Friendly Society, Annual Movable Conference held in Drill Hall, St Mary's Road, Southampton, May 16-19, 1910, pp. 146-7.

[47] Annual Meeting of the N.C. of F.S., 1910. Report of the Executive Committee, p. 32.

[48] Report of the meeting of the High Court of the Ancient Order of Foresters, speech by William Marlow, quoted in The Depositor, The Official Organ of the National Deposit Friendly Society, XIV (September, 1910), 156.

After the meeting of mid-June for the discussion of the actuaries' report, Lloyd George again broke communication with the National Conference, reiterating at the same time his promises that the Government would take no action on sickness insurance unless the friendly societies had the opportunity to discuss the measure. His reason on this occasion, not revealed at the time, was the beginning of a series of meetings with the Unionist opposition to search for a compromise agreement on the constitutional position of the House of Lords. These constitutional conferences were the result of the death on May 6 of King Edward VII and the decision by the leaders of both parties not to inject his inexperienced successor, George V, into the unprecedented constitutional crisis in which the prestige of the crown might easily become involved. Lloyd George was one of the four Liberal Party leaders appointed to negotiate. Between the middle of June and its last meeting on October 21, the constitutional conference met twenty-two times.

During this period the Chancellor saw no friendly society leaders, but at some time during the busy summer—probably after July 29 when Parliament and the constitutional conference both recessed for over two months, and certainly before August 17—he found time to meet members of another powerful group whose importance in national insurance was ultimately as great as that of the friendly societies themselves. These were the representatives of the industrial insurance industry, and at this meeting Lloyd George learned for the first time that he faced an enemy who might be able to force a complete reconstruction of his projected plan of sickness insurance.

4

Like the friendly society movement with which it competed, industrial insurance represented a response to the British workmen's fear of the deterrent poor law. But whereas the friendly societies sought to keep their members out of the poor house during life, and to secure them from a pauper's grave with the death benefit—besides normally offering medical care and maternity benefits—the customary industrial insurance policy provided death benefit only. On this slender basis had grown by the end of the first decade of the twentieth century a gigantic industry with over 30,000,000 funeral benefit policies outstanding and nearly

10,000,000 new ones sold each year. The industry employed about 100,000 men, of whom about 70,000 were the full-time door-to-door sales agents, whose weekly, personal collection of the premium gave industrial insurance its singular character.[49]

The official return for the number of industrial policies in force on the last day of 1910 was 28,541,525, with a total face value of £285,809,757, or about £10 per policy. This figure represented a net increase over 1909 of 727,686, but ten times this number of policies may have been sold during the year.[50] For instance, during 1913 the twelve largest industrial companies sold a total of 9,130,839 new policies, worth together over £101,000,000, a sum slightly larger than half the total national budget of the same year. The difference between the net increase and the total number of new policies sold indicates that for each ten new policies sold in a year, there were about nine lapses.

In the years immediately before World War I there were about seventy-five industrial insurance organizations. Of these, fifty were organized as collecting friendly societies, but most of this group were small local organizations, usually known as 'Burial Societies,' employing few collectors and usually devoting themselves to a particular geographic locale or economic interest. Ninety per cent, if not more, of the huge business of collecting insurance, the 'industrial insurance industry,' was monopolized by twelve companies. Of these, nine were limited liability corporations and three were the so-called 'collecting' friendly societies.[51]

By far the largest of the twelve companies was the Prudential.

[49] An easily accessible discussion of the industrial insurance industry by a recognized expert may be found in the Beveridge Report: Appendix D, The Problem of Industrial Assurance, *Cmd. 6404*, 'Social Insurance and Allied Services,' 1942, pp. 249–76. A more complete, if unfriendly, report on industrial insurance in the years immediately after the passage of the National Insurance Act is in the 'Special Supplement on Industrial Insurance,' in the *New Statesman*, March 13, 1915, pp. 1–32. This report was done by Sidney Webb for the Fabian Research Department.

[50] *Post Magazine and Insurance Monitor*, LXXII (January 14, 1911), 33.

[51] It should be remembered that 'collecting' friendly societies, of which the only important ones for this study were the Liverpool Victoria, the Royal Liver, and the Scottish Legal, were scarcely different in organization and aims from the limited companies except that they had no stockholders and were run for the benefit of their officers and agents. They were technically friendly societies, registered under the Friendly Societies Act of 1896, in order to take advantage of tax exemptions available to friendly societies. But their orientation and method of doing business were in every way the same as the limited companies with whom they were allied in 1911 in the struggle with the true friendly societies.

This company had an industrial insurance reserve fund nearly nine times as large as that of its nearest competitor and neighbour in Holborn, the Pearl. The Prudential was the largest private owner of freehold properties in the United Kingdom. It was the largest shareholder of Bank of England stocks, and of Indian and colonial government bonds and stocks. It was a major source for local authority borrowing. Each month its investment committee had to find a profitable situation for about half a million more pounds; its premium income was about one-third of the £20,000,000 per year enjoyed by the twelve largest companies together.[52]

These figures should convey an understanding of the most important fact for the purposes of this study about industrial insurance: that it was an extremely large, profitable, and rather closely controlled business, that it engaged the talents and provided rewards for a great number of very able men, and finally, and most significant, that it had in its collecting agents an army of men in weekly contact with nearly every working-class home in the United Kingdom.

Like the patent non-crushable, non-stainable, detachable collar he wore, or the Coventry bicycle he rode, the industrial insurance collector-salesman was a product of the mature, late-Victorian British industrial society. His equipment was a board school education and the ambition to get on. The sale of funeral policies offered the sharp, unabashed, clever young man from the slums a quick way to the £3 or £4 per week income enjoyed by only one person in six before World War I. With a bowler hat on the back of his head, a straight-steel pen behind his ear, and a bottle of Stephen's Blue-Black Ink in his waistcoat pocket, the collecting agent was an easily-recognizable figure in working-class neighbourhoods. As 'The Man from Prudential,' the symbol of all collecting insurance agents, he was a stock character of music hall satire, and his relations with the housewives he visited each day provided the material for many broad jokes. He was likely to be a radical Liberal in politics and, scorning the commodity he himself sold, a member of a friendly society. The agents had no particular love for the companies that employed them, and were well organized in the National Union of Assurance Agents.[53]

[52] These statistics are largely taken from the *New Statesman*, 'Supplement on Industrial Insurance,' pp. 3, 9.

[53] The huge staff of the Prudential had its own union, the National Association

The policies sold by the collecting agents were calculated not on the round figure of the face value of the policy itself, but rather in multiples of a penny per week premium. For one penny a week, the Refuge Insurance Company, for example, would provide, after a six-month waiting period, a whole life policy on a child aged eleven worth £10 0s. 7d.[54] At age twenty, however, the same penny per week would buy a policy worth only £8 10s. after six months. At age thirty, this figure was £6 6s., and at age forty, £4 12s. Hence a man of thirty, wishing to provide an amount enough for a 'respectable' funeral and calculating that this could not be less than £10, might well buy two one-penny policies which would provide him a funeral benefit of £12 12s.

In canvassing for industrial life insurance, including the worst slums that were absolutely untouched by friendly society activity,[55] the agent's argument was always the same: the last thing a bereaved family could do for the departed was to provide a proper funeral. The English working man did not need to be reminded of the degradation of potter's field. And his wife, who usually bought the policy, understood the honour accruing in a funeral celebration of some proportions. The street's expectation of a pageant had to be considered, and funerals could not be purchased on credit.[56]

of Prudential Agents. Rowntree found that York, with a population of 75,800, of whom 46,800 were workers, had seventy-five full-time and ten part-time insurance agents. Of the full-time agents, forty were from the Prudential. Rowntree, *Poverty*, pp. 364–5.

[54] The company would pay half the amount of benefit between three and six months, nothing before three months. After ten years the face was worth £10 17s.

These figures, not easily available, were given in an article in the *Insurance Mail* by W. H. Altcroft, actuary to the Refuge. *Insurance Mail*, December 10, 1910.

[55] In his survey, Charles Booth discovered that even among his Class B—the poorest class in East London with a fixed address, defined as 'casual earnings—"very poor" '—3½d. a week was saved for industrial insurance. Charles Booth, *Life and Labour of the People of London* (London, 1892), I, 138–9.

[56] Lady Bell recalled the pride of impoverished widows who had been able to achieve some display in the funerals of their husbands killed in the accidents at the Middlesbrough mills. 'I put him away splendid,' said one who had given the funeral party sandwiches. 'I buried him with ham,' said another. For the iron workers, she reported, funerals were one of the principal social opportunities. The budgets of workers with incomes even as low as £1 a week almost always showed at least 7d. for insurance. Part of this, of course, would have been to the sick club. Bell, *Works*, pp. 55–75, 76–7, 83. Rowntree estimated that the average wage-earning family in York paid about 8¼d. for industrial insurance per week. The total amount per week paid by York workingmen, he thought, could be 'not less' than £400. Rowntree, *Poverty*, p. 365.

L

Industrial insurance required no medical examination beyond proof of age of the insured, nor was the consent of the insured required, nor, before 1909, did the agent seek to prove more than a casual insurable interest on the part of the beneficiary.[57] As a result, it was estimated during the debates on the Assurance Companies Act of 1909, as many as one-third of industrial policies in force were illegal.

The commission on existing policies might vary from under 20 to 30 per cent of the amount of the premium. This figure was likely to be larger for agents working for collecting friendly societies where the agents could use their contacts with the insured, who were legally the governors of the society, to bring pressure on management.[58] The total amount of the premiums due an agent from policies in force was termed in the trade the 'book.' Theoretically, the commission was a percentage of the book, although with the exception of the Prudential, companies usually paid only on the basis of the amount of money actually collected. Books could be bought or sold or they could be built up from nothing.[59] The total amount invested in books of 70,000 or more collecting agents could hardly have been less than £15,000,000 and was estimated by Lloyd George in the autumn of 1910 to be twice this amount. The insurance companies were able to use the pro-

---

[57] Insurable interest was first defined in 14 Geo. 3, c. 48. This statute separated insurance from gambling by requiring that the beneficiary of a policy have some pecuniary interest in, or incur some hardship from, the casualty insured against.

[58] The Royal Liver Collecting Society was reported by the Parmoor Committee in 1920 to be almost completely under the control of its agents. '. . . it was admitted that, between one item of remuneration and another, the agents have succeeded in obtaining for themselves about 31 per cent of the weekly premiums paid by the members.' Cmd. 614, 'Report of the Departmental Committee on the Business of Industrial Assurance Companies and Collecting Societies,' 1920, p. 2.

[59] Typical advertisements for sales of books:

'Royal London—£6 book, inclusive two days; West London; 30 times. [i.e. £180] apply Superintendent, 62 Cricklewood Lane, N.W.'

'Liverpool Victoria—good £7 7s. book; full commission; £170; easily and pleasantly collected. Apply E. C. Hoy, Central Buildings, Gallowtree Gate, Leicester.'

Insurance Mail, June 3, 1911.

'Book £8 or part; good business; 25 per cent, collected in three days; 30 times cash [i.e. £240]; Liverpool Victoria, Romford. apply 'H.', 8 Clarissa Road, Chadwell Heath.'

Insurance Mail, July 15, 1911.

tection of this tremendous vested interest to ensure the obedience of their collecting or 'out-door' staffs in the struggle with the Government and the friendly societies during 1911.

Ordinarily, however, the collecting agent spent little more than two or three days per week servicing existing policies. As much time as possible he took for the promotion of new business. Most industrial policies had no value during their first three months in force and paid only half their face for the next three months. During this period, particularly during the first three months, nearly the whole of the premium paid by the insured went to the agent as a bonus for the sale of the policy. Hence for many agents new business was more important, and more profitable, than policies in force. As a consequence, one of the most serious charges brought against industrial insurance was 'over-selling,' which was the chief cause of the extremely high rate of lapse among industrial insurance policies. As policies were sold under the pressure of persuasive salesmanship the tendency was for them to lapse soon after issue, once the original interest stimulated by the agent had died. The Parmoor Committee noted, for instance, that in 1913 nearly five million policies lapsed and that of these, nearly four million had come into force either in 1912 or 1913. The committee concluded that the premiums paid on these four million policies less than a year old must have totalled about £500,000. Of this sum, nearly all would have gone to the agents as new business commissions.[60]

Industrial insurance industry made its money from the improvidence and fecklessness of the British working population. The lower-class housewife who carefully saved pennies in a sugar bowl over the mantelpiece for the weekly call of the funeral benefit collector could not bring herself to carry those pennies a few blocks to the post office savings bank. Still less could she enjoin her husband to become a member of a friendly society. The gigantic industrial insurance industry was in essence a product of the lack of economic self-discipline among the lower levels of the English working class. It justified its existence to the public by the argument that without the weekly appearance of the collector to

[60] *Cmd. 614*, p. 3. The committee suggested that the lapse experience of the Refuge was about average. In the ten years between 1909 and 1918, the Refuge had issued 9,322,336 new policies and had had in the same period 6,426,313 policies lapse. *Ibid.*, p. 3. On the prevalence and profitability of lapsing see also: 'Special Supplement on Industrial Insurance,' *New Statesman*, pp. 10–15.

force savings, most purchasers of industrial insurance would not save at all. But the English poor paid dearly for the luxury of this unofficial inducement to thrift. The size of the industry and its rapid growth, particularly in the twenty-five years immediately before World War I, are testimony to the almost unbelievable profitability of this form of enterprise. This fact in itself was important in directing the Government's attention to it in 1910 and made the companies an almost continual target for nationalization in the period between World War I and World War II. Although the industrial companies sought to disguise their profitability by merging the statistics of their ordinary life insurance business with their industrial life insurance business, some figures are available. These show that in the last four years before the war the industrial life companies alone (collecting friendly societies were subject to more searching inquiry by the Registrar of Friendly Societies and thus were counted separately) had income from premiums and interest on reserves averaging about £20,000,000 per year. Of this sum, an average of no more than 37 per cent was paid to beneficiaries and in surrenders.[61] In contrast, salesmen's commissions, indoor management expenses, and dividends to stockholders in the years 1911–14 averaged more than 43 per cent of company income. Salesmen's commissions alone were more than 22 per cent.[62]

The collecting friendly societies represented a very small proportion—hardly one-seventh in terms of income—of the total industrial insurance business. But, although there were fifty collecting friendly societies, only three controlled three-quarters of the business, and of these, two ranked in size with the proprietary companies. These were the Royal Liver (named after the pub where it had been founded, 'The Liver' in St Anne Street, Liverpool), based in Liverpool, and the Liverpool Victoria, based

---

[61] Under the law, industrial insurance policies had a surrender value to which the companies attached much importance in their public statements. But many policyholders were ignorant of the surrender value, and the amount paid out in any one year rarely exceeded 1 per cent of the company's income.

[62] Cmd. 2849, 'Statistical Abstract for the United Kingdom for each of the fifteen years from 1911 to 1925,' 1927, pp. 194–5. A crude figure of total management expenses as a percentage of premiums for some of the larger individual industrial companies is available for each year under the heading of life assurance in Whitaker's Almanack. It shows that the Prudential, the company usually taken to symbolize the worst in industrial life insurance and the victim in 1911 of a consistent press attack by the popular newspaper John Bull, had by far the lowest management costs as a proportion of total income.

in London. By 1911 the Liverpool Victoria was the largest collecting friendly society, and its secretary, Arthur Henri, was one of the most influential men in the industrial insurance industry. In the last report before the advent of national insurance, the Chief Registrar of Friendly Societies stated that in the year 1908 the Liverpool Victoria had enjoyed an income of £1,199,574 and had spent in that year £390,355 on benefits and £489,606 on management. The remainder had gone to swell a £3,471,460 reserve.[63] Because of the influence of the agents on management policies in the collecting friendly societies, agents' commissions in these organizations tended to take a substantially larger proportion of the total management expenses than they did in the companies.[64] In 1920 the Liverpool Victoria reported to the Parmoor Committee that it had spent 45 per cent of its premium income on salesmen's commissions and indoor managerial expenses between the years 1909 and 1913. It spent 31 per cent of its premium income on agents' commissions alone.[65]

Potentially, the political power of the industrial insurance

[63] 'Report of the Chief Registrar of Friendly Societies,' 1909, Appendix C, pp. 15, 92. *Parliamentary Papers*, 1910, No. 171. In collecting societies generally, the Chief Registrar estimated, of each £1,000 spent, £444 went in death benefits and £499 went to management expenses. Other benefits, some sick pay, endowments, and policyholders' bonuses took the rest. *Ibid.*, p. 15.

[64] In its report, the Parmoor Committee remarked, '. . . the fact is that the control of the organization in the case of all the large societies, has been secured by the agents, by the servants of the societies. The various committees of management are appointed, to a large extent, from among the agents, and are, apparently, more accountable for their actions to the associated agents than to the members.' This was particularly true in societies governed by delegates, for the delegates, nominally elected by policyholders, in fact, were nominees of the agents. *Cmd. 614*, p. 4.

[65] *Cmd. 614*, Appendix A, p. 21, Table V. The Royal Liver declined to give any confidential data on operations to the Parmoor Committee, but the committee stated elsewhere that it estimated salesmen's commissions in the Liver to be about equal to those in the Liverpool Victoria. Comparable figures for some of the limited companies to be mentioned most frequently in this study show the following percentages for 1909–13: (1) for salesmen's commissions and new business bonuses alone; and (2) indoor and outdoor administrative costs combined.

Company Name	(1)	(2)
British Legal and United Provident	30%	51%
Pearl	34%	45%
Prudential	27%	39%
Refuge	27%	49%
Royal London	32%	46%

Cmd. 614, Ibid.

industry was far greater than that of the friendly societies, and it represented more than simply the power of organized wealth. If it could be induced to act, the leaders of industrial insurance had in their disciplined army of collectors a legion of political canvassers that Liberal or Unionist election agents could only admire. No government, least of all Asquith's Liberals, who in January, 1910, had seen their overwhelming majority of 1906 reduced to near equality with the Unionists, could afford to disregard the constituency influence of the industrial insurance agent.

5

Lloyd George's meeting with representatives of the industrial insurance industry, probably occurring in early August, 1910, marks the beginning of a new phase in the growth of national health insurance that would end with a virtual reconstruction of the scheme. At the meeting, the Chancellor learned of the effect his proposals for widows' and orphans' pensions would have upon the industrial insurance industry. Even though the plan itself did not include a funeral benefit, the widows' pension would lessen, if not destroy, the appeal of such a benefit. The gigantic investment in books would be lost, wiped out by government competition. Lloyd George was reportedly surprised at this information. He had not known about book interest. Perhaps, he suggested, the agents could be offered compensation for their loss. No doubt 'a few tens of thousands would satisfactorily settle the matter. He was told, to his surprise, that in one great Society alone, adequate compensation would amount to between two and three million pounds.'[66]

Faced by the threat of resistance from industrial insurance, the Chancellor attempted to remove his sickness programme from politics. On August 17 at Criccieth, Lloyd George drafted a long memorandum, subsequently corrected by Charles and Lucy Masterman, proposing a ministerial coalition with the Unionists to solve the problems that 'affect the health, the vitality, the efficiency, and the happiness of the individuals who constitute the races that dwell in these islands.' Of the twelve specific problems

[66] G. B. Wilkie, *Nationalization of Insurance*, London, 1931, p. 36. There is no contemporary account of the meeting, although, clearly, one occurred. The source cited above is a sixpence pamphlet, a reprint of a series of articles that had appeared in the *Insurance Guild Journal* inspired by the Labour Party's adoption in 1929 of a resolution calling for nationalization of insurance companies.

dealt with, by far the longest section—occupying nearly as much space as all the other sections combined—was devoted to an attack on the industrial insurance industry and its resistance to his attempt to provide widows' and orphans' pensions. The Chancellor dwelt at length on the pitiful condition of a widow with young children, whose husband had died in the prime of life.

She suddenly finds herself without any adequate means, very often with all her means exhausted by medical and funeral expenses, face to face with the task of having not merely to attend to her household duties and the bringing up of the children, but also with that of earning a livelihood for herself and for them. In Germany they contemplate adding provision for widows under these conditions to their ordinary invalidity insurance. It is relatively easy to set up a system of that kind in Germany; but here one would have to encounter the bitter hostility of powerful organizations like the Prudential, the Liver, the Royal Victoria [sic, Royal Liver and Liverpool Victoria], the Pearl, and similar institutions, with an army numbering scores, if not hundreds of thousands, of agents and collectors who make a living out of collecting a few pence a week from millions of households in this country for the purpose of providing death allowances. The expenses of collection and administration come to something like 50 per cent. of the total receipts, and these poor widows and children are by this extravagant system robbed of one half of the benefits which it has cost the workman so much to provide for them. Sometimes these agents and collectors sell their books and sub-let them and make hundreds of pounds out of the transaction, all at the expense of the poorest and most helpless creatures in the land. This system ought to be terminated at the earliest possible moment. The benefits are small, costly, and precarious, for if a man is unable, owing to ill health or lack of employment, to keep up his payments, his policy is forfeited. State insurance costs 10 per cent. to administer, and, inasmuch as the state and the employer both contribute, either the premium is considerably less, or the benefits are substantially greater, than with the insurance companies. But however desirable it may be to substitute state insurance, which does not involve collection and therefore is more economical, any Party that attempted it would instantly incur the relentless hostility of all these agents and collectors. They visit every house, they are indefatigable, they are often very intelligent, and a government which attempted to take over their work without first securing the co-operation of the other Party would inevitably fail in its undertaking; so that, if a scheme of national insurance is taken in hand by any Party Government, it must be confined to invalidity, and the most urgent and pitiable cases of all must be left out. I may add that compensation on an adequate scale is well-nigh impossible, inasmuch as it would cost something like 20 or 30 millions at the very least to buy off the interest of these collectors, and such a payment would crush the scheme and destroy its usefulness. On the other hand, the agents cannot be absorbed within the new system, there being no door-to-door collection contemplated.[67]

Although it is frequently argued that the only concern of industrial insurance was to prevent the inclusion of a State funeral benefit there is nothing to indicate that at this time the Chancellor of the Exchequer was considering the institution of a funeral benefit. The question of whether a death grant was ever seriously projected during the planning of national sickness insurance can perhaps never be satisfactorily answered. There is strong evidence to show that during the early discussions such a benefit was deliberately excluded, partly at the insistence of the friendly societies, but also to prevent competition with the industrial

[67] The entire coalition memorandum is printed as an appendix in Sir Charles Petrie, *The Life and Letters of the Right Hon. Sir Austen Chamberlain* (London, 1939), I, 381-8. One of the innumerable minor mysteries of recent British historical writing is the consistent misinterpretation of this section of the coalition memorandum. It is invariably referred to as a section on 'unemployment' because inexplicably the Chancellor chose to head his attack on industrial insurance with these words. One recent author, who deals fully with the coalition proposal, has assumed that the industrial insurance collectors were opposed to unemployment insurance. In fact, they supported this portion of the National Insurance Act as providing a way for working-class families to maintain the payment of premiums on their funeral insurance while out of work. Roy Jenkins, *Mr Balfour's Poodle*, London, 1954, p. 110. Lloyd George himself helped to divert attention from this section of the memorandum. Assuming, perhaps, that no copy of the memorandum existed, he stated in his *War Memoirs* that the purpose of the memorandum had been chiefly the promotion of national defence and compulsory military service. David Lloyd George, *War Memoirs* (Boston, 1933), I, 33-9. In fact, his entire discussion of national defence in all aspects occupied a single, short paragraph in more than eleven pages.

insurance industry. Certainly Lloyd George's memorandum deals with widows' and orphans' pensions and the plan that the Government had then at hand, coming out of the actuaries' report of March 21, 1910, provided these benefits only. A funeral benefit would have taken an insignificant part of the worker's contribution and would have been easy to administer, but it would have had little social utility.[68] It would have accomplished little toward relieving the hardship of widows and orphans which had been part of Lloyd George's aim from the beginning. Customarily the entire benefit was spent on a respectable funeral.[69] The conclusion can only be that while Lloyd George may have toyed with the idea of a funeral benefit during the last days of November after the breakdown of the constitutional conference, he never seriously took up the proposal. The provision to which the insurance companies objected was widows' and orphans' pensions. From their point of view this was as dangerous as a funeral benefit. Moreover, the conclusive evidence appears to be that with a widows' and orphans' pension, a funeral benefit was relatively unnecessary, certainly not socially useful enough to risk arousing the opposition of the industrial insurance companies. Therefore, a funeral benefit would scarcely be investigated seriously as long as the widows' and orphans' pension was part of the programme; and this benefit was not definitely dropped until early January of 1911, while Lloyd George had made a public promise well over a month before to do nothing that would harm industrial insurance.

The only contemporary source to mention funeral benefits, as opposed to widows' pensions, is Lucy Masterman's diary-biography of her husband, Charles Masterman. She says that Lloyd George discovered during the constitutional conference, while working on his insurance scheme, that 'it would be possible for the

[68] Tatham's English Life Table No. VI, based on mortality between 1891 and 1900, showed that a man of twenty could expect to live to be 62·02 years of age. Assuming that after the beginning no one would enter State insurance at a later age than twenty, a ½d. contribution per week for forty years compounded at 3 per cent interest would yield an available death benefit of £8·41. This may be taken as the basic cost of the death benefit. The Refuge Insurance Company sold an £8·5 death benefit at age twenty for 1d. per week, in effect, almost precisely twice the cost of pure insurance. The Manchester Unity offered at age twenty an £8 death benefit for 2⅛d. every four weeks, that is, 0·531d. per week.

[69] A second actuaries' report rendered on August 27, 1910, after the Criccieth memorandum, did not mention a funeral benefit and represented only an addendum to the first report. Braithwaite Papers, Part II, Item 4.

L*

Government to include insurance against death in its scheme and, with no government grant whatever, to give the insurers double the amount at present given by industrial insurance companies *nearly two-thirds of whose takings are absorbed in expenses.*'[70] This it certainly would have been possible for the Government to do, and no doubt any actuary could have told the Chancellor these facts. Mrs Masterman continues to say that during the general election of December, 1910, candidates were hounded for pledges against 'Death Insurance.' Against Mrs Masterman's account two things must be said. While the relevant section is headed 'Diary, dated October 12th, 1910,' the passages that follow are clearly written out of recollection after that date. Second, although Mrs Masterman writes a great deal about the Insurance Bill—her husband was second in importance only to Lloyd George himself in the formulation and establishment of national insurance—she appears to be altogether unaware that widows' and orphans' pensions were a part of the scheme, even though these two were by far the most important and expensive benefits, having been calculated by the actuaries to take about one-half the total contribution.

The story about death benefits, however, appears not to have come from Mrs Masterman, but from Sidney Webb's survey of industrial insurance for the *New Statesman* in 1915. Here he stated that the Prudential 'is reported to have driven the Government sternly from the original project of including Funeral Benefit in the state scheme. . . .'[71] This statement, although not unnoticed in the next twenty years, was widely publicized by Arnold Wilson and Hermann Levy in their attack on industrial insurance in 1937.[72] Levy then repeated the story in his excellent history of the health scheme, the basic source for most modern writers on the subject.[73]

The public announcement that the industrial insurance industry was concerned about the Government's social insurance plans came on September 27, 1910, in a paper delivered to a meeting of the Law Society at Bristol by Howard Kingsley Wood, then a rising insurance solicitor. Kingsley Wood warned that the State was planning soon to introduce measures of unemployment,

[70] Lucy Masterman, *C. F. G. Masterman*, London, 1939, p. 163.

[71] 'Supplement on Industrial Insurance,' p. 9n.

[72] *Industrial Assurance: An Historical and Critical Study*, London, 1937, pp. x–xi, 78.

[73] Hermann Levy, *National Health Insurance, A Critical Study*, Cambridge, 1944, p. 12.

invalidity, and life insurance. There could be no objection to the first two, but the last would cause grave difficulties for the 80,000 collecting insurance agents. He noted that 'two months ago' Winston Churchill had boasted that his friend Lloyd George would soon introduce into Parliament measures to enable 'householders to guard themselves against sickness, against invalidity, and against the death of the breadwinner. That was to say, a provision for widows and orphans to an extent and a degree which had never yet been dreamt of as practical in the history of our country.' This, said Kingsley Wood, was in fact an attempt 'to foist on the country a scheme of State Life Insurance.' It would 'cut out the heart of voluntary life insurance.'[74] Kingsley Wood's information about government plans for the insurance scheme was always excellent. But ten days later, Mrs Emmeline Pethick-Lawrence, speaking to a suffragist meeting at the Pavilion Theatre, announced that a friendly society journal had reported that the Government had given up widows' pensions. The Chancellor, she said (who with Winston Churchill was a favourite target for suffragist demonstrations), was now considering a very different Bill from the one he had discussed previously with the friendly societies.

> Instead of providing that a weekly allowance of 5s. should be paid to every widow having a child or children under 16 years of age and that a weekly allowance of 5s. should be paid to the man in sickness, as agreed by the friendly societies, Mr Lloyd George struck the widow out of the Bill altogether, and instead of giving 5s. to the man, as suggested by the friendly societies, gave 10s. to the man and nothing to the widow. It was done because Mr Lloyd George had to make his Bill as attractive as possible to the working man, especially the aristocracy of labour in this country, and he thought it would be a better bribe, a draw for the working man if he increased the insurance of the man and withdrew the insurance of the widow.[75]

It is extremely unlikely that Mrs Pethick-Lawrence's intelligence on government intentions would be better than that of Kingsley Wood and the industrial insurance companies, and there is no

[74] 'State Insurance,' *Post Magazine and Insurance Monitor*, LXXI (October 1, 1910), 792.
[75] *The Times*, October 10, 1910.

other evidence that the Chancellor had at that time given up widows' pensions. Indeed, all available evidence is to the contrary. Yet, precisely as Mrs Pethick-Lawrence predicted, widows' pensions eventually were dropped, and the money saved by deleting this expensive item was used to raise the sickness benefit from 5s. to 10s.

Mrs Pethick-Lawrence's statement provides one of the few supporting pieces of evidence for the consideration, at some period, of a government funeral benefit. The Chancellor may have examined, early in October, the possibility of dropping widows' pensions and using the money to increase the sickness benefit to 10s. But this would leave his plan offering nothing for widows. He may therefore have considered instituting a funeral benefit, not a particularly useful, but still a relatively inexpensive, sop to his original intention. If this is the case, he quickly returned to his old plan, for he did not announce his final decision to drop widows' pensions until early in 1911.[76]

Widows' pensions, with or without the addition of a funeral benefit, remained a political possibility so long as Lloyd George's coalition proposal was under consideration, and despite Asquith's remarks years later that he had never paid much attention to it, the proposal was debated seriously, and indeed favourably, by Liberal leaders until very nearly the end of October.[77] However, when the constitutional conference, which had provided the political climate that made coalition appear feasible, reported failure on November 10, any possibility of a coalition died with it. Asquith announced almost immediately that Parliament would be dissolved on November 28. In the hectic atmosphere of a general election, Lloyd George knew well his plan was virtually at the mercy of the friendly societies and the commercial insurance companies. Perhaps on this account—the coincidence of dates is too strong to be altogether disregarded—the Chancellor agreed now to meet leaders of the friendly societies and industrial insurance companies, both of whom he had avoided—with the exception

[76] MS notes by W. J. Braithwaite, corrected by John Bradbury, January 21, 1911, Braithwaite Papers, Part II, Item 11.

[77] See: Lloyd George to Lord Crewe, October 20, 1910, quoted in James Pope-Hennessy, *Lord Crewe, 1858–1945, The Likeness of a Liberal*, London, 1955, p. 119; Lord Crewe to H. H. Asquith, October 22, 1910; Edward Gray to H. H. Asquith, October 26, 1910, Asquith Papers, Box 12, ff. 197, 198, 214, 215.

of the secret meeting early in August—for the past six months. On November 2, Lloyd George conferred with the leaders of the Manchester Unity and a few weeks later with the representatives of the insurance companies. What occurred at these meetings is not altogether clear except that the meeting with the Manchester Unity officials was acrimonious. Although the leadership of the friendly societies was bound to a pledge of secrecy, their subsequent oblique references to dislike of 'compulsion' suggest they had been informed that the orientation of national insurance was slowly changing. Whereas at first the working population had been given the choice of membership in a State scheme or a voluntary friendly society, now they were virtually forced to become members of friendly societies.[78]

The industrial insurance industry was no less discontented with what it heard. The Chancellor still intended to pay a sum at death, reported Arthur Henri to the annual conference of the Liverpool Victoria at Leicester. The payment would not, of course, be in a lump sum, 'but more in the way of a permanent provision during widowhood . . .' plus a payment for children to a given age. Clearly, Lloyd George had returned to the idea of widows' pensions, if he had ever left it. As a result of this, the Liverpool Victoria resolved to join with the rest of the industrial insurance industry in demanding a pledge from all candidates in the coming election to oppose any government action that would harm the insurance companies.[79]

The pledge referred to, and the largely favourable response to it that the collecting industry was able to force from unhappy Liberal M.P.s fighting to maintain a thin majority in an apathetic electorate, would become one of the most potent weapons in the insurance industry's long struggle with the Government and with the friendly societies. The pledge began to circulate in the last week of November. It demanded:

Will you pledge yourself to oppose any measure of State Insurance which is likely prejudicially to affect the interest of the great affiliated orders and friendly and collecting societies and companies, or to jeopardize the livelihood of the very many thousands of persons engaged in the business of industrial life

[78] See the statement of Mr T. Barnes, Grand Master of the Manchester Unity, *The Times*, November 3, 1910.
[79] *Assurance Agents' Chronicle*, XXII (December 10, 1910), 598.

assurance, and will you oppose any exceptional treatment of any order, society, or company to the prejudice of others.[80]

What 'measure of State Insurance' the Government was planning that might 'jeopardize the livelihood of the very many thousands of persons engaged in the business of industrial life assurance' was undefined. Nevertheless, in the last days of November there occurred a flurry of reports in newspapers. Some of these were completely erroneous; some were based on misinformation, containing perhaps a germ of truth; but all together had a considerable public effect. The spokesman for the leaders of the industrial insurance industry was the *Insurance Mail*, published in those days by the Insurance Publishing Company (now Stone and Cox) which printed also rate books, mortality tables, and many of the innumerable forms required by the industry. The *Mail*'s editorial policy reflected the wishes of insurance officials, and in the months that followed, it would be the ordinary channel by which the insurance company authorities spoke to their out-of-door staff on political matters. Describing rather mysterious happenings at the end of November, the *Mail*'s editor stated:

> On Saturday, November 26th, it came to my ears on exceptional authority that the Government intended to introduce a state-aided scheme, which was practically industrial life insurance. On the following Monday morning the 'Daily Express' contained an article which was obviously based on the same knowledge. On the next day 'The Financier' had a similar article. Wednesday morning brought a protest on political grounds, from the 'Daily News,' and Thursday produced a letter from Mr Lloyd George which was apparently a blank denial.[81]

What really happened in that week, the editor concluded; was there really a threat?

The article referred to in the *Financier* had concluded: 'Unless the industrial insurance workers wake up—unless they, through their respective Members of Parliament, prevent unwarranted

---

[80] *The Financier*, December 2, 1910. The 'great affiliated orders,' i.e., the true friendly societies, were not, of course, involved in the circulation of this pledge. The *Assurance Agents' Chronicle* noted this in a lead article and described it simply as a 'bit of swank.' *Assurance Agents' Chronicle*, XXII (December 10, 1910), 598.　　　　　　　　　　　　[81] *Insurance Mail*, December 17, 1910.

interference with their business—their vital interests will be imperilled.' The correspondent reported that he had heard it on the highest authority that the government was going to enter into competition with collecting societies.[82] Whether or not the ripple of fear that swept through the insurance world in the last days before the general election had any foundation in fact, it is clear there was a rumour, fanned and supported by some leaders of the collecting agents' unions, that the Government planned to nationalize one or more industrial insurance companies.[83] David Lloyd George was forced to act quickly.[84] On December 1, 1910, he issued a letter denying that the Government intended in any way to interfere with industrial insurance.

> The proposed benefits do not include the provision of a funeral benefit or any immediate money payment on the death of a contributor or his relatives, nor, of course, will there be any endowment for children on attaining a certain age. The whole of this field will still be left open to the existing agencies.
>
> . . . .
>
> I have given a pledge on behalf of the government that no scheme dealing with sickness or invalidity will be submitted to the House of Commons until all societies having any interest in the matter have been consulted.

To that pledge I adhere. The reason why the representatives

---

[82] *The Financier*, November 29, 1910. The article in the *Daily News* was based on that paper's inability to distinguish between friendly societies and collecting friendly societies. The editor remarked that Lloyd George had after all met the collecting friendly societies on November 2 (the date he met the Manchester Unity), that he had promised repeatedly always to protect friendly society interests, and that the sellers of funeral benefits need not be concerned. *Daily News*, December 1, 1910. Apparently the *Daily News* had mistaken the attackers for the defenders, jeered the *Financier* the next day.

[83] One history of the Prudential, written by a company official, asserts that David Jones, secretary of the National Association of Prudential Assurance Agents, was attempting to promote nationalization of insurance. H. Plaisted, *The Prudential Past and Present*, London, n.d. [1917], pp. 94–103. A letter in the *Assurance Agents' Chronicle* of November 26, 1910, tends to confirm this. The letter, signed only 'Common Sense,' said that Prudential agents 'supported by some socialist members of Parliament,' were 'clamouring for state purchase.' *Assurance Agents' Chronicle*, XXII (November 26, 1910), 568. A letter in the *Mail* later in the month, referring to the rumours, noted that speculation eventually had settled on government purchase of the Prudential and the Liverpool Victoria. *Insurance Mail*, December 31, 1910.

[84] *Daily News*, December 2, 1910.

of some of these societies have not yet been consulted is that the Government saw no prospect this year of putting forward their plan. Every consideration will be given to the views of every kind and class of society before the proposals take their final shape. Yours faithfully, D. Lloyd George.[85]

Temporarily the insurance companies appeared to have won. The Chancellor had promised to do nothing that would hurt them, and unquestionably had restricted his freedom of action for the future. The insurance companies succeeded, they reported later, in extracting 490 pledges from a House of Commons numbering, in those days, 670.[86] On the same day that it printed the letter, the *Mail* congratulated 'all those who have worked so earnestly during the past three weeks. . . .'[87]

But the battle was not quite over, or at least industrial insurance was not certain of the extent of its victory. Immediately after the last returns were reported from the general election on December 19, Lloyd George, whose voice had almost entirely given out (it was feared that he had cancer) went to the Riviera, not to return to London until January 8. During this period, indeed until well into February, the insurance world remained in a state of apprehension. Probably most of this suspicion was groundless, for one of the Chancellor's first acts after returning to England was to order the reconstruction of his plan without widows' pensions; but insurance men could not know this and so, even with the Chancellor's pledge to do nothing to harm them a matter of record, the companies began to organize on a permanent basis machinery which could be used to put pressure on the Government.

Basically the insurance companies distrusted the wording of Lloyd George's pledge. He had promised that there would be no 'immediate' payment upon the death of the breadwinner. Did this, the *Insurance Mail* asked, also rule out a widows' pension to begin some time later?[88] The industry leaders decided that it did not, and the weeks around the Christmas and New Year holidays saw insurance publications exhorting the collecting agents to organize themselves and prepare for a struggle. The greatest danger was complacency, trumpeted the *Insurance Mail*:

[85] *Insurance Mail*, December 17, 1910. Extracts from this letter appeared in most daily newspapers on December 2. Only the *Mail* appears to have printed the letter in full.
[86] *Ibid.*, June 24, 1911.   [87] *Ibid.*, December 17, 1910.   [88] *Ibid.*

We are able to state that the activity which has been evident in the insurance world for some weeks is not the activity of hysteria, or of a foolish scare founded on nothing. It is a definite and deliberate movement for mutual protection against a positive menace. The Chancellor of the Exchequer intends to make provision for widows and orphans in the near future. The benefits may be called pensions to the widow on the death of the breadwinner, but they are payments following death—and so are indistinguishable from industrial life insurance.

The great need now, the journal continued, was for organization. The companies would soon ask their superintendents' fraternals (district supervisors' organizations) to act as local committees. Most important,

the powerful organization of industrial offices and collecting societies, popularly known as the 'Combine,' has been actively at work for some time, and will meet to form a kind of Parliamentary committee, and to determine a course of action within the next few days.[89]

The 'Combine' was the popular title for the Association of Industrial Assurance Companies and Collecting Friendly Societies (now usually called 'the Associated Offices'). It had been organized in 1901 and announced as its first object: 'The carrying out of any lawful thing which shall tend to promote the principles, practice, and business of Industrial Assurance and for mutual protection against unfair or prejudicial legislation.' Its executive committee of eleven was dominated in 1911 by the Liverpool Victoria and the Pearl. Its secretary was F. D. Bowles, managing director of the Pearl. Other members of the executive committee usually present at negotiations with the Government were Thomas Neill of the Pearl, F. T. Jefferson of the Britannic, Arthur Henri of the Liverpool Victoria, and Edward Smith of the Royal London.[90] However,

[89] *Insurance Mail*, January 14, 1911.
[90] Thomas Neill, 1856–1937, born, Cookstown, Tyrone, Ireland; father a land agent; Protestant; became insurance agent; went to Pearl, 1910; executive, Industrial Life Offices' Association, 1902–12 (founding member); left the Combine to become one of first National Health Insurance Commissioners, 1912–16; Chairman, National Amalgamated Approved Society, 1916–36; succeeded F. D. Bowles as Honorary Secretary of the Combine, 1920–6; Chairman, Combine, 1928–36 (retired). K.B., 1920.
Arthur Henri, 1859–1923, born, Liverpool; joined Liverpool Victoria (then

the ordinary spokesman for the Combine and certainly one of the most able lobbyists of the pre-war period in Great Britain was a smiling, clever, chubby little man who was, at the time of his death, Chancellor of the Exchequer in Winston Churchill's World War II coalition, Howard Kingsley Wood.[91] Until his appointment as standing counsel for the Combine, Kingsley Wood had been a solicitor for the Liverpool Victoria and the Royal London Mutual. Although nominally a Conservative, Kingsley Wood, like all successful lobbyists, insisted that the interests he represented were non-political,[92] and indeed the *Insurance Mail*, the Combine's voice, made much of the diversity of political opinion among the insurance company leaders.[93]

It would appear that Kingsley Wood's first act as salaried adviser to the Combine was to propose that the industrial insurance companies demand the right to participate in State insurance. The fear that the Government might at some future time expand the service to include widows' pensions was probably the reason. The companies themselves had no interest in the administration of sickness benefits and, with the exception of a few collecting friendly societies, had never found it profitable even to engage in this form of business.[94] But if the scheme were to change or expand, Kingsley Wood felt industrial insurance would be better able to

based in Liverpool) at age 17; made reputation in New Business Department; became Secretary in 1896. Instrumental in the establishment of the Combine. A devout Methodist.

[91] For Braithwaite's comments on these men, see Bunbury, ed., *Ambulance Wagon*, pp. 97–8.

[92] Howard Kingsley Wood, 1881–1943, born, Hull; father a Methodist minister; educated, Central Foundation Boys' School, London; solicitor, 1903; member, London County Council; M.P., Cons., Woolwich West, 1918–43; private secretary to Christopher Addison as Minister of Health, 1919–22; Parliamentary Secretary, Ministry of Health, 1924–9; Parliamentary Secretary, Board of Education, 1931; Postmaster-General, 1931–5; entered Cabinet, 1933; Minister of Health, 1935–8; Secretary of State for Air, 1938–40; Lord Privy Seal, 1940; Chancellor of Exchequer, 1940–3. Firm of Kingsley Wood, Williams and Murphy represented Combine after 1911. In 1935 George Williams of firm became secretary of Combine. Kt. 1918.

[93] See, for instance: *Insurance Mail*, January 21, 1911, January 28, 1911.

[94] In 1908, sixteen of each £1,000 spent by the fifty collecting friendly societies went for sickness benefits. 'Report of Registrar,' 1909, p. 151. On the usual attitude (pre-Insurance Act) of the industrial companies towards sickness insurance, see the speech of C. F. Norman of the Law Integrity. Friendly society members had a 'proprietary interest' in keeping down sickness claims, but a company 'having neither a soul to be saved or a body to be kicked' could not control malingering. *Insurance Mail*, November 19, 1910.

protect itself inside the programme than out of it.[95] At any rate, the societies insisted upon being received on January 12. At this time they made it clear to the Chancellor's representative, Rufus Isaacs, that they desired statutory recognition of their right to participate in the administration of national insurance, even though no companies might actually make use of this right.[96]

The Chancellor had not been present at the January 12 meeting because of a recurrence of the throat trouble that would plague him throughout the whole of 1911 and then magically disappear. Isaac's assistant for this meeting, and the chief architect of national insurance, was William John Braithwaite, who had been appointed to the task only three weeks before. For Braithwaite the sickness scheme would combine the elements of public triumph and personal tragedy. For almost precisely a year, from December 1910 to December 1911, he worked at building the scheme, not, to be sure, single-handedly, but as Lloyd George's most important professional adviser and the only adviser with personal experience in insurance. Then when the measure was complete the Chancellor, with the singular callousness that was as much a part of his nature as his charm, appointed Robert Morant to supervise the establishment of the service, a post Braithwaite had confidently expected to be his.[97]

[95] See: Bunbury, ed., *Ambulance Wagon*, p. 96.

[96] Rufus Daniel Isaacs, 1860–1935, born, London; Jewish parentage; father a fruit merchant in the City; educated, University College School and Brussels and Hanover; called to the Bar, 1887, Q.C., 1898; entered Parliament (L.) for Reading, 1904–13; Solicitor-General, 1910; Attorney-General, 1910–13; Lord Chief Justice, 1913–21; President, Anglo–French Loan Mission to U.S.A., 1915; Special Envoy, U.S.A., 1917; High Commissioner and Special Ambassador, U.S.A., 1918; Viceroy and Governor-General of India, 1921–6; Secretary of State for Foreign Affairs, 1931. Represented railroads, winning side in Taff Vale litigation, 1902; took active part piloting N.H.I., 1910–11, through Parliment. P.C., 1911. Kt., 1910; Baron, 1914; Earl, 1917; Marquess, 1926.

Bunbury, ed., *Ambulance Wagon*, p. 96. The Braithwaite memoirs suggest that the companies had already decided to enter national insurance at the time of the January 12 meeting. Other evidence indicates that this decision on the part of most companies did not come until May.

[97] William John Braithwaite, 1875–1936, born, Great Waldingfield, Suffolk; father a minister; educated, Winchester and Oxford; resident, Toynbee Hall, 1898–1903; assistant secretary, Board of Inland Revenue, 1910–12; secretary, National Health Insurance Joint Committee, 1912; Commissioner for Special Purposes of Income Tax, 1913.

Morant's fulsome biographer, Bernard Allen, did not mention Braithwaite's name and many works, from R. J. Minney's ridiculously inaccurate biography of Lord Addison to William Frazer's sober and otherwise excellent history of

In the days after the January 12 meeting with the Combine, State insurance underwent a crucial transformation. First of all, widows' pensions finally were dropped from the scheme. No doubt Lloyd George had intended this since his letter of December 1, but the general election and his absence abroad had prevented any action being taken.

But perhaps more important than the dropping of one benefit was the decision to use the proportion of the contribution thereby freed to increase the sickness benefit from 5s. to 10s. a week.[98] This, as W. G. Bunn correctly diagnosed in June in a letter written in anticipation of his death, was a great and important change in the orientation of national insurance. No longer was it a programme to extend the friendly society principle; rather the plan had become a full-fledged and competing State programme, which any group of men who cared to form themselves into an insurance society would be permitted to administer.[99] Friendly society acquiescence in this change was purchased for the moment by the Government concession of its claim to such friendly society reserves as would be released when the artificially-created State insurance reserve took over the payment of benefits to the elderly friendly society members. The Government's eventual plan was to give each society a credit equal to the amount necessary to provide

English public health, state that Morant wrote the National Insurance Act. R. J. Minney, *Viscount Addison: Leader of the Lords*, London, 1958, p. 129. Minney asserts that the National Insurance Act was passed in 1912. *Ibid.*, p. 130; Frazer, *English Public Health*, p. 306.

[98] Bradbury wrote to G. F. Hardy the day after the meeting with the Combine leaders to ask what would be the effect of increasing the sickness benefit from 5s. to 10s. for the first thirteen weeks of sickness and introducing a three-day waiting period before beginning payment. He asked the actuary to hurry. The Chancellor was anxious to get on with the scheme. J. S. Bradbury to G. F. Hardy, January 13, 1911, Braithwaite Papers, Part II, Item 9.

[99] The alteration of the benefit from 5s. to 10s. changes the whole character of the scheme.

. . . .

It was originally intended that the main object of the scheme should be to meet the lower orders of the poorer section of the working classes, a large proportion of whom, it was hoped, would be able to pay the contribution necessary to provide the minimum benefit of 5s., and it was also understood should the insurers be in a position to pay a higher rate of contribution they could assure additional benefits through one or the other of the approved societies.

Letter by W. G. Bunn, June 9, 1911, 'Original Scheme of Insurance,' Del. Min., H. of O., 1910–12, p. 35.

all its members, young and old, with the required minimum benefits from the beginning. For the many insolvent societies national insurance, therefore, was a way of averting bankruptcy. For the more solvent ones, the State reserve released large society funds, estimated by Lloyd George later at ten to twelve million pounds, which could be used to pay extra benefits to their existing, prenational insurance members. This bribe prevented a friendly society revolution at the time of the dropping of widows' and orphans' pensions and the raising of the sickness benefit.[100]

The third important change of January, 1911, came as a result of the Chancellor's decision to give industrial insurance companies and collecting societies the right to become approved societies.[101] This decision, taken after the January 12 conference, met strong resistance from Braithwaite and John Bradbury. J. Lister Stead, Secretary of the Foresters, who had earlier become an adviser to the two men, threatened to resign. Braithwaite and Bradbury cast about for some means of excluding the societies by regulation.[102] Eventually they hit upon what would be, with the exception of the

[100] At the present moment the proposals reported out by the Actuaries have been modified by dropping out the provision for widows and orphans [inserted in Bradbury's MS, 'subject to further negotiations with the Societies.'] and by giving up the State's claim upon the friendly Societies for an apportionment of their existing funds. This latter modification [both 'would' and 'will' here] form part of the negotiations with the Societies, who are not aware this may be proposed. [The preceding sentence from 'This' to 'proposed' lined out by Bradbury's pen.] The position of the Trade Unions in the scheme is not settled.

The sickness benefit will probably be 10s. for men and 7s. 6d. for women, for either thirteen or twenty-six weeks, dropping to 5s. in each case after the period fixed. The Chancellor is also considering a proposal for providing a marriage portion for women. . . .

MS notes by W. J. Braithwaite, corrected by John Bradbury, January 21, 1911, Braithwaite Papers, Part II, Item 11.

[101] The so-called 'approved societies,' which at the beginning would have been only registered friendly societies, were to be the ordinary contributor's chief contact with State insurance. He would receive his benefit as a member of an approved society which would have its own reserves—except for the special reserve previously referred to, created on behalf of elderly members—and would make its own scale of payments under its own supervision.

[102] Their first proposal, apparently overruled by the Chancellor, was to stipulate that all approved societies should be organizations already paying sickness benefits. This definition, wrote Bradbury, 'excludes most of the Trade Unions but it is not close enough to exclude the Collecting Societies, unless this paying of sickness benefit is defined in some way as forming the principal or one of the principal objects of the Societies.' 'Introduction to accompany memorandum on scheme prepared for draftsmen,' Bradbury MS, February, 1911, Braithwaite Papers, Part II, Item 14.

medical benefit, perhaps the most hotly-contested single clause in the Bill. Friendly societies were all highly democratic organizations, a fact that caused many of their difficulties. Industrial insurance companies were autocratically controlled business organizations and even the collecting friendly societies, although theoretically run by their members, were always managed by ordinary authoritarian business methods. The aim of the insurance Bill was to extend the friendly society principle to those portions of the population not covered. Perhaps, thought Braithwaite, the provisions regulating approved society government could be drawn so as to make it impossible for industrial insurance organizations to qualify. 'Provisions will be inserted requiring all Approved Societies to have self government,' he wrote Lloyd George on March 10, 1911,

> and to adopt the mutual principle. The trouble is that Self Government in the case of the Collecting Societies is a 'farce.' The only bond of connection between the members is the Collector, and though the law now forbids the Collector to be the delegate on the representation of the members, he can still control the vote by using his influence on the voter. To prevent this occurring under the State Scheme, all Societies managed by delegates [that is, centralized societies without branches] might be required to set up local Committees for managing the local business. Doctors, appeals, etc. . . .

The central office could still retain a veto over local affairs, Braithwaite continued. There might be one committee for, perhaps, each 250 members who are more than three miles from the nearest branch office. Members, he thought, could thus get to know each other as in a true friendly society. 'If the Chancellor thinks some proposition of this sort worth proceeding with it would be desirable to consult the Hearts of Oak . . .' or some other centralized friendly society.[103]

After the flurry of activity around the first of the year, the insurance industry's preoccupation with Lloyd George's sickness scheme declined, even though the suspicion and hostility of its leaders did not. The *Insurance Mail* and Kingsley Wood worked

[103] W. J. Braithwaite to D. Lloyd George, Braithwaite MS, March 10, 1911, Braithwaite Papers, Part II, Item 34; see: Bunbury, ed., *Ambulance Wagon*, p. 119.

hard to keep interest alive by warning the collectors that widows' pensions were not dead, only delayed. For his part in the agitation, Kingsley Wood produced two pamphlets: *State Insurance vs. The Industrial Insurance Institutions*, published in February, and *The National Insurance Bill and the Industrial Insurance Agent*, published immediately after the Bill's introduction in June.[104] But, in general, industrial insurance agents' interest turned elsewhere. The most noteworthy public statement during the period came from T. C. Dewey, chairman of the giant Prudential, which was not in fact a member of the Combine, although it co-operated fully with that organization on national insurance. At the annual meeting of this organization on March 2, Dewey voiced what would become the most important area of struggle after the introduction of the Bill: the insurance industry's fear, not of government competition, but of friendly society competition should the societies become the administrators of insurance. If payments under insurance, said Dewey, are to be made by other than government officials, 'we feel we ought to be given the option of employing our staff for that purpose, at any rate so far as our own policyholders are concerned.'[105]

6

Meanwhile, Braithwaite and Bradbury, aided by surprisingly few other civil servants, were working in almost frantic haste to put together what had now become Part I of the National Insurance Bill. The Cabinet had decided on January 20 to join sickness insurance and unemployment insurance in a single Bill, which, after the second reading, would be referred to a select committee of the House of Commons, which would take evidence from friendly societies and all other interested bodies.[106] In this way Lloyd George's reiterated promise not to let his measure take its final form without a solicitation of the views of all affected parties would be fulfilled. And the charge that national insurance should at least

[104] It may be worth noting that neither of these pamphlets is available in any British national library, nor are they in the files of their publisher's successor, Stone and Cox. The February pamphlet consisted mainly of quotations from speeches of Lloyd George and Winston Churchill mentioning widows' and orphans' pensions. The July pamphlet dealt chiefly with the importance of the entry of industrial insurance into the State scheme.

[105] See: *The Times*, March 3, 1911; *Insurance Mail*, March 11, 1911.

[106] H. H. Asquith to George V, January 20, 1911, Asquith Papers, Box 6, ff. 1, 2.

have the benefit of a royal commission investigation to some extent would be met.[107]

One of Braithwaite's early decisions was to drop the awkward phrase 'invalidity insurance,' and the pessimistic one, 'sickness insurance,' as the titles of the plan. Reasoning that as life insurance was in reality insurance against death, insurance against sickness could be designated health insurance. In this way Lloyd George's project acquired the name by which it customarily has been known.[108]

In the last weeks of January and the first weeks of February Lloyd George was almost continually out of London, either in Wales or on the Continent, attempting to recover his voice. Braithwaite and Bradbury, assisted frequently by C. F. G. Masterman and the Chancellor's private secretary since 1910, R. G. Hawtrey, and occasionally by Rufus Isaacs, began to draw together the outlines of the insurance scheme. Not until after the middle of February, on Saturday and Sunday, February 18 and 19, were they able to meet Lloyd George for a full-dress conference. Typically for the Chancellor, the conference met not in London but at the Albion Hotel in Brighton. In addition to Braithwaite, Bradbury, Masterman and Hawtrey, Rufus Isaacs and L. T. Hobhouse, Professor of Sociology at London University, attended the meeting.

Generally conversation during the two days centred on three problems, each of them basic to any scheme of national health insurance. The first was the question of personal eligibility. Who beyond compulsorily insured manual workers might be eligible to become insured voluntarily? This question would become critical in negotiations with the doctors, who were loath to see large numbers of relatively well-to-do patients become members of the hated friendly societies.

The second question concerned selection of those insurance institutions that would be eligible to become approved societies. The Chancellor had already given his promise on January 12 that industrial insurance organizations could gain approval under certain conditions. At Brighton Braithwaite attempted to induce

---

[107] In the event, these sensible plans were never carried out. Unemployment insurance was handled quickly and quietly by a Grand Committee and Part I was examined in the full public glare of the Committee of the Whole House.

[108] Bunbury, ed., *Ambulance Wagon*, p. 129.

acceptance of his provision that approved societies be only organizations already paying sickness benefit. This was, of course, rejected.

The third question turned on the matter of approved society reserves and involved, but by no means settled, the much larger matter of the basic nature of health insurance finance. Ought health insurance to be run like private insurance, with the accumulation of an interest bearing reserve that would be spent during the later years of the contributor's life when the amount of money paid out to him in benefits outstripped his premiums? Or, alternatively, would it be possible to manage health insurance, as unemployment insurance was to be managed, simply by paying current benefits from current contributions, depending on the fact that unlike a private insurance organization a compulsory government scheme could depend on a continuous and predictable flow of new entrants whose contributions would maintain its solvency?[109]

The importance of the eventual decision to employ a reserve system for national health insurance benefits is frequently missed. Braithwaite considered it one of his important contributions to the scheme and, as in so much else, the pattern established in 1911 was followed in Great Britain as the welfare state grew. On the other hand, social welfare programmes of the United States and to some extent Germany have followed the lateral, or as Braithwaite called it, 'the dividing out' system of insurance. The lateral plan has the advantage that the State never becomes the custodian of a huge sum of money, which could in a very large programme have an effect on the economy, and would in a programme of any size raise political problems of investment. Contributions by men at work are immediately spent in benefits. A workman builds up no credit on his behalf to be spent in times of sickness, unemployment, or old age. During his active period of life he simply pays for those unable to work on account of these contingencies, secure in the knowledge that contributions collected from those who follow him will similarly take care of him. The advantage of this system is that benefits bear no relation to the amount of a reserve already accumu-

---

[109] These points were discussed in a memorandum drawn up by Braithwaite for the consideration of the Brighton Conference. His memoirs give an extended summary of the memorandum. Bunbury, ed., *Ambulance Wagon*, pp. 109–12. He had also produced for the conference a rough outline of the Bill. 'Draft of a Bill to Provide for Insurance Against Invalidity,' February 16, 1911. Braithwaite Papers, Part II, Item 19.

lated, but only to the total amount of contributions being paid at any one time. Thus benefits may be increased simply by increasing contributions. But of particular importance for the problem of national health insurance, a dividing out scheme would have covered the older worker, while at the same time avoiding the £60,000,000 debt Lloyd George's programme acquired in creating the artificial reserves made necessary by the acceptance into health insurance of many millions of hitherto uninsured old people.

In addition to the contention that accumulating insurance was the invariable practice of the true friendly societies and that dividing societies ordinarily were despised in friendly society circles, Braithwaite's principal argument for an accumulating or lineal system of insurance was that the interest paid on a worker's reserve fund during his active lifetime would permit him to enjoy much larger benefits for the same amount of contribution.[110] A 9d. insurance premium (during the Brighton conference the premium under discussion was 8d.) would buy 10½d. in benefits throughout the life of a boy of sixteen just entering insurance. In effect, by permitting his payments to accumulate as a reserve and receiving the 3 per cent interest that the State undertook to pay, 16½ per cent more money was available for benefits.[111]

The rebuttal of the contention that under dividing out insurance the workman is defrauded of the interest on his contributions would seem to lie in a consideration of the singular nature of State insurance. Because practically the only field for the investment of national insurance funds is government bonds, the benefit enjoyed through theoretical interest is in reality only a larger Treasury contribution to the insurance fund. In addition, because national insurance is compulsory insurance, and as the British practice has always been a flat rate contribution, in effect a regressive tax, political expediency and social utility alike would seem to dictate that the insurance scheme should be constructed so as to assure, in times of inflation, a return to the working man approximating in

[110] Braithwaite's arguments against a dividing out scheme are printed in full in Appendix B of his memoirs. Bunbury, ed., *Ambulance Wagon*, pp. 311–12. See also Arthur S. Comyns Carr, J. H. Taylor, and W. H. Stuart Garnett, *National Insurance*, London, 1912, p. 97.

[111] For an excellent discussion and defence, in layman's language, of the accumulating reserve system of national insurance, see: W. H. Stuart Garnett, 'The National Insurance Bill, The Financial Basis,' *Westminster Gazette*, November 6, 1911.

real terms the amount of value he has been forced to put in.[112] This is far more difficult when benefits are paid from a reserve that has been accumulated over a long period of years than when they are simply proportionate to an easily altered contribution.

At the Brighton conference the strongest spokesman against the accumulative principle was John Bradbury. In this he was supported by the Chancellor. Bradbury noted that the German system was about half lineal and half lateral and that the Germans, as would the English, found difficulty in the investment of accumulated funds.[113] The Chancellor remarked that national health insurance funds could perhaps be used for housing. Bradbury retorted that consols (government bonds) could also be used for subsidizing housing and in any event the accumulating principle was simply like adding £100,000,000 to the national debt. Nevertheless, it may well be that Lloyd George's eventual conversion to the accumulating system—the decision 'to be virtuous' which permitted Braithwaite to plan for a conventional insurance reserve fund—was based on the realization that in this way he would have available a sum to underwrite a programme that had been in his mind even longer than health insurance, the repopulation of the English land. In a Cabinet memorandum little more than three weeks after Lloyd George's agreement to the accumulating principle there appeared after the statement that 'any sums standing to the credit of a Society shall be invested with the National Debt Commissioners . . .' the words: 'It is proposed to use part of the funds for making loans under the Housing Acts.'[114] Here lay the germ of a third great welfare project that evolved in the Chancellor's mind from national health insurance as health insurance had been a logical extension of pensions.

In two and a half months, between the middle of February and the end of April, most of the health insurance portion of the huge National Insurance Bill took shape. It would be tedious and of little value to catalogue the innumerable drafts, Cabinet memoranda,

[112] For a statement of this point of view see: Allen T. Peacock, 'The National Insurance Funds,' *Economica*, XVI (August, 1949), 228–42.

[113] Stenographic notes of most of the discussion at the Brighton conference are available in Braithwaite Papers, Part I, 'Memoirs, 1910–1912,' Part 3, typescript, thirty-nine pages, unnumbered.

[114] Cabinet Memorandum, 'Insurance Scheme,' April 13, 1911, Braithwaite Papers, Part II, Item 57, p. 12. See also: Bunbury, ed., *Ambulance Wagon*, pp. 124–7.

and departmental notes that went into its construction. Some of the basic problems—the criteria for admission as an approved society, the amount of the sickness benefit, and the decision on the funded benefit—have already been discussed. Of these, the question of the reserve fund may serve as an introduction to a description of the problems that faced Braithwaite and his co-workers in the production of the national health insurance scheme.

First, if the scheme was to accumulate a claims reserve in the conventional way, then the very large number of elderly people who would be among the ten million workers insured for the first time under health insurance—men and women who had made no payments to friendly society reserves on their own behalf—somehow would have to be provided with reserves to take into the approved societies they joined. This could be accomplished by (1) requiring the new elderly members to pay higher contributions than younger members, which would be administratively difficult and unfair, or (2) by giving them smaller benefits, against which the same argument could be made, or (3) by artificially providing the societies they joined with a reserve. Eventually both the second and the third options were employed. The debt based upon the total amount of deficit incurred by each society computed on the basis of the number of its members over the age of seventeen was made up for the society by a paper credit, 'the reserve value,' granted to the society's reserve. Each society thus became technically solvent, though the scheme as a whole was in debt in the amount of £66,000,000.[115] This paper debit would be extinguished in sixteen years, as the elderly members who caused it died or passed from insurance at age seventy. The Government planned to divert a portion of each workman's contribution, $1\frac{5}{8}$d. per week for men and $1\frac{1}{4}$d. per week for women, to redeem the reserve values.[116]

This diversion was possible because, as originally calculated, the real cost of all benefits under the Act was considerably less than the total benefit each contribution ought to have been able to provide. As an illustration, the plan as a whole was in the position of a friendly society that had allowed its older members to use up their reserves (as many societies had) and then had raised rates of

[115] Men and women over age fifty received slightly lower sickness benefits, although all other benefits remained the same. The amending Act of 1913, however, abolished this distinction.

[116] On raising the employers' contribution, see: Bunbury, ed., *Ambulance Wagon*, pp. 149–51.

contributions so high that younger members were paying enough to provide their own benefits for life and to rebuild also the wasted reserves of the elders. At the time of introduction the benefits specified in the Bill and their costs were:

(a) The medical benefit: This was medical attendance of the insured by a general practitioner who would be an employee of the approved society. In all early calculations it had been assumed the doctor would be paid 4s. per year for each contributor he treated. This would take 1·5d. of the contribution.

(b) The sickness benefit: This was a payment for the maintenance of the wage earner and his family during a period of illness. Although adjusted several times during the formulation of the Bill, when the measure was introduced it amounted to 10s. per week for men and 7s. 6d. per week for women during the first thirteen weeks of illness and 5s. per week for both for the next thirteen weeks. It would begin after the fourth day of illness and would cost 2·2d. per week per insured.

(c) The disability benefit: This began when the sickness benefit ran out. It amounted to 5s. per week and might continue indefinitely. This was expected to take 0·8d. of the insured's contribution.

(d) The maternity benefit: This was the only benefit paid directly to a member of the insured's family who was not a contributor. It amounted to 30s. paid to the insured's wife at the time of childbirth. If both husband and wife were contributors, the payment was doubled. The wife, however, unless she was a contributor, received only the maternity benefit; medical or midwife attendance was not included in the Act. Most friendly societies gave a maternity benefit on similar terms. It was calculated to cost 0·6d. per week per contributor.

(e) Finally the Bill included a sanatorial benefit. This gave the insured, and eventually members of his family, the right to treatment in a sanatorium for tuberculosis. These institutions were to be built and maintained by a 1s. 3d. annual payment (that is, 0·3d. per week) from the insurance fund for each contributor, plus 1d. per year from funds voted by Parliament.

The total cost of the benefits outlined above was 5·4d. per week per male contributor. (Because of the 7s. 6d. sickness benefit for women, the total cost for women would be slightly lower.) With 0·9d. added for administration, the total cost of benefits was 6·3d.

per week. Until nearly the end of April the 'employed contribution' toward unemployment insurance had been calculated to be 6d.: 4d. paid by the workman and 2d. by his employer. The State contribution would be for working men one-quarter of the amount of the cost of benefits, not quite 2d. Taken together this sum left a comfortable margin of nearly 2d. per male contributor which was to be used for the redemption of reserve values. Then just before the Bill was introduced, the employed contribution was raised to 7d., with the employer paying 3d. instead of 2d. At the same time the State's proportion was decreased slightly to two-ninths of the cost of the benefit rather than one-quarter. This gave the famous 9d. contribution, the 'ninepence for fourpence' of which Lloyd George was so proud, although in fact the State contribution, calculated on the cost of benefits rather than on a fixed rate, was not quite 2d.[117] During the first sixteen years of the scheme's operation, most of the benefit of the State's contribution would go to make up the $1\frac{5}{9}$d. diverted to maintaining elderly workers or, more accurately, to paying off the debts incurred by their acceptance, and only after sixteen years would national health insurance benefits begin to reflect the total 9d. contribution. (As benefits rose, the State contribution to national health insurance, which was keyed to their cost, would also rise.) Young men and women were in effect bearing the burden of the inclusion of the elderly, although they did receive nearly, but not quite, the benefit of their own employed contribution.

This, then, was the price paid for the determination to set up national health insurance on an accumulative basis. The result was the awkward scheme of central reserve values established to make certain that no approved societies received an advantage by accepting only younger members. The aim, in every case, within the necessities of the plan, was to give societies as much freedom as possible in managing their own affairs. The extension of friendly society principles had been one of Lloyd George's

---

[117] The burden of the elderly workers continually bedevilled the planners of national health insurance. On March 24, Lloyd George wrote briefly noting that the report on the poor laws, which he had now begun to read, showed that the State was offering for 8d. what a healthy youth of twenty-one could receive in any good friendly society for $3\frac{3}{4}$d. Braithwaite Papers, Part II, Item 46. After the Bill's introduction when the total contribution was 9d., *The Times* pointed out that the insured would get for that 9d. only about one-half the benefits the same amount would bring in the best friendly societies. *The Times*, August 3, 1911.

original goals and the widespread acceptance of the fraternal idea, he felt, was absolutely necessary for State insurance. On this matter he wrote to the Cabinet on March 30. If the State could not enlist the support of the insured in the maintenance of the insurance fund, he said, the scheme would soon be bankrupt. Malingering was the greatest evil of all benefit schemes, and even the friendly societies had not been able to stamp it out altogether. The only really effective check upon it was to engage the self-interest of the workers by making each worker understand that any deficiency would have to be made up by all. Once the workers knew this, he thought, malingering would become unpopular among them and they would take the surest and the shortest way to discourage it. This was, he wrote in a private explanation of his Bill for the Cabinet soon after its introduction, the real reason for the local committees which had now appeared as Clause 21 (2) (3) (4) of the Bill.

> Experience shows that the business of controlling sick claims cannot be properly managed without local interest and cooperation of members of a society. It is therefore proposed in this clause that the societies administering benefits under the Bill should set up local committees practically in the way in which the great friendly societies and trade unions with one or two exceptions now conduct their business. . . .
>
> It is hoped that the local committees will also accomplish the object of enabling members in a district to know each other and to take greater interest in the management of their society. There is always a danger with a centralized society that members may feel no personal interest in the way in which the affairs of the society are conducted. A local committee will stimulate interest in the management of societies and prevent malingering.[118]

The overriding desire to leave as much independence as possible to the friendly societies meant particularly that the Government would have to accede to the societies' often-repeated demand for the power to reject applicants on any grounds except that of age. The many peculiar society requirements for membership—

---

[118] 'Notes on Clauses,' June 2, 1911, p. 8. Bill File, National Insurance Bill, 1911, 'Part 2, Committee Stage (Commons),' Ministry of Pensions and National Insurance.

temperance, protestantism, and above all, health—would have to be left intact. It followed, then, that under a compulsory scheme in which all the population were covered, there would be many in the early days of the scheme, particularly those at the lower end of the economic scale, who would be unable to gain admission to any society. What to do with this class of people—no one knew how large it would be—was one of the most serious questions occupying the planners of national health insurance. In the original plan, national health insurance had envisioned a compulsory State society providing small benefits for a minimal contribution. This would encourage membership in true friendly societies, which would offer more generous benefits for a higher contribution. Those few too feeble to join even the State society, the friendly societies had assumed, would be left to a revised poor law.[119] But with the reconstruction of the plan after the deletion of widows' pensions and the improvement of State benefits, the State society, which in any event never had been fully worked out, disappeared also. Now for a time it was thought that such people might be exempted from contributions altogether. The obvious difficulty here was that by contriving to fail to be accepted by an approved society, one could avoid paying national insurance contributions altogether and hence the scheme would become voluntary. Finally, on March 10 Braithwaite suggested keeping money from contributors unacceptable to all societies in a special fund at the post office, which had been designated as the ordinary agency for collection of contributions. These people would, in fact, not be under insurance at all. There would be no mutualization of funds. This programme would be simply a form of savings in which each contributor would have to his credit his own and his employer's contribution, plus the government contribution and interest. This part of the health scheme came to be known ambiguously as 'deposit insurance.'[120]

The insurance scheme in relatively completed form, although

[119] See Bunn letter, Hearts of Oak Benefit Society delegate minutes, June 9, 1911, p. 36.

[120] See: W. J. Braithwaite to D. Lloyd George, March 10, 1911, Braithwaite Papers, Part II, Item 34. See also: Bunbury, ed., *Ambulance Wagon*, p. 123. On earlier thinking for approved society rejects see: 'Scope of Scheme,' type script, unsigned, undated, unpaged (appearing after 'Draft A' of March 17, in the M.P.N.I. Bill File, but it is obviously several weeks earlier), Bill File, National Insurance Bill, 1911, 'Part 1, to Second Reading (Commons).'

still with an employed contribution of 6d. per week rather than 7d., was approved by the Cabinet on April 5, 1911.[121] Part II, the unemployment scheme, had already been approved in principle, but the cost of administration was considered high and this portion of the Bill was referred back to the Board of Trade for further consideration.[122] On that day Asquith closed his letter to the king with an uncharacteristic outburst of enthusiasm for social reform.

> The two schemes taken together with the Old Age Pensions Act, will, in the opinion of the Cabinet, form the largest and most beneficent increase in social reform yet achieved in any country.[123]

7

In the period between the formal announcement of the National Insurance Bill in the king's speech on February 6, and the first reading debate on May 4, 1911, the details of the scheme remained unusually secret. Even the friendliest administration newspapers, Spender's *Westminster Gazette* and Massingham's *Nation*, could offer little beyond the bare outlines that were known to all.[124] This may no doubt be accounted for by the fact that the details of the Bill changed from day to day, and there was little solid news to leak even to the most trusted editor. As mid-April came and went, time was growing short. The House of Commons' preoccupation with the Parliament Bill must eventually end; 1912 certainly would be devoted to Irish home rule. The *Westminster Gazette* speculated that Wednesday evenings either April 19 or 26 would see the introduction of national insurance.[125] At last on

---

[121] The plan discussed by the Cabinet is printed in: Cabinet Memorandum, 'Insurance Scheme, D. Ll. G., March 30, 1911,' Bill File, National Insurance Bill, 1911, 'Part 1, to Second Reading (Commons).' M.P.N.I.

[122] H. H. Asquith to George V, April 5, 1911, Asquith Papers, Box 6, ff. 24-5. Braithwaite noted happily in his diary that the Cabinet had 'thrown out' the unemployment scheme. In view of Sir Hubert Llewellyn Smith's 'insolent superiority,' the reception of his measure was especially comforting. Bunbury, ed., *Ambulance Wagon*, p. 141.

[123] Asquith to George V, April 5, 1911.

[124] See, for instance: *Westminster Gazette*, April 18, 1911.

[125] On the 26th, the Chancellor thought it expedient to explain publicly that his doctor had ordered him to make no long speeches until at least the week after next. *Westminster Gazette*, April 27, 1911. In fact, the decision to change the employed contribution from 6d. to 7d. had been made only two days before

M

Thursday, May 4, at a little after four o'clock in the afternoon the Chancellor rose and in a quiet voice, begging the members' pardon for his inaudibleness, asked leave to introduce the National Insurance Bill.[126]

Lloyd George explained his Bill principally as a measure for reducing pauperism. He stressed the relatively small number of working men who had been able to join friendly societies, even though the disastrous economic effect of the illness of the wage earner was well known. Generally the Chancellor's speech was accounted far more successful than his introduction of the 1909 budget and the reception given by party leaders was uniformly favourable. Austen Chamberlain, answering for the Unionists, welcomed this brief moment when 'the housebreakers' among the Liberals allowed the Chancellor to do some constructive work.[127]

As introduced, Part I of the National Insurance Bill provided the familiar friendly society benefits of medical treatment, a sickness benefit of 10s for thirteen weeks for men and 5s. for the next thirteen weeks to begin on the fourth day of illness (in place of 10s., women received 7s. 6d.), a 5s. disability benefit, a maternity benefit of 30s., and the right to treatment in a sanatorium. The 7s. employed contribution (6s. for women) was to be paid by means of revenue stamps, normally procured by the workman's employer, who would purchase the stamps at the post office and affix them to a card provided him by the workman. At the end of each three months, the workman would carry his card filled with stamps to the approved society of his choice where it would represent the workman's contribution for that quarter of the year. The govern-

and the new estimates on the cost of benefits were not completed. Bunbury, ed., *Ambulance Wagon*, p. 150.

[126] *H. of C. Deb.*, XXV (May 4, 1911), col. 609.

[127] *Ibid.*, col. 645. Privately Chamberlain was even more complimentary and not so even tempered. He wrote: 'Confound Ll. George. He has strengthened the Government again. His sickness scheme *is* a good one, and he is on the right lines this time. I must say I envy him the opportunity, and I must admit he has made good use of it.' Petrie, *Austen Chamberlain*, I, 277.

Joseph Austen Chamberlain, 1863–1937, born, Birmingham; son of Joseph Chamberlain; educated, Rugby and Trinity College, Cambridge; M.P., Liberal Unionist, East Worcester, 1892–1914; Birmingham, 1914–37. Civil Lord of Admiralty, 1895–1900; Financial Secretary to Treasury, 1900–1902; Postmaster General, 1902–3; Chancellor of the Exchequer, 1903–5 and 1919–21; Secretary of State for India, 1915–17; member, War Cabinet, 1918; Lord Privy Seal and Leader of the House of Commons, 1921–2; Secretary of State for Foreign Affairs, 1924–9; First Lord of Admiralty, 1931; Chairman, Court of Governors, London School of Hygiene and Tropical Medicine.

ment's contribution of two-ninths of the cost of benefits—about 2s. in the case of men—was paid directly to the society on the basis of the number of cards they held and the benefits they gave.

All workmen over sixteen years of age earning less than £160 per year, the income tax limit, were compulsorily insured, and all manual labourers were compulsorily insured whatever their income. Moreover, anyone of any income could insure voluntarily, which would mean that he paid both the employer's and the employee's contribution. Except for the deposit contributors, who were to be handled by the post office, the chief administrative agencies of the scheme were the approved societies who were required, unless they were already organized with branches, to set up local committees to provide personal contact with the insured. The societies employed the doctors whose service constituted the medical benefit.

The Bill provided for the appointment of 'local health committees' whose membership of between nine and eighteen was to be appointed one third by the approved societies, one third by local sanitary authorities, and one third by the post office contributors. Besides administering the sanatoria and providing for representation of the post office contributors in the official hierarchy, the local health committees (not to be confused with local management committees) were given large but unspecific duties to look into local health conditions, provide lecturers on health, to investigate whether a given local authority was inadequately enforcing sanitary legislation and thus increasing the amount of sickness in the community, and generally to symbolize the rather slight interest of the Bill's planners in the larger aspects of public health and sanitary science.[128]

The Newsholme–Newman–Webb-medical officer of health alliance had continually urged Braithwaite to raise the status of the local health committee to that of a statutory committee of the county councils, and so, presumably, to provide an entré for the

---

[128] Clause 46 of the Bill gave power to the insurance administration to recover extra costs of sickness from a local authority if it could prove that the insurance scheme had been subject to unusual expense because of local authority inefficiency. This clause, which proved to be totally unworkable, took up as much time during planning as any other single provision of the Bill. It was stoutly resisted throughout by the Local Government Board and the local authority lobbying agencies: the Association of Municipal Corporations and the County Councils Association.

medical officer of health and the prevention of destitution social philosophy.[129] At a breakfast on February 28 at 11 Downing Street, apparently the only meeting between the Webbs and Lloyd George during the planning of national health insurance, the Webbs had extracted from the Chancellor a promise that he would consult Newsholme in the planning of the Bill. This Braithwaite did and received much useful advice, particularly on the administration of the medical benefit, and doctors' relations with friendly societies. But on the whole, Fabian influence on national health insurance was smaller than on any other establishment of the New Liberalism.[130]

Government administration of national health insurance for the three kingdoms and Wales was to be handled by a board of commissioners appointed by the Treasury. The chief duty of this board was the inspection of the approved societies, and many clauses of the Bill dealt with supervision, conditions for approval, and methods for valuation of the societies.

Despite the almost universal public approval expressed by politicians, and indeed by the press generally, two important bodies expressed reservations. These two were the collecting insurance industry and the British Medical Association. Although they had little in common, they became allies in the struggle against the one group at least partially satisfied with the insurance Bill as it stood—the friendly societies.

The passage of the National Insurance Bill provides an almost classic history of lobby activity. On one side were the doctors and the industrial insurance industry seeking to modify the Bill in their own interest. On the other were the friendly societies trying

[129] See: Arthur Newsholme to W. J. Braithwaite, March 28, 1911, and Memorandum, Arthur Newsholme, March 31, 1911. Bill File, National Insurance Bill, 1911, 'Part 1, to Second Reading (Commons);' 'Memorandum by Sir George Newman,' June 15, 1911, Braithwaite Papers, Part II, Item 78; and see also: Beatrice Webb, *Our Partnership*, London, 1948, p. 472.

[130] During the February 28 breakfast, Beatrice Webb terrified Braithwaite by talking to him about venereal disease, and Sidney Webb wasted his time with Lloyd George attacking the friendly societies. For Braithwaite's description of the breakfast see: Bunbury, ed., *Ambulance Wagon*, pp. 115, 117; see also: Appendix A, pp. 307–10, Sidney Webb's memorandum on the insurance scheme. This shows surprisingly little acquaintance with government plans as they had progressed by early March. Mrs Webb assumed she had made a considerable impression on Lloyd George and noted in her diary that the front bench Liberals seemed to be 'softening' towards herself and her husband. Webb, *Partnership*, pp. 469–70.

to maintain what was left of their original privileged position. Between the lines, working first with one side, then with the other, never permitted to forget that industrial insurance held pledges from two-thirds of the House of Commons, and as time went on finding it necessary to depend more and more upon industrial insurance support, was David Lloyd George. Compared to this, the formal political debate was of little interest. The Parliament Bill held the centre of the scene at Westminster during the summer months of 1911. During the critical committee stage of national health insurance when the doctors and insurance companies gained their first victory over the friendly societies in the so-called Addison amendment, public interest was focused on the House of Lords, where the Unionist Party leaders, under the threat of a massive creation of peers, struggled with their own following to secure the passage of the Parliament Bill.

Finally, with the Lords' veto abolished, the Unionist rank and file vented the residue of their anger on national insurance. The original cordiality of the opposition turned to irresponsible obstruction. More than five hundred amendments were offered. Perhaps more characteristic, part of the decline of parliamentary standards of the period, was the willingness of the official opposition to turn to obstruction outside the normal political arena. Like franchise for women, abolition of the Lords' veto, and finally, almost disastrously, Irish home rule, much of the important political activity surrounding national health insurance was extraparliamentary. The unwillingness of Englishmen in the strange days before World War I to obey the enactments of a lawful Parliament seemed likely for a time to turn Lloyd George's health plan into a terrible, and expensive, joke. This period of opposition began with the fatuous anti-stamp-licking campaign before the Bill became law and culminated in late 1912 in the revolt of the doctors. Although it has been given much attention by historians, the public controversy that raged about the requirement that mistresses affix insurance stamps on the contribution cards of their servants—which perhaps could be termed the revolt of the duchesses—had little real importance so far as the progress of Lloyd George's Bill was concerned. Its only effect was to force Lloyd George to depend more heavily upon the well-organized opinion-moulding machinery of the industrial insurance companies, and so, in the long run, to undermine further the position of the friendly societies in national health insurance. The revolt of the doctors was far more serious and will be discussed in the next chapter.

Spokesmen for the collecting insurance industry admitted rather pleasant surprise when the terms of the national health insurance scheme became known. As it stood the Bill would not hinder the funeral benefit business, and by protecting the income of contributors might cut down on lapsing. 'The Bill itself contains much that is good,' said the *Mail*, 'and excepting the fear of the "thin edge of the wedge," there appears to be little to object to in it.'[131] But within two weeks insurance opinion changed. Insurance men remembered that although there would be no funeral benefits under the plan, the friendly societies, which would become the approved societies under the Act, invariably offered funeral benefits as a normal part of their private business. Hence there was the danger that the friendly societies might use the government programme to undermine the commercial funeral benefit industry. 'What is there to prevent the approved societies from circularizing every one of their new members to the effect that the State scheme does not give death benefits, but by paying, say, another sixpence a week they can have double sick pay plus a sum at death?' asked the *Mail* on May 27. Friendly society officials as agents of the State would now be entering the houses of families covered by industrial insurance companies and because the societies employed no collectors they could offer better terms than the commercial industry.[132]

> The matter is causing a state of unrest, and various meetings have been called to discuss it. As we write the Association of Industrial Companies and Collecting Societies is meeting for the purpose. The Association has been debating this grave subject for the last three days. We greatly hope that a suitable and fair solution of the difficulty will be found.[133]

---

[131] *Insurance Mail*, May 13, 1911. See also: *Assurance Agents' Chronicle*, XXIII (May 13, 1911), 222–3.

[132] While the Refuge, for instance, gave a death benefit of £8·41 for 1d. per week contribution at age twenty, the Manchester Unity for 3½d. per month, that is, 0·88d. per week, would give, at age twenty, a £10 benefit upon the death of the member and a £5 benefit upon the death of his wife.

[133] *Insurance Mail*, May 27, 1911. Funeral benefits under national health insurance were no longer an issue. On May 17, F. Handel Booth, who ordinarily acted for the Combine in the House of Commons, noted that the Act as written

By the end of May the unrest in the insurance world was being heard politically. The Bill, it was felt, 'would drive members into what were called "approved" societies.' If it passed in its present form 'insurance agents might as well emigrate.'[134]

The Combine's decision was announced to the world towards the end of June by Arthur Henri of the Liverpool Victoria. Writing in his company's magazine, he announced:

> We may say that under suitable machinery it is our intention to step forward and work this sick business; and a paramount reason for doing so is that thereby we shall most effectually conserve our existing business, and, correspondingly, the collecting interest also. The more of our present members can be got to join the Victoria sickness section the more secure our staff will be in respect of such business. Obviously where our members join the large 'orders' there enters a new and subtle form of competition with our death benefit and endowment business.
>
> . . . .
>
> Hence our intention to become a recognized authority under the Bill; and from this intention arises our reasonable claim that the conditions of 'approval' shall be suitable to our organization and not adapted exclusively to the far different organization of the 'orders.'[135]

This decision marked the end of the original conception of national health insurance. Although the Chancellor had long since agreed that an approved society could be a section of a collecting society or industrial insurance company, the clauses thoughtfully introduced by Braithwaite and Bradbury after the January 12 conference would have made it virtually impossible for a society

---

might make it possible for approved societies to give death benefits out of surpluses arising from insurance contributions. He asked the Chancellor whether this could be excluded by a separate amendment. Lloyd George replied casually saying, 'Certainly, I will.' *H. of C. Deb.*, XXV (May 17, 1911), col. 1988. The result was Section 37 (3) of the Act, 'no surplus and no part of any surplus shall be applied for the purpose of paying any benefits payable on death . . .' or any other benefits not specified. This unimportant amendment has received far too much attention.

[134] See reports of conferences at Wolverhampton and Walthamstow, Essex. The latter was John Simon's constituency. *Insurance Mail*, June 17, 1911.

[135] *Liverpool Victoria Record*, June, 1911, quoted in *Assurance Agents' Chronicle*, XXIII (July 1, 1911), 304.

run for profit or a society using collectors to become approved. At issue were two related sets of requirements. The first was Clause 21 (2) (3) (4) of the Bill as introduced requiring the establishment of local management committees unless the society already had branches in each locality where it had members. The second was Clause 18 (2) (ii) (iii) (iv). These dealt with the government of an approved society. The first required that an approved society

> must be precluded by its constitution from distributing any of its funds otherwise than by way of benefits (whether benefits under this Act or not) amongst its members. . . .

The second subsection (iii) stipulated that 'its affairs must be subject to the absolute control of its members;' and the last (iv) said that 'its constitution must provide for the election of all its committees, representatives, and officers by its members.'

All this was, of course, normal practice in true friendly societies, but the industrial insurance organizations were pre-eminently profit-making institutions run by autocratic business methods. Clause 18 (2) (ii) would probably have prohibited the payment of any company funds to stockholders. Certainly it would have made impossible the use of collectors and the requirements for local committees would have made them unnecessary. Finally, the requirement for the election of highly-paid insurance company officials by hundreds of thousands of the working-class members of approved societies was unthinkable. Thus without the elimination of these clauses industrial insurance's formal right of entry into the health scheme meant nothing, and well before Henri's announcement the companies set to work to force their deletion from the Act. Correspondingly, although slower to react, the friendly societies fought to see them retained. The last weeks of June and all of July, while public attention was distracted by the unprecedented disorder attending the progress of the Parliament Bill through the House of Commons, the insurance industry devoted itself to national health insurance.

At this time the companies ordered into the struggle the vast army of collecting agents who were told to make certain that every home in the United Kingdom knew of their cause. A 'recent' meeting reported in the *Mail* of four hundred insurance workers in South London, the richest insurance market in the kingdom, at the Surrey Masonic Hall, Camberwell, may provide an illustration of the employment of agents. The chairman of the meeting was A. Hartwell, a director of the London and Manchester. Also on the platform were officers of the Refuge, the United Friendly, Liverpool Victoria, and the Royal Liver. Mr Hartwell opened the meeting:

> Gentlemen, we want you to thoroughly understand your position in the matter of the Insurance Bill. Our standpoint is not a political one. . . . There are a number of clauses that, if they see the light of day, will be a menace. They should be entirely eradicated from the Bill. We have 490 letters from Members of the House of Commons, promising they will not support death benefits in this Insurance Bill. We want more than this. Only last week the secretary of the Odd Fellows said that this Bill would be the death of industrial insurance. At the eleventh hour we have the orders against us. It lies now in your hands to show Mr Lloyd George and to show every Member of Parliament that we are determined to stand for our own interests. It is our bread and butter.

Edwin R. Balding, Managing Director of the United Friendly, closed the meeting with an appeal to the agents in the simplest economic terms:

> What may be the effect on your books in the course of the next two or three years? How many books now fetch 40, 30, or 25 times? Well, I say that you will have a difficulty in disposing of them at a much smaller amount than this. The scheme is being rushed through, and yet all of our interests are at stake. I hope that all of you will do your utmost to bring your local Members to reason.[136]

The insurance men did their utmost. In the next few weeks through lobby delegations, at constituency meetings, in letters, and in private conferences, members of the Government and distracted M.P.s were reminded of the power of industrial insurance. The insurance workers, it was reiterated,

> are only too anxious to meet and afford their Member the benefit of their experience. The insurance agent goes into practically every house in the land. He is looked upon as a member of the

[136] *Insurance Mail*, June 24, 1911.

M*

family, consulted on many matters quite apart from his business, and, oftener than not, stands in the relationship of guide, philosopher and friend to his members. Such a man knows not only his particular business, but has of necessity acquired a very deep and considerable knowledge of human nature as well. Use him, ask his help, it will willingly be at your service.[137]

At the end of June the insurance industry won an important concession with Lloyd George's agreement to delete the prohibitive Clause 18 (2) (ii) on the distribution of any society funds in any way other than in benefits. This change does not appear to have been opposed by the societies at the time, although later it appeared as one of their complaints.[138]

By the end of July insurance men were claiming victory. The insurance men, bragged a speaker at Wakefield with two M.P.s on the platform,

> were satisfied that never before had the Government realized the power and strength of insurance men. And any Government that dared play the knave with us would find that we could play the deuce with them. And besides this, the present Bill would act as a warning as to the difficulties that would be found in dealing with any further scheme of insurance. (Applause)[139]

Braithwaite recalls Kingsley Wood leaning over to him and whispering: 'We have got Ll. G. there (putting his thumb on the desk) and shall get our own terms!'[140]

Kingsley Wood had found an ally for industrial insurance in the British Medical Association. Through the first six months of 1911 the doctors watched the growth of Lloyd George's health plan with a great deal of suspicion. They had been put off early in the year by what can be designated only as a deliberate untruth. On the same day the *Manchester Guardian* and *The Times* both published

---

[137] Letter sent by secretary, J. Walsh, of Rochdale (Lancashire) Fraternal to Members of Parliament: H. T. Cawley, Heywood; Sir W. R. D. Adkins, Middleton; A. G. C. Harvey, Rochdale (all Liberals), n.d., quoted in *Insurance Mail*, July 22, 1911.

[138] Bunbury, ed., *Ambulance Wagon*, pp. 181–2.

[139] Meeting of Yorkshire Fraternals at Wakefield Social Institute, July 22, 1911, quoted in *Insurance Mail*, August 5, 1911.

[140] Bunbury, ed., *Ambulance Wagon*, p. 168. Surprisingly, Braithwaite professes to be unsure whether the activity of the collectors was organized by the companies. *Ibid.*, p. 169.

what purported to be an outline of the health plan stipulating that the scheme would include no medical benefits because the £160 income limit would, in many parts of the country, deprive doctors of much of their private practice.[141] The appearance of virtually the same notice in two extremely well-informed newspapers within a few hours of one another suggests that the information was given out to both and that it was not simply the result of speculation in one being picked up and reprinted as fact in the other.

Certainly the Chancellor of the Exchequer consulted the doctors as little as possible during the formulation of the Bill, although exact evidence is conflicting on how many meetings took place.[142] Privately Lloyd George professed a low opinion of medical deputations which, one may suspect, coloured all his thinking about doctors during the passage of the Bill and afterwards. '. . . it is difficult to ascertain the true feelings of doctors as a whole on any proposal affecting them,' he said during the Brighton conference, 'since a Deputation of Doctors is always a Deputation of swell Doctors: it is impossible to get a Deputation of poor Doctors or of slum Doctors.'[143] This statement may account for his persistent assumption throughout 1912 that the doctors' public pronouncements did not represent the consensus of the profession, no matter how strongly they were worded.

The form of medical attendance planned under national health insurance was closely tied to the whole question of the sickness benefit and to the control of malingering. Friendly society practice had always made the doctor the principal officer responsible for the award of sickness certificates, the presentation of which was necessary to claim the sickness benefits. It followed that a doctor dependent upon his patients' good will for his income could not be properly stringent in the award of certificates, and so friendly societies almost never permitted free choice of a doctor.

[141] *The Times*, January 4, 1911; *Manchester Guardian*, January 4, 1911.

[142] In 1912 Lloyd George told the House of Commons he met the medical profession four times in 1911 before the Bill was introduced—three times during April and May and once at the beginning of the year. *H. of C. Deb.*, XXXVIII (May 6, 1912), cols. 178–9. On the other hand, the *British Medical Journal* stated that although the Chancellor had consulted with the friendly societies for two years, he had heard the B.M.A. only once 'for an hour or so,' just before the Bill was introduced. *B.M.J.* Supp., June 17, 1911, p. 441.

[143] 'Brighton Conference,' Braithwaite Papers, Part I, 'Memoirs, 1910–1912,' Part 3.

Society members in a given area had to accept the doctor under contract to their society in that area. If dissatisfied their only recourse was to attempt to induce their lodge to change doctors, but as members of the society themselves, as lodge members rather than doctors' patients, their interest was in maintaining stringent control of the sickness costs. Lloyd George's original plans for handling the medical benefit, fully discussed at the Brighton conference, had been to leave the matter to the societies. But by the end of March, under the influence of Masterman and Arthur Newsholme, he had begun to change his opinion. On March 30, he wrote to the Cabinet:

> I have interviewed a large number of doctors on the medical side of this scheme. They all agree in denouncing the present system of medical relief as organized by the friendly societies.

Fees were too small, the Chancellor continued, about 4s. including drugs and appliances. For the health scheme, he said, he would like to see the medical benefit handled by the local health committees.

> But compulsorily to transfer the medical work now undertaken by Friendly Societies, medical clubs, and Works Clubs to the Health Committee would at this stage provoke formidable opposition.
>
> I propose, however, to give the Societies the option of handing over this part of their duties to the Health Committee, the latter charging them 5s. per member. An advantage of this transfer, beside severing the connection between the doctors and the despised societies would be facilitation of the movement toward a system of salaried doctors and the eventual final control of the problem of malingering.

'Free choice of Doctors promotes malingering,' wrote Lloyd George.

> That is the experience of Germany. It is equally the experience of our own Friendly Societies. The medical profession like it, and we shall have to encounter a certain measure of opposition amongst a class of doctors if we set our face against free choice. I would not recommend the Government to forbid it altogether, but rather to make arrangements in the Bill which will tend gradually and eventually to eliminate it. This, I hope, will be

accomplished if we can make it worth the Friendly Societies' while to transfer the duty of providing medical relief for their members to the Health Authority proposed to be set up in this Bill. As the leaders of the Friendly Societies are fully alive to the inroads made on their funds by this evil, and to the extent to which it is fostered by free selection of doctors, they will not be averse to a restriction of this right.[144]

Medical reaction to the national health insurance scheme after its first authoritative public description by Lloyd George on May 4 was immediate and violent.[145] Partly this was the result of an apparent mistake made by the Chancellor during his opening speech. Describing the administration of the medical benefit, Lloyd George had suggested that it would be desirable to separate the costs for the prescription of drugs from the doctors' capitation fee so that there would be no inducement for the medical man to economize on drugs. This, he said, was done in the friendly societies.

> In addition to that, I think there ought to be provision for improvement in the standard of payment to the doctors. Sometimes, no doubt, they are quite adequately paid, but sometimes they certainly are not, and I think financial provision ought to be made in the scheme for raising the level to 4s. I have done so, and I hope that this will meet the views of the House.[146]

Dr G. F. McCleary, who became eventually senior medical officer in national health insurance, wrote in his history of the service in 1932 that this small mistake—the reference to raising the medical benefit 'to 4s.' which should have read 'of 4s.'—turned many doctors against the service before they had examined the Bill.[147] Whether or not it was this error, the small size of the medical

[144] 'Insurance Scheme, D. Ll. G.,' March 30, 1911, pp. 18, 22. Bill File, M.P.N.I. Belatedly the profession itself had begun to look into various plans for State medical care. This investigation, including a long questionnaire to ascertain professional opinion, was not complete when national health insurance was introduced. See: 'Report on the Organization of Medical Attendance on the Provident or Insurance Principle,' *B.M.J.* Supp., March 4, 1911, pp. 81–122.

[145] This excepts the *British Medical Journal* itself, which welcomed the Bill in a mildly laudatory leader taken almost *verbatim* from Austen Chamberlain's speech. ¡The magazine was immediately deluged by letters of protest from doctors. See: *B.M.J.*, May 13, 1911, p. 1137, and May 20, 1911, pp. 1191–4.

[146] *H. of C. Deb.*, XXV (May 4, 1911), col. 629.

[147] George F. McCleary, *National Health Insurance*, London, 1932, pp. 88–9.

benefit caused an outcry, and following the opening speech the doctors acted swiftly in organizing their opposition to the Bill.[148] On May 31, only two weeks after the first printed text of the Bill became available, the British Medical Association held a special representative meeting in the examination hall of the Royal Colleges' building on the Victoria Embankment. The profession had originally intended to ask the Chancellor to receive a delegation during the meeting. Lloyd George asked in return whether the meeting might receive him and permit him to explain his measure. The Chancellor appeared the following evening, June 1, and in one of his most effective platform performances, convinced the doctors not to oppose his Bill.

'I was one of those present when the Chancellor met the delegates of the British Medical Association,' wrote a well-known specialist, Dr Herbert Woodcock.

The bright-eyed, alert, popular politician, courageous, ready and good humoured, was a glorified example of the witty, business-like market practitioner compelling his wares on a circle of admiring but doubting critics. He was just the man to

---

[148] The actuarial memorandum of March, 1910, and many subsequent documents had calculated the cost of the medical benefit as 4s. per contributor per year.

In view of the discussions in February and March about the doctors' attitude towards the friendly societies suggesting the possible transfer of medical benefits to the local health committees, it would seem unlikely that Lloyd George and Masterman were 'a good deal taken aback' by Christopher Addison's revelation that friendly society medical administration 'stank in the nostrils' of the profession. Addison's presentation of himself, reinforced by a careless biographer, as the only interpreter of medical opinion to insurance planners, is wildly inaccurate. Christopher Addison, *Politics From Within*, 1911–1918 (London, 1924), I, 20–21.

Christopher Addison, 1859–1951, born, Lincolnshire; educated, Trinity College, Harrogate; received medical training at St Bartholomew's Hospital; taught at Medical School, Cambridge, and Medical School, University of London; lecturer, St Bartholomew's Hospital; Editor, *Quarterly Medical Journal*. M.P., Liberal, Hoxton Division, Shoreditch, 1910–22; M.P., Labour, Swindon Division, Wiltshire, 1929–31 and 1934–5; Parliamentary Secretary to Board of Education, 1914–15; Parliamentary Secretary to Ministry of Munitions, 1915–16; Minister of Munitions, 1916–17; Minister of Reconstruction, 1917–19; President, Local Government Board, 1919; first Minister of Health, 1919–21; Minister without Portfolio, 1921; Parliamentary Secretary, Ministry of Agriculture, 1929–30; Minister of Agriculture and Fisheries, 1930–31; Secretary of State for Commonwealth Relations, 1945–7; Lord Privy Seal, 1947–51; Lord President of Council, 1948; Leader of House of Lords, 1945–51; Baron Stallingborough, 1937, Viscount, 1945.

make us forget that the Cabinet Minister in charge of a Bill is a man who has to strive strenuously to pass his measure whatever its value. This particular Bill, however, was a bad one.[149]

Lloyd George's great political achievement before the doctors was to transform their opposition to himself into an opposition to the friendly societies. He convinced the profession that it should support the transfer of the medical benefit to the local health committees, a change he had already decided was necessary. For years, he said, he had been a careful student of the conditions of medical practice and the doctors had a genuine grievance.

> I can tell you this; that I am entirely with you in this . . . and if you can persuade the House of Commons to consent to the transfer of the whole medical attendance, including maternity, to the Local Health Committees you will find me an enthusiastic supporter of that proposal. (Loud applause) But you must remember there are two sides to this question, and that the Approved Societies will not readily resign this power. You have brought a good deal of pressure on me during the last few days, and I want you to transfer that pressure from me to the House of Commons. I am entirely of your view as to this; I do not believe you will ever get a satisfactory medical service until you do transfer it to the Local Committees.[150]

The Chancellor pointed out that one important friendly society, the Hearts of Oak, had already agreed, had indicated indeed that it desired, to pass administration of the medical benefit to the local health committees. As a centralized society with no local branches, the Hearts of Oak had never administered the medical benefit itself and had used salaried local sickness visitors for the purpose of certification for the sickness benefit. The Hearts of Oak therefore had protested also Clause 21 (2)(3) and (4) requiring the formation of local management committees, saying that in their organization, with neither the experience nor the desire to handle the medical benefit, local committees were unnecessary. The day before, a delegation of the Hearts of Oak had visited the Chancellor

[149] Herbert DeCarle Woodcock, *The Doctor and the People*, London, 1912, p. 77.
[150] 'Report of Special Representative Meeting held in Examination Hall of the Royal Colleges of Physicians and Surgeons, Victoria Embankment, London, May 31, June 1, 1911,' *B.M.J.* Supp., June 3, 1911, p. 354.

and had received his promise that if they transferred the medical benefit to the local health committees the requirement for formation of local management committees would be lifted.[151] Toward the end of his speech, the Chancellor proposed that the doctors make common cause with the Hearts of Oak friendly society, suggesting that all of them together bring pressure on their Members of Parliament.[152]

The doctors' hatred of the friendly societies and the defection of the Hearts of Oak on the matter of local committees gave industrial insurance its first great parliamentary victory. The doctors did not want to work for the approved societies; the industrial insurance industry did not want local management committees. Local committees were useful only if the doctors did work for approved societies. On behalf of the Combine, Kingsley Wood gave up the administration of the medical benefit, of little interest to industrial insurance in any case, and the British Medical Association supported the abolition of the management committees. On August 1 Kingsley Wood consented to an interview with the *Insurance Mail* to explain his compromise. 'It is an open secret,' said the *Mail*, 'that he has been acting for our offices in the recent negotiations connected with the National Insurance Bill and has been advising them . . . on points arising out of the Bill. . . .' The original Bill, explained Kingsley Wood to the readers of the *Mail*, made it possible for any 250 contributors in a locality to require the formation of a local management committee, which would for all practical purposes supersede the work of the insurance agent. 'In insurance circles,' he said, 'this has been thought to be an unnecessary interference not only with the management of societies which might be formed, but also with their superintendents and agents.'

---

[151] *Cd. 5869*, 'Reports of Deputations to the Chancellor of the Exchequer,' 1911, pp. 3–4. See also Braithwaite's comments on this decision. Bunbury, ed., *Ambulance Wagon*, pp. 175–6.

[152] 'Report of Special Representative Meeting,' *B.M.J.* Supp., June 3, 1911, pp. 354–5. As almost its last act, the representative meeting passed unanimously the famous 'Six Cardinal Points,' which would become the basic medical platform in the struggle over national insurance. One of these, free choice of doctor, would be incorporated in the same amendment that accomplished the transfer of medical benefit from the friendly societies. The rest belong to a later portion of this study. Immediately after the representative meeting adjourned, the Medical Secretary of the B.M.A., Dr James Smith Whitaker, began to collect promises from all doctors in the United Kingdom not to work under national health insurance until the six points were agreed to. J. Smith Whitaker, 'Circular Letter,' June 3, 1911, printed in *B.M.J.* Supp., June 10, 1911, p. 404.

The amendments announced by the Chancellor that day would end approved society administration of the medical benefit and end also the requirement for local management committees. No doubt all insurance men would approve of this change, remarked the Combine's solicitor dryly, and it would also save 'a considerable amount of friction with the medical profession.'[153] On the day of the interview the Commons sitting in Committee of the Whole House voted 387 to 15 to deprive all approved societies of supervision over insurance medical practice and to vest it in the local health committees. These would establish a list or 'panel' of all doctors in the community who chose to apply, from which the insured could select his physician. Lloyd George sought to avoid the wrath of the friendly societies by the paltry subterfuge of removing the Whips, permitting thus a technically free vote. At the same time he warned the societies not to oppose the change too strenuously. There will be many new approved societies under health insurance, he said in an oblique reference to industrial insurance, 'and I venture to predict the vast majority . . . will hand over the medical benefit to the local health committees.'[154] On October 27, Clause 21 disappeared from the National Insurance Bill without debate.

'A much improved outlook,' announced the *Insurance Mail*, referring to the Kingsley Wood interview. Insurance companies would now be able

> to escape the interference of local tradesmen with our methods of conducting the State sickness insurance scheme. We get this concession by placing in the hands of the local health committee the administration of the medical benefit provided by the Bill, a matter that has just been dealt with by the House of Commons.

But, continued the *Mail*, 'we are not yet out of the wood.' The friendly societies were still fighting hard and the Chancellor 'may still need considerable support in Parliament, and agents who have the opportunity might do worse than recommend—we might say urge—their local members to support the amendments in the Chancellor's name.'[155]

---

[153] *Insurance Mail*, August 12, 1911.

[154] *H. of C. Deb.*, XXIX (August 1, 1911), col. 318.

[155] *Insurance Mail*, August 12, 1911. The same issue of the *Insurance Mail* printed a letter from the management of the Prudential to its agents announcing

For the friendly societies the loss of the administration of the medical benefit was a harsh blow. The Chancellor of the Exchequer, whom they had regarded as their champion, was now an object of loathing. On August 4, meeting at the Westminster Palace Hotel, the board of directors of the Manchester Unity passed a resolution demanding that national health insurance be postponed until the next year. At the same time the Grand Master, A. H. Warren, made a speech virtually charging the Chancellor with dishonesty.[156]

But the societies were only beginning to understand their position. On August 8 at Burton, the Foresters, riding a crest of angry speeches filled with phrases such as 'broken faith' and 'election promises,' began to debate whether it would not be better for the friendly societies to withdraw from the Bill altogether. J. Lister Stead, whose personal disappointment may be imagined, led the fight against the amendment, reminding the delegates that there were bodies outside the friendly society movement waiting only for the chance to take over the Bill with all of its imperfections. In answer to shouts of 'Let them have it,' he pointed out that to give away the administration of health insurance meant to give away also most Forester members. Eventually the conference demanded that either the medical benefit be restored to the societies or, if it remained with the local health committees, that the approved societies be given a majority of the membership on those bodies.[157] Two days later Alfred Watson supported Stead's obviously official position in a letter to *The Times*.

> If the Hearts of Oak or the Foresters or the Manchester Unity stand outside the Bill, their members, however much they may dislike it, will have to go to other societies to obtain State insurance benefits, and vast numbers will consequently be gone away from their original society. This would mean the speedy decline of any society which, however powerful it may be today, stood outside the Bill. In other words, decay is the unhappy prospect which faces any great friendly society if in the exercise

a special bonus of 20 per cent of the regular commission for the out-of-doors staff. The letter remarked upon 'special difficulties of work this year . . .' and that 'staff have been largely employed in affording advice and information to policyholders.' *Ibid.*

[156] *The Times*, August 4, August 5, 1911.
[157] *Ibid.*, August 9, 1911.

of self-government, . . . it should decide to remain independent instead of becoming an agency of the State.[158]

The friendly societies were trapped.

Precisely as these letters were being written, on August 9, the final debate occurred in the House of Lords on whether to accept the Commons' disagreement with Lord Lansdowne's amendment to the Parliament Bill. On the tenth with Lord Lansdowne not voting for his own amendment and thirty-seven Unionists dividing against their own party, the Parliament Bill was accepted by the narrow majority of seventeen. On August 22, Parliament recessed until October 24.

During the interval the insurance Bill inherited the unexpended anger built up among the Unionists by their failure over the Parliament Act. The Opposition attitude towards health insurance had been conditioned at first by Austen Chamberlain's genuine liking for the scheme[159] and A. J. Balfour's inability to take the trouble to master the details of the measure, coupled with the rest of the party's unwillingness to do anything that might oppose the friendly societies.[160] However, as the privileged position of the friendly societies began to decline, the Unionists found it possible to attack the Bill on behalf of the societies, as they had old age pensions, without seeming to oppose a measure of popular welfare. This change in position was not immediately apparent within the House of Commons, for the party remained officially friendly and did not force divisions on either the first or second reading. But a new tone was manifest in the press and at by-elections.[161]

The changing Opposition attitude began to evidence itself late in August with a series of letters to the press from a group of young Unionists, nearly all of whom had come into Parliament in 1910, had been active in the fight against the Parliament Act, and were known as convinced tariff-reformers. Among those who

[158] *The Times*, August 11, 1911. Just a month later Watson was hired by the Government. Bunbury, ed., *Ambulance Wagon*, pp. 202–3.

[159] Austen Chamberlain, *Politics From the Inside*, London, 1936, pp. 336–7.

[160] See: Memorandum, A. J. Balfour, typescript with MS corrections, n.d. (before committee stage), Austen Chamberlain Papers, Box 9, Bundle 18. Alfred Cox, who visited Balfour to attempt to rally support for the British Medical Association position, came to the conclusion that he 'wasn't particularly interested' in the problem of national health insurance. Cox, *Doctors*, p. 91.

[161] *Westminster Gazette*, July 17, 1911. At the Luton by-election on July 20, electors were urged to vote Unionist 'and save the Friendly Societies.' Herbert Du Parq, *The Life of David Lloyd George* (London, 1912), III, 579.

would be better known were Leopold Amery, Henry Page Croft, and Laming Worthington Evans, who had led what organized opposition the party had offered to the National Insurance Bill. The letters remarked upon Lloyd George's smug speech of August 4 on a motion to report progress, in which he thanked the House of Commons for its cooperation on national health insurance. The note of extreme optimism and self-congratulation was unwarranted, the letters argued. The amendments permitting the entry of industrial insurance into the health scheme had scarcely been discussed and certainly not voted on outside of committee. To suggest that the Opposition was satisfied was a mistake. It had only begun to fight.[162]

By the end of September the discontent over Unionist weakness on the insurance Bill had spread to the highest ranks of the party.[163] This discontent was by no means a result solely of Balfour's lack of leadership over national insurance, but the full parliamentary effect of a changing Unionist attitude would not be felt until the former Prime Minister's resignation on November 14. The rumblings of August and September were followed, in the final portion of the committee stage, by opposition both in and out of Westminster.

With the parliamentary opposition stiffening, the medical profession by no means yet satisfied, and the friendly societies approaching open revolt, the sponsors of the insurance Bill were forced to ask for support from the only friendly force available, the industrial insurance companies. In unmistakable terms, Kingsley Wood warned his party of the dangers of too open an alliance with the friendly societies. In a letter to *The Times* on August 24, writing, he said, as a Unionist, he reminded the opposition that the industrial insurance companies had over thirty million policies outstanding, insuring the sum of £285,000,000. '. . . it is possible to estimate the folly of provoking their antagonism,' he concluded, 'by resisting the claims of those bodies for what is only a demand for equal recognition and treatment.'[164] A few days later he

---

[162] *The Times*, August 24, 1911; *National Review*, LVII (September, 1911), 157–60.

[163] See the note from Walter Long to Balfour complaining of the party's difficulties as a result of the 'absurd and wholly unjustifiable welcome' given the insurance Bill. W. Long to A. J. Balfour, September 29, 1911, quoted in Sir Charles Petrie, *Walter Long and His Times*, London, 1936, pp. 165–7.

[164] *The Times*, August 28, 1911.

announced that he and F. Handel Booth, M.P. for Pontefract, intended to begin an extensive speaking tour around the country to explain the national insurance Bill and to protest friendly society claims for exclusive administration of the measure.[165]

For the friendly societies the period of the parliamentary recess was critical. Health insurance, which they had helped plan, was slipping from their control. Yet they could not withdraw from the programme. They could only try to change it, or to defeat it.[166] Early in September the directors of the Manchester Unity began a public attack on national health insurance with a pamphlet sent to every one of the society's nearly 800,000 members, *The National Insurance Bill as It Affects You as a Member of the Manchester Unity of Odd Fellows.* The Chancellor of the Exchequer, said the pamphlet, has gone 'too far to recede,' and the directors had every reason to believe that in the collecting societies' drive for the extension of the Act 'practically all Members of Parliament have had such pressure brought upon them that extension is inevitable.' The result is that the industrial insurance companies 'will not only come into the scheme, but come in on their own terms.' The pamphlet protested the concessions made to the companies in Clause 18 and Clause 21—those diluting the non-profit require-

---

[165] *The Times*, August 30, 1911. Booth was designated by the *Insurance Mail* as 'The Insuranceman's M.P.' His chief function appears to have been to put down questions in the House of Commons that the Combine wished to have asked. He was frequently a member of delegations to the Chancellor. See the tribute to the insurance industry's 'fearless friend in Parliament,' *Insurance Mail*, June 10, June 17, 1911.

Frederick Handel Booth, 1867–1947, born near Manchester; received high-school education; became an ironmaster; contested King's Lynn, 1900, and Wentworth, 1918; M.P., Liberal, for Pontefract, 1910–18. Director, British Legal Insurance Company which had once employed Lloyd George as solicitor.

The House of Commons that assembled on January 31, 1911, included 87 members who were directors of insurance companies. Among these were 47 Unionists, 38 Liberals, and 2 Irish Nationalists. But only four were directors of industrial companies. These, in addition to Booth, were Jonathan Samuel, Liberal, like Booth a director of the British Legal and United Provident; Sir J. Henry Dalziel, Liberal, Deputy Chairman of the Liverpool Victoria; and W. E. Horne, Liberal Unionist (i.e. Unionist), a director of the Prudential. *Post Magazine Almanack*, London, 1912, pp. 16–17.

[166] The elder statesman of the friendly society movement, J. Frome Wilkinson, wrote a long and thoughtful article for the *Contemporary Review* in September, 1911, already cited, accusing the societies of selfishness, and saying that if they had not attempted to monopolize the programme, their present position might have been better. Wilkinson, 'National Insurance,' *Contemporary Review*, September, 1911.

ment for approved societies and abolishing local committees—and urged all friendly society members to organize so that 'an unceasing shower of protests should fall upon the head of every Member of Parliament.'[167]

The Manchester Unity pamphlet began the friendly societies' battle against their dual adversaries, the medical profession and the insurance industry. This struggle reached a climax in the first three weeks of October before the reassembly of the House of Commons. Everyone understood that in the short period remaining in the session there would be no time for negotiation. Any ground regained had to be conquered in October.

The opening event of this month came on October 9 with the first of two meetings, a week apart, between the friendly societies and the medical profession. Nothing illustrates better the endless complexity and almost unbelievable complication inherent in a broad measure of social welfare than the attempts to provide medical treatment under national health insurance. The old system, abhorred by the doctors, of contract practice under the friendly societies had been theoretically ended on August 1 with the agreement to take the medical benefit from the approved societies and give it to the local health committees. From the list published by the committees each insured person would choose his doctor. In this way one of the principal medical aims, that of free choice of doctor, presumably had been accomplished. But this concession was seriously diluted by the so-called 'Harmsworth amendment,' which stipulated that any insured who were 'entitled to receive medical attendance and treatment under any system or through any institution existing at the time of the passage of this Act,' should be permitted to continue to do so. This referred specifically to the approximately 100 'medical institutes,' usually formed by association of friendly society members in a given area, who had banded together to hire a full-time physician. Altogether about 300,000 people received medical benefits in this way. One of the largest and best-conducted medical institutes was in Luton, Bedfordshire, Mr Harmsworth's constituency.[168]

---

[167] For opposing opinions of the pamphlet, see *The Times*, September 13, 1911, and the *Insurance Mail*, September 23, 1911. It was apparently in a letter by Lloyd George's secretary, R. G. Hawtrey, to a David Williams of Bridgend, commenting upon this pamphlet, that the famous phrase, 'ninepence for fourpence' was first used. *Westminster Gazette*, September 6, 1911.

[168] W. G. Bunn of the Hearts of Oak, which gave no medical benefit, had been

The conferences of October 9 and October 16 between the friendly societies and the medical profession dealt with the profession's dislike of the Harmsworth amendment and with the friendly societies' concern for the substantial number of their present members over sixty-five years of age, or above the insurance income limit, who would not be eligible for insurance under the State scheme. A friendly society, by turning itself into an approved society, did not lose responsibility for its old members, yet by the terms of the Bill many would be excluded from State insurance.[169] The meetings of October 9 and October 16 were long and, as might have been expected, acrimonious. Representing the doctors were Ewen Maclean, Chairman of the Representative Body of the B.M.A. and brother of Donald Maclean, a prominent Liberal M.P. and later leader of the party; J. A. Macdonald, Chairman of the Council of the B.M.A.; and J. Smith Whitaker, the Medical Secretary of the association. Present for the friendly societies were R. W. Moffrey, the new president of the National Conference, John McNicol, its secretary, William Marlow, and J. Lister Stead, among a number of others. Also present was H. Kingsley Wood. Besides Lloyd George, Braithwaite and Bradbury were in attendance.

Except as a demonstration of the depth of the ill feeling between the friendly societies and the medical profession, the conferences were inconclusive. Much of the discussion turned on the necessity and importance of the panel system, with Lloyd George asserting he had had nothing to do with the amendment of August 1, and that it had been a free vote. The societies reminded the profession that a doctor who dared to refuse a certificate for sickness benefit would probably lose a patient. The doctors replied that the societies were interested only in the protection of their funds and required a doctor to give 'satisfaction, not to his patient, but to the majority of the . . . lodge meeting.'[170] Several times during the two days the

an early promoter of the institutes. Cecil Harmsworth was no relation to Alfred Harmsworth, the proprietor of *The Times* and the *Daily Mail*. He had come into Parliament only in July, and protection of friendly societies had been an important factor in the election contest. For an extended discussion, almost the only one available, of the important concession of the Harmsworth amendment, see: Comyns Carr, *National Insurance*, pp. 61–3, 192–4.

[169] On the background of these meetings see: Bunbury, ed., *Ambulance Wagon*, pp. 205, 207–9.

[170] 'Conference on National Insurance Bill, *Private and Confidential*,' October 9, October 16, 1911 ('Transcript of shorthand notes of R. D. Shedlock'), p. 10, Bradbury Papers, Public Record Office, T.170/6.

stenographic report noted interruptions which had to be quieted by the Chancellor. The meetings decided nothing except to add a few words to the end of what became eventually Section 15 (4) of the Act insuring that 'no person shall be deprived of the right . . . of selecting the duly qualified medical practitioner by whom he wishes to be attended,' instead of accepting treatment through a medical institute.[171]

The doctors came from these meetings dissatisfied; the Harmsworth amendment remained in the Bill. They could not get an agreement on a solid income limit above which a contributor could not claim medical benefit. Their growing resentment after the single victory of August 1 presaged trouble for the future.

Between the first and second meetings of the doctors and the societies, on October 12 and 13, the National Conference of Friendly Societies held its annual conference in Free Gardeners' Hall, Edinburgh. In his presidential address on October 12, R. W. Moffrey urged moderation upon the friendly society movement. He pointed out that between the medical profession and the industrial insurance companies, the companies were the more dangerous enemy. The transfer of the administration of the medical benefit to the health committees might after all be a good thing. Probably on this the societies should compromise. But with the demands of collecting insurance the case was otherwise. The societies had no right to claim a monopoly, said Moffrey, but 'they should object to the Bill being so amended as to render the self-government of an "approved society" a mythical privilege to the members by virtually placing it in the hands of a committee of management which could be made permanent and identical with the directorate of an industrial assurance company.'[172] Following this, Moffrey announced the first of 'eleven minimum demands,' which the National Conference passed the next day 48 to 38 with the stipulation that if demands were not conceded the friendly society movement would refuse to administer national health insurance. The first demand specified: 'That approved societies shall be constituted on the basis of self-management by the members.'[173]

[171] 'Conference on National Insurance Bill, *Private and Confidential*,' October 9, October 16, 1911, p. 44.

[172] *The Times*, October 13, 1911.

[173] The other ten demands were of unequal importance for the purposes of this study, although each was in itself a serious matter for the societies. Several will be dealt with below. Basically the first four constituted demands to retain

The National Conference received Lloyd George's answer even before their meeting had ended. On October 14, in a public speech at Whitefield's Tabernacle in Tottenham Court Road, he told the world of the financial weaknesses of the friendly societies. In 1905, he said, two-thirds of the societies in the United Kingdom had deficiencies, that is, they were giving benefits they could not pay for. State supervision, he said, would be a good thing. Referring to Moffrey's speech two days before, he noted that the National Conference president had admitted the societies were making no progress in number of members. In Moffrey's own society, the Manchester Unity, the Chancellor pointed out, national insurance would release reserves of £3,500,000. He was growing tired of friendly societies' complaints, he continued,

> . . . you inquire of the Foresters, the Hearts of Oak, the Shep-
> herds, the Druids, the Rechabites, the Sons of Temperance
> (laughter), I have got them all here; I can roll them off by the
> yard. (laughter) I have been thinking friendly societies, talking
> friendly societies, and dreaming friendly societies except when
> after a very bad supper the doctor turns up (laughter).[174]

If there were any doubt after the derisive speech at Whitefield's Tabernacle about what the Chancellor would do in the face of the friendly society ultimatum, the *Nation* dispelled these in a leading article published on the same day. The Government, said Massingham's journal, had only two alternatives in the face of the 'most exacting' minimum terms from the friendly societies. 'The Chancellor could either fall back on the collecting societies as his main agents . . .' or he could honourably withdraw his Bill, having already committed the Government to it. But Lloyd George, the article concluded, was not the type to withdraw the Bill.[175]

the medical benefit, to give societies a majority of representatives on local health committees, to prevent health committees from being transferred to county or borough authorities, and to give local committees of doctors advisory power only. The remaining demands generally aimed at insuring that the societies had financial autonomy and retained the surplus funds set free by the credit of reserve values. A convenient full statement of the demands is available in Appendix D, in Bunbury, ed., *Ambulance Wagon*, pp. 318–22.

[174] *The Times*, October 16, 1911. The Hearts of Oak had reported the first deficit in its history six months earlier. *Insurance Mail*, April 22, 1911.

Two weeks before, the directors of the Grand United Order of Odd Fellows had voted 'in consequence of existing circumstances,' not to publish their valuer's report. *Assurance Agents' Chronicle*, XXIII (September 30, 1911), 467.

[175] 'Insurance and Disablement,' *The Nation*, October 14, 1911.

By the beginning of the third week of October, the friendly societies had clearly received notice that the Government was determined to permit the entrance of the industrial insurance companies into the national health scheme. Moreover, if forced to do so, the Chancellor, at least, was prepared to try to work the scheme without the cooperation of the friendly societies. The leaders of the Combine themselves were by now aware that their own position in the scheme was safe. 'I think the sick societies are now convinced that the public will not agree to special privileges for any one body,' said Kingsley Wood to the editor of the *Insurance Mail* about the middle of October.

At any rate, the public is showing that spirit, and the Members of Parliament are pledged to such an extent that the societies have awakened to the fact that their claims are not likely to be granted. In short, the friendly societies have practically all given way and have agreed that the Bill must be made universal as regards administration.[176]

There remained one obstacle to industrial insurance's complete satisfaction with the health insurance Bill. It was contained in Clause 18 (2) (iii) and (iv) specifying that all committees, representatives, and officers of approved societies should be chosen through election by their members. The friendly societies had made 'self-management by the members' the first of their eleven minimum demands at Edinburgh. Now the Combine intended to secure the deletion of this requirement from the national insurance Bill. For industrial insurance this was an awkward project because in this the collecting friendly societies were not involved, only the limited companies. For the companies the danger in Clause

[176] *Insurance Mail*, October 21, 1911. This interview was occasioned by the completion of the series of promotional meetings that Kingsley Wood, F. Handel Booth and Percy Rockliff had held throughout the United Kingdom during the Parliamentary recess on behalf of the insurance Bill. Rockliff was secretary of the National Association of Registered Friendly Societies, which despite its name was mainly an association of non-registered marginal friendly societies. Rockliff's task had been to obtain the right of approval for these organizations. By holding tight to the hand of Kingsley Wood he achieved this. He is responsible for one of the most fanciful of the many imaginative accounts of the reasons for the entrance of the industrial insurance industry into national health insurance. *Cmd. 6405*, 'Social Insurance and Allied Services, Appendix G, Memoranda from Organizations,' 1942, p. 99. Of him, Braithwaite remarked, 'I . . . warned the 1912 officials never to interview him except with a witness.' Bunbury, ed., *Ambulance Wagon*, p. 97.

18 (2) (iii) (iv) lay not in the possibility that the contributors themselves might gain some real control in the management of the
approved society, but that the society would fall under the domination of its own collectors. This had already occurred in several of
the collecting societies. Braithwaite hoped that this weakness in the
Combine might be exploited to force some comprise. 'They were
very frightened of their own collectors,' he wrote early in October,
'who had a Trade Union, and the weakest point in their armour
was the threat of a delegate system.'[177] To be sure, the rules of
some collecting societies, like the Liverpool Victoria, made it
possible for the company directors to pack any meeting,[178] but the
Royal Liver was almost completely under the management of its
agents,[179] as were many other of the smaller collecting friendly
societies. For companies like the Prudential, the danger from its
own sales force was hardly less than the danger of friendly society
competition or of a Government-sponsored death benefit. The
specific requirement for election had to be deleted.

This apparently was the consideration behind the hastily
organized meeting that convened at the Treasury on Thursday
morning, October 19. Nearly a month before, the friendly
societies had scheduled a mass meeting for Albert Hall to be held
that evening. At Edinburgh they had made clear that at this time
they would make their decision on whether or not to enter the
national health insurance programme. Lloyd George had agreed to
meet them to discuss their minimum demands on the afternoon
before the meeting. As the first and most critical friendly society
demand was the requirement for approved society self-government, which the industrial insurance companies were determined
to eliminate, this had to be disposed of first. October 19, therefore,
was the critical day in the planning of national health insurance.
Although he had decided to dispense with the friendly societies if
forced to do so, there were many, W. J. Braithwaite the most
influential, who felt he should maintain a place for them in the
scheme. A unanimous friendly society withdrawal might well
mean the delay of the Act and would certainly mean, as the
societies had been warned many times, the eventual decay of the
movement. Most of the advantages of State insurance would be

---

[177] Bunbury, ed., *Ambulance Wagon*, p. 206.
[178] Braithwaite had pointed this out to Masterman on October 14. *Ibid.*, p. 209.
[179] *Cmd. 614*, p. 2.

lost if its enactment destroyed the provident societies. With their disappearance might go also the Chancellor's reputation as a friend of the working class. A private conference between opposing factions with himself as mediator was his customary solution for all such problems.

On October 19, the men of industrial insurance and the men of the friendly societies faced each other for the first and only time. Representing the Combine were its old leaders, Smith of the Royal London, Neill of the Pearl, Jefferson of the Britannic, and Henri of the Liverpool Victoria, who were supported by the far less familiar figures controlling the giant machine of the Prudential, Alfred C. Thompson, the general manager, Frederick Schooling, the chief actuary, and Arthur Rhys Barrand, the assistant manager. But present also were David Jones of the National Association of Prudential Agents and Henry Brown of the National Union of Life Assurance Agents, in whose hands Clause 18 could become a dangerous weapon. On the other side of the table were Moffrey and A. H. Warren of the Manchester Unity, C. W. Burns of the Hearts of Oak, Lister Stead, Marlow, and John McNicol, secretary of the National Conference. (W. G. Bunn had died a month before.) Lloyd George had Braithwaite with him. Also present, among others, was Kingsley Wood.

Generally the spokesmen for the companies were Neill, Henri, and Schooling. Neill opened the discussion, explaining why the companies wished to enter the scheme. Now that the State had taken upon itself the task of looking after the children and wives of men who were incapacitated, he said, its interest would not end when the breadwinner died.

> There must be some provision made for the widow and orphans, sooner or later, and we hope sooner rather than later. That will mean, with the licking on of this postage stamp or that insurance stamp, the absolute annihilation and termination of the employment of the collector.

When this occurred, he concluded, the companies could better protect their interest inside the scheme than out of it.[180] Therefore,

[180] 'Conference on the National Insurance Bill (Clause 18),' October 19, 1911, p. 4 ('Transcript from shorthand notes of R. D. Shedlock'), typescript, 31 pages, p. 4, Braithwaite Papers, Part I, 'Memoirs, 1910–1912,' Part 3, following page 79. Neill spoke with some warmth, announcing that he had not received an invitation to the conference until ten that morning.

the companies wanted to come in and they wanted to come in under rules appropriate to their form of business. They wanted 'liberty in management.'

The leaders of the agents' unions, Jones and Brown, argued for a delegate system, which, of course, the collectors would control. In this demand they were supported by the friendly society representatives for whom the imposition of a delegate requirement represented the last chance to exclude industrial insurance. Faced by this unusual alliance, the arguments of the industrial insurance representatives grew heated. Arthur Henri taunted the friendly societies, saying that they had about 'got to the end of their tether. (Cries of "no").'[181] Lloyd George's sympathies clearly were with the companies. It would not do, he argued, to force a system of contributor representation upon the industrial insurance companies simply because it suited the friendly societies. Friendly societies did not have collectors; insurance companies did.

> There is a danger that collectors undoubtedly would, in the vast majority of cases, be elected as delegates, and once being there it would be too much to ask of human nature that they should not be there occasionally to advance their own interests as well as the interests of the rank and file members.[182]

The eventual compromise came with a proposal by Mr E. Goodship of the Royal Liver to amend paragraphs iii and iv of Clause 18 to read simply that the affairs of a society should be under the 'absolute control of its members,' that boards of management in societies having systems of elected delegates would be chosen by the delegates, and 'in societies where the delegates are not so appointed, by the members under the rules of such societies.'[183] Because another part of Clause 18 already provided that the rules

[181] 'Conference on the National Insurance Bill (Clause 18),' October 19, 1911, p. 8. The Liverpool Victoria itself, although a collecting friendly society, did not have a delegate system. Rather, it had what would become the pattern for the industrial insurance approved societies, an open meeting. This was described during the conference as 'shadowboxing.' A hall was engaged; notices were sent out to all members inviting them to come, but no one ever did. *Ibid.*, pp. 9–10, 16–17.

[182] *Ibid.*, p. 19. The Chancellor apparently had forgotten that since 1896 insurance collectors had been forbidden by statute to serve as delegates in collecting friendly societies, although they did in fact make their will effective by choosing those who were elected delegates through their influence on the contributors.

[183] *Ibid.*, p. 17.

of all societies were under the control of the insurance commission, the effect of the amendment was to leave the determination
of the form of new societies to the insurance commissioners without
any statutory requirement.

Debate on the Goodship amendment became angry and Lloyd
George, who had accepted the proposal immediately, tried to call
the conference to order with the reminder, which would have
astounded admirers of the ideal of parliamentary government, that
'at the present moment we are making law.'[184] Barrand of the
Prudential, still fearful of his own agents, asked whether the
amendment might not give the commissioners the right to insist
upon a delegate system. The Chancellor answered that it did not,
for the second part of the amendment could not mean the same as
the first. In the face of further objections from the Prudential
men, who hoped to get a delegate system prohibited by statute,
Lloyd George, in a sudden obeisance to the authority of Parliament, reminded them that they would have to have a compromise
of some sort to take into the House of Commons when it reconvened the next Tuesday. 'And you must remember,' he remarked
piously, 'it is a jury that neither you nor I can control. And it is
better to go there with an agreement.'

'I am certain I cannot,' Schooling retorted, 'but I thought you
could.'[185]

In the end Kingsley Wood, Barrand, Marlow, Moffrey, and
Braithwaite were appointed a committee to draft the wording for
Parliament to approve. The friendly societies were defeated. The
privileged party in national health insurance was now the industrial
insurance industry. The extent of the societies' frustration was
apparent in a statement by John McNicol, who had been associated with the planning since the autumn of 1908. McNicol said:

Pardon me for saying this: so far as the friendly societies are
concerned, I think, Mr Chancellor you will bear me out in this
respect: that in our preliminary conversations with you prior to
the introduction of the Bill, we excluded a death benefit
altogether in order that there might be no complaint from the
societies that are represented here today about your entering
their field, and I trust you will pardon me for expressing regret

[184] 'Conference on the National Insurance Bill (Clauge 18),' October 19,
1911, p. 20.
[185] Ibid., p. 24.

that having been so careful in our attitude and action in this matter they should desire to come into competition with us.[186]

W. J. Braithwaite recorded his anger in his diary. Self-government, he thought, had become a political and not a legal matter.

> . . . from this moment, at the bottom of my heart, I lost a great deal of my interest in the Bill. I regarded the whole transaction as a betrayal of the spirit of the Bill, for whilst these Collecting Societies were entitled to come in, they should have done so under control and not as controllers. The fight lost that day (it had really been lost some months before in the House of Commons) will have to be renewed at some time in the future, when Industrial Insurance is either bought out or confiscated.[187]

8

After the friendly societies' surrender to industrial insurance, there was little chance that they would revolt on any other matter. The Chancellor therefore could safely dictate his own terms on the other nine of the ten 'minimum demands.' Only three, numbers two, three, and four, were of great importance. All of these dealt with the medical benefit. Number two demanded the return of the administration of the medical benefit to the societies and that the medical benefit be given to existing members of friendly societies excluded from the State scheme. Number three demanded that the majority of the local health committees be representatives of the approved societies, and number four demanded the payment of sickness benefit from the first, rather than from the fourth, day of illness, which was normal friendly society practice. The societies argued that their present members expected this benefit, that without it health insurance would give smaller rather than larger coverage, and that therefore they would have to pay the first three days sickness benefit from their own funds.

After the conference on Clause 18 concluded, the industrial insurance representatives withdrew and the rest of the afternoon was spent in debate on these demands. The Chancellor rejected all

---

[186] 'Conference on the National Insurance Bill (Clause 18),' October 19, 1911, p. 30.
[187] Bunbury, ed., *Ambulance Wagon*, p. 212.

suggestions to return the medical benefit to the approved societies, although he did agree that present members who did not qualify for the State scheme would continue to receive medical attendance. In addition, much to the disgust of the medical profession, he agreed that approved societies and the post office deposit contributors together should appoint three-fifths of the members of the greatly enlarged local health committees (which were eventually renamed Insurance Committees). He categorically refused, indeed declined to discuss further, the payment of sickness benefit from the first day of illness.

After the resolution of the industrial insurance crisis, payment for the first three days of illness became a major demand of the friendly societies. The issue did eventually result in an important change in the measure and therefore ought to be examined briefly. Because the census figures for 1911 were not available when they began their work, Hardy and Wyatt, in making their calculations for national health insurance, had used Tatham's English Life Table No. VI, based on mortality in England and Wales between 1891 and 1901. For rates of sickness they had used the Manchester Unity experience between 1893 and 1897, published by Alfred Watson in 1903. The rationale of this was that the Manchester Unity constituted the largest society in the country with a national membership that could be reasonably compared to the population coming under national health insurance. But because the Manchester Unity selected its membership fairly rigorously and national health insurance would not, the actuaries assumed a sickness incidence 10 per cent above the Manchester Unity experience. On the other hand the Manchester Unity compensated for accident, while national health insurance would not, and so they hoped to recover their 10 per cent. Thus far, the claims experience of national health insurance should have been the same as the Manchester Unity.

But the Manchester Unity tables referred only to men, while 30 per cent of the workers covered under national health insurance would be women. The difficulty was that few friendly societies admitted women, for whom there were no applicable experience tables. The actuaries were in a position comparable to the dilemma of the planners of the universal old age pension. Women's sickness insurance would be expensive, but no one knew how expensive. Hardy and Wyatt could only assume that sickness claims from women would be the same as men, while fearing that they would not be. This made a margin of safety absolutely essential. The margin of safety achieved by not compensating the first three days of illness would save money both on men's and women's illnesses, would help prevent malingering, and would exclude the frequent short-term illnesses to which the actuaries assumed women were liable.[188]

But while refusing to consider using his three-day margin to compensate an unknown but very large amount of short-term female sickness, the Chancellor made a major concession in agreeing to maintain the full sickness benefit for a second thirteen weeks and to count all sickness periods within a twelve-month period as continuous. The difference appears to have been that during the first three days the female liability to sickness would use proportionately a far larger part of the total amount expended on sickness than the percentage of women in the insured population. At the end of the sickness period, on the other hand, most of the extra money would go to men. Whether or not this decision was of greater social utility, it was certainly more expedient actuarily.[189] In addition, this alternative was calculated to be less expensive by about £100,000 per year. It may be significant that during the planning of the Bill early in 1911, Lloyd George had investigated the possibility of maintaining the full sickness benefit for twenty-six weeks.

The final event of this crowded Thursday was the great Albert Hall meeting. The building was packed and colourful with sashes, scarves, and banners of the societies. A. H. Warren of the Man-

---

[188] Much of this data comes from a paper read before the Birmingham Insurance Institute in March, 1913. J. Murray Laing, *A Few Notes on the National Insurance Act*, Birmingham, 1913. Laing was actuary of the Britannic Assurance Company.

[189] The actuaries calculated that to insure for the first three days would cost £384,000 per year for men and £120,000 for women, even though women accounted for only about 30 per cent of the insured and received 7s. 6d. sickness benefit instead of 10s. But to continue the 10s. and 7s. 6d. sickness benefit for an extra thirteen weeks, that is, for twenty-six weeks altogether, would cost £350,000 per year for men, and only £60,000 for women. Hence at the beginning of the period the women's benefit would amount to 23·8 per cent of the total cost, but at the end of the period it would be 14·6 per cent of the total cost. For a discussion see: Letter from G. F. Hardy and F. B. Wyatt, October 30, 1911, in *Cd. 5930*, 'Copy of Memorandum Explanatory of the Principal Amendments which it is Proposed to Incorporate in the National Insurance Bill,' 1911, pp. 5–6.

N

chester Unity addressed the meeting and did his best to convey an impression of personal satisfaction with the friendly society achievements. Some other leaders, notably William Marlow, displayed the resentment that all society leaders must have felt, and in the end the meeting refused to agree to the denial of the sickness benefit during the first three days and instructed the leaders to re-open the question. In view of the fact that the National Conference had voted only a week before to reject all participation in national health insurance unless the 'minimum demands' were accepted, this decision by the Albert Hall meeting should have carried a good deal of weight. But the next day Lloyd George declined even to see any friendly society leaders, nor would his private secretary, who turned the men away, promise to raise the question with him. The friendly societies were reduced to sending him a letter pointing out that the alternatives offered on October 19 had not been accepted by the Albert Hall meeting. This letter was never answered.[190]

On the day he refused to see the friendly societies, Lloyd George spoke to a dinner at Holborn Hall sponsored by the association of non-registered friendly societies in the company of its secretary, Percy Rockliff, and F. Handel Booth. Both *The Times* and the *Westminster Gazette* noted his good spirits. The Bill now, he said, was 'absolutely safe' and would become law before Christmas. It would be 'a great Christmas gift' for the people.[191] On the same evening Liberal M.P.s had received a two-line whip (the two lines ruled under an item of business on the House of Commons agenda meant that the individual Member's attendance was 'particularly requested' and that the item was one of exceptional importance). The business at hand was a Government motion asking for the full time of the House of Commons with the adoption of closure for the passage of national health insurance. The note concluded by saying that since adjournment the Chancellor had been in almost continuous consultation with accredited representatives of interests concerned with the Bill 'with the result that most of the difficulties have been and are being satisfactorily adjusted.'[192]

[190] Executive Committee's Report, *Resolutions of the National Conference of Friendly Societies*, held in the Geographical Institute, St Mary's Place, Newcastle-on-Tyne, September 26–7, 1912, pp. 15–17. On the Albert Hall meeting see *The Times*, October 20, 1911.
[191] *The Times, Westminster Gazette*, October 21, 1911.
[192] *Ibid.*, October 20, 1911.

The last six weeks of the National Insurance Bill's progress through Parliament were marked by almost complete sterility of debate in the House of Commons. A nadir was reached on November 30 with the disposal of 470 amendments without discussion under closure. Outside of Parliament, the industrial insurance industry congratulated itself upon a task fully and satisfactorily accomplished while the friendly society movement rumbled with unhappiness and division. On November 9 the directors of the Manchester Unity, unable to meet with the Chancellor, passed a resolution demanding that no provision other than sick pay from the first day 'will be satisfactory.'[193] Early in December the Hearts of Oak and the Manchester Unity boards of directors forwarded resolutions to the House of Lords asking them to amend the Bill to provide sick pay from the first day.[194] This action was immediately followed by a letter from the National Conference of Friendly Societies to Lloyd George assuring him of the executive committee's support for national health insurance, despite reports 'boomed in the press' of what the Manchester Unity and Hearts of Oak were doing. Through it all the industrial insurance interests constantly urged the Chancellor to disregard friendly society demands and to depend fully on their support.[195]

One matter frequently mentioned by the friendly societies as a weakness of national insurance was the failure to provide a hospital benefit. Compared to some other questions this omission received little public attention during the passage of the Bill, although it grew to be of great importance later and would finally be regarded

[193] *The Times*, November 10, 1911. This action was followed by a flurry of letters in *The Times*, first from Lister Stead announcing that friendly society hostility to the Bill was diminishing, followed by a letter from J. Harford Hawkins of the Manchester Unity saying that he was astonished at Stead's statement, and that the Bill was 'disliked by the doctors, it is disliked by the friendly societies, it is disliked by employers, by the hospitals, and by the nation generally. . . .' *The Times*, November 20, November 22, 1911.

[194] *Ibid.*, December 8, 1911. The vote in the Manchester Unity was six to five. The next spring a special conference of the organization severely criticized the directors for this action. *Oddfellow's Magazine*, XLIII (March, 1912), 116.

[195] The Chancellor has made a good bargain with our industrial assurance institutions, and thus has the support of 100,000 practised insurance men. He need fear no threats. We believe that he will stick to his bargain with us, and we believe that the sick clubs know he will. It is this knowledge which has cleared the air.

Lead article, 'Gathering Up the Threads,' *Insurance Mail*, October 28, 1911.

as the chief weakness of the scheme.[196] The division of the British hospital system, if the word 'system' may be used, into two competing branches—the voluntary hospitals, small in number and great in prestige, and the poor law hospitals, many times larger but altogether without either social or medical status—complicated any provision for institutional treatment under national health insurance. Moreover, there was in the Bill the basic irrationality that the Chancellor had determined early to offer institutional treatment for a single disease—tuberculosis. The Bill specified that local health committees were to 'make arrangements' with local authorities or private persons, including those operating sanatoria for profit, for the care of tuberculosis among the insured. Immediately the question arose of what existing institutions might be available for this. The most extensive public provisions for treatment of tuberculosis were maintained by the poor law guardians. Certainly it would be ridiculous to duplicate facilities, some of which were expensive and modern, simply because the existing ones were tainted by parochial relief, yet any connexion with the poor law would be politically disastrous to the health scheme. There were very few immutable rules in the planning of national health insurance, but one was that at no point would the insurance administration touch the poor law. But because there would be £1,500,000 available for building sanatoria, the Local Government Board was anxious to get some recognition as a provider of sanatorial facilities. 'I do not suppose that the Committees [the local health committees] would wish to send their cases to the Boards of Guardians if they could accommodate them elsewhere,' wrote the permanent secretary of the Local Government Board, Sir Horace Munro, to the powerful head of the poor law division, Sir James Davy, on November 10, 'but it may possibly happen that, at any rate at first, there may be nowhere else to send them, and it may therefore be unwise definitely to exclude poor law authorities from institutions in which the sanatorium benefits may

---

[196] For instance: Frazer, *Public Health*, p. 310.

[197] There were 34,414 deaths from tuberculosis among people between the ages of fifteen and sixty-five in England and Wales in 1909. Of these, about 20 per cent, slightly less than 7,000, occurred in poor law infirmaries. For London alone, 2,495 of 6,337 deaths from tuberculosis occurred in poor law infirmaries in 1909. Arthur Newsholme, 'Estimate as to number of Beds required for Pulmonary Tuberculosis in England and Wales,' April 5, 1911. Bill File, National Insurance Bill, 1911, 'Part 1,' M.P.N.I.

be afforded.'[198] But throughout the guardians were rigorously excluded from the Bill and each clause mentioning local authorities included always the phrase 'other than poor law authorities.' Until 1929 poor law hospitals by definition remained accommodation for paupers. Ten days later Munro, still hoping to divert some of the largess of national health insurance towards the Local Government Board, asked Newsholme whether tuberculosis could be classed as a 'fever,' within the meaning of Section 80 of the Public Health (London) Act of 1891. Newsholme replied seriously that without doubt some cases did fall within this category but that unfortunately many people needing sanatorium treatment had no fever.[199]

The basic problem for insurance planners in the consideration of institutional medical treatment was not the scheme's relation to the poor law infirmaries, but to the voluntary hospitals. Should the scheme undertake some form of hospital treatment? How could it be handled? How could fifteen million members of the working class, the great majority of whom were now provided for the first time with regular financial support for medical treatment, be insinuated into a hospital system that offered practically nothing between poor law infirmaries, theoretically for paupers, and voluntary hospitals, reserved for charity? At bottom, it was the failure to find an answer to this question, rather than any serious lack of money, that kept the national health insurance planners from incorporating some forms of institutional treatment into their scheme. The matter had been thoroughly discussed at the Brighton Conference. Braithwaite, Bradbury, and Masterman were against any connexion with the hospitals. The aim of the plan, they felt, was to keep the wage earner and his family from the poor house, not to take him to the hospital. Bradbury added that 'hospitals, like the medical men, would be out for plunder.' Lloyd George, on the other hand, noted that many friendly societies made block grants to voluntary hospitals for the care of their members. This might be continued under State insurance. Many of the hospitals, he thought, would welcome, say, £5,000 a year.[200]

Far more critical than the question of how the Act could make

---

[198] H. C. Munro to James Davy, November 10, 1911, Bill File, National Insurance Bill, 1911, 'Part 3, Report to Third Reading (Commons),' M.P.N.I.

[199] Arthur Newsholme to H. C. Munro, November 20, 1911, MS, Bill File, National Insurance Bill, *Ibid*.

[200] Brighton Conference, February 19, 1911, Braithwaite Papers, Part I. This provision eventually was incorporated in the Act.

use of voluntary hospitals was the harm that might be done to the hospitals by the Act. There was the fear among hospital administrators, much exaggerated as it turned out, that the required contributions demanded for medical care would end any further donations among the working class to the funds of voluntary hospitals. Even more perplexing, how could a voluntary hospital, theoretically run for charity, admit without payment a national health insurance contributor with an assured income of 10s. per week? Obviously this person could not be considered indigent. Yet if the hospital, upon the recommendation of its almoner, were to demand part of his sickness benefit, what would become of his family, for whom the sickness benefit represented their only income? But then how could the voluntary hospital prevent a lazy national health insurance doctor from referring troublesome, or simply chronically ill, patients to their out-patient wards, even though their ailments were well within his capacity to treat? This already occurred too frequently among friendly society practitioners.

At his meeting with the British Medical Association on June 1, the Chancellor had been asked what national health insurance intended to do about the hospitals. Lloyd George answered that he was aware that friendly societies presently helped voluntary hospitals with collections, made contributions to them, and asked for special arrangements for their members. He did not think he should do more, he concluded, and adopting by instinct the line that would serve him best, remarked that to do more would require interference in hospital management.[201]

The spokesman for British voluntary hospitals during 1911 was Sir Henry Burdett, a retired member of the stock exchange, member of the boards of several London hospitals, and founder and editor of the professional journal, *The Hospital*. Burdett had long been interested in social reform, and had in fact presented one of the four plans on old age pensions that the terms of reference of the Rothschild Committee had permitted that body to examine.[202] Burdett was by all odds the most influential, non-medical interpreter of the hospital point of view. He differed from the

[201] Special Report of Representative Meeting, *B.M.J.* Supp., June 3, 1911, p. 358.

[202] Henry C. Burdett, 1847–1920, born, Broughton near Kettering; father a minister; had an early interest in medicine, hoped to be a physician; secretary, Share and Loan Department, London Stock Exchange, 1883–97; wrote widely on finance and municipal taxation, colonial affairs, nursing, public health, and

honorary medical staff of the hospitals he served as a board member over the question of whether the hospitals should accept payment from the national health service for work done for insurance patients. Generally, the consultants and specialist who controlled the beds in the voluntary hospitals, who constituted the members of the royal colleges, and who were the public voice of the British Medical Association, opposed the proposition that they be paid for services rendered to health insurance patients, even though there was the likelihood that insurance would greatly increase their load of work. The fact was that there was little precedent for a paying working-class patient in a voluntary hospital. The English middle class and upper class were treated either at home or in profit-making nursing homes—Burdett had been active in founding the first of these in Fitzroy Square—or occasionally in the new pay beds in the voluntary hospitals. Here they were treated by specialists and consultants accredited to the hospitals who received fees far beyond the competence of the insured working class to pay. Other than this there was practically no way to enter a voluntary hospital except as a charity patient. The status of an honorary appointment would decline if the holder took small, regular fees for his services and, more important, his control over the admission of patients to his beds would disappear.[203]

Burdett's contention, first made clear at the second annual conference of the British Hospital Association, held September 28 and 29 in Manchester, was that voluntary hospitals could and should come into national health insurance on the same basis as sanatoria. He hoped to see what was then Clause 15 of the Bill, which provided the sanatoria, altered to include the voluntary institutions. The conference declined to demand this, and eventually passed a resolution simply calling on the Government 'so to amend the Bill that the continued existence of the voluntary hospitals may be safeguarded financially. . .' without giving a plan.[204] Nevertheless the inclusion of the hospitals became

social reform; submitted a plan for contributory old age pensions to the Rothschild Committee. Superintendent, Queen's Hospital, Birmingham; Seaman's Hospital, Greenwich; K.B., 1897.

[203] For a discussion of the place of hospitals under national health insurance, see: Brian Abel-Smith, *The Hospitals in England and Wales*, 1800–1948, Cambridge, Mass., 1964, pp. 233–51.

[204] *Lancet*, October 7, 1911, pp. 1044–5. See also the report of Burdett's speech in *Westminster Gazette*, September 29, 1911.

Burdett's chief proposal for national health insurance. In it he received little support from medical and hospital groups. The doctors were far more concerned with the effect of national insurance on their own profession; and the honoraries in the hospitals, who were the leaders of the medical profession but who would not be working under the Act themselves, were concerned chiefly with inciting the opposition of the general practitioner and with keeping the status of 'honorary' clean. Hospital boards of trustees, while constituting an extremely influential group of laymen, were unable ever to evolve a plan that would permit the acceptance of government money without the inevitable concomitant of government control. So Burdett went ahead virtually alone with his demand to put the hospitals into the scheme in the place of the tuberculosis sanatoria. The hospitals, he thought, ought to share in the 1s. 3d. per year from the contributors and the 1d. per contributor provided by Parliament as set out in Clause 15 (2) (a) (b) of the Bill. Hospitals would then set aside beds for the insured and would charge the insurance fund the cost plus 10 per cent. For the inevitable expansion of accommodations that would come, Burdett proposed that the insurance commission establish a sinking fund from which it would lend money to the hospitals at a rate of not less than 3 per cent. In this way there would be no direct charge upon the Treasury and hospitals would, technically at least, receive no government money, other than the 1d. for research already provided to the sanatoria.[205]

By this time Lloyd George had surmounted the crisis of the friendly societies and with insurance industry support he had no fear of other quarters. The long reasoned argument from Sir Henry Burdett apparently was never answered, and on November 25, writing now to John Burns, Burdett threatened political reprisal. Saying that he had not 'received any intimation from Mr Lloyd George' on his intentions on the hospital benefits, he was now asking Burns, the Cabinet member most intimately associated with hospitals, to bring some facts before his colleagues.

[205] This plan is fully set out in a memorandum: 'The National Insurance Bill and Hospital Benefit,' November 9, 1911, Bill File, National Insurance Bill, 1911, 'Part 3,' M.P.N.I. Burdett accompanied this memo with a printed copy of Clauses 1 to 17 of the Bill, all that the House of Commons had worked through before its August recess, in which he had inked out the word 'sanatorial,' wherever it appeared, and inserted the word 'institutional.'

This is a most unusual step to take, but the crisis is acute, the time is short, and the alternative of arousing the country from end to end is not one which is desirable to enter upon, or one to which I will be any party, unless or until it is made inevitable in defence of the defenceless sick and breadwinners of the nation.

After repeating the familiar assertions that national health insurance would reduce the income of voluntary hospitals by one half and that 500,000 of the 15,000,000 insured would need hospital treatment each year, Burdett ended his long letter with the announcement that a special representative meeting of all United Kingdom voluntary hospitals was to be held at the Westminster Palace Hotel. 'By the time the meeting assembles it will be known whether the hospitals and the insured are safeguarded under the insurance Bill or not. . . . Speaking from forty-five years of active association with successive British Governments, from that of Lord Palmerston downward. . . . he could not believe that the Government would disregard the interest of the British worker.[206]

Burns appears to have sent the letter on immediately to Lloyd George, diluting any effect it may have had by adding a protest of his own against a recent decision of the Chancellor letting Welsh insurance commissioners distribute sanatorial money in place of the Local Government Board.[207] Lloyd George answered with a short, curt note on the sanatorial money, saying that he could not resist so overwhelming an expression of the wishes of the Welsh Members of Parliament, and on Burdett's letter that he would give it 'careful attention.'[208]

The great meeting at the Westminster Palace Hotel was disappointing and inconclusive. Burdett, as Lloyd George no doubt realized, could not bring forward his proposal to put the hospitals into the scheme in place of the sanatoria. And so, while the conference heard many speeches, and many warnings of danger, it offered no plan. Burdett's rather pathetic threat to 'raise the country' came to nothing.[209]

It should be pointed out, although Lloyd George never appears

[206] Sir Henry C. Burdett to John Burns, November 25, 1911, Bill File, National Insurance Bill, 1911, *Ibid.*

[207] At the last moment, Lloyd George had ended the system of a single insurance commission for the entire nation and had permitted the establishment of four separate insurance commissions for each of the three kingdoms and Wales.

[208] Bill File, National Insurance Bill, 1911, *Ibid.*

[209] *The Times*, December 2, 1911.

N*

to have mentioned it, that the Act did provide in Section 8 (1) (*b*) for treatment of the insured in 'sanatoria or other institutions or otherwise when suffering from tuberculosis, or other diseases as the Local Government Board with the approval of the Treasury may appoint. . . .' Clearly this could have become a hospital benefit. This was mentioned in a letter to the *Spectator* by H. W. Burleigh on December 9, 1911, and, more important, was commented upon by Carr, Garnett, and Taylor in their massive reference book for insurance administrators.[210]

9

One of the reasons for the negligible impact of Sir Henry Burdett's campaign against national health insurance was that by November the programme was under far more clamorous attack from several other directions. The most important of these, certainly the best known, was the ludicrous anti-stamp-licking campaign which grew during the Bill's last days in the House of Commons, at the end of November and early December. This agitation might have been altogether comic were it not for the fact that it stimulated the climate of extraparliamentary resistance in which the far more dangerous revolt of the doctors later occurred. Moreover, the campaign in London, chiefly a project of the Northcliffe Press, promoted other attacks around the country that led to an astonishing series of Liberal by-election defeats.

The Unionists first received notice that national insurance, unlike old age pensions, was not popular with the electorate in the Oldham by-election on November 13, when a Liberal majority of 3,501 in December 1910 became a Unionist majority of 1,632. The victor, E. R. B. Denniss, announced that he felt the most important factor in his success was the National Insurance Bill.[211] This was quickly followed on November 22 with the announcement of the result in South Somerset where a Unionist won a seat that had been consistently Liberal for a quarter of a century. There had been some doubt at Oldham whether the National Insurance Bill or a superior Unionist organization was more important in influencing votes. But in South Somerset, the *Westminster Gazette* admitted sadly, the defeat was clearly the result 'of Tory misrepresentation

[210] Carr, *National Insurance*, p. 87.
[211] *The Times*, November 13, 14, 15; *Westminster Gazette*, November 14, 1911.

with regard to the Insurance Bill. . . .'[212] On the day of the election, Lloyd George had rejected an amendment put down by the Opposition that would have made insurance optional with household servants. The Chancellor argued that to permit this would be virtually to exclude serving girls from insurance, for the mistress could easily influence them. Also, he said, the percentage of former female household servants among the elderly paupers was higher than that of any other category.

In anticipation of the rejection of this amendment, the *Daily Mail*, early in the month, had called for correspondence on the subject of insurance of serving girls. By the twenty-first, it reported that 'never in its history' had it received so much correspondence. A 'Litchfield Matron' wrote that the Chancellor 'forgets that if he gets this silly Insurance Bill through Parliament he has to meet a whole army of indignant women who will simply laugh in his face and refuse to obey him.' A Kensington mistress 'of twenty years' experience' said, 'we are ready to fight for our homes. My orderly life shall not be interfered with and upset by a tyrannical law.' A St John's Wood matron wrote that insurance contributions were really being used to pay for old age pensions.[213] 'Resistance' wrote,

> I have seen no reference in the course of this correspondence to the pathetic case of the nursery governess. Why should she— who has perhaps seen better days, who is perhaps a *lady* (think of it!)—be dragged through the weekly ordeal of plastering nasty stamps on a grimy card? My blood boils when I think of the blush of shame mantling her humble brow, the more so as this duty will doubtless have to be performed in the presence of that vast army of prying, peering, callous, gossiping new officials which is growing every day—the minions of a radical government.[214]

As the end of the month approached *The Times* noted that the Unionists were reported being 'snowed under' by letters and postcards of protest on national health insurance—ten mail sacks on November 28, nine on November 29. This, said the journal,

[212] *Westminster Gazette*, November 22, 1911.
[213] *Daily Mail*, quoted in *Westminster Gazette*, November 21, 1911.
[214] *Westminster Gazette*, November 22, 1911.

represented an informal referendum or vote of protest against national health insurance.[215]

November 29 saw the climax with the famous Albert Hall rally, mainly under the sponsorship of the *Daily Mail*, in which mistresses and maids were invited to come and demonstrate that they would not submit to tyranny. The vitality of British democracy was manifest by the appearance of the Dowager Countess Desart and her maid on the same platform. *The Times* reported that the vast auditorium was filled and thousands of women stood outside. 'The night was raw and foggy but it made no difference. The girls were determined to show their feelings on a matter which they consider vitally affects their interests. . . .' Before the meeting an organist maintained enthusiasm playing popular airs. Unfortunately he hit upon 'March of the Men of Harlech.' 'Immediately there was a tornado of hissing, which changed to enthusiastic cheers as the music of "Rule Britannia, Britons Never Shall Be Slaves" broke upon the ears.'[216] Lady Desart made the featured address of the evening, concluding a violent attack upon the Welsh Chancellor of the Exchequer with the reminder that England

> . . . never did nor never shall
> Lie at the proud foot of a conqueror.

The meeting continued with fiery speeches from a number of other titled ladies and from Hilaire Belloc. It concluded with a carefully-worded resolution protesting health insurance only as it applied to domestic servants and condemning the hordes of politically-appointed inspectors who would soon invade the homes of free-born Englishmen to force housewives to lick stamps for David Lloyd George. The only untoward occurrences were persistent questions from the floor demanding to know why the Unionists had not come out flatly against health insurance.

The Albert Hall rally seriously worried the Government. 'There can, I think, be no doubt that the insurance Bill is (to say the least) not an electioneering asset,' wrote Asquith to Crewe the next day.

'The Daily Mail' has been engineering a particularly unscrupulous crusade on behalf of mistress and maid,' and one hears from all constituencies of defection from our party of the small class of employers. Nor is the situation likely to improve,

---

[215] *The Times*, November 29, 1911.   [216] *Ibid.*, November 30, 1911.

a year hence, when the contributions are in full blast, and the 'benefits' remote and sporadic. The Lords will not reject the Bill and it seems doubtful now whether they will seriously amend it. A 'wash our hands' policy seems likely to be professed.[217]

Although there were suggestions after the rally that the next logical step was straightforward refusal to pay the national insurance contribution, and Lady Desart established the 'Tax Defence Association' in South Molton Street, which continued well into spring to collect postcard pledges to disobey the law, more thoughtful Unionists were becoming fearful. A. V. Dicey, whose reflections on other programmes of the New Liberalism have already been adduced as representing the best of philosophical Conservatism, wrote to *The Times* on December 2, deploring the irresponsibility of members of his party, even as he deplored the National Insurance Bill.

> In common fairness even the present ministry ought not to be attacked, first for rejecting the contributory system in regard to old age pensions, and next for attempting to introduce the contributory system as the basis for their scheme of national insurance.

The Bill, said Dicey, has not been considered, not understood, and is badly drawn. It should be given to a referendum, or the House of Lords should reject it, but the party of the constitution could not conscientiously urge violation of the law. There may be a time, he concluded, to resist the enactments of a lawful Parliament that has 'lost its moral authority,' but this time has not yet come.[218]

The insurance Bill received its third reading in the House of Commons on December 6 after a reasoned amendment for its postponement had been defeated. The Unionists, beginning to believe their own propaganda that the Bill was genuinely unpopular, tried, as Asquith had predicted, to disassociate themselves from it. The new Opposition leader, Andrew Bonar Law, announced early in 1912 that his party, when they returned to power, would repeal national health insurance, and then under pressure from Austen Chamberlain's supporters disavowed his

[217] H. H. Asquith to Lord Crewe, November 30, 1911, Asquith Papers, Box 46, f. 193.
[218] *The Times*, December 4, 1911.

previous statement.[219] But any interest in the parliamentary progress of national health insurance had long since disappeared. The House of Lords took less interest in this last measure of Liberal social reform than in any of its predecessors and on December 16, 1911, the National Insurance Bill received the royal assent.

It may be useful here to summarize briefly the terms of the measure as they had been altered by the House of Commons. In addition to the major changes already discussed—the transfer of the medical benefit, the institution of the panel system, the admission of industrial insurance and the extension of the full sickness benefit to twenty-six weeks—Parliament had ended the general acceptance of voluntary contributors with incomes over £160, admitted dependants of the insured to the sanatoria, decreed that deposit insurance would end in 1915, divided the governmental administration of insurance into four national boards supervised by a joint committee, and had exempted from the payment of all contributions workers earning less than 2s. per day. Finally, under pressure from the Irish Nationalist Party, citizens of the other island were removed from the coverage of the medical benefit, and the money thus saved was added to the sickness benefit, providing in effect a cash subsidy from the insurance fund to Irish contributors. The Government lamely explained this change by saying that the extensive system of poor law dispensaries in Ireland made national health insurance medical service unnecessary. To some extent this was true. Nearly one-half the general practitioners in Ireland did some work for the poor law guardians—obtaining better terms of service for its members was the chief duty of the Irish Medical Association—and perhaps one-quarter of the population received its ordinary medical care through this agency. But in reality the substitution of the cash payment was the result of demands by the Irish labour movement and the hierarchy of the Roman Catholic Church.[220] The Irish medical profession itself had not supported the change.

[219] H. of C. Deb., XXXIV (February 14, 1912), col. 35. See also: Robert N. W. Blake, The Unknown Prime Minister, The Life and Times of Andrew Bonar Law, London, 1955, pp. 139–40. The Liberals lost a third by-election on December 2, This was in North Ayrshire, where the new Solicitor General, A. M. Anderson. failed to win re-election after his appointment.

[220] George Dangerfield quotes the following excerpt of a poem that was current in Irish labour circles:

With the first administrative step under national health insurance, the appointment of the joint insurance committee and the English insurance commission at the end of November, began the revolt of the doctors. This came as a result of the appointment of the Medical Secretary of the B.M.A., Dr James Smith Whitaker, to both committees. And so while the Government worked to turn an Act that was a bundle of contradictions and compromises into an efficiently working administrative machine, the battle over the principle of State medicine, which should have ended with the royal assent on December 16, continued. The political phase of the evolution of national insurance was not yet over.

'The Charge of the Sick Hundred'

With money to pay the rent
Which Lloyd George has kindly lent,
Happy sick hundred!
And tho' they are badly crushed,
Into the pub they rushed,
Later with faces flushed,
Homeward they went.

George Dangerfield, *The Strange Death of Liberal England*, London, 1936, p. 305.

7 The Establishment of National Health Insurance

'THE STATE INSURANCE DOCTOR'

When responding to a call by night
How oft he longs for his vanished right
To refuse attendance—as he might
    When he was a Private Doctor.

But now alas! he doth well know
That Nolens Volens he must go;
And should he hesitation show,
    That patient may change his doctor.

For wasn't this 'free right of choice'
Urged by the BMA's joint voice?
Therefore *must* the heart rejoice
    Of the State Insurance Doctor.

Chorus:

Oh, who'd not be a medical man
On Lloyd George's great Insurance Plan
Which such a glorious time began
    For the State Insurance Doctor?

DR JOHN JOHNSON of Bolton, *British Medical
Journal*, December 23, 1911.

The story of the two and one-half years between December 16, 1911, when the National Insurance Act received the royal assent, and the outbreak of World War I falls into three distinct, almost unrelated, parts. First there was the organized resistance of the medical profession to the terms of service offered by the Act. The suppression of this revolt, for it can be described in no other terms, was the work of David Lloyd George. No other man in the Cabinet could have accomplished it. By January 15, 1913, when the medical benefit took effect, he had shattered the solid front of medical opposition and had inflicted a defeat upon the British Medical Association from which that organization did not recover in membership and prestige until the twenties.

The second part of this story deals with the mechanics of the establishment of the health insurance service. As Lloyd George's defeat of the doctors was a political victory, the construction in seven months of an administration that could begin the collection of insurance contributions on July 15, 1912, was no less an organizational victory. Here the credit belongs to Sir Robert Morant, who was appointed to head the insurance scheme at the end of November, 1911, under circumstances discussed in Chapter III.

The third portion of this chapter covers the eighteen months between January 15, 1913, when insurance benefits became payable, and the outbreak of war. It will survey briefly several of the more important administrative problems encountered at this time, notably the surprisingly high incidence of sickness discovered among women, which seemed to threaten the solvency of insurance. Perhaps as important, certainly more interesting for the historian of social politics, were the beginnings in 1913 of Lloyd George's third great programme of reform, envisioned as a complement to the 1909 budget and health insurance: the repopulation of the English countryside. This 'land campaign,' as it was usually called, appeared to have grown naturally in the Chancellor's mind from a contemplation of the taxation of the increment of land values enacted in the 'people's budget' and of the money that would become available for housing in the national insurance reserve. This reform was the logical culmination of a series that aimed at forcing down the price of unimproved land and providing the funds for workers to build upon it.

I

As almost its last act, the special meeting of the British Medical Association of May 31–June 1, to which Lloyd George had spoken, had passed unanimously the 'Six Cardinal Points' which were to be the minimum conditions under which the profession would take service under national health insurance. The six points were:

1. An income limit of £2 a week for the insured: no one earning more should be permitted to receive medical benefit without extra payment to the doctor.

2. Free choice of doctor by the patient, subject to the doctor's consenting to act.

3. Medical and maternity benefits to be administered by the local health (later 'insurance') committees, not the friendly societies, and all questions of medical discipline to be settled by medical committees composed entirely of doctors.

4. The method of payment in the area of each insurance committee to be decided by the local profession.

5. Payment should be 'adequate'; this later was defined as a capitation fee of 8s. 6d. per head, per year, excluding the cost of medicine.

6. The profession to have adequate representation upon the various administrative bodies of national health insurance.

During his speech and in the subsequent discussion, Lloyd George had mentioned all of these points, among many others, and had readily agreed to all of them except the income limit and the remuneration of 8s. 6d. Free choice of doctor and the administration by insurance committees of the medical benefit, although not the maternity benefits, had, of course, been guaranteed in the amendment moved by Dr Christopher Addison on August 1. Nevertheless, beginning immediately after the special representative meeting and continuing through the summer and autumn of 1911, the Medical Secretary of the association, Dr James Smith Whitaker, was busy mobilizing professional opinion against health insurance. This involved obtaining signatures to a declaration stipulating that the undersigned agreed 'that in the event of the National Health Insurance Bill becoming law, I will not enter into any agreement for giving medical attendance and treatment insured under the Bill, excepting such as shall be satisfactory to the medical profession and in accordance with the declared policy of the B.M.A. . . .' By the end of the year the association claimed it had collected over 27,000 signatures.[1]

The profession's growing discontent following upon the approved societies' recovery of partial control of the medical benefit through the Harmsworth amendment, heightened by its

---

[1] Paul Vaughan, *Doctors' Commons, A Short History of the British Medical Association*, London, 1959, pp. 200–3.

James Smith Whitaker, 1866–1936, born rural Yorkshire; educated Manchester Grammar School and Owen's College, Manchester; engaged in general medical practice, Great Yarmouth, 1892–1902; Medical Secretary of B.M.A., 1902–11; deputy chairman, English insurance commission, and member of joint insurance committee, 1911–19; senior medical officer, Ministry of Health, 1919–32. Kt. 1931.

inability to arrive at an accommodation with the societies during the meetings of October 9 and 16, has been described. This hostility to the insurance scheme and to Lloyd George personally was notably apparent in the conduct of Sir James Barr, an Ulsterman and ardent Unionist, who was president-elect of the association.[2] Even before taking his largely honorary office, Dr Barr began to attempt to rally medical opinion against the Bill. At Edinburgh on October 13, while the National Conference of Friendly Societies was meeting in the same city, he denounced Lloyd George's plan in most uncompromising terms. National health insurance, he said, 'would impair the independence, increase sickness, and hasten the degeneracy of a spoon-fed race.' It was a great step down the path to socialism. It would lower the standard of medical education and discourage intelligent young men from entering the medical profession.[3]

Although the doctors' hostility grew more intense in the autumn of 1911, Lloyd George's optimism after the October 19 conference demonstrated his conviction that by finding the solution to the problem of the relationship of industrial and friendly society insurance, he had removed the last serious obstacle to the easy passage of the Bill. The doctors indeed were placated to some extent on the matter of the income limit by the imposition of a £160 maximum income for voluntary insurers, although it was provided that after five years on insurance a contributor might continue as a voluntary insurer, even though his income came to exceed that amount. Local medical committees, made up entirely of doctors, were instituted to handle questions of medical discipline. If the doctors in an area chose to reject payment by capitation fee, the local medical committees would co-operate with the insurance committees in determining the method of payment. In summary, by the end of November nearly all the six cardinal points had been met or at least given recognition, except the 8s. 6d.

[2] Alfred Cox, *Among the Doctors*, London, 1950, p. 87.

James Barr, 1849–1938, born Claremont, Tyrone; father a J.P.; educated Londonderry, and Glasgow University; consulting physician, Liverpool Royal Infirmary; specialist in circulatory disease; President, Lancashire and Cheshire Branch of the B.M.A.; President, Liverpool Medical Institute; President of B.M.A., 1912. Kt. 1905; C.B.E. 1920.

[3] *The Times*, October 14, 1911. Barr's antagonism toward anyone connected with the Chancellor appears also to have diminished Christopher Addison's usefulness as a mediator between the doctors and the Government. Cox, *Doctors*, p. 91.

capitation fee. Medical opinion seemed unsure and unformed. Although the doctors did not like the Act, there was no suggestion they would resist it. The great outburst of anger that followed the appointment of J. Smith Whitaker to the joint insurance committee and to the English insurance commission took the Government, and the British Medical Association, by surprise.

The possibility of such an appointment had been clear at least since November 20, when Lloyd George had consulted the Chairman of the Representative Body, Ewen Maclean, about it. A week later the Chancellor had interviewed the Medical Secretary, and on November 30 Vaughan Nash made the formal invitation on behalf of the Prime Minister.[4] Without replying, Smith Whitaker placed the entire matter in the hands of the B.M.A. Council. On December 2 the Council met, and after a long discussion voted thirty-eight to three to endorse the appointment of their Medical Secretary for the posts.[5] This did not imply, the Council specified, that the doctors were satisfied with national health insurance, although in view of the doctors' persistent demand for representation at all levels in the insurance administration, the approval of Smith Whitaker's appointment appeared to the press to be entirely justified.[6]

On December 6, the day after the public announcement of the B.M.A.'s approval of Smith Whitaker's appointment, the belief of the profession's leaders that they had won an important, if modest, victory was rudely shattered. Dr Fred J. Smith, a leading consultant at London Hospital, published in *The Times* a letter entitled 'The Great Betrayal.' Although admitting that the Bill probably would not affect him personally, he denounced the 'shameful . . . betrayal' of British doctors by 'politicians (ordinary

---

[4] Vaughan, *Doctors' Commons*, p. 206; Sir John Conybeare, 'The Crisis of 1911–13, Lloyd George and the Doctors,' *Lancet*, May 18, 1957, p. 1033.

[5] Two factors commended approval of the appointment: that Smith Whitaker would be the deputy chairman of the English insurance commission and that J. Lister Stead had already been made a commissioner. The most vocal opponent of approval was Dr Major Greenwood, who reminded the others of the agreement not to accept service under insurance until all the cardinal points were achieved. 'Minutes of Special Meeting of B.M.A. Council, December 2, 1911,' *British Medical Journal*, Supplement, December 9, 1911, pp. 586–90.

[6] *The Times*, December 2, December 5, 1911; *Westminster Gazette*, December 2, 1911. Smith Whitaker's salary was to be £1,500, the amount received in those days by a deputy secretary in the Civil Service, although technically he was not a part of it.

and medical).' He noted that the announcement of Smith Whitaker's appointment made no mention of the six cardinal points, which had not yet been achieved, and that it had been this same Smith Whitaker who since June had been circulating among the doctors the pledge to take no service under the Act until all the cardinal points were conceded.[7]

By the end of the first week of December the B.M.A. Council began to react to the totally unexpected excoriation it was receiving. It hurriedly published the minutes of its meeting of December 2 and Sir Victor Horsley published a letter in *The Times* signed by all metropolitan members of the Council, saying that the pledge referred only to medical service, not to administrative service under national health insurance.[8] Nevertheless the doctors would not be placated. With the appointment of Smith Whitaker, all the vague uneasiness and the unfocused dissatisfaction of the previous months came to a head. The National Medical Union, a rival professional association which would refuse to work the Bill, was organized on December 14. Five days later on the nineteenth at Queen's Hall, London, another organization, 'the British Medical Association Reform Committee,' pledged to 'end or mend the B.M.A. Council,' was established. When he tried to remind the doctors at Queen's Hall that most of the six cardinal points had been conceded, Sir Victor Horsley himself was shouted down with cries of 'Traitor!' 'What is the price of your peerage?' 'Go to your Lloyd George!'[9]

The medical profession was now in open revolt against its own leadership. In rebellion it was supported and encouraged by the Northcliffe newspaper chain, particularly the *Daily Mail*, which slipped easily into the sponsorship of the doctors' revolt as the anti-stamp-licking campaign dwindled. The *Mail* reported wholesale resignations from the British Medical Association and

[7] *The Times*, December 6, 1911. Smith followed his first letter with a second, on December 9, amplifying the points first made.

[8] *Ibid.*, December 11, 1911. Meanwhile *The Times* was warning the doctors not to undermine the leadership of the association. *Ibid.*, December 9, 1911.

[9] Conybeare, 'Crisis,' *Lancet*, May 18, 1957, p. 1033; Cox, *Doctors*, p. 95; Vaughan, *Doctors' Commons*, pp. 204–5. Besides being the first Chairman of the Representative Body, Horsley was a well-known political radical and was a prospective Liberal candidate for London University. His attempt to defend the Council's policy destroyed his position as a leader of the British medical profession. In February Dr Ewen Maclean also retired as Chairman of the Representative Body and was replaced by Sir Jenner Verrall.

denied the right of the *Journal* to speak any longer for the British medical profession. The *Journal* retorted by suggesting that the Unionist press had no real interest in the doctors' problems, but was using the profession as a political weapon or, even more likely, as a circulation builder.[10]

Clearly if the leadership of the B.M.A. were to maintain a position as the spokesman of the profession, it would have to demonstrate its firmness on the six cardinal points and show that it would not co-operate with the Government on any other than its own terms. This thinking was behind a letter to *The Times* on December 26 by Sir James Barr, in which the president-elect of the association, even though on December 2 he had himself voted in favour of Smith Whitaker's appointment, sought to prove the Council's new determination. Sir James wasted no time in complaining about the unwillingness of the health programme's administration to negotiate with the profession. He attacked the health Act in principle. It was a step towards socialism, he asserted, too expensive, and not actuarily sound. Both the medical service and hospital treatment were inadequate. It showed the deterioration of British character that the nation was willing to submit to it. He attacked the provision for sanatorial treatment of tuberculosis in astounding terms for one dedicated to the saving of life and the arts of healing. Sir James quoted the director of the Royal Albert Asylum, who had said that:

> Many an imbecile owes his existence to the fact that his parents failed to die of tuberculosis. Hitherto medical men have been devoting all their energies to the environment, adapting the environment to the individual, not the individual to the environment, thus not assisting nature to take care of itself.

Towards the end of the long letter Barr suggested that the weapon for the doctors was passive resistance. If the medical profession could unite against national insurance, he concluded his letter, 'Mr Lloyd George could retire with his Act to the obscurity from which he should never have emerged. I quite agree with the

---

[10] *B.M.J.*, December 16, 1911, p. 1614. It may be worth noting that during this period of extreme journalistic violence, immediately after Christmas, David Lloyd George himself was vacationing on the Riviera in the villa of Lord Rothermere, brother of Lord Northcliffe, and business manager of the newspaper chain. Arthur C. Murray, *Master and Brother, The Murrays of Elibank*, London, 1945, p. 90.

Standard that it is nothing short of a national calamity that such a man should hold any office in any government.'[11]

Thus, at the end of the year, the battle was joined. A portion of the membership of the British Medical Association had forced the organization into a position of stern intransigence.[12] At the time, however, it was unnoticed, or at least uncommented upon, that the writers of the innumerable open letters in the month after the Smith Whitaker appointment were not ordinarily those who would be working under the national health insurance scheme. Beginning with Dr Fred Smith himself, many signatures subscribed to denunciatory letters in lay and professional periodicals carried with them the initials M.D., F.R.C.P., or F.R.C.S. The consultants and specialists urging the B.M.A. forward at the beginning of 1912 would find by the end of the year that they had left behind the lowly, voiceless general practitioner for whom national health insurance promised a larger and steadier income than he had ever known.[13] The division of the medical profession, finally exploited with great skill by Lloyd George in the autumn of 1912, had its origin in the uncompromising position to which the leading members of the medical profession drove the B.M.A. at the beginning of the year.

The association began the new year by voting at a special representative meeting to call upon all medical men to resign any posts held in the national health administration. Some doctors did withdraw from government service as a result. But James Smith Whitaker, whose resignation would have meant the most, remained loyally at work and suffered subsequently a professional and social boycott that wounded him severely.[14]

During the first six months of 1912 there was no negotiation and virtually no contact between the joint insurance committee and the medical profession. The doctors assumed they could win their

[11] *The Times*, December 26, 1911. The letter was widely reprinted and commented upon. For representative opinions, see *Westminster Gazette*, December 28, 1911, and *B.M.J.*, December 30, 1911, pp. 1713-15.

[12] In the first issue of the new year the *Journal* admitted having failed 'to give expression to the wishes of the bulk of the profession,' and promised to mend its ways in the future. *B.M.J.*, January 6, 1912, p. 41.

[13] 'What annoyed me most at these meetings,' commented Dr Alfred Cox, who succeeded Smith Whitaker as Medical Secretary in December and was himself a G.P., 'was that some of the most prominent of the diehards were consultants and others not directly affected. . .' by the Bill. Cox, *Doctors*, p. 91.

[14] *Ibid.*, p. 94.

battle by waiting. Contributions under national health insurance would begin in mid-July; the insured could claim medical service and other benefits in return for their contributions on January 15, 1913. If the profession could only hold together and refuse service, the outcries of the insured would cause the Government to grant all demands. Not until June 7 did the Chancellor of the Exchequer meet representatives of the medical profession. In the discussions on this occasion he immediately pointed out that four of the six cardinal points had been conceded virtually in every detail and that the income limit for the insured was fixed by statute and not likely to be changed. At the same time both sides agreed that, despite continuous discussion of the matter for a year, there was very little data available about how much doctors in the United Kingdom were actually earning.[15]

With the consent of both parties a well-known chartered accountant, Sir William Plender, was asked to investigate the remuneration of British general medical practitioners. Six towns—Darwen, Darlington, Dundee, Norwich, St Albans, and Cardiff—were taken as representative. In these areas were 265 practitioners. Of this number, fifty-one refused to submit their records for scrutiny. Forty of these, from a total of ninety-six, lived in Cardiff, and consequently that city had to be dropped from calculations. Plender made his report on July 11, 1912. His findings were a shock, and should have been a warning, to the distinguished members of the medical profession who were responsible for the position now held by the B.M.A. In the five towns of his sample, Plender discovered, the ordinary general practitioner received an average of 4s. 5d. per patient per year for medical attendance upon all classes of the population.[16]

Plender's report demonstrated conclusively a fact well known to

[15] Unquestionably the best source for the story of the Government's negotiations with the medical profession after the passage of national health insurance is: *Cd. 6907*, 'Report for 1912–1913 of the Administration of the National Insurance Act, Part I,' 1913. This document, Dr Cox remarks, is 'a very fair and complete, though necessarily concise, statement of the position, and should be studied by all who wish to know the details of the introduction of the Act and its administration in its earlier stages.' Alfred Cox, 'Seven Years of National Health Insurance in England,' *Journal of the American Medical Association*, LXXVI (May 7, 1921), 1309.

[16] *Cd. 6305*, 'Existing Conditions in Respect of Medical Attendance and Remuneration in Certain Towns,' 1912. On the effect of the Plender report on the doctors, see Cox, 'Seven Years,' *J.A.M.A.*, May 7, 1921, p. 1310.

the rank and file of British medicine, but so far unconsidered by both the B.M.A. leaders and the general public: that the approximately 6s. per contributor that Lloyd George proposed to allot to the insurance committees as medical remuneration represented a considerable increase not only over what doctors usually received from friendly societies, but also upon what they earned from the public at large.[17] The lesson here was explicit. The Harley Street leadership of the B.M.A. was out of touch with its own following. It had been talking of 'clinical freedom' and of 'conditions of mutual trust between doctor and patient' to a body of men who, however honourable and devoted, had to think first of all of a living wage. Certainly Sir William's report told the ordinary general practitioner in a working-class neighbourhood nothing he did not already know. But it had a profound effect on public opinion and startled, but failed to influence, Barr and his colleagues.[18]

Plender's report was laid before the medical association, which replied by reiterating its earlier demand for an income limit and a basic 8s. 6d. capitation fee, and asking for an immediate decision. The joint insurance committee answered, saying that further negotiations were possible only if commissioners with plenary powers were appointed. Upon receipt of this ultimatum, the association, on July 19, 1912, broke off all negotiations and requested again the resignation of all doctors on government administrative boards. At the same time a new covenant was circulated, a so-called 'pledge complementary to the undertaking' (of June, 1911), which bound the signatories to place at the disposal of the association's State Sickness Insurance Committee their resignations from all forms of contract practice. Most affected by this would be the existing friendly society practitioners. Meanwhile

[17] The cost of medical benefits had been calculated at £4,200,000, which amounted to 6s. per head including the cost of drugs, medical appliances, and doctors' pay. Assuming that the doctor's prescribing cost no more than 1s., this left a 5s. capitation fee. This amount, however, was not fixed by Parliament. Rather the planners of the Act had always assumed that the administrators of the medical benefits, first the approved societies and then the insurance committees, would pay only what was necessary to hire a sufficient number of doctors to fill the panel in their particular area. For a well-informed temperate discussion of the medical benefits from the doctors' point of view, see: J. Dyer Bray, *The Doctors and the Insurance Act: A Statement of the Medical Men's Case Against the Act*, Manchester, 1912, pp. 63–6.

[18] Mrs Masterman states that Plender's report turned public opinion clearly against the doctors. Lucy Masterman, *C. F. G. Masterman*, London, 1939, p. 242.

professional leaders began to bring organized pressure on recalcitrant colleagues. Consultants with honorary appointments in hospitals were urged to limit the house staff to signers. It was suggested that general practitioners appoint only resisters as assistants and *locum tenens*.[19] Since July 15 contributions were being collected from the working population; benefits were to become payable in five months. The medical profession clearly assumed time was on its side.

But the Government had at hand a powerful weapon, which if used with skill might easily destroy the doctors' resistance. This was the bitter antagonism between the profession and the friendly societies. The concession to the doctors of insurance committee administration of the medical benefit and the panel system could be reversed and the administration of the medical benefit returned to the friendly societies on terms that would make an underpaid young general practitioner in a working-class neighbourhood forget all appeals about medical solidarity. 'The Chancellor within twelve months, if he chose,' commented the *National Insurance Gazette*, noting the B.M.A.'s decision to break off negotiations with the insurance commission, 'could guarantee £350 per annum to over 12,000 medical men with leave to conduct general practice.' This would be, the magazine remarked, a State medical service to which, nevertheless, thousands of young underpaid doctors would flock. Or, alternatively, the approved societies 'are quite willing to take over the 6s. per year and make their own arrangements.'[20]

This only slightly veiled threat of either a salaried State medical service or a return to approved society administration was repeated in the clearest possible terms little more than a week later in the *Nation*. Here in a special 'Medical Supplement' to Massingham's journal, David Lloyd George himself warned the doctors that previous government concessions had been made not out of weakness but out of justice and that many alternatives to the present arrangements for the medical benefit were available. The

---

[19] Conybeare, 'Crisis,' *Lancet*, May 18, 1957, p. 1034. For a good picture of the operation of professional pressure on a single doctor, see the novel: Francis Brett Young, *Doctor Bradley Remembers*, New York, 1938, pp. 497–502.

[20] *National Insurance Gazette*, July 27, 1912. The *National Insurance Gazette* began publication on April 1, 1912. Like the *Insurance Mail*, it was published by the Insurance Publishing Company, whose successors are Stone and Cox. It devoted itself to matters of interest to the approved societies.

Government, said the Chancellor, had at its back the organized power of the friendly societies. He had

> risked the hostility of these very powerful organizations, and the measure was for some time put into jeopardy owing to the opposition of these societies to the control of the medical benefit being vested in Committees on which the Municipalities and the medical profession were represented.

But the societies, he reminded the doctors, were still quite anxious for the return of the medical benefit. Finally, he said,

> there are other alternatives which are being increasingly pressed upon us by very influential quarters for dealing with this momentous question of medical care of the industrial population of this country. . . . My only reluctance up to the present to consider the practicability of these suggestions has been due to the hardship that would undoubtedly be inflicted by their realization upon a large number of General Practitioners.

He did not, of course, want to hurt the doctors if it could be avoided, but: 'The supreme consideration of every Government must, however, be the well-being of the people as a whole.'[21]

While on one hand threatening the doctors with more onerous terms of service in case of a medical strike, the Chancellor at the same time began to prepare a gigantic new financial inducement that would effectively destroy whatever unity the medical profession had thus far been able to maintain. On October 22, with less than three months left before the beginning of the medical benefit and with over £4,000,000 of insurance contributions already collected, Lloyd George received Cabinet permission to increase the total cost of the medical benefit to 9s., including drugs and appliances. This was not equal to the 8s. 6d. excluding drugs demanded by the medical association, but it did amount to a straight 2s. 6d. increase per head per year in the cost of the medical benefit and was calculated by the Cabinet to involve a charge upon the Exchequer of about £1,500,000.[22]

The intention was to give all doctors a minimum income of 7s. per patient per year, excluding the cost of drugs. If the doctor

---

[21] *Nation*, August 3, 1912, 'Medical Supplement,' pp. i–ii.
[22] H. H. Asquith to George V, October 23, 1912, Asquith Papers, Box 6, ff. 168–9.

supplied the drugs, he would receive an allowance of 8s. 6d., while if he regularly did not do so, 1s. 6d. would be applied to medicine. The remaining 6d. was taken from a special fund reserved at the beginning of the Bill for medical treatment of tuberculosis patients. This would be used for contingencies either in drugs or medical service. A doctor could expect, therefore, a capitation fee of at least 7s. per year and perhaps as much as 9s. when supplying medicine. In addition there would be a grant of £30,000 by Parliament to be used for drugs in areas of epidemic or disaster.

Pressure to reopen negotiations now was growing inside the medical association, and on November 4 the B.M.A. restored informal contact with the Government in a letter requesting information concerning plans for certain provisions of the medical benefit, such as the hiring of assistants, the paying of mileage, and the method by which administrators proposed to satisfy themselves that medical service was being properly given.[23] Communications on these and other points followed, the results of which were embodied in a government memorandum on December 3. The memorandum stipulated that a simple daybook kept by the doctor would be sufficient evidence of proper performance of duties, that assistants in certain capacities could be used, and that mileage would be paid.

Although the association had not yet replied to the memorandum, it appeared that negotiations were closed. The Government recognized the right of doctors to payment in forms other than a capitation fee if they so desired. Doctors were to be remunerated for work done beyond their ordinary professional capacity, such as emergency operations. Early in December, substantive regulations for the administration of the medical benefit were circulated and insurance committees began to issue letters to the doctors in their areas inviting them to join the scheme.

'It now appears to be fairly certain that the doctors will work the Act,' noted the *Insurance Gazette* on December 4, as the British Medical Association Council was meeting to consider the new government proposals. The friendly societies were unhappy, noted the *Gazette*. They were disappointed that the administration of the medical benefit had not been restored to them. They were now protesting

---

[23] *Official Report, House of Commons Debates*, Series 5, XLIV (December 5, 1912), cols. 2486–7.

against the concessions to the doctors. . . . If the House of Commons and the Chancellor had known, twelve months ago, what would happen, we think the Societies' demands to have the administration of the medical benefit left in their hands, would have been conceded. The whole business has been a sorry and a disastrous one—entailing moreover, much unnecessary expense.[24]

Thus there was considerable surprise, and much consternation both in and out of the medical profession, when on December 21, 1912, three weeks before the medical benefit was due to take effect, a special representative meeting voted by a majority of over four to one not to accept the Government's terms. This was more than an act of unwisdom; it was an act of folly. 'On the morning of this meeting,' recalled Dr Cox sadly, 'I had in my possession scores of letters and telegrams from our local secretaries which showed that in some areas a majority of men had already joined the panel, in spite of the fact that nearly 100 per cent had signed a pledge that they would not do so until released by the Association. More telegrams to the same effect came in during the meeting.' Some doctors in the poorest areas, noted the Medical Secretary, found their income would be doubled under national health insurance.[25]

The association put forward a plan by which the doctors' terms of service would be negotiated between the profession and representatives of the insured. The doctors, apparently, were basing their legal case on Section 15, Subsection 3 of the National Insurance Act, which gave local insurance committees the power to set income limits for certain groups of insured above which the insured would be permitted to make their own arrangements for medical benefit. The intent of this provision was to avoid hardship in cases where the contributor travelled continuously and was unable to arrange with a particular panel doctor, or in the case of chronic illness, or in case of need for specialists when the amount of the medical benefit would prove inadequate. These provisions, however, had been inserted to cover special situations and had never been intended as an alternative to the normal operation of the Act. The Government immediately replied, saying it could

---

[24] 'The Administration of the Medical Benefit,' *National Insurance Gazette*, December 7, 1912.
[25] Cox, *Doctors*, p. 97.

sanction no arrangement in which the State would be committed
to the payment of money by other than its own agents. With twenty-
three days left before medical service under the Act commenced,
the medical profession and the joint insurance committee broke
contact for a second time.

The Government accepted the situation complacently. Lloyd
George knew well that the medical profession was seriously split
over the question of accepting service under the Act and had
assumed from the beginning that the well-paid consultants and
specialists who supported the B.M.A. in its intransigence knew
less about the opinions of the rank and file of the medical profession than he did himself.[26] Also the Government had been
planning for precisely this emergency, while dropping public hints
about the manifold advantages of a salaried medical service.[27]
Throughout the struggle with the doctors, indeed throughout the
several struggles connected with the passage and establishment of
national health insurance, the Chancellor of the Exchequer's use
of the public press to suggest points of view he could not himself
officially hold or to spread a terrifying rumour, suggests a pre-
cocious understanding of the now well-developed art of political
propaganda.

For providing the medical benefit in case of a boycott by the
British Medical Association the Government proposed to transfer
the administration of this service from the local insurance committees to the four national insurance commissions. The insurance
commissions would hire doctors on salary where they could get
them, and transfer them into areas needing medical service. In
these areas the government doctors would have a monopoly not
only of insurance practice, but of such private practice as they cared
to undertake among the families of the members of the approved
societies, whom the Government was certain would willingly
co-operate in this.[28]

[26] See, for instance: D. Lloyd George to H. H. Asquith, December 28, 1912,
Asquith Papers, Box 13, ff. 110, 111. In this letter, concerning the possibility
of a general election in the spring or summer of 1913, Lloyd George argued for
the later date, saying that the benefits of the Act would be more apparent in
June and the division in the doctors was so serious that it would not be healed
by then.

[27] See, for instance C. F. G. Masterman's statement in the House of Commons.
H. of C. Deb., XLV (December 18, 1912), cols. 1508–9.

[28] This plan was communicated early and secretly to the approved societies.
See: Minutes of the General Committee, December 12, 1912, National Deposit

Lloyd George made public the Government's plan on January 2, 1913, in a speech to the Insurance Advisory Committee. Here he dilated on the advantages of a salaried medical service. It would not necessarily be full time, he said. Doctors would be free to attend members of the family of the insured, but would not work outside the family. As an example, he cited Bradford, which had about 100,000 insured. This number could be taken care of, he thought, by fifty doctors at £500 per year each.[29] 'Salaried service,' concluded Lloyd George cheerfully, 'I think in many cases would be better for the patient.'

> For the approved societies it would be infinitely better from a financial point of view, because you will have a perfect check on malingering in those cases, for after all there is one weakness in the panel system, that if you allow a man to change his doctor it is very difficult for a doctor to be exceedingly stern in the matter of certificates. . . .[30]

The Chancellor's smiling threats were unnecessary. The doctors' revolt had already collapsed when he made his speech. The same issue of the *National Insurance Gazette* that reported the speech noted briefly that 'about 11,000 doctors have joined panels.' When the local insurance committee advertised for doctors in Bradford, it got three times as many applications as were needed. In Sheffield the local medical ranks held until the word was quietly passed that Scottish doctors would be brought in on salary to take their places. Immediately 100 doctors appeared at the town hall to register with the local insurance committee. In the New Forest doctors were stampeded into joining panels by the rumour of an omnibus with drawn blinds heading towards Lymington filled with Scottish doctors.[31] By January 10, nearly 15,000 doctors had signed contracts with the insurance committees, and by the fifteenth so many panels were complete that it was necessary to institute monopolies in only five areas.

Friendly Society, Item 3419. See also memo from the N.D.F.S. Secretary, C. Tuckfield, December 11, 1912. Tuckfield was a close personal friend of W. J. Braithwaite.

[29] The Plender investigation had shown that the average private general practitioner served 2,320 people to earn £493 per year. *Cd. 6305*.

[30] *National Insurance Gazette*, January 11, 1913. See also: *Cd. 6907*.

[31] E. S. Turner, *Call the Doctor, A Social History of Medical Men*, New York, 1959, pp. 259–60.

The British Medical Association was defeated and crushed. A representative meeting on January 17 passed the following resolution: 'That this meeting, recognizing the force of present circumstances and consulting the best interests of the Association and the unity of the profession now releases all practitioners from their pledges.'[32]

The result of the battle with the Government was a heavy decline in B.M.A. membership that was not fully restored until 1923. '. . . it was a long time,' remarked Dr Cox, 'before I could forgive those who had led the Association into a humiliating Debacle, when we might have claimed a substantial victory—and all, at the end, for the sake of sixpence. We had in fact "won on points." '[33] The British Medical Association had no experience in fighting the Government, said Cox. It is impossible to exaggerate the importance of carrying public sympathy in such a fight, he warned American doctors immediately after World War I. 'We had it with us all the time when we were fighting for "free choice of doctor," adequate remuneration, and a reasonable voice in the way the professional side of the Act was to be worked. We lost much of it when people began to think that we were irreconcilable and unconstitutional.'

> The government . . . astutely fostered the idea that the profession was attempting to upset the decision of Parliament, and gained the sympathy of the public who had hitherto regarded the profession with the admiration the British public always shows for a good fighter.

The public, he concluded, 'loathed' direct action.[34]

2

The establishment of the national health insurance administration, an evolution which occurred simultaneously with the battle against the doctors, constitutes an entirely separate story. In the place of leadership, instead of David Lloyd George, was Sir Robert Laurie Morant. Instead of January 15, 1913, the critical date, by which time all problems had to be solved, was July 15, 1912, when the collection of contributions began. Rather than having to deal

---

[32] *B.M.J.* Supp., January 25, 1913, p. 97.   [33] Cox, *Doctors*, p. 99.
[34] Cox, 'Seven Years,' *J.A.M.A.*, May 7, 1921, p. 1310.

with the opposition of men who, however wealthy, conservative and well-entrenched, were at least reasonable and intelligent people from whom one could expect concession and compromise, the opponent for Morant and his colleagues was the gigantic, internally contradictory, frequently self-defeating Part I of the National Insurance Act of 1911.

The political head of the national health insurance administration was Charles Masterman. He had been Lloyd George's chief political aide virtually from the beginning of insurance planning, and had understood at least from 'early in the autumn of 1911' that he would take over the defence of the administration in the House of Commons once the measure was passed.[35] The choice of Morant as permanent chief of the insurance administration was Masterman's decision. Mrs Masterman reports her husband had 'great admiration' for the man. Moreover, since the Holmes Circular his usefulness as permanent secretary at the Board of Education had clearly come to an end.[36] Accordingly, Masterman got in touch with Morant almost immediately after his own verbal appointment and asked the education secretary to assume the task of putting national health insurance into operation. (There is absolutely no evidence that Braithwaite was ever considered for this post.)

Morant appears to have accepted the national health insurance post willingly enough. He had a love of power for its own sake and a penchant, easily developed in civil servants, for being at the centre of affairs. Certainly the prospect of constructing from the beginning an administrative machine many times larger, with a far wider scope of activity than the mainly supervisory functions of the Board of Education, must have appealed to him.

On the other hand he was taking charge of a programme disliked by most people in whose opinions he had confidence. National health insurance symbolized a far greater violation than the school medical service of the neat principles of unification of health functions under the local authorities. The unconditionality of insurance itself had been condemned many times by the Webbs, and the Act's passage was for them an important defeat. With national health insurance the campaign for the prevention of destitution had come to an end, and the Webbs went off for a trip

[35] Masterman, *C. F. G. Masterman*, p. 220.
[36] A devout churchman, Masterman, unlike many other Liberals, had not opposed the Education Act of 1902.

O

around the world. 'All the steam went out of the movement for extinguishing the Boards of Guardians and transferring their powers to the County and Municipal Authorities and to the National Government...' remarked Sidney Webb in his history of English local government.[37] George Lansbury, Mrs Webb remarked, told her that Masterman had come up to him after the introduction of the scheme on May 4 'with a pleasant jeering expression: "We have spiked your guns, eh?" ' At the same time John Burns was going about saying that 'insurance has finally "dished the Webbs." '[38]

Morant therefore displayed a proper reluctance at leaving the friends who had supported him at the Board of Education and who felt he was betraying them by going to national health insurance.[39] 'Please do not think I have basely deserted what you care about,' he wrote to Margaret McMillan shortly after his appointment was announced.

> I have not taken the Insurance Commission Chairmanship from choice. I would *rather* have stayed at the B. of E. especially as we may now at last get some money wherewith to give a big stimulus to clinics.

But he found he was no longer trusted in education and of no help to the president. The people for whom he had been 'loyally working' had driven him away. When Lloyd George had said to him, 'I want your energy and strength and force to help push my Insce. Bill,' he could not plead he was needed at the Board of Education.

> I must just hope that I may have a little chance occasionally in my new chairmanship to bend the work under this amazing Insurance Bill into wise Public Health channels....[40]

[37] Sidney and Beatrice Webb, *English Local Government, English Poor Law History: Part II: The Last Hundred Years* (London, 1929), II, 723.

[38] Beatrice Webb, *Our Partnership*, London, 1948, p. 475.

[39] Morant was appointed chairman of the English insurance commission, one of the four national commissions Lloyd George permitted to be written into the Bill. He was also deputy chairman of the joint insurance committee, which was made up principally of the chairmen of the English, Scottish, Welsh, and Irish commissions.

[40] R. L. Morant to Margaret McMillan, n.d., 'Tuesday, 2 a.m.' Morant's appointment appeared in the papers on November 29, 1911. This letter was apparently written soon afterwards. Albert Mansbridge, *Margaret McMillan, Prophet and Pioneer*, London, 1932, p. 70.

The reference to 'wise Public Health channels' suggests the line of evolution Morant hoped national health insurance would take. Following Fabian doctrine, his aim in the long run was to transfer as many of the functions of health insurance as possible to county and borough councils. During the planning of Part I Sir Arthur Newsholme had attempted to have the insurance committees (then called local health committees) made statutory committees of the local authorities. This had been firmly resisted by Lloyd George, Masterman, and Braithwaite. The prevention of this transfer had been one of the minimum demands of the friendly societies—one which Lloyd George had accepted with alacrity and for which he had invited friendly society support. Nevertheless Morant and the Webbs remained great personal friends, and Morant, surprisingly for a civil servant of his rank, was an inveterate gossip. As a result the Webbs knew the problems of health insurance and had perhaps too great an influence on the permanent head of the programme. Still worse, said Mrs Masterman:

> Neither of them had any respect for the word 'confidential,' and difficulties inside the office came rapidly to the knowledge of those whose chief desire was to destroy the Act and Government together. I was present at a rather disagreeable scene at which Masterman assailed his subordinate on a rumoured comment of the Webbs': 'Insurance will be all right. We have put in Morant,' and told him bluntly that his first duties were to the Commission.[41]

Morant's name at the head of the insurance administration, commented *The Times* in a lead article, would be received with 'general astonishment . . . to put it mildly.' The rest of the commissioners, the paper remarked, were men identified with the various interests upon which the insurance Act had infringed.[42] This assessment was perfectly correct. Nearly every member of the English insurance commission had been a participant in the struggles that had surrounded the construction of national health insurance. Besides Morant and Smith Whitaker, there were John

[41] Masterman, *C. F. G. Masterman*, p. 232.

[42] *The Times*, November 29, 1911. The *Lancet*, it should be remarked, highly approved of the choice. Morant 'may be implicitly trusted to see fair-play and fairly assumed to be conversant with, and sympathetic towards, professional ideals.' *Lancet*, December 2, 1911, p. 1565. The promotion of good relations with the medical profession may have been a factor in Morant's appointment.

Bradbury, who maintained a link with the Treasury; Thomas Neill, lately of the Combine and the Pearl Insurance Company; David Shackleton of the Trades Union Congress; J. Lister Stead of the National Conference of Friendly Societies and the Foresters; and, taking note of the growing place of women in politics, Mona Wilson, secretary of the Women's Trade Union League. Finally, as an *ex-officio* member on each of the national commissions, appeared the Chief Registrar of Friendly Societies since 1912, George Stuart Robertson. On the Scottish Commission was John McNicol of the National Conference. The deputy chairman of the Welsh Commission was Dr H. Meredith Richards, a leading medical officer of health and one of the principal spokesmen for Morant and Newman in the struggle with the London School Board and Dr James Kerr. The secretary of the Welsh Commission was Thomas Jones, later deputy secretary of the Cabinet and a friend and biographer of Lloyd George.

To serve the semi-political appointees on the national boards and the joint committee, Morant collected in the next few months an astonishingly brilliant staff of young civil servants, many of whom would contribute to making the decades after World War I the Augustan age of the British civil service. To assist Braithwaite in the secretariat of the joint committee were Richard W. Harris, Braithwaite's friend, defender, and successor as clerk (the new title for the secretary's post) to the joint committee, and Alfred Watson as chief government actuary. Finally, Masterman's private secretary was James Arthur Salter, now Lord Salter and one of Britain's most eminent government servant-academician-politicians.

By private arrangement the staff of the English insurance commission served also the joint committee. Here the secretary was Claud Schuster, a friend of Morant's from the Board of Education who had served briefly as Registrar of Friendly Societies. In 1915 he would become permanent secretary to the Lord Chancellor. The rest of the commission bristled with names of future permanent secretaries and ministers: John Anderson, Warren Fisher, Henry N. Bunbury, Wilfred Greene, Ernest Strohmenger, and Sylvanus Vivian.[43]

[43] As evidence of the level of ability in the insurance commission, Wheeler-Bennet points out in his biography of Anderson that by the autumn of 1912 four fellows of All Souls' College were employed there at one time. John

The rapid expansion of the insurance administration and the fact that a large portion of its income was not under Treasury control were bound to bring charges of political favouritism and patronage in appointment. These rumours continued until the outbreak of the war and were stimulated by Morant's weakness for gossip. Unfortunately he did not restrict his confidences to the Webbs, but communicated his frustrations also to Sir Almeric Fitzroy, an old friend from his first days in the education department, who was Clerk of the Privy Council and a staunch Unionist. With the permanent chief of the insurance administration denouncing his own superiors for allowing the health scheme 'to sink to the level of a political machine,' and saying that 'Masterman was a wire-puller,' the opposition was bound to react.[44] One early casualty of the continuing political difficulties of national health insurance was C. F. G. Masterman.[45]

The appointments that were causing so much comment in the political world were made for a programme having as yet no being. The Insurance Bill that became law on December 16, although over one hundred pages long, was little more than a declaration of intent by Parliament. Unlike any of the other measures so far discussed in this study, including unemployment insurance, it did not provide a new duty for an existing department. Rather it created the duty and left the administrators to create the department. The administrative machinery, the departmental regulations, the premises, and the staff, all had to be acquired and set in motion before July 15, 1912. Lucy Masterman's journal records a well-known incident related by her husband that illustrates the situation in which the insurance administrators found themselves about a week after the Bill received the royal assent. Masterman recalled that he and Morant had spent an evening

Wheeler-Bennet, *John Anderson, Viscount Waverley*, London, 1962, p. 32. Braithwaite noted in his memoirs that six of the new first-class clerks had been at Toynbee Hall, in addition to Llewellyn Smith and Beveridge in unemployment insurance. Sir Henry Bunbury, ed., *Lloyd George's Ambulance Wagon, The Memoirs of W. J. Braithwaite*, London, 1957, p. 282. Sir Henry Bunbury himself spent several years at Oxford House.

[44] Almeric Fitzroy, *Memoirs* (London, 1925), II, 499, 527–8.

[45] For a defence see: 'The Spoils System,' *Nation*, February 24, 1912. The notice inviting applications for staff positions under national health insurance, signed by Morant, included the singular warning: 'Any attempts to enlist support for applications on political grounds or for political purposes, whether through members of Parliament or otherwise . . .' would disqualify the candidate. *Westminster Gazette*, December 16, 1911.

walking up and down Whitehall outside the Government buildings. We went through all the insuperable difficulties and foolishness of action. The Bill had been a year in passing. He was called in only a week after it had passed. The German Insurance Scheme had taken twenty-five years to complete. We were asked to complete a far more complicated scheme in six months. Half the clauses were highly technical, many contradicted each other, some rendered necessary action obviously illegal. The German scheme was carried out with the general good [will]; ours was to be launched amid a hurricane of abuse and hatred, with everyone doing everything legally possible to hinder and check its construction. There was no office, no staff, no address, no telephone. I remember his increasing anger as we summarized all the difficulties 'til he stopped at midnight outside the Treasury and sweeping his stick around us two on the pavement [he] declared fiercely: 'Here is the National Insurance Office.' Then the absurdity of the situation struck me and we burst into laughter, and laughing, went home.[46]

There is no need to recount in detail the complex story of the preparations for the collection of insurance contributions. An office for the national insurance commissions and joint committee was eventually acquired in February in a block of flats near Buckingham Gate, renamed Wellington House. Endless codes of administrative regulations were drafted and printed and circulated to the approved societies. The societies themselves had to be valued and their rules approved. In this connexion R. W. Harris recalled the difficulty caused by the fictitious requirement for democratic control for industrial insurance approved societies that had been agreed upon at the conference of October 19, 1911. '... we were greatly exercised in our own mind,' he remarked, 'as to how the appearance of [democratic] control could be secured, even though the substance admittedly would remain as remote as the moon.' Someone suggested that if one of the Prudential approved societies actually was ever forced to hold an annual meeting, the company would have to hire the Albert Hall.[47] As the years passed, requirements were even further diluted. Professor Alexander

[46] Masterman, *C. F. G. Masterman*, p. 223.
[47] Richard W. Harris, *Not So Humdrum, The Autobiography of a Civil Servant*, London, 1939, p. 115. The Prudential alone formed six separate approved societies for different classes of risks.

Gray, a member of the English insurance commission staff in 1911, wrote in 1923:

> It is no secret that although in the matter of quorums the rules of societies have been reduced to the verge of absurdity, nevertheless a very large number have the utmost difficulty in getting a quorum, where it is not possible to mobilize a solid phalanx of typists for the purpose.[48]

A basic problem, indigenous to all social legislation, was the communication of the citizen's rights and duties in the immensely complicated national insurance scheme to virtually every working-class home in the kingdom. To explain the Act and answer questions about it the insurance administration assembled a staff of lecturers, who were immediately attacked as having a Liberal political bias. Finally, in March, the joint committee was reduced to ordering a huge printing of twenty-five million circulars explaining the Act in the simplest possible terms. These were to be distributed by the Post Office to every residence in the British Isles. Unfortunately, in the inevitable haste, R. W. Harris, who drew up the circular, neglected to indicate whether the sevenpenny employed contribution was paid weekly, monthly, or when the insured chose to pay it. For this error the insurance administration was roundly denounced in the press.[49]

Towards the end of April, Morant nearly broke down and appealed to the Cabinet to postpone the date of the beginning of the collection of contributions. This appeal was overruled, but the crisis resulted in the assignment of a number of extra first-class clerks to the insurance administration.[50]

The first list of approved societies appeared on June 7, and the first issue of cards took place the next day. There was more than a little fear among the administrators that because of the unpopularity of insurance by this time, large numbers of people would heed the advice of the Northcliffe press and refuse to pay contributions.

[48] Alexander Gray, *Some Aspects of National Health Insurance*, London, 1923, p. 18.

[49] Harris, *Humdrum*, pp. 158–9.

[50] Bunbury, ed., *Ambulance Wagon*, pp. 287–8; Masterman, *C. F. G. Masterman*, p. 236. Charles Masterman himself felt that the help given by Warren Fisher, who came in at this time, was of critical importance in meeting the July 15 deadline. The insurance administration received some respite from newspaper attacks in this period because of the diversion created by the sinking of the *Titanic* on April 15.

But July 15 came and went quietly enough, and at the end of the first week the Post Office had in hand over 90 per cent of the money the actuaries had calculated would be due.[51]

By October 1 the sale of stamps indicated that about 12,300,000 contributions were being paid each week. It had been expected that 75 per cent of the adult male population, or 9,200,000 men, and 25 per cent of the adult female population, or 3,900,000 women, would come under national health insurance, not counting voluntary contributors. From this had to be deducted for any given week the unemployed, the sick, and those on vacation. As a result the actuaries had calculated 12,080,000 contributions per week. Thus the figures showed income running slightly above this expectation.[52]

On the number of deposit contributors the calculations of the actuaries proved to be entirely wrong. The friendly societies had always prided themselves on their rigorous selection of applicants both on grounds of character and of physical condition. Therefore, without any precise data whatever, the actuaries had assumed that a substantial proportion of the total insured would be contributors at the post office. By little more than guesswork, Hardy and Wyatt had set the figure of deposit contributors at between eight and nine hundred thousand. Instead, by 1913, there were 320,000, which itself represented a decrease from 1912. Moreover most of these were not the unhealthy, but the ignorant and confused, or opponents of the Act, or people who felt themselves above the status of friendly society member.[53] The small demand for the post office scheme was a totally unexpected development. It was a consequence of the fierce competition for new members between the approved societies of the friendly societies and of the industrial insurance companies, which made most societies willing to accept applicants in any physical condition, without regard to the prospective member's character or interest in the organization's principles or welfare.[54]

[51] Bunbury, ed., *Ambulance Wagon*, p. 289.

[52] *National Insurance Gazette*, October 19, 1912.

[53] See: Ioan G. Gibbon, 'The Working of the Insurance Act,' *Economic Journal*, XXIII (December, 1913), 627–32. The proportion of deposit contributors would, of course, decline after the beginning of the scheme when all the new entrants would enter insurance between the ages of sixteen and twenty.

[54] Masterman reported in 1913 that two of the largest insurance organizations in the United Kingdom, one a friendly society and one an industrial insurance

At a conference early in December the industrial insurance industry had tried to arrive at an agreement with the friendly societies for regulating competition for new members under health insurance and particularly for controlling transfers among societies. Such understandings were customary in industrial insurance, and indeed the Combine had been established, among other reasons, to prevent transfers from one industrial insurance company to another.[55] A. H. Warren of the Manchester Unity answered Kingsley Wood's invitation immediately and curtly by saying that the friendly societies had already 'been interfered with quite enough.' Other friendly society speakers at the meeting reiterated this point of view. Hence the proposal for an arrangement with the friendly societies to abolish transfers came to nothing. In June, 1912, most of the large industrial companies formed the National Amalgamated Approved Society, which quickly agreed with the few important industrial societies remaining outside—the Liverpool Victoria, the Royal Liver, the London and Provincial, the Prudential, and eventually the Hearts of Oak—to refuse transfers from each other.[56]

Even while they attempted to arrange a truce with the friendly societies, the industrial insurance companies turned the great force of collectors—the force that had won the industry its predominant place in health insurance—to enlisting a majority of the new entrants to approved societies. Since the introduction of the Bill, as a means of stimulating activity among them, the *Insurance Mail* had been suggesting ways for the agents to use health insurance as a canvassing device. During the early days of the passage of the Bill, the *Mail* proposed that the agent might say:

> As of course you know there are no death benefits under the State Scheme. Our business is so extensive, our offices so safe,

company, had asked to be allowed to take over all deposit contributors and operate them as an approved society. *H. of C. Deb.*, LV (July 15, 1913), col. 1109.

[55] See the report of a meeting in Essex Hall, December 7, 1911, under the chairmanship of H. Kingsley Wood. *The Times*, December 8, 1911. For an insurance company a transfer was far more serious than a lapse. With a lapse the accumulated reserve of the insured remained with the company unless the individual realized that his policy had a surrender value and chose to claim it, which few did. In a transfer the insured normally took nearly the whole of his reserve with him to the new company.

[56] See letter to the *National Insurance Gazette* from Alfred C. Thompson, general manager of the Prudential, September 17, 1912, *National Insurance Gazette*, September 28, 1912, p. 339.

O*

and we do our work so honestly and well, that the Government does not propose to interfere with us. Mr Lloyd George has gone fully into the matter, and if there had been anything even doubtful about our business he would have included death benefits in his Bill.

This argument, said the editor, 'is unanswerable and will stand a little elaboration.'[57] After the October 19 conference with the place of the collecting industry in national insurance safe, the *Mail* devoted several columns in each issue to urging the solicitation of members for the industrial insurance approved societies. Agents should remember, said the editor,

that their administration of State benefits will give them a more permanent, and a semi-official position in the members' houses; and . . . that the arrears on the life policies will likely be less in times of sickness, for in such times the members will be in receipt of State sick pay. If the agents take around the sick pay, as appears probable, there will be an opportunity of peaceful persuasion in the direction of preventing arrears on the life business, but any excessive pressure by the agent, to this end, will probably have a disastrous effect, for the State will insist more strongly on full sick pay being handed to the claimant. We shall all have to be very careful on this point.[58]

The *Mail* also suggested that agents attempt to extract a promise from their life policy customers to insure for State benefits with the approved society that the agent himself represented. It printed a suitable form for the householder to sign.

It may be said that this promise is useless. From a legal point of view it is. But from a moral or effective point of view, it is anything but useless. A number of men signing that form would feel bound to live up to it, especially if they are likely to get the same benefits from one society as another.[59]

Inevitably, with this form of pressure on the agents, and with the companies using their huge resources to offer special benefits before the legal commencement of insurance, there were bound to be complaints of abuse of the State system.[60] B. Seebohm Rown-

---

[57] *Insurance Mail*, May 27, 1911.
[58] *Ibid.*, November 4, 1911.   [59] *Ibid.*, October 28, 1911.
[60] The Act stipulated a six-month waiting period, i.e. from July 15, 1912 to

tree reported to the *Yorkshire Herald* in May, 1912, that an agent of a 'well known insurance company' had called at his house and asked the maid at the door how many servants lived there. She was told, he stated, that they would all be required to join an approved society under the insurance Act. 'He then handed application forms to her and asked her to sign them and get the others to sign as well. She told him she did not wish to do this. The agent said, however, that whether it was liked or not, it was necessary to join a society, and that he had been sent by the Government, implying that there was no choice as to which society had to be joined.'[61]

In this form of competition the friendly societies were bound to lose. The pathetic reward of the right to hang the lodge banner in the parlour window for a week for the recruitment of five members could never overtake the technique of a trained salesman stimulated by a new business bonus. Two months after the beginning of contributions the industrial insurance approved societies reported their membership had passed the friendly society membership, whose size remained practically as it had been when they were voluntary organizations. The trade union approved societies had sunk to about one-fourth of their previous numerical strength.[62]

The stagnation that overtook the old friendly society movement with the advent of national health insurance was not confined to the rate of growth. The new State members had no interest whatever in the fraternal aspects of the societies and the tendency apparent for a quarter of a century to regard friendly society membership in purely economic terms now predominated in most lodges. Walter P. Wright, the Grand Master of the Manchester Unity, testified to a departmental committee in 1914 on the disappearance of the old friendly society spirit in his own organization. 'There used to

January 15, 1913, for the payment of State benefits. But many companies offered at least partial coverage of the sickness benefit during this waiting period and the huge resources of the Prudential made it possible to offer the full sickness benefit after one payment. The best the Manchester Unity could promise, on the other hand, was the sickness benefit after a 5s. payment, or fifteen weekly 4d. contributions. *National Insurance Gazette*, July 27, 1912.

[61] *Yorkshire Herald*, May 23, 1912, quoted in *National Insurance Gazette*, June 8, 1912.

[62] Industrial insurance approved societies had about 6,500,000 members, the friendly societies about 6,000,000, and the trade unions only about 500,000. *National Insurance Gazette*, September 28, 1912. The friendly society figure includes also members of the collecting friendly societies. Thus the true friendly society figure would be smaller.

be a sing-song in the lodge room in a public house,' said Wright.

> Of course many lodges have moved to unlicensed premises, and there has not been that same sort of social intercourse that there used to be, but I do not know that that has altogether had a bad effect.

But when State insurance was introduced, Wright continued, it was expected

> that all the State members would be induced to take an interest in the society apart from their State insurance, and would be induced to insure for additional benefits. That view has not been borne out by what has happened. We find that the State members are practically taking no interest whatever in the affairs of the society, and that lodges composed entirely of State insured members—and we have many lodges, of women particularly, composed of State insured members only—have to be conducted by independent members who are not members of the lodge at all. It has been an absolute failure in the Manchester Unity, the effort to get the State insured persons to take an interest in the affairs of the society.[63]

The decline of the true friendly societies, both in membership and in vigour, continued at an increasing rate through the period of national health insurance, and their revival became one of the important aims of the Beveridge report. At the beginning of World War II the friendly societies were not only relatively far behind the collecting organizations in size, but the movement was now losing members in absolute figures.[64]

[63] *Cd. 7690*, 'Report of the Departmental Committee on Sickness Benefit Claims Under the National Insurance Act,' Appendix, Vol. III, 1914, p. 64.

[64]

Membership in Thousands at Various Dates

	1912	1923	% Inc. or Dec. in 1923 over 1912	1938	% Inc. or Dec. in 1938 over 1912	1923
Industrial Life Companies	5,143	6,870	+33·6%	8,470	+64·7%	+23·3%
Friendly Societies w/o Branches (includes Collecting Societies)	2,826	3,550	+25·7%	5,140	+81·9%	+44·8%
Friendly Societies with Branches	2,935	3,150	+ 7·3%	3,000	+ 2·2%	− 4·8%
Trade Unions	1,418	1,510	+ 6·5%	1,480	+ 4·4%	− 1·9%

These calculations are taken from figures in the Beveridge report. *Cmd. 6404*, 'Social Insurance and Allied Services,' 1942, p. 25.

With the advent of State insurance in 1948 the societies were cut adrift. Since then, particularly in the heart of the old movement, the decentralized orders, the decline in membership has continued, although the societies now are wealthy. In 1952 the decentralized societies had 1,792,000 members. Ten years later this membership had fallen 32 per cent to 1,218,000, scarcely more than a quarter of the membership in 1911.[65]

A last event of the early period of the national health insurance administration, occurring just before the commencement of benefits, was the ejection of W. J. Braithwaite from the English insurance commission. Braithwaite's departure had been foreshadowed by the appointment of Morant to manage the scheme. The clash of temperaments between the two, R. W. Harris reports, was immediate.[66] Morant was not one to brook a possible rival, and Braithwaite was worn out, on the verge of a nervous collapse.[67] Morant quickly destroyed the younger man's position with both Lloyd George and Masterman, and in December, 1912, he was transferred to the sinecure of Special Commissioner of Taxes. As a result, for the next thirty years the insurance Act was generally assumed to be Morant's creation, a belief he never troubled to contradict during his lifetime, and which was carried on in many writings about him by men who must have known better. Except for a generous mention of Braithwaite's work by Lucy Masterman,[68] R. W. Harris's obituary of his friend in *The Times*, and Lord Salter's comments upon Braithwaite's unrewarded service as an illustration of the character of David Lloyd George,[69] Braithwaite's great contribution remained practically unknown until the publication of his memoirs in 1957.

3

In the eighteen months after the beginning of the payment of benefits, the health insurance administrators were preoccupied by a single but highly complex problem: the unexpected high claims for sick pay. A drain upon the reserves for sickness benefit was

[65] *Economist*, July 24, 1965, Supplement on Insurance, pp. xxii–xxvi.
[66] Harris, *Humdrum*, p. 160.
[67] See also, Arthur Salter, *Memoirs of a Civil Servant*, London, 1961, pp. 59–60.
[68] Masterman, *C. F. G. Masterman*, p. 182.
[69] Arthur Salter, *Personality in Politics*, London, 1947, p. 49.

reported almost immediately by societies with a large proportion of women, although no one could say whether the claims technically were 'excessive' because there existed no record of friendly society experience against which to compare them. Another possible cause of sickness claims was the separation of the doctors who certified for the benefit from the approved societies who paid the benefit. Dr Addison's amendment creating the panel system under the management of the local insurance committees had largely relieved the doctors from any responsibility for society funds. As they had insisted be the case, physicians were not connected with the societies which paid the money that the sickness certificates entitled the insured to collect. From the contributor's point of view the panel doctor had a blank cheque on the society treasury and any doctor who acquired a reputation for refusing certificates quickly lost patients. Consequently it cost a doctor a good deal in capitation fees if he refused certificates, but nothing if he gave certificates freely. It was not his money that was spent.[70]

The problems of the panel physician had been fully explored during the revolt of the doctors, when a salaried service was under consideration. Now the warnings of the friendly societies in that controversy seemed to be fully vindicated. By the beginning of May, with the medical benefit in effect only a little over three months, the problem of malingering began seriously to concern the officials of the approved societies.[71] The solution demanded by the approved societies—one that some friendly societies such as the Hearts of Oak had long used—was a system of medical referees. The referee could either take over entirely the certification of patients for sickness benefit, or simply confirm a certificate upon the request of an approved society official. In either case, he lifted from the shoulders of the doctor the onus of refusing certificates while having nothing to do himself with the course of medical treatment.

[70] In an early test case on malingering resulting from a suit by a woman against a Prudential approved society in the City of London court on November 27, 1913, it developed that a doctor had been signing blank certificates with a rubber stamp and permitting them to be distributed by his house maid. The court in this case found for the plaintiff and gave costs as well. There was nothing in regulations, it said, requiring doctors to sign certificates personally. *National Insurance Gazette*, December 6, 1913.

[71] *National Insurance Gazette*, May 10, 1913.

A second factor besides the apparent unwillingness of medical men to refuse certificates to valued patients was the continuing competition among approved societies for members. The industrial insurance approved societies had begun the practice of paying a sickness benefit claim on the spot. The agent would pay the benefit from his funeral policy collections and present a voucher for the contributor's signature. On the basis of the voucher he was reimbursed by the company. For an agent the well paying funeral benefit business was the real inducement to work national health insurance. Thus the unnecessary exasperation of a potential customer through the refusal of a sickness certificate was a thing to be avoided. This was particularly true as that customer might well transfer to another approved society if his present one appeared to be unnecessarily stringent in the allowance of claims. Therefore, as had long been customary with funeral benefit premiums, an agent might pay the sickness benefit for several weeks from his own pocket if the contributor failed to produce the necessary sickness certificate.[72]

By summer of 1913 the problem of the control of sickness benefits was approaching a crisis. Officials, particularly of the industrial insurance approved societies, were demanding action. 'The Government has introduced a National Insurance scheme, and has embodied it upon the statute book. . . ,' wrote James Redman Ormerod, formerly manager of the Pioneer Life, now vice-chairman of the Lancashire insurance committee and member of the managing board of the National Amalgamated Approved Society.

It is costing something approaching £30,000,000 per annum in one way or another. The actuarial calculations upon which the scheme was based are in virtually every society being falsified by the experience of sickness being greatly in excess of expectations. The *character* of sickness insurance was altered when it was changed from the voluntary to the compulsory principle. We are hearing every day of excessive sickness claims through alleged malingering, and money is being poured out to the extent of thousands of pounds every week, and some of it is going to idlers and impostors. The dishonest persons are

[72] It was noticed quite early that reports of excessive sickness claims, to be sure consistently denied, were associated with the industrial insurance approved societies. *National Insurance Gazette*, June 28, 1913.

endangering the very existence of the approved societies and the probability of the honest members deriving ordinary benefits in due course. I repeat that the malingering apparent imperils the existence of the whole scheme. It is, therefore, the duty of the Government and of the Commissioners to INQUIRE INTO THE FACTS AT ONCE, and if they do so, they will no longer hesitate about providing the comparatively small sum of money necessary to provide State medical referees or judges for alleged malingering cases.[73]

The issue of the *National Insurance Gazette* carrying Ormerod's front page article printed also a letter from the grand master of an unnamed friendly society indicating that societies were likewise beginning to feel the effect of excessive sickness benefits. The letter stated also the ordinary approved society attitude on the reason for malingering: it was the doctors' fault. Doctors, said the society official, were 'practically allowing the malingerer to choose his own time for starting work. In the old days, a word to the doctor and an intimation to the "sick" one invariably had the desired effect.'[74]

By this time it had become clear—although there were no statistics available because no society wished to admit that it was itself in any financial danger—that much of the unexpected cost of the sickness benefit was the result of excessive sickness claims among women.[75] But it was not clear how much represented malingering, how much resulted from genuine unhealthiness, or what proportion was caused by employers who had previously paid wages during sickness but who now encouraged employees to collect State benefits.[76]

By mid-summer Ormerod's demand for an official investigation of excessive sickness claims was echoed in many quarters. As a result, on August 22, 1913, a departmental committee was

[73] *National Insurance Gazette*, June 14, 1913.

[74] *Ibid.*

[75] From the desire to maintain approved society independence and to leave the administration, good or bad, to society leaders who would be responsible to their own members rather than to the government, national health insurance maintained no centralized records. There was no way to ascertain easily the amount or the duration of sickness except through the compilation of the individual records of 23,500 different organizations.

[76] This was a widespread grievance among domestic servants, nurses, shop assistants, clerks and teachers. J. Murray Laing, *A Few Notes on the National Insurance Act*, Birmingham, 1913, pp. 11–13.

appointed under the chairmanship of Claud Schuster which included Alfred Watson, J. Smith Whitaker, Mary Macarthur, A. C. Thompson, Walter Wright, A. H. Warren, and several other industrial insurance and friendly society officials. This committee met for nearly a year. Its report, signed on July 24, 1914, the day after Austria-Hungary presented her ultimatum to Serbia, provides the researcher with a vast source of information not only on sickness benefits but on the general operation of health insurance and on the impact of the scheme on the friendly society movement.[77]

Although the presentation of the departmental committee report was completely obscured by Britain's entrance into World War I— the document was not even published until December, 1914—it deserves considerable notice. Taking together the majority report and the several reservations appended by individuals, it illuminated most of the inherent defects of national health insurance. In this way it served as a precursor for the royal commission of 1924, and indeed for the Beveridge report eighteen years later.

The committee discovered to be sure that payments of sickness benefits to women were running far ahead of expectations. Whether this was caused by malingering on the part of women, or was simply the result of inadequate statistics available during the drawing of the Act, or of both of these combined with a large amount of very real ill health among working-class women, the committee found it difficult to say. The Manchester Unity for instance submitted data on its sickness experience in England only for the nine months down to October 12, 1913. It had expected to spend £213,196 on men's sickness benefits. It had in fact spent £196,628. For women, on the other hand, the organization had estimated a cost of £42,296 but had spent in the nine months alone £48,303.[78] The experience of the Liverpool Victoria approved society, one of the largest of the independent collecting society approved sections, showed even a greater variation from expectations. For the first nine months it had estimated men's sickness among its 350,000 members to cost £80,606. It received claims totalling £62,262 for 77 per cent of the estimate. For women it

[77] Cd. 7687, 'Report of the Departmental Committee on Sickness Benefit Claims Under The National Insurance Act,' 1914. See also: Cd. 7688, Cd. 7689, Cd. 7690, 'Appendix, Vols. I, II, III.'

[78] Cd. 7690, p. 61.

estimated £39,202 and in fact spent £49,755 for 127 per cent of the estimate.[79]

Paradoxically the possibility that the excessive sickness claims were genuine made the problem more dangerous than if they were not. If large numbers of women actually were malingering, the increasingly serious approved society deficits could be diminished by stricter administration of the sickness benefit or by appointment of medical referees or by a number of other relatively simple controls. If, on the other hand, the apparent liability to sickness among working women, especially mothers, was a fact inherent in English working-class life, it could mean that women were basically not an insurable risk under the health scheme as then constituted. The writers of the official report of the departmental committee assumed that the former alternative was the case, and recommended the establishment of a widespread system of official medical referees. They chose also to criticize, in rather strong terms for ordinarily docile civil servants, the separation of the doctors who in effect granted the sickness benefit from the approved societies who paid it.

It is scarcely necessary to observe that what has been found necessary in the past practice of friendly societies is even more necessary under present conditions when the introduction of a large section of the population to insurance has at least for a time deprived the societies of that intimate knowledge of all their members which previously existed in many cases, and when simultaneously there has been introduced to the work of certifying a large body of doctors who have not been trained to the knowledge of the conventions and practice of friendly society work.

. . . .

In the course of our inquiry, . . . overwhelming testimony has been advanced in support of the view that unaided, the panel practitioner experiences difficulty in discharging satisfactorily his duties of certification, and that therefore it is desirable in certain cases that a second . . . medical opinion should be available.

. . . .

Every man, it is said, is afraid of getting the name, 'do not go

[79] *Cd. 7688*, pp. 46–7.

to Dr ——. He will not put you on the club.' It is a very important factor in doubtful cases.[80]

In opposition to the committee majority, Mary Macarthur, the Webbs, the medical officers of health with whom they were in contact, and most important, Sir Robert Morant, were all convinced by early 1914 that the unhealthiness of British working-class women prevented their medical attendance from being an insurable proposition.[81] The fact was, said the reformers, that the working wife and mother in the English industrial slums was never really well. Women were not malingering, Sidney Webb told the departmental committee on February 25, 1914; they were subject to more illnesses than men. With characteristic diffidence, insisting he knew little of actuarial science and was only 'guessing,' he told the departmental committee that the deficit on women's costs alone was already probably £700,000, that it was growing at the rate of between £60,000 and £70,000 a month, and would no doubt be £1,500,000 by the end of 1914.[82]

Women's benefits, he felt it was generally agreed, could scarcely be reduced further. They paid eight-ninths of the men's contribution and received only three-quarters of the men's sickness benefit. The only alternative was the reconstruction of the plan. This the Webbs were already proposing. Women's sickness in effect seemed to have provided the weapon with which Fabian ideas could breach the defences that social insurance had provided for Liberal reform. The 'magic of averages,' it had begun to appear, was not the answer to everything after all.

A few days after Sidney Webb testified, Beatrice Webb presented Robert Morant with the draft of a report on national health insurance that would appear the next month in the *New Statesman* advocating, among other things, the transfer of all medical care connected with birth, pregnancy, and tuberculosis

[80] *Cd. 7687*, pp. 9, 34, 35.

[81] See: Mary Agnes Hamilton, *Mary Macarthur*, London, 1925, pp. 116–17. As a pioneer in the fight for women's economic rights, Mary Macarthur's appearance as a member of a departmental committee concerned chiefly with ill-health among women had special poignancy. Her first baby had been born dead only four months before the committee convened. Soon after, she had broken down and cried while addressing a public meeting and had vowed not to speak publicly again. Her participation in the work of the departmental committee marked her reappearance in politics. *Ibid.*, pp. 127–8.

[82] *Cd. 7689*, p. 382.

to a local government public health authority. To her great joy Morant informed her that Lloyd George had agreed to consider this possibility if it would make health insurance sounder financially. [83]

Two months later, after meeting Lloyd George and Herbert Samuel, presumably accidentally, at a performance of *Parsifal* and arguing with the Chancellor about female sickness during the intermission, Mrs Webb, with Margaret Bondfield, Mary Macarthur, and Dr Addison, attended a breakfast at 11 Downing Street. Here she discovered that the opponent of her plans was the 'lost soul,' Charles Masterman, to whom Lloyd George was deferring on decisions on health insurance. Nevertheless, her diary entry concluded, the reformers were hopeful. 'We are anxious to make the deficit the occasion for a big scheme for maternity and infancy under the Public Health Authority.' Samuel was for it. National health insurance was in a 'financial hole' because the actuaries had forgotten the 'risk of pregnancy.' [84]

On this occasion Beatrice Webb's inevitable optimism for the success of her plans seems more than usually justified. Masterman's period of effective political power was coming to an end, as was the only important portion of his career in the House of Commons. On February 19 he had failed to gain re-election in Bethnal Green after being appointed to the Cabinet as Chancellor of the Duchy of Lancaster. Three months later he was defeated again at Ipswich, and although he remained in the Cabinet until February, 1915, without a seat in the House of Commons he was politically impotent. By this time Lloyd George's reforming energies were diverted into the land campaign, and Churchill was at the Admiralty. With Masterman's departure from the House of Commons the old conception of social insurance as the staple of Liberal reform lost its most dedicated partisan on the front bench. [85] Had the war not intervened to restore approved society

[83] Margaret I. Cole, ed., *Beatrice Webb's Diaries, 1912–1924*, London, 1952, p. 19. See also: 'Special Supplement on the Working of the Insurance Act,' *New Statesman*, March 14, 1914, pp. 1–31. The *New Statesman* report anticipated many recommendations of the departmental committee. It proposed the appointment of medical referees, which had long been standard in Germany, and advocated for the future, as did Mary Macarthur's reservation in the departmental committee reports, the abolition of the approved society system. On the importance of referees, see: Sir John Collie, *Malingering and Feigned Sickness*, London, 1917, pp. 608–14. Nevertheless the widespread appointment of referees for certification decisions did not begin until after the war.

[84] Cole, ed., *Webb Diaries*, p. 22.

[85] After the humiliating defeat in Ipswich on May 23, 1914, Masterman wen

solvency, the Webbs, through their intimacy with a Morant now unchecked by a powerful political chief, might well have presided over the complete reconstruction of national health insurance.[86]

4

The most important matter of contention in the debates over malingering and the control of the sickness benefit was the effect on health insurance of independent panel medical practice. The transfer of the administration of the medical benefit from the approved societies to the insurance committees, and the concessions that had followed it, had given the doctors—although they refused to admit it—a privileged place in national health insurance. Such consideration for medical convenience, the friendly societies maintained, jeopardized the welfare of the scheme as a whole. In view of this controversy, the position and conditions of service of the approximately 14,000 British general practitioners who chose to inscribe their names on the lists of local insurance committees may bear some examination.

In 1912 there were 41,053 medical practitioners of all kinds on the *British Medical Register*. Of these, about 9,000 were abroad or in the services. Of the remaining 32,000 approximately 12,000 were consultants, registrars, teachers, public health physicians, or retired. This left about 20,000 general practitioners to serve a population of approximately 45,000,000. Assuming equal distribution, which did not of course exist, each G.P. had about 2,250 patients. On the basis of the calculation made in Chapter 6, between four-fifths and five-sixths of the British population could be designated as of the working class. One could estimate that up-

abroad for a holiday. One of his last services to health insurance was a plea to Lloyd George to refuse Morant's proposal to transfer the maternity benefit to the county councils. Masterman, *C. F. G. Masterman*, p. 264. The loss of this, the most popular benefit, might well have begun the break-up of the unified health insurance administration.

[86] Probably attempting to allay demands for a more comprehensive health scheme, Masterman had been suggesting for some time the extension of national health insurance. In April, 1913, for instance, he stated unequivocally in the presence of both F. Handel Booth and Kingsley Wood that 'life insurance would in the future be added to sickness insurance.' Speech to the Faculty of Insurance, *National Insurance Gazette*, April 12, 1913. When the war broke out he was working on plans for a medical consultant service and a rural nursing service. Masterman, *C. F. G. Masterman*, p. 264.

wards of 36,000,000 people would be affected by health insurance, either directly or by having some member of the family as a contributor. Before health insurance perhaps half this number received general practitioner service on a regular basis through a friendly society or club.[87] However, the four-fifths to five-sixths of the British population who made up the working class employed no more than three-quarters of the twenty thousand G.P.s in the country.[88]

William A. Brend, whose important full-scale survey of health insurance in 1917 has become a source for much subsequent writing on the subject, concluded that the competition for patients among doctors was one of the principal causes of malingering. Brend told of spending a winter evening in the surgery of a Glasgow panel physician who saw over seventy patients in the course of three hours. At the end of the evening some who had been waiting hours were ushered into the surgery three at a time. Brend said he knew of a very capable doctor living a short distance up the street who saw perhaps a dozen patients during the same evening. Such a doctor, he thought, was hardly in the position to refuse a sickness certificate. Yet as long as free choice was to be observed, Brend concluded, the State could not put any limit on the doctors' practice. Conversely, if excessive numbers were to be prevented, free choice would have to be abandoned.[89]

Although the doctors' fears of the effect of national health insurance upon themselves were probably the most widely publicized aspect of all the agitation against the insurance Act, there is no question that Lloyd George's plan raised considerably the standard of living of the average British general practitioner. For the slightly more than 14,000 panel practitioners before World War I, there were somewhat fewer than 14,000,000 health insurance contributors.[90] This gives a basic ratio of about one panel

[87] Conybeare, 'Crisis,' *Lancet*, May 18, 1957, p. 1032.

[88] This assumption is based on the fact that somewhat more than fourteen thousand doctors accepted panel practice. Presumably any physician whose regular patients, no matter how few, became insurance contributors would himself take on panel practice at least for those patients.

[89] William A. Brend, *Health and the State*, London, 1917, p. 180. Brend's book generally was most critical of health insurance for lack of attention to the wider aspects of public health and preventive medical care. The author showed considerable sympathy for the Fabian point of view on health insurance. Brend was not a doctor, but a barrister and a specialist in forensic medicine.

[90] *National Insurance Gazette*, May 10, 1913. As with other national health insurance statistics, figures on the number of doctors on panels are unreliable. The insurance commissions of England, Wales, and Scotland reported in the

practitioner per one thousand of the insured. But this figure by itself means very little. Certainly many panel practitioners, particularly those whose patients were well-to-do, took very few insurance contributors. Some doctors were surprised to discover that their insurance patients insisted upon paying fees for medical attendance, although they brought at the same time sickness certificates for the doctor to sign so they could collect the sickness benefit.

At the other end of the scale a few doctors had very large insurance practices. The *Lancet* discovered a single-handed practitioner in Bradford with a list of over four thousand, and Dr Harry Roberts reported himself to have the largest insurance practice in Great Britain in Harford Street, Stepney. With two assistants he handled over six thousand insurance patients.[91] A *Lancet* survey in Bradford of ninety-eight doctors with panel practices concluded that the average doctor in that city had from slightly fewer than eight hundred to about one thousand panel patients, and that he earned between £300 and £500 per year from national health insurance. There were, of course, wide variations from this figure. Twenty-nine doctors earned fewer than £50 from national health insurance, while seven doctors in Bradford earned between £1,000 and £1,500 from the service.[92]

first six months of 1914 a total of 20,040 doctors on the registers of local insurance committees. But this is a larger figure than the estimated number of general practitioners for the entire United Kingdom including Ireland, which had no medical benefit. Clearly many doctors had registered on more than one panel, and so were counted twice. The Scottish insurance commission, which reported 2,735 doctors' names on panels, discovered that this figure represented only about 1,790 individuals. (Cd. 7496, 'Report for 1913–14 on the administration of National Health Insurance,' 1914, pp. 176, 539, 574.) Probably the correct estimate was close to the figure published in the *National Insurance Gazette* just after the war began. The *Gazette* announced, without citing a source, that there were 14,522 panel practitioners in Great Britain: 11,825 in England, 901 in Wales, and 1,796 in Scotland. At the same time a total of 4,422 doctors had remained outside national health insurance. *National Insurance Gazette*, August 29, 1914.

[91] Winifred Stamp, '*Doctor Himself*,' *An Unorthodox Biography of Harry Roberts, 1871–1946*, London, 1949, pp. 75–6.

[92] 7 doctors earned from £1,000 to £1,500 from N.H.I.

2	,,	,,	,,	800 to 1,000	,, ,,
15	,,	,,	,,	500 to 800	,, ,,
32	,,	,,	,,	300 to 500	,, ,,
13	,,	,,	,,	250 to 300	,, ,,
19	,,	,,	,,	50 to 250	,, ,,
29	,,	,,	£50 or less from N.H.I.		

Lancet, March 14, 1914, p. 789.

An important factor in all calculations about medical income under national health insurance was that many panel practitioners regarded their insurance work chiefly as an entré for gaining the practice of the rest of the family, while others devoted themselves to insurance work. Hence in each town there would be a tendency for a substantial portion of the panel practice to slip into the hands of a few doctors. This had been noticeable also in Germany where in many communities one-fifth of the doctors had over one-half of the insurance patients. The average income, therefore, of £320 from national insurance for the hypothetical average doctor would be considerably less than half the amount of money he actually was earning if his entire practice in and out of insurance approached the national mean of somewhat over two thousand patients.

All evidence points to a rapid rise in the value of medical practice. Dr Cox, in a rather caustic interview with a correspondent from the *National Insurance Gazette* towards the end of the first benefit year, stated that a serious effect of the Act had been to cause a shortage of doctors for educational and institutional authorities. Young doctors just out of training who had hitherto been happy enough to accept salaries ranging up to £300 per year could now earn nearly twice that amount with a panel practice. Established practitioners noted the same difficulty in advertising for assistants at increasingly high salaries. The *Gazette* in its own survey discovered that fees for assistants and *locum tenens* had gone up about 50 per cent. Still more important, thought the *Gazette*, the going price for the sale of practices had increased by about the same amount and non-panel doctors had increased their fees as well.[93] A working-class medical practice had become at last a worthy investment for the purchase of which a young doctor could now borrow money.[94] Although the effect of this sudden prosperity among working-class doctors was not altogether healthy in the long run, without question Lloyd George's Act reversed decisively and permanently the trend, several decades old, towards a steadily declining economic position among general practitioners.

For England as a whole the English insurance commission estimated the average list to be 750 and calculated that 50 per cent of the doctors had fewer than 500 insurance patients. *Cd. 7496*, p. 176.

[93] *National Insurance Gazette*, December 13, 1913.

[94] Donald McI. Johnson, *The British National Health Service*, London, 1962, pp. 460–7.

Before concluding the discussion of the conditions of medical practice two items with less happy issue deserve note. Doctors in southern Lancashire, after long and bitter experience with club practice, had elected, as they were entitled to do under Section 15 of the Act, to be paid on the basis of treatment rendered to the insured rather than by capitation fee. The Act stipulated that doctors in any area in agreement with the local insurance committee could elect their method of payment subject only to the fact that the insurance committee had only 9s. per head per insured available for payment, no matter how it was divided. At the beginning of the century the Manchester Medico-Ethical Association had drawn up a tariff of professional fees that had been widely accepted by the local profession, based roughly on the rental value of the patient's house. The Manchester doctors now demanded they be paid according to this scale of fees. Within four months it was apparent that payment by attendance would not work. Under such a system the doctor's economic interest was to see the patient as frequently as possible, precisely the opposite motive to that of the capitation fee. As a result, by the beginning of May the doctors had overspent the amount available for their payment by over 50 per cent, so that the medical benefit fund in the hands of the insurance committee eventually was able to meet claims only to the extent of 12s. 6d. in £1.[95]

A second item suggesting an abuse of the Insurance Act by the medical profession was a stipulation appearing in the National Insurance Amending Act of 1913. This clause, reproduced in the standard contract between the insurance committees and the panel physicians, forbade doctors to accept any fee, or any other remuneration, for the treatment of panel patients. The doctors brought it upon themselves, remarked the *Insurance Gazette*, by giving poor treatment to some panel patients and intimating that the treatment would improve if the patient paid an extra fee.[96] This change in the uniform contract caused some unhappiness among the doctors as a reflection upon their professional ethics.[97]

The National Insurance Amending Act of 1913 illustrates, by the matters with which it deals, the various difficulties that health insurance had encountered. The amending Act's original purpose

[95] *National Insurance Gazette*, May 10, 1913.
[96] *Ibid.*, December 13, 1913.   [97] *Ibid.*, December 20, 1913.

had been to give statutory authority for the 2s. 6d. increase in the medical benefit that Lloyd George had promised on October 23, 1912. But the Government took the occasion to remove also a number of anomalies and injustices that had appeared in health insurance administration. The Act ended the reduced benefit that the original measure had provided for entrants to national insurance over the age of fifty and gave them henceforth the standard benefits. It made statutory the promise for the continuation of the medical benefit to friendly society members not under national health insurance. The amending Act gave reduced benefits to some eighty thousand British workers who for one reason or another—under age sixteen, over age sixty-five, or receiving more than £26 unearned income—were not compulsorily insured under health insurance. In order to avoid putting a premium on the employment of these people, the original Act had required the employer to pay his portion of the contribution for them even though the worker would not receive any benefit from this payment. The amending Act now gave these exempt workers the medical and sanatorial benefits, the cost of which approximately equalled their employers' contribution.

The amending Act also specified that a worker who had fallen into arrears in his insurance contribution because of unemployment would have to make up only his own contribution before being reinstated in insurance at full benefit. As originally passed the insurance Act had required both the employer and employee arrears to be made up, with the result that many employers of casual labour refused to hire a worker unless he could produce a fully-stamped card. This meant, in effect, that many of the worst paid of the British workers were bearing the full cost of the insurance contribution.[98] This injustice was one of several serious Labour Party complaints about the Insurance Act. On January 31, 1913, the party's annual conference had unanimously adopted a resolution demanding that the National insurance Act should be repealed and re-established on a non-contributory basis. This action had followed a speech by Beatrice Webb calling attention to the casual labourer's difficulty with insurance.[99]

Finally, the amending Act excluded from the medical benefit, voluntary contributors earning more than £160 a year, and

---

[98] *National Insurance Gazette*, October 12, 1912.
[99] *Ibid.*, February 8, 1913.

reduced their contribution at the same time by one penny. Thus with the single exception of a compulsorily insured manual worker, the doctors had finally succeeded in establishing a £3, if not a £2, income limit.

The fact that the amending Act made no change in the relation of national health insurance to the nation's hospitals caused some comment. The truth was that British hospitals had suffered far less from health insurance than Sir Henry Burdett or anyone else had believed would be possible. The predictions that the working class would give up any subscription to the voluntary hospitals proved to be incorrect. In his year-book for 1915 Sir Henry conceded generously that 'the greater London hospitals . . . have fortunately been in a position up to the present to bear the burden of National Insurance without grievous injury.'[100]

The other observable trend, certainly a desirable one from a clinical point of view, was a marked decrease in hospital out-patient attendances and an increase in in-patient activity. St Bartholomew's, for instance, had 120,834 out-patient attendances in 1912 and 78,783 in 1913.[101] Birmingham General had 16,261 out-patient attendances in the thirteen weeks before January 15, 1913, and 13,511 in the thirteen weeks following.[102] But equally there was a mounting demand for in-patient services, presumably the result of panel physicians discovering ailments that would otherwise have gone untreated. The growth of the demand for this type of highly specialized service would continue after the interval of the war in a nation far less able to support through individual philanthropy the improving level of medical care that health insurance had taught the British working population to expect.

Health insurance seems to have had far less effect on the other great system of working-class medical care, the poor law. After 1912 the number of men and women receiving both indoor and outdoor medical relief, which had been climbing steadily since the eighties, began to drop. The reversal of this trend was, however, by no means dramatic. No doubt many who were accustomed to

[100] *Burdett's Hospitals and Charities, 1915*, pp. 96–8, quoted in Brian Abel-Smith, *The Hospitals in England and Wales, 1800–1948*, Cambridge, Mass., 1964, p. 246.
[101] *Ibid.*
[102] *National Insurance Gazette*, May 3, 1913.

using the poor law medical facilities were not in any case eligible for insurance.[103]

National health insurance did not reduce dramatically the numbers of English poor who had to resort to the poor law for medical care. But the planners had never intended that it should. The aim of health insurance had not been to provide an alternative to poor law medical facilities, but rather, so far as possible, to enable the English working class to avoid the poor law, and pauperism, altogether. The imminence of pauperism in any time of family sickness was a threat in the lives of all English workmen, but nowhere more than in rural districts where the level of cash wages and the consequent opportunity to save were the lowest. Here, far more than in the cities, national health insurance, like old age pensions, had been greeted with enthusiasm. To an agricultural labourer earning 18s. a week, the assurance of 10s. per week when he was sick was unheard of munificence. Because their paltry incomes made any other form of savings impossible, many agricultural families carried substantial amounts of funeral and endowment insurance even to the extent of depriving themselves of a balanced diet in order to meet premiums.[104]

The problem of the agricultural labourer and of the British land had troubled Lloyd George, as it had many Englishmen, well before the advent of national insurance. He had never been an important supporter of the agricultural colony schemes early in the century, but in numerous speeches he had remarked upon the irony of hunger, idle men, and unused land in a nation striving to build a vigorous imperial race.[105] In the middle of 1912, well before health insurance was fully launched, he turned without pause to the problem of the British countryside.

The insurance Act as finally passed specified in Section 54 that

[103] Helen L. Witmer, 'English Health Insurance and the Poor Law,' *Social Service Review*, VI (March, 1932), 83–107.
[104] See: B. Seebohm Rowntree and May Kendall, *How the Labourer Lives, A Study of the Rural Labour Problem*, London, 1913, pp. 219, 251, 275, 311. Rowntree's book contains much to indicate that contrary to popular opinion, agricultural labourers did not even eat well. National health insurance also extinguished many of the small, unregistered, rural benefit societies and gave unwitting help to the cause of agricultural trade unionism by driving thousands of labourers into the National Agricultural Labourers' Union to register for benefits. Frederick E. Green, *A History of the English Agricultural Labourer 1870–1920*, London, 1927, p. 182.
[105] See speech at Chester, July 28, 1905.

in the investment of reserve funds the insurance commissioners were to give preference to loans to local authority housing. This appears indeed to have been one of the arguments that brought the Chancellor to agree to an accumulating insurance system. But even without this, the solution to the land problem seems to have commended itself to Lloyd George as the natural complement to national insurance. The insurance Act had been designed particularly to handle the problems of an industrial society. Yet there remained in the land the last great stronghold of privilege, the last remnant of feudalism.[106] The Chancellor's attack on landlords begun in the budget of 1909 would be continued, in fact had to continue, for a small effect of old age pensions noted by agricultural labourers was the increase in cottage rentals.[107]

Toward the end of 1911, when the insurance Bill was in its last stages, Lloyd George took the opportunity, while accepting a three-year limitation on the post office deposit scheme, to announce that the two great measures of Liberal social legislation that lay ahead were the reconstruction of the poor law—which would be accomplished in 1913–14 within the three-year limitation—and a full-scale reform of housing, which had not been accomplished by the Housing and Town Planning Act of 1909. Three weeks later, before the National Liberal Federation at Bath, he specified that his particular area of interest was the countryside. National health insurance would clean up the slums in the cities through the powers of insurance commissioners to force local sanitary authorities to do their duty. But rural Britain could not be handled this way, and this, he announced, was the next project.[108]

The story of the land campaign may be told quickly. Lloyd George's principal adviser on the subject appears to have been B. Seebohm Rowntree, whom he appointed to a privately-financed committee headed by Arthur H. Dyke Acland to investigate the conditions of poverty in both rural and urban districts. The rural

[106] The insurance Act comes between two great measures of emancipation, wrote Charles Masterman in the *Nation*, the destruction of the power of the House of Lords and 'the coming changes in our land system.' *Nation*, July 13, 1912.

[107] See: Letter, *Nation*, May 13, 1911.

[108] 'The Next Reform Bill,' *Westminster Gazette*, November 25, 1911. On Lloyd George's personal attitude towards the land problem see Harold Spender, *The Prime Minister*, London, 1920, pp. 175, 356, and George Allardice, Baron Riddell, *More Pages From My Diary, 1908–1914*, London, 1934, pp. 63–6, 151–2.

report was finished in the summer of 1913, and was eventually published in October. By this time Rowntree and the Chancellor were close friends and Lloyd George leaned heavily on his knowledge of poverty.[109]

The Chancellor looked forward to the establishment of a system of land tribunals for setting rents similar to those established in Ireland in 1881. By pulling down the price of agricultural land he would make it possible for labourers to buy their homes with money borrowed from the national health insurance administration. He received official Cabinet approval for his programme on October 16, 1913,[110] and the autumn of 1913 saw the Chancellor laying the lash of his oratory upon the landlords as three years earlier he had denounced the dukes.[111]

The land campaign was cut short by the war, but it appears to have generated little popular enthusiasm. The Liberals made a serious attempt to use the land as an issue in the by-election at Reading on November 8, 1913, when the Chancellor's inaugural promotion of his scheme was at its height. The Reading seat had been vacated by Rufus Isaacs when he was appointed Lord Chief Justice and the Liberal candidate to take his place was the historian, G. P. Gooch, an old friend of Masterman's and an early member of the Christian Social Union. With Gooch, the Liberals lost by a heavy majority a seat they had held since 1900. The Unionst candidate gained more votes than Gooch and the Labour candidate combined.[112]

[109] Asa Briggs, *A Study of the Work of Seebohm Rowntree, 1871–1954*, London, 1961, pp. 62–6. Part of Lloyd George's plan was to make land reform the main issue in the election of 1915. Many rural seats had been lost in 1910 and hopefully would be recaptured. *Ibid.*, p. 66.

[110] Riddell, *Diary*, p. 181.

[111] See the reports of Lloyd George speeches at Bedford, October 11, 1913, regarded by the *Spectator* as the beginning of the land campaign (*Spectator*, October 18, 1913): Swindon, October 22, 1913, Middlesbrough, November 8, 1913; Holloway, November 29, 1913. At Swindon the Chancellor had said that he planned to use national insurance money as capital to build houses for agricultural labourers, who would be charged only the State interest rate of 3 or 3½ per cent. The savings, he said, would go to the labourers. The *Gazette* estimated at that time there were about £10,000,000 in the insurance reserve fund. *National Insurance Gazette*, November 1, 1913.

[112] *The Times*, November 3, November 5, November 10, 1913. The land campaign revived the popular animosity towards health insurance, which had begun to decline. It was at this time that the insurance contribution acquired the name by which it would be known through the twenties and thirties, the 'Lloyd George.' In the autumn of 1913 the *National Insurance Gazette* thought it

By this time all domestic issues were subordinated to Irish home rule. Ulster was preparing rebellion, the South was arming, the British nation appeared to be on the verge of civil war, and Liberalism was dying.[113] The British parliamentary system eventually was able to survive the violence that surrounded the great constitutional and social reform measures of the New Liberalism, but the party itself could not. In attempting to shore up its own political fortunes, Liberalism may have attempted too much. In its social legislation it had ended the inviolability of personal wealth as its reform Bills of the nineteenth century had destroyed the political power of the land. Henceforth, society could call on a man's wealth not only to defend the realm or to promote the welfare of the nation, but to better the economic status and living conditions of specific individuals whom the donor himself did not choose. At bottom this was a project of which too many Liberals, both in and out of the Government, disapproved. The party of the industrial revolution, of economic and political individualism, of peace, retrenchment, and reform, refused to accept enthusiastically the programmes that might have saved it. And the Labour voter, whom Lloyd George and Churchill hoped to gain for it, could never be brought to trust the old leaders of Liberalism. The party of Gladstone had waited too long. The horizontal division of politics, the 'cleavage of classes' that Harcourt had predicted before the turn of the century, could not be papered over by even the most comprehensive programme of social reform.

of interest to print the reply to the magistrate of a man in the South Shields Police Court. When asked the amount of his wages, he answered: 'Twenty-five shillings, less Lloyd George.' *National Insurance Gazette*, October 11, 1913.

[113] Lisle March Phillipps had warned the Government towards the end of 1912 against undertaking land reform on the basis that Liberalism could not stand another period of strain like national health insurance. 'Mr Lloyd George and the Country,' *English Review*, XII (November, 1912), 631–42.

CONCLUSION

In any attempt to deduce a theme from the Liberal experiments in social reform the student realizes first that there are really two epochs of reform in the Edwardian period. Of the six measures discussed in this study, three—feeding of school children, the school medical service, and old age pensions—were reforms not necessarily Liberal in origin. These measures had long been under discussion if not by the public at large at least among a considerable group of enthusiasts. Their political story repeats the familiar history of such nineteenth-century reforms as Penny Postage, repeal of the corn laws, or free education: extraparliamentary discussion, petition, lobby delegations, waiting upon ministers and M.P.s, until one party or the other became convinced of political profit to be garnered from the measure in question. Only when this occurred did the proposal become political in the technical sense.

The second triad of Liberal reforms, labour exchanges, unemployment insurance, and health insurance, was as removed in origin from the first three as if the measures had been enacted in another country. In fact these owed more to Germany than to any British model. The impulse behind this second phase of reform activity can hardly be described as philanthropic. National insurance was the Liberal response to the threat of socialism. The emergency had its origin in the decay of the deterrent principle of poor relief. This had been inevitable since the enactment of household franchise in 1885, when the poor, for whom parochial relief was supposed to be a salutary and disciplining force, obtained the vote. In effect the choice of the warden had been turned over to the prisoners. The breakdown of the deterrent system was as clear in 1908 as the pernicious effects of rate-aided wages had been in 1832 but Asquith's Government unlike its Whig predecessor, was faced by a democratic franchise. On one hand it could not leave the national provision for distress as it was without losing the votes of labour and inviting still more consideration of a full-fledged socialist alternative. But neither would the old Gladstonians among the Liberals permit the abolition of the poor law.

The Government's option then—it can hardly be said there was a decision—was to do nothing about the poor law but to erect beside it, although totally separated, a series of new institutions that hopefully would obviate the need for it. One may imagine that in the distance there glimmered for Lloyd George and Masterman the ideal of a framework of contributory insurance institutions by which the city labourer, the agricultural labourer, the aged, and the children would have available such an apparatus for the prevention of distress that the poor law would become redundant and, like State machinery under pure communism, would wither away. Certainly Lloyd George was not planning for this day; but he never planned for anything. He proceeded by intuition and flashes of insight. In his mind, one programme suggested another. Emotionally he knew the world he wished to see. His route there would be determined by circumstances along the way.

As it turned out he never reached his goal. The violence of British politics in the last years before the war, to which he himself contributed so much, made impossible any further work on reform even after the parliamentary phase of Irish home rule was concluded. In the war the man himself was changed, like many others. He wasted the four years given him after the peace when he could have begun the reconstruction planned during the conflict and when he might have given the returning soldier a few elements of the better world he had promised.

A second point to be made about the beginnings of British social reform is the noticeable distortion in political processes caused by welfare legislation. Since the days of the Roman republic, politicians have discovered that State measures for popular welfare were difficult to oppose. During the nineteenth century the two leading British parties had refrained, by implicit agreement, from competing openly in measures that would fall within the definition of social legislation. In a nation where both parties were dominated by aristocracy or near aristocracy, with a limited franchise, this compromise was easy to maintain. But after 1885, as Sidney Webb had warned the Royal Commission on the Aged Poor, it was inevitable that the labouring man would begin to use his vote, not on matters of war and peace, or even the party affiliation of the ambassador at Paris, but to determine questions of far greater concern to him, the conditions under which he lived and worked.

P

As a result, in the last quarter century before the war, national politics operated at two levels. One, the traditional level, concerned the ancient affairs of State—war and peace, foreign policy, or oil-fired battleships and army reserves. Also included in the traditional politics were the more prosaic matters customarily associated by the Liberals with the word 'reform,' the Irish union, the Church of England, the House of Lords, and most of all, the land. Here lay the only form of wealth the traditional Liberal could attack, as hereditary privilege was the only form of privilege. For most members of Campbell-Bannerman's and Asquith's Cabinets, for most of the leaders of the Liberal constituency associations, and for many traditional Liberal voters in the professions, in business, and in the civil service, these questions constituted the whole substance of politics. Economic liberty meant the right to enter the civil service without an aristocratic patron or to receive compensation for improvements made on rented land; it did not mean that the State had an obligation to help a worker find a new job or to support him while he looked. Because one did not wish to be represented in Parliament by the heir of a county family, it did not follow that his choice would be a trade union secretary.

Thus for many Edwardian Liberals, and for many of their historians, the politics of the people, as it was beginning to be called, was not only of little interest, but positively distasteful. But precisely in this area lay the concern of the Labour Representation Committee, the Liberal radical, and the occasional surviving Tory democrat such as Sir John Gorst. On this account there could occur the political paradox seen in the Debate on the Address in 1907, when a Government with a newly-elected and overwhelming majority in the House of Commons narrowly escaped defeat over old age pensions, a proposal that had been entirely absent from the official manifestoes of both parties during the general election in 1906.

Because of this studied disregard, welfare legislation never figured as an electoral issue in the years before World War I. Nor was it debated within Westminster Palace upon the ground of whether as a principle it was a desirable or an undesirable thing for the British population. The Unionists never opposed national health insurance as they opposed Irish home rule, the reform of the House of Lords, the restriction of pub licences, or the elimination of the Church from public education. Only on the single occasion of the debate on the feeding of school children was the principle of the measure discussed with intelligence and enthusiasm. On all other reform measures the opposition either simply failed in its duty to oppose, as in school medical inspection, or sought to extend coverage and benefits to make the proposal ruinously expensive as in old age pensions and to some extent in national health insurance. Lloyd George described this tactic as sinking the ship by overloading it. Consequently the political story of Liberal social legislation, and to a great extent the history of all social legislation, cannot be written in terms of parliamentary debate or even in the ordinary extraparliamentary partisan intrigue. Social legislation is the one form of legal enactment that an opposition responsible to a democratic electorate dare not fight. Indeed almost the only way that a minority party can defend itself against bread and circuses is by killing their sponsor. As the careers of C. F. G. Masterman, Winston Churchill, David Lloyd George, and for that matter Franklin Delano Roosevelt, demonstrate, the political life of a proposer of social legislation is singularly dangerous.

These reflections upon the lives of the men who first received effective political power in the New Liberalism lead to the third major conclusion of this study. Considering the size of the group of Liberal radicals and moderate Labourites who were involved, the magnitude of the achievement can be described only as stupendous. Great Britain was diverted from a socialist solution to the problem of poverty and was turned instead to the establishment of the institution of social insurance. The profit system, with its vagaries and caprices, was left intact. Taken altogether the group was far smaller, and more homogeneous, than the House of Commons. The early architects of the welfare state, including even David Lloyd George, were not at the centre of the Liberal establishment. Asquith's confidants were Gray and Haldane, Crewe and J. A. Spender, not Churchill, and certainly not Lloyd George. These two represented, virtually alone in the Cabinet, the cause of reform. To support them, they had in the House of Commons, in the civil service, and in the serious political press, a small number of young men who had been concerned with the condition of the people long before it became an important formal political matter. Held together by backgrounds in the university settlements and the friendship of H. W. Massingham, Samuel

Barnett, and H. Scott Holland, these men were able to achieve within a few years a legislative revolution. They took the British State into an entirely new field of activity and although by no means solving the problem of the condition of the people, they settled the lines upon which the eventual solution would be found. They discovered and navigated the narrow channel between rigid and authoritarian Fabian dogmatics and emotional, irresponsible Toryism, which looked for an answer to social questions in the return to a hierarchical society that had never existed. In the end, even though Liberalism died as a political force, its moderate and essentially British ideal remained alive. The architects of the modern welfare state accepted the British worker as the frequently improvident and self-indulgent man he was. They did not seek to provide him with charity, and they tried to reform neither the worker nor the economic system in which he made his living. Rather they required him by law to provide for himself and his family so that he could better withstand the vagaries of capitalism. The British working man remains therefore at liberty, free from both the paternal factory owner and the omnipotent relieving officer. Social insurance, compulsory self insurance, has provided the armour that allows the increasingly desperate, but still free, human atom to live in an ever more complex and oppressive industrial society.

BIBLIOGRAPHY

The following items represent the most valuable sources for the purposes of this study. The list includes in addition a few works that the researcher should perhaps avoid. A number of extremely useful but well-known general surveys of the period have been omitted in the interest of brevity. Omitted also are several standard statistical references, notably *Whitaker's Almanack*, which contains more history than almost any other source. For some reason a few otherwise well-run libraries throw away the superseded copies of this invaluable work.

CONTEMPORARY MATERIALS

UNPUBLISHED SOURCES

(A) Letter Collections

1. Asquith Papers—New Bodleian Library.

   These papers reflect Asquith's general lack of interest in social reform other than old age pensions. They contain an extremely useful, hitherto unworked, box of letters and government documents on pensions.

2. Balfour Papers—British Museum.

   Very little on social reform except for the Education Act of 1902, but contain many letters from the Webbs, Morant, and Joseph Chamberlain.

3. Beveridge Papers—London School of Economics.

   Extremely useful on the background of labour exchanges, both for the public campaign and the preparation of the Bill and for the preparation of the unemployment insurance scheme. Contain much correspondence from Winston Churchill illuminating his thinking during his life as a Liberal radical.

4. Bradbury Papers—Public Record Office.

   Of little use but contain some important unpublished printed memoranda on the National Insurance Bill.

5. Braithwaite Papers—London School of Economics.

   Extremely useful. The collection follows Braithwaite's memoirs, but contains a great deal of material unprinted in that book.

6. Burns Papers—British Museum.

   Useful for the correspondence from the Webbs and George Bernard Shaw. The collection demonstrates Burns' separation from the central activity of social reform.

7. Campbell-Bannerman Papers—British Museum.
   Little on Liberal reform. Useful for the politics of national efficiency.

8. Austen Chamberlain Papers—University of Birmingham.
   Some material on the background of national health insurance.

9. Joseph Chamberlain Papers—University of Birmingham.
   Contain some material, not so much as one would expect, on old age pensions.

10. Ripon Papers—British Museum.
    Little on reform. Useful for tracing the thoughts and activities of Campbell-Bannerman with whom Ripon was intimate.

11. Webb Papers—London School of Economics.
    The Webbs wrote voluminously to everyone. However, one feels, after using this correspondence, that he has learned more about the Webbs than about the topics that interested them.

This writer, like others, regrets the inaccessibility of the Lloyd George Papers. But he feels that Lord Beaverbrook's long closure of them has practically destroyed their usefulness for the historian of the New Liberalism. Certainly the books of the two writers who claim to have used them recently, R. J. Minney and Frank Owen, did not demonstrate much knowledge that would not be available through a careful perusal, which neither of them made, of printed sources.

(B) Unpublished Government Materials

1. Education, Ministry of
   a. *Bill File: Education (Provision of Meals) Bill, Papers Leading up to the Bill.*
   b. *Private Office Papers.*

2. Pensions and National Insurance, Ministry of
   a. *Bill File: Old Age Pensions, 1908, S. B. Provis.*
   b. *Bill File: National Insurance Bill, 1911, Part 1—to Second Reading (Commons).*
   c. *Bill File: National Insurance Bill, 1911, Part 2—Committee Stage (Commons).*
   d. *Bill File: National Insurance Bill, 1911, Part 3—Report to Third Reading (Commons).*

3. Public Record Office, *Cabinet Papers, 1880–1914, Cab. 37.*

4. Trade, Board of, Central Offices for Labour Exchanges and Unemployment Insurance, Unemployment Insurance 191, 'Repayments to Associations Under Section 106,' June, 1913.
   Subtitled: 'Particulars of Associations Which Have Given Notice

of Their Intention to Apply for a Repayment Under Section 106 of the National Insurance Act, 1911, Which Have Adopted Systems Deemed by the Board of Trade to Be Satisfactory' (scrapbook with printed insertions).

PRINTED SOURCES

(A) Periodicals, Newspapers, and Yearbooks

1. *Assurance Agents' Chronicle.*
   Organ of the National Union of Life Assurance Agents.

2. *Daily News.*
   A. G. Gardiner, editor.

3. *The Times* (London).

4. *Commonwealth, A Christian Social Magazine.*
   Henry Scott Holland, editor.

5. *Contemporary Review.*
   Sir Percy W. Bunting, editor.

6. *Depositor.*
   Organ of the National Deposit Friendly Society.

7. *Edinburgh Review.*
   A. R. D. Ellis, editor.

8. *English Review.*

9. *Fabian Quarterly.*

10. *Financier and Bullionist.*
    Incorporated into the *Financial Times* after World War I.

11. *Fortnightly Review.*
    Editors: Frank Harris, 1886–94; W. L. Courtney, 1894–1928.

12. Hearts of Oak Benefit Society, *Annual Statement*, 1908–11.

13. Hearts of Oak Benefit Society, *Delegate Minutes*, 1910–12.

14. Independent Order of Odd Fellows, Manchester Unity, Friendly Society, *Quarterly Reports*, 1908–12.

15. Independent Order of Odd Fellows, Manchester Unity, Friendly Society, *Reports of Annual Movable Conference*, 1908–12.

16. *Insurance Mail*, 'A Weekly Review Devoted Chiefly to Industrial Life Insurance Affairs.'

17. *Manchester Guardian.*

18. *Medical Directory*, 1911, 1912.

19. *Medical Register*, 1911, 1912.

20. *Nation.*
    Henry W. Massingham, editor.

21. National Conference of Friendly Societies, *Resolutions of the Annual Meeting*, 1909–12.

22. National Deposit Friendly Society, 'Minutes of the General Committee,' 1910–12.

23. *National Insurance Gazette.*

24. *National Insurance Yearbook.*

25. *National Review.*
    Leo Maxse, editor.

26. *Nature.*

27. *New Age.*
    Joseph Clayton, editor, 1906–7, succeeded by A. R. Orage.

28. *New Statesman.*
    Clifford Sharp, editor.

29. *Nineteenth Century.*
    James Knowles, to 1908; William Roy Skilbeck, 1909–19.

30. *Oddfellows' Magazine.*
    Organ of the I.O.O.F., Manchester Unity.

31. *Post Magazine Almanack, The Insurance Directory, Reference and Yearbook*, London, 1912.

32. *Post Magazine and Insurance Monitor.*

33. *Quarterly Review.*

34. *Speaker.*
    Henry W. Massingham, editor.

35. *Spectator.*
    J. St Loe Strachey, editor.

36. Toynbee Hall, *Annual Reports.*

37. *Westminster Gazette.*
    J. A. Spender, editor.

38. *Westminster Review.*

39. *Labour Annual.*

40. *Liberal Yearbook.*

(B) *Published Government Documents*
1. Parliamentary Papers.
    a. Papers by Command.
    b. Other Parliamentary Papers.

No. 444, 1881, 'Paupers, Indoor (Members of Benefit Societies.)' Local Government Board return, March 31, 1881.

No. 366, 1891, 'Paupers, Indoor (Members of Benefit Societies.)' Local Government Board return, July 24, 1891.

No. 265, 1892, 'Poor Law (Indoor and Out-door Relief.)' Local Government Board return, June 14, 1892.

No. 171, 1910, 'Report of the Chief Registrar of Friendly Societies for the year ending 31st December, 1909.'

'Special Report and Report from the Select Committee on the Education (Provision of Meals) Bill, 1906; and the Education (Provision of Meals) (Scotland) Bill, 1906,' *P.P.*, Reports from Committees, 1906, VIII, Part 3, 288.

2. *Hansard, Parliamentary Debates*, Series 3, Series 4.

3. *Official Report, House of Commons Debates*, Series 5.

4. *Official Report, House of Lords Debates*, Series 5.

(C) Contemporary Books or Pamphlets of a Polemical, Didactic, or Partisan Nature

1. Alden, Percy. *Democratic England*. New York, 1912.
   Introduction by C. F. G. Masterman. Alden formerly Warden of Mansfield House. A good statement of the Liberal radical point of view on reform.

2. ——. *The Unemployed, A National Question*. London, 1905.
   Foreword by Sir John E. Gorst. An early demand for unemployment insurance.

3. Barnett, Samuel A. and Henrietta O. *Towards Social Reform*. New York, 1909.
   A collection of magazine articles written between 1895 and 1908, some in otherwise unobtainable journals.

4. Bell, Mrs Hugh (Lady Bell). *At the Works: A Study of a Manufacturing Town*. London, 1907.
   Dedicated to Charles Booth. Result of interviews in Middlesbrough in North Yorkshire. Very useful. One of the early attempts at systematic social research stimulated by Booth and Rowntree.

5. Belloc, Hilaire. *The Servile State*. Boston, 1912.
   An attack on the New Liberalism, particularly health insurance.

6. Blackley, M. J. J. *Thrift and National Insurance as a Security Against Pauperism, With a Memoir of the Late Rev. Canon Blackley and a Reprint of His Essays*. London, 1906.
   A paperback pamphlet aimed at reviving the Blackley scheme put together by Blackley's wife and several members of Chamberlain's pension committee.

P*

7. Blatchford, Robert. *Britain for the British*. London, 1902.
Very influential in its day.

8. ——. *Dismal England*. London, 1899.
The poor's world.

9. Booth, Charles. *Life and Labour of the People of London*. I (London, 1892).

10. ——. *Old Age Pensions and the Aged Poor*. London, 1899.
The first detailed statement of Booth's plan for pensions.

11. ——. *Pauperism, A Picture and the Endowment of Old Age, An Argument*. London, 1892.

12. Booth, William. *In Darkest England and the Way Out*. New York, 1891.
The original proposal for land colonies. Very influential.

13. Brabrook, Sir Edward W. *Institutions for Thrift*. London, 1905.
Paperback pamphlet, a reprint of two lectures given at the University of Liverpool School of Training for Social Work.

14. ——. *Provident Societies and Industrial Welfare*. London, 1898.
Extremely useful. Much statistical data on the condition of friendly societies. Contains some early charges against industrial insurance.

15. Bray, J. Dyer. *The Doctors and the Insurance Act: A Statement of the Medical Man's Case Against the Act*. Manchester, 1912.
Paperback pamphlet. No indication of any connexion with the British Medical Association. Generally a moderate and informative statement.

16. Bray, Reginald A. *The Town Child*. London, 1907.
Exposé of the physical conditions among slum children. Draws much material from the Interdepartmental Committee on Physical Deterioration.

17. Burgess, Joseph. *John Burns: The Rise and Progress of a Right Honourable*. Glasgow, 1911.
A Labour attack on Burns' record as a Labour leader and Cabinet Minister. Went through four printings in 1911.

18. Charity Organization Society. *Miscellaneous Pamphlets, 1870–84*.
A useful collection bound together by the British Museum.

19. Churchill, Winston S. *Liberalism and the Social Problem*. London, 1909.
Collected speeches, 1905–9. Introduction by Henry W. Massingham in which the phrase 'the new liberalism' occurs for the first time.

20. Coulton, G. G. *Public Schools and Public Needs*. London, 1901.
An attack on the English public schools in the name of national efficiency.

21. Cramb, John Adam. *Reflections on the Origins and Destiny of Imperial Britain*. London, 1900.
Lectures delivered at Queen's College. A textbook of late Victorian imperialism.

22. Drage, Geoffrey. *Public Assistance*. London, 1930.
Collection of Drage's writings. The author was an influential pre-Webbian social thinker of the C.O.S. school. Gave his name to the Drage reports on the annual cost of social services.

23. ——. *The State and the Poor*. London, 1914.

24. Engels, Frederick. *The Condition of the Working-Class in England in 1844*. London, 1892.
First edition published in Great Britain in English. One had been published in the U.S.A. in 1886.

25. Evans, Laming Worthington, ed. *The National Insurance Bill, 1911*. London, 1912.
Pamphlet published by the National Conservative Union apparently in response to Lloyd George's *The People's Insurance*.

26. Gibbon, Sir Ioan Gwilym. *Medical Benefit: A Study of the Experience of Germany and Denmark*. London, 1912.

27. ——. *Unemployment Insurance, A Study of Schemes of Assisted Insurance*. London, 1911.
Gibbon's doctoral dissertation written before the National Insurance Bill was presented.

28. Gorst, Sir John E. *The Children of the Nation*. New York, 1907.

29. Greville, Frances Evelyn, Countess of Warwick. *A Nation's Youth*. London, 1900.
Foreword by Sir John E. Gorst.

30. Hobson, John A. *The Crisis of Liberalism: New Issue of Democracy*. London, 1909.
A statement to rank with Massingham's introduction to Churchill's *Liberalism and the Social Problem* as an exposition of the New Liberalism.

31. Horsfall, T. C. *The Example of Germany*. Manchester, 1904.
Horsfall wrote for the *Workingmen's Times*, which competed with Blatchford's *Clarion*. The book was influential in turning popular British attention, as opposed to professional reformers, to German social legislation.

32. Lloyd George, David. *The People's Insurance.* London, 1911.
A pamphlet made up of selections from speeches, letters, and a copy of the Bill as passed by the House of Commons. No original material.

33. Loch, Sir Charles S. *Charity and Social Life.* London, 1910.
A good summary of the C.O.S. position on most things.

34. ——. *The National Insurance Bill.* London, 1911.
Pamphlet, published in October, 1911. An attack on health insurance warning, among other things, of the danger of malingering after the transfer of the medical benefit.

35. McCurdy, C. A. and Lees Smith, H. B. *The People's Guide to the Insurance Act.* 3rd ed. London, 1912.
A pamphlet of the Liberal Insurance Committee by two M.P.s.

36. Macnamara, Thomas J. *The Great Insurance Act. Addresses to the Working Man.* London, n.d. (preface dated January, 1912).
Addresses to Macnamara's constituents in North Camberwell.

37. Massingham, H. J., ed. *H. W. M., A Selection From the Writings of H. W. Massingham.* London, 1925.

38. Masterman, Charles Frederick Gurney. *The Condition of England.* 7th ed., London, 1912.
Extremely influential. A gloomy apocalyptic discussion of the decadence of English society. Went through seven editions between 1909 and 1912.

39. ——, ed. *The Heart of the Empire.* London, 1901.
An attack on imperialism and a call for reform.

40. Mearns, Andrew. *The Bitter Cry of Outcast London: An Inquiry Into the Condition of the Abject Poor.* London, 1883.
'Published on behalf of the London Congregational Union, sponsored by the Rev. Andrew Mearns.' Sometimes attributed to William Preston.

41. Money, Sir Leo G. Chiozza. *A Nation Insured.* London, 1912.
Pamphlet published by the Liberal Publications Department.

42. ——. *Riches and Poverty.* 10th ed. London, 1911.
Extremely influential. Went through ten editions between October, 1905, and March, 1911.

43. ——. *The Truth About Insurance.* London, 1912.
Pamphlet published by the *Daily Chronicle.*

44. Newman, George. *The Health of the State.* London, 1907.
One of a series of 'Social Service Handbooks' edited by Percy Alden, attempting to direct attention to social problems.

45. Paulin, Sir David. *Old Age Pensions and Pauperism*. Edinburgh, 1896.

46. Pease, Edward R. *The Municipal Public House*. London, 1904.

47. Raine, G. E. *Lloyd George and the Land, An Exposure and an Appeal*. London, 1914.
    Paperback pamphlet. Raine was a Unionist hack writer.

48. ——. *The Real Lloyd George*. London, 1913.

49. 'A Ratepayer.' *National Efficiency and the Drink Traffic*. London, 1906.
    Preface by R. B. Haldane.

50. Robertson, John M. *Wrecking the Empire*. London, 1901.

51. Rowntree, Arnold S. *The Insurance Act Explained*. Darlington, 1912.
    Liberal pamphlet, published by the *Northern Echo*.

52. Rowntree, B. Seebohm. *Poverty, A Study of Town Life*. London, 1901.
    Of first-rate importance. In many ways more useful for this study than Booth's investigation.

53. —— and Kendall, May. *How the Labourer Lives, A Study of the Rural Labour Problem*. London, 1913.
    Extremely useful. Gives information on the effect of Liberal reform legislation on the land. Part of the research for the land campaign.

54. —— and Lasker, Bruno. *Unemployment, A Social Study*. London, 1911.

55. Samuel, Herbert. *Liberalism, An Attempt to State the Principles and Proposals of Contemporary Liberalism in England*. London, 1902.
    Introduced by H. H. Asquith.

56. Schloss, David F. *Insurance Against Unemployment*. London, 1909.
    Very informative. A well-organized survey of European unemployment insurance programmes extant in 1909.

57. Shadwell, Arthur. *Industrial Efficiency, A Comparative Study of Industrial Life in England, Germany and America*. 2 Vols. (London, 1906).
    Very well reviewed at the time of publication but not a very scientific study. Much generalization from personal impression.

58. Shaw, George Bernard. *A Plea for Municipal Trading*. London, 1904.

59. Strachey, J. St Loe, ed. *The Manufacture of Paupers: A Protest and a Policy*. London, 1907.

A collection of articles that appeared in the *Spectator* between May and July, 1906. Many of the writers, such as W. A. Bailward and William Chance, were connected with the Charity Organisation Society.

60. Watson, Alfred W. *An Account of the Investigation of the Sickness and Mortality Experience of the I.O.O.F., Manchester Unity, During the Five Years 1893–1897*. Manchester, 1903.

A huge, invaluable, statistical analysis of friendly society difficulties. Nothing else like it exists. Introduction by R. W. Moffrey.

61. Webb, Sidney and Beatrice. *Industrial Democracy*. London, 1920.

First published in 1897.

62. White, Arnold, *Efficiency and Empire*. London, 1901.

An exemplary Kiplingesque attack by an imperialist on softness behind the lines. 'Things aren't what they used to be,' 'Smart Set.' Foreign blood diluting the race.

63. ——. *The Great Idea*. London, 1909.

Story of the Salvation Army.

64. ——. *The Problems of a Great City*. 3rd ed. London, 1895.

One of the many lurid descriptions of the London slums.

65. ——. *Tries at the Truth*. London, 1891.

A volume of essays on social reform.

66. Woodcock, Dr Herbert De Carle. *The Doctor and the People*. London, 1912.

An attempt by a well-known specialist to make a balanced assessment of national health insurance.

SECONDARY MATERIAL

SCHOLARLY OR TECHNICAL MATERIAL ON SPECIALIZED TOPICS

(A) Periodicals

1. *American Historical Review.*
2. *American Medical Association, Journal.*
3. *American Political Science Review.*
4. *British Medical Journal.*
5. *Chartered Insurance Institute, Journal.*
6. *Economica.*

7. *Economic History Review.*

8. *Economic Journal.*
   The journal of the Royal Economic Society, which had a very influential membership. The editor after 1911 was John Maynard Keynes.

9. *Economic Review.*
   'Published quarterly for the Oxford Branch of the Christian Social Union.'

10. *Historical Journal.*

11. *Institute of Actuaries, Journal.*
    Extremely useful and difficult to obtain. Many of the leaders of industrial insurance, although none of the friendly society leaders, except Alfred Watson, were members of the Institute.

12. *Insurance Institute of London, Journal.*

13. *Journal of Economic History.*

14. *Journal of Modern History.*

15. *Journal of the History of Ideas.*

16. *Lancet.*
    Far more moderate and in many ways better informed than the *British Medical Journal* during the period of national health insurance.

17. *Political Quarterly.*

18. *Political Science Quarterly.*

19. *Practitioner* (London).
    Had a brief period of prosperity as the resort for many rebels from the British Medical Association.

20. *Public Health.*
    The journal of the medical officers of health. Arthur Newsholme, editor until 1908. G. F. McCleary, editor after February, 1908.

21. *Royal Statistical Society, Journal.*
    A rarely used, and invaluable, source of specialized numerical data on all problems of social conditions and social reform.

22. *Social Service Review.*

23. *Toynbee Record.*
    Edited by W. H. Beveridge during his stay at Toynbee Hall from 1903 to 1907.

(*B*) *Books or Pamphlets.*

1. Armstrong, Barbara N. *The Health Insurance Doctor, His Role in Great Britain, Denmark and France.* Princeton, 1939.
   A published doctoral dissertation with some useful statistics.

2. Barnard, R. W. *A Century of Service, The Story of the Prudential, 1848–1948.* London, 1948.
   Mostly on the Prudential before 1900. A publicity puff.

3. Beveridge, William H. *Unemployment, A Problem of Industry.* Rev. ed. London, 1931.
   Contains a valuable history, added to the 1909 edition, of labour exchanges and unemployment insurance. Many useful statistics.

4. ——. *Voluntary Action, A Report on Methods of Social Advance.* London, 1948.
   Part of Beveridge's fight to retain a place for friendly societies in the welfare state. A good description of friendly society work and an attack on industrial insurance.

5. Brown, Charles and Taylor, Joseph. *Friendly Societies.* Cambridge, 1933.
   A pamphlet published by the Institute of Actuaries Students' Society.

6. Brown, E. H. Phelps. *The Growth of British Industrial Relations.* London, 1959.
   An important study.

7. Bryant, Louise S. *School Feeding, Its Origin and Practice At Home and Abroad.* Philadelphia, 1913.
   Contains much information on British activity.

8. Clegg, Cyril. *Friend in Deed.* London, 1958.
   The history of the Refuge Assurance Company.

9. Cohen, Joseph L. *Insurance Against Unemployment.* London, 1921.
   Deals with the United States and the United Kingdom, a standard work.

10. Cohen, Percy. *The British System of Social Insurance.* London, 1932.
    Chiefly a description of the system as it existed in 1932.

11. Collie, Sir John. *Malingering and Feigned Sickness.* 2nd ed., London, 1917.
    A standard work. Deals mostly with workman's compensation cases.

12. Collis, Edgar L. and Greenwood, Major. *The Health of the Industrial Worker.* London, 1921.
    A basic textbook on industrial working conditions.

13. Dublin, Louis I. and Lotka, J. *Length of Life, A Study of the Life Table.* New York, 1936.

14. Finer, S. E. *Anonymous Empire, A Study of the Lobby in Great Britain.* London, 1958.

15. Gosden, P. H. J. H. *The Friendly Societies in England, 1815–1875.* Manchester, 1961.
    A useful study that should be carried forward.

16. Hoffman, Frederick L. *More Facts and Fallacies of Compulsory Health Insurance.* Newark, New Jersey, 1920.
    Hoffman was a vice-president of the Prudential of America.

17. ——. *Poor Law Aspects of National Health Insurance.* Newark, New Jersey, 1920.
    Paperback pamphlet, a reprint of a paper given at the National Conference of Social Work in New Orleans.

18. Hogarth, Archibald H. *Medical Inspection of Schools.* London, 1909.
    Chiefly a handbook for inspectors.

19. Humphreys, Noel A., ed. *Vital Statistics: A Memorial Volume of Selections from the Reports and Writings of William Farr.* London, 1885.

20. Industrial Life Offices' Association. *Jubilee Brochure, 1901–1951.* London, 1951.
    A pamphlet published in the fiftieth anniversary of the founding of the Combine. One of the few sources for personal data on the members of that organization.

21 Kelynack, T. N., ed. *Medical Examination of Schools and Scholars.* London, 1910.

22. Little, Ernest M. *History of the British Medical Association.* London, 1932.
    Slightly useful. The chapter on national health insurance was written by Alfred Cox.

23. Moffrey, R. W. *A Century of Odd Fellowship.* Manchester, 1910.
    A history of the Manchester Unity by a Grand Master of the order.

24. Morrah, Dermot. *A History of Industrial Life Assurance.* London, 1955.
    To be avoided. Commissioned by the Associated Offices.

25. Mowat, Charles Loch. *The Charity Organization Society, 1869–1913, Its Ideas and Works.* London, 1961.
    Very useful. Written from Loch's papers.

26. Newman, Sir George. *The Building of a Nation's Health*. London, 1939.
   The life work of a great public servant.

27. Newsholme, Sir Arthur. *Fifty Years in Public Health*. London, 1935.
   Should be read with Newman above.

28. Plaisted, H. *The Prudential, Past and Present*. London, n.d. [1917].
   The author was an officer of the Prudential.

29. Potter, Allen. *Organized Groups in British Politics*. London, 1961.
   An excellent study of lobbying.

30. Roberts, Dr Harry. *A National Health Policy*. London, 1923.
   A species of political pamphlet by a highly successful East End panel practitioner.

31. Rooff, Madeline. *Voluntary Societies and Social Policy*. London, 1957.
   Has a useful chapter on the development of maternity and child welfare services, mostly taken from McCleary.

32. Sandall, Robert. *The History of the Salvation Army*. Vol. III: *Social Reform and Welfare Work, 1883–1953*. (London, 1955.)
   A bad history of a great organization that needs a good history. Chiefly an advertisement for William Booth.

33. Sinclair, J. G. *Evils of Industrial Assurance, An Examination of the Secret Methods Used in the System*. London, 1932.
   An attack on the companies by a former agent. Some useful information on the handling of books and on sales methods.

34. Stewart, J. P. *British Pressure Groups, Their Role in Relation to the House of Commons*. Oxford, 1958.
   Sociological.

35. Turner, E. S. *Call the Doctor, A Social History of Medical Men*. New York, 1959.
   Useful.

36. Vaughan, Paul. *Doctors' Commons: A Short History of the British Medical Association*. London, 1959.
   The author was the publicity officer of the B.M.A. Nevertheless this is a good book, by no means uncritical of association policy.

37. Whitelegge, Sir Arthur and Newman, Sir George. *Hygiene and Public Health*. 12th ed. London, 1911.
   A standard textbook for medical officers of health.

38. Wilson, Sir Arnold and Levy, Hermann. *Industrial Assurance: An Historical and Critical Study*. London, 1937.

A violent attack on industrial insurance, well informed, but slipshod in scholarship.

GENERAL SECONDARY SOURCES

(*A*) *Biographies, Memoirs, Edited Diaries, Biographical Sketches, and Autobiographies*

1. Adams, William S. *Edwardian Portraits*. London, 1957.

Contains a caustic chapter on Baden-Powell.

2. Addison, Christopher. *Politics From Within, 1911–1918*. I (London, 1924).

During the enactment of national health insurance Addison was by no means so close to the centre of affairs as he was later.

3. Allen, Bernard M. *Sir Robert Morant, A Great Public Servant*. London, 1934.

A basic source in the 'Morant legend.'

4. Amery, Leopold S. *My Political Life*. I (London, 1953).

5. Anderson Mosa. *Noel Buxton*. London, 1952.

Foreword by G. P. Gooch. Contains a good deal about the Christian Social Union.

6. Ausubel, Herman. *In Hard Times: Reformers Among the Late Victorians*. New York, 1960.

Not a very good book. Suffers from too great a reliance on primary material.

7. Barnes, George N. *From Workshop to War Cabinet*. New York, 1924.

Contains some useful material on old age pensions.

8. Barnett, Henrietta O. *Canon Barnett, His Life, Work, and Friends*. 3rd ed. 2 Vols. (London, 1921).

A useful, but badly edited, collection of letters with a running commentary by Mrs Barnett. Has become an important source since the Toynbee Hall library was destroyed by bombing.

9. Bennett, Arnold. *The Journal of Arnold Bennett*. New York, 1933.

10. Beveridge, William H. *Power and Influence: An Autobiography*. New York, 1955.

Very useful for early agitation on reform. Unfortunately marred by special pleading on the Beveridge Report.

11. Birrell, Augustine. *Things Past Redress*. London, 1937.

12. Blake, Robert N. *The Unknown Prime Minister: The Life and Times of Andrew Bonar Law, 1858–1923.* London, 1955.
    Useful on politics. Tends, like the biographies of other leading political figures of the period, to disregard social reform.

13. Blatchford, Robert. *My Eighty Years.* London, 1931.
    Concentrates on Blatchford's life before the turn of the century. Understandably, there is very little on his later life.

14. Anon. (Mrs Charles Booth). *Charles Booth, A Memoir.* London, 1918.

15. Briggs, Asa. *A Study of the Work of Seebohm Rowntree, 1871–1954.* London, 1961.
    A workmanlike biography.

16. Bunbury, Sir Henry N., ed. *Lloyd George's Ambulance Wagon: Being the Memoirs of William J. Braithwaite, 1911–1912.* London, 1957.
    Extremely valuable but must be used with care. Braithwaite's knowledge of politics was limited, his prejudices were strong and his recollections, even based on his diary, not always accurate.

17. Carter, Violet Bonham. *Winston Churchill, An Intimate Portrait.* New York, 1965.
    A fascinating book with little new political information.

18. Chamberlain, Sir Austen. *Politics From Inside.* London, 1936.
    Useful, but selective in topics covered.

19. Cole, Margaret I., ed. *Beatrice Webb's Diaries, 1912–24.* London, 1952.

20. ——. *The Webbs and Their Work.* London, 1949.
    Contains an extremely useful essay by R. C. K. Ensor.

21. Cox, Alfred. *Among the Doctors.* London, 1950.
    Cox was assistant and Medical Secretary of the British Medical Association during the passage of national health insurance, yet of very humble origins himself and sympathetic with the general practitioner.

22. Cresswell, D'Arcy. *Margaret McMillan, A Memoir.* London, 1948.
    Not to be used if anything else is available.

23. Crewe, Marquess of. *Lord Rosebery.* II (London, 1931).
    The standard biography.

24. De Mendelssohn, Peter. *The Age of Churchill: Heritage and Adventure, 1874–1911.* New York, 1961.
    A large book containing little information.

25. Dugdale, Blanche E. C. *Arthur James Balfour*. 2 Vols. (London, 1936).

26. Du Parq, Herbert. *The Life of David Lloyd George*. 4 Vols. (London, 1912).

27. Ervine, St John. *God's Soldier, General William Booth*. 2 Vols. (New York, 1935).

28. Fels, Mary. *Joseph Fels, His Life-Work*. New York, 1916.
    Careless with facts but containing useful material on land colonies and children's welfare.

29. Fitzroy, Sir Almeric. *Memoirs*. II (London, 1925).
    The Greville Diaries of the Edwardian period. Fitzroy was not important but was acquainted with people who were.

30. Fox, Alice Wilson. *The Earl of Halsbury, Lord High Chancellor*. London, 1929.
    A balanced picture of a leader of the die-hards.

31. Gardiner, Alfred G. *John Benn and the Progressive Movement*. London, 1925.
    Much useful material on London government at the turn of the century.

32. ——. *The Life of George Cadbury*. London, 1923.

33. ——. *The Pillars of Society*. London, 1916.

34. George, William. *My Brother and I*. London, 1958.
    Lloyd George's brother. Contains a large number of direct quotes from the Chancellor's letters. Contains also some surprising mistakes. Confuses the opposition to the 1909 budget and opposition to health insurance.

35. Gollin, Alfred M. *The Observer and J. L. Garvin, 1908–1914*. London, 1960.

36. ——. *Proconsul in Politics, A Study of Lord Milner in Opposition and in Power*. London, 1964.
    A full and careful story of the neglected later period of Milner's life.

37. Gooch, George P. *Under Six Reigns*. London, 1958.

38. Gulley, Elsie E. *Joseph Chamberlain and English Social Politics*. New York, 1926.
    Excellent in its time but now outdated. Needs to be done again.

39. Gwynn, Stephen and Tuckwell, Gertrude. *The Life of the Right Hon. Sir Charles Dilke*. 2 Vols. (London, 1917).

40. Haldane of Cloan, Viscount. *Richard Burdon Haldane: An Autobiography*. London, 1929.

41. Hamilton, Lord George. *Parliamentary Reminiscences and Reflections*. II (London, 1922).
Contains nothing on the Royal Commission on the Poor Laws.

42. Hamilton, Mary Agnes. *Arthur Henderson*. London, 1938.
A useful biography but Henderson deserves another one.

43. ——. *Mary Macarthur*. London, 1925.
More a memoir than a biography.

44. ——. *Sidney and Beatrice Webb*. London, 1933.
In some ways this book, written while both the Webbs had more than a decade to live, is the most useful study of the couple yet available. It has received much unjustified criticism.

45. Hammond, John Lawrence. *C. P. Scott of the Manchester Guardian*. London, 1934.

46. Harris, Richard W. *Not So Humdrum: The Autobiography of a Civil Servant*. London, 1939.
More of a reminiscence than an autobiography but contains material on the administration of national health insurance.

47. Holland, Bernard. *The Life of Spencer Compton, Eighth Duke of Devonshire*. II (London, 1911).

48. Holland, Henry Scott. *A Bundle of Memories*. London, 1915.
Material on the Christian Social Union.

49. Hughes, Emrys. *Keir Hardie*. London, 1956.

50. Hyndman, Henry M. *The Record of an Adventurous Life*. London, 1911.

51. James, David. *Lord Roberts*. London, 1954.
Traces the campaign for national service.

52. James, Robert Rhodes. *Rosebery*. London, 1963.
Not an important improvement upon Crewe.

53. Jenkins, Roy. *Asquith*. London, 1964.
A competent summary of the Prime Minister's life. Leans too heavily on Spender and on Jenkins' previous work. Used the Asquith papers at the Bodleian, although clearly not all of them. Mentions health insurance only once, in connexion with the labour alliance, and pensions only in reference to the budget.

54. Jermy, Louise. *The Memories of a Working Woman*. Norwich, 1934.
A fascinating bit of ungrammatical prose by a woman born in the 1880's who spent most of her life as a ladies' maid. Appears to be entirely genuine.

55. Jones, Thomas. *Lloyd George*. London, 1951.
    Thin, but the only biography of Lloyd George worth purchasing.

56. Kekewich, Sir George. *The Education Department and After*. London, 1920.
    The permanent secretary who preceded Morant. A partisan of the National Union of Teachers. Hostile to Morant.

57. Kent, William. *John Burns: Labour's Lost Leader*. London, 1950.

58. Lockhart, J. G. *Cosmo Gordon Lang*. London, 1949.
    Lang was Bishop of Stepney from 1901 to 1909.

59. Lowndes, George A. *Margaret McMillan, 'The Children's Champion.'* London, 1960.
    A collection of reminiscences, without identification of origin. A poor piece of scholarship.

60. Mansbridge, Albert. *Margaret McMillan, Prophet and Pioneer*. London, 1932.
    Not very complete but the best available.

61. Markham, Violet. *Friendship's Harvest*. London, 1956.
    Contains a useful and admiring profile of Morant.

62. Marsh, Edward. *A Number of People, A Book of Reminiscences*. New York, 1939.
    Marsh was Churchill's secretary during the period at the Board of Trade and the Home Office. Highly entertaining reading, the origin of many Churchill stories.

63. Martin, Hugh, ed. *Christian Social Reformers of the Nineteenth Century*. London, 1927.
    A collection of essays.

64. Masterman, Lucy. *C. F. G. Masterman*. London, 1939.
    An invaluable source although Mrs Masterman occasionally rounds out her diary entries from memory.

65. Masterman, N. C. *John Malcolm Ludlow, The Builder of Christian Socialism*. Cambridge, 1963.
    Better on the early and middle period of Ludlow's long life than on his career as Registrar of Friendly Societies.

66. Maurice, Major-General Sir Frederick. *The Life of Viscount Haldane of Cloan*. 2 Vols. (London, 1937).

67. McKenna, Stephen. *Reginald McKenna, 1863–1943*. London, 1948.
    Thin, but had access to the McKenna papers.

68. Minney, R. J. *Viscount Addison, Leader of the Lords*. London, 1958.
    Addison did nothing to deserve such a bad biography.

69. Morley, John, Viscount. *Recollections*. II (New York, 1918).

70. Nevinson, Henry W. *Changes and Chances*. London, 1923.
    One of Massingham's group. An important journalist.

71. Newsholme, Sir Arthur. *The Last Thirty Years in Public Health*. London, 1936.
    Autobiographical account of Newsholme's activities at the Local Government Board and after.

72. Newton, Thomas, Baron. *Retrospection*. London, 1941.

73. Olland, S. L., ed. *A Forty Years' Friendship, Letters from the Late Henry Scott Holland to Mrs Drew*. New York, 1919.

74. Petrie, Sir Charles. *The Life and Letters of the Right Hon. Sir Austen Chamberlain*. I (London, 1939).

75. ——. *Walter Long and His Times*. London, 1936.

76. Pope-Hennessy, James. *Lord Crewe, 1858–1945, The Likeness of a Liberal*. London, 1955.

77. Postgate, Raymond. *The Life of George Lansbury*. London, 1951.

78. Reffold, Albert E. *Wilson Carlile and the Church Army*. 3rd ed. London, 1928.

79. Riddell, George, Baron. *More Pages from My Diary, 1908–1914*. London, 1934.
    Not very full until 1912 but otherwise an excellent source on Lloyd George.

80. Rogers, Frederick. *Labour, Life and Literature, Some Memories of Sixty Years*. London, 1913.
    An indispensable source on the origin of old age pensions and on the early days of political labour. Rogers was first chairman of the Labour Representation Committee.

81. Sadleir, Michael. *Sir Michael Sadler, 1861–1943*. London, 1949.
    A memoir of Michael Sadler by his son. A polemic against Morant. Contains information on the politics of education.

82. Salter, Arthur, Baron. *Memoirs of a Civil Servant*. London, 1961.

83. ——. *Personality in Politics*. London, 1947.

84. Scott, J. W. Robertson. *The Life and Death of a Newspaper*. London, 1952.
    A careless pasting together of reminiscences and documents concerned with the *Pall Mall Gazette* with, however, some useful source material.

85. Simey, T. S. and M. B. *Charles Booth, Social Scientist*. London, 1960.
   A short workman-like biography.

86. Simon, John, Viscount. *Retrospect: The Memoirs of the Rt Hon. Viscount Simon*. London, 1952.
   A masterpiece of the art of using words to conceal information.

87. Snowden, Philip, Viscount. *An Autobiography*. I (London, 1934).

88. Spender, Edward Harold. *The Fire of Life*. London, 1926.

89. ——. *The Prime Minister*. London, 1920.
   Completely uncritical, almost a memoir. Admits he received help in the writing from Lloyd George.

90. Spender, John Alfred. *The Life of the Right Hon. Sir Henry Campbell-Bannerman*. 2 Vols. (Boston, 1924).

91. —— and Asquith, Cyril. *The Life of Lord Oxford and Asquith*. I (London, 1932).

92. Stamp, Winifred. *'Doctor Himself.' An Unorthodox Biography of Harry Roberts, 1871–1946*. London, 1949.
   Roberts was a prolific writer on medical subjects and claimed to have the largest panel practice in Great Britain.

93. Summer, Dudley. *Haldane of Cloan, His Life and Times*. London, 1960.
   Little new material.

94. Tallents, Sir Stephen. *Man and Boy*. London, 1943.
   Very useful on the early administration of labour exchanges. A good, not altogether flattering, picture of Tallents' chief, William Beveridge.

95. Thomas, Malcolm. *David Lloyd George, The Official Biography*. London, 1948.
   Disappointing. Jones' is a far better and shorter study.

96. Tsuzuki, Chushichi. *H. M. Hyndman and British Socialism*. London, 1961.

97. Webb, Beatrice. *My Apprenticeship*. 2nd ed. London, 1945.

98. ——. *Our Partnership*. London, 1948.
   These two edited diaries are indispensable sources for any writing on British social conditions or reform legislation before World War I. They must, however, be used with care. Beatrice Webb did not always know as much as she assumed she did.

99. Wells, Herbert George. *Experiment in Autobiography*. New York, 1934.

100. Wheeler-Bennett, Sir John. *John Anderson, Viscount Waverley*. London, 1962.
    A good professional biography.

101. White, William Allen. *The Autobiography of William Allen White*. New York, 1946.
    White knew and liked John Burns who gave him the Burns-eye view of British politics.

102. Whyte, Frederic. *The Life of W. T. Stead*. II (New York, 1925).

103. Winnington-Ingram, Arthur Foley, Bishop. *Fifty Years' Work in London*. London, 1940.
    Winnington-Ingram was head of Oxford House for ten years and Bishop of Stepney from 1897 to 1901.

104. Wolf, Lucien. *The Life of the First Marquess of Ripon*. II (London, 1921).

105. Young, Kenneth. *Arthur James Balfour*. London, 1963.
    Contains some surprising mistakes, not only of interpretation but of fact.

(B) *Histories of Special Programmes and Acts.*

1. Abel-Smith, Brian. *The Hospitals, 1800–1948. A Study in Social Administration in England and Wales*. Cambridge, Massachusetts, 1964.

2. Ashworth, William. *The Genesis of Modern British Town Planning*. London, 1954.

3. Brend, William A. *Health and the State*. London, 1917.
    Important. A first full-scale survey of health insurance. Critical of the programme and widely quoted in later studies.

4. Bruce, Maurice. *The Coming of the Welfare State*. London, 1961.

5. Bulkley, M. E. *The Feeding of School Children*. London, 1914.
    A good history of the Provision of Meals Act.

6. Carr, Arthur S. Comyns, Garnett, W. H. Stuart, and Taylor, J. H. *National Insurance*. London, 1912.
    A massive legal interpretation of each clause of the National Insurance Act. The first edition contained also nearly one hundred pages of general summary of the Act's administrative and financial specifications. Indispensable for any study of health or unemployment insurance.

7. Chegwidden, T. S. and Mynddin-Evans, G. *The Employment Exchange Service of Great Britain*. New York, 1934.
    Chiefly a survey of the working of the service in the twenties but with some history.

8. Clark, Frederick Le Gros. *Social History of the School Medical Service*. London, 1948.
A pamphlet published by the National Council of Social Service. Well done. Short, but informative.

9. De Schweinitz, Karl. *England's Road to Social Security, 1349–1947*. Philadelphia, 1947.

10. Eckstein, Harry. *The English Health Service, Its Origins, Structure, and Achievements*. Cambridge, Massachusetts, 1959.
Better on structure and achievements than origins.

11. Frazer, Dr William M. *A History of English Public Health, 1839–1939*. London, 1950.
A first-class history dealing with the medical rather than the political side of public health.

12. Gibbon, Sir Ioan Gwilym and Bell, Reginald W. *The History of the London County Council, 1889–1939*. London, 1939
A good comprehensive study.

13. Gilson, Mary Barnett. *Unemployment Insurance in Great Britain*. New York, 1931.
Chiefly on the working of unemployment insurance after World War I.

14. Gray, Alexander. *Some Aspects of National Health Insurance*. London, 1923.
A pamphlet. A reprint of a lecture given to the Glasgow School of Social Study and Training, November, 1922. Professor Gray had been a civil servant in the early days of national health insurance administration.

15. Harris, Richard W. *National Health Insurance in Great Britain, 1911–1946*. London, 1948.
Disappointing. Memories and some badly digested evidence.

16. Hill, Arthur C. C. and Lubin, Isador. *The British Attack on Unemployment*. Washington, 1934.

17. Hoare, H. J. *Old Age Pensions, Their Actual Working and Ascertained Results in the United Kingdom*. London, 1915.
An administrative handbook. The author was a clerk for the Pension Committee of Camberwell and Lewisham.

18. Hoffman, Frederick L. *National Health Insurance and the Friendly Societies*. Newark, New Jersey, 1921.
This book attempts to show the evil effect of national insurance upon private thrift.

19. Hohman, Helen Fisher. *The Development of Social Insurance and Minimum Wage Legislation in Great Britain*. Boston, 1933.
A soundly researched, first-class history, attempting to cover, perhaps, too wide a field.

20. Johnson, Dr Donald McI. *The British National Health Service*. London, 1962.
A short well done history of national health insurance and the national health service.

21. Lafitte, François. *Britain's Way to Social Security*. London, 1945.
Essentially a hard cover pamphlet, one of the 'Target for Tomorrow' series.

22. Laing, J. Murray. *A Few Notes on the National Insurance Act*. Birmingham, 1913.
Pamphlet. A reprint of a paper read before the Birmingham Insurance Institute, March, 1913. A good explanation of the Act by an insurance company actuary.

23. Laski, Harold J., ed. *A Century of Municipal Progress, 1835–1935*. London, 1935.
A collection of essays on various aspects of social reform, some hardly municipal, good essays by George Newman and Gilbert Slater.

24. Leff, S. and V. *The School Health Service*. London, 1959.

25. Levy, Hermann. *National Health Insurance, A Critical Study*. Cambridge, 1944.

26. Lowndes, George A. M. *The Silent Social Revolution*. London, 1955.
A useful study of the history of education, not clearly written.

27. McCleary, Dr George F. *The Early History of the Infant Welfare Movement*. London, 1933.

28. ——. *The Maternity and Child Welfare Movement*. London, 1935.
McCleary writes with special knowledge. He began his professional career as Medical Officer of Health for Battersea in 1902.

29. ——. *National Health Insurance*. London, 1932.

30. MacKintosh, Dr James M. *Trends of Opinion About the Public Health, 1901–51*. London, 1953.
Draws conclusions from interest in health matters shown in periodicals and newspapers.

31. Norwood, Cyril. *The English Tradition of Education*. London, 1929.

32. Pimlott, Sir J. A. R. *Toynbee Hall*. London, 1935.

33. Raynes, Harold E. *Social Security in Britain, A History*. 2nd ed. London, 1960.

34. Seymour, John Barton. *The British Employment Exchange*. London, 1928.

35. Stead, The Rev. Francis Herbert. *How Old Age Pensions Began to Be*. London, n.d. [1910].
    With Frederick Rogers' and Barnes' memoirs, the indispensable source on pensions.

36. Tillyard, Sir Frank and Ball, F. N. *Unemployment Insurance in Great Britain, 1911–1948*. Leigh-on-Sea, 1949.
    Contains a useful analysis of the Act, very little on politics, misses the importance of William Beveridge.

37. Wickwar, Hardy and Margaret. *The Social Services, An Historical Survey*. 2nd ed. London, 1949.
    Cursory, some mistakes in fact.

38. Wilkie, G. B. *Nationalization of Insurance*. London, 1931.
    A paperback pamphlet opposing nationalization but with some facts on the pre-war history unobtainable elsewhere.

39. Williams, J. H. Harley. *A Century of Public Health in Great Britain*. London, 1932.

40. Wilson, Sir Arnold and MacKay, G. S. *Old Age Pensions, An Historical and Critical Study*. London, 1941.
    Depends heavily on a few sources, very little on pensions before 1908. Uses an International Labour Office publication of 1933 to survey pensions in foreign countries. Appears never to have heard of the United States Social Security Act.

(C) *General Histories, Economic, Political, Social; and Political and Social Philosophy*

1. Adams, William Scovell. *Edwardian Heritage: A Study in British History, 1900–1906*. London, 1949.
   Much concerned with impact of big business on Edwardian England.

2. Armytage, W. H. G. *Heavens Below, Utopian Experiments in England, 1560–1960*. London, 1961.

3. Bealey, Frank and Pelling, Henry. *Labour and Politics, 1900–1906*. London, 1958.
   Very useful.

4. Checkland, S. G. *The Rise of Industrial Society in England, 1815–1885*. New York, 1964.

5. Clapham, John H. *An Economic History of Modern Britain*. III (New York, 1938).

6. Clayton, Joseph. *The Rise and Decline of Socialism in Great Britain, 1884–1924*. London, 1926.

7. Cole, George D. H. *British Working Class Politics, 1834–1914*. London, 1950.

8. ——. *A Short History of the British Working Class Movement*. II (London, 1926); III (London, 1927).

9. —— and Postgate, Raymond. *The British Common People, 1746–1946*. University Paperback Edition. London, 1946.

10. Cole, Margaret. *The Story of Fabian Socialism*. London, 1961.

11. Dangerfield, George. *The Strange Death of Liberal England*. London, 1936.

12. Dicey, Albert V. *Law and Public Opinion in England*. 2nd ed. London, 1917.

   The introduction to the second edition contains a lucid statement of the nineteenth-century individualistic ideal to which the New Liberalism was a reaction.

13. Elton, Godfrey. *England Arise, A Study of the Pioneering Days of the Labour Movement*. London, 1931.

   A book still worth consulting.

14. Ensor, R. C. K. *England, 1870–1914*. Oxford, 1936.

15. Finer, Herman. *The Theory and Practice of Modern Government*. II (London, 1932).

16. Ginsberg, Morris, ed. *Law and Opinion in England in the Twentieth Century*, London, 1959.

   Contains provocative essays on insurance and pensions, among other things.

17. Green, Frederick E. *A History of the English Agricultural Labourer, 1870–1920*. London, 1927.

18. Gretton, R. H. *A Modern History of the English People, 1880–1922*. London, 1930.

   Written principally from newspapers.

19. Halevy, Elie. *A History of the English People in the Nineteenth Century*. V, VI (University Paperback Edition, New York, 1961).

   These two volumes, originally entitled *Epilogue* (Vols. I and II) covering British political history from 1895 to 1914, remain the fullest and most reliable general analysis of the period.

20. Hutchison, Keith. *The Decline and Fall of British Capitalism*. London, 1951.

   An interesting interpretation that has been widely quoted.

21. Inglis, K. S. *Churches and the Working Class in Victorian England.* London, 1963.
   Excellent coverage of the Salvation Army, Christian socialism, and the settlement movement.

22. Inman, Walter Grant. 'The British Liberal Party, 1892–1939.' Unpublished Ph.D. dissertation, Clark University, 1939.
   Contains a good survey of the rise and decline of the party of national efficiency. Written entirely from secondary material.

23. Jenkins, Roy. *Mr Balfour's Poodle.* London, 1954.
   A first-class study of the Liberal attack on the House of Lords.

24. Jennings, William Ivor. *Parliament.* New York, 1940.
   Perhaps the best modern analysis.

25. Lynd, Helen Merrell. *England in the Eighteen Eighties, Toward a Social Basis for Freedom.* New York, 1945.
   An extremely important book now too frequently neglected.

26. McBriar, A. M. *Fabian Socialism and English Politics, 1884–1918.* London, 1962.
   Uneven, not always well informed.

27. Maccoby, Simon. *English Radicalism: The End?* London, 1961.
   Unevenly written, over-detailed and yet with many blank spots. Good on labour politics in the North.

28. McDowell, Robert B. *British Conservatism.* London, 1959.

29. Newman, Sir George. *Health and Social Evolution.* London, 1931.
   The Halley Stewart lectures for 1930.

30. Newsholme, Sir Arthur. *Medicine and the State.* London, 1932.
   A good statement of the application of Fabian principles to government medical care.

31. ——. *Public Health and Insurance.* Baltimore, 1920.
   Contains some rather strong criticism of the insurance Act and of its administration.

32. Owen, David. *English Philanthropy, 1660–1960.* Cambridge, Mass., 1964.
   Contains useful chapters on the Charity Organisation Society and the Royal Commission on the Poor Laws.

33. Pelling, Henry. *A Short History of the Labour Party.* London, 1961.

34. Pipkin, Charles W. *Social Politics and Modern Democracies.* I (New York, 1931).
   Painstakingly researched but Hohman is to be preferred. Volume II on France.

35. Playne, Caroline E. *The Pre-War Mind in Britain, An Historical Review*. London, 1928.
    Devoted mostly to attitudes towards Germany and the war, but helpful.

36. Poirier, Philip P. *The Advent of the Labour Party*. London, 1958.
    A good book, better in some ways than Bealey and Pelling.

37. Roberts, B. C. *The Trades Union Congress, 1868–1921*. London, 1958.
    Disappointingly narrow in orientation.

38. Semmel, Bernard. *Imperialism and Social Reform: English Social-Imperial Thought, 1895–1914*. Cambridge, 1960.
    Useful, more a collection of essays than a connected study.

39. Slater, Gilbert. *Poverty and the State*. London, 1930.
    A good, though old, comprehensive survey.

40. Slesser, Sir Henry. *A History of the Liberal Party*. London, 1943.
    A defence of Campbell-Bannerman.

41. Stead, The Rev. Francis Herbert. *The Story of Social Christianity*. II (London, 1924).
    Far less useful than his history of pensions.

42. Tillyard, Sir Frank. *The Worker and the State*. 3rd ed. London, 1948. Chiefly a survey of labour law.

43. Wagner, Donald O. *The Church of England and Social Reform Since 1854*. New York, 1930.
    A doctor's dissertation.

44. Webb, Sidney and Beatrice. *A Constitution for the Socialist Commonwealth of Great Britain*. London, 1920.

45. ——. *English Local Government: English Poor Law History: Part II: The Last Hundred Years*. 2 Vols. (London, 1929).

46. Young, G. M. *Victorian England, Portrait of an Age*. Oxford Paperback edition. London, 1961.

FICTIONAL MATERIALS

1. Disraeli, Benjamin. *Sybil: Or, The Two Nations*. London, 1881. First published 1845.

2. Galsworthy, John. *The Forsyte Saga*. New York, 1922.

3. Shaw, George Bernard. *The Doctor's Dilemma*. New York, 1911.

4. Wells, Herbert George. *The New Machiavelli*. New York, 1908.

5. Young, Francis Brett. *Doctor Bradley Remembers*. New York, 1938.
   Dedicated to David Lloyd George.

INDEX

Q*